T0340354

# Demystifying Fixed Income Analytics

This book discusses important aspects of fixed income securities in emerging economies.

## Key features

- Clarifies all conceptual and analytical aspects of fixed income securities and bonds, and covers important interest rate and credit derivative instruments in a simple and practical way.
- Examines topics such as classifications of fixed income instruments; related risk-return measures; yield curve and term structure of interest rates; interest rate derivatives (forwards, futures and swaps), credit derivatives (credit default swaps); and trading strategies and risk management.
- Provides step-by-step explanation of fixed income products by including real-life examples, scenarios and cases, especially in the context of emerging markets.
- Presents consistent reference of actual market practices to make the chapters practice oriented while maintaining a lucid style complemented by adequate reading inputs and clear learning outcomes.
- Includes complete solutions of numericals and cases for all chapters as an eResource on the Routledge website to aid understanding.

The book will serve as a ready guide to both professionals from banking and finance industry (fixed income/bond dealers; fund/investment/portfolio managers; investment bankers; financial analysts/consultants; risk management specialists), and those in academia, including students, research scholars, and teachers in the fields of business management, banking, insurance, finance, financial economics, business economics, and risk management.

**Kedar Nath Mukherjee** is Assistant Professor at the National Institute of Bank Management, Pune, Maharashtra, India. He has extensive experience in providing training to senior and middle-level executives in treasury and risk management departments of commercial, investment, and cooperative banks, primary dealers, insurance companies, pension funds, public sector undertakings, corporate treasuries, etc., on the topics of fixed income securities, bond portfolio management, investment management, risk management, and financial derivatives. Besides professional training, he also teaches courses in PGDM programmes and undertakes consultancy activities. He has published research papers in various journals, and the monograph *Fixed Income Securities: Valuation, Risk and Risk Management*.

# Demystifying Fixed Income Analytics
## A Practical Guide

Kedar Nath Mukherjee

Routledge
Taylor & Francis Group

LONDON AND NEW YORK

First published 2021
by Routledge
2 Park Square, Milton Park, Abingdon, Oxon OX14 4RN

and by Routledge
52 Vanderbilt Avenue, New York, NY 10017

*Routledge is an imprint of the Taylor & Francis Group, an informa business*

© 2021 Kedar Nath Mukherjee

*British Library Cataloguing-in-Publication Data*
A catalogue record for this book is available from the British Library

*Library of Congress Cataloging-in-Publication Data*
A catalog record has been requested for this book

ISBN: 978-1-138-35881-2 (hbk)
ISBN: 978-0-367-51479-2 (pbk)
ISBN: 978-1-003-04516-8 (ebk)

Typeset in Sabon
by Apex CoVantage, LLC

Visit the eResources: www.routledge.com/9780367514792

To my 'Baba'
Late Purnendu Mukherjee

# Contents

**11  Interest rate options and structured products**                337

**12  Credit default swaps**                                         351

# Figures

# Tables

# Case studies

# Foreword

The Indian economy has been through a period of significant economic reforms ever since the early 1990s. One aspect which many of us fail to look at in the context of economic reforms is the fact that the political dispensation has gone through several changes in the last three decades but what has remained constant is the reforms narrative across the ruling political parties. Thus, forging a political consensus has been a milestone achievement for India, and there is no longer any debate on the need for reforms. The debate has clearly centered around the content of reforms and the pace. Given this milestone achievement in terms of real sector reforms, it is no surprise that the steps to liberalize the financial markets and put Indian financial markets on a global map have been policymakers' contemporaneous focus for the last few years.

Financial market reforms started with freeing up the administered interest rate regime in the 1990s. Simultaneously, an avalanche of reforms hit the money, bond, currency, and capital markets in India in terms of expanding the product space as well as the participant space. The strengthening of the market infrastructure across the market segments has also been the key focus area of policymakers at the same time. Despite these focused efforts, it is not a great commentary that the bond market development in India is still a work in process and the unfulfilled agenda hangs on – and it has been hanging on for almost one generation of stakeholders spanning almost 25 years. There is still no clear answer to this question as to why bond market development has been in the slow lane. If I have to find an answer to this question of slow pace of bond market development, I would actually put my finger on lack of awareness about bond markets amongst several stakeholders, including market practitioners. Bond as a financial instrument remains a kind of enigma to many investors. Bond mathematics continues to scare away a large number of beginners. There are very many investors who shun bonds due to this reason of complexity.

This is where I feel that this practical guidebook by Dr Kedar Nath Mukherjee has a significant role to play and will stand out.

It is not that there are no good books on markets in the world today. There are – but the books relating specifically to Indian bond markets are very few. Even amongst these few, not many of them make the subject matter look easy, interesting and readable, and hence many a reader is scared off by the complexity of the narrative adopted. Dr Kedar Nath Mukherjee has adopted a refreshingly simple approach to explain the most difficult topics in this practical guide, and that is what sets this book apart from the rest. The book has focused on the Indian scenario all through its contents. The initial chapters which touch upon the conceptual aspects of bonds are an essential reading for anybody getting initiated in the bond space. The ease with which the author explains the concepts and draws illustrations from India will certainly be very useful to any reader making a serious effort to understand this market.

In any book on bonds, the chapters on term structures of interest rates, pricing, and valuation are acid tests for the author's capacity for simplicity and clarity. Dr Mukherjee comes through with flying colors in these acid tests; in fact, he leads the reader through a garden path even on difficult concepts. Certainly, this practical guide, therefore, is an important companion for any serious student.

The instrument specific chapters, like interest rate futures, FRAs, IRSs, and interest rate options, are really helpful for Indian market practitioners because they clearly lay out the product specifications, supplemented by practical exercises, very lucidly in front of the reader. Credit default swaps have been a non-starter in India so far, and I am sure this book will facilitate better understanding of the product.

The section on trading and management strategies dwells at length on several practical and effective ways of running a bond portfolio and will be a very useful aid for any portfolio manager. This section will certainly help any trader to adopt a prudent approach in bond markets.

The section on risk management is an essential primer for any middle office practitioners.

All in all, I feel that the book, with its refreshingly lucid approach on a complex subject, will be an essential guide and companion for students and researchers as well as market practitioners.

G. Mahalingam
Whole Time Member, Securities and Exchange Board of India (SEBI)
Executive Director (Retd.), Financial Markets Department,
Reserve Bank of India (RBI)

# Preface

"Why this book, especially when there are many titles available on the same subject by eminent authors internationally?" This may be a genuine question in the mind of the readers who are looking to gain reasonable insights on any topic or subject. This makes the job of authors much more challenging in proposing a new title on a standard subject that already has good references in existing literature. But a general statement always remains valid – "Even if there are lots of alternatives available, a single item may not be the best for everyone".

As a faculty member in the areas of finance, teaching subjects like fixed income securities, securities analysis and portfolio management, risk management, financial derivatives, etc. for more than a decade, addressing both fresh postgraduates and market practitioners in the areas of fixed income securities market in emerging economies such as India, I sensed a vacuum in the understanding of analytical aspects of the concerned subject in simple language with effective step-by-step guidance. Here is where the thought process for this small piece of effort started. Lots of queries and requests emerged from postgraduate students and practising bankers and financial experts to suggest a good book in the areas of fixed income securities, especially at the intermediate level, mostly focusing on the emerging markets. This made my determination stronger to introduce a practical guide restricted to a few simple fixed income products but with an in-depth understanding.

The content and coverage of this book is designed primarily keeping in mind the analytical skills and understanding that is required to successfully analyze and manage a fixed income portfolio, especially in the context of emerging fixed income markets like in India, and other Asian and African emerging economies. An attempt is made to demystify the complete cycle of a few standard fixed income products, with a brief description about the fixed income market in some developed and emerging economies, classification of fixed income products under various categories, their properties, users, and usefulness; issuance of such products in the primary market and subsequent trading in the secondary market; pricing and valuation of various fixed income products, giving due concerns to actual market practices and regulatory guidelines; use of various measures to estimate the yield on fixed income security/portfolio; analyzing the term structure of interest rates; measuring sensitivity of fixed income securities/portfolio, majorly due to change in interest rates; use of interest rate derivatives (viz. forwards, futures, swaps, and options), contracts, their structures, pricing, valuation, settlement, usefulness in trading, and risk management; practical strategies to trade in and manage fixed income portfolios; optimization of fixed income portfolios; and finally, the use of appropriate practices to manage the risk of fixed income securities/portfolios with a special reference to banking. This book is written keeping in mind the knowledge requirements of both academics and professional experts from banking and finance industries, and I hope this will be useful to readers.

# Acknowledgements

First, I would like to acknowledge the contribution of my better half Shatabdi, and our daughter Ayushi in both my professional and personal life. Without their whole-hearted support and patience, nothing significant would have been possible at this stage. I dedicate this piece of my prolonged effort to my father, the late Purnendu Mukherjee, who has been the biggest source of inspiration from my childhood till today, when I miss him. My father had never set a very big target for me since my childhood. The only thing that he always used to remind me of at every stage is that, "Just try if you could achieve something that makes you satisfied and makes me feel proud of you".

I thank everyone concerned at my institute, National Institute of Bank Management (NIBM), Pune, all my programme participants from banks and other financial institutions in India and abroad, my PGDM students at NIBM, and my close friends and well-wishers, who have encouraged me to finally materialize this initiative after a prolonged effort.

Finally, I acknowledge the sincere efforts made by all concerned from the publishers Routledge, Taylor & Francis Group, in giving my manuscript a final shape.

# Abbreviations

| | |
|---|---|
| ABS | Asset Backed Securities |
| AFS | Available for Sale |
| ALM | Asset Liability Management |
| ASEAN | Association of Southeast Asian Nations |
| BCBS | Basel Committee on Bank Supervision |
| BSE | Bombay Stock Exchange |
| CBOT | Chicago Board of Trade |
| CCF | Credit Conversion Factor |
| CCIL | Clearing Corporation of India Limited |
| CCP | Central counterparties |
| CD | Certificate of Deposits |
| CDO | Collateralized Debt Obligation |
| CDS | Credit Default Swap |
| CF | Conversion Factor |
| CFTC | Commodity Futures Trading Commission |
| CLN | Credit Link Notes |
| CMB | Cash Management Bills |
| CME | Chicago Mercantile Exchange |
| CP | Commercial Papers |
| CPI | Consumer Price Index |
| CRAR | Capital to Risk-weighted Assets Ratio |
| CRR | Cash Reserve Ratio |
| CSA | Credit Support Annex |
| CTD | Cheapest to Deliver |
| CY | Current Yield |
| DCF | Discounted Cash Flows |
| DEAR | Daily Earning at Risk |
| ECB | External Commercial Borrowings |
| ES | Expected Shortfall |
| EWMA | Exponentially Weighted Moving Average |
| FBIL | Financial Benchmark India Limited |
| FCCB | Foreign Currency Convertible Bonds |
| FCD | Fully Convertible Debentures |

| | |
|---|---|
| FII | Foreign Institutional Investors |
| FIMMDA | Fixed Income Money Market and Derivatives Association |
| FPI | Foreign Portfolio Investors |
| FRA | Forward Rate Agreement |
| FRB | Floating Rate Bond |
| FRN | Floating Rate Loan |
| FV | Future Value |
| GARCH | Generalized Autoregressive Conditional Heteroscedasticity |
| GDP | Gross Domestic Product |
| GMRCC | General Market Risk Capital Charge |
| GOI | Government of India |
| HFT | Held for Trading |
| HS | Historical Simulation |
| HTM | Held till Maturity |
| IAS | International Accounting Standard |
| IIB | Inflation Indexed Bonds |
| IMA | Internal Model Approach |
| IMF | International Monetary Fund |
| INBMK | Indian Benchmark |
| IRDA | Insurance Regulatory and Development Authority |
| IRF | Interest Rate Futures |
| IRR | Internal Rate of Return |
| IRS | Interest Rate Swap |
| ISDA | International Swaps and Derivatives Association |
| LAF | Liquidity Adjustment Facility |
| LIBOR | London Interbank Offered Rate |
| MBS | Mortgage Backed Securities |
| MCS | Monte Carlo Simulation |
| MCX | Multi Commodity Exchange |
| MIBOR | Mumbai Interbank Offered/Outright Rate |
| MIFOR | Mumbai Interbank Forward Rate |
| MOF | Ministry of Finance |
| MRCC | Market Risk Capital Charge |
| MTM | Marked to Market |
| NAV | Net Asset Value |
| NBFC | Non-Banking Financial Companies |
| NCD | Non-Convertible Debentures |
| NCDEX | National Commodity and Derivatives Exchange |
| NDTL | Net Demand and Time Liabilities |
| NII | Net Interest Income |
| NIM | Net Interest Margin |
| NMCE | National Multi Commodity Exchange |
| NPV | Net Present Value |
| NSCCL | National Securities Clearing Corporation Limited |
| NSE | National Stock Exchange |

| | |
|---|---|
| NSS | Nelson-Siegel-Svensson |
| OCD | Optionally Convertible Debentures |
| OIS | Overnight Index Swap |
| OMO | Open Market Operation |
| OTC | Over-the-Counter |
| PCD | Partly Convertible Debentures |
| PD | Primary Dealers |
| PDO | Public Debt Office |
| PFRDA | Pension Fund Regulatory and Development Authority |
| PLR | Prime Lending Rate |
| PV | Present Value |
| PV01 | Price Value of 1 Basis |
| PVBP | Price Value Basis Point |
| QFI | Qualified Foreign Investors |
| RBI | Reserve Bank of India |
| RSA | Risk Sensitive Asset |
| RSL | Risk Sensitive Liability |
| RWA | Risk Weighted Asset |
| SDL | State Development Loans |
| SEBI | Securities and Exchange Board of India |
| SEC | Securities and Exchange Commission |
| SGL | Subsidiary General Ledger Account |
| SIFMA | Securities Industry and Financial Markets Association |
| SLR | Statutory Liquidity Ratio |
| SMM | Standardized Measurement Method |
| SPV | Special Purpose Vehicle |
| SRCC | Specific Risk Capital Charge |
| STRIPS | Separate Trading of Registered Interest and Principal of Securities |
| VCV | Variance Co-Variance |
| VAR | Value at Risk |
| VWAP | Volume Weighted Average Price |
| WPI | Wholesale Price Index |
| YTB | Yield to Best |
| YTC | Yield to Call |
| YTFC | Yield to First Call |
| YTFP | Yield to First Put |
| YTM | Yield to Maturity |
| YTP | Yield to Put |
| YTW | Yield to Worst |
| ZCB | Zero Coupon Bond |
| ZCYC | Zero Coupon Yield Curve |

# 1 Fixed income securities market

## An overview

**Key learning outcomes**

At the end of this chapter, the readers are expected to be familiar with:

- Nature of fixed income securities market worldwide and within India
- Operations in primary and secondary debt markets
- Primary issuance (auctions, public issue, private placements)
- Secondary market trading in government and non-government securities
- Settlement of trades in debt securities
- Role of major players in Indian debt market

## Fixed income securities market – an introduction

Equities and debts are two important categories of instruments available in the financial market, a key driver of national and international economy. Equities are perpetual liability, and they connote owner's legal claim, after all liabilities are met, upon the available assets of the entity in which the equity shares are held. On the other hand, bonds are debt instruments, in which the legal bond issuer owes the bond holders a debt, depending on the terms of the bond, and are obliged to pay regular *coupon* and/or to repay the principal at a later date, commonly known as *maturity*. Government and non-government entities worldwide meet their financial requirements by issuing these instruments, which are subscribed to by different types of investors: Institutional and/or retail. Equity and debt markets in most of the economies worldwide are well developed capture important shares of their respective GDPs.

The debt market is the financial market for issuance, trading and settlement in fixed income securities of various types.[1] Fixed income securities are issued by various organizations, i.e. central and state governments, public bodies, statutory corporations, banks, financial institutions, and corporate bodies. These markets are an important source of funds, especially in developing economies like India. In order to finance its fiscal deficit, the government (central and state) borrows money from the market by issuing government securities (G-Secs.), which are sovereign securities issued by, say, the central bank of the country (e.g. Reserve Bank of India or RBI) on behalf of the government. The role of fixed income markets as an efficient tool to raise money for government projects (national and local) has been considered and appreciated worldwide for centuries.

## Global debt markets – a review

The financial market of an economy gets the status of developed market if it is characterized by proper financial, legal, and regulatory frameworks. Even if the equity markets of the financial system in most of the world economies, including India, are well developed, the same may not be valid in case of the bond market, especially the market for non-government securities. The following section deals with a broader overview of the debt market (government and non-government) in some of the developed and emerging, especially Asian, economies which have experienced a significant growth over the years in developing their debt (government and corporate) market.

### US debt market

The bond market in the United States is the largest market in the world, with a total outstanding of USD 37.0 trillion at the end of 2017. The proportion of debt securities in the US securities market is almost equal to that of equities, reflecting an equal importance of their debt market (162% and 198% respectively for equities and debts as a percentage share of US GDP during the end of 2017) comparative to other economies, where concentration of equities is more than the debts. The corporate bond market in United States is again the largest market (22% of the total bond issuance in US) in the world, not only in terms of outstanding volume (USD 9 trillion during the end of 2017), but also in terms of annual turnover in the secondary market. The US debt market is a very well-developed and efficient market with a high level of liquidity in the secondary markets (USD 764 billion of daily trading volume, of which USD 505 billion was in Treasury securities during 2017). The reason for this being that the interest of not only the corporate but also the banks and other institutions tapping the debt market, rather than seeking loans or deposits to meet their financial requirements (10% of loan financing vs. almost of 70% of financing through capital markets). The US bond market is also well diversified and consists of several instruments, such as Treasury bills and bonds, federal agency securities, municipal bonds, corporate bonds, mortgage backed securities (MBS), asset backed securities (ABS), etc. In order to strengthen the demand for corporate bonds, a developed market like the US has experienced a significant demand from financial institutions like banks, mutual funds, insurance companies and pension funds. The US corporate bond market has experienced a wider investor base that also includes retail investors. Mortgage-related debt captures the maximum market share (annual average: 26–27%), followed by the Treasury issues and corporate debts, respectively, with an annual average of close to 24 and 20%. Domestic and foreign investors play a dominant role in the world's largest debt market. The annual average participation of FIIs in the US Treasury market is almost 38.50% out of total outstanding Treasury debts. But in terms of average daily trading volume in US debt market, the Treasury market captures more than 60% of the secondary market trading, followed by the MBS (28%), and others. The development and growth in the US debt securities market are presented in the following tables (Table 1.1 to 1.3).

## European debt market

Although individual countries in European region have their own domestic bond markets, the European bond markets are also increasingly acting like a single market. In Europe, bonds are about two-thirds of the total volume of securities outstanding in the financial market (bonds and shares). Apart from vanilla bonds issued by governments and non-government entities, other types of fixed income securities commonly popular in European markets are: collateralized debt obligations (CDOs), structured products, covered bonds, etc., issued by governments and other entities like: monetary financial institutions (MFIs), financial corporations other than MFIs[2] and non-financial corporations, as given in the following table (Table 1.4).

About 45% (last 10-Year Average) of the European bond market is government (central and general) debt, followed by debts issued by the MFIs (35%), and financial and non-financial corporations (20%). In terms of the maturity of debt instruments in the European region, 90% are long-term debts and the rest (10%) account for the short-term instruments. At the same time, 75% (25%) of the total debt issue in the European region are fixed rate (floating rate) in nature. Bond markets in European countries, e.g. France, Germany, London, Italy, Spain, Switzerland, etc., are reasonably well developed, where the majority of market participants are institutional investors, for example: pension funds, insurance companies and banks. Exposures in bonds by various institutional investors, however, differ between European countries.

An important feature of the European corporate bond market, which is in contrast with many emerging markets including in India, is that most of the bonds are listed in exchanges, but a significant proportion of secondary market trading takes place through OTC platforms. This practice signifies that listing is preferred not to facilitate trade through exchanges, but to enable institutional investors and fund managers with restrictions to invest

*Table 1.1* Outstanding volume in US debt market

Outstanding Volume in U.S. Debt Market (Percentage Share and Total in USD Billions)

| | Municipal | Treasury | Mortgage Related | Corporate Debt | Federal Agency Securities | Money Markets | Asset-Backed | Total |
|---|---|---|---|---|---|---|---|---|
| 2000 | 9.16% | 18.25% | 25.47% | 21.32% | 11.46% | 9.98% | 4.36% | 16171.71 |
| 2001 | 9.12% | 16.87% | 26.78% | 21.96% | 12.26% | 8.38% | 4.63% | 17590.64 |
| 2002 | 9.29% | 16.89% | 27.87% | 21.42% | 12.53% | 7.24% | 4.77% | 18982.12 |
| 2003 | 9.29% | 17.47% | 27.93% | 21.29% | 12.83% | 6.32% | 4.87% | 20463.27 |
| 2004 | 12.55% | 17.23% | 27.51% | 20.01% | 11.79% | 6.11% | 4.81% | 22905.90 |
| 2005 | 12.55% | 16.90% | 29.25% | 18.85% | 10.60% | 6.66% | 5.20% | 24680.69 |
| 2006 | 12.10% | 15.94% | 30.91% | 18.02% | 9.70% | 7.21% | 6.11% | 27144.14 |
| 2007 | 12.05% | 15.36% | 31.88% | 18.09% | 9.87% | 6.08% | 6.67% | 29441.07 |
| 2008 | 11.79% | 18.62% | 30.48% | 17.71% | 10.34% | 5.15% | 5.90% | 31056.65 |
| 2009 | 11.97% | 22.60% | 29.11% | 18.95% | 8.49% | 3.54% | 5.34% | 32126.33 |
| 2010 | 11.67% | 26.12% | 27.32% | 19.83% | 7.49% | 3.12% | 4.45% | 33892.69 |
| 2011 | 11.37% | 28.83% | 26.36% | 19.93% | 6.76% | 2.81% | 3.95% | 34435.31 |
| 2012 | 11.06% | 31.24% | 25.00% | 20.46% | 5.93% | 2.69% | 3.62% | 35359.15 |
| 2013 | 10.56% | 32.57% | 24.02% | 21.04% | 5.65% | 2.61% | 3.54% | 36392.33 |
| 2014 | 10.13% | 33.36% | 23.59% | 21.42% | 5.41% | 2.48% | 3.60% | 37479.94 |
| 2015 | 9.90% | 34.28% | 23.12% | 21.46% | 5.19% | 2.45% | 3.60% | 38476.37 |
| 2016 | 9.71% | 35.06% | 22.73% | 21.78% | 4.97% | 2.23% | 3.52% | 39670.87 |
| 2017 | 9.42% | 35.29% | 22.69% | 21.94% | 4.72% | 2.36% | 3.59% | 41005.37 |
| **Avg.** | 10.76% | 24.05% | 26.78% | 20.30% | 8.67% | 4.86% | 4.59% | 29848.58 |

*Source:* SIFMA Database

Table 1.2 Average daily trading volume in US debt market

*Average Daily Trading Volume in US Debt Market (Percentage Share and Total in USD Billions)*

| Year | Municipal | Treasury | Agency MBS | Non-Agency MBS | ABS | Corporate Debt | Federal Agency Securities | Total |
|---|---|---|---|---|---|---|---|---|
| 2000 | 2.45% | 57.76% | 19.43% | – | – | | 20.36% | 357.6 |
| 2001 | 1.73% | 58.54% | 22.00% | – | – | | 17.73% | 508.9 |
| 2002 | 1.70% | 58.04% | 24.47% | – | – | 2.83% | 12.96% | 631.2 |
| 2003 | 1.68% | 57.66% | 27.40% | – | – | 2.40% | 10.87% | 751.8 |
| 2004 | 1.81% | 61.05% | 25.38% | – | – | 2.12% | 9.65% | 817.3 |
| 2005 | 1.84% | 60.37% | 27.41% | – | – | 1.80% | 8.58% | 918.6 |
| 2006 | 2.59% | 58.71% | 28.49% | – | – | 1.89% | 8.32% | 893.7 |
| 2007 | 2.48% | 56.19% | 31.54% | – | – | 1.61% | 8.18% | 1,014.9 |
| 2008 | 1.87% | 53.38% | 33.29% | – | – | 1.38% | 10.08% | 1,036.1 |
| 2009 | 1.52% | 49.88% | 36.67% | – | – | 2.44% | 9.50% | 817.8 |
| 2010 | 1.49% | 59.10% | 35.87% | – | – | 2.29% | 1.25% | 893.7 |
| 2011 | 1.32% | 66.14% | 28.33% | 0.52% | 0.17% | 2.41% | 1.12% | 858.5 |
| 2012 | 1.33% | 61.13% | 33.03% | 0.53% | 0.18% | 2.66% | 1.14% | 849.0 |
| 2013 | 1.37% | 66.83% | 27.30% | 0.50% | 0.16% | 3.03% | 0.81% | 816.1 |
| 2014 | 1.35% | 69.14% | 24.41% | 0.51% | 0.20% | 3.66% | 0.73% | 729.2 |
| 2015 | 1.18% | 67.25% | 26.49% | 0.42% | 0.20% | 3.83% | 0.62% | 728.8 |
| 2016 | 1.37% | 66.94% | 26.65% | 0.37% | 0.17% | 3.81% | 0.69% | 775.5 |
| 2017 | 1.41% | 66.14% | 27.37% | 0.33% | 0.19% | 4.02% | 0.54% | 763.8 |
| **Avg.** | 1.69% | 60.79% | 28.09% | 0.46% | 0.18% | 2.64% | 6.84% | 786.81 |

*Source:* SIFMA Database

*Table 1.3* Participants-wise distribution of US treasury securities

Participants-wise Distribution of US Treasury Securities (Percentage Share and Total in USD Billions)

| Year | Individuals | Mutual Funds | Banking Institutions | Insurance Companies | Monetary Authority | State & Local Govt. | Foreign and International | Pension Funds | Others | Total |
|---|---|---|---|---|---|---|---|---|---|---|
| 2000 | 14.50% | 5.28% | 2.57% | 2.89% | 12.60% | 7.63% | 27.46% | 25.32% | 1.76% | 4,062.7 |
| 2001 | 10.69% | 6.21% | 2.13% | 2.86% | 13.40% | 7.97% | 29.11% | 25.85% | 1.78% | 4,118.5 |
| 2002 | 6.50% | 6.23% | 2.32% | 3.81% | 14.30% | 8.06% | 31.87% | 24.61% | 2.29% | 4,400.1 |
| 2003 | 8.59% | 5.70% | 3.28% | 3.52% | 13.82% | 7.76% | 32.07% | 23.30% | 1.95% | 4,823.2 |
| 2004 | 9.09% | 5.13% | 1.02% | 3.67% | 13.73% | 7.59% | 35.23% | 22.53% | 2.00% | 5,226.6 |
| 2005 | 7.20% | 5.02% | 0.45% | 3.69% | 13.38% | 9.38% | 36.19% | 22.03% | 2.67% | 5,560.9 |
| 2006 | 5.53% | 4.82% | 0.37% | 3.44% | 13.48% | 10.04% | 37.25% | 22.21% | 2.88% | 5,780.4 |
| 2007 | 2.85% | 6.52% | 0.24% | 2.42% | 12.24% | 10.82% | 39.77% | 21.97% | 3.16% | 6,051.2 |
| 2008 | 1.94% | 11.20% | 3.54% | 2.52% | 6.47% | 8.00% | 44.72% | 19.33% | 2.27% | 7,353.5 |
| 2009 | 9.50% | 8.46% | 3.03% | 2.52% | 8.77% | 6.67% | 42.08% | 16.98% | 2.01% | 8,859.2 |
| 2010 | 10.32% | 7.78% | 3.36% | 2.42% | 9.72% | 5.76% | 43.03% | 15.55% | 2.07% | 10,504.4 |
| 2011 | 5.69% | 8.51% | 3.46% | 2.58% | 14.29% | 4.90% | 43.50% | 15.17% | 1.90% | 11,642.0 |
| 2012 | 7.12% | 8.55% | 4.04% | 2.28% | 12.99% | 4.68% | 44.05% | 14.86% | 1.44% | 12,822.9 |
| 2013 | 8.39% | 7.54% | 2.85% | 1.97% | 16.15% | 4.40% | 42.83% | 14.60% | 1.28% | 13,680.6 |
| 2014 | 5.54% | 8.16% | 3.59% | 2.12% | 17.07% | 4.34% | 43.10% | 14.77% | 1.32% | 14,416.7 |
| 2015 | 7.79% | 9.22% | 3.58% | 2.01% | 16.26% | 4.30% | 41.05% | 14.37% | 1.42% | 15,141.1 |
| 2016 | 8.76% | 11.24% | 4.10% | 2.05% | 15.41% | 4.46% | 38.17% | 14.37% | 1.43% | 15,983.8 |
| 2017 | 8.32% | 11.72% | 4.23% | 2.26% | 14.94% | 4.40% | 39.01% | 13.78% | 1.35% | 16,430.9 |
| Average | 7.68% | 7.63% | 2.68% | 2.72% | 13.28% | 6.73% | 38.36% | 18.98% | 1.94% | 9269.9209 |

*Source:* SIFMA Database

*Table 1.4* Nominal value of bond outstanding in EURO region issued by governments and other institutions (in EURO billions)

Bond Outstanding in EURO Region (in EURO Billions)

| Month-Year | Total Economy | MFIs | FIs | Non-FIs | Central Govt. | Other General Govt. |
|---|---|---|---|---|---|---|
| Dec-00 | 7237.2 | 2777.3 | 374.5 | 426.8 | 3542.4 | 116.1 |
| Dec-01 | 7778.9 | 2990.3 | 485.2 | 513.5 | 3649.0 | 141.0 |
| Dec-02 | 8194.1 | 3129.8 | 590.4 | 507.8 | 3759.2 | 206.9 |
| Dec-03 | 8847.4 | 3383.6 | 737.7 | 556.6 | 3921.8 | 247.7 |
| Dec-04 | 9548.2 | 3756.8 | 818.0 | 557.2 | 4109.2 | 307.0 |
| Dec-05 | 10372.4 | 4149.6 | 1011.1 | 576.5 | 4281.2 | 354.0 |
| Dec-06 | 11182.7 | 4596.8 | 1236.6 | 589.8 | 4374.6 | 385.0 |
| Dec-07 | 12156.7 | 5087.1 | 1552.7 | 633.0 | 4486.2 | 397.6 |
| Dec-08 | 13508.9 | 5306.5 | 2213.5 | 689.7 | 4877.6 | 421.6 |
| Dec-09 | 15257.0 | 5410.6 | 3155.5 | 788.6 | 5432.5 | 469.8 |
| Dec-10 | 15835.9 | 5282.7 | 3215.0 | 838.7 | 5944.8 | 554.7 |
| Dec-11 | 16482.4 | 5564.4 | 3202.5 | 859.9 | 6230.5 | 625.1 |
| Dec-12 | 16699.8 | 5445.0 | 3329.6 | 918.4 | 6315.9 | 690.9 |
| Dec-13 | 16417.7 | 4928.9 | 3223.1 | 987.6 | 6597.6 | 680.4 |
| Dec-14 | 16449.0 | 4591.9 | 3288.5 | 1052.9 | 6822.7 | 693.1 |
| Dec-15 | 16518.8 | 4303.1 | 3432.4 | 1122.0 | 6958.9 | 702.4 |
| Dec-16 | 16638.7 | 4212.9 | 3368.7 | 1245.5 | 7108.1 | 703.5 |
| Dec-17 | 16592.7 | 4079.4 | 3296.1 | 1260.1 | 7257.3 | 699.8 |
| **Average** | **13095.47** | **4388.71** | **2140.62** | **784.70** | **5314.97** | **466.48** |

*Source*: European Central Bank Database

in un-listed securities. European markets have several trading platforms, like EUROMTS and EUREX-BOND, efficiently providing trading solutions to all such OTC trades.

### Japanese debt market

Japan raises significant amount of debt capital, offering a wide range of financial tools to meet a range of issuer and investor requirement, to finance government expenditures and to meet the financing requirement of other non-government entities. Domestic credits, debts and equity financing are roughly estimated to 48, 37, and 15% respectively of the total domestic finance requirement in Japan. This figure ensures that the debt market in Japan is equally important, like domestic credit, to the government and non-government entities to meet their financing requirements. Various types of securities traded in the Japanese market include: central government securities, local governments bonds, government agency bonds, local public corporation bonds, local governments agency bond, corporate bonds (e.g. straight corporate bonds, ABS and convertible bonds), bank debentures, and non-resident bonds. Out of roughly USD 10,200 billion (210% of Japan's GDP) of outstanding debt in Japan's local currency bond market during 2017, the government and non-government debts respectively captured 93% (196% of Japan's GDP) and 7% (14% of Japan's GDP). The recent data on the share of government debts with respect to Japan's GDP shows that it is almost 10% higher than the annual average, depicting significant growth in the government debt market, and a relative fall in the corporate debt market (from an annual average of 16% to 14% in 2017). At the same time, out of roughly USD 11,100 billion trading in Japanese secondary debt market during 2017, more than 99% of the trades happened in government securities, exhibiting a liquid secondary market mostly for the government. securities, which is almost consistent over the years, as reflected from the annual average figures (99.50%). The central bank, general governments, banks, financial and non-financial institutions, foreign investors and others, including households, are the major participants in Japanese debt market. Even if banks capture the maximum share in government debts (annual average of 30%), this share is showing a decreasing trend (from 42% in 2010 to 17% in 2017). This gradual fall in the banks holding in government securities is supplemented by a continuous rise in the share of the central bank (from less than 9% in 2010 to 41% in 2017). The share of contractual savings institutions (e.g. insurance, pension funds, mutual funds, etc.) and other holders, including foreign and retail holders, mostly remains the same, respectively in the range of 22 and 16%.

### Republic of Korea's debt market

Before the Asian financial crisis in the late 1990s, the Korean bond market comprised mostly corporate bonds, as experienced from the fact that there is almost an equal share (36–37%) from the domestic credit and debt market in Korea to meet the financing needs of the Korean economy. But during the financial crisis in 1998, the IMF bailout prompted the Korean government to encourage the Govt. bond market. Accordingly, primary dealers (PDs) were introduced in 1999, and the inter-dealer market (IDM) was opened in the Korea Exchange (KRX). The Korean bond exchange market is comprised of the inter-dealer market and the retail market. Bonds publicly offered in the Korean market include Government securities, Municipal bonds, Special bonds (monetary stabilization bond [MSB], bank bonds and other financial bonds), corporate bonds and ABS. The over-the-counter (OTC) market accounts for almost 80% of the Korean bond market.

Korea is one of the few economies where, out of roughly USD 2000 billion (125% of Korea's GDP) of total outstanding domestic debts, the non-government debt captures almost 60% (74% of the GDP), followed by the government debt with a share of 40% (51% of GDP) during 2017. Despite several deficiencies present in the Korean corporate bond market, it has experienced a remarkable growth, especially after the 1997 financial crisis. Among all possible variants of fixed income instruments available, the market for ABS is one of the important attractions of the Korean debt market. Like the European market, even if most of the securities are listed in the Korean stock exchange, more than 95% of trades in bonds take place over-the-counter. Even if the Korean secondary bond market experienced liquidity constraints because of the strong presence of institutional investors, most preferring a buy-and-hold investment strategy, several initiatives have contributed to building greater depth and liquidity in in the market, which can be experienced from the percentage share of government and non-government debts respectively to the tune of 73 and 27% of the total trading volume in the secondary domestic debt market during 2017.

## Malaysian debt market

The Malaysian bond market is one of the most developed and vibrant bond markets in the East-Asian region and is the largest local currency bond market in the Association of Southeast Asian Nations (ASEAN). The remarkable development of the Malaysian bond market has largely been achieved through the exceptional growth of corporate bonds and *Sukuk*[3] markets. Malaysia's well-developed government bond market is complemented by a sizeable corporate bond market. The market also offers a wide range of instruments, considering the fact that it has the largest *Sukuk* market in the world. *Sukuk*, or Islamic bonds which are issued on Islamic principles, play a major role in Malaysia's capital market development.

The total outstanding domestic debt market volume of USD 318 billion (95% of Malaysian GDP) during 2017 is shared by 57% (50% of Malaysian GDP) in government debts and 43% (45% of Malaysian GDP) in non-government debts. The secondary debt market in Malaysia shows a higher trading volume of 83% for government debts and 17% for non-government debts during 2017, showing a growth in the corporate bond trades (from an annual average of 11%). The nature of bond market and its development over the years in ASEAN economies may be captured through the statistics given in the following tables (Table 1.5 to 1.6).

## Debt markets in India

The Indian debt market is one of the largest in Asia. The total size (total debt outstanding) of the domestic government debt market in India is approximately close to INR 5,049,107 crore (i.e. USD 701.26 Billion at an USD/INR exchange rate of 72), stood at 33.30% of India's GDP, during 2016–17. The government securities. (central and state) are the most dominant category of debt markets and form a major part (roughly 70%) of the market in terms of market capitalization, while approximately 30% of the market capitalization goes to non-government securities (PSU's, Bank/FI,

*Table 1.5* Local currency bond outstanding in ASEAN economies

| Economy | Year | Govt. Security | Corporate Bond | Total (USD billions) | Economy | Year | Govt. Security | Corporate Bond | Total (USD billions) |
|---|---|---|---|---|---|---|---|---|---|
| China | 2010 | 78.84% | 21.16% | 3054.03 | Malaysia | 2010 | 58.99% | 41.01% | 246.55 |
| | 2011 | 73.56% | 26.44% | 3453.29 | | 2011 | 59.84% | 40.16% | 263.19 |
| | 2012 | 68.16% | 31.84% | 4067.8 | | 2012 | 59.89% | 40.11% | 326.93 |
| | 2013 | 65.59% | 34.41% | 4684.14 | | 2013 | 58.45% | 41.55% | 312.05 |
| | 2014 | 63.25% | 36.75% | 5272.17 | | 2014 | 58.63% | 41.37% | 315.53 |
| | 2015 | 65.08% | 34.92% | 6248.47 | | 2015 | 54.66% | 45.34% | 260.58 |
| | 2016 | 69.77% | 30.23% | 7128.86 | | 2016 | 54.28% | 45.72% | 260.2 |
| | 2017 | 72.39% | 27.61% | 8739.49 | | 2017 | 52.32% | 47.68% | 317.86 |
| | Avg. | 69.58% | 30.42% | 5331.00 | | Avg. | 57.13% | 42.87% | 288.00 |
| Hong Kong | 2010 | 53.34% | 46.66% | 163.3 | Philippines | 2010 | 88.00% | 12.00% | 73.11 |
| | 2011 | 53.75% | 46.25% | 168.48 | | 2011 | 87.14% | 12.86% | 77.31 |
| | 2012 | 52.66% | 47.34% | 177.49 | | 2012 | 87.06% | 12.94% | 99.12 |
| | 2013 | 55.73% | 44.27% | 194.66 | | 2013 | 86.49% | 13.51% | 99.48 |
| | 2014 | 56.37% | 43.63% | 194.23 | | 2014 | 83.53% | 16.47% | 104.26 |
| | 2015 | 57.38% | 42.62% | 208.49 | | 2015 | 82.90% | 17.10% | 101.48 |
| | 2016 | 58.11% | 41.89% | 236.19 | | 2016 | 81.70% | 18.30% | 98.17 |
| | 2017 | 60.48% | 39.52% | 244.04 | | 2017 | 81.38% | 18.63% | 109.83 |
| | Avg. | 55.98% | 44.02% | 198.00 | | Avg. | 84.78% | 15.23% | 95.00 |
| Indonesia | 2010 | 88.03% | 11.97% | 106.62 | Singapore | 2010 | 60.97% | 39.03% | 169.08 |
| | 2011 | 85.21% | 14.79% | 109.59 | | 2011 | 62.10% | 37.91% | 190.65 |
| | 2012 | 82.80% | 17.20% | 111.31 | | 2012 | 61.31% | 38.69% | 230.81 |
| | 2013 | 83.34% | 16.66% | 107.6 | | 2013 | 61.40% | 38.60% | 243.71 |
| | 2014 | 85.43% | 14.57% | 123.49 | | 2014 | 60.09% | 39.91% | 243.83 |
| | 2015 | 85.73% | 14.27% | 126.94 | | 2015 | 56.68% | 43.32% | 227.85 |
| | 2016 | 85.77% | 14.23% | 162.57 | | 2016 | 57.45% | 42.55% | 232.31 |
| | 2017 | 84.49% | 15.51% | 184.22 | | 2017 | 61.13% | 38.87% | 271.57 |
| | Avg. | 85.10% | 14.90% | 129.00 | | Avg. | 60.14% | 39.86% | 226.00 |

**Japan**

| Year | | | |
|------|------|------|------|
| 2010 | 90.51% | 9.49% | 11,718.41 |
| 2011 | 90.94% | 9.06% | 12,707.99 |
| 2012 | 91.52% | 8.48% | 11,656.31 |
| 2013 | 92.13% | 7.87% | 9987.4 |
| 2014 | 92.42% | 7.58% | 8969.55 |
| 2015 | 92.65% | 7.35% | 8928.16 |
| 2016 | 93.04% | 6.96% | 9631.54 |
| 2017 | 93.22% | 6.78% | 10,212.1 |
| Avg. | 92.05% | 7.95% | 10,476.00 |

**Thailand**

| Year | | | |
|------|------|------|------|
| 2010 | 81.44% | 18.56% | 224.63 |
| 2011 | 80.78% | 19.23% | 225.34 |
| 2012 | 79.35% | 20.65% | 278.48 |
| 2013 | 77.68% | 22.32% | 275.11 |
| 2014 | 75.06% | 24.94% | 281.32 |
| 2015 | 74.86% | 25.14% | 277.87 |
| 2016 | 73.11% | 26.88% | 302.96 |
| 2017 | 72.67% | 27.34% | 346.25 |
| Avg. | 76.87% | 23.13% | 276.00 |

**Korea**

| Year | | | |
|------|------|------|------|
| 2010 | 42.83% | 57.17% | 1149.15 |
| 2011 | 41.47% | 58.53% | 1229.01 |
| 2012 | 38.90% | 61.10% | 1470.97 |
| 2013 | 38.16% | 61.84% | 1641 |
| 2014 | 41.18% | 58.82% | 1702.82 |
| 2015 | 40.68% | 59.32% | 1719.51 |
| 2016 | 41.01% | 58.99% | 1713.72 |
| 2017 | 40.95% | 59.05% | 2019.77 |
| Avg. | 40.65% | 59.35% | 1581.00 |

**Vietnam**

| Year | | | |
|------|------|------|------|
| 2010 | 75.88% | 24.18% | 16.25 |
| 2011 | 80.77% | 19.23% | 18.41 |
| 2012 | 91.11% | 8.93% | 25.41 |
| 2013 | 93.94% | 6.06% | 31.52 |
| 2014 | 96.07% | 3.93% | 41.46 |
| 2015 | 94.79% | 5.21% | 41.04 |
| 2016 | 94.06% | 5.94% | 43.96 |
| 2017 | 93.44% | 6.56% | 47.29 |
| Avg. | 90.01% | 10.01% | 33.00 |

*Source:* AsianBondsOnline

Table 1.6 Selected bond market characteristics in ASEAN economies

| Economy | Year | Bond Outstanding in Percentage of GDP | | | Bond Outstanding as per Maturity | | | | Trading Volume in Secondary Market | | |
|---|---|---|---|---|---|---|---|---|---|---|---|
| | | Govt. (% GDP) | Corporate (% GDP) | Total (% GDP) | 1–3 years (% of Total) | 3–5 years (% of Total) | 5–10 years (% of Total) | >10 years (% of Total) | Govt. Bonds (%) | Corporate Bonds (%) | Total (USD billions) |
| CN | 2017 | 49.77 | 18.98 | 68.75 | 26.73 | 29.18 | 35.46 | 8.63 | 93.04 | 6.96 | 2280.88 |
| | Average | 37.64 | 16.47 | 54.11 | 28.73 | 23.67 | 33.85 | 13.75 | 76.24 | 23.76 | 2400.734 |
| HK | 2017 | 43.34 | 28.32 | 71.66 | 61.52 | 13.44 | 22.93 | 2.11 | | | |
| | Average | 38.96 | 30.60 | 69.56 | 55.75 | 19.06 | 20.67 | 4.52 | | | |
| ID | 2017 | 15.53 | 2.85 | 18.38 | 16.53 | 14.28 | 28.15 | 41.04 | 89.17 | 10.83 | 74.15 |
| | Average | 12.64 | 2.21 | 14.84 | 16.28 | 12.26 | 27.97 | 43.49 | 93.02 | 6.98 | 59.00875 |
| JP | 2017 | 196.27 | 14.26 | 210.54 | 31.92 | 13.85 | 23.40 | 30.82 | 99.74 | 0.26 | 11115.06 |
| | Average | 187.93 | 16.17 | 204.10 | 32.22 | 16.75 | 24.50 | 26.52 | 99.51 | 0.49 | 11328.17 |
| KR | 2017 | 51.02 | 73.57 | 124.59 | 31.70 | 14.88 | 24.46 | 28.97 | 72.87 | 27.13 | 465.98 |
| | Average | 48.09 | 70.33 | 118.42 | 39.80 | 20.10 | 20.44 | 19.67 | 78.53 | 21.47 | 603.7688 |
| MY | 2017 | 49.72 | 45.32 | 95.04 | 24.24 | 21.01 | 31.73 | 23.03 | 83.30 | 16.70 | 39.82 |
| | Average | 55.22 | 41.39 | 96.61 | 26.75 | 23.86 | 34.19 | 15.20 | 88.69 | 11.31 | 79.17 |
| PH | 2017 | 28.19 | 6.45 | 34.64 | 20.26 | 20.74 | 22.84 | 36.17 | | | |
| | Average | 30.56 | 5.46 | 36.02 | 17.76 | 16.14 | 27.37 | 38.73 | | | |
| SG | 2017 | 49.59 | 31.53 | 81.11 | 25.70 | 20.54 | 29.78 | 23.98 | | | |
| | Average | 46.28 | 30.70 | 76.98 | 27.44 | 19.35 | 29.83 | 23.38 | | | |
| TH | 2017 | 53.04 | 19.95 | 72.99 | 29.69 | 19.17 | 18.61 | 32.52 | 94.33 | 5.67 | 145.75 |
| | Average | 53.15 | 16.16 | 69.31 | 36.71 | 18.12 | 22.62 | 22.56 | 96.93 | 3.07 | 139.15 |
| VN | 2017 | 20.03 | 1.40 | 21.43 | 32.14 | 27.00 | 16.38 | 24.47 | | | |
| | Average | 17.52 | 1.77 | 19.29 | 48.19 | 30.15 | 13.60 | 8.06 | | | |

*Source:* AsianBondsOnline

and corporate bonds). Even if India boasts of a world-class equity market, its bond market segment is still emerging and is mainly dominated by government securities. Even if the government bond market in India captures a significant position of its GDP, the value of corporate bond (bonds issued by FIs and corporate entities) outstanding in India account for not more than 20.00% of its GDP, compared to Korea (74%), Malaysia (45%), Singapore (32%), Hong Kong (28%), China (19%), Thailand (20%), Japan (14%) during end of 2017 (*as per the figures given by AsianBondsOnline*).

### Government debt market in India

Government securities are tradable instrument issued by the central government or the state government, acknowledging the government's obligation to make the payment of interim coupons at a fixed interval (e.g. in every 6 months), and/or to make the final payment of the principal amount at the maturity, without any possibility to default in either of its dues or obligation. Government securities broadly can be of two types: Short term, usually with an original maturity of less than 1 year and commonly known as *Money Market Instruments*, and long term, usually more than of 1-year maturity and known as *Capital Market Instruments*. Money market instruments issued by the central government are known as Treasury bills, having three different maturities: 91 days, 182 days, and 364 days. On the other hand, long-term securities issued by the government of India (GOI) are called as *Dated Securities* (with a maximum maturity of 40 years). Other than T-bills and dated securities, in order to meet the temporary cash requirement of the government, GOI also issues a new short-term instrument, similar to T-bills but with a maturity of less than 91 days, known as *Cash Management Bills* (CMBs). State governments of different states in India also issued long-term bonds or dated securities, commonly known as *State Development Loans* (SDLs, mostly with 10-years of maturity). Besides dated securities, the government of India also issues several savings instruments (e.g. savings bonds, national savings certificates (NSCs), etc.), or special securities (e.g. oil bonds, Food Corporation of India bonds, fertilizer bonds, power bonds, etc.) with a guarantee from the GOI.

### Non-government securities/corporate bond market in India

Like government agencies, corporate borrowers may also issue debt securities to meet their financing requirement. The corporate bond market, an alternative to bank financing, provides a substitute means of long-term resources to corporations. The size and growth of this market depends upon several factors, including financing patterns of companies. A liquid corporate bond market can play a crucial role in supporting economic development as it supplements the banking system to meet the requirements of the corporate sector for long-term capital investment and asset creation.

It provides a stable source of finance when the equity market is volatile. Corporate bond markets can also help firms, reducing their overall cost of capital by allowing them to tailor their asset and liability profiles. The non-government debt market, with its significant and meaningful presence, also helps an economy to overcome or to withstand a market downturn by spreading the risk to a wide range of investors, instead of concentrating the same within the banking industry, which would otherwise be the case if the majority of corporate financing were done through bank credit.

Undoubtedly, the equity market in India has experienced an incredible growth over the last few decades and has significantly contributed to the GDP of the economy. In regard to the bond market, the government securities market in India is reasonably well developed in comparison with other developed economies, but the same is not true in case of non-government securities market. The insufficient development of the corporate bond market in India is clearly reflected through the substantial financing gap in corporate sectors, especially for infrastructure development, a crucial factor for maintaining and enhancing overall growth of an economy.

Presently, the corporate debt market in India is in its infancy both in terms of market participation and owing to many structural inadequacies. While the primary corporate debt market issuance has been significant, most of these were accounted for by public sector financial institutions and relatively very small amounts of funds are raised by manufacturing and other service industries through this market. Most of them are again issued on a private placement basis to institutional investors. The low level of activity in corporate bonds in secondary markets in India is due to the fact that the market is dominated by a limited number of players and inadequate disclosure about the securities which are issued mainly through private placement route. There is very little retail interest in corporate debt due to the institutional structure of the market. Corporate bonds in India are normally issued by public sector undertakings (e.g. Rural Electrification Corporation – REC, Karnataka Power Corporation Limited – KRCL, National Thermal Power Corporation – NTPC); state-level undertakings (e.g. Power Transmission Corporations, Power Finance Corporation, Road Transport Corporation); municipal bodies; public or private sector banks (State Bank of India, Bank of Baroda, Punjab National Bank, Bank of India, Union Bank of India, HDFC Bank, etc.); non-banking finance companies (e.g. Tata Capital, Reliance Capital); all India financial institutions (e.g. Infrastructure Development Finance Company – IDFC, Export-Import Bank – EXIM, National Bank for Agricultural and Rural Development – NABARD); private sector entities (e.g. Reliance Industries, Tata Motors, ACC); and housing finance companies (e.g. Housing Development Finance Corporation – HDFC, National Housing Bank – NHB). Non-government entities can also issue debt instruments with different ranges of maturities and with different features. Short-term money market instruments issued by banks and corporate entities are respectively known as certificates of deposit or commercial papers.

### Primary debt market in India (government vs. non-government debts)

The primary market enables the government as well as non-government or corporate entities in raising the required capital to meet their financing requirements. A well-developed primary market is very important for the prosperity of an economy.

The primary debt market in India consists of securities issued by the government (both central and state) and various non-government entities, including public and private sector undertakings, banks, NBFCs, etc. The total market borrowings from the government (central and state) through the bond market during 2016–17 is roughly USD 167 billion, which is the highest since 2010–11, as indicated in the following table (Table 1.7). Even if central government borrowing has come down over the years, state government borrowing has experienced an increasing trend, almost by USD 14 billion from 2015–16 to 2016–17.

Similarly, if the share of government and non-government entities in the primary market in India is considered together, as reflected in the following table, the total primary issuance by the government is significantly larger than the total primary issuance by the non-government entities over the years, excepting the year 2016–17. The Indian corporate bond market has experienced a significant growth, both in terms of issuance in the primary market and secondary market turnover during 2016–17, as exhibited in the following table (Table 1.8).

The percentage share of different types of non-government issuers in the primary market in India over the last few years, as captured in the following table (Table 1.9), can also be taken into consideration to understand the presence of different types of issuers and their trend over the years in the primary non-government debt market in India. Among two major non-government issuers, public sector financial institutions and private sectors (NBFC and others), the table clearly exhibits a downward trend in the share of issuance of the former and an increasing trend in the issuance of debt securities by the private sector, possibly reflecting less dependence on bank credit and more interest on market borrowing in India.

*Table 1.7* Market borrowings of central and state governments

| Issuer/ Securities | Gross Borrowings (USD Billion) | | | | | | |
|---|---|---|---|---|---|---|---|
| | 2010–11 | 2011–12 | 2012–13 | 2013–14 | 2014–15 | 2015–16 | 2016–17 |
| Central Govt. | 108 | 117 | 127 | 117 | 122 | 112 | 109 |
| State Govt. | 23 | 31 | 33 | 33 | 39 | 44 | 58 |
| Total | 131 | 148 | 160 | 150 | 161 | 156 | 167 |

*Source*: RBI Database; NSE Indian Securities Market Review

*Table 1.8* Indian debt market – selected indicators

| Issuer/Securities | Amount Raised From Primary Market (USD Billion) | | | | | Turnover in Secondary Market (USD Billion) | | | | |
|---|---|---|---|---|---|---|---|---|---|---|
| | 2012–13 | 2013–14 | 2014–15 | 2015–16 | 2016–17 | 2012–13 | 2013–14 | 2014–15 | 2015–16 | 2016–17 |
| Government | 160 | 150 | 161 | 156 | 167 | 2,209 | 2,715 | 2949 | 108 | 116 |
| Corporate/ Non-Govt. | 68 | 52 | 72 | 78 | 111 | 37 | 37 | 47 | 154 | 222 |
| Total | 227 | 202 | 233 | 234 | 278 | 2,246 | 2,752 | 2996 | 262 | 338 |

*Source*: Indian Securities Market Review; Prime Database, RBI and NSE.

*Table 1.9* Percentage break-up in corporate bond issuance in India by issuer type

| Issuer Type | 2012–13 | 2013–14 | 2014–15 | 2015–16 | 2016–17 |
|---|---|---|---|---|---|
| Public Sector Financial Institutions | 52.46% | 53.49% | 54.13% | 40.56% | 27.27% |
| State Financial Institutions | 1.53% | 0.55% | 0.20% | 0.00% | 0.04% |
| Public Sector Undertakings | 11.24% | 11.53% | 7.22% | 6.56% | 9.55% |
| State Level Undertakings | 2.44% | 1.36% | 1.40% | 4.85% | 2.91% |
| Private Sector-NBFC & Others | 32.33% | 33.07% | 37.05% | 48.04% | 60.23% |

*Source*: Prime Data Base; Indian Securities Market Review

*Table 1.10* Instrument-wise % of traded volumes in government securities in India

| Period (Quarter) | % of Traded Volumes | | |
|---|---|---|---|
| | G-Secs. | SDL | T-Bills |
| 2014–15Q4 | 90 | 2.5 | 7.5 |
| 2015–16Q1 | 89.1 | 2.2 | 8.7 |
| 2015–16Q2 | 87.6 | 3.1 | 9.2 |
| 2015–16Q3 | 86.3 | 3.9 | 9.7 |
| 2015–16Q4 | 88.7 | 3.9 | 7.4 |
| 2016–17Q1 | 89.1 | 3.5 | 7.4 |
| 2016–17Q2 | 91.8 | 3.3 | 4.9 |
| 2016–17Q3 | 91.9 | 2.9 | 5.3 |
| 2016–17Q4 | 84.8 | 5.3 | 9.9 |

*Source*: CCIL; Indian Securities Market Review

### Secondary market trading in government securities

Once the debt securities are issued in the primary market, the same are thereafter eligible for trading in the secondary market. Even if the primary market in India, both for government and non-government securities, is reasonably developed, both in terms of number of securities issued and the total size or volume of issue, the same is not the case for the secondary debt market, as observed from the following Table (Table 1.10).

The above table clearly indicates the tradability of dated securities issued by the government of India, especially in comparison with similar securities issued by various state governments, and also short-term instruments issued by the central government. As far as the tradability of government securities of various maturity segments are concerned, it is again clear from the following table that securities of all possible tenors/maturities are not equally tradable/liquid in the Indian market. As expected from the continuous trend of popularity in the 10-year benchmark, government securities maturing within 7–10 years experience maximum liquidity (quarterly average of 44.50% of total trades), followed by securities with a residual maturity in the range

*Table 1.11* Historical tenor-wise traded volumes in government securities in India

*Tenor-wise Distribution of Traded Volumes in Government Securities in India*

| Periods | Total Trade (INR crores) | <5y | 5–7y | >7–10y | >10–15y | 15–20y | >20–40y |
|---|---|---|---|---|---|---|---|
| 2014–15Q4 | 2,285,028 | 13.31% | 1.40% | 42.90% | 38.58% | 1.10% | 2.72% |
| 2015–16Q1 | 2,280,747 | 16.97% | 1.52% | 49.97% | 27.99% | 1.48% | 2.07% |
| 2015–16Q2 | 2,154,202 | 11.44% | 2.52% | 66.64% | 16.03% | 1.28% | 2.09% |
| 2015–16Q3 | 1,931,992 | 14.68% | 13.13% | 41.27% | 26.09% | 2.59% | 2.23% |
| 2015–16Q4 | 2,190,725 | 25.30% | 9.41% | 31.67% | 30.29% | 1.65% | 1.69% |
| 2016–17Q1 | 2,827,816 | 20.44% | 10.72% | 31.96% | 34.10% | 1.31% | 1.47% |
| 2016–17Q2 | 5,205,353 | 9.94% | 8.75% | 36.66% | 42.32% | 1.15% | 1.18% |
| 2016–17Q3 | 4,592,866 | 7.45% | 8.27% | 45.49% | 36.11% | 1.30% | 1.38% |
| 2016–17Q4 | 2,572,437 | 12.34% | 6.44% | 53.29% | 25.15% | 1.05% | 1.74% |
| Quarterly Avg. | 2,893,463 | 14.65% | 6.91% | 44.43% | 30.74% | 1.43% | 1.84% |

*Source:* CCIL, Indian Securities Market Review, NSE, 2017

of 10–15 years (roughly around 31%), and securities maturing in less than 5 years (around 14.50%). The following table (Table 1.11) clearly exhibits the fact that long-term securities are hardly traded in the Indian market.

### Secondary market trading in non-government securities

Even if there are a limited number of corporates that primarily prefer to tap the debt market, at least through private placements, there happens to be hardly any significant trading volume in the Indian secondary market, neither through recognized exchanges nor through OTC. The secondary corporate bond market in India is still in the very nascent stage, compared to other developed economies worldwide. Predominance of private placements in the Indian corporate bond market might possibly lead to narrow down the scope for secondary market trading. Further, whatever public issues come in the market, they hardly are used for trading in the secondary market. Once a large corporate issues some securities, some trading is observed for a few days, especially due to the existence of the underwriter as the market maker. Most of such bonds are purchased by investors through the primary issue, with the intention of holding till maturity, leading to a severe problem of illiquidity in the secondary market.

With the initiatives taken by SEBI during April 2007, launching trading and reporting platforms in BSE and NSE, the market has experienced an efficient price discovery and reliable clearing and settlement of all trading. Even if these platforms exist, the majority of the trading happens through OTC, where trades are executed mostly through brokers. Irrespective of the platform through which trades are executed, all trades, including from the OTC segment, need to be mandatorily reported on an available reporting

*Table 1.12* Growth of secondary corporate bond market in India

*Secondary Market Trade in Corporate Bonds*

| Year | No of Trades | Volume of Trades (INR Billion) |
|---|---|---|
| 2007–2008 | 19079 | 959 |
| 2008–2009 | 22683 | 1,482 |
| 2009–2010 | 38230 | 4,012 |
| 2010–2011 | 44060 | 6,053 |
| 2011–2012 | 51533 | 5,938 |
| 2012–2013 | 66383 | 7,386 |
| 2013–2014 | 70887 | 9,708 |
| 2014–2015 | 75791 | 10,913 |
| 2015–2016 | 70123 | 10,224 |
| 2016–2017 | 88495 | 14,707 |

*Source*: SEBI; Indian Securities Market Review

platform within a specific time frame. All commercial banks, primary dealers, NBFCs, and selected All India Financial Institutions (AIFIs) were specially required to report their OTC secondary market transactions in the FIMMDA platform within 30 minutes from the closure of the deal, and the settlement of the same needed to be reported within 1 trading day from the completion of the settlement. But according to an *RBI circular dated 24 February 2014, reporting of a secondary market transaction in corporate bonds in the FIMMDA platform has been discontinued with effect from 1 April 2014. Therefore, presently, NSE and BSE are the only two trading and reporting platforms for corporate bonds in India.*

Even if the secondary market trading for non-government securities in India is still insufficient, especially in comparison with the developed markets, but there is no doubt that India is experiencing a growth in its corporate bond market (both in terms of total number and volume of trades), as exhibited in the following table (Table 1.12).

Corporate bond trading in India is again depending largely on the credit quality of the bonds, as reflected through the credit rating, given by the external rating agencies. Concentrations of trading volume in various corporate debt issues, depending on their credit rating, are reported in the following table (Table 1.13). The table exhibits the fact that the highest concentration is always observed in bonds with highest safety (an annual average of more than 60%), followed by high safety (between 10–15% over the years). Whereas trading in securities below a AA rating just account for roughly below 10% of the total trading volume over the years, at the same time, the following table also supports the growth of the Indian corporate bond market in recent years, especially for relatively low rated securities, where the presence of low rated (below AA) securities just got doubled in 2015–16, from less than 10% to more than 20%.

*Table 1.13* Rating profile of the corporate bond issuer in India

| Rating | 2012–13 | 2013–14 | 2014–15 | 2015–16 | Average |
|--------|---------|---------|---------|---------|---------|
| AAA | 64.32% | 69.90% | 64.79% | 56.05% | 63.77% |
| AA+ | 15.47% | 13.55% | 13.97% | 11.05% | 13.51% |
| AA | 7.21% | 5.64% | 5.63% | 6.09% | 6.14% |
| AA- | 4.69% | 3.47% | 6.09% | 5.93% | 5.05% |
| Others | 8.32% | 7.44% | 9.52% | 20.88% | 11.54% |

*Source*: Prime Date Base; Indian Securities Market Review

## Issuance and settlement of debt securities in India

### Primary issuance and settlement in government securities

Dated securities, issued by both central and state governments, are primarily issued through auctions, conducted by the Reserve Bank of India. At the beginning of every half of the financial year viz. April – September and October – March, a half yearly *Auction Calendar* is issued in case of central government dated securities, indicating the amounts, the period within which the auction will be held, and the tenor of the security, which is made available on the Reserve Bank's website. The government of India and the RBI also issue regular press releases to announce the issuance a few days before the date of issue.

Government securities, state development loans, and T-bills are regularly sold by RBI through periodic public auctions. While 91-day T-bills are auctioned every week on Wednesdays, 182-day and 364-day T-bills are auctioned every alternate week on Wednesdays. The Reserve Bank of India issues a quarterly calendar of T-bill auctions, which is available at the RBI website.

Auctions are conducted electronically on the Reserve Bank of India's Core Banking Solution (*E-Kuber*) System, facilitating the trading members to electronically submit their bids (both competitive and non-competitive bids) for primary issuance of securities or T-bills. An investor can submit more than one competitive bid at different yields/prices. The Government Stocks are issued by crediting the subsidiary general ledger account (SGL) of parties maintaining such an account with RBI or in the form of a stock certificate. All non-members, including non-scheduled urban cooperative banks, can participate in the primary auction through scheduled commercial banks or primary dealers by maintaining a security or gilt account with them. Auctions for government securities are normally either yield based or price based.

### Yield based auction

When the government issues a new security, the same is based on yield based auction. In this type of auction, RBI announces the issue size or notifies the

*Table 1.14* Process of arriving at cut-off yield in primary auction

*Details of Bids Received in the Ascending Order of Bid Yields*
*(Notified Amount = 1000 Crore, Maturity = 10 Years, say 28 July 2024)*

| Bid No. | Bid Yield | Amount of Bid (Rs. Crore) | Cumulative Amount (Rs. Crore) | Securities Allotted (Rs. Crore) |
|---|---|---|---|---|
| 1 | 8.20% | 200 | 200 | 200 |
| 2 | 8.25% | 250 | 450 | 250 |
| 3 | 8.30% | 200 | 650 | 200 |
| 4 | 8.35% | 200 | 850 | 200 |
| 5 | 8.40% | 150 | 1000 | 90 |
| 6 | 8.40% | 100 | 1100 | 60 |
| 7 | 8.42% | 150 | 1250 | 0 |
| 8 | 8.45% | 100 | 1350 | 0 |
| 9 | 8.47% | 150 | 1500 | 0 |
| 10 | 8.50% | 100 | 1600 | 0 |

*Source*: Self-created by the author

amount and the tenor of the paper to be auctioned. The bidders submit bids in terms of the yield (up to 2 decimal points, e.g. 8.40% or 8.83%) at which they are ready to buy the security. Bid yields are arranged in ascending order and Treasury will choose the cut-off yield at which the aggregate demand (notified amount) exhausts the net supply under competitive bids, as shown in the following table (Table 1.14). Bidders, quoted at or below the cut-off yield, become successful, and quoted above the cut-off yield, are unsuccessful and therefore get rejected.

The issuer would get the notified amount by accepting bids up to 5, where the notified amount of Rs.100 crore gets exhausted. Since the bid number 6 also is at the same yield, bid numbers 5 and 6 would get the allotment on pro-rata basis, so that the notified amount is not exceeded. In the above case, the 5th and 6th bidder respectively would get Rs.90 crore {balance left after allotment till bid 4, i.e. Rs.150 crore × (bid amount by the 5th bidder at the cut-off yield, i.e. Rs.150 crore/total bid amount at the cut-off yield of 8.40%, i.e. Rs.250 crore)} and Rs.60 crore. Bid numbers 7 to 10 are rejected as their bid yields are higher than the cut-off yield of 8.40%.

### Price based auction

This method of auction is normally used in case of reissue of existing government securities. In this type of auction, RBI announces the issue size or notified amount and the tenor of the paper to be auctioned, as well as the coupon rate of the concerned security, which is already fixed through the yield-based auction when the security was issued for the first time in the market. The bidders here submit bids in terms of the price. First of all, the cut off price is decided where the total notified amount gets exhausted. Bids at a lower price than the cut-off price are rejected and bids higher than the cut-off price are accepted.

This price-based auction can be again *Uniform-Price/Single-Price* based Auction (*French Auction*), and *Variable/Multiple-Price* based auction (*Dutch Auction*). In a uniform-price based auction, all the successful bidders are required to pay for the allotted quantity of securities at the same auction cut-off price, irrespective of the actual price quoted by all of them. On the other hand, in a multiple-price based auction, the successful bidders are required to pay for the allotted quantity of securities at the respective price they have bid, irrespective of the auction cut-off price.

Suppose the government may decide to reissue one of its existing securities (8.40 GS 2024), offering a coupon of 8.40% p.a. and a residual maturity of 9.5 years, for a notified amount of another 1000 crore. The details of the price-based auction of this existing security are as follows:

*Table 1.15* Process of arriving at cut-off price in primary auction

*Details of Bids Received for 8.40 GS 2024 in the Descending Order of Bid Prices (Notified Amount = 1000 Crore, Maturity = 9.5 Years)*

| Bid No. | Bid Price | Amount of Bid (Rs. Crore) | Implicit Yield | Cumulative Amount (Rs. Crore) | Securities Allotted (Rs. Crore) |
|---------|-----------|---------------------------|----------------|-------------------------------|--------------------------------|
| 1 | 105.50 | 200 | 7.58% | 200 | 200 |
| 2 | 105.25 | 250 | 7.61% | 450 | 250 |
| 3 | 105.00 | 200 | 7.65% | 650 | 200 |
| 4 | 104.75 | 200 | 7.69% | 850 | 200 |
| 5 | 104.56 | 150 | 7.71% | 1000 | 90 |
| 6 | 104.56 | 100 | 7.71% | 1100 | 60 |
| 7 | 104.25 | 150 | 7.76% | 1250 | 0 |
| 8 | 104.00 | 100 | 7.80% | 1350 | 0 |
| 9 | 103.85 | 150 | 7.82% | 1500 | 0 |
| 10 | 103.50 | 100 | 7.87% | 1600 | 0 |

*Source*: Self-created by the author

Since the total notified amount of Rs.1000 crore towards the reissuance of 8.40 GS 2024 gets exhausted at a price of Rs.104.56/-, as shown in the Table 1.15, the cut-off price will be the same and any bid above the cut-off price will be accepted, and any bid lower than the cut-off price will be rejected. Accordingly, bid number 7 to 10 will be rejected. Now, similar to the yield-based auction system, all bidders who quote the same cut-off price will get the allotment on a pro-rata basis, as shown in the above table. Depending upon the nature of the price-based auction (uniform or multiple price), the allotment of securities will be made to the successful bidders, either uniformly at the single cut-off price of Rs.104.56/- or at the actual prices (equal to or higher than the cut-off price) quoted by the respective bidders.

The auction conducted by RBI for such reissuance is usually a variable price auction (*French Auction*). At times, as part of some signalling, RBI may indicate a cut-off (a higher price or lower yield) wherein the bids may not result in the issue being fully subscribed. In such case, the issue may partially or fully devolve on RBI. These securities may be later sold by RBI to market based on market movements of rate.

### Underwriting in auction

Being an important part of the primary auction of securities, underwriting requires primary dealers to quote their bids, indicating the amount they are willing to underwrite, and the fee expected, one day prior to the auction. Upon examination of the bid on the basis of the market condition, the auction committee of RBI takes a decision on the amount to be underwritten and the fee to be paid. In case of devolvement, the bids put in by the PD's are set off against the amount underwritten while deciding the amount of devolvement. In case the auction is fully subscribed, the PDs need not subscribe to the issue unless they have bid for the same.

### Different types of bidding

The processes of bidding are of two types: competitive and non-competitive. In *Competitive Bidding*, an investor is expected to bid at a specific price/yield and successful bidders are allotted securities accordingly. Competitive bids are generally made by well-informed investors such as banks, financial institutions, primary dealers, mutual funds, insurance companies, and other major FIs. The minimum bid amount in case of a competitive bidding is Rs.10,000/- and in multiples of Rs.10,000/- thereafter. Multiple bidding is also allowed, wherein an investor is allowed to give several bids at various prices/yield levels.

Unlike well-informed and major institutional investors, small institutional and retail investors, wishing to invest in government securities but at a smaller level, may not have the sufficient skills and expertise to participate in the auction process through competitive bidding. In order to facilitate such a requirement, the government has started the scheme of *Non-Competitive Bidding* in dated securities, through which co-operative banks, RRBs, firms, companies, corporate bodies, institutions, provident funds, HUFs, trusts, individuals, etc. get an opportunity to enter into the government securities market in India. Under this scheme, eligible investors may apply for a certain amount of securities in an auction without quoting a specific yield/price. Such bidders are finally allotted securities at the weighted average yield/price quoted by different competitive bidders in the auction. Five percent of the total notified amount in any issue is reserved for such non-competitive bidding. Participants eligible for non-competitive bidding, except co-operative banks and RRBs, are required to hold a gilt account with a bank or a PD. A non-competitive bidding scheme is also available for state government securities (SDLs), with a cap of 10% of the notified amount at the aggregate level, and 1% of the notified amount at an individual level, as against Rs.2 crore in case of securities issued by the central government.

### Settlement of primary issuance of government securities in India

Once the allotment process in the primary auction is finalized, the successful participants are advised to pay the consideration amounts to the government on the date of settlement. The settlement cycle for a dated security (central and state governments) and T-bills auction is T+1. On the date of settlement, the fund accounts of the participants are debited by their respective consideration amounts and their securities accounts (SGL accounts), or the gilt account maintained with the banks or PDs in case of transaction through non-competitive bids, are credited with the amount of securities that they were allotted.

### Issuance and settlement in non-government securities

Non-government debt instruments issued by different entities in India can be issued through two different processes: public issue and private placements.

### Public issue

A public issue is an offer made to the public in general to subscribe to the bonds. In public issue, the bond issuer, before issuing the bond, has to issue a prospectus containing details about the company and the bonds to be issued. After the public issue, bonds are listed on recognized stock exchange(s) in India. In the case of a listed bond, the investor can buy the bonds in the public issue at face value or from the exchange at a premium or discount. Public issue, even if it involves a more stringent process, provides better publicity for the issuance and therefore offers the advantage of wider investor participation and thus a better diversification of risk in the financial system.

### Private placements

The majority of the primary issuances in the non-government securities market takes place through private placements. Private placement is broadly defined as the process of issuing securities or invitation to subscribe securities by a company to a selected group of persons, as per the relevant sections of the Indian Companies Act. As per Section 42 of Indian Companies

Act 2013, "The offer of securities or invitation to subscribe securities, shall be made to not more than 200 persons in the aggregate in a financial year (excluding qualified institutional buyers and employees of the company being offered securities under ESOP)". Because of its flexibility and operational ease for the bond issuers, it continues to be a preferable option for them to raise money from the market in India.

Even if the issuers of non-government securities or corporate debts in India prefer to go for private placements rather than public issues, SEBI has made it mandatory to report all the trades in corporate bonds, even if issued through private placements, at least in one of the platforms, viz. NSE, BSE, and FIMMDA. Even if there is a growing trend in the total size of public issues in the Indian corporate debt market over the years, the same is still very insignificant when it is compared with the issue size through private placements, exhibiting the relative popularity of private placements among the bond issuers in India.

*Settlement for secondary market trading in debt securities in India*

Secondary market transactions in government securities in India are generally settled through the member's securities/current accounts maintained with the RBI, with delivery of securities and payment of funds being done on a net basis. The Clearing Corporation of India Limited (CCIL), considered as the major settlement agency for trade in government securities in India, guarantees settlement of trades on the settlement date by becoming a central counterparty to every trade through the process of *Novation*.[4]

Delivery versus payment (DvP) is the mode of settlement of securities wherein the transfer of securities and funds happens simultaneously, eliminating the settlement risk in such transactions. There are three types of DvP settlements in India: DvP-I, DvP-II, and DvP-III.

*DvP-I:* The securities and funds legs of any transaction are settled on a gross basis, where the settlements occur separately for each transaction, without netting the payables and receivables of the participant.

*DvP-II:* This method follows two different approaches to settle the security leg and the fund leg. The securities are settled on gross basis, and the funds are settled on a net basis, wherein the funds payable and receivable of all transactions of a party are netted to arrive at the final payable or receivable position which is finally settled.

*DvP-III:* In this method, both the securities and the funds legs are settled on a net basis and only the final net position of all transactions undertaken by a participant is settled.

As far as the settlement of secondary market transaction in corporate bonds in India through the stock exchanges (NSE and BSE) is concerned, the respective clearing houses opened by the stock exchanges, National Securities Clearing Corporation Limited (NSCCL) of NSE and Indian Clearing Corporation Limited (ICCL) of BSE, undertake the entire settlement activity. Any OTC trades in corporate bonds also have to be mandatorily cleared and settled through these clearing houses. Settlements of corporate bond trades shall be carried out between Monday to Friday for three settlement cycles viz., T+0, T+1, and T+2.

## Various participants in the debt securities market

There are a number of participants who take part in the debt market, either in the form of issuer or investor of debt securities, or in the form of some intermediaries, or regulatory bodies, as briefed in the following table (Table 1.16). Issuers issue debt securities to borrow money to fund their capital or liquidity needs. Investors invest their savings or capital by purchasing debt securities in primary and secondary markets. Intermediaries assist buyers and sellers by making markets, underwriting, and providing risk management services. And finally, regulators ensure a well and healthy functioning of the market within the stipulated norms and conditions. The following table clearly exhibits the key players in the fixed income markets under three broad categories.

### Major investors in Indian debt market

Both institutional and retail investors can participate in the Indian debt (government and non-government securities) market. Institutional participants include: banks (Reserve Bank of India, commercial banks, co-operative banks, regional rural banks), primary dealers, insurance companies, mutual funds, provident funds, pension funds, etc. Investors can also be classified as general investors, like commercial and retail banks, government institutions, private corporations, as well as retail investors. Investors falling

*Table 1.16* Key players in fixed income markets

| Issuers | Intermediaries | Investors |
| --- | --- | --- |
| Central Government & Its Agencies | Investment Banks | Government & Sovereign Wealth Funds |
| State Government and Municipalities | Commercial Banks | Pension Funds |
| Commercial Banks | Dealers | Insurance Companies |
| Corporations (Public & Private) | Primary Dealers | Mutual Funds |
| Foreign Institutions | Interdealer Brokers | Commercial/Investment Banks |
| Special-Purpose Vehicles (SPVs) | Credit Rating Agencies | Asset Management Firms |
| | | Households |

*Source*: Self-created by the author

*Table 1.17* Holding pattern (%) in government securities in India

Holding Pattern (%) in Government Securities

| Types of Investors | 2014 | 2015 | 2016 | Average |
|---|---|---|---|---|
| Commercial Banks | 42.77 | 43.59 | 40.92 | 42.43 |
| Non-Bank PDs | 0.34 | 0.35 | 0.28 | 0.32 |
| Insurance Companies | 21.02 | 21.9 | 22.55 | 21.82 |
| Mutual Funds | 1.68 | 2.52 | 1.96 | 2.05 |
| Co-operative Banks | 2.57 | 2.71 | 2.63 | 2.64 |
| Financial Institutions | 0.73 | 0.68 | 0.86 | 0.76 |
| Corporates | 1.12 | 0.86 | 1.05 | 1.01 |
| Foreign Portfolio Investors | 3.62 | 3.68 | 3.13 | 3.48 |
| Provident Funds | 7.47 | 7.11 | 6.24 | 6.94 |
| RBI | 14.5 | 12.07 | 14.61 | 13.73 |
| Others | 4.18 | 4.51 | 5.77 | 4.82 |
| State Governments | 0 | 0 | 1.8 | 0.60 |

*Source*: RBI

under asset pooling industries, such as government pension schemes, private pension funds, insurance companies, mutual funds, and asset management companies, etc. also have significant exposure in the debt market in India. These investors can again be domestic as well as foreign investors. The following table (Table 1.17) highlights different types of investors in the government securities market and their holding pattern over the years.

## Banks

Among all possible institutional investors, banks are the largest group of investors in this market, but are highly regulated by RBI, both in terms of investment in government securities and investment in corporate bonds. The investment portfolio of Indian banks mainly consists of various debt instruments, and equities and related products. The overall investment portfolio again is classified as held till maturity (HTM), held for trading (HFT), and available for sale (AFS). HFT and AFS taken together are known as the trading portfolio, the securities under which are intended to be held by banks for trading (buy-sell) intentions, depending upon their requirements and market movements. Several debt instruments again are classified as SLR approved and non-SLR securities. The Reserve Bank of India has defined several restrictive norms for banks in regard to investment in SLR approved and non-SLR securities. All dated securities issued by the central government and various state governments, and Treasury bills issued by the central government, are categorized as SLR approved securities. All other debt securities issued by the government under a special programme (e.g. oil bonds, fertilizer bonds, etc.) and all securities issued by non-government entities are called non-SLR securities. Commercial banks, in order to meet the minimum statutory requirement, such as the statutory liquidity ratio (SLR), which is presently 18.75% (as of September 2019) of banks net demand and time liabilities (NDTL), are required to invest only in SLR approved securities, which they can park in a special portfolio called held till maturity (HTM), that avoid any kind of revaluation of securities and, therefore, the price risk for the investors. Investment in SLR approved securities can also be a part of banks' trading portfolios (held for trading and available for sale). Compulsory investment in these SLR approved securities is primarily to ensure sufficient demand of government securities in the domestic market so that government can raise money from the market to meet its deficit and also to ensure sufficient liquidity in the banking system of the economy. All primary (urban) co-operative banks, rural co-operative banks, and regional rural banks are also supposed to maintain the minimum SLR and therefore required to invest a part of their NDTL in such SLR approved securities.

The above table (Table 1.17) shows the strong presence (more than 40% of the total outstanding till 2016) of scheduled commercial banks in the government securities market in India over the years. The percentage share of cooperative banks in holding government securities ranges between 2.5 to 3.0%.

### Central bank (RBI in India)

Being the central bank of the country, the Reserve Bank of India also holds a reasonable share (around an annual average of 14% over the years) in the outstanding volume of government securities market in India. But the purpose of holding a significant percentage of such securities by the central bank is neither for any statutory requirement nor for any investment. The central bank participates in this market essentially to manage the liquidity condition in the Govt. securities market.

This liquidity management can be done through a practice called *Open Market Operation* (OMO). OMO is an activity conducted by the central bank to buy or sell government securities from/to the open market, with an objective to adjust the rupee liquidity conditions in the market on a durable basis. Central banks use these operations as the primary means of implementing monetary policy. In presence of an excess liquidity in the market, RBI resorts to sale of securities, thereby sucking out the rupee liquidity. On the other hand, in case of a tight liquidity condition, the RBI can purchase/buy-back securities from the market, thereby injecting liquidity into the market.

Unlike the system of long-term liquidity management through OMO, the RBI may also like to enable the same on a day-to-day basis. This short-term liquidity is generally managed by the RBI through a process called *Liquidity Adjustment Facility* (LAF), where commercial banks and PDs can avail liquidity whenever required against the government securities posed with the RBI as collateral. Under the same LAF system, it is also possible to park excess funds with the RBI in case of excess liquidity in the system.

*Insurance companies, provident and pension funds, and mutual funds*

Other than banks, insurance companies, provident funds, and pension funds also invest in short- and long-term debt instruments issued by government (central and state) and non-government entities. But these institutions are mostly interested into long-term products, due to their long-term investment requirements, in order to meet long-term liabilities. As a result, most of the central government securities with very long maturities are subscribed by these institutions. The above table (Table 1.17) shows the significant average percentage share of insurance companies (roughly around 22%) and provident funds (roughly at 7%) in total outstanding government securities in India as on a certain date. These institutions are also subject to several restrictions imposed by their respective regulators.

As per the consolidated investments made by all the life insurance companies in India during 2016–17, as released by the IRDA, the regulatory body of the insurance industry in its Annual Report 2016–17, the majority of the total investable funds (almost 65%) are parked in central government, state government, and other approved securities. Investment in other approved instruments, including shares, corporate bonds/debentures, mutual funds, derivatives, investment in subsidiaries, etc., made by the life insurers in India during the same period also account for more than 30% of their total investments. The majority of these actually went to debt instruments issued by several non-government entities. Similarly, the consolidated investments made by the non-life insurers in India in the central government, state government, and other approved securities during 2016–17 is almost 37% of their total investments, followed by another 30% in other approved instruments including non-government debt products. Therefore, the insurance industry in India also holds a significant share of the debt (government and non-government) market, and therefore can play a vital role for the development of the entire debt market in India.

*Foreign institutional investors (FIIs)*

Foreign Institutional Investors[5] (FIIs) play a very important role in the growth of the capital market of an economy. FIIs always try to invest in several securities in several markets worldwide to diversify their massive portfolio. As in the case of many economies, FIIs also play a significant role in the development of the Indian capital market as well. But the way they are involved in the equity segment is not the same as observed in the debt segment, especially the corporate debt segment. India has been gradually liberalizing its capital account to foreign participation. One of the key such liberalization measures is the gradual increase of FII's limit in the debt markets. FII's limits, both for government securities (Dated securities and T-Bills) and corporate bonds

*Table 1.18* Quarterly investments of foreign portfolio investors in debt securities in India

*FPI Investments in Debt Securities (INR billion)*

| Period (Quarter) | Govt. Securities | Corporate Bonds | SDL |
|---|---|---|---|
| Mar-14 | 847 | 840 | 0 |
| Jun-14 | 1052 | 915 | 0 |
| Sep-14 | 1396 | 116 | 0 |
| Dec-14 | 1503 | 1438 | 0 |
| Mar-15 | 1529 | 1890 | 0 |
| Jun-15 | 1516 | 191 | 0 |
| Sep-15 | 1528 | 1869 | 0 |
| Dec-15 | 1617 | 1793 | 36 |
| Mar-16 | 1657 | 1689 | 45 |
| Jun-16 | 1645 | 1613 | 39 |
| Sep-16 | 1804 | 1704 | 15 |
| Dec-16 | 1508 | 1621 | 11 |

*Source*: NSDL; Indian Securities Market Review, NSE

(listed non-convertible debentures, corporate bonds, commercial papers, etc.), are prescribed separately and are non-fungible.

SEBI registered foreign institutional investors (FIIs), qualified foreign investors (QFIs), and long-term investors may purchase, on a repatriation basis, government securities and non-convertible debentures (NCDs)/bonds issued by an Indian company subjected to the terms and conditions as stipulated and updated by RBI and SEBI from time to time.

Unlike in the US Treasury securities market, where the last few years' share of Foreign and International Investors stood at more than 48% of the total outstanding (annual average since 2000 stood at 43.77%), the similar figure, as described in the above table (Table 1.17), in Indian government securities market is quite insignificant and stood at an annual average of 3.5% only. The following table (Table 1.18) also exhibits the investment of foreign portfolio investors in various segments of the debt securities market in India over the last three years.

## Retail investors

India's gross domestic savings, presently at almost 30% of India's GDP during March 2017, where the contribution of the household sector, majorly intermediated by banks and other non-banking financial entities, in total savings during the said period stood at roughly 61% (16.3% of India's GDP). At the same time, the financial savings of India's households as a percentage of total household savings is roughly around 40%. As far as the financial savings of India's households are concerned, the same is broadly invested in bank deposits (46% in 2016–17), small savings schemes, provident and pension funds (9%), mutual funds (12%), and life insurance policies (20% in 2016–17). Retail investors' investment in securities (equity and debts), especially debt securities issued by the government (central and state) and various non-government entities, is relatively very marginal, especially in comparison with the developed economies like the US, where the share of individuals' in the total outstanding volume of the US Treasury market is roughly around 7–8%.

Major factors driving the quantum of retail investment in the debt market segment are tax benefits, returns, liquidity, and safety. If we look into the investment needs of individuals in emerging economies like India, the needs are adequately met through bank deposits and the small savings schemes offered by other government agencies. Besides this, participating in the equity and debt market through several intermediaries also makes such investment channels uncomplicated for the general public who otherwise may like to park a part of their savings in those instruments. On the other hand, most of common people may be ready to accept a comparatively lower return from their investment, but what they would prefer is to ensure that their investment is reasonably safe and guaranteed.

### Intermediaries in Indian debt market

In addition to the end participants in the debt markets (the issuers and the investors), there is another group of participants who facilitate the entire process, starting from the issuance of the debt securities, followed by investing and trading in such security. These intermediaries are involved in the issuance, sale, trade, and settlement of deals towards debt securities in both primary and secondary markets. Some of the major important intermediaries in the debt market are described in the following section.

### Primary dealers

Intermediaries like primary dealers (PDs) are involved in the issuance, sale, and trade of debt securities in both primary and secondary markets. Primary dealers assume a major role in government securities markets. They are normally required to tender for all primary issues and also to deal with central banks in open market operations from time to time. PDs play a very crucial role in market making for government securities in most of the economies by way of underwriting the issue of securities. PDs can also take a leading role in market making for corporate bonds as well, at least for securities qualifies for minimum criterion. The presence of these intermediaries makes the debt market more liquid.

In the year 1995, the Reserve Bank of India (RBI) introduced the system of primary dealership only in the government securities market, selecting independent entities to undertake primary dealer activity. Subsequently, in the year 2006–07, in order to broad base the PD system in India, banks were permitted to undertake the primary dealership business departmentally, and the standalone PDs were permitted to diversify into business activities other than the core PD business, subject to certain conditions. The broad objectives of the primary dealer in India are to:

1   Strengthen the infrastructure in the government securities market in India in order to make it vibrant, liquid, and broad based.
2   Ensure development of underwriting and market making capabilities for government securities outside the RBI, so that the central bank of the country can be gradually free from these functions.
3   Improve the secondary market trading system, contributing to better price discovery, enhancing liquidity and turnover, and encouraging voluntary holding of government securities amongst a wider investor base.

Presently there are 7 Standalone PDs and 14 (with the recent addition of YES Bank in the list) Bank PDs in India dealing with underwriting and trading in government debt instruments, both T-Bills and Dates Securities. At this time, the average participation of the non-bank PDs in the government securities market is roughly around 0.30% of the total outstanding.

### Rating agencies

Debt securities issued by non-government entities are considered to be riskier than government securities, as reflected by the credit rating: internal rating or external rating offered by external credit rating agencies. There can be global as well as domestic rating agencies. The rating of a security exhibits the credit worthiness of the issuer and/or a particular issue and is generally used by investors to take investment decisions. The process of arriving at a rating, considering all possible factors related to the credit worthiness of a corporate, varies from one agency to other, as possibly reflected from differences in the rating of the same corporate. Even if there may be some inconsistency in the credit rating provided by more than one rating agency, the same if duly mapped, should not be significantly different. A typical rating methodology uses financial reports as a starting point for the assessment of credit worthiness of the debt issuer.

Some of the global rating agencies include: Standard & Poor, Fitch; whereas CRISIL, ICRA, and CARA are three major domestic rating agencies in India. In order to facilitate the development of a vibrant primary market for corporate bonds in India, the relevant rating and issuance norms for corporate bonds keep getting amended by the concerned regulatory bodies. In order to reduce the cost of issuance of debt instruments, issuers can get their rating from only one credit rating agency as against the earlier stipulation of not less than two rating agencies. Ratings assigned to various corporate issues are broadly divided into five categories: Highest Safety (AAA), High Safety (AA), Adequate Safety (A), Moderate Safety (BBB), and

Non-Investment Grade (lower than BBB). Such rating classification can be further extended by allotting a positive or negative sign in it (such as AA+, AA, AA–, etc.). Trading in corporate bonds, especially in countries like India, is mainly concentrated in the bonds with highest safety (AAA), and the high safety (AA) issues, majorly due to insufficient liquidity in low-rated securities even within the investment grades.

## Clearing Corporation of India Limited (CCIL)

The Clearing Corporation of India Ltd. (CCIL), set up in 2001 primarily as the clearing agency for government securities in India and started operating from February 2002, provides an institutional infrastructure for the clearing and settlement of transactions in government securities, money market instruments, and also for foreign exchange and other related products. It acts as a central counter party (CCP) for all transactions in government securities by positioning itself between two counterparties by way of becoming the nearest counterparty to both the buyer and seller of the actual transaction. All outright trades, undertaken on the NDS-OM platform and in the OTC market, are cleared and settled through the CCIL. After receiving the trade information, CCIL works out participant-wise net obligations on both the securities leg and the funds leg, reflecting the payable/receivable position of the gilt account holders against their respective custodians. Accordingly, the settlement file, containing the net position of both the participants, is forwarded to the RBI, where settlement takes place by simultaneous transfer of funds and securities under the delivery versus payment (DvP) system. The CCIL also provides the service of guaranteeing the settlement of all trades in govdernment securities in India by collecting margins from all participants and maintaining the *Settlement Guarantee Fund.*

## Fixed Income Money Market and Derivatives Association (FIMMDA) and Financial Benchmark India Pvt. Ltd. (FBIL)

The Fixed Income Money Market and Derivatives Association of India (FIMMDA), an association of scheduled commercial banks, public financial institutions, primary dealers, and insurance companies, dealing with the money (T-bills, CPs, CDs, and other products), securities (Bonds), and derivatives markets, was incorporated as a company under section 25 of the Companies Act, 1956 on June 3, 1998. FIMMDA presently (as on October 2018) has a list of 120 members representing all major institutional segments of the market, including the nationalized banks in India (21 banks), private sector banks (21 banks), foreign banks (31 banks), financial institutions (6 FIs), insurance companies (18 ICs), all primary dealers (7 Standalone PDs), and small finance companies (12 SFCs).

The FIMMDA represents market participants and aids the development of the bond, money, and derivatives markets. It acts as an interface with the regulators, including RBI, SEBI, MoF, IMF, World Bank, etc. on various issues impacting the functioning of these markets. It also undertakes developmental activities, such as the introduction of benchmark rates and new derivatives instruments, etc. FIMMDA releases rates of various government securities, corporate bonds, and securitized papers that are used by the market participants for the valuation of investment portfolios held by the banks and PDs. FIMMDA also plays a constructive role in the evolution of best market practices by its members so that the market as a whole operates transparently as well as efficiently.

The FBIL, jointly owned by FIMMDA, FEDAI, and IBA, was formed in December 2014 as a private limited company under the Companies Act 2013, majorly aiming to develop and administer financial benchmarks. *Financial Benchmarks* are indices, values, or reference rates used for the purpose of pricing, settlement, and valuation of financial contracts relating to money market, government securities, and foreign exchange in India.

REGULATORY BODIES (RBI & SEBI)

The regulator for central and state government securities is the Reserve Bank of India. A corporate operating in India may be classified into two categories on the basis of regulatory jurisdiction – listed and non-listed. All corporates by and large are administered by the Companies Act 1956 and the regulatory administration is carried out by Department of Company Affairs (DCA), Ministry of Finance. Listed corporates are overseen by the Securities and Exchange Board of India (SEBI) through listing agreements and exchanges. Listed corporates are required to follow elaborate corporate governance principles, accounting standards, disclosure norms, and continuous disclosure statements incurring additional cost. Unlisted corporates, however, enjoy regulatory arbitrage over listed corporates.

Keeping in view the rapidly evolving global developments, the Reserve Bank of India has given sufficient focus on how to ensure the development of financial markets in India. Well-developed financial markets are not only important for the critical role they play in the transmission of monetary policy, but they also facilitate price discovery in the market, which leads the market to grow significantly and contributes to the overall growth of the economy. The Reserve Bank of India pursues its efforts to impart sufficient liquidity in the government (both central and state) securities market, while trying to diversify the investor base, so that the systemic risks can be successfully spread across the economy.

As far as the corporate debt market in India is concerned, it is primarily regulated by two institutions: RBI and SEBI, with the active involvement of the Insurance Regulatory and Development Authority (IRDA). Being the monetary authority in India, one of the primary interests of RBI is to ensure an adequate flow of credit in the economy. In addition, SEBI's outlook is to ensure the sufficient development and regulation of non-government securities' markets in India, keeping the investors' interests protected. Since insurance companies are one of the largest investors in the corporate debt market in India, it is essential to involve the IRDA in reforming the supply side of the corporate bond market initiated by RBI and SEBI.

## Bibliography

### Reports

*Creating Green Bond Markets – Insights, Innovations, and Tools from Emerging Markets*. Prepared by IFC and the Climate Bonds Initiative (CBI) for the SBN Green Bond Working Group, October 2018. Washington, DC. Source: www.ifc.org/wps/wcm/connect/55e5e479-b2a8-41a6-9931-93306369b529/SBN+Creating+Green+Bond+Markets+Report+2018.pdf?MOD=AJPERES

*Debt Capital Markets 2017 Review and 2018 Forecast*; Société Générale – Corporate and Investment Banking, November 2017. Paris. Source: https://cib.societe generale.com/uploads/tx_bisgnews/SG_CIB_-DCM_2017_Review_and_2018_Forecast.pdf

*Development of Corporate Bond Market in India*; Report of the Working Group, Reserve Bank of India, August 2016. India. Source: www.pfrda.org.in/writeread data/links/corporate%20bond%20market984d464f-b7cb-4cd1-a193-a79b 685bb115.pdf

*Government Securities Market in India – A Primer*; Reserve Bank of India, July 2018. India. Source: https://rbi.org.in/scripts/PublicationsView.aspx?id=16413

*Indian Debt Market*; CRISIL Year Book, 2018. India. Source: file:///C:/Users/mukherjee/Downloads/crisil-yearbook-on-the-indian-debt-market-2018.pdf

*Indian Securities Market: A Review*; National Stock Exchange of India Limited (NSE), Vol. XX, 2017. India. Source: www.nseindia.com/content/us/ismr_full2017.pdf

*India's Debt Markets: The Way Forward*; Asia Securities Industry & Financial Markets Association (ASIFMA), July 2017. Hong Kong. Source: www.asifma.org/wp-content/uploads/2018/05/asifma-indias-debt-markets-the-way-forward1.pdf

### Research articles/working papers

Mukherjee, K. N. (2012). *Corporate Bond Market in India: Current Scope and Future Challenges*. Working Paper. United States. https://papers.ssrn.com/sol3/papers.cfm?abstract_id=2171696

### Data sources

Asia Securities Industry and Financial Markets Association (ASIFMA): www.asifma.org/publications/

Asian Bonds Online (ABO): https://asianbondsonline.adb.org/data-portal/

Clearing Corporation of India Limited (CCIL): www.ccilindia.com/Research/Statistics/Pages/Infovendors.aspx

European Central Bank (ECB): www.ecb.europa.eu/stats/financial_markets_and_interest_rates/html/index.en.html

Fixed Income Money Markets and Derivatives Association (FIMMDA): http://fimmda.org/modules/content/?p=1009

National Stock Exchange of India Limited (NSE): https://nseindia.com/products/content/derivatives/irf/irf.htm

Reserve Bank of India (RBI):
https://dbie.rbi.org.in/DBIE/dbie.rbi?site=statistics

Securities and Exchange Board of India (SEBI): www.sebi.gov.in/sebiweb/home/HomeAction.do?doListing=yes&sid=4&ssid=32&smid=0

Securities Industry and Financial Markets Association (SIFMA): www.sifma.org/resources/archive/research/

## Notes

1 Fixed Income Securities are of different types, depending on their issuers (Govt. and Non-Govt. entities) and different features (such as types of coupons, embedded options, taxability, currency, issuing market, etc.).

2 MFIs are central banks, resident credit institutions as defined in community law, and other resident financial institutions whose business is to receive deposits and/or close substitutes for deposits from entities other than MFIs and, for their own account (at least in economic terms), to grant credits and/or make investments in securities.

3 SUKUK is an Islamic Financial Certificate, similar to a bond, issued in compliance with Islamic religious laws, where investors carry an ownership in the issuing firm/entity, not any claim of interest, as in the case of bonds.

4 "Novation" is a netting scheme, adopted by the CCIL, where the clearing corporation interposes as central counterparty upon acceptance of the trades by replacing the existing obligations with the new obligations. Under this novation scheme, the bilateral relationship between the two participants/members is substituted with bilateral contracts between each participant/member and the CCIL, and is generally in effect from the moment a trade is accepted by CCIL for settlement.

5 As per the definition of SEBI, "Foreign Institutional Investor means an institution established or incorporated outside India which proposes to make investment in India in securities". FIIs investment in debt and equity in India are subjected to the prescribed limit set by the concerned regulatory bodies.

# 2 Fixed income instruments
## Various classifications

**Key learning outcomes**

At the end of this chapter, the readers are expected to be familiar with:

- What are the basic features of fixed income or debt securities that make them different from other asset classes in the financial market?
- What types of instruments are available in the fixed income securities market, especially in emerging countries?
- How domestic market issues are different from international market issues.
- How debt instruments are classified as per their important features.
- What kind of securities are issued by the government bodies (central government/state government/municipalities) and non-government entities (banks/PSUs/FIs/NBFCs/corporates)?
- How debt securities are different based on the currency in which they are issued.
- How SLR approved securities are different from non-SLR securities.

## Basic features of fixed income security

All fixed income/debt securities or bonds have some basic features, based on which they are classified under various sub-categories. Analysis of these basic features is very important to understand the complete dynamics of fixed income/debt securities. The following section describes some of the basic features applicable to any type of fixed income security.

### Issuer

The most important feature of a fixed income security is the type of entity/institution which has issued the security in the market. Securities can be broadly issued by supranational organizations (e.g. World Bank, IMF), governments, and non-government entities. Government issuers include the central government, state government, municipal bodies, etc.; whereas, non-government issuers are: banks and other financial institutions, non-banking financial companies, public sector undertakings/entities, and private companies. Fixed income securities or bonds, almost in all markets, are broadly classified based on their issuers. Securities issued by the central government are commonly known as *Government Securities* or *Treasury Bonds*, whereas bonds issued by all other entities other than the government (central and state) are known as *Corporate Bonds*. A list of fixed income securities issued by different types of issuers are given in the following table (Table 2.1).

Risk and return on a fixed income security, finally leading to its demand in the market, largely depends on the issuer of that security. Any security issued by the central government of an economy seems to be completely

*Table 2.1* Example of fixed income securities issued by different types of issuers in India

| Issuer | Fixed Income Security/Bond Details |
|---|---|
| Supranational Organization | *World Bank Green Bond*, issued on 27 May 2016, maturing in 2021, paying a coupon of 5.6%; with a volume of INR 300 Million, JP Morgan as the lead manager. |
| Central Government | *091 DTB 08112018* (ISIN: IN002018X211); 91-Day Treasury Bill (zero coupon) issued by the government of India, maturing on 8 November 2018. |
|  | *7.17% GOI 2028* (ISIN: IN0020180174); Dated Security issued by government of India, paying a coupon of 7.17% p.a., maturing on 8 January 2028. |
| State Government | *8.31% UTTARPRADESH SDL 2025* (ISIN: IN3320150250); Dated Security issued by Uttar Pradesh State Govt., paying a coupon of 8.31% p.a., maturing on 29 July 2025. |
| Bank | *ICICI BANK LIMITED CD 03DEC18* (ISIN: INE090A166Q8); Certificate of Deposit (zero coupon), issued by the ICICI Bank Ltd, maturing on 03-December-2018. |
|  | *7.95% HDFC BANK LIMITED 2026* (ISIN: INE040A08369); Dated Security issued by HDFC Bank Ltd., paying a coupon of 7.95% p.a., maturing on 21 September 2026. |
| Public Sector Undertaking/ Enterprise | *7.54% REC Bond 2026* (ISIN: INE020B08AC9); Dated Security issued by Rural Electrification Corporation Ltd., paying a coupon of 7.54% p.a., maturing on 30 December 2026. |
| Financial Institution | *IFCI-SR54–9.75%-16–7–2030-PVT* (ISIN: INE039A09MD2); Dated Security issued by the IFCI Ltd., paying a coupon of 9.75% p.a., maturing on 16 July 2030. |

(*Continued*)

*Table 2.1* (Continued)

| Issuer | Fixed Income Security/Bond Details |
| --- | --- |
| Non-Banking Financial Company | *8.73% LIC HOUSING FINANCE LIMITED 2018* (ISIN: INE115A07HD4); Dated Security issued by the LIC Housing Finance Ltd., paying a coupon of 8.73%, maturing on 15 May 2018.<br>*HDFC LTD 135D CP 14DEC18* (ISIN: INE001A14TI6); 135 Days Commercial Paper (zero coupon) issued by Housing Development Finance Corporation Ltd., maturing on 14 December 2018. |
| Private Corporates | *8.07% TATA SONS LIMITED 2021* (ISIN: INE895D08600); Dated Security issued by Tata Sons Ltd., paying a coupon of 8.07% p.a., maturing on 5 August 2021. |

*Source*: All tables in this chapter are created by the author unless otherwise stated

risk-free, at least to the domestic investors, and therefore offers a lower return. On the other hand, securities issued by any non-government entities are relatively risky, depending upon their respective credit rating, and therefore may offer some spread above the risk-free return. In India, as per RBI-FIMMDA norms, especially for the valuation purpose, the entire range of fixed income securities are broadly classified into five categories: government securities (securities issued by the central government), state development loans (securities issued by various state governments), securities issued by banks/PSUs/FIs, securities issued by NBFCs, and securities issued by private corporates. Accordingly, the investors, especially those regulated by the RBI, need to analyze their investments in fixed income securities issued by different categories of issuers with different levels of credit risk by looking at the risk of failing in the payment of interim and final dues on time.

## Maturity

Unlike equities, all fixed income securities have a specific life, within which all dues (interim cash flows and final principal) are expected to be settled by the issuers of securities. This fixed life is called Maturity or Tenor of a fixed income security. Maturity, normally expressed in terms of years, is another key feature of fixed income securities. In general, there can be two concepts of maturity related to fixed income securities. One is the *Original Maturity* and the other is *Residual Maturity*.

Maturity is the time gap between the first date when the security is issued in the primary market and the last date when the security is matured and the final due(s) are settled by the issuer. Original maturity is considered to classify fixed income securities into money market products (e.g. Treasury bills, commercial papers, and certificates of deposits with original maturity of less than 1 year) and capital market products (e.g. dated securities with original maturity of more than 1 year). Original maturity of most of the dated securities available in the Indian market is normally in the range of more than 1 year till 40 years. But there are securities with undefined maturity, known as *Perpetual Bonds*. Even if the maturity of such securities is not pre-specified, the market may prefer to consider the last available tenor point of the yield curve, say 40 years, as its maturity, especially to deal with the concerned analytics related to the security.

On the other hand, residual maturity of a fixed income security, on a given trading/settlement/valuation date, refers to the time gap between that specific date and the date when the security matures. In fixed income parlance, maturity of a fixed income product normally refers to its residual maturity. Even if the original maturity of a security remains static during its entire life, the residual maturity continuously reduces as time goes on. Calculation of residual maturity is again based on various day count methods/conventions.[1] There are four such conventions: 30/360, 30/365, Actual/365, and Actual/Actual, applicable to different types of securities, as per the respective market practices. The number of future cash flows due from a fixed income security, and therefore the price/value of the same, the yield/return from the security, and its price sensitivity due to change in interest rates, largely depends upon its residual maturity along with other factors. The traded yield of various dated securities of different residual maturities is generally used to construct the term structure of interest rates or yield curve.

For example, consider the value of a GOI security (*6.79% GS 2029*) on 7 June 2017 that was issued by the government of India on 26 December 2016, and maturing on 26 December 2029. Here, the original maturity of the security is 13 years (time difference between 26 December 2029 and 26 December 2016). The residual maturity of the same security will always be smaller than the original maturity, depending upon the date when the residual maturity is estimated, and therefore continuously reduces as time passes until the maturity date. The residual maturity of the same security again depends upon the applicable market practices in terms of day count method/convention. The residual maturity of 6.79% GS 2029, on 7 June 2017, following different day count methods, is briefed in the following table (Table 2.2).

The above table (Table 2.2) clearly demonstrates that the residual maturity for the same security may vary, maybe in small fraction, depending upon the day count method selected, as per the common market practice in the respective markets.

### Principal value

The principal value, alternatively known as the face value/par value/nominal value/maturity or redemption value, is the amount that the issuer of

*Table 2.2* Residual maturity under different day count methods

| Residual Maturity with Different Day Count Method | Residual Maturity on 7 June 2017 (in Years) | Excel Function Used |
|---|---|---|
| Residual Maturity (Actual/Actual) | 12.5537 | =YEARFRAC(Start Date, Maturity Date, 1 as Day Count Method) |
| Residual Maturity (Actual/360) | 12.7361 | =YEARFRAC(Start Date, Maturity Date, 2 as Day Count Method) |
| Residual Maturity (Actual/365) | 12.5616 | =YEARFRAC(Start Date, Maturity Date, 3 as Day Count Method) |
| Residual Maturity (30/360) | 12.5528 | =YEARFRAC(Start Date, Maturity Date, 4 as Day Count Method) |

a security agrees to repay to the security holder at the time the security is matured. This is the value at which a security is generally issued in the primary market, especially the first time of issuance. The principal or face value of a security can be any amount, as given in the bond indenture. Generally, the face value of a bond (govt. or non-govt.) issued in the Indian market is INR 100. A bond holder gets the coupon on a debt security, always estimated on the principal/face value, irrespective of the price (premium, par, or discount) which is paid to purchase the security from the secondary market.

### Currency denomination

Fixed income securities can be issued in any currency: domestic or foreign. If an issuer based in India wants to tap the domestic market, securities may be preferably issued in Indian Rupees (INR). Here, money will be raised in domestic currency, and payments (interim and final) will also be made in the same currency. Alternatively, a domestic issuer may also issue securities in attractive foreign currencies, like US Dollars, Euros, Pound Sterling, Yen, etc. Due to the lack of sufficient demand in the domestic market, an issuer may prefer to issue bonds in different foreign countries at their respective currencies to tap international investors.

This arrangement is beneficial to both issuer and investors. Issuers with better credit worthiness may end up paying a lower interest, and therefore may reduce their borrowing cost if the prevailing interest rates are relatively lower in the foreign markets in comparison with the domestic interest rates. On the other hand, foreign investors get a natural hedge on their investment against any unfavorable movement in the foreign exchange rate (i.e. currency risk) by way of receiving all (interim and final) cash flows in their respective domestic currencies. But obviously, there is a cost involved to both the issuers and investors with this arrangement. Foreign investors, especially when their domestic interest rates are very low in comparison with the same in the issuer's market, may suffer an opportunity loss. At the same time, natural hedge from the currency risk, enjoyed by the foreign investors, comes by way of transferring the risk in the books of the issuer.

## Coupon

Coupon is the periodic interest that a bond holder/investor (i.e. lender of money) earns for lending money to the bond issuer (i.e. borrower) till the time the final amount (last coupon and principal) is returned back to the lender on or before maturity. The rate at which the periodic coupon is calculated (on the principal amount) and paid is known as the coupon rate or nominal yield. Bonds are generally described with the coupon rate (e.g. 6.79% GS 2029, 8.07% TATA SONS LIMITED 2021). The coupon rate of a bond is generally quoted for a full year but may be paid in different frequency (annually, semi-annually, quarterly, etc.). Coupons are commonly paid on a semiannual basis. The coupon rate may be fixed for the whole life of a bond till its maturity (*Fixed Rate Bond*), or it may vary from period to period, depending upon the prevailing market rate of interest (*Floating Rate Bond*). The coupon rate of a fixed rate bond is decided when the bond is issued in the primary market and remains fixed for its entire life. Whereas, the coupon rate of a FRB or floater is reset at designated dates (known as coupon reset dates) based on some reference rates prevailing in the market, pre-specified in the bond indenture. For example, the government of India has issued an FRB (ISIN: IN0020160084) on 7 November 2016, maturing on 7 November 2024, where the semiannual coupon is based on the prevailing Treasury-bill (182 days) rate as on the reset dates. Even if there are different types of coupons offered in debt securities worldwide, the market is predominantly captured by securities offering a fixed coupon, as described in the following table (Table 2.3).

Even if an FRB offers a variable coupon rate, there may be some restriction in terms of offering a maximum (cap) or minimum (floor) coupon at any reset date. Certain bonds may not offer any periodic coupon, known as *Zero Coupon Bond*, where the earning for the bond holder/investor is the discount in the price which is offered while buying a security which subsequently gets redeemed at par on maturity.

There may be certain security, where the coupon is linked to some inflation index, known as *Inflation Indexed Bond*. These types of security protect the bondholders from the erosion of purchasing power of fixed nominal coupon payments caused by rising inflation. Some securities may offer a fixed coupon, but not till the maturity. There may be a *Step-up* or *Step-down* feature, where the fixed coupon gets revised (up or down) after certain interval(s). Some securities may offer a *Deferred Coupon*, where the issuer may not pay any coupon or may pay a lower coupon for the first few years/periods, and subsequently offer a higher coupon thereafter.

Table 2.3 Instrument-wise outstanding volume in central government securities in top 10 bond markets (2016 figures)

| Year | Type of Security | US | UK | Germany | Brazil | Spain | India | Korea | Canada | Belgium | Australia |
|---|---|---|---|---|---|---|---|---|---|---|---|
| 2010 | Floating rate | 0.00% | 0.00% | 4.86% | 33.82% | 1.68% | 2.38% | | 0.00% | 1.25% | 0.00% |
| | Straight fixed rate | 91.30% | 78.04% | 91.32% | 37.09% | 98.32% | 97.62% | 99.19% | 92.27% | 96.53% | 91.62% |
| | Inflation indexed | 8.70% | 21.96% | 3.56% | 28.52% | 0.00% | 0.00% | 0.81% | 7.73% | 0.00% | 8.38% |
| | **Total (in USD Billion)** | **7080.50** | **1589.26** | **1420.77** | **953.46** | **589.93** | **463.31** | **323.20** | **394.68** | **363.42** | **138.44** |
| 2011 | Floating rate | 0.00% | 0.00% | 9.95% | 31.93% | 1.37% | 1.52% | | 0.00% | 1.23% | 0.00% |
| | Straight fixed rate | 91.21% | 77.58% | 85.82% | 37.53% | 98.63% | 98.48% | 98.98% | 92.48% | 96.62% | 92.06% |
| | Inflation indexed | 8.79% | 22.42% | 3.85% | 29.96% | 0.00% | 0.00% | 1.02% | 7.52% | 0.00% | 7.94% |
| | **Total (in USD Billion)** | **8407.93** | **1780.05** | **1522.61** | **943.42** | **662.57** | **598.68** | **342.42** | **424.67** | **376.08** | **178.08** |
| 2012 | Floating rate | 0.00% | 0.00% | 6.13% | 23.06% | 0.36% | 1.45% | | 0.00% | 1.65% | 0.00% |
| | Straight fixed rate | 90.98% | 76.83% | 88.33% | 40.41% | 99.64% | 98.55% | 98.21% | 92.27% | 96.52% | 92.73% |
| | Inflation indexed | 9.02% | 23.17% | 4.59% | 35.95% | 0.00% | 0.00% | 1.79% | 7.73% | 0.00% | 7.27% |
| | **Total (in USD Billion)** | **9417.12** | **2055.46** | **1557.79** | **923.16** | **837.58** | **542.65** | **397.50** | **452.72** | **400.92** | **229.89** |
| 2013 | Floating rate | 0.00% | 0.00% | 3.41% | 20.59% | 2.47% | 1.14% | | 0.00% | 2.48% | 0.00% |
| | Straight fixed rate | 90.52% | 76.93% | 90.58% | 41.61% | 97.53% | 98.67% | 98.26% | 92.12% | 95.91% | 92.73% |
| | Inflation indexed | 9.48% | 23.07% | 4.51% | 37.22% | 0.00% | 0.19% | 1.74% | 7.88% | 0.00% | 7.27% |
| | **Total (in USD Billion)** | **10262.49** | **2258.40** | **1629.19** | **833.75** | **986.90** | **556.00** | **443.64** | **441.79** | **435.69** | **225.16** |
| 2014 | Floating rate | 1.48% | 0.00% | 2.96% | 20.28% | 2.10% | 0.88% | | 0.00% | 2.54% | 0.00% |
| | Straight fixed rate | 88.76% | 75.38% | 89.94% | 41.18% | 96.21% | 98.95% | 98.35% | 91.69% | 95.72% | 92.53% |
| | Inflation indexed | 9.75% | 24.62% | 5.37% | 37.93% | 1.69% | 0.17% | 1.65% | 8.31% | 0.00% | 7.47% |
| | **Total (in USD Billion)** | **11046.89** | **2238.20** | **1458.84** | **796.45** | **889.52** | **615.88** | **467.10** | **407.60** | **391.23** | **257.41** |

*(Continued)*

Table 2.1 (Continued)

| Year | Type of Security | US | UK | Germany | Brazil | Spain | India | Korea | Canada | Belgium | Australia |
|---|---|---|---|---|---|---|---|---|---|---|---|
| 2015 | Floating rate | 2.81% | 0.00% | 2.49% | 25.03% | 1.10% | 0.52% | | 0.00% | 2.36% | 0.00% |
| | Straight fixed rate | 87.19% | 74.12% | 89.11% | 38.53% | 96.24% | 99.40% | 98.58% | 91.46% | 95.90% | 92.42% |
| | Inflation indexed | 10.00% | 25.88% | 6.38% | 35.73% | 2.66% | 0.08% | 1.42% | 8.54% | 0.00% | 7.58% |
| | **Total (in USD Billion)** | 11677.54 | 2181.25 | 1301.33 | 641.90 | 850.74 | 649.82 | 481.25 | 349.30 | 359.67 | 265.07 |
| 2016 | Floating rate | 2.77% | 0.00% | 2.28% | 30.05% | 0.36% | 1.29% | 0.00% | 0.00% | 1.43% | 0.00% |
| | Straight fixed rate | 86.91% | 74.38% | 89.52% | 35.57% | 96.08% | 98.68% | 98.18% | 91.59% | 96.07% | 92.73% |
| | Inflation indexed | 10.32% | 25.62% | 5.79% | 33.87% | 3.56% | 0.02% | 1.82% | 8.41% | 0.00% | 7.27% |
| | **Total (in USD Billion)** | 12090.28 | 1861.98 | 1245.68 | 898.92 | 853.06 | 684.27 | 502.13 | 385.31 | 361.77 | 299.99 |
| 2017 | Floating rate | 2.74% | 0.00% | 1.77% | 32.86% | NA | NA | 0.00% | 0.00% | 1.26% | 0.00% |
| | Straight fixed rate | 86.65% | 74.05% | 89.26% | 35.88% | 95.14% | NA | 98.37% | 91.78% | 96.16% | 93.29% |
| | Inflation indexed | 10.61% | 25.95% | 6.26% | 30.82% | 4.86% | NA | 1.63% | 8.22% | 0.00% | 6.71% |
| | **Total (in USD Billion)** | 12512.85 | 2105.57 | 1429.43 | 1030.27 | 1032.27 | NA | 602.69 | 444.77 | 414.27 | 388.72 |

*Source:* BIS Statistics

The coupon rate of a bond, fixed or floating, decided at the time of issuing the bond or on any of the coupon reset dates, generally depends upon the market expectation from the respective bond issuers as per their credit worthiness, and also for the respective maturity of the bond. Since there is no doubt in the credit worthiness of the central government of an economy, securities issued by the central government are completely risk-free, and therefore expected to offer the lowest coupon rate for any maturity. Bonds issued by various state governments, even if risk-free, need to offer slightly higher coupons based on the market expectation towards the financial strength and many other parameters of the respective states. Coupon rates applicable to securities issued by non-government organizations/institutions are expected to be with a spread/premium above the coupon rate of similar risk-free bonds, depending upon the issuers' credit worthiness as reflected from their credit rating.

The maturity of the bond may also play an important role to fix the coupon rate. If short- and medium-term securities are more relatively liquid than the long term, the market may expect the illiquidity premium from long-term bonds, leading to a higher coupon for bonds with longer maturities, irrespective of similar credit worthiness. Similarly, the longer the maturity, the higher would be the possibility for a non-government issuer to default in its payment obligations, leading to a higher market expectation. Therefore, if a non-government issuer issues two bonds of similar liquidity but of different maturity, the bond with higher maturity is likely to offer a higher coupon rate, especially to cover the high credit risk.

Coupon rate of a security is very important not only to estimate its market value, but also to understand the sensitivity of its value towards change in interest rates.

## Yield

The coupons of a bond is the nominal return that an investor earns till the maturity and remain fixed. Whereas, the yield of a bond, in simple terms, is the return that the market expects from a specific security at a given point of time, and therefore changes from time to time, depending upon the change in market conditions. There are different concepts of yield in the context of debt securities, but the most common bond yield measure is *Yield to Maturity* (YTM). YTM of a bond is the average return that the market expects from a trade in that security at a given market price. Alternatively, YTM of a bond is the internal rate of return (IRR) from an investment, at the current market price, in that security. There are different yield measures, depending upon the nature of debt securities, discussed separately in subsequent chapters. The yield of a fixed income security is a comprehensive measure to analyze the security, especially for an investor/trader to take an investment/trading decision.

## Debt market instruments: classification

Debt instruments or securities available in the financial market can be presented under different classifications. Such classification can be based on:

1   Markets (domestic or international markets).
2   Features of the debt instrument (e.g. maturity, type of coupons, optionality, convertibility, etc.).
3   Issuing sectors and sub-sectors (resident, central government, state government, municipal bodies, non-government entities, non-resident sector).
4   Currency of debt issue (domestic, foreign currency).
5   Regulatory classification, etc.

### *Classification of debt instruments based on markets*

Debt instruments, irrespective of their nature and properties, can be issued either in the issuer's domestic market or in the international market. This classification allows analyzing the relative attractiveness of the domestic debt market in comparison with the international markets.

This classification is particularly important for emerging market economies and indicates the strength and viability of the economy to raise funds domestically through debt issues. Resident institutions in emerging economies, in the absence of reasonable access to the international markets, generally raise funds in their domestic market. But at the same time, financial liberalization allows financial markets to become more open to foreign issuers and investors. Therefore, many economies attract foreign investors by way of issuing securities in the international markets. This international debt issuance induces inflow of relatively cost-effective foreign capital, leading to facilitate the domestic institutions with a lower borrowing cost, and accordingly may promote economic growth.

Any debt issue can be classified as a domestic market issue depending upon the *Residence of Issuer* or *Location of Issue*. When a resident of an economy issues certain debt products in the same economy, the market for such security, regardless of the currency of the issue, can be classified as domestic market. At the same time, if the location of the issue is important, all debt securities issued in a specific economy, either by residents or non-residents, and irrespective of the currency of issue, can be classified as domestic market issues. Once securities are issued by a resident of an economy, the classification (domestic vs. international) can be broadly based on:

• The recognized exchange (domestic or international) in which the security is listed.
• The availability of a security identification number, an International Security Identification Number (ISIN) with a country code, or a domestic security code.
• The currency (domestic vs. foreign) at which the security is issued.

## Classification of debt instruments based on their feature

Depending on the nature and characteristics (e.g. coupon, maturity, additional features like options, risk, currency, etc.) of the instruments, debt securities can be classified as follows:

### Fixed rate bonds/straight bonds/plain vanilla bonds

These bonds have the coupon rates fixed for their entire life or maturity. Most government bonds are issued as fixed rate bonds. Most of the popular corporate bonds are also of similar type, paying a semi-annual but fixed coupon over their life and the principal at the end of the maturity.

For example: 7.80% GS2020 was issued on 3 May 2010, for a tenor of 10 years maturing on 3 May 2020. Coupons on this security are paid half-yearly at 3.90% (half-yearly payment being the half of the annual coupon of 7.80%) of the face value on November 3rd and May 3rd of each year, till the maturity. Similarly, *7.54% REC Bond 2026* is a corporate bond, paying a fixed coupon rate of 7.54% per annum but payable semiannually, and matures on 30 December 2026.

### Floating rate bonds/floaters

These bonds have a coupon rate that is not fixed throughout the life and varies over time with reference to some benchmark/reference rate of interests, even if the coupons are usually paid semi-annually. These types of bonds may have some floor or cap attached to them, representing that even if the benchmark rate changes by any value, the coupon rate, even if floating, will always lies within the range of floor and cap rate. Some of the well-known benchmark rates used in Indian market are: government of India yield, Mumbai (London) Interbank Offer Rate (MIBOR/LIBOR), call rate, T-bill rate, prime lending rate (PLR), etc.

For example, FRB 2020, issued on 21 December 2009, and maturing on 21 December 2020, paying a semi-annual coupon in every six months depending on some reference rate, is one of the FRB issued by the government of India. In the case of most floating rate bonds issued by the government of India so far, the base/reference rate is the weighted average cut-off yield of the last three 182-day Treasury-bill auctions preceding the coupon re-set date and with a zero initial spread. For example, the last coupon payment date of the above Floating Rate Bond FRB 2020 was 21 June 2018, when the base rate on the bond for the coupon payments was fixed at 6.87%, being the weighted average rate of implicit yield on 182-day Treasury bills during the preceding three auctions. Hence, the coupon rate applicable on 21 June 2018 would be 6.87%.

Unlike in case of a simple floating rate bond or *Floaters*, there are also certain floaters whose coupon rate moves in the opposite direction from the reference rate. These securities are called *Inverse Floaters* or *Reverse*

*Floaters.* Issuers (investors) may like to use this kind of a structure in a rising (falling) interest rate scenario to reduce the cost of raising funds (generate higher return on investment). The coupon of an inverse floater is the difference between a fixed rate and a floating benchmark rate, say MIBOR. Most non-banking finance companies (NBFCs) in India, such as Mahindra and Mahindra Finance, Rabo India Finance, Cholamandalam Finance, and Sundaram Finance, etc. have issued inverse floaters to raise funds. Suppose Hindalco, one of the largest aluminum makers in India, wants to float a Rs.100 crore bonds issue, with a "AAA" rating from CRISIL, with an inverse floating interest rate structure on 27 February 2015. Suppose the bond is of 5-year maturity, with a call/put option at the end of 3 years. The floating coupon will be the difference between a fixed rate of 17.04% and the NSE 3-month MIBOR, a benchmark for the call money in India, and is payable semi-annually. If the 3-month MIBOR as on the issue date is 8.54%, the semi annualized rate applicable to the inverse floater for calculating the nearest coupon would be 8.50% (17.04–8.54%). If the 3-month MIBOR is expected to rise (fall) at 9.04% (at 8.04%), HINDALCO the bond issuer (any investor) is likely to pay less (receive more) by 50 basis points. That's how the bond issuer or investors/traders benefit from these kinds of issues, depending upon their view on interest rates.

## Zero coupon bonds

Zero coupon bonds (ZCBs) are bonds with no coupon payments. Like Treasury bills, they are issued at a discount to the face value. Instead of paying any periodic coupons, the ZCB holder gets the price discount in the beginning itself. Therefore, ZCBs are alternatively known as *Deep Discount Bonds*. The government of India issued such securities in the nineties. It has not issued zero coupon bonds after that. All Treasury bills issued by the government of India are the only zero coupon debt instruments, which are essentially short-term money market instruments. Such ZCBs, if not available in the market, can be created by government dealer firms, known as primary dealers (PDs) in India, under the Treasury's Separate Trading of Registered Interest and Principal Securities (STRIPS) Program. These zero coupon instruments are called Treasury STRIPS.

In the case of ZCB issued by any non-government entity, since the issuers do not pay any interest regularly, the credit risk of such bonds gets un-recognized till the maturity, and therefore carries a significant amount of credit risk for the investors. Because of this high credit risk, RBI has stringent norms for Indian banks to invest in such ZCBs. However, as per RBI norms, banks can invest in zero coupon bonds, provided the issuer creates a sinking fund and keeps it in liquid investments or government securities. These types of debt instruments in India are normally offered to retirement funds, such as exempted provident funds, gratuity funds, and superannuation funds. ZCBs are generally issued at the shorter end of the maturity, say up to two years.

## STRIPS

Separate Trading of Registered Interest and Principal of Securities *(STRIPS)* are a special form of zero coupon securities. STRIPS are instruments wherein each cash flow of the fixed coupon security is converted into a separate tradable zero coupon bond. For example, when Rs.100 of the 7.80% GS 2020 is stripped, each cash flow of coupon (Rs.3.90/- in each half year) will become a coupon STRIP and the principal payment (Rs.100 at maturity) will become a principal STRIP. These cash flows are traded separately as independent securities in the secondary market. STRIPS in government securities are expected to ensure availability of sovereign zero coupon bonds, which will facilitate the development of a market-determined zero coupon yield curve (ZCYC). STRIPS also provide institutional investors with an additional instrument for their asset-liability management. Further, as STRIPS have zero reinvestment risk, being zero coupon bonds, they can be attractive to retail/non-institutional investors. Unlike ZCBs issued by non-government entities, such Treasury STRIPS are free from any credit risk.

### Bonds with embedded options

Bond may have an option (call or put) embedded in it, giving certain rights to the issuers and/or investors. The more common types of bonds with embedded options are: callable bond, puttable bond, and convertible bond. *Callable* bonds give the issuer the right to redeem or buy-back them prematurely on certain terms. The call option can be an American or a European option. The purpose of such an option is to reduce the cost to the issuer in the regime of falling interest rates. On the other hand, a *Puttable* bond gives the investor the right to prematurely sell it back to the issuer on certain predefined terms. Puttable bonds safeguard the interest of bond holders when interest rates rise in the market. *Convertible* bonds, alternatively known as *Hybrid Securities*, give the bond holder the right to convert them into equity shares on certain terms. Such bonds can be fully or partly convertible. In the case of partly convertible, investors are offered equity shares for the part that is redeemed, and the other part remains as a bond. Callable (puttable) bonds are generally traded at a lower (higher) price in comparison with the similar option-free bonds. Since the call/put option can be exercised after the specific lock-in period but on some specific call/put date (1st call date/2nd call date/. . ./nth call date), the prices at which the bond will be called-off or sold-off in all possible call/put dates are also specified in the bond indenture. This schedule of alternative prices is called the *Call/Put Schedule.*

A 6.72% GS2012 was issued on 18 July 2002, for a maturity of 10 years, maturing on 18 July 2012. The optionality on the bond could be exercised after the completion of a 5-year tenure from the date of issuance on any coupon date falling thereafter. The government has the right to buy-back the bond (call option) at par value (equal to the face value) while the investor has the right to sell the bond (put option) to the government at par value at the time of any of the half-yearly coupon dates starting from 18 July 2007. Even if presently there is no such callable/puttable GOI bond outstanding in the market, these types of instruments are very common in the non-government securities market. Many corporates in India presently issue such bonds with a higher coupon rate to attract investors but may like to include a call and/ or put option, to ensure an exit route the moment the market moves against the bond issuer and/or holder. For example, say, IDFC LIMITED SR-PP 2/2015 OPT II 9.6 NCD 29AP24 FVRS10LAC (ISIN: INE043D07GK9), a secured non-convertible debenture issued by IDFC Limited with a face value of Rs.100/- and a fixed coupon of 9.60% p.a., payable annually, issued on 29 April 2014, and maturing on 29 April 2024, has an embedded call option where the option can be exercised on 29 April of every year after a lock-in period of 4 years, i.e. on 29 April 2019, 29 April 2020, 29 April 2021, 29 April 2022, and 29 April 2023.

### Step-up/step-down bonds

Partly similar to a fixed rate bond, a step-up bond pays a specific coupon rate for the initial period, followed by a higher coupon rate for the subsequent periods. Therefore, a step-up bond, even if offered at a lower coupon during the initial period of its issuance, always offers higher but predetermined coupons during the later periods. In other words, the coupon income in a step-up bond steps-up from one period to another. For example, NIRMA, during the year 2017, has issued 60-years (maturity) step-up callable corporate bonds having a coupon rate of 9.5% p.a., with a call option after 5th year and every year thereafter. The coupon will step up by 150 basis points if the call is not exercised after the 5th year and will step up further by 25 basis points each at the end of 6th and 7th year.

The initial coupon in this type of bond is generally lower than the coupon of a similar fixed rate bond, where the motivation for the investors is to earn more in the coming years, but at the cost of lower earnings during the initial periods. Many step-up bonds are callable, giving the issuers some protection against falling interest rates. On the other hand, step-down bonds or notes are structured to offer a higher coupon in the initial period, followed by a lower coupon in the subsequent periods. This type of instrument motivates the investor to subscribe such issue to get a better immediate return in comparison with the similar fixed rate instrument, and therefore can strengthen the demand for such instruments in the market. Step-down bonds may be issued with some put option, giving the buyers a chance to exercise their put option when they find a rise in the market rates.

The major advantages from investing in step-up bonds include: exposure to high-quality issuers, availing a higher coupon payment to offset inflation, benefits of higher liquidity, and a lower level of interest rate risk in rising interest rate environment. However, the promise of higher future earnings from high future coupon payments really may not make any sense, especially when the step-up bond has a call option. The callability nature of most *step-up bonds* make the higher future returns elusive, and the promise for offering a higher future coupon may not materialize if the call option is exercised. Since issuers of step-up bonds are often found to exercise their call option even if interest rates remain flat, perhaps to avoid the higher future coupon payment, callable step-up bonds have more call risk than traditional callable bonds. Step-up bonds are generally more attractive to the investors when rates are expected to rise quickly and to a level above the step-up rates, leading to demotivate the issuers to exercise the call option.

### Asset backed/mortgage backed securities

Mortgage backed securities[2] (MBS) and asset backed securities (ABS) are two important debt instruments, especially in developed markets like USA. Securities created by a third-party entity, or a special purpose vehicle (SPV), from a pool of mortgages of different quality originated by a single or multiple originator(s) are called mortgage backed securities. Once the securities are created, the same is sold to general investors with a different risk-return profile. Whereas, asset backed securities are of similar nature and are created through almost the same process but are created from non-mortgage related assets, such as auto loans, credit card loans, student loans, etc.

As far as the structure of MBS or ABS is concerned, there are broadly three parties involved: originator/seller, issuer, and investor. Besides originating the mortgages or the loan assets, and thereafter selling them to the issuers, sellers of such assets may also act as a service agent, in terms of collection of regular interest payments on the loan and its principal in due time from the borrowers. This process enables the originators/sellers to off-load these exposures from their balance sheet and allows them to take fresh exposures. Issuers, who can be third-party entities or SPVs, acquire the assets from sellers, pool them together, and issue the securities to investors, and can earn their commission. Institutional investors, like investment banks, commercial banks, other non-banking financial institutions, insurance companies, etc., may like to invest in these securities, with the expectation of earning a relatively higher yield and also to diversify their existing portfolio. Investors are also exposed to two major risks: prepayment risk and default risk. Early payment of the loan-principal by the original borrower, leading to a reduction in the future interest components which are the major sources of earnings for the issuer to provide return to the security holders/investors, may finally cause a fall in the yield on such securities, exposing the investors to a risk of lower earning. Similarly, non-payment of any dues (periodic interest and/or principal) by the original borrower may also lead to a credit risk losses to the issuers, which may be finally passed on to the security holders/investors, as experienced in the 2008 US sub-prime crisis. These securities, depending on the risk-return profile, are categorized into three tranches:

senior tranche (low risk – low return), mezzanine tranche (moderate risk – moderate return), and junior/equity tranche (high risk – high return). The losses incurred by the security issuers due to any credit risk on part of the original borrowers are primarily borne by the holder of the junior tranche, and thereafter the remaining losses (if any) are passed on to the other two categories of investors, depending upon the risk profile of their investment.

### Tax-saving infrastructure bonds

Tax-saving infrastructure bonds are proposed by the Indian government to channelize retail and institutional savings into the infra sector. To make these bonds attractive and widen the investor base, the government may allow full tax exemptions to interest income from these bonds. To make these instruments even more attractive to retail investors, infra companies may offer an extra margin to investors for a limited amount of investment.

Even if the actual earning from these instruments is the tax-free coupon, the same is not the true yield effective on these kinds of securities. The effective yield can be calculated by considering the tax rate applicable to the investor. The effective yield is calculated as: *Effective Yield = Coupon Rate/ (1-Tax Rate)*. Therefore, for an investment in a tax-free bond with 8% coupon p.a., an investor in the 30.9% tax bracket will have an effective yield of 11.58%. The cash flow in the hands of the investor is only Rs.8.00/- p.a. for every Rs.100/- invested in the bonds. However, if it is assumed that the investor has to pay the tax at 30.9% on the coupon income, the before-tax coupon could have been 11.58%, leading to an after-tax income of 8% p.a. Therefore, effectively, if the tax-savings bonds are compared with other bonds the coupon income of which is taxable, the tax-savings bond generates the effective yield, not the actual coupon. Any change in tax rate applicable to the concerned investor will change the effective yield on the tax-free bonds.

A number of such tax-free bond issues are slated to hit the stands in the Indian market. Entities commonly very active in issuing tax-free bonds in India include: India Infrastructure Finance Co (IIFCL), National Highways Authority of India (NHAI), Housing and Urban Development Corp. (HUDCO), Power Finance Corp. (PFC), Rural Electrification Corporation (REC), Indian Railways Finance Corporation (IRFC), National Housing Bank (NHB), National Thermal Power Corporation (NTPC), etc.

### Perpetual bonds

Perpetual bonds, having no specific maturity like equity, are classified as hybrid instruments because they have both equity and debt features. These bonds, usually issued by banks, are not redeemable unless the issuer desires, and therefore are treated as equity. RBI considers such bonds as part of banks' Tier-I capital, which traditionally comprised equity instruments.

Some of the perpetual bonds presently outstanding in Indian market are: UNITED BANK OF INDIA 12% PERPETUAL BOND Callable on 29 March 2022, SYNDICATE BANK 11.25% PERPETUAL BOND callable on 15 July 2021, BANK OF INDIA 11.50% PERPETUAL BOND callable on 22 June 2021, etc.

### Junk bonds

Any bond issued by a corporate having a credit rating below investment grade is known as junk bond. Due to poor credit worthiness, the issuer of such a bond offers a very high yield, comparative to a high rated bond of similar tenor, to compensate the bond holder for the additional risk.

### Covered bonds

Covered bonds are debt issued by banks that are fully collateralized by residential or commercial mortgage loans or by loans to public sector institutions and typically have the highest credit ratings. The notes offer an additional protection to bondholders to asset-backed debt because, in addition to looking at the collateral pool as an ultimate source of repayment, the issuing bank is also liable for the repayment. Covered bonds are the second largest segment of the European bond market after government bonds.

### Secured/unsecured bonds

Corporate bonds can be either secured against assets of the corporates or can also be unsecured. Holders of secured corporate bonds, in the event of closure of the company, can be repaid by selling off the assets against which the bonds were secured. Holders of senior secured bonds are ranked higher than the holders of subordinated secured bonds and unsecured bonds in repayment of dues in case of closure of the company. Unsecured bond holders are paid off before any payment is made to the holder of preference shares issued by the corporation.

### Inflation indexed bonds

The principal of these bonds is linked to an accepted index of inflation with a view to protecting the holder from inflation. Inflation indexed bonds (IIBs) were issued in India in the name of capital indexed bonds (CIBs) during 1997, providing inflation protection only to principal and not to interest payment. But IIBs are expected to provide inflation protection to both principal and interest payments. With an inflation indexed bond, the real rate of return is known in advance, and the nominal return varies with the rate of inflation realized over the life of the bond. Hence, neither the purchaser nor the issuer faces a risk that an unanticipated increase or decrease in inflation will erode or boost the purchasing power of the bond's payments. Investors who desire predictable real cash flows can now include indexed bonds in their portfolios. The certain real return will be attractive to investors who are particularly risk averse. It will also be attractive to savers who want to protect their savings from being eroded by inflation. Since inflation-indexed bonds remove the investor's inflation risk, by issuing indexed bonds, the Treasury can avoid paying the inflation risk premium found in nominal interest rates on conventional bonds and can thereby lower its borrowing costs.

The inflation component on principal will not be paid with interest but the same would be adjusted in the principal by multiplying the principal with the index ratio (IR), ratio of recent inflation index to the base index. At the time of redemption, the adjusted principal or the face, whichever is higher, would be paid. The interest rate will be provided protection against inflation by paying a fixed coupon rate on the principal adjusted against inflation. The consumer price index (CPI) reflects inflation to the larger extent, and therefore, globally CPI or the retail price index (RPI) is used for IIBs. Since all India CPI has been released since January 2011, and it will take some time to stabilize, it has been decided to consider WPI for inflation protection in IIBs. For example, if the annual coupon is 8% and the principal is Rs.100/-, the investor will be paid Rs.8/- per annum. If the inflation index rises 10%, the principal will become Rs.110/-. The coupon will remain 8%, resulting in an interest payment of Rs.110 x 8 per cent = Rs.8.8/-

### Basel III bonds

The Basel Committee on Bank Supervision (BCBS),[3] in its latest accord known as Basel-III Accord, a global standard for banks, sets out minimum requirements for capital, liquidity, and leverage, basically designed to rectify some of the blunders and irrational market practices that led to the 2008–09 global financial crisis, has proposed an additional tier I (core capital) and tier II (subordinated debts) capital instruments or bonds issued by banks, requiring absorption of principal losses at an objective pre-specified trigger point through either (i) conversion into common shares or (ii) a write-down mechanism, allocating losses to the instruments. These bonds are commonly known as Basel III bonds. A survey estimate says that Indian banks will require an additional Rs.5 trillion (equity/tier I capital of Rs.1.75 trillion and non-equity/tier II capital of Rs.3.25 trillion) of capital to be Basel III compliant by 2019. In case there is no injection of fresh capital from the government of India, the entire non-equity capital and a significant part of the equity capital may have to be accumulated through these Basel compliant bonds. Other than the Bank of India, IDBI Bank, several other Indian banks are also exploring the issuances of Basel III bonds.

This loss-absorption clause makes such bonds costly for the bank to issue as they have to pay extra interest to cover the additional risk borne by investors. For example, the Bank of India in July 2014, raised Rs.1,250 crore through

Basel III bonds at a coupon rate of 11%, roughly 100–150 basis points higher than normal bonds without the Basel III clause. These bonds can be issued to both institutional and retail investors. To broaden the investor base, the minimum maturity of the bonds has also been relaxed from 10 to 5 years.

## Green bonds

Just like any other bonds where securities are issued by different types of entities for raising funds from investors, *Green Bonds*, alternatively known as *Climate Bonds*, are also fixed income securities, where funds are raised from investors, but are exclusively earmarked for funding greener and environmental projects, such as renewable energy, low carbon transport, sustainable water management, climate change adaptation, energy efficiency, sustainable waste management, biodiversity conservation, etc. An important feature of green bonds is that the responsibility of repayment is with the issuer and not with the firm that is utilizing the funds in green projects. Higher credibility of issuers like supranational bodies (like World Bank, IMF) and major financial institutions make it possible to mobilize the required funds through these bonds from the global markets at cheaper rates.

Combating climate change is one of the greatest challenges these days, but it is increasingly considered as a business opportunity, and it also requires much more financing than governments alone can provide. A large amount of surplus funds are available with many institutional investors in global capital markets who are looking for opportunities that carry the right risk-reward profiles and meet specific criteria for rating, tenor, yield, and also geographical diversity. The green bond market has seen an enormous growth in the past decade, with issuance of USD 74.6 billion globally from around 156 issuers during the first half of 2018, representing an increase of 4% from the similar period (H1) in 2017, with deals primarily coming from Australia, Belgium, China, New Zealand, Norway, etc. The percentage share of the emerging market in the overall issuance size has increased from 25% in H1 2017 to 28% during H1 2018.

As far as the green bond market in India is concerned, these securities are very important fundraising options to manage funds for financing the country's ambitious renewable energy target of 175 GW by the year 2022 with an estimate of about USD 200 billion to finance the renewable energy sector. At the same time, the higher interest rate regime in the domestic market tempts financial institutions to issue dollar denominated green bonds in overseas markets. In March 2015, the EXIM Bank issued USD 500 million worth of green bonds overseas at a coupon rate of 2.75% with an oversubscription by 3.2 times, the proceeds from which are given by the EXIM Bank to companies to finance renewable energy projects. The cumulative issuance size of green bonds in India till July 2018 is around USD 6.5 billion, the majority of them from public sector entities, making India 8th in the world ranking for climate aligned bond issuance.

## Issuing sectors and sub-sectors wise classification of debt instruments

Debt securities available in the financial market of an economy can be classified based on different issuing sectors (resident and non-resident sectors), and sub-sectors. If not from an investor's perspective, but from the monetary policy and financial stability perspective, it is important to understand and analyze the sector-wise debt markets in the country. The presence of non-residents in the domestic debt market may indicate the openness of the national capital market for international players.

Resident sectors can again be sub-classified as: general government, financial corporations, non-financial corporations, households, and non-profit institutions serving households. Debt securities are predominantly issued by the first three sectors. The general government sector includes the central government, state government, and local government or municipal bodies. Financial corporations refer to the central bank, other money issuing corporations (if any), and other financial corporations. Non-financial corporations include all other public and private entities, including banks, NBFC, PSUs, corporates, etc.

Debt securities, within the resident sector, issued by different sub-sectors are described in the following section.

### Central government dated securities

Long-term (more than 1-year of original maturity) debt instruments issued by the central government (government of India), are called as dated government securities. These securities may carry a fixed or floating coupon (interest rate), which is paid on the face value, payable at fixed time periods (usually half-yearly). The tenor of dated securities can be up to 30 years. The nomenclature of a typical dated fixed coupon government security contains the following features – coupon, name of the issuer, maturity, and face value. For example, 7.17% GS 2028 would mean: a fixed income security issued by the government of India on 8 January 2018 with a coupon of 7.17% paid on face value, payable half-yearly (8 July and 8 January) every year till the maturity of the security on 8 January 2028, and redemption of the face/par value at maturity. Presently (as on August 2018), there are a total of 84 such government securities with different coupon and maturity profiles that are outstanding in the market, with a total outstanding volume of roughly INR 52809.50 billion.

### Special securities

In addition to its traditional issues (dated securities and Treasury bills), the government of India, under the market borrowing programme, also issues, from time to time, some special securities to entities like oil marketing companies, fertilizer companies, the Food Corporation of India, etc. as a compensation to these companies in lieu of cash subsidies. In other words, the losses incurred by these companies while offering the concerned products to the general public at subsidized rates decided by the government are not compensated by the government in cash but by issuing bonds guaranteed by the central government. These securities are usually long dated securities carrying a coupon with a spread of about 20–25 basis points over the yield of the dated securities of comparable maturity. These securities are, however, not eligible SLR securities but are eligible as collateral for market repo transactions. The beneficiary, like oil marketing companies, may divest these securities in the secondary market to banks, insurance companies/primary dealers, etc. for raising cash. A few examples of such special bonds issued by the government of India and are presently outstanding in the market are: *08.13% OIL SPL 2021, 08.40% OIL SPL 2026, 9.75% GOI (IFCI) SPL SEC 2021, 7% FERT COS GOI SPL BOND 2022,* etc.

Other than the aforesaid special securities issued by the central government, another type of special security issued by the government of India, and getting special attention these days, are *Recapitalization Bonds.* As a part of the plan to recapitalize the public sector banks in India, the central government has decided to infuse fresh capital (of INR 800 billion) through issuance of recapitalization bonds to all the eligible public sector banks. These securities, normally in the range of 10 – 15 years of maturities and offering coupons in the range of 7.35% – 7.68%, slightly lower than the closing rates of similar maturity benchmark papers, are: issued at par, non-transferrable/non-tradable, non-SLR, but eligible for HTM without any limits. Examples of such securities include: *07.35 Special GOI Security 2028, 07.42 Special GOI Security 2029, 07.48 Special GOI Security 2030, 07.55 Special GOI Security 2031, 07.61 Special GOI Security 2032, 07.68 Special GOI Security 2033,* maturing on the 29th of January in the respective year of maturity.

### Treasury bills (T-bills)

Treasury bills, or T-bills, are money market instruments, which are short term debt instruments issued by the central government (government of India). These instruments in India are presently issued in three tenors, namely, 91 days, 182 days, and 364 days. Treasury bills are zero coupon securities and do not pay any interim coupon/interest. They are issued at discount and redeemed at face value at maturity. For example, a 91-day Treasury bill of Rs.100/- (face value) may be issued at say Rs.98.20/-, that is, at a discount of say, Rs.1.80/- and would be redeemed at the face value of Rs.100/- at maturity. The return to the investors is the difference between the maturity value or the face value and the issue price, i.e. the discount amount. The Reserve Bank of India conducts auctions usually every Wednesday to issue T-bills. Payments for the T-bills purchased are made on the following Friday. The 91-day T-bills are auctioned on every Wednesday. The Treasury bills of 182-day and 364-day tenures are auctioned on alternate Wednesdays. T-bills of 364-day tenure are auctioned on the Wednesday preceding the reporting Friday, while 182-day T-bills are auctioned on the Wednesday prior to a non-reporting Fridays. The Reserve Bank releases an annual calendar of T-bill issuances for a financial year in the last week of March of the previous financial year. The Reserve Bank of India announces the issue details of T-bills through a press release every week. Treasury bills are short-term (up to 1 year) borrowing instruments of the government of India which enable investors to park their short-term surplus funds while reducing their market risk. T-bill auctions are held on the *Negotiated Dealing System (NDS)*[4] and the members electronically submit their bids on the system. Non-competitive bids are routed through the respective custodians or any bank or PD which are NDS members.

### State development loans (SDL)

State Development Loans (SDLs) are market borrowings by state governments. RBI coordinates the actual process of selling these securities. Each state is allowed to issue securities up to a certain limit each year. Generally, the coupon rates on state development loans are higher than those of central government securities of the same maturity. This shows that the central government is considered more creditworthy than state governments. Interest payment frequency is half yearly and other modalities are similar to GOI Securities. They are issued in dematerialized form. State government securities can be issued in the physical form (in the form of a stock certificate) on separate request and are transferable. State development loans are traded in a secondary market but are much less liquid than GOI Securities. Few SDL presently outstanding in the market are: *08.73 UP SDL 2028*, issued by the government of Uttar Pradesh, *08.63 RJ SDL 2028*, issued by the government of Rajasthan, *08.15 TN SDL 2028*, issued by the government of Tamil Nadu, etc.

The State development loans are normally sold through the auction process. All the auctions are multiple price auctions, through competitive bidding, conducted by the Reserve Bank of India and the allotment procedure is similar to that for GOI Securities. Non-competitive bidding has been introduced in the auction of SDL. One day prior to the auction, bids are submitted by primary dealers (PD) to RBI indicating the amount they are willing to underwrite, and the fee expected. RBI, along with state government representatives, then examine the bids on the basis of market conditions and take a decision on the amount to be underwritten and the fee to be paid.

### Other approved securities (OAS)

These securities are generally issued by a central or state government undertakings. The issuers mention in the offer document that particular security is eligible for SLR purposes and permission to that effect has been obtained from central government. The repayment of interest and principal of the security is guaranteed by central or state governments. The coupon rate offered is generally higher compared to government securities and SDL of similar maturities. These securities are not active in the secondary market. The issuers of such securities in the past were ICICI, IDBI, NABARD, SIDBI, HUDCO, State Financial Corporation, and State Electricity Boards. However, similar types of issuance have not been observed in recent years.

### UDAY bond

The term "UDAY" represents *Ujwal DISCOM Assurance Yojana*, a package initiated by the government of India to revive the electricity distribution companies in India from the financial crunch they were facing. UDAY bonds are state government bonds, issued under the UDAY scheme, intended to revive power distribution companies and likely to be placed with investors directly through private placement.

Under the UDAY programme, it is agreed by the respective states to convert 75% of their debt on the books of their respective power distribution companies into state government bonds of 10–15 years maturity, proposed to be issued directly in the market to the respective banks and FIs holding DISCOM debts, with a non-SLR status and an eligibility to be placed as part of HTM and proposed to be priced at not more than 75 basis points above the prevailing 10-year benchmark government security. Examples of such Special SDL or UDAY bonds include: *08.41 RJ SDL SPL 2028, 08.49 AP SDL SPL 2029, 07.93 MP UDAY 2032*, respectively issued by the state governments of Rajasthan, Andhra Pradesh, and Madhya Pradesh.

Since UDAY bonds come with an implicit guarantee from the issuing state government, which need to include the interest and principal due in such bonds as a part of their respective budget, these bonds possess a very low level of credit risk but have an attractive spread, and therefore become a very good investment option for the investors, even in comparison with corporate bonds with AAA ratings. Since insurance companies (life and non-life) in India necessarily need to have a significant exposure in corporate bonds, they may find it more attractive to invest in such bonds rather than investing in corporate bonds of investment grades.

### Municipal bonds

Municipal bonds are debt obligations issued by states, cities, and other government bodies to meet the financial requirement of any public infrastructure projects like school building, highways, hospitals, sewage systems, etc. The interest of such bonds is paid through the revenue generated from the business that backs the obligation. These types of bonds, even if very popular in developed economies like the US, are hardly issued in India. In order to meet the challenges created by growing urbanization, municipal corporations in India will incur huge expenditures to support urban infrastructure in the coming decades. Municipal bonds have advantages in terms of the size of borrowing and the maturity period, often 10 to 20 years. Both these features are considered ideal for urban infrastructure financing. If appropriately structured, municipal bonds can be issued at interest costs that are lower than the risk-return profile of individual Urban Local Bodies (ULBs).

There are basically two types of municipal bonds: general obligation bonds and revenue bonds. In case of the first, the principal and interest both are secured by the full faith and credit of the issuer and usually guaranteed by either the issuer's unlimited or limited tax paying power. In case of revenue bonds, principal and interest are secured by revenues of the ULBs derived from tolls, charges, or rents from the facility built with the proceeds of the bond issue. Major public projects financed by revenue bonds include toll roads, bridges, airports, water and sewage treatment facilities, hospitals, etc.

### Public sector undertaking bonds (PSU bonds)

Due to the reduction in the central government funding to public sector undertakings (PSUs) through the general budget, PSU bonds issue has become an important fundraising programme adopted by public sector undertakings. Accordingly, like other entities, PSUs also issue bonds in the primary market to raise funds, especially to meet their regular working capital and/or capital expenditure requirement. The market for PSU bonds in India has grown substantially over the past decade. All PSU bonds have a built-in redemption, may be within a maturity period of 5 to 10 years, and some of them are embedded with put or call options. The majority of the PSU bonds, issued by state-owned undertakings and carrying interest and principal payment guaranteed by the respective state government, are privately placed with banks or large institutional investors. Historically, default rates of PSU bonds are negligible, and PSUs are perceived as quasi-sovereign bodies

PSUs are permitted to issue two types of bonds: *Tax-free Bond* and *Taxable Bond*. Tax-free bonds are bonds for which the amount of interest is exempted from the investor's income. PSUs issue tax-free bonds or bonds with certain exemptions under the Income Tax Act with prior approval from the government through the Central Board of Direct Taxes (CBDT) for raising funds. This feature was introduced with the purpose of lowering the interest cost for PSUs which were engaged in businesses that could not afford to pay market determined rates of interest. Therefore, there are both taxable coupon PSU bonds and tax-free coupon PSU bonds. PSUs which have raised funds through the issue of tax-free bonds are central PSUs such as MTNL and NTPC, and state PSUs such as state electricity boards (SEBs) and state financial corporations (SFCs). The bonds issued by the state financial corporations are SLR eligible for cooperative banks and non-banking finance companies (NBFCs). PSUs are allowed to issue floating rate bonds, deep discount bonds, and a variety of other bonds. All new issues have to be listed on a stock exchange. Investors in PSU bonds include banks, insurance companies, non-banking finance companies, provident funds, mutual funds, financial institutions, and individuals.

## Corporate bonds/debentures

A debenture is a debt security issued by a corporation that may or may not be secured by specific assets, but rather by the general credit of the corporation. Corporate treasuries use this as a tool to raise medium/long-term funds that become a part of their capital structure. But unlike a debenture, corporate bonds are a form of loans, secured by stated assets, and are typically issued by financial institutions, government undertakings, and large companies. These two terms are used interchangeably in the Indian debt market.

A corporate bond/debenture is a debt security issued by a private company, which offers to pay interest in lieu of the money borrowed for a certain period. In essence, it represents a loan taken by the issuer who pays an agreed rate of interest during the lifetime of the instrument and repays the principal normally, unless otherwise agreed, on maturity.

These are debt instruments issued by private sector companies, having maturities mostly ranging between 1 to 10 years. Long maturity bonds/debentures are rarely issued, as investors are not comfortable with such maturities, especially in order to avoid the credit risk involved in corporate bonds. Generally, corporate bonds/debentures are less liquid as compared to PSU bonds and the liquidity is inversely proportional to the residual maturity. Debenture gives the investors the dual benefit of adequate security and good returns. Debentures are transferrable instruments and may be transferred from one party to another by using a transfer form. Debentures are not negotiable and are issued in physical and dematerialized form. Year-wise outstanding volume in different types of corporate bonds in India are presented in the following table (Table 2.4).

## Types of corporate bonds/debentures

- *Secured Debentures* are those which are secured by a charge on the fixed assets of the issuer company. In case the issuer fails to pay the principal or interest, the liability of the investors will be repaid by selling the charged assets.
- *Unsecured Debentures* are not secured by charge over any assets of the company. In case of any default of interest and principal, the investors will be treated as unsecured creditors of the company.
- *Non-Convertible Debentures (NCD)* are instruments which retain their debt character and cannot be converted into equity shares of the company.

*Table 2.4* Instrument-wise outstanding corporate debt in India

Total Outstanding Corporate Debt in India

|  | Type of Instruments | No. of Instruments Outstanding | Net Outstanding Amount (Rs. In Crores) |
|---|---|---|---|
| December-11 | Fixed Rate | 73.91% | 91.81% |
|  | Floating Rate | 8.77% | 2.34% |
|  | Structured Notes | 6.83% | 0.48% |
|  | Others | 10.49% | 5.37% |
|  | **Total** | **13176** | **983425.8** |
| December-12 | Fixed Rate | 73.67% | 92.54% |
|  | Floating Rate | 7.58% | 1.88% |
|  | Structured Notes | 5.77% | 0.31% |
|  | Others | 12.98% | 5.26% |
|  | **Total** | **15257** | **1211579** |
| December-13 | Fixed Rate | 75.09% | 93.62% |
|  | Floating Rate | 7.54% | 1.70% |
|  | Structured Notes | 5.67% | 0.29% |
|  | Others | 11.70% | 4.39% |
|  | **Total** | **15793** | **1402741** |
| December-14 | Fixed Rate | 72.32% | 91.92% |
|  | Floating Rate | 8.97% | 3.11% |
|  | Structured Notes | 5.26% | 0.53% |
|  | Others | 13.45% | 4.43% |
|  | **Total** | **18664** | **1648456** |
| December-15 | Fixed Rate | 72.20% | 90.66% |
|  | Floating Rate | 9.00% | 3.53% |
|  | Structured Notes | 5.47% | 1.09% |
|  | Others | 13.33% | 4.72% |
|  | **Total** | **21434** | **1911226** |
| December-16 | Fixed Rate | 71.25% | 90.30% |
|  | Floating Rate | 10.30% | 3.68% |
|  | Structured Notes | 6.35% | 1.31% |
|  | Others | 12.11% | 4.70% |
|  | **Total** | **24357** | **2276996** |
| December-17 | Fixed Rate | 71.78% | 90.03% |
|  | Floating Rate | 10.95% | 4.83% |
|  | Structured Notes | 6.35% | 0.64% |
|  | Others | 10.92% | 4.50% |
|  | **Total** | **25414** | **2647034** |

*Source*: SEBI Statistics on Corporate Bonds

- *Partly Convertible Debentures (PCD)* are those where a part of which can be converted into equity shares of the company at a future date at the notice of the issuer. The issuer decides the date and ratio of conversion usually at the time of seeking subscription.
- *Optionally Convertible Debentures (OCD)* are those where the investor has the option to convert the debentures to equity shares at a price decided by the issuer and agreed upon at the time of issue of the debenture.

- *Fully Convertible Debentures (FCD)* are those which are fully convertible into equity at the issuer's notice. The ratio of conversion is decided by the issuer.

The debenture and bond holders have, like other creditors, prior legal claim over the equity and preference stockholders on the assets of the company. The issuer appoints a trustee who acts in fiduciary capacity to protect the interests of the debenture/bond holders. The trustee, by virtue of the trust deed executed by the issuer, holds charge of the security and would be instrumental in initiating legal action for recovery of principal/interest in case of default. The trustees, as per SEBI guidelines, are vested with requisite powers for protecting the rights of the debenture/bond holders and have a right to appoint a nominee director on the board of the issuing company.

### Commercial papers & certificates of deposit

Commercial papers (CPs) are short-term debt instruments issued by non-bank entities like manufacturing companies, NBFCs, primary dealers, etc. It is a popular instrument for financing working capital requirements of companies and can be issued either in the form of a promissory note or in a dematerialized form through any of the depositories approved by and registered with the SEBI. Similar to Treasury bills, CPs can be issued for a minimum period of 7 days and maximum period of 1 year at a discount to face value and redeemable at par to the holder on their maturity. CPs must be issued by private placement only, with a minimum size of Rs.5 lakhs and in the multiples of Rs.5 lakhs thereafter. All CPs in India need to have a minimum credit rating provided by the external rating agencies.

On the other hand, Certificate of Deposits (CDs) are short-term instruments, essentially issued by the commercial banks and special financial institutions (SFIs), and can be issued to individuals, cooperatives, and companies. CDs are freely transferable from one party to another. Similar to T-bills and CPs, the maturity period of CDs ranges from 91 days to 1 year. After issuing CDs, banks cannot buy-back their own CDs before the maturity date. Banks are allowed to issue CDs at a floating rate, provided the methodology of computing the floating rate is objective and transparent and market based, where the issuing bank/FI are free to determine the discount/coupon rate. Banks have to maintain SLR and CRR on the issue price of CDs.

### Classification of debt instruments based on currency of debt issue

Debt issues can be classified based on the currency (domestic/local vs. foreign) at which a debt security is issued. Currency-wise compositions of debt securities are helpful for analyzing the financial stability of an economy. It is again important to distinguish between the currency of denomination and currency of settlement. The currency of denomination (domestic or foreign) is determined by the currency in which the value of positions and all cash flows for the issues are determined. Even if the value of positions and all cash flows for a debt issue are denominated in one currency, the respective settlement may occur in a different currency. The currency of settlement refers to the currency into which the value of positions and flows for debt securities are converted during the time of settlement.

### Foreign currency convertible bonds (FCCB)

In order to raise money in foreign currency, corporates may issue certain bonds in currencies different from the issuers' domestic currency, retaining all features of a convertible bond. Several multinational corporations tap the foreign bond markets by issuing FCCBs, which are quasi-debt instruments and tradable in stock exchanges. FCCBs are attractive to both issuers and investors. Investors get the safety of guaranteed payments on the bonds and are also able to take advantage of any price appreciation in the company's stock. FCCBs may also carry an option feature (call or put) and normally offer an interest (if any) lower than a normal debt paper or foreign currency loans or external commercial borrowings (ECBs). FCCBs have been extremely popular with Indian corporates for raising foreign funds at competitive rates.

### Masala bonds

The corporate sector, including banks and other financial institutions, of an economy, subjected to the fulfillment of certain criterion, may have various channels, like ECBs and FCCBs, to borrow money from overseas markets. But under such circumstances, overseas borrowings happen in globally accepted currencies like dollars, Euros, etc. The Indian corporate sector regularly taps the overseas market with a sizable amount through these borrowing programs. Other than borrowing and repaying in a foreign currency, in which the borrower faces the currency risk of domestic currency being depreciated against the major currency in which the borrowing takes place, it may also be possible for corporate sectors to borrow from the overseas market, but at their domestic currency, especially to avoid the risk of huge losses due to the future possible depreciation of the domestic currency against the major foreign currency, say the US dollar. In other words, say Indian corporates can borrow in INR from the overseas market by issuing INR-denominated bonds to the overseas buyers/investors, and thereby avoid the currency risk. Even if the interest rates applicable to ECBs and other similar overseas borrowing are significantly low, the negative impact of INR being depreciated may overwhelm the benefit of lower interest rates applicable to such borrowings. Therefore, there is an increasing demand in many economies, including India, for such overseas borrowing through domestic currency denominated bonds. These bonds in the Indian market are known as *Masala Bonds.*, just to bring out the Indian culture and cuisine, which is very popular worldwide because of its traditional spices or masalas.

The International Finance Corporation (IFC), the investment arm of the World Bank, had issued an INR 1,000 crore bond in November 2015, basically to fund infrastructure projects in India. The Housing Development and Finance Corporation (HDFC), after RBI's approval in September 2015, is the first company to raise INR 3000 crore by issuing such bonds (3-year maturity and 8.33% coupon) during July 2016, followed by the National Thermal Power Corporation (NTPC) raising INR 2000 crore (5-year maturity and 7.40% coupon) during August 2016 to finance clean energy projects. As per the recent guidelines issued by RBI, the concerned regulator to oversee external borrowings in India, in August 2016, banks are allowed to issue masala bonds to meet their capital needs (tier I and tier II capital) and to finance infrastructure projects. Indian corporates eligible to raise ECB are also allowed to issue such Masala bonds with or without RBI permission, depending upon their status of availing ECBs under approval route or automatic route.

### Regulatory classification of debt instruments (in India)

As per RBI norms, debt instruments in available in India can be categorized as: (A) SLR approved securities, and (B) non-SLR securities. SLR securities are comprised of: dates securities issued by the central government (i.e. govt. securities) and state government (SDL), Treasury bills issued by the central government, and other approved securities (OAS). RBI fixes SLR (statutory liquidity ratio) from time to time – currently (December 2019), it is at 18.50%. RBI requires banks to maintain 18.50% of their *Net Demand and Time Liabilities (NDTL)*, which is to be maintained on a daily basis by investment in cash (other than CRR) and in the prescribed securities. These securities are approved securities for SLR purposes under section 24 of the Banking Regulation Act, 1949, and Indian Trust Act, 1882, and are issued under Public Debt Act, 1944.

### SLR securities

*Statutory Liquidity Ratio* refers to the amount that the commercial banks require to maintain in the form of gold or government-approved securities before providing credit to the customers. SLR is determined and maintained by the Reserve Bank of India in order to control the expansion of bank credit, to ensure the solvency of commercial banks, to compel the commercial banks to invest in government securities like government bonds, and is determined as a percentage of *Net Demand and Time Liabilities* (NDTL). The minimum limit of SLR is presently (as on December 2019) 18.50% of NDTL. However, the average limit maintained by the banks in India is significantly higher than the statutory requirement, maybe more than 25% of NDTL. If any Indian bank fails to maintain the required level of standard liquidity ratio, then it becomes liable to pay a penalty to the Reserve Bank of India. The defaulter bank pays a penal interest at the rate of 3% per annum above the bank rate on the shortfall amount for that particular day. However, on account of default continuing to the next succeeding working day(s), the penalty rate may be increased to a rate of 5% per annum above the bank rate for the concerned days of default on the shortfall. The RBI can increase the SLR to contain inflation, suck liquidity in the market, tighten the measure to safeguard customers' money, or vice versa.

### Non-SLR securities

Indian banks, as institutional investors in the financial market targeted to earn reasonable returns within a tolerable level of risk and to create a well-diversified portfolio, make their Treasury investments not only in SLR approved securities, but also in another range of securities available in the market, subjected to fulfilling some regulatory norms as set by the central bank (RBI). Any investments made by banks in India, other than in SLR approved securities, are classified as non-SLR securities, which are comprised of: non-SLR government (central and state) securities, debentures and bonds of PSUs, corporate bonds and debentures, floating rate bonds, equity and preference shares, mutual funds and venture capital funds, post office deposit schemes, etc. Banks are free to invest in such securities but should undertake the usual due diligence in respect of investments in non-SLR instruments.

Banks can invest both in listed and non-listed securities, subjected to the specified norms. The board of directors of banks should fix a prudential limit for their total investment in non-SLR securities and several sub-limits in different classes of non-SLR investments. Banks must not invest in unrated debt securities. Debt securities should carry a credit rating of not less than investment grade from a credit rating agency registered with the SEBI.

## Self-learning exercise

1   Even if equities and bonds are two important financial market instruments, both are significantly different from each other. Explain.
2   Why are bonds called as fixed income securities?
3   How are debt securities different from one another, depending upon their features?
4   What is the cash flow of a 10-year bond position, paying a coupon interest of 8.4% p.a., payable semiannually, and having a face value of INR 10 crore?
5   What is the cash flow of a 7-year bond that pays no coupon interest and has a face value of INR100.00?

6 Give three reasons why the maturity of a bond is important.

7 Explain whether or not an investor can determine today what the cash flow of a floating rate bond will be.

8 Suppose that a coupon reset formula for a floating rate bond is: 6-month LIBOR + 100 basis points, payable semi-annually. (a) What is the reference rate? (b) What is the quoted margin? (c) Suppose that on the coupon reset date that the 6-month LIBOR is 2.8%. What will the coupon rate be for the period?

9 What is an inverse floating rate bond?

10 What is a bond with an embedded option?

11 What does the call feature in a bond entitle the issuer to do?

12 (a) What is the advantage of a call feature for an issuer? (b) What are the disadvantages of a call feature for the bondholder?

13 What does the put feature in a bond entitle the bondholder to do?

14 Does an investor who purchases a zero coupon bond face reinvestment risk?

15 What are special securities issued by the government (central and state)? Explain.

16 What is a recapitalization bond? How is it different from other special securities issued by the central government?

17 What do you mean by masala bond? How are they useful to the issuer and investors?

18 What is meant by marking a position to market?

19 How are a fixed coupon bond and a zero coupon bond different to an investor in terms of interest rate risk (if any), even if both the bonds are expected to hold till the maturity?

## Notes

1 A day-count convention is a standard convention used in the fixed income securities market basically to estimate the interest accrues on various debt investments. It is used to determine the number of days and the amount of accrued interest between two coupon dates. Since there is no central authority to define day-count rules across all securities worldwide, there are no standard practices to apply at all situations. However, the International Swap Dealers Association (ISDA) has specified some conventions known as: "30/360", "Actual/360", "Actual/365", and "Actual/Actual".

2 Mortgage backed securities are a type of security which are created and secured by a pool of mortgages through a process called securitization. A best example of such securities is the one that caused the 2007–08 US subprime crisis. In this case, securities are created out of pool of subprime mortgage loans through securitization and are sold to investors like Lehman Brothers. The value of those securities largely depended upon the value of those subprime mortgages, which subsequently started falling, causing a subsequent fall in the value of all those MBS, leading to the collapse of Lehman.

3 Basel Committee on Bank Supervision (BCBS) disseminates guidance on critical issues to ensure healthy banking systems across the world, issues international

norms, called the Basel Accord, and sets minimum capital standards for banks. BCBS has produced three such accords, Basel III being the most recent (in 2010).

4 The Negotiated Dealing System (NDS), introduced in the year 2002, is an electronic trading platform operated by the Reserve Bank of India to facilitate dealings in government securities and other types of money market instruments available in India. The Negotiated Dealing System-Order Matching system (NDS-OM) is an electronic, screen-based, anonymous, order-driven trading system for dealing in government securities. It was subsequently introduced in 2005. This screen-based online trading platform has made a remarkable change in the secondary market trading in government securities in India.

## Bibliography

Choudhry, M. (2006). *An Introduction to Bond Markets* (3rd edn.). John Wiley & Sons, Inc., Hoboken, NJ.

Fabozzi, F. (2007). *Fixed Income Analysis* (2nd edn.). John Wiley & Sons, Inc., Hoboken, NJ.

Fabozzi, F. (2013). *Bond Markets, Analysis and Strategies* (8th edn.). Pearson Education India, India.

Fabozzi, F. (ed.). (July 2017). *The Handbook of Fixed Income Securities* (8th edn.). McGraw Hill Education, New York.

Mukherjee, K. N. (2014). *Fixed Income Securities: Valuation, Risk and Risk Management* (1st edn.). Monograph, Published by National Institute of Bank Management (NIBM), Pune, India.

Petitt, B. S., Pinto, J. E., and Pirie, W. L. (2016). *Fixed Income Analysis* (3rd edn.). CFA Institute Investment Series, John Wiley & Sons, Inc., Hoboken, NJ.

Rajwade, A. V. (2008). *Handbook on Debt Securities and Interest Rate Derivatives* (2nd edn.). Tata McGraw-Hill, India.

Sundaresan, S. (2009). *Fixed Income Markets and Their Derivatives* (3rd edn.). Elsevier India Pvt. Ltd., India.

# 3 Basic statistics

**Key learning outcomes**

At the end of this chapter, the readers are expected to be familiar with:

- Descriptive statistical measures required to analyze financial market data
- Correlation and regression analysis required to understand and analyze the interrelationship between various segments of financial markets and between financial products.
- Theory of probability and some important probability distributions that some financial data are expected to follow to understand and analyze the statistical behavior of financial products using their historical observations.
- Testing the statistical significance of necessary statistical estimates required to analyze the financial market data.

## Measures of central tendency

A large volume of data in itself is of very little use in arriving at any meaningful conclusions. Therefore, it becomes necessary to obtain a single number to represent a whole mass of data. This single figure would describe an entire series of observations of varying sizes. Such a typical value usually occupies a central position, so that some observations are larger and some smaller than it. There are various measures to convert a huge mass of data into a single representative figure, commonly known as *Measures of Central Tendency* and include mean, median, and mode.

### Arithmetic mean/average

Arithmetic mean is considered to be the easiest and simplest measure of central tendency that fulfills all the criteria of a satisfactory average measure.

This measure is based on all observations and is also easy to calculate. As far as sample fluctuations are concerned, arithmetic mean has been found to be the most stable measure of central tendency. In other words, if many samples are drawn from the same statistical population, arithmetic mean will be found to fluctuate less than any other measures of central tendency.

The arithmetic mean of a set of observations is defined as their sum, divided by the number of observations. If $X_1, X_2, \ldots, X_n$ are the values of a variable with frequencies $f_1, f_2, \ldots \ldots, f_n$ respectively, then the arithmetic mean of these values, denoted by $\bar{x}$, is given by

Simple A. M. $\qquad \bar{x} = \frac{1}{n} \sum_{i=1}^{n} x_i$ $\hfill$ (3.1)

Weighted A. M. $\qquad \bar{x} = \frac{1}{N} \sum_{i=1}^{n} f_i x_i$ $\hfill$ (3.2)

where, $N = \sum_{i=1}^{n} f_i$

## Moving average

Moving average, also known as *Rolling Average*, refers to a statistical technique used to analyze a set of data points by creating an average of subsets out of the full data set. In a set of say 100 data points, with rolling window of 25 data points, the 1st (2nd) value of the moving average might be the arithmetic average of data points 1 through 25 (2 through 26) and so on. Such an averaging method helps to smoothen the original series of observations and also to find the trend in the observations by eliminating the cyclical, seasonal, and random variations in time series data. The choice of the length of a moving average also plays a significant role. This average measure allows an investor to look at smoothed data rather than focusing on day-to-day price/rates fluctuations that are inherent in almost all financial markets data. The important types of moving average are discussed in the following section.

## Simple moving average

A simple moving average is calculated by adding say the closing prices (interest rates) of a particular security (maturity) for a number of time periods and then dividing the total by the number of time periods. A simple moving average (SMA) is the unweighted mean of the previous $n$ data points. When calculating successive values, a new value comes into the sum and an old value drops out. A SMA can be disproportionately influenced by old data points. Short-term averages respond quickly to changes in the price/rates of the underlying, while long-term averages are slow to react.

*Weighted moving average*

A weighted average is any average that has multiplying factors to give different weights to different data points. A weighted moving average (WMA) has the specific meaning of weights that decrease *arithmetically*, such that:

$$WMA_M = \frac{nP_M + (n-1)P_{M-1} + ... + 2P_{M-(n-2)} + P_{M-(n-1)}}{n + (n-1) + ... + 2 + 1} \tag{3.3}$$

*Exponential weighted moving average*

In the case of assigning the same weight to every data, it is hard to capture extraordinary events and effects. The problem of assigning linear weight is addressed by using the exponentially weighted moving average (EWMA), where the weight assigned to the older data reduces exponentially. The EWMA model assumes that the weight of the last days is more than old days. The EWMA introduces lambda ($\lambda$), called *Decay Factor* or smoothing parameter, having a value less than one. Under such a condition, each value is weighted by a multiplier, such that the necessary weights for recent to older values are respectively: *(1-$\lambda$) $\lambda^0$, (1-$\lambda$) $\lambda^1$, (1-$\lambda$) $\lambda^2$*, etc. The EWMA volatility measure is such that:

$$\sigma = \sqrt{(1-\lambda)\sum_{t=n}^{1} \lambda^t (x_t - \mu)^2} \tag{3.4}$$

In the case of daily data, $\mu$ is expected to be zero, and therefore the volatility measure can be based on a daily squared return. JP Morgan's RiskMetrics model uses the standard decay factor value of 0.94 for daily and 0.97 for monthly volatility estimations.

*Median*

The median of a set of observations is the value of the middle most item when they are arranged in order of magnitude. It is a special case of percentile ranks and it is the value of the 50th percentile rank. The median is, in a certain sense, the real measure of central tendency, as it gives the value of the most central observation. It is unaffected by extreme values and can be easily calculated from frequency distribution with open end class. The median is the only average to be used while dealing with qualitative data which cannot be measured quantitatively but still can be arranged in ascending or descending order of magnitude.

The median from a grouped frequency distribution can be calculated either (i) by using simple interpolation in a cumulative frequency distribution, or (ii) by using the following formula:

$$Median = l_1 + \frac{(N/2) - F}{f_m} \times c \qquad (3.5)$$

Where, $l_1$ = lower boundary of the median class; $N$ = total frequency; $F$ = cumulative frequency corresponding to $l_1$ cumulative frequency of the pre-median class; $f_m$ = frequency of the median class; and $c$ = width of the median class.

## Mode

The mode of a set of observations is that value which occurs most frequently or the value corresponding to the highest frequency. In other words, mode is the value of the variable which is predominant in the series and around which other values of the series cluster densely. In the case of simple series, the mode can be found by inspection only. However, in the case of a grouped frequency distribution, the mode can be calculated with the following formula:

$$Mode = l_1 + \frac{d_1}{d_1 + d_2} \times c \qquad (3.6)$$

Where, $l_1$ = lower boundary of the model class; $d_1$ = difference of frequencies in the model class and the preceding class; $d_2$ = difference of frequencies in the model class and the following class; and $c$ = common width of classes.

It is to be noted here that the above formula is applicable only when all classes have the same width. When all observations occur with equal frequency, mode does not exist. However, there may be two modes (bi-model) or many modes (multi-model).

The relations between mean, median, and mode is represented by the following equation:

$$Mean - Mode = 3 \times (Mean - median) \qquad (3.7)$$

## Example

Suppose the 10-year monthly GOI risk-free yield over the last four years (2014–2017) is given in the following table (Table 3.1).

*Table 3.1* 10-year GOI risk-free yield

| Months | 2014 | 2015 | 2016 | 2017 |
|---|---|---|---|---|
| **10-Year GOI Risk-free Yield:** | | | | |
| January | 8.8698 | 7.6873 | 7.5187 | 7.1485 |
| February | 8.9384 | 7.7655 | 7.6385 | 7.0912 |
| March | 8.8776 | 7.7991 | 7.4025 | 7.0563 |
| April | 8.8902 | 7.8904 | 7.8721 | 7.2155 |
| May | 8.6867 | 7.6433 | 7.4650 | 6.5111 |
| June | 8.7536 | 7.8697 | 7.7834 | 6.5899 |
| July | 8.4928 | 7.8050 | 7.4091 | 6.5521 |
| August | 8.6252 | 8.0541 | 7.1140 | 6.5426 |
| September | 8.5270 | 7.5300 | 6.8096 | 6.8192 |
| October | 8.2997 | 7.9202 | 6.8216 | 7.0257 |
| November | 8.1234 | 8.0698 | 6.3049 | 7.2457 |
| December | 7.9171 | 8.0940 | 7.1725 | 7.5236 |

*Source*: RBI Database

Now, based on these 48 yield data, we can calculate different measures of central tendency for the monthly risk-free yield in India.

*Arithmetic Mean*

$$\text{Simple A.M.} = \bar{x} = \frac{1}{n}\sum_{i=1}^{n} x_i = \frac{1}{48} \times (367.7632) = 7.6617$$

Similarly, following the moving average method, considering a fixed rolling window of 12 months, the simple moving average of the aforesaid GOI yield can be estimated as:

$$\text{Simple Moving Average} = \bar{x} = \frac{1}{n}\sum_{i=1}^{n} x_i = \frac{1}{37} \times (281.2194) = 7.6005$$

It may be noted here that, using 48 monthly observations and considering a rolling window of 12 months, only 37 average numbers can be estimated.

The weighted moving average, weights being decreased arithmetically, may also be estimated, such that:

$$\text{WMA}_M = \frac{nP_M + (n-1)P_{M-1} + \ldots + 2P_{M-(n-2)} + P_{M-(n-1)}}{n + (n-1) + \ldots + 2 + 1}$$

$$= \frac{5537.9899}{703} = 7.8777$$

The median value of the GOI yield may be simply estimated by arranging the yield data in descending/ascending order, and thereby taking the average of the two middlemost values (because of even number of values), i.e. the average of 7.6433 and 7.6873, coming to 7.6653%. At the same time, the model value can also be estimated by identifying the value with the highest frequency. Since none of the monthly yield data over a period of four years have any single repetition, the yield data cannot be arranged as a frequency distribution table discussed above, so any model value may not be identified.

### Excel functions

These central tendency measures of any sample data may be directly estimated in Excel by using the respective functions, given below:

| | |
|---|---|
| For Arithmetic Mean or Simple Average | =AVERAGE(B2:B49) |
| For Median | =MEDIAN(B2:B49) |
| Fore Mode | =MODE(B2:B49) |

Here, it is assumed that there are 48 monthly observations in the sample data, the central tendency measures of which are expected to be estimated, and the data is available in Excel in column B (B2 to B49), the reference of which needs to be given before estimating the desired statistical measures.

## Measures of dispersion

Many times, a single number is not sufficient to represent the entire mass of data and it becomes necessary to obtain some additional numerical description of the data to represent it more meaningfully. In such a situation, when the original data are spread over a wide range, the average has to be supplemented by some information on how widely the numbers are spread. The quantitative measures of the extent of spread are known as the *Measures of Dispersion*. The word "dispersion" is used to denote the "degree of heterogeneity" in the data set. It is an important characteristic, indicating the extent to which observations vary among themselves. When the values of a given set of observations are equal, the dispersion will be equal to zero. The wider the divergence from one observation to another, the larger will be the dispersion.

For any set of data, the measures of central tendency (mean, median, and mode) tells us only a part of what we need to know about the characteristics of the data set. Therefore, to have some more clear understanding of the pattern of the data, it is important also to measure its spread or variability from the average. If the data are widely dispersed, the central location is less representative of the data as a whole than it would be for the data more closely centered around the mean. A measure of dispersion is designed to state numerically the extent to which individual observations deviate from the average. Such dispersion measures can be an absolute measure or a relative measure.

Absolute measures are expressed in the same unit in which the observations are given, while relative measures are obtained by expressing an absolute measure as percentage of a measure of central tendency. Therefore, relative measures are independent of the units of measurement. Absolute measures are used to measure the amount of dispersion. But in order to compare the dispersion in different series, relative measures are used. Apart from this, if there are two sets of data and both are of dissimilar units, then the relative measures are expected to be the only alternative for comparison among the sets.

### Absolute measures of dispersion

#### Range

The range of a set of observations is the difference between the maximum and the minimum values.

$$Range = Maximum\,Value - Minimum\,Value \tag{3.8}$$

It represents the maximum possible difference between any two observations. The simplicity of its calculation is perhaps the main advantage for its application in statistics. But the main drawback of this measure of dispersion is that it does not depend on all observations. This measure is highly affected by extreme values.

#### Mean deviation (or mean absolute deviation)

The mean deviation of a set of observations is the arithmetic mean of absolute deviations from mean or any other specified value. Mean deviation is usually calculated about the arithmetic mean and therefore commonly refers to *Mean Deviation about Mean*. The formula of M.D. is such that:

$$Mean\,Deviation\,(about\,mean) = \frac{1}{n}\sum|x_i - x|; \;\; or \; = \frac{1}{N}\sum f_i|x_i - \bar{x}|; \tag{3.9}$$

#### Standard deviation

The most comprehensive descriptions of dispersion are those that deal with the average deviation from some measure of central tendency. Variance and standard deviation are two of these important measures in statistics. Variance of a set of observations is the average of squares of deviation from the arithmetic mean and is denoted by $\sigma^2$. Standard deviation is nothing but the square root of the variance, i.e. the square root of the average of squares of deviation from the mean value, and is denoted by σ such that:

$$Standard\ Deviation\,(\sigma) = \sqrt{\frac{1}{n}\sum(x_i - \bar{x})^2}\,,$$

$$or\ (\sigma) = \sqrt{\frac{1}{N}\sum f_i\,(x_i - \bar{x})^2} \tag{3.10}$$

Where, [Insert Equation Here] and $N$ represent the arithmetic mean and the total frequency of the set of observations. The above measures of standard deviation represent the population, but in the case of the sample measure, the value of n or N will be replaced by (n-1) or (N-1) respectively. There is some statistical reason to use (N-1) instead of N and it is well proved. Suppose if we take some sample from a given population and estimate the variance of all the samples, then the average of all the sample variance tends to be equal to the variance of the population only when we use (N-1) as the denominator while calculating the sample variances.

USES OF STANDARD DEVIATION

The main use of standard deviation is to determine, with a great deal of accuracy, where the values of a frequency distribution are located in relation to the mean. According to the Russian Mathematician Chebyshev, whatever be the shape of the distribution, at least 75% of the values will fall within ±2 standard deviation from the mean of the distribution, and at least 89% of the values will lie within ±3 S.D. from the mean. The percentage values can be measured even with more precision to lie within a specific range under a symmetrical, bell-shaped curve in the following way:

i)   About 68% of the values in the population will fall within ±1 S.D. from the mean
ii)  About 95% of the values in the population will fall within ±2 S.D. from the mean
iii) About 99% of the values in the population will lie within ±3 S.D. from the mean

The standard deviation is also useful in describing how far an individual value in a distribution departs from the mean of the distribution. A measure called the *Standard Score* gives the number of standard deviations for a particular observation lie below or above the mean. The standard score computed from a set of observations is given by:

$$Standard\ Score = \frac{x - \Box}{\Box}\text{(for Population Data); or}$$

$$= \frac{x - \bar{x}}{s}\text{(for Sample series)} \tag{3.11}$$

*Portfolio/joint standard deviation*

Portfolio standard deviation or joint variation of more than one data series captures the degree of fluctuation within the values of all data series from their respective averages. This shows the interrelationship in the fluctuation or variations of all the data series. The degree of such joint variation largely depends on the co-movement among the values of different data series. The individual importance or weight of different data series also plays a major role in deriving the common variation among them. Joint variation may be higher or lower than the individual variations, depending on co-movement and relative importance. If three data series, A, B, and C, with the weights of $W_A$, $W_B$, and $W_C$ have a variance equal to $Var._A$, $Var._B$, and $Var._C$ and a correlation coefficient between them as $r_{AB}$, $r_{BC}$, $r_{AC}$, then the joint variation is represented as:

$$Var\left(\sum_{i=1}^{n}x_i\right) = \sum_{i=1}^{n}VarX_i + 2\sum_{i<j}\sum cov\left(X_iX_j\right)$$

$$= \sum_{i=1}^{n}VarX_i + 2\sum_{i<j}\sum P_{ij}\sigma_i\sigma_j \qquad (3.12)$$

$$\sigma_P = \sqrt{\begin{array}{c}w_A^2\sigma_A^2 + w_B^2\sigma_B^2 + w_C^2\sigma_C^2 + 2w_Aw_Br_{AB}\sigma_A\sigma_B\\ +2w_Aw_Cr_{AC}\sigma_A\sigma_C + 2w_Bw_Cr_{BC}\sigma_B\sigma_C\end{array}} \qquad (3.13)$$

*Example*

Suppose the monthly interest rates, 10-year GOI yield, 91-day T-bill rate, and average call monthly rate for a period of 4 years (2014–2017), are given in the following table (Table 3.2):

Now, based on the above data, the absolute measures of dispersion can be calculated as shown in the following table (Table 3.3):

*Excel Function* used to measure the standard deviation is equal to: *STDEV(B2:B49)*

The joint variation of all the three series, assuming equal weightage for all (i.e. 1/3), using the variance and standard deviation measures of all the individual series, and the pair-wise correlation measures, is such that:

$$\sigma_P = \sqrt{\begin{array}{c}w_A^2\sigma_A^2 + w_B^2\sigma_B^2 + w_C^2\sigma_C^2 + 2w_Aw_Br_{AB}\sigma_A\sigma_B\\ +2w_Aw_Cr_{AC}\sigma_A\sigma_C + 2w_Bw_Cr_{BC}\sigma_B\sigma_C\end{array}} = 0.82\%$$

*[Correlation (10-Y GOI & 91-D T-bill), Correlation (91-D T-bill & Call Money Rate), Correlation (10-Y GOI & Call Money Rate) are respective + 0.8885, + 0.9841, and + 0.8637]*

The above joint variation measures indicate that the joint variation form their respective averages. In other words, the monthly average estimates for

*Table 3.2* Historical monthly interest rates in India

*Monthly Interest Rates in India*

| Months | 2014 | | | 2015 | | | 2016 | | | 2017 | | |
|---|---|---|---|---|---|---|---|---|---|---|---|---|
| | 10-Y GOI | 91-D T-bill | Call Rate | 10-Y GOI | 91-D T-bill | Call Rate | 10-Y GOI | 91-D T-bill | Call Rate | 10-Y GOI | 91-D T-bill | Call Rate |
| January | 8.87 | 8.48 | 8.19 | 7.69 | 8.03 | 7.89 | 7.52 | 7.02 | 6.81 | 7.15 | 6.13 | 6.04 |
| February | 8.94 | 9.06 | 8.21 | 7.77 | 8.26 | 7.69 | 7.64 | 7.20 | 6.77 | 7.09 | 6.11 | 6.01 |
| March | 8.88 | 8.50 | 8.37 | 7.80 | 7.78 | 7.58 | 7.40 | 6.87 | 6.93 | 7.06 | 5.70 | 5.97 |
| April | 8.90 | 8.82 | 8.36 | 7.89 | 7.87 | 7.44 | 7.87 | 6.78 | 6.47 | 7.22 | 6.17 | 5.93 |
| May | 8.69 | 8.42 | 8.00 | 7.64 | 7.79 | 7.47 | 7.47 | 6.73 | 6.44 | 6.51 | 6.28 | 6.04 |
| June | 8.75 | 8.47 | 8.08 | 7.87 | 7.60 | 7.11 | 7.78 | 6.58 | 6.33 | 6.59 | 6.30 | 6.08 |
| July | 8.50 | 8.57 | 8.27 | 7.81 | 7.32 | 7.04 | 7.41 | 6.46 | 6.36 | 6.55 | 6.20 | 6.06 |
| August | 8.63 | 8.53 | 7.98 | 8.05 | 7.35 | 7.07 | 7.11 | 6.55 | 6.40 | 6.54 | 6.08 | 5.90 |
| September | 8.53 | 8.41 | 7.80 | 7.53 | 7.03 | 7.14 | 6.81 | 6.41 | 6.42 | 6.82 | 6.07 | 5.88 |
| October | 8.30 | 8.36 | 7.94 | 7.92 | 7.04 | 6.72 | 6.82 | 6.39 | 6.21 | 7.03 | 6.06 | 5.87 |
| November | 8.12 | 8.21 | 7.83 | 8.07 | 7.11 | 6.78 | 6.30 | 5.94 | 6.14 | 7.25 | 6.05 | 5.87 |
| December | 7.92 | 8.30 | 8.11 | 8.09 | 7.11 | 6.73 | 7.17 | 6.25 | 6.12 | 7.52 | 6.12 | 5.91 |

*Source:* RBI Database

*Table 3.3* Absolute measures of dispersion for different variables

| Variable | Range | Mean Deviation | Std. Deviation |
|----------|-------|----------------|----------------|
| 10-Year GOI Yield | 8.94–6.30 = 2.63% | 0.57% | 0.71% |
| 91-Day T-bill Rate | 9.06–5.70 = 3.36% | 0.85% | 0.98% |
| Call Money Rate | 8.37–5.87 = 2.50% | 0.75% | 0.85% |

*Source*: All tables in this chapter are created by the author unless otherwise stated.

the 10-year GOI yield, 91-day T-bill rate, and the call money rate are respectively 7.6617%, 7.1845%, and 6.9328%. These monthly interest rates are expected to jointly vary (rise or fall) on an average of 0.82% from their respective mean values.

### Relative measures of dispersion

Neither the mean nor the standard deviation can be the sole basis for comparing two distributions. Suppose in a set observations with S.D. and mean equal to 10 and 5, the values vary by an amount twice as large as the mean itself. At the same time, in another set of observations with S.D. of 10 and a mean of 1000, the variation relative to the mean is totally insignificant. Therefore, it is very difficult to have an idea about the dispersion of a given set of observation until we know about the S.D. or other measures of dispersion, mean, and the comparison between the measures of dispersion and mean.

Relative measures of dispersion give the idea about the magnitude of the deviation relative to the magnitude of some central measure. There are three important relative measures of dispersion. Two of such measures are: coefficient of variation and coefficient of mean deviation.

Coefficient of variation relates the standard deviation and the mean by expressing the S.D. as a percentage of the mean. The unit of measure, then, is "percent" rather than the same units as the original data. The formula of this measure is given by

$$\text{Coefficient of Variation} = \frac{S.D.}{Mean} \times 100 = \frac{\sigma}{\mu} \times 100 \quad (3.14)$$

Coefficient of mean deviation (about mean or median) is derived by the measure of mean deviation as a percentage of mean or median, and is given by

$$\text{Coefficient of Mean Deviation} = \frac{MeanDeviation}{MeanorMedian} \times 100 \quad (3.15)$$

*Example*

Using the aforesaid example of 10-year GOI yield, 91-day T-bill rate, and call money rate, the relative dispersion measure can be estimated such that:

$$\text{For 10-Year GOI Yield, C. V.} = \frac{S.D.}{Mean} \times 100 = \frac{\sigma}{\mu} \times 100 = 9.25$$

$$\text{For 91-Days T-bill, C. V.} = \frac{S.D.}{Mean} \times 100 = \frac{\sigma}{\mu} \times 100 = 13.57$$

$$\text{For Call Money Rate, C. V.} = \frac{S.D.}{Mean} \times 100 = \frac{\sigma}{\mu} \times 100 = 12.30$$

As suggested by the standard deviation measures, the relative measures also support that the 10-Year GOI yield is relatively the most stable (minimum variation) interest rate among the three, followed by the call money rate and 91-day T-bill rate.

## Skewness and kurtosis

There is no doubt that various measures of central tendency and of dispersion can focus light on the nature of a set of observations. But they cannot reveal the entire story about the data series. There are two other important characteristics called skewness and kurtosis, measuring the asymmetricity in the distribution of a set of observations. Two distributions, with the same mean and standard deviation, may differ widely in their overall appearance. Dispersion is concerned with the amount of variation rather than with its direction. Skewness tells us about the direction of the variation or the departure from symmetry, whereas kurtosis talks about the concentration of variations.

### Skewness

"Skewness", in single word, refers to the "asymmetry" or lack of symmetry in the shape of a frequency distribution. A frequency distribution is said to be symmetrical if the frequencies are symmetrically distributed about mean, i.e. when the values of the variable equidistant from the mean have equal frequencies. Measures of skewness tell us the direction and the extent of skewness. The more the mean moves away from the mode, the larger the asymmetry or skewness. Therefore, when a distribution is not symmetrical, it is called a skewed distribution. In case of positive skewness, the frequencies in the distribution are spread out over a greater range of values on the high-value end of the curve (i.e. the right-hand side) than they are on the low-value end. If the curve is normal, the spread will be the same on both sides of the center point and the mean, median, and mode will all have the same value. The importance of skewness lies in the fact that statistical theory is often based upon the assumption of the normal distribution. A measure of skewness is therefore necessary in order to guard against the consequences of this assumption.

Skewness has benefits in many areas. Many simplistic models assume normal distribution, i.e. data is symmetric about the mean. But in reality, data points are not perfectly symmetric. So, an understanding of the skewness of the dataset indicates *whether deviations from the mean are going to be positive or negative.*

There are various methods to measure the skewness, suggested by a great British Statistician Karl Pearson, such as: *Karl Pearson's Coefficient of Skewness*, and moment measure of skewness. These measures may be estimated as:

$$Skewness = \frac{(Mean - Mode)}{Std.Deviation} = \frac{3(Mean - Median)}{Std.Deviation}; or$$

$$= \sqrt{\beta_1} = \frac{\mu_3}{\left(\sqrt{\mu_2}\right)^3} = \frac{\mu_3}{\sigma^3} \tag{3.16}$$

$\mu_3$ and $\sigma$ are respectively the third moment against mean and the standard deviation.

Though theoretically, there is no limit to this measure, the value given by this formula is rarely very high and usually lies between $\pm 3$; however, in practice, it is rare to exceed $\pm 1$. Based on the symmetric nature of the distribution, the value of this measure would be zero, positive, or negative respectively for symmetrical, positively skewed, and negatively skewed distribution. This measure gives both the direction as well as the extent of skewness or asymmetricity.

*Excel Function* used to capture this asymmetricity measure is equal to: *SKEW(B2:B49)*

## Kurtosis

*Kurtosis* refers to the degree of flatness or peakedness in the region about the mode of a frequency curve. In other words, kurtosis refers to the concentration of values in the tails of a distribution. The tails of a probability distribution function contain the extreme values. Two distributions may have the same average, dispersion, and skewness; yet, in one, there may be a high concentration of values near the mode showing a sharper peak in the frequency curve than in the other. The degree of kurtosis of a distribution is measured relative to the peakedness of normal curve. In other words, the measure of kurtosis tells us the extent to which a distribution is more peaked or flat-topped than the normal curve. If a curve is more peaked than the normal curve, it is called *'leptokurtic'*. In such a case, observations are more closely bunched around the mode. On the other hand, if a curve is more flat-topped than the normal curve, it is said to be *'platykurtic'*. The normal curve itself is known as *'mesokurtic'*.

The only measure of kurtosis is based on moments and is measured by the coefficient $\beta_2$. The value of kurtosis is given by

$$Kurtosis(\gamma_2) = \beta_2 - 3 = \frac{\mu_4}{(\mu_2)^2} - 3 = \frac{\mu_4}{\sigma^4} - 3 \qquad (3.17)$$

Therefore, the value of kurtosis depends upon the value of $\beta_2$. If $\beta_2$ is equal to 3, the value of kurtosis will be equal to zero. On the other hand, a value of $\beta_2$, greater than or lower than 3 represents positive or negative kurtosis respectively. Here $\gamma_2$ is known as *'Excess Kurtosis'*.

*Excel Function* used to capture kurtosis is: *KURT(B2:B49)*

*Example*

Considering the aforesaid example of three different interest rates in the Indian debt market: 10-year GOI yield, 91-day T-bill rate, and call money rate, we may explain the asymmetricity in the distribution of the said time series. The measure of skewness and kurtosis, estimated through the moment measure as described in the above section, using the respective MS-Excel functions are:

|  | 10-Year GOI Yield | 91-Days T-bill Rate | Call Money Rate |
|---|---|---|---|
| Skewness | +0.0941 | +0.2975 | +0.3119 |
| Kurtosis (Excess) | −0.7290 | −1.3459 | −1.4051 |

The above estimates show that all the three interest rate series are slightly positively skewed, exhibiting that at least for the T-bill and call money rates, more than 50% of the time, the historical monthly rates falls below their respective averages, indicating a similar possibility in the future as well. On the other hand, the excess kurtosis for all the three interest rates are negative, indicating that all the three series are leptokurtic and the rates are mostly very close to their model values. Alternatively, this also exhibits that the tails of the distribution are not fat, leading to a lower tail risk where the chances for a larger deviation from the average are relatively higher.

## Correlation and regression

Statistical measures described so far, are used to exhibit the characteristics of a single variable only, e.g. mean, standard deviation, skewness, etc. But in practice, many situations arise in which we have to deal with multiple (two or more) variables simultaneously. If the values of two variables vary in such a way that movements in one variable are accompanied by movements in the other, then there may be some association between those two variables. Financial parameters related to various instruments in the financial market are generally associated to each other and may be with different degree of association. In that case, it is interesting to numerically measure the strength of this association between the variables. The degree of association between the variables under consideration is measured through the *Correlation* analysis. The measure of correlation is known as *Correlation Coefficient*.

After having established the fact that two variables are closely related, we may be interested in predicting the value of one variable given the value of the other. *Regression Analysis* reveals the average relationship between two or more variables and makes for possible estimation or prediction. The mathematical equation used to make the estimates or a prediction regarding the principal variable is known as a *Regression Equation*.

## Correlation

The word "correlation" is used to denote the degree of association between variables. If two variables, say x and y, are so related that variations in the magnitude of one variable tend to be accompanied by variations in the magnitude of the other variable, then they are said to be correlated. For example, yields on government securities of various maturities tend to change (positive or negative) as there is any change in the policy rates set by the central bank of an economy. Accordingly, both the variables, policy rate and yield on government securities are said to be correlated. This correlation is expected to be positive, as any market interest rates are broadly driven by the policy rates. At the same time, when the rate of interest charged by a bank tends to increase, the total amount of loans and advances of that bank tends to come down, indicating a negative correlation between the interest rate and the amount of loans and advances. Likewise, when there is no relation between two variables, e.g. between the number of employees in a bank and the risk-free yield on government securities, then these two variables are said to be uncorrelated.

Correlation may also be linear or non-linear. If the amount of change in 1 variable tends to bear a constant ratio to the amount of change in the other variable, then the correlation is said to be linear; on the other hand, if the ratio is not constant, the correlation is considered as non-linear. The linearity of the association between two variables can be shown through a diagrammatic representation, called *Scatter Diagram*. Here, we are restricted to linear or simple correlation only. This simple correlation is measured by the *Correlation Coefficient*.

There are different ways to ascertain whether two variables are correlated or not. A few of them are: scatter diagram, graph, Karl Pearson's coefficient of correlation, etc. The Pearson coefficient of correlation between two variables – x and y, denoted by the symbol $r_{x,y}$ – is defined as

$$r_{x,y} = \frac{Cov(x,y)}{\sigma_x \sigma_y} \tag{3.18}$$

Where, $\sigma_x$ and $\sigma_y$ are the standard deviations of the variables x and y respectively. $Cov(x, y)$ denotes the covariance of x and y. The correlation coefficient $r_{x,y}$ is a pure number and is independent of the units of measurement. Its value lies between -1 and +1, such that $-1 \le r \le 1$, i.e. the value of r cannot exceed 1 numerically. If it is exactly 1, the variables are said to be perfectly correlated (positive or negative). If it is less than 1, there may a significant correlation, but the same is imperfect. There is a rule of thumb to interpret the value of the correlation coefficient. If the value of $r_{x,y}$ is less than ±0.3, the association between the variables is *Negligible*. If the value is between ±0.3 to ±0.5, the correlation is considered to be *Low*. If the number falls in the range of ±0.5 to ±0.7, and ±0.7 to ±0.9, the degree of association is respectively considered to be *Moderate* and *High*. Any correlation estimate with a value higher than ±0.9 exhibits a very high degree of association.

The function used in Excel to estimate the coefficient of correlation is: =CORREL(B2:C49), assuming that it is required to estimate the correlation between two variables (say, 10-year GOI yield and 91-day T-bill rate in India), with 48 values available for each variable, and are placed in Excel in column B2:B49 and C2:C49.

Even though the coefficient of correlation is one of the most widely used statistical measures, the same may be equally abused. Some major limitations of such coefficient of correlation measures include:

i)   In simple correlation, the basic assumption is that the association between two variables is linear. Therefore, a small value of r indicates only a poor linear relationship between the variables. This, however, does not rule out the possibility that the association may be very close. A small value of r only indicates a poor linear relationship, but the association may be non-linear that cannot be captured by this r. Therefore, before using r as a measure of association between two variables, it is always advisable to look into the scatter diagram to know whether the association is linear or non-linear.

ii)  A high value of r does not imply that there is any direct cause-effect relationship between the variables. The high value of r may be generated due to some other reasons: influence of a third variable affecting both, small size of the sample, mutual influence among both the variables, etc.

iii) Sometimes, it may so happen that two series of observations show a high correlation coefficient even though there is no logical basis for any relationship between them. Such correlation is said to be *Spurious* or *Nonsense* correlation.

### Example

Considering the same example of monthly 10-year GOI risk-free yield, 91-day T-bill rate, and average call money rate in India for last 4 years (2014–2017), used in the previous sections, we may estimate the degree of associations between the three types of interest rates representing the Indian debt market.

As measured through the aforesaid coefficient of correlation equation or using the given MS-Excel function, the degree of association between the three given interest rates are found to be strong enough (0.89, 0.98, and 0.86, respectively between 10-year GOI risk-free yield and 91-day T-bill rate; 91-day T-bill rate and average call money rate; and between 10-year GOI risk-free yield and average call money rate). As per the common rule of thumb, there is a very high (close to or more than 0.90) degree of association between the movements of interest rates in India. As far as the sign and degree of these associations are concerned, the observations are quite expected. Even if all interest rates in an economy are expected to be positively correlated, the association between the interest rates of similar or closer tenors are expected to be relatively higher, as exhibited from the highest degree of association between the 91-day T-bill rate and the average call money rate, relative to the other two pairs (one long term and one short term).

### Regression

The word '*Regression*' is used to denote estimation or prediction of the average value of 1 variable for a specified value(s) of other variable(s). It is concerned with the prediction of the most likely value of 1 variable when the value(s) of other variable(s) is (are) known. The mathematical equation used to make such a prediction regarding the principal variable is known as a *Regression Equation* and its geometrical representation is called a *Regression Curve* or *Lines*.

The variables used to form a regression equation are mainly divided into two – one is dependent variable, and the other is independent variable. The variable whose value is influenced or estimated or forecasted is called the dependent variable or, alternatively, the response variable and is generally denoted by Y. On the other hand, the variable which is used to estimate the value of the dependent variable is termed as the independent or explanatory variable and is generally denoted by $X_i$ (i = 1, 2, . . ., n).

In linear or simple regression, the relationship between the dependent and say an explanatory variable is assumed to be linear, such that: $Y = a + bX$.

*Steps involved in fitting simple regression equation*

Step1:

The first thing required to fit a regression equation is a set of observations on the cause, i.e. explanatory variable, and on the response variable, i.e. dependent variable.

Step 2:

After identifying the set of observations, the next step is to plot the data on a graph paper in the form of a scatter diagram with values of dependent variables along the Y-axis and the corresponding values of independent or explanatory variables along the X-axis.

Step 3:

Decide about the type of curve to be fitted depending upon the shape of the curve around which the points in the scatter diagram are clustered. For example, when the scatter diagram depicts a straight line pattern, simple regression of Y on X is to be fitted.

Step 4:

If Y and X are the ultimate variables for fitting the straight-line regression, then the least square regression equation expressing Y in terms of X is given by

$$Y = a + bX \qquad (3.19)$$

where, $b = \dfrac{Cov(x,y)}{\sigma_x^2} = r\dfrac{\sigma_y}{\sigma_x}$; and $a = \bar{Y} - b\bar{X}$

Step 5:

After getting the values of "a" and "b", the value of the dependent variable, i.e. of Y, can be estimated just by substituting the known value of X in the regression equation.

*Example*

Suppose we want to know the co-movement between interest rate and foreign exchange rate, and also the cause-effect relationship between them. Accordingly, a correlation-regression analysis may be performed with a set of relevant monthly data, say 10-year GOI yield and USD-INR foreign exchange rate, over a period of four years (2014–2017), given in the following table (Table 3.4).

Fundamentally, the risk-free yield of an economy (say 10-year GOI yield in India) and an exchange rate (say USD-INR exchange rate) are supposed to be interrelated and should exhibit some cause-effect relationship between them. A simple coefficient of correlation measure and graphical movement of the rates, as shown in the following section, may establish some statistically significant relationship between the two sets of information. The coefficient of correlation between the bond yield and the exchange rate has

*Table 3.4* Historical monthly GOI yield and USD-INR exchange rate

*Monthly 10-Year GOI Yield and USD-INR Exchange Rate*

| Months | 2014 | | 2015 | | 2016 | | 2017 | |
|---|---|---|---|---|---|---|---|---|
| | 10-Y GOI Yield | USD-INR FX Rate | 10-Y GOI Yield | USD-INR FX Rate | 10-Y GOI Yield | USD-INR FX Rate | 10-Y GOI Yield | USD-INR FX Rate |
| Jan-14 | 8.87 | 62.08 | 7.69 | 62.23 | 7.52 | 67.25 | 7.15 | 68.08 |
| Feb-14 | 8.94 | 62.25 | 7.77 | 62.04 | 7.64 | 68.24 | 7.09 | 67.08 |
| Mar-14 | 8.88 | 61.01 | 7.80 | 62.45 | 7.40 | 67.02 | 7.06 | 65.88 |
| Apr-14 | 8.89 | 60.36 | 7.89 | 62.75 | 7.87 | 66.47 | 7.22 | 64.51 |
| May-14 | 8.69 | 59.31 | 7.64 | 63.80 | 7.47 | 66.91 | 6.51 | 64.42 |
| Jun-14 | 8.75 | 59.73 | 7.87 | 63.86 | 7.78 | 67.30 | 6.59 | 64.44 |
| Jul-14 | 8.49 | 60.06 | 7.81 | 63.63 | 7.41 | 67.21 | 6.55 | 64.46 |
| Aug-14 | 8.63 | 60.90 | 8.05 | 65.07 | 7.11 | 66.94 | 6.54 | 63.97 |
| Sep-14 | 8.53 | 60.86 | 7.53 | 66.22 | 6.81 | 66.74 | 6.82 | 64.44 |
| Oct-14 | 8.30 | 61.34 | 7.92 | 65.06 | 6.82 | 66.75 | 7.03 | 65.08 |
| Nov-14 | 8.12 | 61.70 | 8.07 | 66.12 | 6.30 | 67.63 | 7.25 | 64.86 |
| Dec-14 | 7.92 | 62.75 | 8.09 | 66.60 | 7.17 | 67.90 | 7.52 | 64.24 |

*Source*: RBI Database

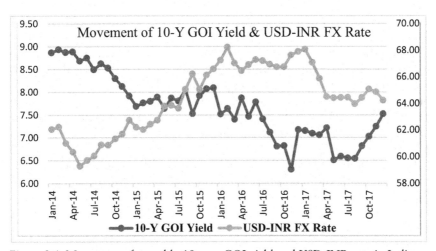

*Figure 3.1* Movement of monthly 10-year GOI yield and USD-INR rate in India

*Source:* All figures in this book have been created by the author unless otherwise stated.

come out to be moderately negative ($r_{xy}$ = *-0.6621*), giving an indication of some possible cause-effect relationship between the variables. The combined line diagram shown in the following figure (Figure 3.1) also indicate some co-movement between the variables.

Considering 10-year GOI yield as the dependent variable (Y variable) and USD-INR exchange rate as an independent variable (X variable), including

*Table 3.5* Summary output of regression results

| Summary Output of Regression Results (Regressing Bond Yield on Exchange Rate) | | | | | | |
|---|---|---|---|---|---|---|
| Overall Significance Statistics | | | Marginal Significance Statistics | | | |
| Multiple R | 0.6621 | | Coefficients | Standard Error | t Stat | P-value |
| R Square | 0.4384 | Intercept | 19.6350 | 1.9994 | 9.8203 | 0.0000 |
| Adj. R Square | 0.4262 | X Variable | -0.1860 | 0.0310 | -5.9928 | 0.0000 |
| Standard Error | 0.5367 | | | | | |
| Observations | 48 | | | | | |

a constant or intercept (C) in the regression equation ($Y = a + bX$), the simple regression analysis is performed in MS-Excel, and the summary output is shown in the following table (Table 3.5).

The above summary has two important sets of information: overall statistical significance of the statistical estimates and marginal statistical significance of the statistical estimates representing the independent variable(s) in explaining the movement of the dependent variable. The overall significance of the regression results is mostly denoted by the R Square and Adjusted R Square values, whereas the marginal significance of each independent or explanatory variable is represented by the values of individual coefficients, t-statistics, and probability values. The above results show that the overall regression model is not robust enough (with small Adj. R Square of 0.4262), probably due to non-inclusion of other important explanatory variable(s). The intercept and the only explanatory variable selected in the regression model are found to be statistically significant, at 99% confidence level or at 1% level of significance.

Regression analysis may be of different types, depending on the nature of the data and the model selected justifying the mathematical relationship between the dependent variable and independent variable(s), broadly establishing the cause-effect relationship between the variables, subjected to necessary statistical tests to ensure the model's goodness-of-fit (overall and marginal).

## Probability distribution

### Types of random variables

A random variable is a variable that can take on a given set of values. It can take any possible value and is unknown till it is observed. There are two fundamental types of random variable, discrete and continuous. A discrete random variable may take on a countable number of distinct values. These are usually measurements or counts and take on integer values such as 0,1, 2, 3, and 4. A continuous random variable is one that can take on any real value, that is, a variable that can take any real number in a given interval. An example of a continuous random variable of interest to the banking and finance industry is the future risk-free rate of interest expected to prevail in the economy.

## Probability

We use probability to characterize the extent to which an event is likely to occur. Intuitively, a probability should lie between 0 and 1. An outcome or event that cannot occur should have a probability of 1. What is the probability that the number of trades that fail to settle when expected today will be the same as yesterday, equal to yesterday, or more than yesterday? Since one of these outcomes is certain to occur, the probability is 1. Probability values indicate the likelihood of an event occurring. The closer the probability is to 1, the more likely the event is to occur. For example, suppose completion, within the next three days, of projects A and B is uncertain, but we know the probability of completion of project A is 0.6 (60 percent) and the probability of completion of project B is 0.25 (25 percent). These probability values provide a numerical scale for measuring our uncertainty in the sense that they inform us that project A is more likely to be completed within the next three days' time than project B. More formally, we say that probability provides a numerical scale for measuring uncertainty.

## Probability functions

Probability functions give a complete representation of the possible outcomes of a random variable. They inform us what outcomes are possible and how likely they are. This is important because once we have knowledge of the possible outcomes and their probability of occurrence, we can quantify the potential risks that we may have to face.

## Method of counting

Counting techniques are used to deal with the problem of selecting items from a large sample, with or without having regard to the order in which they appear in the sample. There is a common mathematical notation that is used to represent the total number of ways that a given choice could occur. This notation is defined as n! (referred to as n factorial) which represents n (n-1) (n-2) . . . 1. Therefore, if n is positive, then n! = n (n-1)!. Further, the initial value, zero factorial, is defined as having the value 1 (0! = 1).

Below are the two important methods of counting:

*Combination*

A combination is a group of items selected from a larger set regardless of the order in which they appear. The number of ways to select r items from a set of n unlike items is written as

$$^nC_r \text{ and is equal to } \frac{n!}{r!(n-r)!}$$

The above way works because there are n ways of choosing the first item, n-1 for the second, and n-r for the rth item. However, since the order is unimportant, a factor r! is introduced as a divisor to allow for all the possible orderings of the selected items.

If for example, the problem of selecting 4 debtors from a group of 20 is considered, then there are $^{20}C_4$ ways of making the choice. Using the equation $n!/r!(n - r)!$ with $n = 20$ and $r = 4$, this gives 20!/4!(20 − 4)!. After simplification, the value comes to 4845. This means that there are 4845 different ways that a sample of 4 debtors may be selected from a list of 20 debtors.

*Permutation*

There are also some occasions when the order of the items in a sample is important. In such cases, the possible way of counting is referred to as permutation and is written as $^nP_r$ which takes the value of $n!/(n - r)$ where r number of items are selected from a set of n items. Here, the link between permutation and combination is such that $^nP_r = r!* \, ^nC_r$.

For example, consider the problem of awarding three team bonuses (first, second, and third) to the treasury of a bank, where there are seven desks in the treasury. The remaining four teams do not receive any team bonus at all. Here, the focus is on the number of possible groups of three different teams along with the positions held by the bonus awarded teams, i.e. the ordering of the teams in the group. Therefore, the required number of arrangement would be $^7P_3$ which comes to 7!/(7 − 3)! = 210. There are, therefore, a total of 210 ways of giving the bonus awards to three teams out of seven.

*Probability distribution*

The decision-makers always face some degree of risk while selecting a particular decision (course of action or strategy) to solve a decision problem. It is because each strategy can lead to a number of different possible outcomes (or results). Thus, it is necessary for the decision-makers to enhance their capability of grasping the probabilistic situation so as to gain a deeper understanding of the decision problem and base their decisions on rational considerations. For this, the knowledge of the concept of probability, probability distributions, and various related statistical terms is needed. The knowledge of probability and its various types of distributions help in the development of probabilistic decision models.

A probability distribution is a graphical representation of all the possible values that a random variable can take on with the probability associated with each value. Probability distribution identifies all the possible outcomes for the random variable with their respective probabilities. Probability density function or probability mass function are used to assign a probability measure to a random variable. Probability distribution of a specific risk indicator is significantly used to capture the future uncertainty. A financial model, used in risk estimation and forecasting, largely depends on the type of distribution that the risk indicator closely follows. Probability distribution depends on the statistical characteristics of the risk indicator. Probability distribution, depending on the type of random variable, is broadly of two types: discrete probability distribution and continuous probability distribution. Some of the popular probability distributions (both discrete and continuous) describing a large set of financial data are described in the following section.

## Binomial probability distribution

This type of distribution is applicable in an experiment of multiple trials with only two possible outcomes, success and failure. It describes discrete or non-continuous data resulting from an experiment called *Bernoulli Process,* *"The occurrence of a success or a failure in a particular trial does not affect, and is not affected by, the outcomes in any previous or subsequent trials".* Outcomes of such a process can be represented by Binomial P. D.

$$P(x = r) = {}^nC_r p^r q^{n-r} = \frac{n!}{r!(n-r)!} p^r q^{n-r} \tag{3.20}$$

Mean and variance for a binomial dist$^n$ are $\mu = np$ and $\sigma = \sqrt{npq}$. Important Assumptions: mutually exclusive outcomes, constant probability of outcomes, and independent outcomes among trial. How to construct a graphical representation of a probability distribution? The shape of a binomial distribution depends on the value of "p & q" for symmetricity and on 'n' for peakedness.

## Poisson probability distribution

Applicability: an experiment of a large number of trials with a very small chances of occurrence of a specific outcome. Mean and variance for a p dist$^n$. is $m = \sigma^2 = n \times p$. Probability mass function of a Poisson distribution with the only constant parameter (m = mean = variance) is given by:

$$f(x) = \frac{e^{-m}.m^x}{x!}; (x = 0,1,2,\ldots\ldots,\infty); e = 2.718 \tag{3.21}$$

The Poisson distribution of recovering 100 loans sanctioned to SMEs, provided the probability of recovering is 0.04. Unlike binomial P.D., Poisson P.D. is not limited to two mutually exclusive outcomes. Though probabilities in a Poisson distribution approach to zero after first few values, the number of possible values is infinite.

### Normal probability distribution

In most of the cases, the basic assumption is that the underlying probability distribution follows a normal distribution. To honor the contribution made by Karl Gauss in the development of normal distribution, it is also termed as Gaussian distribution. The probability function of a random variable x following normal probability distribution with two parameters, mean (μ) and S.D. (σ), is such that:

$$f(x) = \frac{1}{\sigma\sqrt{2\pi}}\exp^{-(x-\mu)^2/2\sigma^2}; -\infty < x < \infty; \pi = 3.1416 \tag{3.22}$$

A normal P.D. with μ=0 and σ=1 is known as standard normal probability distribution. In the case of a normal P.D. where the S.D. is more than 1, the observations are expected to be more dispersed from the expected value. The normal P.D. of a risk parameter with a specific mean and S.D. can be used to find out the chances of generating the value of the concerned parameter with a given deviation (e.g. 1σ, 2σ, 3σ, etc.), as shown in the following figure (Figure 3.2). It is used to understand the maximum periodic loss that an organization can suffer in *Normal* condition and also in *Stressed* scenarios.

## Properties of normal distribution

- Normal distribution has two parameters μ and σ.
- The point in the middle of the normal curve is the expected value [E(x)] for the distribution.
- The normal curve is symmetric around the expected value, i.e. bell shaped, and thin tailed.
- Because of the symmetric nature of the normal curve, Mean = Median = Mode.

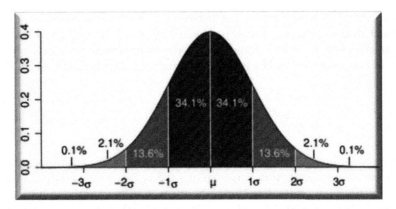

*Figure 3.2* Areas under normal curve

- Two tails of normal curve extend indefinitely and never touch the horizontal axis.
- The probability of obtaining an outcome greater or less than the mean is 50%.
- The probability that the actual outcome will be within ± 1 S.D. from the mean is 68.3%.
- The probability that the actual outcome will be within ± 2 S.D. from the mean is 95.5%.
- The probability that the actual outcome will be within ± 3 S.D. from the mean is 99.7%.

Normal distribution is a closer fit for those parameters or data where the possible deviation are assumed to be within a specific range. But it is quite common to see a persistent departure from normality, especially in the value of most of the risk parameters. A normal curve assumes a thin tail, whereas fat tail is an important property of some other probability distribution, termed as heavy tail distributions, exhibiting extremely large kurtosis. So, whenever a risk parameter is approximated with normal P.D., it is important to recognize the fact that such distribution underestimates the probability of extreme values

### Lognormal probability distribution

Lognormal distribution is widely used to model the P.D. of financial asset's price. An R.V. follows a lognormal distribution if its natural logarithm, rather the variable itself, is normally distributed. Unlike normal P.D., the lognormal distribution exhibits a bounded lower side by 0 and positive skewness. Because of these specific properties, lognormal distribution is found to be accurate to fit the distribution of financial asset prices. As of normal distribution, the lognormal distribution is also described by two parameters – mean and variance. Lognormal distribution takes on several shapes depending on σ. The P.D.F. of a lognormal distribution is given by:

$$f(x; \mu, \sigma) = \frac{1}{x\sigma\sqrt{2\pi}} \exp\left(\frac{-(\log x - \mu)^2}{2\sigma^2}\right); x > 0 \qquad (3.23)$$

Where μ and σ are the mean and S.D. of the variable's natural logarithm, the mean of a lognormal R.V. is [exp (μ + 0.5 σ²)] and the variance is [{exp (2μ + σ²)} × {exp (σ²) – 1}]. Therefore, if the security return (continuously compounded) is found to be normally distributed, the security price is necessarily to be lognormally distributed.

## Test of hypothesis

In many circumstances, statisticians need to take some decisions about a statistical population on the basis of sample observations. While attempting to reach such a decision, it is necessary to make certain assumptions about the characteristics of the population. Such an assumption or statement about the population is called a *Statistical Hypothesis*. Setting up and testing hypotheses is an essential part of statistical inference. In order to formulate such a test, usually some theory has been put forward, either because it is believed to be true or because it is to be used as a basis for argument but has not been proved. For example, claiming that a new drug is better than the current drug for treatment of the same symptoms. The validity of such an assumption needs to be tested by analyzing the sample. The procedure which enables us to check the truth of a certain hypothesis is known as the *Test of Hypothesis* or *Test of Significance*.

In each problem considered, the question of interest is simplified into two competing claims/hypotheses between which we have a choice: the *Null Hypothesis*, denoted $H_0$, against the *Alternative Hypothesis*, denoted $H_1$. These two competing claims/hypotheses are not, however, treated on an equal basis; special consideration is given to the null hypothesis.

### Null hypothesis

The statement that we initially put forward about the characteristic of the population, subject to proper validation, is designated as null hypothesis. The word "null" is used here because an effort is made to nullify this hypothesis based on the collected sample. The same hypothesis is accepted if there is a lack of sufficient evidence from the sample to nullify the initial statement. This is similar to a situation when, say, a borrower defaulted in his/her payments due to a commercial bank (willful defaulter) and is presented by the police before the judge for prosecution. Suppose the judge starts with the presumption that "the accused is not a willful defaulter". Suppose the police have accumulated some relevant facts and evidence which can be placed before the judge to nullify the presumption made by the judge. But if the facts and evidences collected by the police are not sufficient enough to prove that the borrower is a willful defaulter, the police have to accept the presumption made by the judge that "the accused is not a willful defaulter".

In this context, the null hypothesis is such that:

$H_0$: The accused is not a willful defaulter

We give special consideration to the null hypothesis. This is due to the fact that the null hypothesis relates to the statement being tested, whereas the alternative hypothesis relates to the statement to be accepted if/when the null is rejected.

The final conclusion, once the test has been carried out, is always given in terms of the null hypothesis. We say either, "Reject $H_0$ in favour of $H_1$," or "Do not reject $H_0$"; we *never* conclude, "Reject $H_1$", or even "Accept $H_1$". If we conclude, "Do not reject $H_0$", this does not necessarily mean that the null hypothesis is true; it only suggests that there is not sufficient evidence against $H_0$ in favour of $H_1$. Rejecting the null hypothesis. then, suggests that the alternative hypothesis *may* be true.

### Alternative hypothesis

Any hypothesis which differs from the null hypothesis can be called an *Alternative Hypothesis*. The alternative hypothesis, denoted as $H_1$, is a statement of what a statistical hypothesis test is set up to establish. For example, suppose the Reserve Bank of India has proposed to issue a new policy in regard to the long-term deposit rate. Now it has been proposed to test the effect of such an amendment on the depositors. In this context, the null hypothesis can be such that, "The two different policies do not have any different effect on the depositors". Accordingly, the alternative hypothesis might be that the new policy has a different effect, on average, compared to that of the current policy; or the new policy may be better than the existing one. Therefore, the alternative statement can be made in different ways, such that

$H_1$: The two policies have different effects, on average; or
$H_1$: The new policy is better than the current policy, on average.

Though focus is given to prove or disprove the null hypothesis, the alternative hypothesis also needs to be clearly specified because the null hypothesis is put forward for validation only against the alternative hypothesis.

*Type I and type II errors*

In statistics, the terms *Type I error* (also, $\alpha$ *error*, or *false positive*) and *Type II error* ($\beta$ *error*, or a *false negative*) are used to describe possible errors made in a statistical decision-making process, such that:

($\alpha$) Rejecting null when null is true, and
($\beta$) Retaining/Accepting null when null is false

Two important considerations to be kept in mind are: (1) we should reduce the chance of rejecting a true hypothesis to as low a value as desired; (2) the test must be so devised that it will reject the hypothesis tested when it is likely to be false.

## In summary:

- Rejecting a null hypothesis when it should have been accepted creates a *Type I Error*.
- Accepting a null hypothesis when it should have been rejected creates a *Type II Error*.
- In either case, a wrong decision or error in judgment has occurred.
- Decision rules (or tests of hypotheses), in order to be good, must be designed to minimize errors of decision.
- Minimizing errors of decision is not a simple issue because for any given sample size, any effort to reduce one type of error is generally associated with an increase in the other type of error.
- In practice, one type of error may be more serious than the other.
- In such cases, a compromise should be reached in favor of limiting the more serious type of error. Here, an effort can be made to fix the Type I error and to minimize the Type II error.
- The only way to minimize both types of error is to increase the sample size; and such a move may or may not be feasible.

For *example*, suppose we are going to test whether the average savings deposits of a bank as a whole, with the help of a sample of branches, are exactly the same as we are expecting. Suppose we have drawn, randomly, a sample of branches of a bank whose actual average savings deposits are Rs.50,000. Now, in order to validate the value of the population parameter, we have made a null statement that $\mu$ is equal to 50 ($H_0$: $\mu = 50$). Suppose, while testing its validity, we have found that the value of the test statistic falls within the critical region, thereby leading to reject the null hypothesis although it is true. Here we are committing an error by rejecting a statement which is actually true. This is Type I error.

On the other hand, considering the same example as above, suppose that the actual mean of the population is different from 50 and we are again trying to validate whether μ is equal to 50 ($H_0$: μ = 50). Here, let us assume that the value of the test statistic, by chance, fell in the acceptance region, leading to the conclusion that the null hypothesis can be accepted even if it is false in reality. Here, the error that we are committing by accepting a false null hypothesis is Type II error.

### Test statistic

A test statistic is a function of sample observations. Its value is used to decide whether or not the null hypothesis should be rejected in our hypothesis test. Various tests of significance have been developed to meet various types of requirements in social, economic, financial, operational, and business environments. Some of the important tests used to check the significance of the statistical hypothesis include z-test, t-test, chi-square test, f-test, etc. All these tests are based on some assumptions, and therefore are treated as a *Parametric Test*. But there are also some statistical tests to validate the significance of a hypothesis which are free from any pre-specified assumptions, and therefore called a *Non-Parametric Test*.

The applicability of different test statistics depends on the size of the sample. The test normally used for a large sample is different from that for a small sample. If the sample is large, the most common test is a z-test. But a t-test or chi-square test are normally applied for a small sample. Again, the selection of a specific test statistic also depends on the purposes of using such tests, such as testing the expected difference between the sample and population parameters (mean, standard deviation, proportion, etc.), testing the expected difference among the same parameter but of two different populations, testing the interdependence between two variables or attributes, and testing the goodness of fit, i.e. whether the sample observation fits to any given pattern or distribution, etc.

### Significance level

The significance level of a statistical hypothesis test is a fixed probability of wrongly rejecting the null hypothesis $H_0$, if it is in fact true. It is the probability of a type I error and is set by the investigator in relation to the consequences of such an error. That is, we want to make the significance level as small as possible in order to protect the null hypothesis and to prevent, as far as possible, the investigator from unintentionally making false claims. The significance level is usually denoted by α

Significance Level = *p (type I error)* = α

Commonly used levels of significance in practice are 5% (0.05) and 1% (0.01). If a 5% level of significance is adopted, it implies that in 5 samples out of 100, we are likely to reject a true $H_0$. In other words, it can also be said that we are 95% confident that our decision of rejecting $H_0$ is correct. Level of significance is normally set in advance before collecting the sample observations.

### Critical region

The critical region CR, or rejection region RR, is a set of values of the test statistic for which the null hypothesis is rejected in a hypothesis test. That is, the sample space for the test statistic is partitioned into two regions; one region (the critical region) will lead us to reject the null hypothesis $H_0$, the other will not. So, if the observed value of the test statistic is a member of the critical region, we conclude, "Reject $H_0$"; if it is not a member of the critical region then we conclude, "Do not reject $H_0$".

Suppose that $\alpha = .05$. We can draw the appropriate picture and find the z score for -.025 and .025. We call the outside regions the rejection regions.

We call the shaded areas the *rejection region* since, if the value of z falls in these regions, we can say that the null hypothesis is very unlikely so we can reject the null hypothesis

### Example

50 large banks were questioned about the percentage of their capital they keep to meet the regulatory requirements. Here, we want to test the hypothesis that large and healthy banks need less capital to satisfy the regulator, where a bank in general needs an average of 10% regulatory capital. Here, we follow the following steps.

A.  Compute a rejection region for a significance level of 0.05 (5%).
B.  If the sample mean, i.e. the average capital maintained by big and healthy banks is 9% and the standard deviation is 0.5%, what can you conclude?

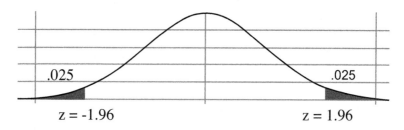

$z = -1.96$                    $z = 1.96$

.025                              .025

*Figure 3.3* Critical region in normal curve

*Solution*

First, we write down the null and alternative hypotheses

$$H_0 : \mu = 10\% \qquad H_1 : \mu < 10\%$$

This is a left-tailed test. The z-score that corresponds to .05 is -1.96. The critical region is the area that lies to the left of -1.96. If the z-value is less than -1.96 there, we will reject the null hypothesis and accept the alternative hypothesis. If it is greater than -1.96, we will fail to reject the null hypothesis and say that the test was not statistically significant. Here, we have

$$Z = \frac{9-10}{0.5 / \sqrt{50}} = -14.14$$

Since -14.14 is to the left of -1.96, it is in the critical region. Hence, we reject the null hypothesis and accept the alternative hypothesis. Here, we can conclude that the large and healthy banks may require less amount of regulatory capital to satisfy the regulator.

## P-value

The probability value (*p*-value) of a statistical hypothesis test is the probability of getting a value of the test statistic as extreme as or more extreme than that observed by chance alone, if the null hypothesis $H_0$ is true.

It is the probability of wrongly rejecting the null hypothesis if it is in fact true. It is equal to the significance level of the test for which we would only just reject the null hypothesis. The *p*-value is compared with the actual significance level of our test and, if it is smaller, the result is significant. That is, if the null hypothesis were to be rejected at the 5% significance level, this would be reported as "$p < 0.05$".

Small *p*-values suggest that the null hypothesis is unlikely to be true. The smaller it is, the more convincing is the rejection of the null hypothesis. It indicates the strength of evidence for say, rejecting the null hypothesis $H_0$, rather than simply concluding, "Reject $H_0$" or "Do not reject $H_0$".

## Example

Suppose that we want to test the hypothesis with a significance level of .05 that the average borrower default rate in banks has changed after Basel II came into effect. Suppose the average borrower default rate in banks throughout the history is 10%. But during the last 10 years, the average default rate has fallen to 8% with a standard deviation of 0.4%. Now what would be conclusion?

We have

$H_0 : \mu = 10$

$H_1 : \mu < 10$

We compute the z score: $Z = \dfrac{8-10}{0.4/\sqrt{10}} = -15.81$

Since the probability value of the above z score is much lower than the specified p-value (0.05), we can conclude that there has been a change in the default status of borrowers after the implementation of Basel II in banking history. Note that small *p*-values will result in a rejection of $H_0$, and large *p*-values will result in failing to reject $H_0$.

### Power

The power of a statistical hypothesis test measures the test's ability to reject the null hypothesis when it is actually false – that is, to make a correct decision.

In other words, the power of a hypothesis test is the probability of not committing a type II error. It is calculated by subtracting the probability of a type II error from 1, usually expressed as:

Power $= 1 - p(type\ II\ error) = (1 - \beta)$

The maximum power a test can have is 1, the minimum is 0. Ideally, we want a test to have high power, close to 1.

### One-sided and two-sided test

A one-sided test is a statistical hypothesis test in which the values for which we can reject the null hypothesis, $H_0$, are located entirely in one tail of the probability distribution. In other words, the critical region for a one-sided test is the set of values less than the critical value of the test, or the set of values greater than the critical value of the test. A one-sided test is also referred to as a one-tailed test of significance.

On the other hand, a two-sided test is a statistical hypothesis test in which the values for which we can reject the null hypothesis, $H_0$, are located in both tails of the probability distribution. In other words, the critical region for a two-sided test is the set of values less than a first critical value of the test and the set of values greater than a second critical value of the test. A two-sided test is also referred to as a two-tailed test of significance.

The choice between a one-sided and a two-sided test is determined by the purpose of the investigation or prior reasons for using a one-sided test.

*Example*

Suppose we wanted to test a depositor's claim that there is, on average, 10% interest given by Indian banks on a term deposit for 5 years.

We could set up the following hypotheses:

$H_0 : \mu = 10\%,$

Against

$H_1 : \mu < 10\%$ or $H_1 : \mu > 10\%$

Either of these two alternative hypotheses would lead to a one-sided test. Presumably, we would want to test the null hypothesis against the first alternative hypothesis since it would be useful to know if there is likely to be less than 10% interest, on average, given by a bank (none of the depositors would complain if they get the correct rate of interest or more in their deposited amount).

Yet another alternative hypothesis could be tested against the same null, leading this time to a two-sided test:

$H_0 : \mu = 10\%,$

Against

$H_1 : \mu \neq 10\%$

Here, nothing specific can be said about the average interest rate in a bank; only that, if we could reject the null hypothesis in our test, we would know that the average rate of interest in Indian banks is likely to be less than or greater than 10%.

## Self-learning exercise

1 What is a statistical average? What are the desirable properties for an average to possess? Mention different types of averages and state why the arithmetic mean is the most commonly used amongst them.
2 What is moving average? How this different from simple arithmetic mean? If you think of applying the moving average on financial asset price data, which specific moving average method you will prefer and why?
3 Classify different measures of dispersion. What are the properties and use of *Standard Deviation*? When do we prefer some relative measures instead of absolute measures like standard deviation?
4 What do we mean by skewness and kurtosis? What is the role of these two measures in non-normal distribution. Briefly explain.

5  How are measures of shape important for a portfolio manager to understand the risk involved in various financial assets?
6  Briefly explain the important properties of correlation and regression. How are both complementary to each other to understand the statistical properties of bivariate or multivariate data?
7  What is the theory of probability? How does probability distribution help to understand the statistical behavior of historical data on interest rates?
8  How do you differentiate between normal and non-normal probability distribution? If a risk manager assumes that the return on a debt security is normally distributed, what conclusions may he draw regarding the prices/returns of that particular security?
9  How are type I and type II errors important, say to a bond trader for testing his null hypothesis that a 10-year bond yield will remain unchanged for next few weeks.
10  How does a bond portfolio manager, having a large set of information on bond, equity, and FX markets (domestic and worldwide), make use of such data to successfully manage his portfolio? Briefly explain how the use of a few statistical measures help the manager to successfully analyze the data.

## Bibliography

Dougherty, C. (2012). *Introduction to Econometrics* (4th edn.). Oxford University Press, Oxford, UK.

Gujarati, D., Porter, D. C., and Gunasekar, S. (2015). *Basic Econometrics* (5th edn.). McGraw Hill Education (India) Pvt. Ltd., India.

Gupta, S. C. (2009). *Fundamentals for Statistics* (6th edn.). Himalaya Publishing House, India.

Levin, D. M., Stephan, D. F., Krehbiel, T. C., and Berenson, M. L. (2009). *Statistics for Managers: Using Microsoft Excel* (5th edn.). PHI Learning Pvt. Ltd., India.

Livin, R. I., and Rubin, D. S. (2008). *Statistics for Management* (7th edn.). Pearson Education Inc., India.

Swift, L., and Piff, S. (2005). *Quantitative Methods for Business, Management, and Finance* (2nd edn.). Palgrave Macmillan, New York.

Tsay, R. S. (2015). *Analysis of Financial Time Series* (3rd edn.). Wiley India Pvt. Ltd., India.

Winston, W. L. (2018). *Microsoft Excel 2016: Data Analysis and Business Modeling* (5th edn.). PHI Learning Pvt. Ltd., India.

# 4   Risk and return measures

Key learning outcomes

This chapter is expected to enable readers to answer the following questions:

- What are the different types of risk associated with investment in fixed income securities?
- How to capture risks in individual debt security and the portfolio.
- What are the different measures to calculate returns from investment in debt instruments?
- How to estimate security-wise and portfolio level returns.
- What are the major advantages and limitations of various risk-return measures?

## Risk and return in bonds: meaning and linkages

Bonds are an important component of investment portfolios for most investors, especially for institutional investors. Bonds reduce the overall risk of a portfolio by introducing diversity. Bonds produce steady current income – income that investors receive, say in every year/six months/quarter. This steady stream of income is important to some investors, depending on their asset-liability structure and their current needs. Bonds are more low-risk investments than stocks, sometimes at the cost of lower returns. The attractiveness of bond investment largely depends upon the future movement of interest rates. Bonds are attractive options when the market anticipates interest rates to fall. As interest rates fall, bond values rise, giving a positive return to the investor. The main sources of return from a bond are: regular (annual/semi-annual) coupon income, reinvestment income (i.e. interest on coupon received), and bond's price appreciation (if any). Even if the coupon rate, the major source of return from a bond, is fixed in a fixed rate bond, there may be several risk factors causing different levels of variation in the returns from a bond. Alternatively, bonds are susceptible to a number of risks, depending on the nature of the bond issue. Like other investment opportunities in the financial market, the risk-return linkage is also applicable in a bond investment. If an investor wants to earn a higher return, he has to compromise with some risk factor(s), such as credit risk, interest rate risk, liquidity risk, etc. There can be different measures available to capture the risk and return from an individual security, or a portfolio of many securities. These are discussed in the following section.

## Risks associated with fixed income securities

Investment in any financial asset generates a return subject to some uncertainty. This uncertainty may be favourable or unfavourable to an investor. Any uncertainty that causes any kind of financial losses for the investor is generally termed as '*Financial Risk*'. In other words, risk refers to the *Chance of Financial Losses* due to unforeseen or random changes in underlying *Risk Factors*. Since the goal of investing is to get the best return possible from the investment, investment risk is the possibility that the investor will get back less than their investment or their expected return, or that they will get less than what they could have had if they had invested their money elsewhere, commonly known as *Opportunity Costs*. Even if investment in fixed income securities like bonds generates a fixed income for the investor, such investments are also exposed to several risk factors and may cause different degree of financial losses for the investor. Some of these important risk factors are discussed in the following section:

### Interest rate risk

Since the value of a bond at any point in time is nothing but the present value (PV) of all the future cash flows due on the security, and the PVs of future cash flows are inversely related to the existing rate of interests of different respective tenors, there is an inverse relation between the price of a bond and the rate of interest. This leads bond investors to be exposed to interest rate risk. Alternatively, in the event of a rise in interest rates, the price of a bond decreases and the investor has to face a capital loss, leading to *Interest Rate Risk*. Risk of a certain fall in the price of a fixed income security only due to a possible rise in interest rate is specifically called the *Price Risk*. Changes in interest rate also lead to another type of risk in bond investment, and is known as *Reinvestment Risk*, as discussed in the next section. There is a possible trade-off between the price risk and reinvestment risk, which arises due to changes in interest rates.

Suppose an investor has bought 06.79 GS 2029, a bond issued by the government of India, paying a coupon of 6.79% per annum, payable semi-annually, maturing in 2029 at par value. Now, suppose the market interest rate has gone up by 21 basis, from 6.79% to 7.00% and the investor wants to sell the bond where the coupon rate would be the same as 6.79%. Since the bond is selling at par, nobody would like to buy the bond at par with a coupon rate of 6.79%, where the market interest rate is 7.00%. Here, neither the investor can change the coupon rate nor can they change the actual maturity of the bond so that the same would be saleable in the market. Here, what the bond seller can do is reduce the bond price so that the amount of coupon received on the bond at the bond's par value would be equal to the amount based on the new or revised interest rate on the new or revised price, so that without changing the original coupon rate, the current market rate can be offered to the prospective buyer of the bond.

The magnitude of interest rate risk largely depends upon the features of a bond issue, such as: maturity, coupon rate, coupon payment frequency, yield, presence of options, etc. In the case of a floating rate bond, even if the coupon rates are adjusted with the prevailing market rates at every coupon reset date (annually, semi-annually), the value of such bond is exposed to interest rate fluctuation during two coupon reset dates. The interest rate risk of a bond can be captured through different measures, such as: Macaulay duration, modified duration (MD), effective duration, key rate duration, price value basis points (PVBP or PV01), and convexity, discussed in detail in the respective chapter.

### Reinvestment risk

*Reinvestment Risk* is based on the assumption that interim cash flows (i.e. coupons) from a fixed income security are reinvested at every interval, so that further interest can be earned on interest. But if the investor fails to reinvest the periodic coupons at a predetermined rate, the actual yield from the bond till its maturity will be different than whatever was expected. *For example*, an investor bought a central government security 6.79 GS 2027 with a face value of INR10 crore, having an annual coupon of 6.79%, say payable annually. Every year, the investor receives INR 67.90 lakhs (6.79% × INR10 crore) which can be reinvested back into another bond. But if over time, the market rate suddenly falls to 6%, then INR 67.90 lakhs received from the bond can only be reinvested at 6%, instead of the 6.79% rate of the original bond. This risk is contrary to price risk, because when interest rates rise, price risk increases, but reinvestment risk declines. Alternatively, due to rise in interest rates, there will be a fall in the price of a security, but the investors can be in a position to reinvest their interim cash flows at a higher rate and thereby can earn some gain, termed as reinvestment gain. Similarly, in the event of a sudden fall in the interest rates, future values of interim cash flows may decline, leading to a risk in the investment, called *Reinvestment Risk*. Since there is no interim coupon payment in the case of zero coupon bonds, such instruments do not have any reinvestment risk. The severity of the reinvestment risk for a fixed coupon bond largely depends upon the maturity and the coupon rate of the bond. The longer the maturity of a bond, the higher will be the likelihood that reinvestment income will be lower (due to a fall in interest rates) for the remaining maturity, and therefore severe would be the impact. On the other hand, the higher the coupon rate of a bond, the bigger will be the coupon payments to be reinvested at a lower rate, leading to a bigger loss due to a fall in interest rates.

## *Yield curve risk*

Maturity of a bond is one of the important factors for its price sensitivity due to a change in the interest rate or the yield. Therefore, the value of a portfolio of bonds with different maturities depends on how the value of individual bonds with different maturity periods changes following the change in interest rates. The rate of interest or the yield of different bonds varies according to their respective maturities, as may be depicted by the yield curve. The graphical relation between the yield on similar types of securities and their respective maturity is known as the yield curve. It is basically assumed that, in the scenario of changing interest rate, the yield of different bonds with different maturities changes by similar basis points, commonly known as a *Parallel Shift* in the yield curve. But in real market conditions, when there is any change in the rate of interest, even if all the rates change in a similar direction (rise or fall), the magnitude of change is not necessarily the same for all bonds with different maturities, which can be represented by a *Nonparallel Shift* in the yield curve. This non-parallel shift may result into *Steepening* of the yield curve where the yield spread between long-term and short-term yields widens, or *Flattening* of the yield curve where such yield spread narrows.

For example, in India, if the 10-year risk-free rate or base yield (i.e. yield on 10-year GOI bond) changes by 50 basis points (bps), yields of all other maturities are expected to experience a positive change, but need not to be exactly 50 bps. As a result, the risk-free yield curve will shift upward, but need not be shifted upward parallel by 50 bps. Due to the nonparallel shift, the yield curve may become *Flatter* or *Steeper*.[1] The price sensitivity of the whole bond portfolio, in the event of change in the interest rates, largely depends on market expectation towards the type of shifts in the yield curve. Accordingly, a portfolio consisting of few short-term securities and some long-term securities, and in a situation where long-term rates increases more than the rise in short-term rates, i.e. in the event of steepening of the yield curve, the fall in the value of long-term securities may be more than the losses incurred in short-term securities, affecting the portfolio loss. Because of these unequal changes in the interest rates of different tenors, a portfolio manager may fail to capture the actual loss in his bond portfolio, assuming a parallel shift in the yield curve, causing a further risk for the institution. Interest rate sensitivity measures, e.g. modified duration and PVBP/PV01, even if they capture how sensitive the bond portfolio is to a future change in interest rates, these measures are based on the assumption of parallel shift in the yield curve. Therefore, bond investors who invest in several bonds throughout the maturity segment and capture interest rate risk through the aforesaid portfolio sensitivity measures, are exposed to another risk, called *Yield Curve Risk*.

*Example*

Suppose an investor has the following five central government securities, of different maturities, in their government securities portfolio, as given in the following table (Table 4.1). Different securities, depending upon their various features, are exposed to different levels of interest rate risk. While estimating the interest rate risk on the entire portfolio, examine the level of yield curve risk on the whole portfolio, depending upon the expected change in interest rates for different tenors, leading to steepening or flattening of the yield curve.

From the given information on all the individual securities in the portfolio, it is possible to revalue the portfolio for any given change in interest rate or yield, assuming that there is a parallel shift in the yield curve, say by 100 basis points. But in reality, interest rates of different tenors may change by different magnitude, resulting to a non-parallel shift (steepening or flattening) in the yield curve, causing a different volume of interest rate risk losses in the bond portfolio. Therefore, assumption of parallel shift, upward or downward, flattening or steepening, in the yield curve may lead to an improper estimation of future losses and may turn out to be risky, termed as yield curve risk.

The following table shows the portfolio losses under different circumstances, such as:

i.   Parallel upward shift in the yield curve, by 100 bps.
ii.  Non-parallel shift in the yield curve, where the YC flattens (between 50–150 bps).
iii. Non-parallel shift in the yield curve, where the YC steepens (between 50–150 bps).

The portfolio losses under different scenarios, as exhibited in the following table (Table 4.2), clearly states the improper estimation of the interest rate risk losses for a simple assumption of parallel shift in the yield curve. The degree of actual portfolio loss (higher/lower) may depend upon the actual shift (steepening or flattening) in the yield curve and also the degree of such shift. In the given example, the portfolio loss is estimated under different circumstances and for a specified degree of change (50 to 150 basis points) in the interest rates of various tenors. Here, the risk is not that the projected losses are overestimated than the actual. This exact situation may vary depending upon the change in market scenarios. The actual risk, as may be defined by the yield curve risk, is the risk arising due to improper (higher or lower) estimation of possible future losses.

*Table 4.1* A sample government securities portfolio held by an investor

Settlement Date = 31-Oct-2018

| Security Description | Maturity | Residual Maturity (Years) | Coupon Rate | Traded Price (INR) | Traded Yield | Face Value (Rs. in Cr.) | Market Value (Rs. In Cr.) |
|---|---|---|---|---|---|---|---|
| 6.05% GS 2019 | 2-Feb-19 | 0.2556 | 6.05% | 99.6900 | 7.13% | 1 | 0.9969 |
| 6.84% GS 2022 | 19-Dec-22 | 4.1361 | 6.84% | 97.1100 | 7.67% | 1 | 0.9711 |
| 7.17% GS 2028 | 8-Jan-28 | 9.1889 | 7.17% | 95.7100 | 7.83% | 1 | 0.9571 |
| 7.95% G.S 2032 | 28-Aug-32 | 13.828 | 7.95% | 99.0700 | 8.06% | 1 | 0.9907 |
| 8.83% GS 2041 | 12-Dec-41 | 23.117 | 8.83% | 106.1300 | 8.23% | 1 | 1.0613 |
| **Portfolio** | | | | | | 5.00 | 4.9771 |

*Source:* All tables in this chapter are created by the author.

*Table 4.2* Portfolio level losses due to various yield curve shifts

Settlement Date: 31-Oct-2018

| Security Description | Residual Maturity (Years) | Market Value (Rs. In Cr.) | Parallel Shift in Yield Curve | | Steepening of Yield Curve | | Flattening of Yield Curve | |
|---|---|---|---|---|---|---|---|---|
| | | | Rise in IR (bps) | Fall in Value (INR) | Rise in IR (bps) | Fall in Value (INR) | Rise in IR (bps) | Fall in Value (INR) |
| 6.05% GS 2019 | 0.2556 | 0.9969 | 100 | 24083.7 | 50 | 11434.03 | 150 | 36701.8 |
| 6.84% GS 2022 | 4.1361 | 0.9711 | 100 | 337320 | 75 | 254767.2 | 125 | 418999 |
| 7.17% GS 2028 | 9.1889 | 0.9571 | 100 | 602958 | 100 | 602957.9 | 100 | 602958 |
| 7.95% G.S 2032 | 13.828 | 0.9907 | 100 | 774337 | 125 | 954767 | 75 | 588764 |
| 8.83% GS 2041 | 23.117 | 1.0613 | 100 | 994336 | 150 | 1436983 | 50 | 516036 |
| **Portfolio** | | 4.9771 | | 2733034 | | 3260909 | | 2163459 |

The above table (Table 4.2) clearly exhibits the fact that actual portfolio level losses due to either steepening or flattening of the yield curve are significantly different from the portfolio level losses estimated assuming a parallel shift in the yield curve. This difference in the loss estimates, just due to different types of shifts in the yield curve, is known as the yield curve risk.

## Liquidity risk

If an investor doesn't want to hold a bond till its maturity and intends to sell the same in between, they are concerned whether the market is liquid enough to offer them a right/fair price. Market liquidity can be measured through a number of dealers, the size of bid-offer spreads, market depth, etc. Alternatively, *Liquidity* refers to the ease with which a reasonable size of a security can be transacted in the market within a short notice, without adverse price reaction. Liquidity risk is the risk that the investor may have to sell their bond at a price which is actually lower than its true market price based on the prevailing interest rate. The liquidity risk can be measured by capturing the size of the spread between the *Bid Price* (the price which a buyer is willing to pay) and the *Ask Price* (the price which the seller intends to receive). The wider the *Bid-Ask Spread*, the greater would be the liquidity risk. One measure of liquidity risk in the government debt market can also be the difference between the volume of trading of newly issued on-the-run security and the volume of trading when the issue becomes old, called off the run. But such measures can be applied only when new securities of very similar maturity are issued in the market, leading to make both on-the-run and off-the-run securities of similar maturities available in the market. Liquidity risk is an important concern for bond investors or traders, especially if the underlying bond market does not experience sufficient number and volume of trading on a regular basis. A player in the fixed income securities market needs to fix the extent of liquidity premium for all illiquid securities in order to undertake any trading on the same, or to calculate how much worth those securities are under such illiquid market conditions. Market players, especially in illiquid markets like in India, face a very significant challenge not only to capture the liquidity risk even in the case of government securities, but also to price the same. Two similar bonds with the same maturity, but with different degrees of liquidity, are expected to be priced differently. Future cash flows of the bond with lesser liquidity are subjected to be discounted at a higher interest rate due to the presence of illiquidity premiums, leading the bond to be traded at a lower price.

## Example

Suppose there are two securities, issued by the government of India and almost of similar maturity currently (say as on 13 July 2017) traded in

*Table 4.3* Details of two government securities of similar maturity

| Description | Maturity Date | Res. Mat. | No. of Trades | Total Volume (F.V. Rs. Cr.) | Wtd Avg Price (Rs.) | Wtd Avg Yield (%) |
|---|---|---|---|---|---|---|
| 6.79% GS 2029 | 26-Dec-2029 | 12.4528 | 1657 | 24134.00 | 100.45 | 6.74 |
| 7.88% GS 2030 | 19-Mar-2030 | 12.6833 | 19 | 530.21 | 106.99 | 7.04 |

*Table 4.4* FIMMDA GOI base yields, as on 13 July 2017

| Tenor (Years) | 12.00 | 12.25 | 12.50 | 12.75 | 13.00 |
|---|---|---|---|---|---|
| GOI Base Yield | 6.69 | 6.66 | 6.75 | 6.93 | 7.10 |

the market. Details of both the securities are given in the following table (Table 4.3):

Suppose the FIMMDA[2] GOI Base yields, as on 13 July 2017, for few relevant tenors are given in the following table (Table 4.4):

Even if both the securities are of similar nature, especially in terms of residual maturity and issuer risk, the yield at which the securities are traded in the market are significantly different, by almost 30 basis points as on a given date. From this actual trade information, how can liquidity risk be captured and on which security?

From the above data, even if both the securities are issued by the government of India and almost of similar maturity (roughly 12.5 Years), both the securities have different levels of market acceptance, i.e. liquidity, as reflected from the data on the number of trades and trading volume. Because of the on-the-run status, the first security (6.79% GS 2029) is much more liquid than the second one, as supported by large number of trades and high trading volume. These different levels of liquidity affect the market of individual securities, especially for a relatively unpopular or illiquid security, causing a liquidity risk for the security. This can be explained in the following section.

From the base (risk-free) yield data provided by the FIMMDA as on the given date, we may compare the fair values and the actual traded numbers, both in terms of the yield and price, for both the liquid and illiquid security on the given date. The weighted average market price and the weighted average yield for the both the securities may be compared respectively with the fair yield of similar tenor, interpolated from the FIMMDA base yield data, and the fair price estimated based on the base yield of the concerned tenor. These comparisons, as given in the following table (Table 4.5), may exhibit the liquidity risk attached to a specific security:

Since the first security is highly liquid, the same is traded at a yield and price which are very close to its fair values, i.e. sellers (buyers) are able to sell (buy) at a price or yield that broadly they expect, and therefore do not

*Table 4.5* Liquidity risk in government security captured through price imperfection

| Security | Tenor (Years) | Fair Yield (%) | Market Yield (%) | Fair Price (Rs.) | Market Price (Rs.) | Price Diff. (Rs.) |
|---|---|---|---|---|---|---|
| 6.79% GS 2029 | 12.4528 | 6.7298 | 6.7400 | 100.4976 | 100.4500 | 0.0476 |
| 7.88% GS 2030 | 12.6833 | 6.8810 | 7.0400 | 108.3471 | 106.9900 | 1.3571 |

have any liquidity risk. But if we see the second security (7.88% GS 2030), the differences, both in terms of yield and price, among fair expectation and actual market values are significant. Based on the prevailing market situation on the given date, when the security is expected to be traded at a price (yield) of Rs.108.3474/- (6.8810% p.a.), the same is actually traded at a reasonably lower (higher) price of Rs.106.9900/- (yield of 7.0400% p.a.). This lower traded price or higher traded yield for the second security is basically due to the liquidity risk, where the buyers are ready to pay a lesser price or to accept a higher yield, in comparison with the similar security but of higher liquidity. This lower price or higher yield for an illiquid security is a compensation given to the buyer for holding an unpopular position or to bear the liquidity risk.

### Call risk (timing risk)

A coupon bond can be issued with a provision of early settlement before its scheduled maturity. In case of a callable bond, the issuer can call back the bond when the interest rate of similar bond available in the market falls below the coupon rate applicable to the original bond. Therefore, the cash flow pattern of a callable bond is uncertain because it is not known to the investor when the bond will be called. If the bond is called due to a fall in the interest rate and accordingly the coupon rate, the investor has to reinvest their proceeding at a lower rate comparative to the original rate of interest, and therefore is exposed to *Reinvestment Risk*. At the same time, the potential for price appreciation, due to fall in the interest rate, will also be lower comparative to a similar but option-free bond. This will lead to insufficient capital gain for the investor because of *Price Compression* due to the embedded option. This reinvestment risk and the risk of price compression can be treated as the *Call Risk*, which is present only in those bonds with an embedded call option.

### Example

Suppose the government of India, as on 13 July 2014, has issued a 10-year 7.50% fixed coupon bond, payable annually, with an option to call back the

*Table 4.6* Risk-free base yield curve, as on 13 July 2017

| Maturity | 1.00 | 2.00 | 3.00 | 4.00 | 5.00 | 6.00 | 7.00 | 8.00 | 9.00 | 10.00 |
|---|---|---|---|---|---|---|---|---|---|---|
| YTM | 6.34 | 6.33 | 6.53 | 6.58 | 6.57 | 6.64 | 6.81 | 6.87 | 6.71 | 6.53 |

issue on any of the coupon payment dates after a lock-in period of the first two years at par value. Accordingly, the first possible call date, after two years of lock-in period, would be 13 July 2017, when the issuer will decide whether to exercise the call option or to go ahead with the issue. Generally, the issuer looks at the prevailing market situation, mainly in terms of the market rate of interest, in all the possible call dates and decides accordingly. Suppose the bond, as on 13 July 2017, is traded at Rs.101.75/-. Suppose the risk-free base yield curve, as on 13 July 2017, is given in the following table (Table 4.6):

Based on the prevailing market situation as on 13-July-2017, the first coupon payment date of the bond with call option after the lock-in-period of first two years, find out whether there is any possibility for the government of India to call back the issue. If the call option is exercised, what will be the call risk to the investor?

Comparing the fixed commitment made by the issuer in the bond and the prevailing market situation as on the first call date, the following observation may be made:

Original Fixed Coupon Paid: 7.5000%
Risk-free Yield for the Residual Tenor (7 Year): 6.8110%

(Maturity Date Minus 1st Call Date)
Opportunity Loss (to the Issuer) p.a.: 7.50% − 6.8110% = 0.6890%

Since the issuer incurs an opportunity loss continuing with the bond issue, it is expected that the issuer will exercise the call option and will call back the entire issue, indicating a call risk for the investor.

Now if the call risk to the investor is divided into reinvestment risk and price risk, the same may be estimated as follows, as shown in the following table (Table 4.7):

Therefore, the call risk for the investor is by way of earning 0.6890% less on their return on reinvestment, and a price loss of Rs.1.7500/- per unit of security due to exercise of the call option at the bond's par value.

### Credit risk

Since the government of India cannot be expected to default on its promised payments of coupons and the principal amount against the central government securities, these securities do not carry any counterparty/credit/default risk. However, there are bonds issued by various non-government entities

*Table 4.7* Estimation of reinvestment & price risk due to call option

| *Investor's Situation if Issuer Exercises the Call Option:* | |
| --- | --- |
| New rate at which fresh investment for the residual tenor (7 year) can be made (extracted from the base yield curve) | 6.8110% |
| Original coupon rate received till the call date from the existing bond issue | 7.5000% |
| Reinvestment risk to the investor, for making new investment at the prevailing market rate, as on the 1st call date | 7.5000% – 6.8110% = 0.6890% |
| Price risk to the investor if the call option is exercised on the 1st call date (market price – call price) | Rs.101.75/- minus Rs.100/- = Rs.1.7500/- |

that carry a significant amount of counterparty/credit risk, in terms of the inability to service all or some of the promised obligations, depending upon their credit worthiness that may change due to financial distress, reorganization, workouts, or bankruptcy.

When an investor buys some bond from a bond issuer other than the government, he is expected to be exposed to some credit risk based on the credit worthiness of the issuer or the specific issue. The major types of credit risk are – default risk, downgrade risk, and credit spread risk. *Default Risk* can be defined as the risk that the issuer will fail to satisfy the terms of the obligation with respect to the payment of interest and principal on time. Default risk can actually be calculated not only by considering the rate of default but also the rate of recovery out of the total default. *Downgrade Risk* refers to the migration of credit quality, as exhibited by the different grade of credit ratings provided by different external rating agencies in the form of *Transition Matrix*, from higher or good rating to lower or bad rating. A credit rating of a bond issue or an entity indicates the potential default risk associated with a particular bond issue or the issuer. This rating migration may lead to a fall in the market value of a bond. It is well known that the price of a bond issue is inversely related with the yield of the bond, which actually comprises of two components – yield on a similar default-free (e.g. government) bond, and the risk premium above such yield to compensate the concerned risk associated with that bond. This risk premium is alternatively known as the *Yield Spread* and the part of this yield spread attributable to the default risk is known as the *Credit Spread*. Since credit spread is an integral part of the yield of a non-government security, any change (e.g. increase) in such spread will lead to an increase in the yield, resulting to a fall in the value of the bond. This expected decline in the value of a bond due to a rise in credit spread is known as the credit risk or *Credit Spread Risk*, in the context of bonds.

*Example*

Suppose a 10-year AAA rated PSU bond with a 7.50% coupon currently sells at Rs.100/-. Suppose the risk-free yield of similar tenor is 7.00% p.a., making a credit spread of 50 basis points for AAA rated PSU bonds. Some investors may invest in the bond because of its AAA rating, considering the highest level of safety. Suppose the revised rating of the same security is now migrated to A. The risk-return ratio that was once attractive to the current bondholders will now become unattractive as the risk has increased without any increase in returns. Even if the spread offered in such a bond is fixed at 50 bps (7.50% minus 7.00%), the market now expects a slightly higher spread due to the downgradation of its credit quality. Suppose the market expects a credit spread of 1% for similar 'A' rated bonds, taking the yield level to 8.00% p.a. (risk-free yield of 7% plus a credit spread of 1%). In such a case, the holders of this bond, if they prefer to sell the bond in the market, will get a lower price due to a rise in yield expectation caused by the pressure of rating downward, and therefore exposed to the credit risk.

### Legal risk

*Legal Risk* refers to the risk of adverse effect in the value of debt securities due to any change in the law in the country. Most legal risk is associated with the tax-exemption status of particular bonds, especially infrastructure bonds and municipal bonds, because these bonds are generally exempted from income tax in India. However, if tax rates decline, the advantage of the tax exemption also declines, and therefore the price of the bond in the secondary market also falls – this is commonly known as tax risk. The second type of legal risk occurs because tax-exempted securities have to satisfy specific legal requirements, and if it is later determined that the security does not satisfy these requirements, its tax-exemption status may be eliminated, which would reduce not only the effective return of the bond after taxes, but it would also reduce the price of the bond in the secondary market as the yield on that particular security would have to be equal with the taxable yield of other comparable bonds available in the market.

### Foreign exchange risk

If an investor holds a bond whose cash flows are not denominated in domestic currency, they are exposed to the risk of unfavorable change in the foreign exchange rate between the two currencies, known as *Exchange-rate Risk* or *Currency Risk*. Though the amounts of cash flows, either coupons or principal, are certain in foreign currency, they are uncertain in domestic currency and depend on the prevailing exchange rate at the time of the cash flows. If the foreign currency depreciates at the time of cash flows, though the investor gets a fixed amount of payment in terms of foreign currency, the amount of payment in terms of domestic currency would be less than whatever was expected. This risk of receiving less (in domestic currency) while investing in any bond issue where payment is made in foreign currency, is represented as exchange-rate risk.

### Volatility risk

Volatility, not of the bond's price but of the yield of the bond, significantly affects the price of a bond issued with some embedded options (call or put). The larger the yield volatility, the higher would be the price for the call and put options embedded with a bond issue. Since the price of a callable (puttable) bond is equal to the price of a similar option-free bond minus (plus) the price of the call (put) option, an increase (decrease) in the yield volatility will lead to rise (fall) in the price of the call and put option. Rise in yield volatility, therefore, leads to a simultaneous fall (rise) in the price of the callable (puttable) bond. This risk of price decline of a bond with an embedded option due to a change in the yield volatility is known as *Volatility Risk*.

### Sovereign risk (country risk, political risk)

*Sovereign Risk*, alternatively known as *Country Risk*, *Political Risk*, is the risk associated with the laws of the country, or to events that may occur there. Particular events that can disturb a bond market are the restriction of the flow of capital, taxation, and the nationalization of the issuer. A particular form of sovereign risk is *convertibility risk*, which represents prohibition of the exchange of the foreign currency for domestic currency. The only solution for an investor in this situation is to accept the local currency or to wait until the rule changes. Similarly, due to inadequate laws regarding financial disclosures or accounting rules in many emerging countries, it may be difficult to assess the true creditworthiness of the bond issuer, resulting in *Disclosure Risk*.

Even if an investment in a fixed income security like a bond may be exposed to all the above risks, call risk, credit risk, volatility risk, foreign exchange risk, and sovereign risk are almost absent in case of any domestic securities issued by the government.

## Return measures for fixed income securities

Given the three important sources of potential return from a fixed income security, such as coupon income, capital gain (loss), and reinvestment income, various yield measures, expressed as a percentage return, can be applied based on a single or all of the above potential sources. Accordingly, different return measures give different information regarding the FI securities in different possible scenarios. These measures may reflect the return for an individual fixed income security or for the portfolio of various FI securities. Return can be calculated for a specific period (monthly, semi-annually, annually), or for the full maturity/holding period. Different such return measures include:

### Nominal return/coupon rate (CR)

Nominal return is nothing but the rate of interest promised to be paid by the bond issuer to the bond holder over a span of time. Nominal return is normally expressed at annual basis but can be expected to be due and received annually, semi-annually, or quarterly. In other words, nominal yield is the stated interest rate of the bond as the percentage of bond's par value. Nominal return can be positive or zero, based on the type of bond. In the case of a zero coupon bond, there is no nominal return. For example, a bond with a par value of Rs.100/- and paying 8% interest pays Rs.8/- per year in two semi-annual payments of Rs.4/- each. Nominal return can be fixed throughout the maturity or can vary based on some benchmark rate, depending upon the nature of the security (fixed or floating rate bond). In the case of floating rate bonds, the nominal yield gets adjusted at every coupon reset date. The nominal yield is therefore calculated as:

$$\mathrm{No\,min\,al\,Yield} = {Annual\,Interest\,Payment}\Big/{Bond's\,Par\,Value} \qquad (4.1)$$

### Current yield (CY)

After their issuance in the primary market, bonds get traded in the secondary market, not necessarily at the par value, but may be traded at a price less or more than the par value, respectively known as trading at discount and at premium. Therefore, the return to an investor on a bond issue purchased from a secondary market need not necessarily to be the nominal return. Investment in the secondary market may yield an interest rate that is different from the nominal yield, called the *Current Yield*, or current return. Movement of such yield measure depends on the movement in the market price of the concerned security, such that:

$$Current\,Yield = {Annual\,Interest\,Payment}\Big/{Bond's\,Current\,Market\,Value} \qquad (4.2)$$

Even if the nominal yield of a fixed rate bond is fixed throughout its maturity, the current yield may be extremely volatile, depending on the price volatility of the concerned bond issue. If a bond is traded at its par value, then the current yield will be equal to the nominal yield. The larger the difference between the current market price of a bond and its par value, the wider would be the difference between the nominal and current yield, such that:

- A Bond Traded at a Discount => Current Yield > Nominal Yield
- A Bond Traded at a Premium => Current Yield < Nominal Yield

Current yield is important and is required to be considered along with the nominal return of a bond issue, especially in the case of a fixed rate bond in order to get the current market condition reflected in the bond price, enabling investors to take their investment decision based on their preference.

*Example*

Suppose a 10% coupon bond with a face value of Rs.100/- is currently traded at Rs.95/-. In such a case, even if the nominal yield is 10%, the current yield of the bond is 10.53% (Rs.10 / Rs.95). Similarly, if the bond is traded at a premium, e.g. at Rs.105/-, the current yield would be 9.52% (Rs.10 / Rs.105). If the bond is still traded at its par value, i.e. at Rs.100/-, there won't be any difference between the nominal and current yield.

The current yield (CY) of a bond portfolio can be estimated by taking the weighted average of the current yields of all the securities in the portfolio, where market values of position in individual securities ($MV_s$) with respect to the market value of the entire portfolio ($MV_p$), as on a given date, can be used as the weights. For example, the current yield of a bond portfolio consisting of the following five government of India (GOI) securities, as on 31 October 2018, can be estimate, as shown in the following table (Table 4.8):

*Table 4.8* Estimation of current yield on a bond portfolio

*Settlement Date = 31-Oct-2018*

| Security Description | Maturity Date | Residual Maturity (Years) | Face Vale (Rs. in Cr.) | Traded Yield (YTM) | Traded Price (INR) | Market Value (INR in Cr.) | Current Yield |
|---|---|---|---|---|---|---|---|
| 6.05% GS 2019 | 2-Feb-19 | 0.2556 | 1 | 7.13% | 99.6900 | 0.9969 | 6.07% |
| 6.84% GS 2022 | 19-Dec-22 | 4.1361 | 1 | 7.67% | 97.1100 | 0.9711 | 7.04% |
| 7.17% GS 2028 | 8-Jan-28 | 9.1889 | 1 | 7.83% | 95.7100 | 0.9571 | 7.49% |
| 7.95% G.S 2032 | 28-Aug-32 | 13.828 | 1 | 8.06% | 99.0700 | 0.9907 | 8.02% |
| 8.83% GS 2041 | 12-Dec-41 | 23.117 | 1 | 8.23% | 106.1300 | 1.0613 | 8.32% |
| Portfolio | | | 5.00 | | | 4.9771 | 7.4019% |

After estimating the current yield for all the five securities, as on 31 October 2018, comparing the annual fixed coupon income of each security with respect to their current market price, the portfolio current yield may be estimated by taking the weighted average of the current yield from all the five securities, such that:

$$
\begin{aligned}
Current\ Yield\ _{Portfolio} =\ & \\
& (CY_{S1} \times MV_{S1} / MV_p) + (CY_{S2} \times MV_{S2} / MV_p) \\
& + (CY_{S3} \times MV_{S3} / MV_p) + (CY_{S4} \times MV_{S4} / MV_p) \\
& + (CY_{S5} \times MV_{S5} / MV_p) \\
=\ & (6.07\% \times 0.9969/4.9771) + (7.04\% \times 0.9711/4.9771) + \\
& (7.49\% \times 0.9571/4.9771) + (8.02\% \times 0.9907/4.9771) + \\
& (8.32\% \times 1.0613/4.9771) \\
=\ & 7.4019\%
\end{aligned}
\tag{4.3}
$$

### Average return or yield to maturity (YTM)

YTM of a bond is the average rate of return that an investor earns from his investment in that bond if the same is held till its maturity. YTM can also be treated as the *Internal Rate of Return* (IRR)[3] or the *Hurdle Rate of Return* required to sell the bond at its ruling market price. Even if the nominal and current yields consider only one source of income, i.e. the coupon income, to estimate the return from a bond, the YTM takes into consideration all the possible sources of income from a bond issue. YTM assumes that bonds are held till maturity and interest receipts are reinvested at the same rate.

Technically, YTM is that single discounting rate that makes the sum of present values of all future cash flows due from a security till its maturity equal with the current market price. Accordingly, once a security is traded, its market price, along with the amount and timing of its interim cash flows due till the maturity, may be used to extract the yield to maturity of that security. Alternatively, if the YTM of a security on a given date is known, the price of that security can be estimated.

### Example

Suppose a GOI bond (7.28 GS 2019), offering an annual coupon of 7.28%, payable semi-annually, maturing on 3 June 2019, is currently (on 11 July 2017) traded at a price of INR 101.6300/-. The market may like to know the YTM or the IRR of that security being traded at the ruling market price (i.e. at Rs.101.6300/-).

Yield to maturity of a bond may be estimated through different approaches or methods. It can be solved manually (in MS Excel) through the bond pricing structure following discounted future cash flow methods, either by a trial-and-error process or with the help of some Excel optimization

*Table 4.9* Estimation of bond price using YTM

| Semi-annual Period (t) | Semi-annual Cash Flows (CF) | Yield to Maturity (YTM) | Discounted CF [DCF = CF/(1+YTM/2)^t] |
|---|---|---|---|
| 0.7889 | 3.64 | 6.3478% | 3.5514 |
| 1.7889 | 3.64 | 6.3478% | 3.4421 |
| 2.7889 | 3.64 | 6.3478% | 3.3362 |
| 3.7889 | 103.64 | 6.3478% | 92.0688 |
| Dirty Price | Σ DCF | | 102.3985 |
| Clean Price | = Σ DCF – AI | | 101.6301 |

technique (e.g. Goal Seek or Solver) or perhaps by using a pre-specified financial function available in MS Excel.

Given the settlement and maturity date for the security, the residual maturity of the given security is estimated as 1.8944 years or 3.7899 semi-annual periods. Therefore, there will be four semi-annual cash flows due in that security till the maturity. The first three will be the semi-annual coupon, followed by the last and final semi-annual coupon plus the principal redemption due at maturity.

Considering the settlement date, maturity date, and day count convention used, the actual due dates for all the four future cash flows may be estimated, which can further be used while discounting the future CFs, at an unknown interest rate known as YTM, as shown in the following table (Table 4.9):

The first and second column of the above table is known and the sum of the DCF (i.e. the dirty price) minus the accrued interest (i.e. the market price) is also known. Therefore, the single unknown (i.e. YTM) to be used to discount all the cash flows may be estimated by using the Excel optimization with the following details:

Objective Function  : Sum of DCF (i.e. Dirty Price) - Accrued Interest

= Market Price (i.e. Clean Price)

= Σ DCF - 0.7684 = 101.6300

Changing Parameter  : YTM

Accordingly, YTM may be estimated, with a close approximation, following a detailed process. The YTM arrived at through this process is 6.3478% per annum.

At the same time, YTM may also be extracted from the price with the help of a single Excel function, given below:

= **YIELD**(*Settlement, Maturity, Rate, Price, Redemption,*

*Frequency, [Basis]*)

Providing details about the above required parameters, such as settlement date (=11 July 2017), maturity date (= 3 June 2019), coupon rate (7.28%), market price (= Rs.101.63/-), redemption value (Rs.100/-), coupon payment frequency (= 2), and day count convention, represented as "Basis" (= 4, to represent 30/36 convention), the YTM of a security may be directly estimated through the MS Excel function "YIELD". The YTM of the above security, extracted by using the Excel function is 6.3479%, which is very close to the YTM estimated above, is similar till the first three decimals.

The yield to maturity of a portfolio of securities may be estimated as the weighted average YTM of all the securities in the portfolio. Weights to be assigned with the security-wise YTM are nothing but the market value of position in the individual security divided by the market value of the whole portfolio. Therefore, the YTM of a portfolio consisting of 'i' number of securities is defined as:

$$YTM_P = \left( YTM_{S1} \times {MV_{S1}}\Big/{MV_P} \right) + \left( YTM_{S2} \times {MV_{S2}}\Big/{MV_P} \right)$$
$$+ \ldots\ldots + \left( YTM_{Si} \times {MV_{Si}}\Big/{MV_P} \right) \tag{4.4}$$

Accordingly, the YTM of a portfolio of five securities, as described in the example of the previous section, may be estimated as:

$$\begin{aligned} YTM_{Portfolio} &= \left( YTM_{S1} \ MV_{S1}/MV_P \right) + \left( YTM_{S2} \ MV_{S2}/MV_P \right) \\ &+ \left( YTM_{S3} \times MV_{S3}/MV_P \right) + \left( YTM_{S4} \times MV_{S4}/MV_P \right) \\ &+ \left( YTM_{S5} \times MV_{S5}/MV_P \right) \\ &= 7.7991\% \end{aligned}$$

When a bond is bought at a discount, yield to maturity will always be greater than the current yield because there will be a gain when the bond matures, and the bondholder receives par value back, thus raising the true yield; when a bond is bought at a premium, the yield to maturity will always be less than the current yield because there will be a loss when par value is received, which lowers the true yield. Interrelation between different yield measures and trading price of a bond may be seen from the following table (Table 4.10):

*Table 4.10* Relationship between bond price and yields

| Price of Bond | Relationship |
| --- | --- |
| Bond Traded at Par | CR = CY = YTM |
| Bond Traded at Discount | CR < CY < YTM |
| Bond Traded at Premium | CR > CY > YTM |

*Return till the call (put) date (YTC/YTP)*

Yield to call (YTC) or yield to put (YTP) is applicable only to callable (put-table) bonds. YTC (YTP) is the rate of interest that equates the PV of all the interim cash flows expected to be received till the possible call (put) date and its call (put) price received when the bond is buy-back (sell-off). Alternatively, YTC (YTP) is the yield that will make the present value of the cash flows up to the concerned (first/second/last) call (put) date equal to the current market price of the bond. Cash flows can be considered till the first call (put) date if the bond is assumed to be held only till the first call (put) date. YTC (or YTP) and YTM differ only due to the difference in the holding period. Just like YTM, these are also measures of internal rate of return (IRR) but are calculated for each of the possible call (put) dates when the bond is expected to be buy-back (sell-off). Yield to first call (yield to first put) is the YTC (YTP) at the earliest possible date when the bond is buy-back (sell-off). There can be as many numbers of YTCs or YTPs as the total number of possible dates when the issuer (holder) is allowed to exercise their call (put) option. In short, YTC or YTP are nothing but the bond's YTM after reducing the maturity to the possible call or put date and after converting the bond's par value to the call (put) price of the bond, as agreed upon in the bond and provided in the *Call (Put) Schedule.*

*Example*

Suppose a 5-year 10% annual coupon payment Treasury callable bond, with a call (at the first call date) price of Rs.105/- and with the first call date after a lock-in period of 2 years, is traded at a market price of 103. What would be the yield to first call? As discussed above, YTFC is nothing but the YTM of the bond after adjusting the bond's maturity to 2 years (i.e. reducing the bond's actual maturity to the first call date) and the redemption value to Rs.105/- (instead of the par value as in the case of an option-free bond due at maturity). Therefore, the YTFC is such that:

$$103 = \{10/(1 + YTFC)^1\} + \{(10 + 105)/(1 + YTFC)^2\};$$
$$\Rightarrow YTFC = 10.63\%$$

Similarly, the YTC for all possible call dates can be calculated by increasing the bond's maturity to that date and by altering the redemption value to the call price of the bond at the respective call date.

*Yield to worst (YTW) and yield to best (YTB)*

Besides YTM, an investor can also calculate the yield measures for all the possible call (put) dates till the maturity. Given a specific YTM and all possible YTCs (YTPs) for a callable (puttable) bond at the respective call (put) price of the bond, the investor can find out the worst or best return that can be generated from such investment. Lowest (Highest) of the YTM and all the YTCs (YTPs) is known as the worst (best) return or yield to worst (yield to best). The holder of a callable (puttable) bond, in the event of falling (rising) market interest rates of concerned tenor, can generate the YTW (YTB) if the call (put) option is exercised in the first call (put) date. Therefore, YTW in the case of callable bond, is supposed to be the yield to first call (YTFC), and YTB in case of a puttable bond, is also supposed to be the yield to first put (YTFP). YTW can be treated as the minimum possible yield that an investor will definitely earn from a callable bond in any possible circumstances. Similarly, YTB is the maximum possible yield that an investor is expected to earn from a puttable bond if the put option is exercised in the right time.

*Example*

Suppose a government of India fixed coupon bond, with a fixed coupon of 8.00% per annum, payable annually, maturing after 6 years, embedded with a call option, to be exercised at the end of every year till the maturity, with a lock-in period of first 2 years, exercisable always at par value (i.e. with a call price of Rs.100/- in any call date), is currently traded at Rs.101.50/-. What will be the minimum yield (i.e. yield to worst) under any circumstances that an investor is expected to earn from this security?

Since the bond, with 6 years of residual maturity, is callable at the end of every year after a minimum lock-in-period of first 2 years, there are three possible call dates. The bond issuer may like to call back the bond in any of these three call dates, depending upon the prevailing market situation, in terms of interest rates, or may like to continue till the maturity (if the market continues to move in his favour).

Accordingly, the investor will at least earn the minimum of all possible yields, which in this case is the yield to first call, as shown in the table (Table 4.11). Therefore, the yield to first call (=7.4240%) is the yield to worst, to the investor, as on the given settlement date.

*Total return (TR)*

Even if there are different return measures used by different types of players involved in the bond market, an investor, in order to calculate the actual and comprehensive return from a fixed income security, needs to be concerned with the following:

- The return should be generated with certainty
- The return measure should consider all possible cash flows (CFs) during the holding, not necessarily till the maturity of the security
- Return measure should undertake the actual rate(s), not some assumed rate, at which the interim CFs can be reinvested

*Table 4.11* Estimation of YTW in bond with call option

| Details of Security with Call Schedule | | Estimation of Yield using the "YIELD" Function in MS Excel | |
| --- | --- | --- | --- |
| Settlement Date (say) | 1-Jan-2017 | **Yield to 1st Call** (YTM, reducing maturity date to the 1st Call Date) | **7.4240%** |
| 1st Call Date (end of 3rd Year) | 1-Jan-2020 | **Yield to 2nd Call** (YTM, reducing maturity date | **7.6280%** |
| 2nd Call Date (end of 4th Year) | 1-Jan-2021 | to the 2nd Call Date) | |
| 3rd Call Date (end of 5th Year) | 1-Jan-2022 | **Yield to 3rd Call** (YTM, reducing maturity date to the 3rd Call Date) | **7.4240%** |
| | | **Yield to Maturity** | 7.4240% |
| Maturity Date | 1-Jan-2023 | **Yield to Worst** | 7.5516% |
| Residual Maturity (Years) | 6.0000 | (Minimum of YTCs & YTM) | |
| Coupon | 8.00% | | |
| Coupon Payment Frequency | Annual (i.e. 1) | | |
| Market Price | INR 101.50 | | |
| Par Value & Exercise Price | INR 100.00 | | |

- Return measure should also consider the actual capital gain (loss) expected to be released from the sale of security at the end of the investment horizon (IH) if it falls before the maturity.

Total return represents the overall return actually generated from a security or portfolio of securities. Total return measure is linked with the actual investment horizon, not the maturity of the security, and therefore alternatively known as *Holding Period Return*. It is the rate of interest that makes the bond's current price equal to the total projected value of the security at the end of the investment horizon. TR largely depends on investment horizon, actual reinvestment rate, and the bond's expected selling price at the end of the time horizon, such that:

*Semi-annual TR = [ { (Total Projected Amount at the*
  *End of IH / Bond's Purchase Price) ^*
  *(1 / Total Semi-annual Period within IH) } – 1]*  (4.5)

The total projected amount expected to be generated at the end of the IH is the sum of coupon cum interest on coupon and the projected selling price of the bond at the end of the IH. Accordingly,

*Annual TR (Bond - equivalent basis) = Semi - annual TR □ 2*  (4.6)

*Example*

Suppose an investor, as on 2 July 2017, is holding a government security (6.35 GS 2020), maturing on 2 January 2020, currently traded at INR 99.7550/-. Suppose the investor may like to hold the security for next 1.5 years.

Compute the total return or holding return period from the specified security, assuming that the investor reinvests all their semi-annual coupons received till the holding period at the same YTM that prevailed today.

All necessary details regarding investments and market rates are given in the following table (Table 4.12).

Considering all possible cash flows (inflows and outflows) till the holding period, the holding period return or total return, as shown in the previous section, can be estimated. Accordingly, the annual return can be estimated as:

*Annual Holding Period Return = [ { (Total Projected Amount at the End of IH / Bond's Purchase Price) ^ (1 / Total Semi-annual Period within IH) } – 1] × 2*

$$= [ \{ (9.8359 + 99.7672) / 99.7550 \} \wedge \{1 / (1.5 \times 2) \} - 1] \times 2 = \mathbf{6.3761\%}$$

*Table 4.12* Details of investment and interest rates

| Details of Security: | | Details of the Bond at the End of the Holding Period: | |
|---|---|---|---|
| Settlement Date | 2-Jul-2017 | Settlement Date | 2-Jan-2019 |
| Maturity Date | 2-Jan-2020 | Maturity Date | 2-Jan-2020 |
| Coupon | 6.35% | Res. Mat. | 1.0000 |
| Market Price | 99.7550 | Coupon | 6.35% |
| YTM (Estimated in MS Excel) | 6.4577% | **Estimation of 1-Year Forward Rate after 1.5 Year:** | |
| Res. Mat. | 2.5000 | Year | YTM |
| No. of CFs | 5 | 1.50 | 6.3189% |
| | | 2.50 | 6.4290% |
| Holding Period (Yrs.) | 1.5 | FR (1.5 Y, 2.5 Y) | 6.5943% |
| | | Bond Price after 1.5 Year | 99.7672 |
| | | **Cash Flows Till the Holding Period:** | |
| | | Coupon Income | 9.5250 |
| | | Future Value of All Coupons | 9.8359 |
| | | Bond Selling Price after 1.5 Year | 99.7672 |

| **FIMMDA-PDAI GOI Base Yields, till a Period of 5 Years** | | | | | | | | | |
|---|---|---|---|---|---|---|---|---|---|
| Maturity | 0.50 | 1.00 | 1.50 | 2.00 | 2.50 | 3.00 | 3.50 | 4.00 | 4.50 | 5.00 |
| YTM | 6.32 | 6.34 | 6.32 | 6.33 | 6.43 | 6.53 | 6.57 | 6.58 | 6.57 | 6.57 |

The total return of a portfolio of various fixed income securities can be calculated differently depending on two possible circumstances:

- When the investment horizon (IH) for all securities are equal.
- When different securities are expected to hold for different periods.

If the IH for all the securities are equal, then the semi-annual TR can be calculated on an aggregate basis, such that:

In the case of different IH, the portfolio TR can be the weighted average of total return of individual securities. Respective weight could be the market value of the total position in individual security with regard to the market value of the total portfolio.

## Limitations of different yield measures

Nominal yield/coupon rate (CR) talks about the contracted rate of return expected to be generated from the FI security throughout the bond holding period. Accordingly, CR may not represent the current market situation. Current yield (CY) talks about only the rate of return generated from the actual investment during the current period, which keeps changing from period to period, even on daily basis, depending upon the change in market price. Therefore, CY fails to give overall information about the return that can be generated from the investment. Even if YTM considers all sources of return generated from the investment till the maturity, it suffers from serious limitations. YTM assumes that the rate at which the interim cash flows can be reinvested is nothing but the same YTM. Therefore, if the actual reinvestment rate differs from the YTM, the concerned YTM may fail to represent the actual return generated from the security till its maturity, which is known as reinvestment risk. YTM also assumes that the security is going to be held till its maturity and accordingly considers all the expected future cash flows. If the security is sold before the maturity, there may be some possibility for some capital loss, known as price risk. This reinvestment risk and price risk make the YTM doubtful.

Yield to call (YTC) or yield to put (YTP) does not represent any certain rate of return. Calculation of YTC (YTP) is based on the assumption that the security may be buy-back (sell-off), depending on the movement of the market rate of interest. Accordingly, there may be different possible YTCs (YTPs). Therefore, YTC or YTP are neither certain nor give a single return measure. Yield to worst (YTW) is again an uncertain return measure, focusing more on a worst situation. YTW may not have any practical implication, except to represent the conservative approach of the investor.

Even if the holding period return, or total return measure, allows the portfolio manager to evaluate which of several potential bonds considered for investment will perform best over the planned investment horizon, it is also not free from certain limitations. The main disadvantage of this approach is that it requires the portfolio manager to make some assumptions about reinvestment rates, future yields, and to think in terms of a specified period or horizon. Since there is a trade-off between the price risk and the reinvestment risk due to a change in interest rates, their overall impact on TR depends on the comparative change in the bond's selling price and the reinvestment income. It, however, enables a portfolio manager to evaluate the performance of a bond under different interest rate scenarios in terms of short-term reinvestment rate and future YTM at the end of the investment horizon, thereby assessing the sensitivity of the bond to interest rate changes. The approach of analyzing the total return of a bond at different scenarios of reinvestment rate and YTM at the end of a specific investment horizon is known as scenario analysis.[4] Scenario analysis helps get an idea about the expected total return in all possible circumstances and can highlight the best and worst possible total return.

## Analysis of returns on a debt portfolio: a case

Suppose a small commercial bank as on 30-Oct-2018 holds a government securities trading portfolio (HFT) consisting of top five liquid GOI securities carrying a market value of INR 97.5770 crores. Details about the bank's position on all these securities are given in the following table (Table 4.13):

*Table 4.13* Composition of government securities trading portfolio of a bank

| Security Description | Maturity Date | Res. Maturity (Year) | Traded Price (INR) | Market Value (INR Cr.) |
|---|---|---|---|---|
| 7.17% GS 2028 | 08-Jan-2028 | 9.19 | 95.71 | 38.2840 |
| 7.37% GS 2023 | 16-Apr-2023 | 4.46 | 98.38 | 29.5140 |
| 7.59% GS 2026 | 11-Jan-2026 | 7.20 | 98.41 | 14.7615 |
| 6.84% GS 2022 | 19-Dec-2022 | 4.14 | 97.11 | 9.7110 |
| 8.83% GS 2041 | 12-Dec-2041 | 23.12 | 106.13 | 5.3065 |
| Portfolio | | | | 97.5770 |

The person managing this trading portfolio in the bank may like to report to his head the kind of return that the portfolio generates as on the given date. The portfolio manager may like to use all possible measures to estimate the return/yield on this portfolio and wants to make a critical presentation to his head of the department. The portfolio manager may also like to estimate the possible yield that is likely to be generated from this portfolio, assuming a holding (for all securities) period of just 1 year. The FIMMDA GOI Yield Curves as on 30-Oct-2018 are given in the following table (Table 4.14).

*Table 4.14* FIMMDA GOI yield curves as on 30 October 2018

| Tenor (Year) | 0.25 | 1.00 | 2.00 | 3.00 | 4.00 | 5.00 | 6.00 | 7.00 |
|---|---|---|---|---|---|---|---|---|
| Par YTM (%) | 6.78 | 7.00 | 7.05 | 7.23 | 7.29 | 7.40 | 7.49 | 7.53 |
| ZCY (%) | 6.84 | 7.00 | 7.05 | 7.25 | 7.31 | 7.44 | 7.54 | 7.58 |
| Tenor (Year) | 8.00 | 9.00 | 10.00 | 11.00 | 15.00 | 20.00 | 25.00 | 30.00 |
| Par YTM (%) | 7.57 | 7.52 | 7.50 | 7.55 | 7.72 | 7.76 | 7.68 | 7.78 |
| ZCY (%) | 7.63 | 7.55 | 7.52 | 7.59 | 7.85 | 7.89 | 7.65 | 7.99 |

## Self-learning exercise

1 What are the various risks that banks or other financial institutions are exposed to on their bond portfolio?
2 How does change in interest rates affect investment in any bond?
3 Explain the interest rate risk of a floating rate security and why such security's price differ from par value.
4 Does an investor who purchases a zero coupon bond face reinvestment risk?
5 How are a fixed coupon bond and a zero coupon bond different to an investor in terms of interest rate risk (if any), even if both the bonds are expected to hold till the maturity?
6 What is liquidity risk, even in a government security?
7 Why is a call risk very common in corporate bonds?
8 How may a bank, investing in government securities with different maturities, be exposed to yield curve risk?
9 What are the various sources of returns from a bond?
10 Interpret the traditional yield measures for fixed rate bonds and explain their limitations and assumptions.
11 Critically evaluate various measures to calculate the return from a bond.

## Notes

1 When a yield curve shifts, the new curve may become flatter or steeper. In case of flattening of the curve, the spread between long- and short-term yield narrows down, while during steepening of the curve, the same spread widens. The yield curve becomes flatter or steeper basically due to different changes in the yields for different tenors.
2 The Fixed Income Money Market and Derivatives Association of India (FIMMDA), an association of Scheduled Commercial Banks (SCBs), Public

Financial Institutions, Primary Dealers, and Insurance Companies, is a voluntary market body for the bond, money, and derivatives market. FIMMDA acts as the principal interface with the regulators towards various issues having impact on the functioning of these markets. It also undertakes various developmental activities, like introduction of benchmark rates and new innovative instruments/products. *(Source: FIMMDA Website)*

3  Internal rate of return (IRR), also known as economic rate of return, is a metric used to estimate the profitability of a potential investment. Alternatively, IRR is a discounting rate that makes the present value (PV) of cash inflows equal with the PV of cash outflows, or the net present value (NPV) of all cash flows from a particular project equal to zero.

4  Scenario analysis, in the context of risk-return analysis, is the process of estimating the expected value of a portfolio after a given period of time, assuming certain unfavorable changes in key factors, such as change in the interest rate. It is very useful for investors to examine a worst-case scenario under uncertain market conditions.

# Bibliography

Bierwag, G. O. (1987). *Duration Analysis: Managing Interest Rate Risk.* Ballinger Publishing Company, Cambridge, MA.

Chambers, D. R., and Nawalkha, S. K. (eds.). (1999). *Interest Rate Risk Measurement and Management.* Institutional Investor, New York.

Fabozzi, F. (2007a). *Duration, Convexity, and Other Bond Risk Measures* (1st edn.). John Wiley & Sons, Inc., Hoboken, NJ.

Fabozzi, F. (2007b). *Fixed Income Analysis* (2nd edn.). John Wiley & Sons, Inc., Hoboken, NJ.

Fabozzi, F. (ed.). (July 2017). *The Handbook of Fixed Income Securities* (8th edn.). McGraw Hill Education, New York.

Martellini, L., Priaulet, P., and Priaulet, S. (2003). *Fixed-Income Securities: Valuation, Risk Management and Portfolio Strategies* (1st edn.). John Wiley & Sons, Inc., Hoboken, NJ.

Veronesi, P. (2011). *Fixed Income Securities: Valuation, Risk and Risk Management.* John Wiley & Sons, Inc., Hoboken, NJ.

# 5 Term structures of interest rates

## Key learning outcomes

At the end of this chapter, readers are expected to be familiar with:

- What are the different concepts of interest rates in the context of the fixed income securities market?
- What are the major factors determining the yield or interest rates on debt instruments?
- How to analyze market news to understand their impact on bond yield.
  How are yield to maturity (YTM), zero coupon yield/ZCY/spot rates, and forward rates extracted from the available market/trade information?
- How are these different rates interrelated and used in the fixed income securities market?
- How to construct term structure of various rates: yield curve, zero coupon yield/spot rate curve, and forward rate curve using different methods.
- Critical analysis of various methods to construct various interest rate term structures.
- How to analyze different types of term structures of various interest rates in India.
- What are the important theories deriving the term structure of interest rates?

## Interest rates: meaning and different types

The interest rate is the rate that is charged or paid for the use of money and is expressed as an annual percentage of the principal. From an investor's perspective, the interest rate is the annual return which he/she generates from her/his investment. Interest rate can be of two types: nominal and real interest rates. Nominal interest rates are normally positive, but real interest rates can be negative, depending upon the economic situation, especially the rate of inflation. The interest rate may change because of several factors; such as: inflationary expectations, alternative investments, risk of investment, liquidity preference, tax implication, and most importantly the maturity or period. Depending upon the length of the period, interest rates could be short term (with less than one-year term) and long term (or a maturity above 1 year). In some cases, there could be some rates of medium term with a maturity between one to 5/10 years. Some important short-term rates are: inter-bank call rates of different maturity (LIBOR/MIBOR with 1-day, 1-month, 3-month, 6-month, 1-year); 1-day, 7-day, 14-day, 1-month repurchase (Repo) rates; 3-month, 6-month, 12-month deposit/lending rates, 91-day, 182-day, 364-day T-bill rates; short-term swap rates, etc. On the other hand, some of the long-term rates include: yield on long-term government securities, corporate bond yields, bank lending rates, long-term swap rates, etc.

## Some important interest rates in Indian debt market

### Benchmark rate

The benchmark interest rate, alternatively known as base interest rate, is the minimum interest rate that investors will demand for their non-governmental investment, say a non-Treasury security. It is also tied to the yield to maturity offered on on-the-run (most recently issued) Treasury security of comparable-maturity. Alternatively, a benchmark rate is an interest rate against which other interest rates are calculated. For example, a benchmark rate could be the interest rate at which the central bank of an economy (here RBI) gives loans (borrows money) to (from) the commercial banks under their jurisdiction, which further can be used as a benchmark by the commercial banks to decide the interest rate for their loan or deposit products of different maturity. The interest rate at which commercial banks and other selected FIs can borrow (lend) money from (to) the Reserve Bank of India is called *Repo Rate* (*Reverse Repo Rate*), which is presently (as on December 2019) at 5.15% (4.90%). At the same time, the other benchmark rate, offered by the central bank, in India is the *Marginal Standing Facility (MSF) Rate*, and Bank Rate, which is presently (as on December 2019) at 5.40%. In the case of borrowing under Repo from RBI through the *Liquidity Adjustment Facility* (LAF) against the excess SLR securities, banks without holding excess SLR securities can still draw down on their holding of SLR securities and borrow from the Reserve Bank of India at the MSF rate, which is the Repo Rate plus 0.25%. MSF is a window for banks to borrow from the RBI in an emergency situation when inter-bank liquidity dries up completely.

Similarly, the benchmark rate can also be an interest rate at which commercial banks are ready to borrow or lend each other. For example, the

*London Inter-Bank Offer Rate* (LIBOR), or the *Mumbai Interbank Offer Rate (MIBOR), Mumbai Interbank Outright Rate (FBIL-MIBOR)*, are other forms of benchmark rate, available internationally and in India. These are widely used benchmark rates to price several financial products, including loans and advances, debt securities, and other financial instruments.

### Government securities yield

The government security yield, or yield to maturity, on a dated (original maturity of more than 1-year) security issued by the central government is the average rate of interest/return that an investor is expected to earn from a risk-free (counterparty risk) investment till the maturity of the security. This yield may vary depending upon the maturity of the debt security. Government security yields of different maturities are extracted from the market prices of various government securities, and therefore are treated as a market-based, risk-free rate of interest that can be further used as a benchmark rate of interest, especially in the non-government securities market. There can be a benchmark risk-free yield of various maturity, extracted from most liquid central government securities of various maturities. But in many developing markets like in India, such benchmark rates may not be available for all possible maturities because of insufficient liquidity for securities of all possible maturities. A 10-year GOI yield (6.7502% as on 18 December 2019) is known to be the true benchmark, risk-free yield in India. Movement in the government security yield is a very good indicator of the expected change (if any) in the domestic economy.

### T-bill rate

Treasury-bill (T-bill) rate is the risk-free rate of interest offered by the central government on its short-term debt obligation having a maturity of less than 1 year. T-bills in India are normally issued with maturities of 91 days, 182 days, and 364 days, which are reasonably liquid short-term financial instruments. T-bill rates (4.9982%, 5.1866%, and 5.2476% respectively for 91 days, 182 days, and 364 days as on 18 December 2019 in India) are very good indicators of short-term risk-free rate of interest in an economy, and therefore can be used as short-term benchmark rates of interest for all non-government debt products.

### Swap rate

It is the interest rate charged to swap a floating rate debt into a fixed interest rate. Alternatively, a swap rate measures the cost for a bank or financial institution to swap or switch from a floating rate agreement to a fixed rate agreement for a specific period, say 3 months to 10 years. Therefore, a swap rate is a fixed rate of interest applicable to swap an asset or liability of a financial institution, linked to a floating rate of interest, say LIBOR/ MIBOR, for a specific maturity. Since swap deals happen between two non-government entities, the rate applicable to such swap contracts, i.e. the swap rate, is not a risk-free rate of interest, and therefore is supposed to be slightly higher than the risk-free government security yield of similar maturity, leading to a positive spread. But there may be some instances, like those observed in India, where the swap rates are consistently below (5.2300%, 5.2840%, and 5.4856% respectively for 3-month, 1-year, and 5-year swap deal as on 18 December 2019 in India) the respective government security yield, leaving a *Negative Swap Spread*, probably due to relatively higher importance given to the non-funding nature of swap deals and ignoring the possibility to charge a higher rate even due to counterparty risk.

## Major determinants of bond yields

In the context of the debt securities market, the rate of interest that is of high importance is the yield on debt security, which may be of different types, such as government security, non-government security with a different level of credit risk, securities with different levels of liquidity, securities with call risk, etc. The yields on government securities of different maturities are considered to be the risk-free rates of interest for the concerned maturity, and all other yields can be subsequently derived from the risk-free yield after adjusting for the credit risk premium, illiquidity premium, and/or call premium. The risk-free interest rate or yield on government securities can be derived through a market-based mechanism, where the same is based on the market demand and supply of debt securities. As applicable to any market-based pricing, the larger the demand, the greater would be the price; and the higher the supply, the lower would be the price. At the same time, as per the basic bond pricing rule, there is an inverse relationship between the price and yield of a security. Accordingly, the higher the price, the lower would be the yield, and vice versa. Therefore, if demands for debt securities are high, it leads to higher prices, finally leading to a lower yield or interest rate, and vice versa. In a market-based economy like in India, interest rates can largely depend upon the factors affecting the demand and supply of debt securities in that economy, including any specific move by the bond market regulator or government as control mechanism. Accordingly, the determinants of yield or interest rate of debt securities can be discussed hereunder:

### Supply or issuance of securities

If the central or state government faces a higher fiscal deficit, and therefore decides to announce a large amount of market borrowing issuing more securities, the supply side is going to be stronger, leading to a fall in price, and therefore a rise in yield or interest rate. Alternatively, if borrowers need more funds from the market, it is quite obvious that they need to pay a higher rate of interest. On the other hand, if an economy is doing well, attempting to reduce the fiscal deficit leads to less borrowing, and therefore less security issuance, causing the price to rise and the yield to fall. Similarly, if any non-government entities need to meet their financing needs through the debt securities market, the rate of interest it has to offer depends upon the relative strength of the supply side in comparison with the demand that may again depend upon some other factor, as well including the credit risk of the issuer.

For example, when the government of India in its Union Budget during February 2018 announced the Mega Health Insurance scheme for 10 crores to poor and vulnerable families, providing a coverage of up to Rs.5 lakh per family per year, it gives a signal to the market that the government fiscal deficit in the coming year is going to increase, leading to a rise in market borrowing through more issuance of debt securities. This possible rise in the supply of central government securities, along with other factors, might also play some role in the hike of the government security yield in India.

### OMO purchase/OMO sale by government

*Open Market Operation (OMO)* is basically a liquidity adjustment mechanism used by the central bank of the country to control the market by way of injecting more liquidity in the system, or sucking liquidity from the system, whenever needed. Under these operations, the central bank may like to buy-back (i.e. OMO purchase) the existing government securities from the market and can inject more liquidity in the system, or may like to sell the securities (OMO Sale) to the market to absorb excess liquidity from the system, and therefore affect the demand and supply of government securities. These regulatory interventions may affect the interest rates that get affected by normal demand and supply forces, or may also remain stable if the market finds it suitable even after the OMO operations.

### Sovereign credit rating

The sovereign rating of an economy is adversely related to the risk-free yield in that economy. If the economy has a poor credit worthiness (say BB credit rating), even if there is no risk for a domestic investor to invest in the securities issued by the central government of that economy, any such investment will be risky for a foreign investors. Therefore, expectation of foreign investors, in terms of sufficient compensation, depending upon the sovereign rating, may also play a significant role in deciding the rate of interest in government securities. The role of the sovereign rating of a domestic economy is relatively significant when there is a strong presence of foreign investors in the domestic securities market, as in the case of USA, where almost half of the Treasury securities are held by foreign investors for whom the US sovereign rating is very important to fix their yield expectations.

For example, when Moody's upgraded India's sovereign credit rating from Baa3 to Baa2, and changed the outlook on the rating to stable from positive during November 2017, it was expected to give a higher confidence to the foreign investors to invest more in securities issued by government of India. This could have led to a higher demand for GOI bonds, causing their prices to rise and the yield to fall, provided such an upgradation of India's sovereign rating strengthened the presence of FIIs in India's debt market.

### Expected future inflation (WPI/CPI)

Expected future rate of inflation is the most crucial factor to determine any rate of interest. Any lender, expecting the rate of inflation to go high in the future, may prefer to lend at an interest rate that is higher than the rate of inflation, and vice versa. Therefore, rising (falling) inflation signals a higher (softer) interest rate regime. Interest rate or yield on debt securities, therefore, largely depends upon the prevailing and future rate of inflation in that economy, as may be indicated by the Wholesale Price Index (WPI), or Consumer Price Index (CPI). Because of its higher importance, the market players always wait for the dates when these inflation numbers are released by the competent authority.

### Growth rate

General economic conditions or the general growth of an economy plays a very crucial role to determine the level of interest rate in that economy. In an economy with an increasing growth rate, the chances for more spending (institutional and retail) increases, leading to more demand of available funds to channelize credit, followed by rising inflation, and may finally lead to a rise in rate of interest. Alternatively, higher growth enhances bank lending and reduces banks' investment in the debt market, thereby reducing the demand for debt securities, followed by a fall in price and rise in interest rates or bond yields.

This situation holds when the economy tends to grow without any intervention from the central bank. On the other hand, if higher growth rate is a result of intervention from the central bank, the high growth may be ensured by injecting liquidity in the system through OMO purchases or cutting the liquidity ratio (SLR), where the price of the bond, and therefore the bond yield, may or may not get affected, depending on the response of major institutional investors like banks towards the demand for concerned securities.

Even if the growth rate and bond yield are generally positively correlated, it may not be always true that the rise in the risk-free yield in an economy is the result of experiencing high growth in that economy. For example, even if such a positive association is presently valid in the US economy, the same may not be true in India. India is experiencing a continuous rise in government security yield even without having a higher economic growth.

## Policy rate

The rate of interests, which are part of the monetary policy issued by the central bank of an economy, are known as *Policy Rates*. The Reserve Bank of India governs monetary activities such as money supply, liquidity, and interest rates through its key policy rates: repo rate and reverse repo rate. Repo or repurchase is a short-term borrowing programme where banks can meet their funding requirement by selling approved government securities to RBI. Repo rate is the discount rate at which banks borrow from RBI. On the other hand, reverse repo rate is the rate at which RBI borrows money from the banks by depositing government securities with them. Thus, the repo rate is always higher than the reverse repo rate. Liquidity can be controlled through these policy rates by the RBI within a system called Liquidity Adjustment Facility provided by the RBI to the banks. Therefore, any fall (rise) in the repo rate allows banks to get money at a cheaper (expensive) rate, thereby controlling the money supply and liquidity in the system.

Policy rates and yield on debt securities are positively interrelated. Any expectation in the rise (fall) in repo rate may lead to a subsequent rise (fall) in the risk-free yield on government securities as well.

For example, the RBI stand on either a hike in the policy rate (RBI Repo Rate) or keeping the same unchanged (from 6.00% during August 2017 to 6.25% during June 2018, and thereafter to 5.15% in December 2019) is expected to have a significant role in keeping the government-security yield in India consistently at a higher level. Lack of any hope from the central bank to cut its policy rate in the near future also gives a signal to the market that the government-security yield in India is not going to soften very soon.

## Reserve/liquidity ratio (CRR & SLR)

Reserve ratios, like cash reserve ratio (CRR) and statutory liquidity ratio (SLR), set by the central bank especially to control the liquidity in the banking system depending upon the economic condition, also play a crucial role in determining the risk-free rate of interest or yield on debt securities. CRR (presently at 4%) is the minimum proportion of bank's total deposits that need to be kept or deposited with RBI in cash. Similarly, SLR (presently set at 18.50% in December 2019) is the minimum percentage of bank's deposits, called net demand and time liabilities (NDTL), which the bank has to maintain internally in form of gold, cash, or other approved securities defined by the RBI.

A change in these policy ratios is actually a regulatory move and may cause a change in the market rate of interest, or the interest rate may remain stable depending upon the reaction of the market and its impact on the demand of debt securities. Any rise in CRR may lead to a fall in the demand for debt securities, causing a fall in the prices of such securities, which may finally take the interest rate or yield at a higher level, and vice versa. On the other hand, if the SLR increases, maybe due to economic instability or a higher fiscal deficit, the demand for SLR approved securities, which are essentially the government securities, increases, causing the bond price to rise and yield to fall. Similarly, under a stable economic condition with a lower fiscal deficit, providing room to free liquidity for the private sector, the central bank may decide to cut the SLR, which may lead to a fall in the demand for such bonds, and therefore the price falls and the yield rises. But under certain market conditions, even if after a change in these reserve ratios, the demand for such bonds may remain stable, and therefore there may not be any change in the rate of interest.

For example, like the current situation in India when banks' deposits are growing at a regular pace, but they are reluctant to extend sufficient credit especially due to the very high level of NPA in the banking system as a whole, this causes a continuous preference towards government securities even after several reductions (20.75 in November 2016 to 18.50 in December 2019) of the minimum statutory requirement of holding such securities (i.e. SLR). Even if the central bank may decide to put a cap on the maximum holding of such securities as held till maturity (HTM),[1] the investors may still show their preference towards such risk-free securities and do not mind keeping them in their trading portfolio (HFT and AFS) and face a regular market-to-market (MTM) in revaluing their investments, even in the regime of continuous rise in the government security yield. Such a situation may incentivize the move of the central bank to control the liquidity, and therefore the interest rates through controlling reserve ratios.

### Global economy

Not only does the economic condition in the domestic economy, but also the global economic condition, especially the US economy, plays a very crucial role in deciding the domestic rate of interest, including the yield on debt securities. The higher the growth possibility for the global economies, especially the large economies, the greater would be the possibility for domestic interest rates, including bond yields, to rise.

For example, when the US Federal Reserve hiked its benchmark interest rate a quarter point, taking the fund rate to a range of 2% to 2.25% during September 2018, with an anticipation of economic growth in the current year and a road map ahead through 2021, it gave a strong signal to the world economy that the economic condition in US was getting normalized. This situation brought back the confidence of global investors in the US economy and financial market, resulting in a regular and significant outflow of funds from many developing economies, including India, affecting their financial market and interest rates.

### FII movements

The domestic rate of interest can get affected by the presence of foreign institutional investors (FIIs). There can be significant inflow and/or outflow of funds by the FIIs, which can affect the domestic market. A significant amount of such FIIs inflows, within the permissible limit, may increase the demand for domestic financial assets, including debts and equities, and therefore can push the prices up, which may finally lead the yield on debt security to fall. On the other hand, in the event of significant FIIs, outflows from the domestic debt market may cause over supply of debt securities in the market, pushing the price to go down and the yield to go up. Therefore, movement of FIIs in the domestic debt market may play a short-term but crucial role in determining the rate of interest or yield on debt securities.

For example, when there was a historic withdrawal of FIIs by more than INR 90,000 crore from the Indian capital market in October 2018 due to several economic developments worldwide, including a rate hike by Federal Reserve, the government security yield in India got a consistent hit, causing the 10-year yield to be at more than 7.80% during end of October 2018, almost 80 basis points higher than the 10-year GOI yield during the same time last year.

### Major exchange rate

The domestic rate of interest, if not monotonically, but up to a significant extent, depends upon the appreciation or depreciation of the domestic currency in comparison with the foreign currency, or alternatively the movement of the exchange rate. If the Indian Rupee appreciates against the US Dollar, the USD-INR exchange rate (presently at a level of 72.75 as on 2 November 2018, meaning USD 1 is equal to INR 72.75) falls. If, however, the INR depreciates, the USD-INR exchange rate increases, meaning more INR need to be spent to get one USD. The domestic rate of interest is significantly influenced by the movement of the major currencies, like US Dollars, Australian Dollar, Euro, GBP, JPY, CHF, etc. against the INR. Any depreciation of INR against these major currencies, leading to a rise in the concerned exchange rate (e.g. USD-INR, AUD-INR, EURO-INR, GBP-INR, JPY-INR, CHF-INR), may finally lead to a hike in the domestic rate of interest, including the yield on debt securities, and vice versa. *Interest Rate Parity*[2] theory may be referred to understand the linkage between the domestic rate of interest and foreign exchange rate to ensure a no interest arbitrage.

A classic example to establish the linkage of exchange rate and interest rate is the current regime in the Indian financial market, where both the exchange rate (say USD-INR) and government-security yield have been increasing for a quite long time. One important reason for the rise in GOI yield in India is the consistent depreciation of INR against USD, and therefore the rise in the USD-INR rate from less than 65 during November 2017 to more than 72 during November 2018. As long as the rupee is expected to depreciate against USD, it is unlikely to expect any fall in the risk-free yield in India.

## Default & liquidity factor

The factors or determinants described above broadly affect the risk-free rate of interests, i.e. yield on government debt securities. As far as the yield on non-government securities are concerned, the same is also driven by the credit worthiness of the issuers of the securities, as defined by various credit rating, such as AAA, AA, A, etc. The lower the credit worthiness of the issuer with lower credit rating, the greater would be the credit risk for the investor, and therefore the higher would be the credit risk premium and therefore the yield, and vice versa. Therefore, the yields on low-rated securities are always higher than the yield on highly rated securities. Not only the existing credit worthiness, but also the expected future migration in the credit quality (if any) should be taken into consideration to understand the future movement in the respective rate of interest or yield. Similarly, liquidity can also be taken into consideration to derive the yield on several debt securities, which may be with different levels of liquidity. Since investors of illiquid securities face some inconvenience to sell their security in the right time and also at a right price, they may like to get compensated by a liquidity premium, which increases the yield or interest rate for that instrument. Therefore, liquidity (liquidity risk) of a debt security has an inverse (positive) relationship with the concerned yield.

For example, when the government of India had issued one of its 10-year securities (*6.79% GS 2027*) on 15-May-2017, maturing on 15-May-2027, the same was considered to be the 10-year benchmark, and a 10-year on-the-run bond, attracting maximum liquidity in the market, and therefore traded at a relatively lower yield, say close to 6.80%. But once the central government issued another 10-year security (*7.17% GS 2028*) on 8-Jan-2018, maturing on 8-Jan-2028, the same became the present on-the-run and had taken over the benchmark status, attracting the maximum liquidity in the market. As a result, the earlier benchmark (*6.79% GS 2027*), almost of similar maturity, has become the off-the-run security with relatively less liquidity, and therefore started trading at a relatively higher yield. If the trade history of NDS-OM as on 30-October-2018 is considered, the last trade in *7.17% GS 2028* and *6.79% GS 2027* happened at a yield of respectively 7.83% and 7.90%. The difference of 7 basis points is just an illiquidity premium attached to the off-the-run security.

On the other hand, let's consider two non-government securities: 8.81% SMALL INDUSTRIES DEVELOPMENT BANK OF INDIA 2022 (AAA rated), and 10.90% IDEA CELLULAR LIMITED 2023 (AA rated), both traded on 30-October-2018 respectively at a yield of 8.81% and 10.87%, and therefore at a yield spread of respectively 109 bps and 288 bps. Both the securities as on the trading date are of closer maturity and are also equally liquid. But the major reason for the difference in their yield spread is the credit/default risk attached to the respective security. Being a relatively low rated (AA) bond, 10.90% IDEA CELLULAR LIMITED 2023 is traded at a higher default risk premium.

### Domestic stock market

Fundamentally, the bond market and the stock market are expected to move inversely to each other. As stocks rise, demand for stocks increases, leading to a fall in the demand for bonds, causing the bond prices to fall and the bond yields to rise, and vice versa. But at the same time, it is not necessary to always establish this linkage between the stock and bond market. A significant exception to this expected co-movement is the current regime in India, where the stock market is experiencing a downward trend and the yield on debt securities are also rising, possibly due to the relatively higher impact of other market forces expected to affect the interest rates.

## Term structure of interest rates: different types

It is well known that, if identical bonds have different terms to maturity, consequently their interest rates differ. Term structure of interest rates is the relationship among yields on financial instruments with identical tax, risk, and liquidity characteristics, but only of different time to maturity. Therefore, the term structure of interest rates can be referred to as the relationship between the yield of various bonds and other fixed income products and their respective time to maturity. The term structure of interest rates is a very important because there is a common belief that the shape of the yield curve reflects the market's future expectation for interest rates and the conditions for monetary policy. Different types of term structure, in the context of the debt securities market, can be constructed depending on the nature of interest rates, such as *Yield to Maturity, Zero Coupon Yield/Spot Rates, Forward Rates*, etc. Depending on the relation between the rate of interest and time, a term structure may be broadly of three different shapes: *Upward Sloping, Downward Sloping*, and *Flat*, as shown in the following figure (Figure 5.1). A Term Structure can be with multiple slopes at different maturity levels, known as *Humped Curve*. In a normal market condition, term structure of interest rates is expected to be an upward slopping curve, where interest rate increases as the maturity increase but at a decreasing rate. Such Term Structure of Interest Rates can again be constructed with different Risk Profile: such as Risk-Free term structure, term structure of interest rates for different category of bond issuer with different level of credit worthiness. The basic term structure of interest rates of an economy is the term structure constructed out of Yield on Central Govt. securities of different maturities, commonly known as the *Base Yield Curve*.

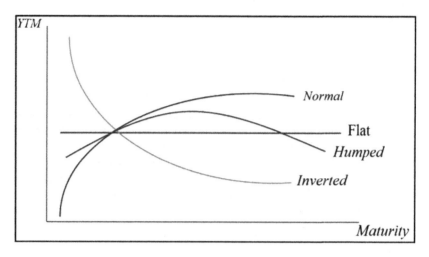

*Figure 5.1* Different possible shapes of yield curve

Based on different types of interest rates, term structure can be broadly classified as: *Yield Curve, Spot Rate Curve*, and *Forward Rate Curve*, which are discussed in the following section.

### Yield curve

The term structure of interest rates basically refers to the relationship between yield to maturity (YTM) of bonds with different terms to maturity. When YTMs of such bonds are plotted against their maturities, it represents the yield curve. The yield curve is also defined as the graphical presentation of yields on bonds with different terms to maturity but with the same risk profile, liquidity, and tax considerations. Such a yield curve can be constructed for particular types of bonds, like government securities and corporate bonds of a particular category (in terms of issuer's segment, credit rating, etc.). Economists and investors believe that the shape of the yield curve reflects the market's future expectation for bond yields/interest rates and conditions for the country's monetary policy.

The yield curve may be graphically classified as: upward sloping, flat, or downward sloping. When the yield curve is upward sloping, the short-term interest rates, such as a 91-day Treasury-bill rate, are below the long-term rates, such as long-term government securities maturing 10 years and above. When a yield curve is flat, the short-term interest rates and long-term interest rates all become the same. When the yield curves are downward sloping, commonly known as inverted, the long-term rates are found to be lower than the short-term rates. Some of the important facts about the yield curve are:

- Interest rates are non-negative; and possess the properties of mean-reverting.
- Interest rates on bonds of different maturities move together over time.
- Changes of interest rates are expected to be correlated, but not perfectly correlated.
- Volatility of short- and medium-term rates are higher than that of long-term rates, mostly due to higher liquidity in short and medium terms.
- When short-term interest rates are low, yield curves are more likely to have an upward slope; when short-term interest rates are high, yield curves are likely to slope forward and be inverted.
- Yield curves usually slope upward.

The possible shapes of yield curves are explained below.

### Normal/upward-sloping yield curve

Upward-sloping yield curves are usually observed in most of the developed nations worldwide. If a yield curve is upward sloped, there exists a positive term premium, resulting in longer-term interest rates being higher than shorter-term interest rates. The positive slope reflects investors' expectations for the concerned economy to grow in the future, which is again expected to cause a higher inflation-risk premium that investors demand for their longer-term investments. This higher inflation expectation may lead the central bank to tighten monetary policy by raising short-term interest rates in the future to slow economic growth and dampen inflationary pressure. Risk arises due to uncertainty in the future rate of inflation, which is further factored into the current yield curve, leading to a higher yields for longer maturities.

In such normal market conditions with higher expectation for long term rates, the shape of the yield curve, even if upward slopping, again depends on the fundamental relation between change in interest rates with respect to change in time or maturity. In other words, for a fixed increase in time, if the interest rate increases at a constant rate, the shape of the yield curve looks like an upward-sloping *Straight Line*. On the other hand, for every positive change in time, if the yield increases but at an increasing rate, the yield curve takes a shape of upward-sloping *Convex Curve*. However, both these situations do not support the fundamental relationship between change in time and change in interest rates. Therefore, in a normal market scenario, when yield movements are positively interrelated with change in time, the yield curve takes the shape of an upward-sloping *Concave Curve*, exhibiting the fact that for every positive change in time/maturity, the change in interest rates/yields are positive, but at a *Decreasing Rate*.

*Inverted/downward-sloping yield curve*

However, the market may always not remain normal and may experience a different shape of a yield curve. There are many economies in the world, including the USA, where the same have experienced a persistent deflation and their bond markets exhibit a downward-sloping or inverted yield curve, reflecting the fact that future cash flows are more valuable than current cash flows. If a yield curve is inverted, bonds with longer maturities are expected to offer lower yields than bonds with shorter maturities. This shape is generally seen when the market expects interest rates to fall in future. Under this abnormal and contradictory circumstance, long-term investors will settle for lower yields now if they think the economy will slow or even decline in the future. An inverted curve may indicate a worsening economic situation in the future.

Like the normal yield curve, the inverted yield curve may also take the shape of a downward-sloping straight line, downward-sloping concave, or downward-sloping convex. If it is assumed that for every positive change in maturity, the yield changes at a lower rate, then an inverted yield curve may take the shape of a downward-sloping convex curve.

*Flat yield curve*

If a yield curve is found to be flat, short-term interest rates are almost equal with the medium- and long-term interest rates. This type of curve indicates that the market environment is sending mixed signals to investors, who are interpreting interest rate movements in various ways. In such an environment, it is difficult for the market to determine whether interest rates will move significantly in either (increase or decrease) direction in the future, resulting in a flat curve. A flat yield curve usually occurs when the market is making a transition that releases different but simultaneous indications towards the movement of interest rates in the economy. In other words, there may be some signals that short-term interest rates will rise, and other signals that long-term interest rates will fall, making the yield curve relatively flatter than the normal positively slopped curve. When the yield curve is flat, investors can optimize their risk/return trade-off mostly by choosing fixed income securities with the least risk, or highest credit quality. Even if rare, but whenever long-term interest rates start declining, a flat curve can sometimes lead to an inverted curve, which may be a matter of concern for the market.

*Humped yield curve*

Even if there are three most usual shapes of yield curves, the relationship between an interest rate and the term to maturity of bonds may not always be consistent and linear. Such a relationship may change at different maturity levels, leading to a single curve with different slopes and curvatures, commonly

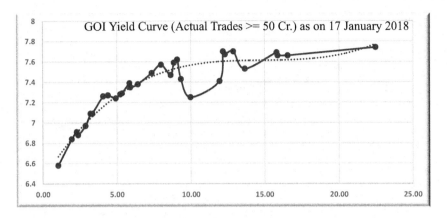

*Figure 5.2* Government of India yield curve (using actual traded yields)

known as a *Humped Curve*. It is often seen that the market expects that interest rates will first rise (fall) during a period and then fall (rise) during another period, or even may remain constant for a certain period. This kind of yield curve, having various slopes during different periods, is known as a *Humped Yield Curve*, as shown in the following figure (Figure 5.2).

As far as any shift in the yield curve is concerned, there may be two broader types of shift in the curve, viz. parallel and unparallel shift. When interest rates change by the same amount for bonds of all terms, the shift in the yield curve is called a *Parallel Shift*. Under such circumstances, the shape of the yield curve remains unchanged, although interest rates are higher or lower across the curve. There may be different types of unparallel shifts in the yield curve. A change in the shape of the yield curve is called a *twist* and means that interest rates for bonds of some maturity change differently than bonds of other maturity. When the difference between long- and short-term interest rates is large, the yield curve is said to be steeper. On the other hand, if such a difference is narrowed down, the new curve becomes flatter. Different types of yield curve shifts are shown in the following figure (Figure 5.3). The lower short-term interest rates exhibit the easy availability of money and low or declining inflation. Higher longer-term interest rates reflect investors' fears of future inflation. Tight monetary policy results in short-term interest rates being higher than longer-term rates.

Even if the yield curve can be theoretically constructed very easily, there may be various issues involved to extract a valid yield curve. Issues required to be addressed before the construction of a valid yield curve include:

- Availability of yields for all required maturity points.
- If required to be interpolated, how accurate is the method of interpolation.

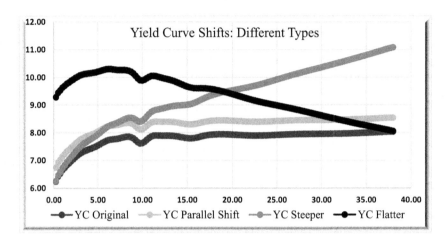

*Figure 5.3* Different yield curve shifts

- Validity of the assumption undertaken in the concerned method.
- Acceptable level of trade-off between the accuracy and smoothness.

### Methods of constructing yield curve

In absence of sufficient yield points throughout all the required maturities, a complete yield curve is constructed through different interpolation methods. Some of the common but important interpolation methods are:

- Linear interpolation method
- Cubic interpolation method
- Cubic spline method

### Linear interpolation method

Under the first method, it is assumed that any unknown rate lies on a straight line between two adjacent known rates on the yield curve. The slope of the segment joining the known lower rate ($R_1$) and the unknown rate ($R_n$) must be equal to the slope of the segment joining the two known rates ($R_1$ and $R_2$). This will ensure that all three points lie on the same line. Accordingly, the unknown rate ($R_n$) for known maturity ($t_n$) can be derived, such that:

$$R_n = R_1 + [\{(R_2 - R_1) / (t_2 - t_1)\} \Box (t_n - t_1)] \tag{5.1}$$

A GOI risk-free yield curve constructed through linear interpolation method, using actual trades in the secondary market as on a given date, is exhibited in the following figure (Figure 5.4).

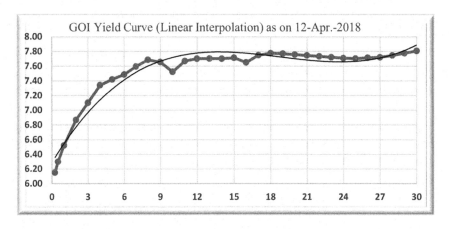

*Figure 5.4* GOI yield curve (extracted through linear interpolation)

*Table 5.1* Actual trades in central government securities

| Res. Maturity | 0.2027 | 0.9644 | 1.2137 | 1.4438 | 2.2000 | 2.2301 |
|---|---|---|---|---|---|---|
| W. Avg. Yield | 7.47 | 7.24 | 7.24 | 7.3 | 7.34 | 7.34 |
| Res. Maturity | 3.3452 | 3.4548 | 3.9288 | 4.2630 | 4.3644 | 4.8685 |
| W. Avg. Yield | 7.45 | 7.47 | 7.54 | 7.62 | 7.58 | 7.62 |

*Source*: All tables in this chapter are created by the author unless otherwise stated.

## Example

Suppose the weighted average yield on a few government of India securities, say till a residual maturity of 5 years, traded in NDS-OM platform, as on 29 January 2016 are given in the following table (Table 5.1).

From the given yields of different maturity, how are yields for different intermediate maturity interpolated following the linear interpolation technique?

## Solution

Since the available market yields are a different fraction of residual maturities, yields of some required maturity, say 3 months, 6 months, 12 months, 2 year, 3 year, and so on, maybe till 30 years, need to be linearly interpolated to construct a yield curve.

From the yield points of two given maturities, the yield of the required intermediate, as shown in the following table (Table 5.2), may be extracted through the linear interpolation technique, as explained above and further shown below.

*Table 5.2* Extraction of missing yield through linear interpolation

| Tenor (Year) | Yield | Tenor (Year) | Yield |
|---|---|---|---|
| 0.2027 $(t_1)$ | 7.47% $(R_1)$ | 1.4438 $(t_1)$ | 7.30% $(R_1)$ |
| 0.25 $(t_n)$ | ? $(R_n)$ | 1.50 $(t_n)$ | ? $(R_n)$ |
| 0.9644 $(t_2)$ | 7.24% $(R_2)$ | 2.20 $(t_2)$ | 7.34% $(R_2)$ |

As per the equation given above, assuming a constant change in the yield points from one maturity to another, the yield for 0.25 years and 1.50 years can be extracted as follows:

$$0.25 \; Year \; Yield = R_1 + [\{(R_2 - R_1) / (t_2 - t_1)\} \times (t_n - t_1)] = 7.47\%$$
$$+ [\{(7.24\% - 7.47\%) / (0.9644 - 0.2027)\}$$
$$\times (0.25 - 0.2027)] = 7.4557\%.$$

Similarly, $1.50 \; Year \; Yield = R_1 + [\{(R_2 - R_1) / (t_2 - t_1)\} \times (t_n - t_1)]$
$$= 7.30\% + [\{(7.34\% - 7.30\%) /$$
$$(2.20 - 1.4438)\} \times (1.50 - 1.4438)]$$
$$= 7.3294\%$$

The same process may be followed to interpolate the yield for all required maturity or maturity.

### Cubic Interpolation Method

The cubic interpolation method assumes that any unknown rate belongs to a cubic polynomial which contains four known rates on the yield curve. There are four unknown parameters in a cubic polynomial function, such that:

$$R_t = a + bt + ct^2 + dt^3 \tag{5.2}$$

't' represents the known maturity. Values of these 4 parameters (a, b, c, and d) can be obtained simultaneously from the known rates. Each segment of the YC is a cubic polynomial whose slope and curvature depend on the known rates and the time points between which the unknown rate is inserted. This yield curve is not smooth but supposed to be more practical comparative to the one extracted by the first method, as supported by more actual trades.

There is no doubt that a non-linear function better captures the movement of interest rates than captured by linear technique. But as far as the selection of the degree of polynomial in the functional form is concerned, the cubic function has a preference over others because of the following:

1　It is possible to capture both the slope and curvature of a curve only if the polynomial is at least of third order. Unless the polynomial is differentiable till second order, it may not be possible to capture both the slope and curvature of the curve, which are required for the necessary optimization to construct the final curve.

2   On the other hand, a higher order, say fourth or fifth order function, even if possibly give a better term structure, may not be possible to consider because of insufficient actual trade data in a relatively illiquid market like in India. Suppose if a fifth order polynomial is considered, at least six pairs (yield and maturity) of trade data are necessary to construct every segment of the curve, which may not be possible in an illiquid market like India, especially while constructing the long-term segment of the curve, say 15–20 years, or beyond 20 years.

Steps required to construct a yield curve through cubic interpolation:

*   Selection of any four points on the available yield curve nearest to the required TTM.
*   Form the TTM and YTM matrices.
*   Multiply the YTM matrix with the inverse of the TTM matrix to compute the coefficients of the cubic polynomial.
*   Use the estimated coefficient values of the polynomial to interpolate the YTM of the required maturity.
*   Follow the same steps to calculate YTMs for all the required TTM.

## Cubic spline method

It is suggested (James & Webber – 2000) that the parametric method may produce a satisfactory overall shape for the term structure, but it is more suitable only where good accuracy is not required. Market practitioners generally prefer an approach that gives a reasonable trade-off between accuracy and ease of implementation. Cubic spline interpolation is a form of interpolation dealing with a special type of piecewise polynomial called a *Spline*. Spline interpolation is preferred over polynomial interpolation because the interpolation error can be made small. Beim (1992) states that the cubic spline method performs at least as satisfactory as any other method.

A spline is a piecewise polynomial, consisting of individual polynomial segments joined by *Knot Points*. Even if different pieces are joined together, several conditions are imposed to ensure the smoothness so as to appear as a graph of a single polynomial. Since while fitting a term structure, importance is given to slope and curvature, the required polynomial needs to be differentiable at least twice, 1st order for slope and 2nd order for curvature. This leads to the requirement of polynomial function of order 3. A polynomial of higher order may be used to ensure varying degrees of accuracy and continuity.

The objective of this method is to produce a continuous curve joining market observed rates as smoothly as possible. Under the cubic polynomial method, several polynomials are joined together, but what is ensured here is the smoothness at the joining points. For continuity and smoothness, the imposed conditions while joining two polynomials are:

- Equal values at the knot points.
- Equal slopes at the knot points.
- Equal curvature at knot points.
- Zero curvature at the end points.

The boundary condition (4th) ensures that the slopes of extrapolated segments (beyond end points) are constant and the YC is linear.

Necessary steps to construct YC through cubic spline:

- Construct the TTM and YTM matrices by inserting known values (known rates with their respective maturities) in the polynomials.
- One knot point (TTM, YTM) will be common to both.
- Augmenting the matrix through:

  ○ Equating 1st derivative at the joint.
  ○ Equating 2nd derivatives at the joint.
  ○ Equating 2nd derivative, at the endpoint of each polynomial, to zero.

- A system of eight equations, representing the aforesaid objective functions and necessary constraints, can be framed to solve the values of eight unknown parameters in the two polynomials.

### *Example*

The actual trade in government of India bonds, excluding in any special security, dated 12 April 2018, may be considered to extract the risk-free yield curve, using both cubic interpolation and cubic spline methods. The above steps are followed to extract the coefficients' values of the concerned cubic polynomial and the same are used to extract the yield for the required maturity (say till 30 years), which are subsequently used to construct the risk-free GOI yield curve using both interpolation method, as shown in the following figure (Figure 5.5).

### *Zero coupon yield/spot rate curve*

Yield to maturity (YTM), even if a very important interest rate or yield measure in the context of the bond market, has certain limitations. YTM as a yield measure, extracted from coupon bearing securities, depends upon the specific maturity and also the reinvestment rates. Therefore, YTM may not be considered to construct a robust term structure of interest rates free from reinvestment risk. This may lead to consideration of a type of interest rates or yields which are extracted from some zero coupon instruments, and therefore free from any reinvestment risk. Yields from zero coupon securities are termed as *Zero Coupon Yield* or *Spot Rates*. The *zero coupon yield*

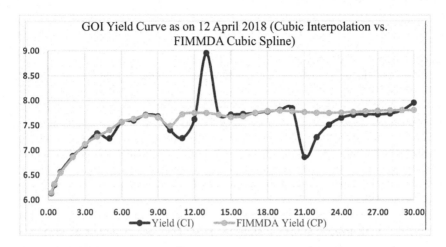

*Figure 5.5* GOI yield curve (extracted through cubic interpolation)

*curve* or *spot rate curve* plots zero coupon yields (or spot rates) against various terms to maturity.

In the first instance, if there is a liquid zero coupon bond market, such a spot rate curve can be easily constructed. However, it is not necessary to have a set of zero coupon bonds available and/or traded in a market in order to construct this curve. There can be many markets where zero coupon instruments are available only for few maturity (like 3 months, 6 months, and 12 months, as in the case of Treasury bills in India), or no zero coupon bonds are traded, where spot rates can be theoretically extracted from the conventional yield to maturity (YTM) curve. These zero coupon yields or spot rates are known as theoretical spot rates and the curve constructed out of those yields is termed as *Theoretical Spot Rate Curve*. Yields of *Treasury Strips*, which are essentially zero coupon securities, of various maturities can be considered as zero coupon yields or spot rates. But in the absence of a developed strip market like in India, various alternative methods can be applied to extract the zero coupon yield or spot rates. One of the important methods is known as *Method of Bootstrapping*. Under this method, the spot rates are theoretically extracted from the available YTM of coupon bearing securities of different maturities, or from the current market prices of such securities. Spot rates can be alternatively extracted from other parametric methods, such as the *Nelson Siegel (NS) Method* or *Nelson-Siegel-Svensson (NSS) Method*, where all the concerned spot rates are modeled in proper functional form and are applied to the market data. Since spot rates are applicable to zero coupon securities, having no reinvestment risk, the spot rate curve is viewed as the true term structure of interest rates. Accordingly, the spot rate for a maturity of n year is regarded as the true n-year rate of interest, and therefore represents the average annual return till the nth year.

## Method of bootstrapping

Bootstrapping is a simple arithmetic procedure for extracting zero coupon yields from available trades in coupon bearing bonds. Any option-free coupon bearing plain vanilla bond can be considered as a package of zero coupon securities, known as Treasury strips. Each zero coupon security in such a package has a face value equal to the regular fixed coupon due in the coupon bond, and maturity equal to the coupon payment dates, and in the case of principal, respectively equal to the fixed principal and the final maturity date. As per the simple bond valuation principal, the value of the coupon bearing Treasury bond should be equal to the value of the package of several zero coupon securities. If this equality does not hold, there would be a possibility to experience some arbitrage in the market.

The basic idea is to start with an initial short-term bond – typically a 6 month- or 12-month bond, which are truly zero coupon bonds, and then calculate their yield. It is typical to observe a 6-month and a 12-month zero, and therefore the first coupon bearing bond matures at month 18. The first two semi-annual ZC yields, easily available from the 6-month (182 Days) and 12-month (364 Days) Treasury bills, denoted as $Z_6$ and $Z_{12}$, can be used to calculate the 18-month spot rate, denoted as $Z_{18}$. Once the 18-month spot rate is derived, it is possible to get $Z_{24}$. The same process can be repeated to extract the desired number of spot rates. Typically, the *par-value* coupon bearing bond can be used, or the yield curve used to extract the zero coupon yield may be assumed to be a *Par Yield Curve*. Given that the values of $Z_6$ and $Z_{12}$ are known, what needs to be done is to find the value of $Z_{18}$ that makes this statement true:

$$100 = \frac{C/2}{\left(1+Z_6/2\right)^1} + \frac{C/2}{\left(1+Z_{12}/2\right)^2} + \frac{C/2}{\left(1+Z_{18}/2\right)^3} \tag{5.3}$$

## Example

Suppose the 182-day and 364-day T-bill rates are: $ZCYC_{6M}=6.9390\%$, $ZCYS_{12M} = 7.3409\%$, and that the coupon on a 1.5-year par-priced coupon bond is 7.4650%. The 18-month zero coupon yield, using the method of bootstrapping as described above, may be extracted as:

$$100 = \frac{7.4650/2}{(1+6.9390\%/2)} + \frac{7.4650/2}{(1+7.3409\%/2)^2} + \frac{100+7.4650/2}{(1+Z_{18}/2)^3}$$

$$\Rightarrow 92.9198 = \frac{103.7325}{(1+Z_{18}/2)^3}; \Rightarrow Z_{18}/2 = \left(\frac{103.7325}{92.9198}\right)^{1/3} - 1;$$

$$Z_{18} = 7.4749\%$$

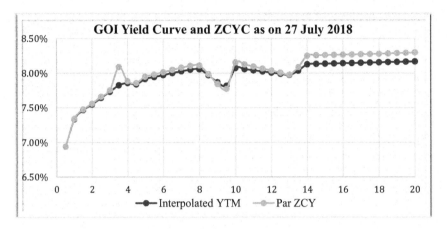

*Figure 5.6* GOI yield curve and zero coupon yield curve

Par ZCYC curve along with the yield curve extracted through linear interpolation, constructed from the actual trades in GOI securities as on 27-July-2018, reported in NDS-OM platform, using the method of bootstrapping, may be considered, as given in the following figure (Figure 5.6).

*Nelson-Siegel (NS) or Nelson-Siegel-Svensson (NSS) model*

Even if zero coupon yield or spot rates can be easily extracted from a nonparametric approach like the bootstrapping method, this method is difficult to adopt maybe because of availability of limited trades in debt securities on a given date. This non-parametric approach to extract the spot rates are easy to understand, and therefore to apply, but may require a lot of trade information, which may not be available in an illiquid securities market like in India. In any illiquid bond market like in India, there is hardly any significant trading beyond for 7 to 10 securities and it is estricted to a particular range of maturity (say close to 10 years), on a regular basis. Therefore, the yields for intermediate maturity required to extract the ZCYC through bootstrapping need to be interpolated form the available trading information. Alternatively, if the yield curve has a large number of holes, too much interpolation might generate a discontinuous and unsmooth graph. This led the ZCYC to highly depend on the type of traded security and the method of interpolation/spline used. In general, interpolation and splines may fail for very short or long-term bonds. At the same time, long-term rates that are very stable could appear very volatile or unbounded. Different interpolation and bootstrapping methods are also sensitive to the process of data filtering used to take care of the relative illiquidity of various securities. These problems led the market to look for some alternative method to extract the zero coupon yields or spot rates.

Parametric models like: *Nelson-Siegel (NS)* and *Nelson-Siegel-Svensson (NSS)* models are the methods for estimating zero coupon yield from the yields observed on Treasury securities under an assumed forward rate function. The N-S model was originally introduced in the year 1987 to construct the ZCYC. The N-S-S model is just a modified version of the former to make the ZCYC more practical and realistic. As per these models, an implied forward rate curve may be constructed for the entire term structure by using a specified forward rate function. Implied forward rates, as generated through the functional form of such parametric models, for various future maturities can be integrated over a specified period to get the necessary ZCYC. The functional forms of such a model are defined by a set of parameters describing the curve. The optimum values of such parameters can be obtained by optimizing some algorithm, such as sum of squares minimization or maximum likelihood. The values of all the parameters can be directly used to derive the zero rates for any maturity, and therefore the ZCYC.

The number of parameters used in the Nelson-Siegel model are 4 ($\beta_0$, $\beta_1$, $\beta_2$, and $\tau_1$) which are subjected to necessary optimization. The above 4 parameters are primarily used in the forward rate function to estimate the forward rates for different future maturities. The integration of such forward rates across a range of maturities till the final maturity point generates the spot rate for the final maturity, given by a specific spot rate function. Therefore, the model consists of two parametric functions: forward rate and spot rate functions. The N-S spot rate function yields a smooth and continuous ZCYC with a *Single Hump* throughout the entire maturity. Nelson-Siegel forward rate and spot rate function are given by:

$$f(m, \beta) = \beta_0 + \beta_1 \times e^{-(m/\tau_1)} + \beta_2 \times (m / \tau_1) \times e^{-(m/\tau_1)} \qquad (5.4)$$

$$r = \beta_0 + (\beta_1 + \beta_2) \times \left(1 - e^{-(m/\tau_1)}\right) \Big/ (m / \tau_1) - \beta_2 \times e^{-(m/\tau_1)} \qquad (5.5)$$

Where $\beta_0$ = Long Term Interest Rate; $\beta_1 + \beta_0$= Short Term Interest Rate; $\tau_1$= Extent or Degree of Hump; $\beta_2$ = Magnitude & Direction of the Hump; and m = Maturity.

Even if the N-S model is simple to derive the ZCYC in the fixed income securities market, it is not flexible enough to consider different shapes across the maturity axis of the ZCYC. Any possible change in the shape (slope and curvature) of the ZCYC along the maturity is not adequately captured in N-S model. Therefore, the N-S model fails to correctly depict the zero rates for different maturity points. This led the market to look for a more realistic version of ZCYC that can ensure the necessary flexibility in the yield curve. The Nelson-Siegel-Svensson version of ZCYC can incorporate more than one hump by adding two more parameters to the N-S model. Accordingly, Nelson-Siegel-Svensson (NSS) forward and spot rate function are given by:

$$f(m, \beta) = \beta_0 + \beta_1 \times e^{-(m/\tau_1)} + \beta_2 \times (m/\tau_1) \times e^{-(m/\tau_1)}$$
$$+ \beta_3 \times (m/\tau_2) \times e^{-(m/\tau_2)} \tag{5.6}$$

$$r = \beta_0 + (\beta_1 + \beta_2) \times \left(1 - e^{-(m/\tau_1)}\right) \big/ (m/\tau_1) - \beta_2 \times e^{-(m/\tau_1)}$$
$$+ \beta_3 \times \left(1 - e^{-(m/\tau_2)}\right) \big/ (m/\tau_2) - \beta_3 \times e^{-(m/\tau_2)} \tag{5.7}$$

Where, $\beta_0$ = Long Term Interest Rate; $\beta_1 + \beta_0$= Short Term Interest Rate; $\tau_1$ ($\tau_2$) = Extent or Degree of 1st (2nd) Hump; $\beta_2$ = Magnitude & Direction of 1st Hump; $\beta_3$= Magnitude & Direction of 2nd Hump; and m = Maturity.

Simplification of the required parameters of N-S/N-S-S Model:

- $\beta_0$ represents the long-term zero rate, therefore will always be +ve.
- $\beta_0$ along with $\beta_1$ determines the short-term zero rate, as exhibited by the vertical intercept of the ZCYC curve.
- $\tau_1$ decides the position of the 1st hump in the ZCYC, which again always needs to be +ve.
- $\beta_2$ determines the magnitude and direction of the 1st hump.
- $\tau_2$ exhibit the positioning of the 2nd hump and must be +ve.
- Similar of $\beta_2$, $\beta_3$ determines the magnitude and direction of the 2nd hump.

NSS ZCYC curve constructed by CCIL as on a given date, using filtered trades in GOI securities, is exhibited in the following figure (Figure 5.7).

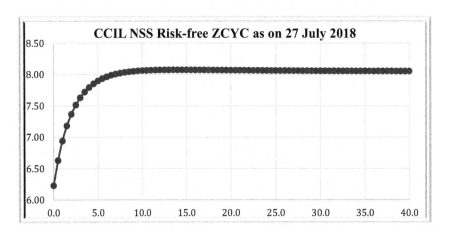

*Figure 5.7* Zero coupon yield curve (extracted through NSS method)

*Forward rate curve*

Forward rates are the future rates of interest for a further future period in time, e.g., 6-month rate 6 months from now. Yield to maturity of various maturities is used to extrapolate the theoretical spot rates, which are again used to extrapolate the forward rates. Forward rates normally represent short-term rates but can be of any period and can be applicable at any certain time in the future. Given the spot rates for two consecutive periods, it is possible to calculate the forward rate between the two periods, such that:

$$F_{m,n} = \left[ \left\{ \left(1 + Z_n\right)^{\wedge n} / \left(1 + Z_m\right)^{\wedge m} \right\}^{\wedge \{1/(n-m)\}} \right] - 1 \tag{5.8}$$

$Z_m$ and $Z_n$ are the two consecutive spot rates (say respectively for 6 months and 12 months), and $F_{m,n}$ is the forward rate for a period of (n-m), say for 6 months, m period (6 months in this case) from now. *Forward Rate* is the rate of interest applicable to an instrument between two future dates (m and n) contracted today. The nth Period Forward Rate (FR) measures the *Marginal Reward* for lengthening the maturity of the investment by n period. The term structure of the forward rate reflects the movement of *Marginal Rate* of interest over future periods, and therefore helps investors to take their investment decisions depending on their views about the interest rates.

*Example*

As per the example in the previous section, the 12-month and 18-month zero coupon yields are respectively 7.3409% and 7.4749%. From these two ZCY, it may be possible to extract the future rate between 1 year and 1.5 year, i.e. the 6-month forward rates 12 months hence. This future rate of interest can be calculated assuming an arbitrage-free market condition, where the proceeds of a straight 1.5-year investment at the end of 1.5 years at S.R.$_{1.5}$ will be equal to the proceeds of the same 1.5-year investment initially made for 1 year at S.R.$_1$ and gradually rolled over for the next half year at the 6-month forward rate 1 year from now, i.e. (F. R.$_{1,15}$). Alternatively, the arbitrage-free conditions are such that:

$$X(1 + S..R._{1.5} / 2)^3 = (1 + S.R._1 / 2)^{\wedge 2}(1 + F.R._{1,1.5} / 2)^{\wedge 1} \tag{5.9}$$

If X represent the principal invested; S.R.$_{1.5}$, and S.R.$_1$ represent the two consecutive spot rates for period 1, and 1.5; and F.R.$_{1,1.5}$ represents the 6-month forward rates at the end of the first year, then the forward rates can be calculated as:

100 (1+7.4749%/2)³ = 100 (1+7.3409%/2)² × (1+F.R.1,1.5/2)¹;
   => F.R.1,1.5 = [{(1+7.4749%/2)³} / {(1+7.3409%/2)²} - 1] × 2;
   => F.R.1, 1.5 = 7.7431%

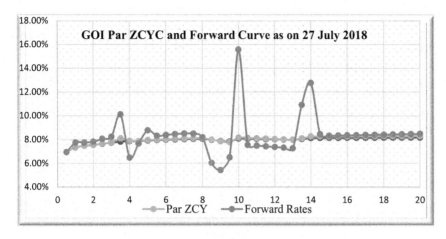

*Figure 5.8* Zero coupon yield curve and forward curve

Following the similar method, all possible 6-month forward rates, starting at all future dates/periods with an interval of 6 months (e.g. $F.R._{1.5,2}$; $F.R._{1.5,2}$; $F.R._{2,2.5}$; $F.R._{2.5,3}$; etc.), may be extracted, which further may be used to construct the forward curve, as shown in the following figure (Figure 5.8).

### The credit spread and non-government security ZCYC

The credit spread, or quality spread, is the additional yield an investor expects for acquiring a non-government security issued by different types of issuers, like banks (public or private), public sector undertakings (PSU), financial institutions (FIs), non-banking financing companies (NBFCs), corporate entities, etc., on and above the risk-free yield on securities issued by the central government. The yield of a non-government security is the sum of risk-free yield plus the credit spread, depending upon the credit worthiness of the concerned entity. Accordingly, the price of a non-treasury bond changes not only due to change in the risk-free Treasury yield, but also due to any change in the concerned spread of the non-Treasury issue. The concerned spread may be nominal spread or Z-spread. The non-Treasury yield curve can be constructed by adding the concerned spread over the Treasury spot rates of respective maturity. The nominal spread changes for different entities and also for different periods. Nominal spreads for Indian non-government entities are regularly (fortnightly and also daily) published by FIMMDA. On the other hand, zero-volatility spread or Z-spread of a non-Treasury issue is the spread that an investor is expected to realize over the entire Treasury spot rate curve if the non-Treasury issue is assumed to be held till maturity. Z-spread is assumed to

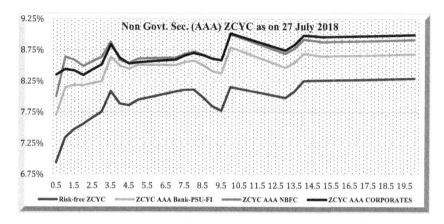

*Figure 5.9* Government securities vs. non-government securities ZCYC in India

be constant over the entire life of the non-Treasury security, and therefore known as *Static Spread*.

Using the risk-free ZCYC curve, extracted through the method of bootstrapping on the GOI par yield curve, as on 27-Jul-2018 and the FIMMDA fortnightly spread matrix published on 13-Jul-2018 (applicable till 28-Jul-2018), the ZCYC for the non-government securities segment (AAA rated) as on 27-Jul-2018 can be constructed, as shown in the following figure (Figure 5.9).

## Theories of interest rate term structure

Economists have developed theories to explain the empirical observations about the shape of the interest rate term structure. Four main theories are: Expectations Theory, Market Segmentation Theory, Liquidity Premium Theory, and Preferred Habitat Theory. These theories are explained in the following section.

### Expectations theory

The expectations hypothesis of interest rate term structure states that the interest rate on a long-term bond will be close to an average of the short-term interest rates that the market expects over the life of the long-term security. For example, if people expect that the average risk-free short-term interest rates say in next 5 years will be 7% per annum, the prediction is that the annual interest rates on a 5-year risk-free security will also be close to 7%. The key assumptions behind this hypothesis are:

(i) short-term and long-term securities can be treated as perfect substitutes; (ii) investors are risk neutral and the shape of the yield curve is determined by investors' expectations of future inflation, and therefore future rate of interests.

According to the expectations theory, where investors are expected to be indifferent to bonds of different maturities, and bonds of any maturity are perfect substitutes to each other, strategies of straightway investing in a longer maturity bond, and alternatively beginning with a shorter maturity bond and gradually rolling over, should yield exactly the same result. Accordingly, the interest rate applicable to the 2-year bond must be equal with the average of the two 1-year interest rates (i.e. 1-year rate as of now, and 1-year future rate after 1 year). For example, assume the current interest rate on the 1-year bond is 7% p.a. and an investor's expectation is that the interest rate on the 1-year bond next year will be 8%. If the investor pursues the strategy of buying the two 1-year bonds, the expected return over the 2 years will equal 7.5%, which is (7%+8%)/2. Under this scenario, the investor will be willing to hold the 2-year bond only if the expected return per year of the 2-year bond is equal to or greater than 7.5% p.a. In other words, the interest rate on the 2-year bond must equal 7.5%, the average interest on the two 1-year bonds.

All these expectation theories share a common hypothesis that the short-term forward rates are closely approximated to the short-term future rates as expected by the market participants, but differ at the influence of other factors, beyond just the market's expectation, in capturing the short-term forward rates. *Pure Expectation Theory* ignores the presence of any systematic factors other than the expected future short-term rates. Pure expectation/hypothesis simply conveys the shape (upward rising, flat, downward sloping) of the term structure based on the markets' expectation about the future short-term rate of interest. Pure expectation theory of having a similar return on investment irrespective of the investment horizon is meaningful not from the angle of a longer investment horizon, but from the angle of a shorter investment horizon, e.g. within a period of 6 months. This theory is actually termed as *Local Expectations* theory, which is nothing but a part of pure expectations.

### Liquidity preference theory

This theory of the interest rate term structure states that the interest rate on a long-term bond not only depends upon the average of short-term interest rates expected to be observed over the life of the long-term bond, but also depends upon a premium or spread that captures the demand and supply conditions for that bond, or in short, the liquidity status of the security. In other words, liquidity premium theory modifies the expectations theory by assuming that investors are risk-averse, and therefore demand a premium for long-term bonds because of interest rate risk, and arises due to locking up funds for a longer period at a fixed rate.

The main assumption behind this theory is that bonds of different maturities are substitutes, but not perfect substitutes. According to the liquidity premium theory, investors have a preference for a bond of some maturity over another. Even if investors tend to prefer shorter-term bonds because of lower interest-rate risk, they may still like to invest in long maturity bonds provided they get a liquidity premium as a compensation for carrying higher risk.

### Market segmentation theory

According to this theory, investors have strong maturity preferences, and therefore there is a different market for bonds of different maturities. This means that markets for bonds of different maturities are completely separate and segmented, and therefore cannot be substitutable. As a result, the demand and supply of bonds of particular maturity are little affected by the bonds of closer maturities, and therefore determined independently. It is assumed that borrowers (i.e. bond issuers) and lenders (i.e. investors) have particular periods in mind for which they want to borrow or lend. Therefore, interest rates of different maturity segments are determined independently.

This theory also explains the reason behind the upward-sloping nature of the yield curve. Investors generally have to decide whether they need short-term or long-term instruments. In such situations, investors may prefer their portfolio to be liquid, and therefore may prefer short-term instruments over long-term instruments, causing a higher demand for short-term instruments. This higher demand causes higher prices, and therefore lower yield. Therefore, short-term yields are lower than long-term yields. However, this theory is silent about the movement of interest rates of all possible maturities together over time.

### Preferred habitat theory

This theory assumes that investors prefer bonds of one maturity over another, i.e. bonds of particular maturity in which they prefer to invest. However, they will be willing to buy bonds that do not have the preferred maturity only if they are compensated with a higher expected return. The investors are likely to prefer the habitat of short-term bonds over that of longer-term bonds; they will only hold longer-term bonds if they have a higher expected return. The above reasoning will lead to the same approach as implied by the liquidity premium theory with a term premium that changes with any change in maturity.

## Term structure of interest rates in India: a case

Suppose a bond portfolio manager, having trading positions in various government and non-government debt securities in India, may like to analyze his portfolio as on 27-July-2018, and therefore may like to construct the useful term structure of interest rates on the same date.

The portfolio manager may require inputs on yield to maturity, zero coupon yield, and forward rates of various maturity, as on the given date, to undertake the risk-return analysis of his portfolio, and therefore may require constructing the following term structures:

i.   Risk-free GOI/Base Yield Curve.
ii.  Risk-free Zero Coupon Yield Curve.
iii. Risk-free Forward Curve.
iv.  Yield Curve and ZCYC Applicable to Various Types of Non-Government Securities.

The portfolio manager may refer to the actual trade history on central government securities as on 27 July 2018, executed in NDS-OM platform, and available from CCIL. They may also use the necessary corporate bond spread data, classified and published by FIMMDA/FBIL on a fortnightly basis, to construct the necessary term structure for non-government securities.

As far as the methodology required to construct the risk-free base yield curve and the risk-free ZCYC is concerned, the portfolio manager may like to use the following methods:

I.   Linear Interpolation, Non-Linear Interpolation, and Spline Method for Risk-free Base Yield Curve.
II.  Method of Bootstrapping for Risk-free ZCYC/Spot Rate Curve.

As far as the non-linear interpolation methods are concerned, the portfolio manager may like to select an optimum order based on the robustness of the method and constraints (if any) towards the availability of minimum trade information, especially in a relatively illiquid market like in India.

The complete trade history on central government securities as on 27 July 2018, are given in the following table (Table 5.3).

*Table 5.3* Actual trades (in NDS-OM) in GOI securities as on 27 July 2018

| Sl. No. | Description | Maturity Date | Residual Maturity | No. of Trades | Total Volume (F.V. Rs. Cr.) | Wtd. Avg. Price (Rs.) | Wtd. Avg. Yield (%) |
|---|---|---|---|---|---|---|---|
| 1 | 7.17% GS 2028 | 08-01-2028 | 9.4472 | 1337 | 11904.55 | 96 | 7.78 |
| 2 | 6.84% GS 2022 | 19-12-2022 | 4.3944 | 159 | 1650 | 96.43 | 7.81 |
| 3 | 7.40% GS 2035 | 09-09-2035 | 17.1167 | 74 | 1402.16 | 93.09 | 8.15 |
| 4 | 6.68% GS 2031 | 17-09-2031 | 13.1389 | 123 | 1015 | 89.59 | 7.97 |
| 5 | 7.59% GS 2026 | 11-01-2026 | 7.4556 | 68 | 845.03 | 97.47 | 8.05 |
| 6 | 7.37% GS 2023 | 16-04-2023 | 4.7194 | 38 | 539.43 | 97.93 | 7.9 |
| 7 | 7.80% GS 2021 | 11-04-2021 | 2.7056 | 12 | 335 | 100.27 | 7.68 |
| 8 | 6.05% GS 2019 | 02-02-2019 | 0.5139 | 14 | 315 | 99.56 | 6.95 |
| 9 | 8.79% GS 2021 | 08-11-2021 | 3.2806 | 11 | 306.8 | 102.89 | 7.76 |
| 10 | 6.97% GS 2026 | 06-09-2026 | 8.1083 | 1 | 195 | 93.68 | 8.05 |
| 11 | 8.60% GS 2028 | 02-06-2028 | 9.8472 | 4 | 80 | 103.46 | 8.08 |
| 12 | 8.33% GS 2026 | 09-07-2026 | 7.9500 | 7 | 45 | 101.54 | 8.06 |
| 13 | 8.08% GS 2022 | 02-08-2022 | 4.0139 | 4 | 40 | 100.75 | 7.86 |
| 14 | 7.72% GS 2025 | 25-05-2025 | 6.8278 | 3 | 37 | 98.44 | 8.02 |
| 15 | 8.20% GS 2022 | 15-02-2022 | 3.5500 | 3 | 35 | 101.1 | 7.84 |
| 16 | 8.27% GS 2020 | 09-06-2020 | 1.8667 | 6 | 35 | 101.26 | 7.52 |
| 17 | 7.94% GS 2021 | 24-05-2021 | 2.8250 | 4 | 25 | 100.55 | 7.71 |

| 18 | 6.65% GS 2020 | 09-04-2020 | 1.7000 | 4 | 25 | 98.64 | 7.51 |
|----|----------------|------------|---------|---|-------|--------|------|
| 19 | 8.32% GS 2032 | 02-08-2032 | 14.0139 | 7 | 24 | 101.57 | 8.13 |
| 20 | 10.03% GS 2019 | 09-08-2019 | 1.0333 | 2 | 20 | 102.58 | 7.36 |
| 21 | 7.5% GS 2034 | 10-08-2034 | 16.0361 | 9 | 17.97 | 94.54 | 8.11 |
| 22 | 8.33% GS 2032 | 21-09-2032 | 14.1500 | 2 | 15 | 101.6 | 8.14 |
| 23 | 7.35% GS 2024 | 22-06-2024 | 5.9028 | 1 | 10 | 97.15 | 7.96 |
| 24 | 8.17% GS 2044 | 01-12-2044 | 26.3444 | 4 | 9.78 | 100.35 | 8.14 |
| 25 | 6.35% GS 2020 | 02-01-2020 | 1.4306 | 1 | 5 | 98.54 | 7.45 |
| 26 | 6.90% GS 2019 | 13-17-2019 | 0.9611 | 1 | 5 | 99.68 | 7.25 |
| 27 | 7.28% GS 2019 | 03-06-2019 | 0.8500 | 1 | 5 | 100 | 7.26 |
| 28 | 8.13% GS 2045 | 22-06-2045 | 26.9028 | 1 | 3.5 | 99.88 | 8.14 |
| 29 | 7.95% GS 2032 | 28-08-2032 | 14.0861 | 2 | 3 | 98.72 | 8.1 |
| 30 | 8.97% GS 2030 | 05-12-2030 | 12.3556 | 1 | 2.31 | 107 | 8.06 |
| 31 | 8.13% GS 2022 | 21-09-2022 | 4.1500 | 2 | 1.46 | 101.05 | 7.83 |
| 32 | 7.80% GS 2020 | 03-05-2020 | 1.7667 | 1 | 1.23 | 100.4 | 7.54 |
| 33 | 8.20% GS 2025 | 24-09-2025 | 7.1583 | 2 | 0.02 | 101.3 | 7.96 |

*Source:* CCIL Website

## Self-learning exercise

1 What is a yield curve? Why is the Treasury yield curve very important not only to the players in financial market, but also for the whole economy?

2 "A yield curve, as on a given date, may not be simply constructed from all the yields on dated securities of various maturities, traded on that date". Do you agree with this statement? If not, why?

3 A newly joined bond trader, expected to trade in government securities in a bank, is trying to understand the movement of risk-free yield in the market. What factors/news/market announcements should he look at to forecast the future movement in the yield, and how do each of these factors affect the yield movement?

4 Explain the basic theories of term structure of interest rates and describe the implications of each theory towards the shape of a yield curve.

5 How is the cubic interpolation method superior to the linear interpolation to construct a term structure of interest rates? Are there any difficulties for a bond portfolio manager, especially in illiquid bond markets like in India, to successfully follow this non-linear method to construct a valid and robust interest rate term structure?

6 On a given date, can a bond trader quickly interpolate the yield for a maturity of 8.85 years from the available yields for 8.60 years and 9.10 years using the linear interpolation technique? Can the application of the same method be justified to interpolate the yield of a specific intermediate maturity from the yield of two far maturities?

7 What is the zero coupon yield or spot rate? How are they different from YTM?

8 Explain why a financial asset can be viewed as a package of zero coupon instruments.

9 Explain why it is inappropriate to use one yield to discount all the cash flows of a financial asset.

10 What actions force a Treasury's bond price to be valued in the market at the present value of the cash flows discounted at the Treasury spot rates?

11 What are the problems with using only on-the-run Treasury issues to construct the theoretical spot rate curve?

12 What is the method of bootstrapping used to construct a ZCYC? How does this method use the market information on coupon bearing securities to construct ZCYC? Is it possible to use this method in the Indian market without any assumption?

13 What are forward rates? How are they extracted from the spot rates?

14 "Forward rates are poor predictors of the actual future rates that are realized. Consequently, they are of little value to an investor." Explain why you agree or disagree with this statement.

15 A bond investor is considering two alternative investments. The first alternative is to invest in an instrument that matures in two years. The second alternative is to invest in an instrument that matures in 1 year and at the end of 1 year, reinvest the proceeds in a one-year instrument. He/she believes that one-year interest rates 1 year from now will be higher than they are today, and therefore is leaning in favor of the second alternative. What would you recommend to the bond investor?

16 Suppose that the coupon rate of a floating rate security resets every six months at a spread of 70 basis points over the reference rate. If the bond is trading at below par value, explain whether the discount margin is greater than or less than 70 basis points.

17 You are a financial consultant. At various times, you have heard comments on interest rates from one of your clients. How would you respond to each comment? (a) "The yield curve is upward-sloping today. This suggests that the market consensus is that interest rates are expected to increase in the future". (b) "I can't make any sense out of today's term structure. For short-term yields (up to three years), the spot rates increase with maturity; for maturities greater than three years but less than eight years, the spot rates decline with maturity; and for maturities greater than eight years, the spot rates are virtually the same for each maturity. There is simply no theory that explains a term structure with this shape." (c) "When I want to determine the market's consensus of future interest rates, I calculate the forward rates."

## Notes

1 One important way to classify the investment portfolio of banks and other financial institutions is to classify them based on the time period and/or purpose of holding such investments. Accordingly, investment portfolios may be sub-classified as: held till maturity (HTM), held for trading (HFT), and available for sale (AFS). As per RBI norms, investments under HTM category need to be held till the maturity. Whereas, any investments made basically for trading purposes can be categorized as HFT or AFS. Securities held under HFT further need to be sold within a maximum period of 90 days. AFS and HFT together are known as a trading portfolio, and therefore need to be Marked to Market (MTM) at regular intervals.

2 Theory of interest rate parity implies the equality of the expected return on domestic assets with the exchange rate-adjusted expected return on foreign currency assets. Interest rate parity (IRP) is a theory in which the interest rate differential between two countries is equal to the differential between the forward (future) exchange rate and the spot (current) exchange rate. An understanding of forward rates is fundamental to the IRP. Interest rate parity plays an essential role in foreign exchange markets, connecting interest rates, spot and forward exchange rates, such that: $F_0 = S_0 \times \left( \dfrac{1 + i_c}{1 + i_b} \right)$. Where $F_0$ and $S_0$ are respectively the forward (future) and spot (current) exchange rates. $i_c$ and $i_b$ are respectively the interest rate in country c and country b.

## Bibliography

Beim, D.O. (1992). Term Structure and the Non-Cash Values in Bonds. Working Papers 92-40. Columbia Graduate School of Business, NY.

Buser, S. A., Karolyi, G. A., and Sanders, A. B. (1996). Adjusted Forward Rates as Predictors of Future Spot Rates. *Journal of Fixed Income*, 6(3), 29–42.

Choudhry, M. (2001). *The Bond and Money Markets*. Butterworth-Heinemann, Oxford, UK.

Choudhry, M. (2004). *Analysing and Interpreting the Yield Curve*. John Wiley & Sons, Singapore.

Choudhry, M. (2006). *An Introduction to Bond Markets* (3rd edn.). John Wiley & Sons, Inc., Hoboken, NJ.

Diebold, F. X., and Li, C. (2003). Forecasting the Term Structure of Government Bond Yields. *NBER Working Paper*. Source: 10048 www.nber.org/papers/w10048

Elton, E. J., Gruber, M. J., Agrawal, D., and Mann, C. (2001). Explaining the Rate Spread on Corporate Bonds. *The Journal of Finance*, 56(1), 247–277.

Fabozzi, F. (November 2002). *Interest Rate, Term Structure, and Valuation Modeling* (1st edn.). John Wiley & Sons, Inc., Hoboken, NJ.

Fabozzi, F. (2007). *Fixed Income Analysis* (2nd edn.). John Wiley & Sons, Inc., Hoboken, NJ.

Fama, E. F. (1984). The Information in the Term Structure. *Journal of Financial Economics*, 13(4), 509–528.

Fama, E. F., and Bliss, R. R. (1987). The Information in Long Maturity Forward Rates. *American Economic Review*, 77(4), 680–692.

Ilmanen, A., and Iwanowski, R. (1997). Dynamics of the Shape of the Yield Curve. *Journal of Fixed Income*, 7(2), 47–60.

James J., and Webber N. (2000). *Interest Rate Modelling*. John Wiley & Sons, Inc., Hoboken, NJ.

Kuttner, K. N. (2001). Monetary Policy Surprises and Interest Rates: Evidence from the Fed Funds Futures Market. *Journal of Monetary Economics*, 47(3), 523–544.

Martellini, L., Priaulet, P., and Priaulet, S. (2003). *Fixed-Income Securities: Valuation, Risk Management and Portfolio Strategies* (1st edn.). John Wiley & Sons, Inc., Hoboken, NJ.

Mukherjee, K. N. (2019). Demystifying Yield Spread on Corporate Bonds Trades in India. *Asia-Pacific Financial Markets*, 26(2), 253–284.

Papageorgiou, N., and Skinner, F. S. (2002). Predicting the Direction of Interest Rate Movements. *Journal of Fixed Income*, 11(4), 87–95.

Ryan, R. J. (1997). *Yield Curve Dynamics: State-of-the-Art Techniques for Modelling, Trading, and Hedging* (1st edn.). Glenlake Publishing Company, Chicago.

Tuckman, B. (2011). *Fixed Income Securities: Tools for Today's Markets* (3rd edn.). John Wiley & Sons, Inc., Hoboken, NJ.

# 6 Pricing and valuation techniques

**Key learning outcomes**

At the end of this chapter, readers are expected to be familiar with:

- How to value fixed income securities, generating a series of future cash flows.
- What are the different steps involved in the valuation process?
- How are the term structure of interest rates and time value of money important in bond valuation?
- How is the yield spread (if any) for various securities arrived at and how is it adjusted while valuing securities?
- How are accrued interest and day count conventions adjusted in valuation of different types of securities?
- How are the valuation of bonds with some special features, e.g. valuation of floating rate bond and bonds with embedded options, different from the valuation of plain vanilla securities?
- What are the market practices towards the valuation of various securities?
- What are the regulatory (RBI, FIMMDA) guidelines for the valuation of different debt instruments in India?

## Valuation of bond: meaning

The value of a financial asset is very important for any market player and concerned entities, such as investors, traders (buyer or seller), dealer/broker, regulator, etc., to deal with that asset. Therefore, an asset may need to be valued at any point of time during the course of its existence. The value of any financial asset represents two values: *Market Value* and *Fair Value*. Market value is the value or price at which the asset is being traded in the market, which broadly depends on the demand and supply of the concerned asset. But fair value represents how much the asset is worth as on the valuation date under the prevailing market condition. There is no doubt that any asset gets traded in the market not at their fair value but at the market value. Market value may be higher or lower than the fair value. The general rule of demand and supply also works here to value a financial asset, that says: The greater the demand, the higher would be the price, and vice versa. A trader (buyer and seller) generally gets an idea of how much price to quote for any asset only after considering the fair value. Therefore, fair valuation of any financial assets, including debt securities, is very important. Besides for trading purposes, whenever any existing positions need to be valued, especially in the absence of the market price, an investor needs to depend on the fair value of the asset. Therefore, fair valuation of a financial asset is one of the important aspects for an investor.

Whenever any amount is invested in some financial asset, like equity shares, bonds, etc., investors expect some returns in the form of some future cash flows from the asset over a certain period of time, as long as the investment holds. In the case of any investment in a debt instrument or bond, the investor gets a certain number and amount of cash flows in the future. The bond investor may like to understand how worthy all those future cash flows are on today's date, which can be arrived at by calculating the present value of all future cash flows, considering the *Time Value of Money*.[1] Fundamentally, the fair value of a bond is nothing but the sum of the present values of all future cash flows expected to be due from the bond, in single or multiple occasions, with or without full certainty. Therefore, broadly, a general debt or bond valuation process involves:

- Estimation of expected future cash flows.
- Calculation of present values of all CFs, after using respective discounting factors.
- Summing up the present or discounted values of all expected future cash flows.

All of the three broader steps again involve several issues to be considered, depending upon the nature of the debt issue, such as: fixed rate, floating rate, zero coupon, callability/puttability, etc.

## Valuation of a bond: broader steps

### Step 1: estimating all future cash flows

In the case of a fixed income security, the possible future cash flows would be either the coupons or the principal, and the treatment of these two types of cash flows is similar except for the time period. Again, as far as the certainty of different cash flows is concerned, cash flows for different government securities are free from any uncertainty or default risk. In the case of zero coupon bond, the cash flow comes only once in its lifetime, i.e. at the time of its maturity. Similarly, coupon-bearing securities provide both coupons at different coupon payment dates (semiannually or annually) until the maturity and the principal payment at the time of maturity. But even if the name "Fixed Income Security" conveyed that the cash flows expected to be generated from such security are certain and fixed, maybe in terms of the amount of cash flows and number of cash flows, there may be a certain complexity in the following circumstances:

- If the coupon payment is not fixed throughout the holding period and is revised at every coupon reset date, referencing to some available market rate of interest, and based on some coupon reset formula, i.e. for *Floating Rate bonds*.
- If some option (*Call Option* or *Put Option*) features are embedded with the bond in regard to changing the contractual due date for the payment of the principal, i.e. in the case of *bonds with Embedded Options*.
- If the investor is given a choice to convert their bond to common stock, i.e. for *Convertible Bonds*.

For example, in case of 7.17 GS 2028, a benchmark GOI dated security with a residual maturity of roughly 9.45 years (as on 27 July 2018), the future cash flows due are: 19 semi-annual coupons of Rs.3.585/- each in every 6 months' time till the maturity, and the single principal amount of Rs.100.00/- due at the maturity. Therefore, there are 20 future cash flows due from this security till the maturity, which are certain both in terms of amount of the CFs and the timing or number of the CFs.

Similarly, GOI FLOATING RATE BOND 2020, maturing on 21 December 2020, offers six (as on March 2018) semi-annual floating coupons linked to the weighted average cut-off yield of the last three 182-day GOI Treasury bill auctions preceding the coupon re-set date, till the maturity, and one principal payment at the maturity. In this case, even if the recent semi-annual coupon, due on 21 June 2018 but reset on 21 December 2017 depending on the then previous three T-bills cut-off yields, is known to the market, the majority of the future cash flows in the form of the following five coupons are still not certain but can be anticipated based on the current market condition and future interest rates expectations. This uncertainty in terms of the amount but not the number of future cash flows may bring some amount of subjectivity in the valuation process and the resultant number, i.e. value of the FRB.

In the case of a callable bond, say, IDFC LIMITED SR-PP 2/2015 OPT II 9.6 NCD 29AP24 FVRS10LAC (ISIN: INE043D07GK9), a secured non-convertible debenture issued by IDFC Limited with a fixed coupon of 9.60% p.a., payable annually, issued on 29 April 2014 and maturing on 29 April 2024, has an embedded call option where the option can be exercised on 29 April of every year after a lock-in period of 4 years, i.e. on 29 April 2019, 29 April 2020, 29 April 2021, 29 April 2022, and

29 April 2023. If the bond is called-off by the issuer on any of these possible call dates, all the interim coupons expected to be due after the option being exercised will be stopped, and the principal amount will be redeemed either at par or as per the call schedule. Therefore, in the case of a bond with an embedded option, even if the amount of future cash flows are fixed and certain, the total number of such cash flows, or the date till which the CFs are expected, are not certain and depend upon the possibility for the issuer to exercise his option and close the debt contract before the scheduled maturity. Even if all possible dates, maybe after a specific lock-in period on which the option (call/put) can be exercised, are clearly specified, the date when the option will be actually exercised is always uncertain and depends upon the prevailing market conditions. This uncertainty needs to be captured in the valuation mechanism to value a debt instrument with some embedded option.

### Step 2: estimating present value of future cash flows

After estimating the expected future cash flows, both in terms of amount of CFs and total number of CFs, the next step is to derive their present values, considering the time value of money theory. The present values of all future cash flows can be estimated through the respective discounting factors applicable to different points of time depending upon the timing of those future cash flows whenever due. The time value of money and method of calculating the discounting factors are discussed in the following section.

### Time value of money and respective discounting factor

In general, money today is not the same as money in 1 year or at any future point of time. This is because if a saver allows someone to utilize their savings of Rs.100/-, say for next 1 year, they will be expecting some value for the time which they have given to the person to utilize their savings for next 1 year. If the saver X has Rs.100 today and gives the same to a borrower Y for next 1 year, they may expect to receive from them Rs.109.00/- at the end of 1 year. This difference in value (Rs.9.00/-) between the money in the future and the money today is the *Time Value of Money*, which again depends upon the rate of interest, timing of cash flows, and frequency of cash flows. This time value can be computed to arrive at either the future value of some present cash flow(s) or to arrive at the present value of some future cash flow(s). These are basically done through compounding (discounting) the present (future) cash flow(s) for a specific period of time and with a specified frequency. The factor which can be used to compound or discount respectively the present and future cash flows is known as the compounding factor and discounting factor, which are a function of rate of interest, timing and frequency of CFs. Alternatively, an nth period discount (compounding) factor is the present (future) value of one unit of currency that is payable at the end (beginning) of period n. The rate of interest to be used depends upon the nature of the cash flows: risk free or risky. Normally, risk-free, short-term, and well accepted in the market, interest rates are used. Timing and frequency of CFs are also equally important to arrive at the compounding or discounting factor, and therefore the time value of money. Depending upon the frequency of CFs, the time value of money can be estimated through a discrete process or a continuous process, respectively, with well-defined (semi-annually, quarterly, monthly, etc.) time intervals, and regular but un-defined time intervals. Therefore, the compounding and discounting factor, under a discrete and continuous process, can be arrived at:

- *Compounding Factor (Discrete)*    $: 1 \times [\{1 + (r/m)\}^{\wedge(t \times m)}]$
- *Discounting Factor (Discrete)*    $: 1 / [\{1 + (r/m)\}^{\wedge(t \times m)}]$
- *Compounding Factor (Continuous)*   $: 1 \times exp^{+(r \times t)}$
- *Discounting Factor (Continuous)*   $: 1 / exp^{(r \times t)}$ or $1 \times exp^{-(r \times t)}$

Where: r = Annualized Interest Rate/Continuously Compounded Interest Rate, m = Frequency of Compounding/Discounting, t = Time Period for the cash flow, exp = Exponential Function

Accordingly, the future (present) value of any present (future) CF can be estimated by adjusting the compounding (discounting) factor with the respective CFs. Now, as far as the discounting of different future cash flows due from a fixed income security or a bond is concerned, a single interest rate can be used or different cash flows can be discounted at different rates of interest applicable to the respective cash flows at the respective time. Accordingly, the entire future cash flows of a bond may be traditionally discounted by using the YTM of the concerned period or maturity, or by using different tenor-specific interest rates, as when the future cash flows are due. Use of these two different approaches by different market players while discounting the future cash flows may create an arbitrage opportunity in the market.

## Example

Suppose an investor wants to buys 7.80% G.S. 2020, maturing on 3 May 2020 and yielding 6.45% p.a. as on 21 July 2017, where the semi-annual future cash flows of Rs.3.90/- each can be discounted with their respective discount-ing (discrete) factor, extracted in the following table (Table 6.1).

The first semi-annual period is just the number of days in between the set-tlement date (21 July 2017) and the date of first CF (i.e. 03 November 2017) out of a total number of days in a semi-annual period (i.e. 180 days as per 30/360 day count convention). This gives the first semi-annual period of 0.5667 years. The subsequent semi-annual periods can be computed just by adding one period every time. This can be discussed in more detail in the following section.

*Table 6.1* Estimation of discounting factor

| Timing of CFs (Semi-Annual Period) | Single IR p.a. (YTM) | Semi-Annual IR | Discounting Factor |
|---|---|---|---|
| 03 Nov 2017 (0.5667) | 6.45% | 3.23% | 1 / (1 + 3.2250%) ^ 0.5667 = 0.9822 |
| 03 May 2018 (1.5667) | 6.45% | 3.2250% | 1 / (1 + 3.2250%) ^ 1.5667 = 0.9515 |
| 03 Nov 2018 (2.5667) | 6.45% | 3.2250% | 1 / (1 + 3.2250%) ^ 2.5667 = 0.9217 |
| 03 May 2019 (3.5667) | 6.45% | 3.2250% | 1 / (1 + 3.2250%) ^ 3.5667 = 0.8929 |
| 03 Nov 2019 (4.5667) | 6.45% | 3.2250% | 1 / (1 + 3.2250%) ^ 4.5667 = 0.8650 |
| 03 May 2020 (5.5667) | 6.45% | 3.2250% | 1 / (1 + 3.2250%) ^ 5.5667 = 0.8379 |

*Source*: All tables in this chapter are created by the author unless otherwise stated.

Once the discounting factors are arrived at, considering the rate of interest (single or multiple) and the timing of the CFs, then the present value of all CFs can be derived just by multiplying the CFs with their respective discounting factors, as shown in the following table (Table 6.2):

*Table 6.2* Estimation of discounting cash flows

| Timing | 3 Nov. 2017 | 3 May 2018 | 3 Nov. 2018 | 3 May 2019 | 3 Nov. 2019 | 3 May 2020 |
|---|---|---|---|---|---|---|
| CF (Rs.) | 3.90 | 3.90 | 3.90 | 3.90 | 3.90 | 103.90 |
| DF | 0.9822 | 0.9515 | 0.9217 | 0.8929 | 0.865 | 0.8379 |
| DCF (Rs.) | 3.8304 | 3.7107 | 3.5947 | 3.4823 | 3.3.35 | 87.0628 |

### Step 3: deriving final value of the security

After discounting all the expected cash flows by using a single interest rate, the final step to value a fixed income security is to add the discounted values of all the expected future cash flows. In the above example, the sum of the six discounted future cash flows or the present value of the six future CFs due at different future point of time from the 7.80% G.S. 2020 till the maturity (3 May 2020) is Rs.105.0544/-, with the accrued interest, discussed in the following section. Even if the amount of each future CF remains the same, the value of the bond will keep changing, depending upon the change in the discounting factor, which again depends upon the concerned interest rate and the timings of the CFs.

Even if every bond has a face value, say Rs.100 per security, it is not necessary to have the same value at any valuation date. The value (market value or fair value) of a bond can be equal to, greater than, or lower than the face value. A bond can be valued and traded at *Par* (i.e. equal to book/ face value), at *Discount* (Less than Face Value), or at *Premium* (More than Face Value). Now the issue is, when is the fixed income security expected to be traded at par, at discount, or at premium? The answer depends on the similarity or dissimilarity between the coupon rate of the security of a specific maturity and the yield to maturity (YTM) for the concerned period at the time of settlement or valuation. Any fixed income security will be valued and accordingly traded at par when there is no difference between the coupon rate and the YTM. Similarly, when the coupon rate is lower (higher) than the yield, the value of the security is expected to be lower (higher) than its par value, and accordingly the security can be traded at discount (premium).

For example, 8.60% G.S. 2028, with a residual maturity of roughly 9.85 years, offering a semi-annual coupon of Rs.4.30/- till June 2028, is traded at a market price of Rs.103.46/- as on 27 July 2018. The bond is traded at premium basically because of lower market expectation (8.08% p.a. as on 27 July 2018) for a risk-free investment for the similar maturity (9.85 years). Similarly, 7.17% G.S. 2028, maturing on 8 January 2028, with a maturity of 9.45 years, is found to be traded at a discounted price of Rs.96/- as on 27 July 2018, because of the lower coupon than the market expectation (7.78% p.a. as on 27 July 2018). Here, even if both the bonds are of almost similar maturity and issued by the same issuer (GOI), the bonds are traded at a different price just because of the difference in the coupon offered by those securities and the market yield for the respective tenors or maturities. The amount of discount (premium) on any bond is broadly the present value of the total opportunity loss (gain) applicable to the bond by way of accepting a lower (higher) coupon on that bond till the maturity. Since market expectation changes on a continuous basis, it is very unusual to see a bond traded at par or very close to par, unless the same is an on-the-run issue offered/issued very recently in the market.

In this context, one fact that is important to note is that though the price of a bond can deviate (higher or lower) from its par value, the extent of deviation tends to reduce as the security moves towards its maturity, and the value of the security will be exactly equal to par at the date of maturity, and therefore is expected to be redeemed only at par. This feature of bond's price movement from any date before maturity till the exact maturity is commonly known as *Pull-to-Par*, as exhibited in the following figure (Figure 6.1).

The valuation of coupon-bearing fixed income security also depends on the frequency of coupon payments, i.e. whether the coupons are paid *Annually* or *Semi-annually*. Accordingly, the actual time when the future cash flows will be due, amount of individual future cash flows, and yield or discount rate(s) applicable to the respective dates need to be adjusted.

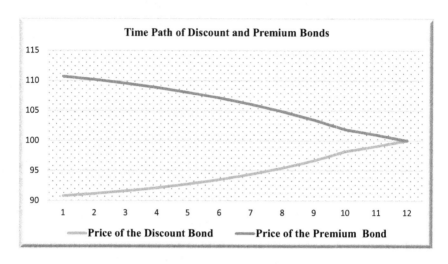

*Figure 6.1* Pull-to-par feature of a coupon bearing bond

Semi-annual coupon payments would be half of the annual coupon, and required yield or discount rate would also be half (as par convention) of the annual rate, and each semi-annual period of 6 months may be treated as 1 period. One of the important facts is that, the larger the frequency of coupon payments in a fixed income security, the higher would be the value for the security. Therefore, the value of a security with semi-annual coupon payments is higher than the value of a similar security but with annual coupon payments. The reason behind this is the higher interest income generated by reinvesting the coupons received at shorter intervals. For example, the price of 7.17 GS 2028, yielding 7.78% p.a. (as on 27 July 2018) and paying Rs.3.585/- semi-annually, as on 27 July 2018, is Rs.95.97/-. A similar bond, all features remain the same but pay an annual coupon, will be priced differently, here Rs.95.96/-, which is almost 1 paisa less than the price of the bond with a semi-annual coupon payment.

The discounted cash flow approach to price a fixed coupon (semi-annually paid) bond, can be summarized in the following section, where the pricing equation can be described as:

$$P = \frac{C_1}{(1+r/2)^1} + \frac{C_2}{(1+r/2)^2} + \frac{C_3}{(1+r/2)^3} + \dots\dots + \frac{C_{2t} + MV_t}{(1+r/2)^{2t}}$$

$$= \sum_{t=0.5}^{n} \frac{CF_t}{(1+r/2)^{2t}} + \frac{MV_n}{(1+r/2)^{2n}} \tag{6.1}$$

Where $C_1$, $C_2$, . . ., $C_t$ are the semi-annual cash flows till the maturity 't' (t = 0.5, 1, 1.5, 2, . . ., n years), $MV_n$ is the redemption price at the maturity (i.e. at year n) which is at par, r is the discounting rate, which can be traditionally the YTM of the concerned maturity.

Since the value of a fixed rate bond has two components, the present value of all fixed semi-annual coupon payments and the present value of maturity/redemption amount, the valuation of such a bond can also be done through the present value of annuity function, such that:

$$Value = Semiannual\,Coupon \times \left[ \frac{1 - \dfrac{1}{(1+r/2)^{2t}}}{r/2} \right]$$

$$+ \,Maturity\,Value \times \left[ \frac{1}{(1+r/2)^{2t}} \right] \tag{6.2}$$

Where '$r$' is the single discounting rate or YTM, and '$t$' is the time to maturity (i.e. residual maturity).

Suppose a bank needs to value the same security (7.80% G.S. 2020, maturing on 3 May 2020) using the present value of annuity formula, as on 21 July 2017. Putting all the necessary components (semi-annual coupon of Rs.3.90/-, rate of interest or YTM of 6.45%, residual maturity of 2.7833 years, and a maturity value of Rs.100/-) in the aforesaid formula, the value of the bond can be estimated. The value of the bond, as on 21 July 2017, giving a yield of 6.45% p.a., is Rs.103.3796/-, which is the *Clean Price* of the bond, subtracting the *Accrued Interest* from the *Dirty Price*, as discussed in the subsequent section.

Since there are no coupon payments in the case of a zero coupon fixed income security, the value of such security is derived only by discounting the maturity value, such that:

$$Value = \frac{Maturity\,Value}{(1+r/2)^{2t}} \tag{6.3}$$

Even if there are no coupon payments in a zero coupon fixed income security, the valuation formula has to consider a semi-annual interest rate and semi-annual periods just to exhibit a uniformity between the valuation process for a coupon-bearing security and a zero coupon security.

The Microsoft Excel Function, used to price a fixed rate option-free bond, is given as:

= **PRICE**(*Settlement, Maturity, Rate, Yld,*

*Redemption, Frequency, [Basis]*)

The inputs required are: the settlement or the valuation date for the concerned bond (*Settlement*), maturity date of the bond (*Maturity*), the coupon rate of the bond (*Rate*), the market rate or the yield to maturity for the concerned tenor (*Yld*), the redemption price which is usually the par value (*Redemption*), the frequency of coupon payments (*Frequency*), and the choice of number of days during a specific period and during a year, alternatively the day-count convention (*Basis*), discussed in the following section. Once this information regarding a bond is given, the bond price can be easily extracted.

For example, the same government of India security (7.80% G.S. 2020, maturing on 3 May 2020) if valued through the MS Excel function, discussed above, with the necessary details on seven parameters, comes out to be Rs.103.3644/-, which is again the clean price of the bond.

## Valuation of bond: important issues

Even if the value of any fixed income security broadly depends upon the present values of all the expected future cash flows till its maturity, as described in the above section, there can be some important issues in terms of amount of expected future cash flows, number and timing of such future cash flows, method of discounting, etc., that may make the valuation process slightly different, and perhaps a little more difficult and exhaustive. Some of these important issues and their respective adjustment in the basic bond pricing/valuation method are discussed in the following section.

### Bond valuation in-between two coupon payment dates/with accrued interest

If the coupon-bearing fixed income security is valued exactly at some coupon payment date, or otherwise if there is no difference between the settlement date and a coupon payment date, then the traditional valuation mechanism, as discussed in the previous section, is applied. But if such a security is traded in the market, and therefore needs to be valued between two coupon payment dates, alternatively, if the settlement date and coupon date date are different, then the valuation process needs separate attention. In this case, the extra component in the valuation formula is the specific portion of a single/first coupon payment, which is actually due to the seller of the security but earned by the buyer or holder of the security, commonly known as *Accrued Interest*. In other words, the portion of the first coupon interest due from the previous coupon payment date till the settlement/valuation date, which is before the next coupon payment date, is known as accured interest (AI). The amount of accrued interest needs to be compensated by the buyer to the seller of the security at the time of buying the security. When a coupon-bearing fixed income security is valued between two coupon payment dates, the valuation is done without considering the portion of accrued interest which is included in the first coupon, and therefore in the price, and such value or price is known as the *Full Price* or *Dirty Price*. This is the price that the buyer needs to pay to the seller, or in short, the *Invoice Price*. But this is not the true price for the security as on the valuation date. The true price, or *Clean Price*, of the security would be the difference between the full price and the amount of accrued interest (if any). In such case, the valuation needs to be done by adjusting the discounting rate(s), the time periods, and the accrued interest, such that:

$$P = \frac{C_1}{(1+r/2)^i} + \frac{C_2}{(1+r/2)^{1+i}} + \frac{C_3}{(1+r/2)^{2+i}} + \cdots + \frac{C_{2t} + MV_t}{(1+r/2)^{t-1+i}} - AI \quad (6.4)$$

Where, i = (days from value date to next coupon date)/days in interest period; depending upon the day count convention followed.

If a bond pays a semi-annual coupon, the accrued interest (*AI*) is calculated such that:

$$
\begin{aligned}
AI = {} & Semiannual\_Coupon \\
& \times \frac{(SettlementDate - LastCouponPaymentDate)}{TotalNo.ofDays\_inSemiannualPeriod}
\end{aligned}
\quad (6.5)
$$

The Microsoft Excel Function directly used to calculate the accrued interest of a coupon bond, is given as:

> = *ACCRINT(Issue, First_interest, Settlement, Rate, Par, Frequency,*
> *[Basis], [Calc_method])*

The inputs required are: the bond issue date or previous coupon payment date (*Issue*), first coupon payment date or the next coupon payment date after the settlement/valuation date (*First_interest*), the settlement or valuation date (*Settlement*), coupon rate of the bond (*Rate*), par/face value of the bond (*Par*), the frequency of coupon payments (*Frequency*), the choice of number of days during a specific period and during a year, alternatively the day-count convention (*Basis*), and a logical function (*Calc_method*) with inputs of TRUE or FALSE, depending upon whether the accrued interest is required to be calculated from the issue date or from the last coupon payment date. The previous and next coupon payment dates, number of days in the coupon period, the settlement date, number of days from the previous coupon payment date till the settlement date, number of days from the settlement date till the next coupon payment date, etc. can also be extracted through the following MS-Excel Functions, such that:

> = *COUPPCD(Settlement, Maturity, Frequency, [Basis])*
> = *COUPNCD(Settlement, Maturity, Frequency, [Basis])*
> = *COUPDAYS(Settlement, Maturity, Frequency, [Basis])*
> = *COUPDAYBS(Settlement, Maturity, Frequency, [Basis])*
> = *COUPDAYSNC(Settlement, Maturity, Frequency, [Basis])*

Even if the amount of accrued interest, expected to be passed on to the bond seller, should be the discounted value of the above AI, discounted for the period between the settlement date and the next coupon payment date, the general market practice/convention is to ignore any discounting of the actual AI, even though the same is paid in advance.

### Selection of day count conventions

Valuation of a bond issue, especially if the valuation is done in between two coupon payment dates, also depends on how the number of days between the settlement date and the last coupon payment date are counted. In other words, while calculating the part of a single coupon, accrued for the period between the last coupon payment date and the settlement/valuation date, there are various conventions used to count the number of days between these two dates, commonly termed as *Day Count Conventions*. There are broadly four such market conventions, such as: Actual/Actual, Actual/365, Actual/360, and 30/360. The numerators represent the number of days in a specific month, while the denominators represent the number of days in a specific year or the specific coupon period (annual/semi-annual). The amount of accrued interest, and therefore the clean price of a bond, depend upon the day count convention followed by the market players for different types of fixed income securities: government, non-government, long-term, short-term, etc.

The day count convention normally followed for a dated government security in India is 30/360, irrespective of the actual number of days, whereas the valuation of dated non-government securities or corporate bonds is based on Actual/Actual. Similarly, the valuation of T-bills, commercial paper, and other short-term or money market instruments having less than 1 year to expiration is based on Actual/Actual or Actual/365 rule. As far as the Actual/Actual convention is concerned, it is exactly similar to the Actual/365 convention, except in the case of leap years.

### Example

Suppose an investor, as on 5 March 2015, may like to value 7.83% G.S. 2018, a fixed rate bond issued by the government of India, offering a fixed coupon of R.3.915/- in every six months for every Rs.100/- investment, till the maturity of the bond, i.e. on 11 April 2018. Will there be any accrued interest? How can the valuation be done considering the accrued interest (if any)? How do the different day count conventions (30/360 and Actual/Actual) affect the value of the bond?

Since the bond is getting matured on 11 April 2018, and the coupons are paid semi-annually, the last date of coupon paid before the settlement/valuation (i.e. before 5 March 2015) and the next date of coupon expected to be paid after the settlement are respectively 11 October 2014 and 11 April 2015. Since the valuation is done in between these two coupon payment dates, i.e. after almost 5 months (just few days less) from the last coupon payment date, there is a majority portion of coupon or interest due on 11 April 2015, accrued for this 5 months to the seller of the bond. Therefore, with the assumption of 30/360 and Actual/Actual day count convention, the amount of accrued interest, the dirty price, and the clean price are calculated below.

Considering the relevant dates (last coupon payment date: 11 October 2014; settlement/valuation date: 5 March 2015; next coupon payment date: 11 April 2015) for the above bond, the number of days between periods under both Actual/Actual and 30/360 day count conventions can be estimated as shown in the following table (Table 6.3):

*Table 6.3* Estimation of number of days under different conventions

| Months | No. of Days (Actual/Actual) | No. of Days (30/360) |
|---|---|---|
| October 2014 (12th Onwards) | 20 | 19 |
| November 2014 | 30 | 30 |
| December 2014 | 31 | 30 |
| January 2015 | 31 | 30 |
| February 2015 | 28 | 30 |
| March 2015 (Till 5th) | 5 | 5 |
| March 2015 | 31 | 30 |
| April 2015 (Till 11th) | 11 | 11 |
| Total Number of Days (11 October 2014 – 05 March 2015) | 145 | 144 |
| Total Number of Days (05 March 2015 – 11 April 2015) | 26 + 11 = 37 | 25 + 11 = 36 |
| Total Number of Days (11 October 2014 – 11 April 2015) | 182 | 180 |

Therefore, the Accrued Interests for 7.83% G.S. 2018 as on 05 March 2015, under different day count conventions, are:

AI (under Actual/Actual) = 1st Semi-annual Coupon after Settlement
× {(October 11 2014 – March 05 2015) /
(October 11 2014 – April 11 2015)}

= {(7.83% × Rs.100/-) / 2} × {145 / 182}

= **Rs.3.1191/-**

AI (under 30/360) = 1st Semi-annual Coupon after Settlement
× {(October 11 2014 – March 05 2015) /
(October 11 2014 – April 11 2015)}

= {(7.83% × Rs.100/-) / 2} × {144 / 180}

= **Rs.3.1320/-**

The period (in semi-annual terms) from the settlement/valuation date till the next coupon date also need to be calculated for the valuation of the bond, and is defined by 'i' such that:

$$i = (Days\ from\ Settlement\ /\ Valuation\ Date\ to\ Next\ Coupon\ Date)$$
$$/Days\ in\ Coupon\ Period$$

Therefore, the value of i required to select the period to discount the respective future CFs, again under different day count conventions, could be:

$i$ (as per Actual/ Actual)  $= 37 / 182 = 0.2033$
$i$ (as per 30 / 360)  $= 36 / 180 = 0.2000$

Now, the 7.83% G.S. 2018, maturing on 11 April 2018 and paying a semi-annual coupon of Rs.3.915/- each, can be valued (dirty and clean price) as on 05 March 2015, as per the different day count conventions. The risk-free YTM for the concerned maturity (3.1041 years) as on the date of valuation is 7.7529% p.a., and therefore the semi-annual YTM stands at 3.8765%. The total number of semi-annual coupons (@Rs.3.915/-) due in this bond are 7, due on 11 April 2015, 11 October 2015, 11 April 2016, 11 October 2016, 11 April 2017, 11 October 2017, and 11 April 2018, and the principal amount of Rs.100/- is due on 11 April 2018.

Therefore, the prices of 7.83% G.S. 2018, under Actual/Actual, as on 05 March 2015 are:

$$DP = \frac{C_1}{(1+r/2)^i} + \frac{C_2}{(1+r/2)^{1+i}} + \frac{C_3}{(1+r/2)^{2+i}} + \frac{C_4}{(1+r/2)^{3+i}}$$
$$+ \frac{C_5}{(1+r/2)^{4+i}} + \frac{C_6}{(1+r/2)^{5+i}} + \frac{C_7 + MV_t}{(1+r/2)^{7-1+i}}$$
$$= \frac{3.915}{(1+3.8765\%)^{0.2033}} + \frac{3.915}{(1+3.8765\%)^{1.2033}} + \frac{3.915}{(1+3.8765\%)^{2.2033}}$$
$$+ \frac{3.915}{(1+3.8765\%)^{3.2033}} + \frac{3.915}{(1+3.8765\%)^{4.2033}} + \frac{3.915}{(1+3.8765\%)^{5.2033}}$$
$$+ \frac{3.915+100}{(1+3.8765\%)^{6.2033}}$$
$$= 3.8848 + 3.7399 + 3.6003 + 3.4659 + 3.3366 + 3.2121 + 82.0760$$

$$DP = Rs.103.3157 / -$$

$$CP = DP - AI = 103.3157 - 3.1191 = Rs.100.1966 / -$$

Alternatively, the prices of 7.83% G.S. 2018, under 30/360, as on 05 March 2015 are:

$$DP = \frac{C_1}{(1+r/2)^i} + \frac{C_2}{(1+r/2)^{1+i}} + \frac{C_3}{(1+r/2)^{2+i}} + \frac{C_4}{(1+r/2)^{3+i}} + \frac{C_5}{(1+r/2)^{4+i}}$$

$$+ \frac{C_6}{(1+r/2)^{5+i}} + \frac{C_7 + MV_t}{(1+r/2)^{7-1+i}}$$

$$= \frac{3.915}{(1+3.8765\%)^{0.2000}} + \frac{3.915}{(1+3.8765\%)^{1.2000}} + \frac{3.915}{(1+3.8765\%)^{2.2000}}$$

$$+ \frac{3.915}{(1+3.8765\%)^{3.2000}} + \frac{3.915}{(1+3.8765\%)^{4.2000}} + \frac{3.915}{(1+3.8765\%)^{5.2000}}$$

$$+ \frac{3.915+100}{(1+3.8765\%)^{6.2000}}$$

$$= 3.8853 + 3.7403 + 3.6008 + 3.4664 + 3.3370 + 3.2125 + 82.0863$$

$$DP = Rs.103.3287 / -$$

$$CP = DP - AI = 103.3287 - 3.1320 = Rs.100.1967 / -$$

### *Selection of single or multiple discounting rates*

Depending on the type(s) of interest rates used to discount the future cash flows due from coupon bearing debt securities, there are two important approaches to value them. These are: traditional approach and arbitrage-free valuation approach. Both approaches have their own significance, and therefore are used by different market players for different purposes.

• *Traditional Approach to Valuation*

As per the first approach, all the expected future cash flows from a coupon-bearing security are discounted at the same rate of interest or discount rate, irrespective of the fact that different cash flows are received at different points of time. Here, the single discounting rate is the yield-to-maturity (YTM) for the concerned tenor/period. YTM is the discount rate which equates the present value of promised payments (coupon plus redemption value at maturity) to the current market price. Alternatively, YTM is the *Internal Rate of Return* (IRR) earned by an investor who buys the bond today at the market price, assuming that the bond will be held until maturity, and that all coupon and principal payments will be made as scheduled. YTM can also be treated as the *Hurdle Rate of Return* required to issue the bond at its ruling market price. Here, the interest rate used for discounting depends on whether the security to be valued is a government security or non-government security. In the case of valuing any government security, the YTM of a risk-free instrument with similar maturity may be used to discount all the expected cash flows. Similarly, some yield spread or yield premium, based on the additional risk, may be added with the concerned risk-free YTM to get the required YTM for the purpose of discounting the expected cash flows of the non-government security. This approach is alternatively known as YTM based valuation, as followed in the previous section to value the government of India security 7.83% G.S. 2018.

- *Arbitrage-free Valuation Approach*

On the other hand, the valuation of a fixed income security would be found to be arbitrage free when the expected future cash flows, received at different points of time, are discounted at the prevailing yields available for those respective periods. Put differently, the coupon-bearing bonds may be viewed as a package of several (equal to the total number of periodic coupon payments) zero coupon issues whose maturity values would be equal to the amount of all expected future cash flows and whose maturity dates would be equal to the future dates when the cash flows are expected to be released. This way of valuing a coupon-bearing security prevents a dealer to earn any arbitrage profit by stripping a coupon-bearing government security and selling off the stripped securities at some higher aggregate value comparative to the cost born by him to purchase the fixed coupon-bearing security. This is the reason why this approach is known as the arbitrage-free valuation approach. In such an approach, multiple interest rates or yields are used for discounting purposes, depending on the actual periods when all the future cash flows are due. These multiple rates are nothing but the zero coupon yields, commonly known as spot rates of different time periods.

In this example, the same as discussed above, 7.83% G.S. 2018 can be considered to understand the arbitrage-free bond valuation, or bond valuation with multiple discounting rates.

*Example*

Suppose an investor, as on 05 March 2015, may like to value 7.83% G.S. 2018, a fixed rate bond issued by the government of India, offering a fixed coupon of R.3.915/- in every 6 months for every Rs.100/- investment, till the maturity of the bond, i.e. on 11 April 2018. How can the bond be valued with multiple discounting rates, assuming 30/360 convention, as followed for government securities in India? Is there any arbitrage opportunity for the trader on 05 March 2015?

The pricing of 7.83% G.S. 2018 as on 05 March 2015 can be done in the similar pricing framework as followed above but just by using different discounting rates, preferably the zero coupon rates for the respective period, available on 05 March 2015. These rates can be extracted from the CCIL NSS ZCYC parameters (*Beta 0* =7.5777, *Beta 1* = 0.3153, *Beta 2* = 1.4161, *Tau 1* =0.2021, *Beta 3* = -0.2810, and *Tau 2* = 1.0001) as on 05 March 2015 provided by the CCIL. The annualized zero coupon rates for all the required tenors (0.20, 1.20, 2.20, 3.20, 4.20, 5.20, and 6.20 semi-annual periods as per 30/360 rule) are estimated from the above parameters and are used in the pricing framework to get the arbitrage-free value of 7.83% G.S. 2018 on 05 March 2015, such that:

$$
\begin{aligned}
DP &= \frac{C_1}{(1+r_1/2)^i} + \frac{C_2}{(1+r_2/2)^{1+i}} + \frac{C_3}{(1+r_3/2)^{2+i}} + \frac{C_4}{(1+r_4/2)^{3+i}} \\
&\quad + \frac{C_5}{(1+r_5/2)^{4+i}} + \frac{C_6}{(1+r_6/2)^{5+i}} + \frac{C_7+MV_t}{(1+r_7/2)^{7-1+i}} \\
&= \frac{3.915}{(1+8.1259\%/2)^{0.2000}} + \frac{3.915}{(1+7.7858\%/2)^{1.2000}} \\
&\quad + \frac{3.915}{(1+7.6543\%/2)^{2.2000}} + \frac{3.915}{(1+7.6143\%/2)^{3.2000}} \\
&\quad + \frac{3.915}{(1+7.5993\%/2)^{4.2000}} + \frac{3.915}{(1+7.5928\%/2)^{5.2000}} \\
&\quad + \frac{3.915+100}{(1+7.5895\%/2)^{6.2000}} \\
&= 3.8839 + 3.7396 + 3.6045 + 3.4738 + 3.3474 + 3.2254 + 82.4881
\end{aligned}
$$

$$DP = 103.7628$$

$$CP = DP - AI = 103.7628 - 3.1320 = 100.6308 / -$$

$$
\begin{aligned}
Arbitrage\_Profit &= Price(Multiple - Rates) - Price(Single - Rate) \\
&= 100.6308 - 100.1967 = Rs.0.4341 / -
\end{aligned}
$$

The arbitrage-free clean price of the bond as on 05 March 2015 is found to be Rs.100.6308/-, which is higher than the value of the same bond, arrived at through single rate based valuation (i.e. Rs.100.1967/-), giving an arbitrage opportunity to market players to make an arbitrage profit of Rs.0.4341/- per Rs.100/- by buying the 7.83% G.S. 2018 and selling the strips created from the same, provided there is a liquid market for such strips as well.

*Presence of some special feature(s)*

Other than a plain vanilla bond with fixed coupon and no other added features, there can be some security bundled with some additional features, like a floating rate of interest or embedded options (call or put). Valuations of such bonds again require some special attention, as discussed in the following sections.

## Valuation of floating rate bond

Floating rate securities/notes (FRN), or *Floaters*, are different from other fixed income securities only in the context of coupon payments. Such coupon payments largely depend on the level of money market interest rates, e.g. LIBOR/MIBOR, T-bill Rate, PLR, call rate, etc. Coupons are normally reset semi-annually/quarterly/monthly. The coupon re-fixation period (e.g. 6 months) and the tenor of the reference rate (e.g. 3-month MIBOR or 6-month T-bill rate) are generally matched but need not necessarily be the same. Periodic coupon resetting makes the FRN relatively insensitive to market yield even in a volatile interest rate scenario. FRN may be issued exactly at some benchmark/reference rate (e.g. 182-day T-bill rate) or may be issued at a certain spread over the benchmark rate, depending on the nature of the bond issuer (government or non-government entity having a different credit rating, liquidity, term to maturity etc.). Therefore, a semi-annual coupon of an FRB can be such that:

*Coupon Rate = Benchmark Rate; or*

*Coupon Rate = Benchmark Rate ± Contracted / Quoted / Initial Spread*

Spreads are normally set at the time of issue and remain fixed until maturity but may be subject to necessary change at some coupon re-fixation date, depending on the concerned factors.

Given the fact that the coupon rate is equal to the prevailing market rate, especially in either of the coupon reset dates, such bonds should be valued and traded at par. Notwithstanding this fact, the valuation of such security largely depends on the level of spread (if any) over the benchmark rate desired by the market participants. In other words, the value of a FRN, at any re-pricing date, does have to compensate for any discrepancy between the contractual and market rate. The larger the deviation between the contracted spread and the desired spread, the more the bond price would diverge from its par value. Therefore, the valuation of a floating rate bond largely depends upon the date of valuation and the nature of spread (if any) added to their reference rate. A spot rate curve or zero swap curve can be used to value a FRN.

*Example*

Consider a bond that pays floating rate coupons semi-annually and that has exactly 2 years to maturity. Further, assume that the present market rates $(R_M)$ for all tenors are flat at 8% p.a. (compounded semi-annually), making all the four semi-annual coupons till the maturity equal with the market rates of 8% p.a. Therefore, the coupon rates on the bond, $R_C$ is also 8% p.a. (compounded semi-annually). What is the value of the bond today? Alternatively, consider an upward-sloping yield curve, where the annualized (compounded semi-annually) market rates $(R_M)$ at which the coupons of the FRB are benchmarked, as on the valuation date, are: 6-M = 8%, 1-Y = 8.5%, 1.5-Y = 9% and 2-Y = 9.5%. What will be the value of the FRB under such circumstances?

The value of the 2-year semi-annually paid FRB (face value INR 100/-), with a current reference rate of 8% p.a. (compounded semi-annually), and with an expectation of interest rates remaining flat at 8% p.a. for the next two years, is such that:

$$Value = \frac{C}{\left(1+R_M/2\right)^1} + \frac{C}{\left(1+R_M/2\right)^2} + \frac{C}{\left(1+R_M/2\right)^3} + \frac{C+FV}{\left(1+R_M/2\right)^4} \quad (6.6)$$

$$Value = \frac{4}{(1+8\%/2)^1} + \frac{4}{(1+8\%/2)^2} + \frac{4}{(1+8\%/2)^3} + \frac{4+100}{(1+8\%/2)^4}$$
$$= 100$$

On the other hand, if the present yield curve is considered to be upward slopping with the given rates of interest for various tenors till 2 years, the FRB gives the first confirmed coupon of INR 4 for every INR 100 (@ 8% p.a.) after the first 6 months, followed by three more semi-annual coupons, the actual amount of which are not known with full certainty, but can be estimated from the present yield curve.

Accordingly, the three future 6-month interest rates, respectively at the end of 6, 12, and 18 months, may be extracted, such that the annualized 6-month future rates are: 9.0012%, 10.0036%, and 11.0072%, respectively at the end of 6, 12, and 18 months from the present coupon-cum-valuation date. These rates can be used to calculate the three expected future coupons of the FRB, which can be further discounted at the market yields for the respective tenors.

Therefore, the bond value is:

$$Value = \frac{(8\%/2)*FV}{\left(1+R_{M,6M}/2\right)^1} + \frac{(9.0012\%/2)*FV}{\left(1+R_{M,12M}/2\right)^2} + \frac{(10.0036\%/2)*FV}{\left(1+R_{M,18M}/2\right)^3}$$
$$+ \frac{(11.0072\%/2)*FV+FV}{\left(1+R_{M,24M}/2\right)^4}$$

$$Value = \frac{4}{(1+8\%/2)^1} + \frac{4.506}{(1+8.5\%/2)^2} + \frac{5.0018}{(1+9\%/2)^3} + \frac{5.5036+100}{(1+9.5\%/2)^4}$$
$$= 3.8462 + 4.1411 + 4.3831 + 87.6297 = 100$$

*The key principal of valuing a FRB, as on any coupon payment-cum-reset date when the coupon rate is expected to be equal to the market rate, especially in the absence of any spreads, is the FRB will always have a par value irrespective of the nature of the yield curve.*

### Example

Consider the 2-year FRB presented in the previous example, where the bond can be valued, just by considering the single known coupon amount and by ignoring the three future coupons. The value of future coupons is extracted from the 6-month future rate of interest, expected to be prevailed at different coupon reset dates till the maturity.

At the beginning of every coupon period, FRBs will always be worth par value, no matter what the future coupons would be, depending upon the movement in future rate of interests. Therefore, while valuing a FRB, instead of considering all the future coupons due on the FRB till the maturity, an alternative approach could be to consider just the immediate/next coupon payment, and the value of that bond as on that specific coupon payment-cum-reset date, which is nothing but the par value. This is again possible when the coupons are linked only to the benchmark rates without any spreads.

Accordingly, the value of the FRB, as per the previous example, would be:

$$Value = \frac{(8\%/2)*FV + PAR}{\left(1+R_{M,6M}/2\right)^1} = \frac{4+100}{(1+8\%/2)^1} = 100$$

### Example

In all cases, following either of the methods, the FRB is valued at par. This is because of the valuation date, which in all the above examples are a coupon payment-cum-reset date, assuming both dates are the same and the market rate benchmarked with the FRB to arrive at the coupons and the discount rate are also the same. But, the value of the same FRB on any dates in-between the two coupon payment/reset dates may differ from the par value, irrespective of the methods followed to value the FRB. Suppose the same FRB but with a residual maturity of 1.75 years and with an immediate semi-annual coupon at 8.20% p.a., re-fixed on the last reset date before 3 months from now, is required to be valued. Let's assume the same upward-sloping yield curve with the following rates of different tenors: 3-M = 7.75%, 6-M = 8%, 1-Y = 8.5%, 1.5-Y = 9% and 2-Y = 9.5%.

Under such circumstances, where the FRB is valued in-between two coupon payment/reset dates, the selection of timings and the respective rates, both to arrive at the future coupons and to discount them, will undergo a change. As on the valuation date, the next three future coupons, other than the immediate next coupon which is known at 8.20% p.a., need to be arrived at with the help of present yield points at 3 months, 9 months, 15 months, and 21 months, instead of 6 months, 12 months, 18 months, and 24 months as followed in the previous example.

Accordingly, the interpolated (linear interpolation) yields and required future rates are shown in the following table (Table 6.4):

*Table 6.4* Interpolated yield and future rates

|  | 3 Months | 9 Months | 15 Months | 21 Months |
|---|---|---|---|---|
| Interpolated Yield | 7.75% | 8.25% | 8.75% | 9.25% |
| Future 6-M Rates (Annualized) |  | After 3-M 8.5005% | After 9-M 9.5023% | After 15-M 10.5052% |

The future 6-month rate and interpolated yields can be used respectively for arriving at the three future coupons, and the rates to discount all the future CFs, due at four different points of time in the future.

Therefore, the bond value would be:

$$Value = \frac{(8.20\%/2)*FV}{\left(1+R_{M,3M}/2\right)^{0.5}} + \frac{(8.5005\%/2)*FV}{\left(1+R_{M,9M}/2\right)^{1.5}} + \frac{(9.5023\%/2)*FV}{\left(1+R_{M,15M}/2\right)^{2.5}}$$
$$+ \frac{(10.5052\%/2)*FV+FV}{\left(1+R_{M,21M}/2\right)^{3.5}}$$

$$Value = \frac{4.1}{(1+7.75\%/2)^{0.5}} + \frac{4.2502}{(1+8.25\%/2)^{1.5}} + \frac{4.7511}{(1+8.75\%/2)^{2.5}}$$
$$+ \frac{5.2526+100}{(1+9.25\%/2)^{3.5}}$$
$$= 4.0228+4.0002+4.2688+89.8481 = 102.1398$$

Alternatively, the same FRB can also be valued by considering the immediate coupon and the value of the FRB expected to be as on the next coupon-payment-reset date, which is the par value, such that:

$$Value = \frac{(8.20\%/2)*FV+PAR}{\left(1+R_{M,3M}/2\right)^{0.5}} = \frac{4.1+100}{(1+7.75\%/2)^{0.5}} = 102.1398$$

Since the market expectation, after the reset of the last coupon 3 months before, has started moving up, as seen from the higher 6-month future rates, the FRB is presently valued at premium, which will again move to the par value just in the next coupon reset date, after which but till the next reset, the value may again change to premium/discount, depending upon the change in market expectations.

It is also seen that the value remains the same, irrespective of the methods of considering all the future coupons or only the next immediate coupon. The valuation of an FRB with/without a contractual spread, but in the presence of a trading spread/margin, may be undertaken in just the similar way the valuation is done for an FRB without any spread, as shown in the previous examples, except adjusting the spread with the cash flows and also with the discounting rates.

## Valuation of bond with embedded options

A bond embedded with a call (put) option is termed as callable (puttable) bond. A call (put) option gives the issuer (holder) the right to buy-back (sell-off) the bond issue before it matures, depending on the movement in the rate of interests. The price of such options needs to be adjusted with the price of similar option-free bonds to derive the value of a callable (puttable) bond. Since in case of callable (puttable) bond, the issuers (holders) enjoy the right to exercise their options, the value of a callable (puttable) bond is expected to be lower (higher) than the value of a similar option-free bond. The price of such an option again depends on the chance of exercising the option, which again depends on the movement in the future rates of interest. In the case of valuing a simple bond, the future interest rates are not expected to be volatile. But the valuation of bonds with embedded options specifically depends upon the volatility in the rates of interest. Therefore, unlike in the case of the valuation of any option-free bond, the framework or mechanism used to value a bond with any embedded options needs to capture the interest rate volatility. Broadly, the value of a callable or puttable bond, in comparison with a similar option-free bond, is such that:

*Value (Callable Bond) = Value (Option - free Bond) – Value (Call Option)*

*Value (Putable Bond) = Value (Option - free Bond) + Value (Put Option)*

*Binomial Option Pricing*[2] model can be successfully used to price bonds with embedded options, based on a binomial interest rate tree framework with due consideration for the following possibility:

- Calling back the bond issue following a fall in yield beyond the coupon rate after a certain lock-in period.

- Selling-off the bond issue following a rise in yield beyond the coupon rate after a certain lock-in period.

Price movements of bonds with embedded options due to a change in yield is not as simple and direct as a similar option-free bond. The impact of a yield change on both the price of a similar option-free bond and on the value of the embedded option need to be considered to value a bond with embedded option. If the interest rate falls (rises), the value of an option-free bond will rise (fall). If the interest rate falls, the value of a call (put) option tends to rise (fall). If the interest rate rises, value of call (put) option will fall (rise). As the interest rate falls (rises), the price of a callable bond will not rise (fall) by a similar amount as in the case of a similar option-free bond. Similarly, as the interest rate rises (falls), the price of puttable bond will not fall (rise) by the similar amount as in case of similar option-free bond.

But as far as RBI-FIMMDA guidelines on valuation of securities with embedded options (call or put) in India are concerned, callable and puttable bonds, because of the uncertainty in the holding period due to its option feature, need to be valued with a conservative approach. Callable bonds are valued at the lowest of the value(s) arriving at all possible call date(s) and also at the maturity. Alternatively, callable bonds are valued at a yield which is higher of all yield to calls and yield to maturities. On the other hand, puttable bonds are valued at the highest of the value(s) arriving at all possible put date(s) and also at the maturity. Alternatively, puttable bonds are valued at a yield which is lower of all yield to puts and yield to maturities.

## Example

Suppose the government of India has issued a government security (6.72%GS2025) with a coupon payable annually, on 18 July 2015 for a maturity of 10 years maturing on 18 July 2025, with a call option. The optionality on the bond could be exercised after the completion of a 5-year tenure from the date of issuance on any coupon date falling thereafter. The government has the right to buy-back the bond (call option) at par value (equal to the face value) on any of the yearly coupon dates starting from 18 July 2020.

Suppose the State Bank of India has invested INR 100 crore in this bond and may like to value its position as on 18 July 2016. The bank needs to value all its positions as per the RBI-FIMMDA valuation norms.

Suppose the FIMMDA base yield curve as on the valuation date is given in the following table (Table 6.5):

*Table 6.5* FIMMDA base yield curve

| Tenor | 1Y | 2Y | 3Y | 4Y | 5Y | 6Y | 7Y | 8Y | 9Y | 10Y |
|---|---|---|---|---|---|---|---|---|---|---|
| Yield (%) | 6.87 | 6.90 | 6.96 | 7.07 | 7.16 | 7.27 | 7.28 | 7.32 | 7.36 | 7.31 |

*Solution*

Since the concerned bond is a callable bond, the same needs to be valued at a yield which is higher of all yield to calls and yield to maturities.

Since the callable bond has a minimum lock-in period of 5 years before which the call option cannot be exercised, the bond has four possible call dates, leading to estimation of four yield to calls (yield to 1st call, yield to 2nd call, yield to 3rd call, and yield to final call), followed by yield to maturity.

The call schedule may be defined as given in the following table (Table 6.6):

*Table 6.6* Details of call schedule attached to a security

| Possible Calls | Date | Call Price |
|---|---|---|
| 1st Call | 18 July 2021 | Rs.100/- |
| 2nd Call | 18 July 2022 | Rs.100/- |
| 3rd Call | 18 July 2023 | Rs.100/- |
| Final Call | 18 July 2024 | Rs.100/- |
| Maturity | 18 July 2025 | Rs.100/- |

In the absence of the actual trade in the concerned security, the same, as per the RBI-FIMMDA valuation norm, may be valued based on the government of India base yield curve. Accordingly, all possible risk-free yield to calls, as on the valuation date, may be derived from the yield to maturity of the respective tenor, equal to the valuation date till the possible call date. In this case, when the bond has a residual maturity of 9 years as on the valuation date, the time between the valuation date till the 1st, 2nd, 3rd, and final call dates are respectively 5 years, 6 years, 7 years, and 8 years. Therefore, the risk-free yield for these tenors, extracted from the base yield curve as on the valuation date, may be considered as the respective yield to call, and the yield for the residual tenor of 9 years may be treated as yield to maturity.

Therefore, four yield to calls and the yield to maturity, as on 18 July 2016, are:

Yield-to-First Call  = 7.16% (= 5-Year YTM);
Yield-to-Second Call = 7.27% (= 6-Year YTM);
Yield-to-Third Call = 7.28% (= 7-Year YTM);
Yield-to-Fourth Call = 7.32% (= 8-Year YTM);
and Yield to Maturity = 7.36% (= 9-Year YTM)

Accordingly, the highest of all the above yields is the yield to maturity, which needs to be considered to value the callable bond by considering all the cash flows till the maturity.

It may be noted here that the YTM, as on the valuation date, turns out to be the highest possible yield because of the consistently upward-sloping base yield curve, indicating a possible rise in future interest rates, making it unfavourable for the issuer to exercise the call option before the maturity. In other words, in a scenario when the yield curve is continuously upward sloping, the issuer is expected not to exercise the call option till the maturity, and therefore to value the callable bond based on the YTM which is the highest of all possible YTCs and YTM. Similarly, if the yield curve is found to be consistently downward sloping, indicating an unfavourable situation for the bond issuer to remain with the bond issue, the issuer is expected to exercise the call option on the very first call date. In such case, yield-to-first call may be found to be the highest possible yield, and therefore may be used to value the callable bond. In case of a humped yield curve, the yield used to value a callable bond need not to be the yield-to-first call or the YTM but may need to be extracted from the yield curve after comparing all the YTCs and the YTM.

Therefore, the value of 6.72%GS2025 as on 18 July 2016 is calculated as:

$$Price = \frac{CF_1}{(1+R)^1} + \frac{CF_2}{(1+R)^2} + \frac{CF_3}{(1+R)^3} + \frac{CF_4}{(1+R)^4} + \frac{CF_5}{(1+R)^5} + \frac{CF_6}{(1+R)^6}$$
$$+ \frac{CF_7}{(1+R)^7} + \frac{CF_8}{(1+R)^8} + \frac{CF_9}{(1+R)^9}$$

The first eight annual cash flows are fixed at Rs.6.72, followed by the final cash flow at Rs.106.72/- (Rs.6.72 + Rs.100). 'R' is the highest possible yield which is fixed at 7.36% p.a. Putting these number in the pricing equation, the value of the callable bond comes out to be Rs.95.8934/-

## Valuation of FI securities: RBI-FIMMDA guidelines

Even if there are various mechanisms to value bonds of different natures, the Reserve Bank of India and Fixed Income Money Market and Derivatives Association (FIMMDA), an association of commercial banks, financial institutions, and primary dealers in India concerned with the domestic market operations, publishes some guidelines, which are consistently followed by the banks and other FIs in India. Valuation of various securities available in the Indian market need to be done as per the FIMMDA guidelines only, summarised below:

- Investments classified under HTM will be carried at acquisition cost. In case the bond is acquired at premium, the premium should be amortized over the period remaining to maturity. The book value of the security should continue to be reduced to the extent of the amount amortized during the relevant accounting period.

- Periodical valuation of investments included in the AFS and HFT would be the market price of the issue as available from the trades/quotes. All AFS and HFT positions need to be market-to-market respectively, at least on a quarterly and monthly basis, especially for reporting purposes. It may be noted here that the book value of the individual securities would not undergo any change after such periodical valuation.
- In respect of unquoted securities, a specific procedure is followed, as suggested by the Reserve Bank of India.
- All unquoted central government securities, qualified for SLR, can be valued from the base yield curve published by FIMMDA.
- Unquoted central government securities, not qualified for SLR, can be valued at the yield from the same base YC plus 25 bps.
- Special securities (oil bonds, fertilizer bonds, IFCI/FCI bonds), directly issued by government of India to the beneficiary entities but do not carry SLR status, are valued at a spread of 25 bps above the corresponding government security or base yield.
- Treasury bills can be valued at carrying cost (for banks) or on a market-to-market basis (for primary dealers), based on the actual traded price (fulfilling some minimum criteria) or the T-bill curve published by FBIL.
- ZCBs should be shown in the books at carrying cost, i.e. acquisition cost plus discount accrued.
- Floating rate bonds, if traded in the market, need to be valued at the traded price. In the absence of any trading, FRB need to be valued by considering all the future CFs (extracted from the forward benchmark rate plus the contractual spread, if any), discounted at the risk-free YTM/ZCYC adjusted with the respective market or *Desired Spread*, if any. The desired spreads added are basically to capture the illiquidity and arise due to the fixation of semiannual coupons of long-term bonds based on the short-term T-bill rates, and are determined based on the simple average of the polled numbers, conducted once in a fortnight, after eliminating the outliers (equals to 2 standard deviations).
- Callable bonds are valued at the yield, the higher of the yield to maturity and all possible yield to calls, adjusting the residual tenor pertaining to the concerned yield. In case the yield levels started falling from the beginning, yield to first call becomes the higher yield and the residual tenor till the nearest call date becomes the tenor used for valuation. On the other hand, if the yield levels remain the same or start rising till the maturity, the YTM becomes the highest yield and the residual tenor till the maturity becomes the tenor used for valuation.
- Puttable bonds are valued at a yield, lower of yield to maturity and all possible yields to put, adjusting the residual tenor pertaining to the concerned yield. In case the market yield starts rising, yield to first put becomes the lowest yield, and the residual tenor till the nearest put date becomes the tenor used for valuation. On contrary, if the yield level remains the same or starts falling till the maturity, the YTM becomes the

lowest yield, and the complete residual tenor till the maturity becomes the tenor used for valuation.

- In case any bond has simultaneous call and put options to be exercised on the same day and with an option of multiple times till the maturity, the nearest call/put date may be considered for valuation.
- Inflation indexed bonds are valued at traded prices (if available), or otherwise at *"Nominal Clean Price"* arrived at by FIMMDA by multiplying its model price, again arrived at by FIMMDA, with the inflation index ratio.
- Non-traded state government securities in India qualified for SLR used to be valued from the base yield curve, but after adding 25 bps with the concerned base yield. But this methodology to value the SDL has undergone a change (from April 2019), where instead of just adding a flat spread of 25 bps on the respective base yield, non-traded SDLs are now valued based on the separate yield curve constructed by the FBIL based on some interpolation/extrapolation techniques applied on the daily actual trades in the SDL segment.
- Valuation of UDAY bonds issued by various state governments in India to repay the DISCOM loans, originally valued at the base yield plus 50 bps, has also undergone a change and is now based on the new method proposed by FBIL. As per the new method, actual trades in all UDAY/DISCOM bonds are initially grouped into different maturity buckets (<1 month, 1 to 3 months, 3 to 6 months, 6 to 9 months, 9 to 12 months, and thereafter all subsequent years like 2020, 2021, . . ., till the longest year of maturity of the outstanding security). YTM of all the outstanding SDLs published by FBIL are now grouped into all these maturity buckets and the average YTM will be arrived at separately for all the buckets. Any UDAY/DISCOM bonds belonging to a particular maturity bucket will be valued at the average YTM of that concerned bucket.
- Perpetual bonds should be valued considering the final maturity as the longest point on the base yield curve (say 40 years, as published by FIMMDA) and the applicable spread for the longest tenor (say 15 years as published by FIMMDA). Accordingly, cash flows of the perpetual bond till the longest point of the base yield curve need to be considered. In case any perpetual bond has a call option, along with a step-up coupon after the call option, the valuation of such security needs to be based on the cash flows with the regular coupon till the call date, followed by the step-up coupon thereafter.
- Any non-government security continuously traded in the last 15 calendar days, with a minimum trading volume of INR 5 crore in any day, can be valued based on the actual traded price.
- Valuation of any rated non-government securities, considering the lowest of available credit ratings not more than 12 months old if given by two or more rating agencies, can be done from the annualized base

yield curve and the required spread, regularly published by FIMMDA, depending upon the nature of issuer (Bank-PSU-FI, NBFC, or corporates), credit rating (AAA to BBB-), and maturity (0.5 to 15 years). Base yield and credit spread for any intermediate tenors may be arrived at through linear interpolation.

- Whenever a corporate bond is traded, the traded spread may be used to value all other non-traded bonds of similar rating and residual tenor, issued by the same entity or issuer.
- Unrated bonds of an issuer may be valued at a spread of an equivalent rated bond of similar tenure from the same issuer, after marking up at least by 25%.
- In case of securities not at all rated by any rating agency, or having a rating older than 12 months, and no corresponding bond of similar valid rating by the same issuer exist, the published credit spread applicable to BBB- for the residual tenor marked up by 25% needs to be used for valuation.
- CPs and CDs, having a residual tenor less than 1 year, should be valued at carrying cost.
- Valuation of Basel III Compliant Perpetual Bond need to be based on the concerned base yield and the qualifying spread published by FIMMDA for two rating grades: AA and Above, and AA- and Below, and for two tenors: 3 to 5 years and 7 to 10 years.

## Bond valuation: a case

Suppose the State Bank of India, as on 27 July 2018, holds AFS positions in 20 dated securities (GOI bonds, SDLs, and non-government securities), both liquid as well as illiquid, as given in the following table (Table 6.7).

The bank may like to value its bond portfolio as on that date, looking at the following parameters, and/or under the following scenarios/ circumstances:

1 MTM values of all the positions (GOI securities and SDL with SLR Status, special SDL, and non-government securities) and of the AFS portfolio as on the given date, considering the necessary regulatory norms or prevailing market practices towards valuation of investments.

2 Base yield curve, as on the given date, needs to be constructed from the available trade data in NDS-OM, with necessary filtration (or removing outliers) where any trades on the same date below a total volume of 20 crores and 50 crores respectively for GOI bonds

*Table 6.7* Composition of bank's AFS portfolio consisting of government and non-government securities as on 27 July 2018

| Sl. No. | Security | Maturity Date | Residual Maturity (in Yrs.) | Coupon (%) | No. of Units Held (in Lakhs) | Face Value (Rs. in Cr.) |
|---|---|---|---|---|---|---|
| 1 | 7.28% GS 2019 | 3-Jun-19 | 0.8500 | 7.28 | 10 | 10 |
| 2 | 6.35% G.S 2020 | 2-Jan-20 | 1.4306 | 6.35 | 10 | 10 |
| 3 | 8.13% GS 2022 | 21-Sep-22 | 4.1500 | 8.13 | 10 | 10 |
| 4 | 6.84% GS 2022 | 19-Dec-22 | 4.3944 | 6.84 | 10 | 10 |
| 5 | 8.20%GS 2025 | 24-Sep-25 | 7.1583 | 8.20 | 10 | 10 |
| 6 | 7.59% GS 2026 | 11-Jan-26 | 7.4556 | 7.59 | 10 | 10 |
| 7 | 7.17% GS 2028 | 8-Jan-28 | 9.4472 | 7.17 | 10 | 10 |
| 8 | 8.97% GS 2030 | 5-Dec-30 | 12.3556 | 8.97 | 10 | 10 |
| 9 | 6.68% GS 2031 | 17-Sep-31 | 13.1389 | 6.68 | 10 | 10 |
| 10 | 7.5% GS 2034 | 10-Aug-34 | 16.0361 | 7.50 | 10 | 10 |
| 11 | 7.40% GS 2035 | 9-Sep-35 | 17.1167 | 7.40 | 10 | 10 |
| 12 | 8.17% GS 2044 | 1-Dec-44 | 26.3444 | 8.17 | 10 | 10 |
| 13 | 6.87% GOI FRB 2020 | 21-Dec-20 | 2.4000 | 6.87 | 10 | 10 |
| 14 | 8.60% Tamilnadu GS 2021 | 20-Jul-21 | 2.9806 | 8.60 | 10 | 10 |
| 15 | 7.82% West Bengal SDL 2023 | 19-Jun-23 | 4.8944 | 7.82 | 10 | 10 |
| 16 | 8.21% Rajasthan Uday Bond 2020 | 31-Mar-20 | 1.6750 | 8.21 | 10 | 10 |
| 17 | 7.21% REC Ltd. 2022 (AAA) | 21-Nov-22 | 4.3167 | 7.21 | 10 | 10 |
| 18 | 7.95% HDFC Bank Ltd. 2026 (AAA) | 21-Sep-26 | 8.1500 | 7.95 | 10 | 10 |
| 19 | 8.32% Reliance Jio Infocom Ltd. 2021 (AAA) | 08-Jul-21 | 2.9472 | 8.32 | 10 | 10 |
| 20 | 8.90% Dewan Housing Finance Corporation Ltd. 2025 (AAA) | 04-Jun-25 | 6.8528 | 8.90 | 10 | 10 |
| | Total G-Sec Portfolio (GOI + SDL + CB) | | | | | 200 |

and SDL are ignored. Linear interpolation method may be followed to construct the base yield curve.

3   Valuation of FRB (if any) may need to be done strictly as per the FIMMDA norm, where all possible coupons till the maturity, the average of three immediate (w.r.t. the valuation date) 182-day T-bill cut-off rates, and the desired (traded/fortnightly polled) spread applicable to the concerned FRB as on the valuation date may require to be considered.

4   Fortnight corporate bond spread matrix, published by FBIL as on the concerned date, may be considered to value all non-government securities.

5   The manager may like to explore the arbitrage opportunity available in all the positions held by the bank, valuing all the securities using the par/base yield curve and the zero coupon yield curve (ZCYC). Accordingly, the manager may like to construct the required term structure of interest rates: yield curve, zero coupon yield curve, and forward curve.

6   Total interest/coupon accrued on the whole portfolio as on the given date.

## Self-learning exercise

1   What are the various sources of returns from a bond and how do these sources affect the current price of the bond?

2   How are the current market price of a bond and its fair price differentiated? What are the factors affecting both the prices and how?

3   How are the coupon rate of a bond and its YTM interrelated and how does this interrelation affect the price difference (if any) between the current price of a bond and its par value?

4   Define the full price, clean price of a bond and the factors causing the differences between these two prices (if any).

5   An investor has invested in 6.90GS 2019 today. He/she is a little doubtful about the movement of its market price and is trying to understand the possible price gain in the future. What could be the maximum price of the bond he/she may think of?

6   What is meant by marking a position to market?

7   Suppose two GOI dated securities (7.80 GS 2021, maturing on 11 April 2021, and 5.87 GS 2022, maturing on 28 August 2022) are presently traded at INR 104.29 and INR 97.16 respectively. How do you think the prices of both the bonds change as they approach their maturity dates?

8 What are the market conventions used to count the number of days in between two dates, in the context of Indian bond market? How do these conventions affect the pricing of a bond?

9 What is accrued interest? How is it adjusted with the price/value of a bond?

10 Explain the arbitrage free valuation approach and the market process that forces the price of a bond towards its arbitrage free value, and also explain how a dealer can generate an arbitrage profit if a bond is mispriced.

11 Identify the types of bonds for which estimating the expected cash flows is difficult, and explain the problems encountered when estimating the cash flows for these bonds.

12 "There is no interest rate risk in case of an investment in a floating rate bond. The yield is always at par with the market, and there is no reason for the value of the FRB to deviate from the par value." Explain whether you agree or disagree with this statement.

13 What is the initial/quoted margin and discount/effective margin in the context of a floating rate bond? Even if the yield curve for the concerned reference rate used to fix the semi-annual coupons of the FRB remain flat, is there any possibility for the FRB to be traded at a price other than the par value, even at any of the coupon reset dates?

14 Identify the relationship between price/value of a callable and put-table bond, price of the similar option-free bond, and the value of the embedded call and put option. Explain with the help of the price-yield curve.

15 How is a callable and a puttable bond valued as per the FIMMDA guideline. How do you justify the valuation methodology?

16 Banks in India are supposed to follow the RBI-FIMMDA norms in terms of valuing their investments, in HTM, AFS, and HFT, in all dated central and state government securities. What are the valuation norms they are supposed to be adhere to?

17 How are banks in India supposed to value their positions in non-government securities to comply with the guidelines suggested by the central bank?

## Notes

1 The time value of money (TVM) is a concept that says that money available now is worth more than the identical sum received at a future date due to its potential earning capacity. Alternatively, with a core principle of finance that money can earn interest, any amount of money is worth more the sooner it is received. A few important aspects of TVM commonly used in financial arithmetic are: present value of future cash flows (inflows, outflows), future value of present cash flows (inflows, outflows), net present value (NPV), all estimated by using relevant discounting or compounding interest rates, with the relevant time period, such

that: $PV = \dfrac{Future\,CF_t}{(1+r_t)^t}$ ; $FV = Present\ CF_t \times (1 + r_t)^t$ ; and $NPV = PV$ of Future

*Inflows – PV of Future Outflows.*

2 The binomial option pricing model is a method to value options contracts. The option pricing model uses an iterative procedure, where the assumptions are that there are two possible outcomes: a move up or a move down. Hence, the binomial part of the model. In contrast to the well-known Black-Scholes model, mathematical simplicity and the option for considering multiple periods are the major advantages of this option pricing model. A multi-period view enables the users to visualize the change in asset price from period to period, and therefore allows them to evaluate the option based on decisions made at different points in time. A binomial tree is constructed, using some predefined probability for each period for success (price moving up) and failure (price moving down), to finally price an option contract. This option pricing model is very useful to price interest rate options and interest rate structured products like caps, floors, collars, etc.

# Bibliography

Elton, E. J., Gruber, M. J., Agrawal, D., and Mann, C. (2004). Factors Affecting the Valuation of Corporate Bonds. *Journal of Banking & Finance*, 28(11), 2747–2767.

Eom, H. Y., Helwege, J., and Huang, J.-Z. (2004). Structural Models of Corporate Bond Pricing: An Empirical Analysis. *The Review of Financial Studies*, 17(2), 499–544.

Fabozzi, F. (2007). *Fixed Income Analysis* (2nd edn.). John Wiley & Sons, Inc., Hoboken, NJ.

Fabozzi, F. (ed.). (July 2017). *The Handbook of Fixed Income Securities* (8th edn.). McGraw Hill Education, New York.

Kalotay, A., Williams, G. O., and Fabozzi, F. J. (1993). A Model for the Valuation of Bonds and Embedded Options. *Financial Analysts Journal*, May–June, 35–46.

Kish, R., and Livingstone, M. (1992). The Determinants of the Call Feature on Corporate Bonds. *Journal of Banking and Finance*, 16, 687–703.

Martellini, L., Priaulet, P., and Priaulet, S. (2003). *Fixed-Income Securities: Valuation, Risk Management and Portfolio Strategies* (1st edn.). John Wiley & Sons, Inc., Hoboken, NJ.

Veronesi, P. (2011). *Fixed Income Securities: Valuation, Risk and Risk Management*. John Wiley & Sons, Inc., Hoboken, NJ.

# 7 Interest rate sensitivity measures

Key learning outcomes

At the end of this chapter, readers are expected to be confident about:

- How do the prices of different bonds respond to a change in interest rate?
- What are the different measures available to capture interest rate sensitivity?
- What is duration, m-duration, PV01/PVBP, and how are these estimated for a single security?
- How is the interest rate sensitivity of a portfolio of various securities estimated?
- How is the IR sensitivity of bonds with embedded options captured, and how is such a measure different from the sensitivity measures applicable to option-free securities?
- What are the usefulness and limitations of various IR sensitivity measures?
- What is convexity, and how is it captured?
- Does convexity truly supplement the m-duration measure to capture bond price sensitivity to interest rates?
- How are these sensitivity measures practically used to successfully manage a bond portfolio of an institutional investor?

## Bond price sensitivity to interest rates: meaning

Prices/values of all types of fixed income securities are sensitive to any change, large or small, in the rate of interests/yield. Since the value of such security at any point of time is broadly the present value (PV) of all the future cash flows due on that security, and the PVs of future cash flows are sensitive to the rate of interests for the respective tenors, the value of any fixed income security is sensitive to any possible change in the rate of interest. Alternatively, there is an inverse relation between the price of a bond or fixed income security and the rate of interest. Any rise (fall) in the rate of interest leads to a fall (rise) in the value of a bond, causing a possible capital loss (gain) for the investor or security holder. Therefore, all investors investing in fixed income securities are said to be exposed to *Interest Rate Risk*. Net gain or loss in the FI portfolio depends on two components: capital gain (loss), and revenue loss (gain). Any change in interest rates affects these two components inversely. Alternatively, the possibility of any capital gain will be supplemented by a revenue loss, and vice versa, but may not completely offset each other. The risk of incurring a capital loss due to a rise in interest rates is known as *Price Risk*, and the risk of earning a lower reinvestment income due to fall in interest rates is termed as *Reinvestment Risk*.

The relation between bond price and interest rate can also be explained with a simple example. Suppose an investor has bought bond X at par value at a coupon rate of 8%. Now suppose, the market interest rate has gone up from 8% to 8.5% and the investor wants to sell the bond where the coupon rate would be same 8%. Since the bond is selling at par, nobody would like to buy the bond at par with a coupon rate of 8%, where the market interest rate is 8.5%. Here neither the investor can change the coupon rate nor can they change the actual maturity of the bond so that the same would be saleable in the market. However, what the bond seller can do is to reduce the bond price so that the amount of coupon received on the bond at the bond's par value would be equal to the amount based on the new or revised interest rate on the new or revised price, so that without changing the original coupon rate, the current market rate can be offered to the prospect buyer of the bond.

The magnitude of interest rate sensitivity/risk of different types of bonds largely depends upon their features (e.g. maturity, coupon rate, coupon payment frequency, yield, presence of options, etc.), as shown in the following figure (Figure 7.1), such that:

- Prices of longer maturity bonds are more sensitive to interest rate changes than a similar bond but with shorter maturity.
- Prices of high coupon bonds or bonds with higher coupon payment frequencies are less sensitive to change in interest rates than the prices of similar low coupon bonds or bonds with lesser coupon payment frequencies.
- The higher the initial YTM of a bond, the lower would be its price sensitivity to change in yield.
- In case of a floating rate bond, even if the coupon rates are adjusted with the prevailing market rates at every coupon reset date, the value of such bond is exposed to interest rate fluctuation during two coupons reset dates, and therefore may get traded at different prices other than the par value.
- In order to understand the sensitivity of bonds with embedded options (call/put) due to a change in interest rates, the same can be achieved by

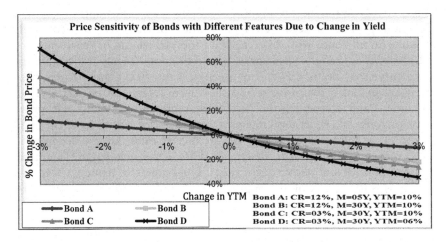

*Figure 7.1* Impact of bonds feature on price-yield relationship

capturing the sensitivity both in the price of similar option-free bond and the price of the option (call/put).

- If the interest rate falls, the chances for the call (put) option holder to exercise their option increases (reduces), and therefore the value of call (put) option tends to rise (fall).
- On the other hand, if the interest rate rises, the chances for the put (call) option holder to exercise their option increases (reduces), and therefore the value of put (call) option will rise (fall).
- Therefore, as the interest rate falls (rises), the value of callable bond will not rise (fall) by the similar amount, as in the case of a similar option-free bond. As the interest rate rises (falls), the value of a puttable bond will not fall (rise) by a similar amount as in the case of a similar option-free bond.

Even if all fixed income securities are individually sensitive to interest rate fluctuations and can be easily captured, the sensitivity of the entire fixed income/bond portfolio needs to be carefully analyzed and estimated. Maturity of a bond is one of the important factors for its price sensitivity due to a change in the interest rate or the yield. Therefore, the value of a portfolio of bonds with different maturities depends on how the value of individual bonds with different maturity periods changes following the change in interest rates. The rate of interest or the yield of different bonds varies according to their respective maturities. The graphical relation between the yield and maturity of different bonds is known as *Yield Curve*. It is basically assumed that in the scenario of changing interest rates, the yield of different bonds with different maturities changes by similar basis points, commonly known as *Parallel Shift* in the yield curve. But in real market conditions, when there is any change in the rate of interest, even if all the rates change in a similar direction (positive or negative), the magnitude of change is not necessarily be same for all bonds with different maturities, which can be represented by a *Unparallel Shift* in the yield curve. Due to this possible unparallel shift, the yield curve may become *Flatter* or *Steeper*. If the yield curve flattens, then the yield spread between long- and short-term interest rates narrows. On the other hand, steepening the yield curve represents widening the spread between long- and short-term interest rates. The price sensitivity of the bond portfolio, in the event of change in the interest rates, largely depends on market expectation towards the type of shifts in the yield curve. Therefore, other than price and reinvestment risk, a bond portfolio manager may also be exposed to the risk of any unparallel shift in the yield curve, commonly known as *Yield Curve Risk*.

## Price/yield relationship

Since interest rates are the major driver of the prices of fixed income securities, it is very important to capture the relationship between the price and yield of a security. The graphical presentation of this relationship is known as *Price-Yield Curve*. The price-yield curve of any option-free bond exhibits a downward-sloping curve which is not linear, and therefore is not a straight line, as exhibited in the following figure (Figure 7.2). The shape of the price-yield curve of any option-free bond is downward slopping and 'Convex'. However, the shape of a price-yield curve of a callable bond is downward sloping but exhibits negative (positive) convexity at a lower (higher) level of yields. On the other hand, the shape of price-yield curve of a puttable bond

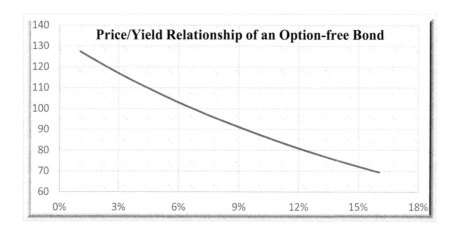

*Figure 7.2* Price-yield relationship of option-free bond

is downward sloping and convex, but with more flatness beyond a certain level of yield (yield > coupon).

Some of the important properties on the relation between the price volatility of an option-free bond and changes in its yield are:

- Even if the yield and price of all bonds move in opposite directions, the percentage change (positive or negative) in the prices or actual price change of different bonds are not similar even though there is a similar change in the yield.
- In case of small changes (positive or negative) in yield, the percentage of price change (in both directions) for a given bond is almost the same, irrespective of the direction of the change in the yield.
- In case of a large change (positive or negative) in the required yield (± X%), the percentage of price change for a given bond is not the same following a positive or negative change in the yield of similar magnitude. A positive percentage change in the price of a bond following a large negative change in the yield is comparatively greater than the negative percentage change in the same bond's price following an identically large but positive change in the yield.
- Assuming other factors remain the same, the longer (shorter) the bond's maturity, the greater (smaller) would be the bond's price sensitivity to interest rates.
- Assuming other factors remain the same, the lower (higher) the coupon rate, the greater (smaller) would be the bond's price sensitivity to interest rates.
- Zero coupon bonds have greater price sensitivity to interest rates than the coupon bearing bond of similar maturity.
- The price of a bond with embedded options (call or put), following a rise or fall in the rate of interest, may not fall (increase) by a similar magnitude as is possible for an option-free bond.

Even if the broader price-yield behavior remains inverse even for bonds with embedded options (call or put), the magnitude of price change or the price impact of a callable or puttable bond, for any given change in yield, may not be same if compared with a similar option-free bond. The price-yield behavior of a callable and puttable bond may be described through the following figure (Figure 7.3).

As shown in the above graph, even if the price-yield behavior for both callable and puttable bonds remains inverse, as depicted through the downward-sloping lines, both the curves, at least at certain segments, are different from the curve depicting the price-yield behavior of an option-free bond. This difference is basically due to the simultaneous impact of any change in interest rate on the value of the options (call or put) embedded in the bond. When there is any change in the interest rate or yield, it affects the value of the options contract as well, depending upon the change in interest

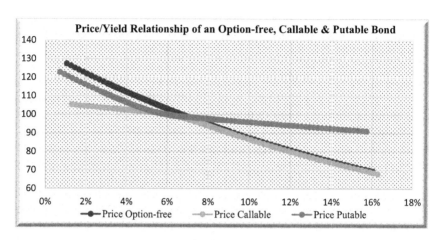

*Figure 7.3* Price-yield relationship of different types of securities

rates, and therefore the possibilities for the option holder to exercise their options.

Let's say there is a callable bond giving a coupon of 6% per annum. Now the moment the yield starts falling below 6%, the issuer will have tendency to exercise the call option. The greater is the fall in yield, the higher will be possibility for the issuer to exercise the option, and therefore the higher will be the value for the option contract, which is subtracted from the value of a similar option-free bond to arrive at the value of callable bond. As a result, whatever is the rise in value of an option-free bond, for a given fall in yield, the value of a similar bond with a call option will rise by a lower amount due to the rise in the call premium, leading to a different shape in the price-yield curve, especially in that segment where there will be a possibility for the bond issuer to exercise the call option. Therefore, the price-yield curve for a callable bond possesses negative convexity or becomes concave in its first segment, exhibiting a scenario where the option may be exercised, followed by normal convex curve in its second segment, similar to the price-yield curve of an option-free bond, representing a situation where there is no incentive for the option holder to exercise the call option. The moment there is hardly any chance for the option holder to exercise the option, the intrinsic value of the option will be close to zero, causing the value of a callable bond to change in a magnitude almost similar to the change in value of an option-free bond for any given change in yield. Therefore, the second segment of the price-yield curve for a callable bond looks almost similar to the price-yield curve of an option-free bond.

Similarly, the holder of a put option, i.e. the bond investor, may have a tendency to exercise their put option when the yield starts rising, say beyond the coupon rate. Therefore, as a result of any rise in the yield, say beyond a level, the chances for the put option holder to exercise the option increases, causing a rise in the put premium that may finally cause the price of the put-table bond to fall but not up to the extent the price of a similar option-free bond falls due to the same rise in yield. As a result, the price-yield curve of a puttable bond, especially in a segment where there are chances for the put option to be exercised, even if it follows the same convex pattern, becomes little flatter, indicating a relatively lower fall in price. As long as the yield level remains low till when the put option holder is not likely to exercise the option, the value of the put premium remains very low, leading the puttable bond to behave just like a similar option-free bond, and therefore almost a similar price-yield curve.

## Various interest rate sensitivity measures

There are some very important basic measures used to quantify the level of bond price sensitivity to change in interest rates/yield. These are *Duration* or *Macaulay Duration, Modified Duration (M-Duration), Price Value Basis Points (PVBP) or PV01, Convexity,* etc. There can be a variety of these measures applicable to different types of bonds.

### Duration or Macaulay duration

Duration (also known as Macaulay duration) of a bond can be expressed in terms of the average life of the security within which the original investment is expected to be recovered. Alternatively, Macaulay duration is the weighted average maturities of all the assumed zero coupon bonds (equal to various cash flows of the coupon bond), where the weights used at different periods are the proportion of PV of cash flows at each period and the full price of the bond (i.e. sum of the PVs of all CFs). In other words, duration is the time period at the end of which the value of all future cash flows will be exactly equal to the current market price of the bond, irrespective of any change (rise or fall) in the yield, making the cash flows insensitive to any change in interest rates. For a zero coupon bond, Macaulay's duration clearly equals the tenor/maturity of the bond. Macaulay's duration can be calculated as:

$$Macaulay\_Duration = \left[ \sum_{i=1}^{n} t_i \times \left( PVCF_i \middle/ \sum_{i=1}^{n} PVCF_i \right) \times 1/k \right] \qquad (7.1)$$

Where $PVCF_i$ represents the present value of cash flows due in period i, and $t_i$ represents the time when various interim cash flows are due till the maturity (n); k is the frequency of interim coupon payments, and therefore is 2 for semi-annual coupon bonds.

Alternatively, Macaulay duration can be represented as:

$$\text{Macaulay Duration} = \frac{\sum_{t=1}^{n} \frac{t \times C}{(1+r)^t} + \frac{n \times M}{(1+r)^n}}{P} \qquad (7.2)$$

Where n = number of cash flows; t = time to maturity; C = cash flow; r = required yield; M = maturity (par) value; P = bond price

This Macaulay duration can also be calculated in MS-Excel by using the following function:

$$= DURATION(Settlement, Maturity, Coupon, Yld. Frequency, [Basis])$$

Where the inputs are the date of settlement/measuring the duration (*Settlement*), date of maturity (*Maturity*), coupon rate (*Coupon*), yield to maturity for the concerned tenor (*Yld*), coupon payment frequency (*Frequency*), with a value of 2 in case of semi-annual bond, and the day count convention followed (*Basis*), the value of which is 4 in case of 30/360 convention, 3 in case of Actual/365, 2 in case of Actual/360, and 1 in case of Actual/Actual convention.

## Example

Suppose there is a government of India dated security (6.90 GS 2019) paying a coupon of 6.90% p.a., payable semiannually, maturing on 13 July 2019, currently (as on 24 July 2017) traded at Rs.100.98/- and at a yield of 6.3610%.

The duration of the bond can be calculated as given in the following table (Table 7.1):

*Table 7.1* Estimation of macaulay duration

| Time period of Cash Flows (half years) | 0.9389 | 1.9389 | 2.9389 | 3.9389 | Total |
|---|---|---|---|---|---|
| Cash Inflows (Rs.) | 3.45 | 3.45 | 3.45 | 103.45 | |
| Discounting Factor | 0.9710 | 0.9411 | 0.9121 | 0.8840 | |
| PV of CFs | 3.3501 | 3.2468 | 3.1467 | 91.4473 | 101.1908 |
| PV × Time | 3.1453 | 6.2952 | 9.2478 | 360.2006 | 378.8890 |

*Source*: All tables in this chapter are created by the author unless otherwise stated.

Duration in number of semi-annual periods = 378.8890/101.1908 = 3.7443
Duration in years = 3.7443/2 = 1.8722 Years.

MS-Excel function, as described above, can also be used to estimate the Macaulay duration measure, straightway in years, by providing the values of the necessary parameters, such that:

$= DURATION(\text{Settlement, Maturity, Coupon, Yld, Frequency, [Basis]})$

$= DURATION(24\text{-Jul-}2017, 13\text{-Jul-}2019, 6.90\%, 6.3610\%, 2, 4)$

$= 1.8722 \text{ Years}$

Therefore, the average maturity of the bond is 1.8722 years, within which the bond investor is expected to get his original investment, i.e. the price of the bond, back, irrespective of the change in the market rate of interest. Throughout the maturity of the bond, any change in rate of interest may cause reinvestment gain and price risk, or reinvestment loss and price gain. But the gain in one may not completely offset the loss in another. If the bond is held exactly till its duration (not till the maturity), the rise (fall) in reinvestment income completely offsets the fall (rise) in the present value of future cash flows due to any rise (fall) in interest rates. Therefore, the Macaulay duration is the average economic lifetime of all future cash flows adjusted for the time value of money.

## Modified duration

Modified duration (MD) is a modified version of Macaulay duration. Modified duration follows the concept that interest rates and bond prices move in opposite direction. It refers to the change in value of the security to one per cent (100 basis points) change in interest rates (yield). A formula that expresses the measurable change in the value of a security in response to a change in interest rates is expressed as under:

$$MDuration = \left[ MacaulayDuration \Big/ \left(1 + \frac{YTM}{k}\right) \right]$$

$$Modified\_Duration = \left[ \left\{ \sum_{i=1}^{n} t_i \times \left( PVCF_i \Big/ \sum_{i=1}^{n} PVCF_i \right) \times 1/k \right\} \times \{1/(1 + YTM/k)\} \right]$$

$$(7.3)$$

Mathematically, m-duration is the relative price change, i.e. the first order differentiation of the bond price function $[P=f(r)]$, and can also be derived as:

$$M - Duration = \frac{1}{P} \times \frac{dP}{dr} = \frac{1}{P} \times \sum_{i=1}^{n} -i \times \frac{C_i}{(1+r)^{(i+1)}} \qquad (7.4)$$

where $P = \sum_{i=1}^{n} \frac{C_i}{(1+r)^i}$

Like Macaulay duration, modified duration can also be calculated in MS-Excel by using the following function230a:

$$= MDURATION(Settlement, Maturity, Coupon, Yld, Frequency, [\textbf{Basis}])$$

Where the inputs are exactly the same as required for estimating the Macaulay duration described in the previous section.

### Example

The above example may be used to estimate the m-duration of the bond (6.90 GS 2019). Accordingly, m-duration may be estimated as:

$$\text{M-Duration} = \text{Duration } (1 + YTM / k) = 1.8722 / (1 + 6.3610\% / 2)$$
$$= 1.8144\%.$$

The same can also be estimated through the MS-Excel function, shown above, such that:

$$= MDURATION(\text{Settlement, Maturity, Coupon, Yld, Frequency, [Basis]})$$
$$= MDURATION(24 - Jul - 2017, 13 - Jul - 2019, 6.90\%, 6.3610\%, 2, 4)$$
$$= 1.8144\%$$

Therefore, the approximate fall (rise) in a bond price due to the possible rise (fall) in yield is such that:

$$\text{Price Change} = (- \text{M-Duration}) * (- \text{Expected Yield Change})$$
$$* \text{Current Market Price}$$

In the present example, the absolute change in price of the concerned bond due to a 2% rise in yield is such that:

$$\text{Price Change} = -1.8144\% \times (+2\% \times 100) \times 100.98 = -\textbf{Rs} \times \textbf{3.6644} / -$$

### Effective duration

Effective duration is like the modified duration measure, but it is used to capture the interest rate risk of a bond, where the number of future cash flows are uncertain, i.e. a bond with an embedded option (call or put). Alternatively, effective duration is the percentage price change of a bond with embedded option (i.e. callable or puttable bond) due to a 1% change in the rate of interest. Effective duration is calculated as:

$$D = \left(P_{-dY} - P_{+dY}\right) / \left(2 \times P_0 \times dY\right) \tag{7.5}$$

Where, $P_{-dy}$, $P_{+dy}$, $P_0$, and $dY$ respectively represent the new price when yield is expected to fall, the new price when yield is expected to rise, original price, and the change in yield. The pricing of a bond with an embedded option cannot be done simply based on the summation of discounted values of future cash flows, as in case of option-free bonds, as is done through the simple *PRICE* function in MS-Excel. The pricing here needs to be based on a framework where interest rate volatility is duly captured in the bond pricing mechanism, preferably through an option pricing framework like binomial option pricing model. It may be noted here that, the modified duration for a simple option-free bond can be alternatively calculated from the above formula by considering the normal bond pricing method. Therefore, effective duration can be used as a proxy measure for modified duration (of an option-free bond), but modified duration cannot capture the effective duration (of bonds with embedded options).

## Example

Considering the above case, a government of India dated security (6.90 GS 2019) paying a coupon of 6.90% p.a., payable semi-annually, maturing on 13 July 2019, currently (as on 24 July 2017) traded at Rs.100.98/- and at a yield of 6.3610%. Effective-cum-modified duration, expected to be almost the same, can be calculated as:

$$ED = \left( P_{-dY} - P_{+dY} \right) / \left( 2 \times P_0 \times dY \right)$$
$$= (102.8379 - 99.1654) / (2 \times 100.98 \times 1\%) = 1.8184\%$$

If values of both the duration measures (m-duration and effective duration) for the given security (6.90 GS 2019) are compared, there is just a small deviation, after two decimal points. The m-duration for the security is 1.8144%, whereas the same through the effective duration, the proxy for m-duration, is 1.8184%. Therefore, the effective duration measure can be used as a reasonable proxy of m-duration.

Effective duration can also be estimated, as commonly observed in the market, through the simple m-duration process, but by reducing the maturity of the bond with call (put) option simply to the first call (put) date, assuming that the option will be exercised in the very first call (put) date. But the reliability of such a proxy measure is really questionable.

## M-duration of floating rate bond

Since the coupon rate of a floating rate bond gets reset in every reset period, for example in every 6 months, it behaves like a zero coupon bond within every reset period. Therefore, the duration of a floating rate bond, without any spread/margin above the reference rate, is just the time period left till the next coupon reset date. Suppose if the coupon rate of an FRB is going to be reset in next 1 month time, the duration of that FRB at that point of time is just 1 month or 0.0833 years. However, a floating rate bond carrying a spread can be represented as a portfolio of two bonds with a coupon equal to the reference rate and the spread over the reference rate. The duration of the second part, i.e. the spread, can be calculated as with other fixed rate bonds. Accordingly, the m-duration can be estimated, considering the market yield for the bond.

### Price value of a basis point (PVBP or PV01

The price value of a basis point (PVBP), alternatively known as PV01, describes the actual change in price of a bond if the yield changes by one basis point (1%/100), such that

$$PVBP \text{ or } PV01 = M - Duration \times 0.0001 \times Price \qquad (7.6)$$

PV01 tells us how much value (in absolute terms) a position or a portfolio will gain or lose for a 0.01% or 1 basis point parallel movement in the yield curve. It therefore quantifies interest rate risk for small changes in interest rates and also in absolute value. It is often used as a price alternative to duration or m-duration (a time or percentage measure). The higher the PV01, the higher would be the volatility (sensitivity of price to change in yield).

### Example

From the modified duration (given in the above example), we know that the security value will change by 1.8144% for a 100-basis point (1%) change in the yield. In value terms, that is equal to 1.8144*(100.98/100) = Rs.1.832 2. Hence, the PV01 = 1.8322/100 = Rs.0.0183/-, which is 1.83 paise. Thus, if the yield of a bond with a modified duration of 1.8144% moves from its present yield of 6.3610% to say 6.4110% (increase by 5 basis points), the price of the bond moves from Rs.100.98 to Rs.100.8884 (reduction of 9.16 paise, i.e. 5 × 1.83 paise).

### Portfolio sensitivity measure

Price sensitivity of individual securities can be ultimately converted into a portfolio measure, known as *Portfolio Modified Duration*, or *Portfolio PV01*. The weighted average of the M-duration of all the securities in the portfolio can be considered to measure the price sensitivity of the bond portfolio to change in interest rates, such that:

$$M \cdot Duration_p = w_1 MD_1 + w_2 MD_2 + w_3 MD_3 + \ldots\ldots\ldots + w_k MD_k$$

Here, m-durations of each security is weighted by the proportion of the portfolio in that security in terms of its current market value. So, if 75%

of a portfolio is in a security with a m-duration of 6%, and 25% is in a security with a m-duration of 8%, then the m-duration of the portfolio is $(6\% \times 0.75) + (8\% \times 0.25) = 6.5\%$. This figure suggests that if there is a 1% rise (fall) in the rate of interest, the value of the portfolio is going to fall (rise) by 6.5% of its current market value. Accordingly, a portfolio manager may construct a bond portfolio that is less sensitive to uncertain fluctuation of interest rates by reducing concentration on securities with higher m-duration. Similarly, security-wise PV01 can be simply added together to get the portfolio PV01, which represents the change in the market value of the entire portfolio due to 1 basis point change in the interest rate. A portfolio manager may like to have an optimum mixture of securities in their portfolio, depending on their concern about both risk and return.

*Example*

Suppose a portfolio manager, as on 17 December 2018, holds a government security portfolio of four very liquid government securities of different maturities with a total market value of INR 949.12 crores (face value of INR 1000 crore). The details of individual positions are given hereunder. The portfolio manager may like to estimate the possible losses on this particular portfolio due to a change in interest rates.

Once the interest rate sensitivity (duration, m-duration, PV01) for individual positions is estimated, the portfolio level sensitivity can be arrived at by taking the weighted average of the individual measure, as estimated below and shown in the following table (Table 7.2):

$$M\text{-}Duration_{Portfolio} = (8.4544 \times 464.10/949.12) + (6.6723 \times 287.22/949.12)$$
$$+ (7.0169 \times 99.45/949.12) + (4.0854 \times 98.35/949.12)$$
$$= 7.3117\%$$

$$PV01_{Portfolio} = 0.3924 + 0.1916 + 0.0698 + 0.0402 = INR\ 0.6940\ Crores$$

$$Alternatively,\ PV01_{Portfolio} = M\text{-}Duration_{Portfolio} \times Market\ Value_{Portfolio} \div 100$$
$$= 7.3117\% \times 949.12 \div 100$$
$$= INR\ 0.6940\ Crores$$

Therefore, the portfolio manager is expected to lose INR 69.3968 crore (7.3117% of INR 949.12 crore) due to 1% rise in the rate of interest, and the same loss will be just INR 0.6940 crore for every one basis point rise in the interest rates. The portfolio loss is estimated to be INR 3.47 crore (INR 0.6940 × 5) for every 5 basis points rise in interest rates. Since m-duration is a percentage measure, the portfolio sensitivity measure can be estimated by taking the weighted average of the security-wise m-duration. But PV01 is an absolute sensitivity measure, and therefore security-wise PV01 can

*Table 7.2* Estimation of portfolio sensitivity measures

Bond Portfolio Composition as on 17 January 2018

| Portfolio | Market Value (Cr.) | Res. Mat. (Years) | Duration (Years) | M-Duration (%) | PV01 (Rs. in Crore) |
|---|---|---|---|---|---|
| 6.68% GS 2031 | 464.10 | 13.6667 | 8.7726 | 8.4544 | 0.3924 |
| 6.79% GS 2027 | 287.22 | 9.3278 | 6.9202 | 6.6723 | 0.1916 |
| 7.17% GS 2028 | 99.45 | 9.9750 | 7.2712 | 7.0169 | 0.0698 |
| 6.84% GS 2022 | 98.35 | 4.9222 | 4.2333 | 4.0854 | 0.0402 |
| Portfolio Measure | 949.12 | | 7.5843 | 7.3117 | 0.6940 |

be simply summed-up to arrive at the portfolio PV01, but with the same assumption of equal change in interest rates for all securities.

## Limitations of duration/m-duration/PV01

Duration, m-duration, and PV01 are widely used as the important bond price sensitivity measures to interest rate fluctuations. There is no doubt that the modified duration measure can easily capture the interest rate risk of a fixed income security. But percentage change in the bond's price due to change in interest rates as captured by these measures and the actual price change may or may not be the same. Such difference, if found to be large, may lead these measures to be un-useful and irrelevant. Consistency between the estimates of price change as depicted by these measures and the actual change depends upon the degree of change in the rate of interest. Bond price sensitivity estimated through modified duration differs significantly with actual in case of large interest rate shock. On the other hand, while measuring the interest rate sensitivity at the portfolio level, it is not justified to expect a similar change in the yield of various tenors. More specifically, the limitations of these sensitivity measures are:

### Linearity in the price-yield relations

Duration, m-duration, and PV01 assume a linear relation between the bond price and yield. Alternatively, the rate of change in the price of a bond is constant for every similar change, irrespective of the direction, in the yield or rate of interest, leading to the price-yield curve as a downward-sloping straight line. But the presence of non-linearity in the price-yield behavior makes this sensitivity measure less useful, especially in certain circumstances. This non-linearity causes a different change in price even if yield is expected to change by a similar amount. The impact of this non-linear price-yield relation is more prominent in case of a large change in the yield, as shown in the following example. A market like in India may comfortably capture interest rate risk in their bond portfolio through these measures only because the interest rates are not sufficiently volatile, and therefore may change by a smaller magnitude.

## Example

Suppose a portfolio manager is trying to understand the non-linearity in the price-yield behavior of 6.79% GS 2027, a government of India security maturing on 15 May 2027, currently (as on 17 January 2018) traded at INR 95.7340 and at a yield of 7.43%; and with m-duration of 6.6722%.

Suppose the manager held a total position of INR 10 crore (face value) in that particular security. In order to show the impact of non-linearity in the estimation of interest rate sensitivity of fixed coupon option-free security, the portfolio manager decided to estimate the change (fall and rise) in the market value of the said position under various interest rate scenarios, as suggested by the m-duration measure, assuming linearity in the price-yield behavior, and also based on the actual change in the value assuming a non-linear price-yield curve. The following table (Table 7.3) clearly exhibits that under the linearity assumption, the fall (rise) in the value of the position due to rise (fall) in yield are going to remain the same, and therefore shows a zero difference under any interest rate scenarios. On the other hand, if the linearity assumption is relaxed, the fall (rise) in value of the position for similar rise (fall) in yield are going to be different under different interest rate scenarios, and such differences increase as the magnitude of change in interest rate increases (from no change to 1% change). This confirms the increasing impact of non-linearity for a larger change in interest rates.

*Table 7.3* Impact of non-linearity for different changes in IR

| Scenarios (Change in IR) | M-Duration | Fall (Rise) in Value due to Rise (Fall) in IR with Linearity | Difference in Change in Value with Linearity | Actual Fall in Value due to Rise in IR | Actual Rise in Value due to Fall in IR | Difference in Change in Actual Value with Non-Linearity |
|---|---|---|---|---|---|---|
| 0.00% | 6.6722% | 0 | 0 | 0 | 0 | 0 |
| 0.01% | 6.6722% | 63876 | 0 | 64629 | 64684 | 55 |
| 0.05% | 6.6722% | 319379 | 0 | 322592 | 323970 | 1378 |
| 0.10% | 6.6722% | 638758 | 0 | 643813 | 649325 | 5512 |
| 0.25% | 6.6722% | 1596895 | 0 | 1599310 | 1633763 | 34453 |
| 0.50% | 6.6722% | 3193791 | 0 | 3164970 | 3302803 | 137833 |
| 1.00% | 6.6722% | 6387581 | 0 | 6198451 | 6750110 | 551659 |

*Parallel shift in yield curve*

For the portfolio sensitivity measures (portfolio m-duration, portfolio PV01) to be meaningful, it needs to be ensured that the interest rate shock should be same for all securities, i.e. the portfolio m-duration measure exhibits the interest sensitivity in the market value of the whole portfolio following a fixed 100-basis-point change in the yield of all the securities, irrespective of their maturities. Alternatively, if there is any change (positive or negative) in the rate of interest for any tenor, all possible rates are expected to change in the same direction and also by a similar magnitude. This property of term structure of interest rates is known as *Parallel Shift* in the yield curve. If the yield points change by different magnitudes depending on their respective maturities, then this bond portfolio sensitivity measure may fail to capture the interest rate risk correctly. In general, short- and medium-term interest rates are expected to be more volatile than the long-term rates in normal market conditions, leading to a different change in the yield points depending on their maturities, and therefore an *Unparallel Shift* in the yield curve. In such case, another sensitivity measure, known as *Key Rate Duration*, may be useful. Key rate duration captures the price effect due to a change in yield for a specific maturity of the yield curve, holding other yields constant. Therefore, there may be several interest rate sensitivity estimates depending on the key yield points on the yield curve, and these multiple risk estimates may be taken into consideration to capture the interest rate risk of a bond portfolio consisting of various securities throughout the yield curve.

## Convexity: a supplement to m-duration

M-duration is a linear measure of how the price of a bond changes in response to any change in interest rates. As interest rates change, the price is not likely to change linearly, instead it would change over some curved function of interest rates. The more curved the price function of the bond is, the more inaccurate m-duration is as a measure of the interest rate sensitivity. This feature of the price-yield curve is known as *Convexity*. Alternatively, *Convexity* is a measure of the curvature of how the price of a bond varies with interest rate. This is the change in m-duration of a bond for per unit change in the bond yield. Presence of convexity makes the modified duration measure overestimate the fall in price due to a certain rise in yield and underestimate the rise in price due to a similar fall in yield, especially for a significant change in the yield. Relative convexity (RC) can be measured as:

$$RC = \frac{d^2P}{dr^2} \times \frac{1}{P} = \frac{1}{P} \times \sum_{i=1}^{n} i \times (i+1) \times \frac{C_i}{(1+r)^{(i+2)}} \tag{7.8}$$

Where, P, r, i, and C respectively represent bond price, concerned yield, time, and cash flows. Convexity can be both positive and negative. A bond with *positive convexity* will not have any option (call or put) features – i.e. the issuer must redeem the bond at maturity. On the other hand, a bond with call features – i.e. where the issuer can redeem the bond early – is deemed to have *negative convexity*. Convexity can be alternatively calculated as:

$$Convexity = \left[ \{P_{-dY} + P_{+dY} - 2P_0\} / \{2 \times P_0 \times dY^2\} \right] \qquad (7.9)$$

Where, $P_{-dY}$, $P_{+dY}$, $P_0$, and $dY$ represent respectively the new price when yield is expected to fall, new price when yield is expected to rise, original price, and the change in yield. Once security specific convexities are estimated, the portfolio convexity can be arrived at by taking the weighted average of individual convexities. The relative convexity measure, once converted into a measure called *Convexity Adjustment* (relative convexity multiplied by the square of change in yield, i.e. RC × Δy^2), can be further used to understand the bond price sensitivity with more accuracy and precision. This is the estimate which needs to be adjusted with the m-duration of the concerned security/portfolio to get the true sensitivity measure, after considering the non-linearity of the price-yield relationship. This measure is known as convexity-adjusted modified duration. Therefore, a change in a bond's price due to any change in yield, after adjusting for the convexity, can be calculated as:

$$\Delta P/P = \{-MD \times \Delta y\} + \{RC \times (\Delta y)^2\} \qquad (7.10)$$

## Example

Suppose, as per the above example, the value of the government security portfolio, consisting of four GOI securities, as on 17 January 2018, stands at Rs.949.12 crore, with a portfolio m-duration and convexity of 7.3117% and 37.7215 respectively. The portfolio sensitivity to any change in interest rates, depending upon only m-duration and m-duration and convexity both, can be estimated as follows:

Fall (rise) in the value of the portfolio due to 1% rise (fall) in interest rates, as per m-duration = 7.3117% × INR 949.12 crore = INR 69.3968 crore.

But after adjusted with the convexity (i.e. convexity adjustment which is 0.3772%), the relative change (fall/rise) in the value of the portfolio, due to rise (fall) in interests is:

$$\Delta P/P = \{-7.3117\% \times (+1)\} + \{37.7215 \times (1\%)^2\} = -6.9345\%$$

$$\Delta P/P = \{-7.3117\% \times (-1)\} + \{37.7215 \times (1\%)^2\} = +7.6890\%$$

The above numbers clearly indicate that the actual fall in the value of securities, and therefore the whole portfolio, due to a certain rise in the rate of interest, is relatively smaller than the rise in their value, due to a similar fall in the rate of interest. Therefore, even if the m-duration measure indicates a similar change (7.3117%) in the value of the portfolio, irrespective of the rise or fall in interest, the convexity adjusted m-durations measure show a 6.9345% fall in the value of the portfolio due to a 1% rise in interest rates, and 7.6890% rise in the value of the portfolio due to a 1% fall in the rate of interests. These clearly indicate that the convexity measure helps to reduce the overestimation of losses under a regime of rising interest rates, and underestimation of gains under a falling interest rate regime, and thereby ensure opportunity gains for the portfolio manager under any circumstances.

Now there may always be a question in the mind of the users, that "*Does this m-duration measure always fail to correctly estimate the possible change in the bond price due to any change in interest rates?*". Alternatively, "*Does this convexity measure always add a significant value by managing overestimation of losses and underestimation of gains due to any change in bond yield?*". The answer is, "*Not necessarily*". If the fall (rise) in value of a position in say a government security, separately estimated through m-duration and convexity adjusted m-duration, is compared with the actual change in the value of that position, under various interest rate scenarios, i.e. for different levels of rise (fall) in the bond yield, as shown in the following table (Table 7.4), we may be in a better position to give a suitable answer. The following table (representing 6.79% GS 2027maturing on 15 May 2027, traded at a yield of 7.43% and at a price of INR 95.7340 as on 17 January 2018) clearly exhibits that, using the m-duration measure, the amount towards overestimation of losses and underestimation of gains respectively due to rise and fall in bond yields is very negligible for a small change in interest rates, and gradually increases as the change in interest rates becomes stronger. The amount of loss (gain) overestimated (underestimated) due to rise (fall) in interest rate by 1 basis point is just INR 276, which may increase to more than INR 2.75 lakhs for a 100-basis-point change in interest rate. This confirms the fact that convexity proves to be a valuable supplement to the m-duration measure while capturing the interest rate sensitivity of any position in bonds when bond yields are expected to change by a relatively bigger number. For any small yield shocks, a bond portfolio manager is indifferent towards selection of m-duration or convexity-adjusted m-duration as a right measure to capture the interest rate sensitivity of his portfolio.

The above facts can also be explained through the following figure (Figure 7.4). The following figure clearly demonstrates the price/yield relationship for different changes in the yield, captured by different sensitivity measures. The lines in the figure are nothing but the price/yield curve, as captured by m-duration (Line capturing Price Movements-Duration Based)), and m-duration adjusted with the convexity (Line capturing Price Movements-Convexity

*Table 7.4* Importance of convexity in measuring IR sensitivity

| Scenarios (Rise in IR) | M-Duration | Convexity | Convexity Adjustments due to change in IR | Convexity Adj. M-Duration (due to Rise in IR) | Convexity Adj. M-Duration (due to Fall in IR) | Overestimated Loss due to Rise in IR (in Rs.) | Underestimated Gain due to Fall in IR (in Rs.) |
|---|---|---|---|---|---|---|---|
| 0.00% | 6.67% | 28.81 | 0.0000% | 6.6722% | 6.6722% | 0 | 0 |
| 0.01% | 6.67% | 28.81 | 0.0000% | 6.6722% | 6.6722% | 276 | 276 |
| 0.05% | 6.67% | 28.81 | 0.0007% | 6.6715% | 6.6729% | 6896 | 6896 |
| 0.10% | 6.67% | 28.81 | 0.0029% | 6.6693% | 6.6751% | 27583 | 27583 |
| 0.25% | 6.67% | 28.81 | 0.0180% | 6.6542% | 6.6902% | 172393 | 172393 |
| 0.50% | 6.67% | 28.81 | 0.0720% | 6.6002% | 6.7442% | 689574 | 689574 |
| 1.00% | 6.67% | 28.81 | 0.2881% | 6.3841% | 6.9603% | 2758296 | 2758296 |

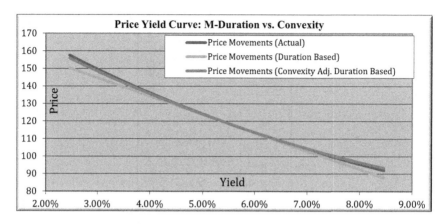

*Figure 7.4* Importance of convexity in measuring IR sensitivity

Adj. Duration Based), which are compared with the actual price/yield curve (Line capturing Price Movements-Actual). It is very clear that there is a significant difference between the m-duration-based price/yield curve and the actual curve, especially when the change (positive or negative) in yield is significantly larger, let's say from an existing level of 5%. However, both curves depict the same picture when the change is relatively very small, say by 100 basis points. On the other hand, if the convexity factor is adjusted with the m-duration, the resultant price/yield curve, due to any change (small or big, and/or positive or negative) in the yield, is very similar and close to the actual price/yield curve. This clearly shows the importance of convexity in capturing the interest rate sensitivity of fixed income instruments without any significant error (overestimation of losses due to rise in yield/underestimation of gains due to fall in yield). It may be noted here that, inclusion of the convexity measure may not add any value in capturing the interest rate sensitivity when the change in interest rates are relatively small. But inclusion of such a measure may lead to some relief in the market risk capital charge required to be maintained on a fixed income portfolio.

## Interest rate sensitivity of a bond portfolio: a case

Suppose the State Bank of India, as on 27 July 2018, holds AFS positions in 20 dated securities (GOI bonds, SDLs, and non-government securities), both liquid as well as illilquid, as given in the case study included in the previous chapter (Chapter 6) on *"Pricing and Valuation Techniques"*.

The risk management department (Treasury Mid Office) of the bank may like to analyze how sensitive their debt portfolio is in the present regime of rising interest rates so that the bank can adopt a better strategy depending upon its future interest rate views. The risk manager may like to consider the following points while analyzing the interest rate sensitivity of the bond portfolio.

1 Various interest rate sensitivity measures (e.g. *duration*, *modified duration*, and *PV01*) may be used to understand the risk that all the individual positions and the whole portfolio are exposed due to change in interest rates or bond yields.
2 Even if the bank presently uses m-duration to estimate the IR risk on its debt portfolio, the risk manager may like to explore the impact of using *Convexity* as a supplement to m-duration in capturing the interest rate risk in the whole bond portfolio. Can the bank get any capital relief in its general interest rate risk capital charge simply after using convexity in capturing the IR sensitivity of the bank's bond portfolio?
3 Since the yield levels are continuously rising for almost a year and are expected to rise further, the risk manager may like to do some scenario analysis where they are interested in estimating the possible amount of losses that the bank is likely to incur in its portfolio due to few possible chan ges (say 10 bps, 50 bps, 75 bps, 100 bps, and 200 bps) in risk-free interest rates/GOI yield, assuming a *Parallel Shift* in the yield curve. The manager may like to estimate these possible future losses using *Various Sensitivity Measures* and would like to justify the current practices presently used by the banking system in India towards the use of a particular measure in capturing the IR risk in debt portfolio.
4 The risk manager may like to do a critical analysis of various sensitivity measures so that they can propose the suitable measure to capture the IR risk of the bank's debt portfolio, especially under very uncertain market conditions, and also in a situation when banks are struggling to manage the required capital under the new Basel norms.

## Self-learning exercise

1 Explain how the basic features of a bond (i.e. maturity, coupon rate, and frequency) affect a bond's sensitivity to any change in interest rates.

2 Distinguish among alternative interest rate sensitivity measures and explain their suitability to capture/manage the interest rate risk in investments in particular and banking business in general.

3 How is the Macaulay duration measure useful to a bond portfolio manager? Other than bond portfolio management, do you think this measure has any other use in commercial banking?

4 How do you differentiate between modified duration and PV01? Which measure is commonly used in the market to measure the IR risk and why?

5 An investor has invested in two GOI dated securities with similar maturities, but of types: fixed and floating rate. How does the IR sensitivity of both the bonds differ from each other? What will be the duration of the FRB?

6 How is the price of a fixed rate option free bond sensitive to change in yield? Does the same relationship hold for a fixed rate bond with a call or put option?

7 Why is effective duration the most appropriate measure to capture interest rate risk in bonds with embedded options?

8 "If two portfolios have the same duration, the change in their value when interest rates change will be the same." Explain why you agree or disagree with this statement.

9 Can there be any possibility of interchangeably when using the m-duration and effective duration measures to capture the IR risk of an option-free bond and a bond with call option?

10 What are the limitations of using m-duration as a measure of a bond's price sensitivity to interest-rate changes?

11 Describe the yield-curve risk and explain why m-duration does not account for yield-curve risk for a portfolio of bonds. Explain with graphs.

12 What is the convexity of a bond and how is it estimated? How is it useful in capturing the IR sensitivity of the bond?

13 How is the convexity measure adjusted with m-duration to estimate the IR risk of a bond?

14 "M-Duration can successfully capture the IR risk of a debt security/ portfolio without considering convexity, as presently followed in developing markets like in India." Is it true under any circumstances?

15 Is it desirable for a bond portfolio manager to use convexity along with m-duration only when the portfolio manager is expected to lose in his/ her bond position due to rise in interest rates?

## Bibliography

Barber, J. R., and Copper, M. L. (1997). Is Bond Convexity a Free Lunch? *Journal of Portfolio Management*, 24(1), 113–119.

Barrett, W., Gosnell, T. Jr., and Heuson, A. (1995). Yield Curve Shifts and the Selection of Immunization Strategies. *Journal of Fixed Income*, 5(2), 53–64.

Bierwag, G. O. (1977). Immunization, Duration and the Term Structure of Interest Rates. *Journal of Financial and Quantitative Analysis*, 12, 725–742.

Bierwag, G. O. (1987). *Duration Analysis: Managing Interest Rate Risk*. Ballinger Publishing Company, Cambridge, MA.

Bierwag, G. O., Kaufman, G. G., and Toevs, A. (1983). Duration: Its Development and Use in Bond Portfolio Management. *Financial Analysts Journal*, 39, 15–35.

Chambers, D. R., and Nawalkha, S. K. (eds.). (1999). *Interest Rate Risk Measurement and Management*. Institutional Investor, New York.

Chance, D. M., and Jordan, J. V. (1996). Duration, Convexity, and Time as Components of Bond Returns. *Journal of Fixed Income*, 6(2), 88–96.

Christensen, P. O., and Sorensen, B. G. (1994). Duration, Convexity and Time Value. *Journal of Portfolio Management*, 20(2), 51–60.

Fabozzi, F. (2005). *Fixed Income Mathematics: Analytical and Statistical Techniques* (4th edn.). McGraw-Hill Companies, Inc., New York.

Fabozzi, F. (2007a). *Duration, Convexity, and Other Bond Risk Measures* (1st edn.). John Wiley & Sons, Inc., Hoboken, NJ.

Fabozzi, F. (2007b). *Fixed Income Analysis* (2nd edn.). John Wiley & Sons, Inc., Hoboken, NJ.

Fabozzi, F. (ed.). (July 2017). *The Handbook of Fixed Income Securities* (8th edn.). McGraw Hill Education, New York.

Grantier, B. J. (1988). Convexity and Bond Performance: The Benter the Better. *Financial Analysts Journal*, 44(6), 79–81.

Ho, T. S. Y. (1992). Key Rate Durations: Measures of Interest Rate Risks. *Journal of Fixed Income*, 2(2), 29–44.

Martellini, L., Priaulet, P., and Priaulet, S. (2002). Beyond Duration. *Journal of Bond Trading and Management*, 1(2), 103–119.

Martellini, L., Priaulet, P., and Priaulet, S. (2003). *Fixed-Income Securities: Valuation, Risk Management and Portfolio Strategies* (1st edn.). John Wiley & Sons, Inc., Hoboken, NJ.

Rendleman, R. J. (1999). Duration-Based Hedging With Treasury Bond Futures. *Journal of Fixed Income*, 9(1), 84–91.

Tuckman, B. (2011). *Fixed Income Securities: Tools for Today's Markets* (3rd edn.). John Wiley & Sons, Inc., Hoboken, NJ.

Veronesi, P. (2011). *Fixed Income Securities: Valuation, Risk and Risk Management*. John Wiley & Sons, Inc., Hoboken, NJ.

# 8 Financial derivative contracts

Key learning outcomes

At the end of this chapter, readers are expected to be familiar with:

- Various concepts of derivatives markets and products: exchange traded vs. OTC market; forwards, futures, swaps, and options (call and put).
- Present status of financial derivatives markets worldwide and in India.
- Role of derivatives as a "useful financial innovation" and as a "weapon of mass destruction".
- Estimation of payoffs to buyer and seller.
- Advantages/uses of derivatives contracts.
- Risks in and risk management of different types of derivative instruments.

## Financial derivatives: meaning & types of contracts

A derivative may be defined as a financial instrument whose value depends on the value of another underlying asset. The International Monetary Fund (IMF) defines derivatives as:

financial instruments that are linked to a specific financial instrument or indicator or commodity and through which specific financial risks can be traded in financial markets in their own right. The value of a financial derivative derives from the price of an underlying item such as an asset or index. Unlike debt securities, no principal is advanced to be repaid and no investment income accrues.

According to the International Accounting Standard (IAS 39):

[A] derivative is a financial instrument: (i) whose value changes in response to the change in a specified interest rate, security price, commodity price, foreign exchange rate, index of prices or rates, a credit rating or credit index, or similar variable; (ii) that requires no initial net investment or little initial net investment relative to other types of contracts that have a similar response to changes in market conditions; and (iii) that is settled at a future date.

Derivatives products can be categorized into different ways, including nature of market where the products are traded, types of underlying on which derivatives are traded, nature of derivative products, etc.

Based on the nature of the markets where the derivative instruments are being traded, they can be classified into two. These are:

### Exchange traded derivatives

A derivative exchange is an organized market where individuals or firms trade derivative products standardized by the exchange. The Chicago Board of Trade (CBOT), being the first derivatives exchange, was established in the year 1848, followed by the Chicago Mercantile Exchange (CME) in 1919. Major exchanges where financial derivatives are traded in India are: *National Stock Exchange* (NSE) of India Ltd., *Bombay Stock Exchange* (BSE), *Multi Commodity Exchange* (MCX), *National Commodity and Derivatives Exchange* (NCDEX), *National Multi Commodity Exchange* (NMCE) of India Ltd., etc. There are two different ways of trading in any exchange: *Open Outcry System* and *Electronic Trading*. Though traditionally the open outcry system was found in most of the exchanges, it has been practically replaced by the electronic trading system in a major number of exchanges all over the world. Exchange traded contracts are standardized, and therefore almost free from counterparty risk. An exchange acts as an intermediary for all transactions, providing a platform to both buyers and sellers where their orders are matched. Once the orders are matched, the exchange becomes the nearest counterparty, i.e. buyer to the seller and seller to the buyer. Since exchanges are a relatively much safer counterparty, such kinds of contracts protect both the buyer and seller against counterparty risk. In order to provide such safety, exchanges take a *Good Faith Deposit*, known as *Initial Margin*, from both the counterparties to ensure that the obligations are duly met by the concerned counterparty. As time passes and the market value of the contract changes, the margin required from the counterparties also undergoes a change, mostly on a day-to-day basis, and the counterparties are also expected to maintain a minimum balance in their margin account. Exchange traded derivatives are usually in the form of a futures or an option contract on various underlying assets, e.g. on equity stocks and indices, commodity, currency, interest rates, etc.

### Over-the-counter derivatives

The over-the-counter market is an important alternative to the formalized exchanges. It is a telephone and computer linked network of dealers who engage in different trades without any physical meeting. Over-the-counter derivatives products are generally traded over the phone and the parties involved in such a trade are usually either two financial institutions, or a financial institution and one of its clients. As far as the most commonly traded instruments are concerned, a financial institution plays the role of a *Market Maker*. In an Over-the-counter market, the telephonic conversations between the two parties are usually taped in order to resolve any future disputes about the agreement made by them. For OTC derivatives, the agreements are usually designed under the framework of an International Swaps and Derivatives Association (ISDA) agreement. Even if counterparty risk is relatively higher in the case of any OTC contracts, possibility of customization, i.e. creating a customized contract depending upon the actual requirement of two counterparties, makes such a contract very popular among the market players. Therefore, the volume of trades in many OTC markets is found to be much larger than the overall trades in the exchange traded market.

As far as the types of underlying are concerned, these are equity, interest rates, currency, commodity, credit, etc. Accordingly, derivatives can also be categorized as equity derivatives, interest rate derivatives, currency derivatives, commodity derivatives, and credit derivatives. These are some broad category of derivative instruments. Each of the above categories may contain different derivative products with a different nature.

The true and final categorization of derivatives is based on the nature of different derivative products traded in the market, either in exchange or at over-the-counter. These are forwards, futures, options, and options on futures and swawps, as shown in the following figure (Figure 8.1). There are again different types of specific instruments under each of these derivative products. A brief about all of these derivatives instruments is discussed in the following sections.

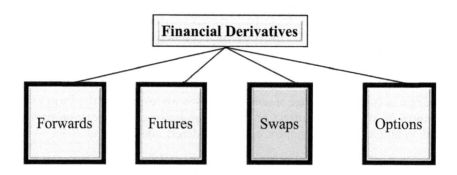

*Figure 8.1* Basic structures of financial derivative contracts

## Forwards

Being the simplest and OTC financial derivative product, a forward contract is a private agreement between two counterparties in which one party (the buyer) agrees to buy from another party (the seller) an underlying asset (e.g. interest rate, foreign currency) on a future date at a price/rate pre-decided at the initiation of the contract. Therefore, it is a commitment between two parties to engage in a bilateral transaction on some future date with a price fixed in advance. The buyer of a forward contract is called the long-position holder, whereas the seller of a forward contract holds the short position.

At the expiry of forward contracts, two possible arrangements can be made to settle the obligation of the counterparties. Accordingly, the two settlement mechanisms are as follows:

- *Physical Delivery*: In this mechanism, the forward contract is settled by the physical delivery of the underlying asset by the seller to the buyer on the agreed upon price while entering into the contract.
- *Cash Settlement*: Alternative to physically settling a forward contract, a long- and short-position holder can settle the net cash value of the position on the delivery date, called cash settlement. There can be three broad possible scenarios at the time of settlement. Depending on what scenario prevails on the expiry date, the net payoffs are determined:
  - Spot Price (ST) > Forward Price (FT): Short holder will pay long holder the difference between spot price and forward price.
  - Spot Price (ST) = Forward Price (FT): The net payoff is zero, i.e. no party needs to pay anything to the other party.
  - Spot Price (ST) < Forward Price (FT): Long holder will pay short holder the difference between the forward price and spot price.

## Futures

Similar to a forward contract, a futures contract is also an agreement between two counterparties wherein the buyer agrees to buy an underlying asset from the seller at a future date at a mutually agreed price decided today. However, unlike forward contracts, futures contracts are traded on recognized stock or derivatives exchanges. In addition, futures contracts are standardized products and can't be customized as in the case of forward deals. Deal specifications, terms and conditions, etc. are all set by the exchange. The buyer and the seller of futures contracts are protected against the counterparty risk by an entity called the Clearing Corporation. Presently, the Indian market experiences financial futures on equities, commodities, foreign currencies (FX) and interest rate products.

The buyer of a futures transaction (called the *Long Position Holder*) agrees to purchase and the seller (*Short Position Holder*) agrees to sell/ deliver a specified item according to the terms of the contract. For example, the buyer of say a "Reliance Industries" stock futures contract commits themselves to purchase at some specified future date (say after one month) a specific number of the "Reliance Industries" shares, paying a price prevailing at the time the contract is purchased.

Forwards and futures contracts are mostly similar, except the fact that the forward contracts are essentially over-the-counter (OTC) contracts traded on a one-to-one basis among the parties involved. The terms of these contracts are decided by the parties mutually at the time of their initiation. If a forward contract is entered into through an exchange, traded on the exchange, and settled through the clearing corporation/house of the exchange, it becomes a futures contract. Futures contracts being standardized contracts appeal to a wide range of market participants, and are therefore very liquid. On the other hand, being a counterparty to all trades in futures deals, the presence of the clearing corporation/house provides an unconditional guarantee for the settlement of all futures deals, thereby ensuring the financial integrity of the entire system. Therefore, although futures contracts take away the flexibility of customization, they offer competitive advantages over the forward contracts in terms of better liquidity and risk management.

### Swaps

A swap is a financial contract exchanging the benefits of two underlying financial contracts for a certain period over the duration of the swap. Periodic payments due to both the counterparties of the contract are based on an agreed-upon amount, called the notional principal amount or simply the *Notional*. Like in the case of other financial derivatives, a swap contract can also be taken on various underlying assets, such as interest rate, foreign currency, commodity, equity, etc. While entering into a swap, the counterparties may (e.g. in case of currency) or may not (e.g. in case of interest rate) exchange the underlying asset (i.e. the principal amount).

### Options

Like forwards and futures contracts, options are derivative instruments that also provide the opportunity to buy or sell an underlying asset on a future date. But unlike forwards and futures, options provide some rights, but only to the buyers. An option is a derivative contract between a buyer and a seller, where one party gives to the other the right, but not the obligation, to buy from (or sell to) the first party the underlying asset on or before a specific day at an agreen-upon price (called the strike price) in exchange of a fee, known as *Option Premium*.

Any option contract has two counterparties: the buyer and the writer.

- The *Buyer* of an option contract has the *Right* to buy/sell an underlying at a pre-decided price (the *Exercise* or *Strike price*) within a certain period of time (*Expiry Date*).
- The *Writer* of an option contract has only the obligation to buy/sell the underlying at a predefined price (the exercise or strike price) within a certain period of time, provided the buyer would like to exercise his/her rights. The writer of an option contract, in return for giving buyer the right, gets a compensation called the option premium.

Options can be of two types: call option and put option. The call option gives the option buyer the right to buy a certain underlying instrument/product from the option seller at the strike price as on the date of expiry. Similarly, the put option gives the buyer the right to sell a certain underlying to the option seller at the strike price at the expiry of the option contract. Option contracts involve three different prices: the price of the underlying known as the spot price, the price at which the delivery or settlement takes place, i.e. the strike price, and the price that is paid to the option writer, i.e. the premium. Options can be again of two types: American and European options. *American* options can be exercised any time up to the expiration date. On the other hand, *European* options can be exercised only as on the date of expiry.

Depending on the price movement of the underlying asset (i.e. P) and its closeness with the strike price (i.e. X), an option contract can again be categorized as:

### In-the-money option

The higher (lower) the price of the underlying, the more likely that $P>X$ ($P<X$), and accordingly, more likely for the call (put) option holder to exercise their rights. The option holder prefers to exercise their option only when the contract generates a positive value to the holder if the same is exercised, and therefore is known as in-the-money option. Therefore, a call (put) option is more likely to be in-the-money, when $P>X$ ($P<X$).

### At-the-money option

The more similar the price of the underlying and the contractual price (i.e. strike price), the more indifferent would be the option holder whether to exercise the option or not. The option holder neither gains nor loses after exercising their rights. If the actual price of the underlying asset at any point of time till the maturity of the contract is not different from the strike price, the option (call and put) is known as an at-the-money option contract.

*Out-of-the-money option*

The lower (higher) the price of the underlying, the less likely that P<X (P>X), and accordingly, unlikely for the call (put) option holder to exercise their rights. The options holder prefers not to exercise their option when the contract fails to generate a positive value (P-X in case of call and X-P in case of put) to the holder if the same is exercised, and therefore is known as an out-of-the-money option. Therefore, a call (put) option is more likely to be out-of-the-money, when P<X (P>X).

## Financial derivatives market: worldwide & in India

The derivatives market worldwide has become an integral part of the financial/capital market, and therefore the financial system of an economy. Even if the derivatives market is not as developed as the underlying securities market in most of the developing or emerging economies, it has gained sufficient popularity, especially after several market crises, including the US subprime crisis. The presence of financial derivatives available on multiple asset classes (e.g. equity, interest rates, currencies, commodities, etc.) in an economy largely depends upon the development and volatility in the underlying market, market awareness of various derivatives products, requirement of institutional investors, necessary financial market regulation, etc. The following tables (Table 8.1 and Table 8.2) exhibit the growth of derivatives market (OTC and Exchange Traded) worldwide and in India. It is invariably observed across the world that the OTC derivatives market, especially after the US subprime crisis, have experiences a slowdown almost in all possible asset classes with some exception. On the other hand, even if exchange traded contracts are not customized, and therefore are not widely popular, still there is positive growth almost for all types of contracts, as experienced from the worldwide figures from the second half of 2017 (H2 2017) to the first half of 2018 (H1 2018).

If we look into the history of the derivatives market in India, it started with equity as the first asset class in June 2000, when the equity index futures were introduced in both the major stock exchanges (NSE and BSE), followed by index options, and then stock options and stock futures all just within a span of almost one and half years. Since then, the equity derivatives market in India has experienced tremendous growth. India is one of the most successful developing countries in terms of a vibrant market for exchange-traded equity derivatives, and presently (in the year 2016) itnstood in the 4th Rank worldwide, after CME Group, EUREX, and CBOE. The following table (Table 8.3) clearly indicates a year-on-year positive growth in equity futures and options segment (in annual turnover) in India, except the year 2015–16. If the latest estimate for the year 2017–18 (till Sep. 2018) is considered, it seems to be quite encouraging, and if the market continues with the same pace, the equity derivatives market in India will

*Table 8.1* OTC derivatives statistics worldwide

Global OTC Derivatives Market

| | Notional Amounts Outstanding (USD Billions) | | | | Gross Market Value (USD Billions) | | | |
|---|---|---|---|---|---|---|---|---|
| | H2 2016 | H1 2017 | H2 2017 | H1 2018 | H2 2016 | H1 2017 | H2 2017 | H1 2018 |
| All Contracts | 482419 | 542439 | 531912 | 594835 | 14948 | 12684 | 10955 | 10326 |
| FX Contracts | 78780 | 88429 | 87117 | 95799 | 3324 | 2627 | 2292 | 2620 |
| Instrument-wise: | | | | | | | | |
| Outright Forwards and FX Swaps | 44226 | 51754 | 50847 | 56416 | 1515 | 1259 | 1111 | 1249 |
| Currency Swaps | 22971 | 24532 | 25535 | 26012 | 1510 | 1160 | 989 | 1155 |
| Options | 11533 | 12088 | 10679 | 13307 | 299 | 208 | 192 | 216 |
| Other Products | 50 | 55 | 56 | 64 | | | | |
| Interest Rate Contracts | 385513 | 435205 | 426648 | 481086 | 10636 | 9046 | 7578 | 6644 |
| Instrument-wise: | | | | | | | | |
| FRAs | 63183 | 75414 | 68334 | 84131 | 243 | 129 | 112 | 107 |
| Swaps | 289103 | 321812 | 318870 | 349761 | 9444 | 8131 | 6747 | 5914 |
| Options | 32823 | 37641 | 39112 | 46833 | 949 | 786 | 719 | 623 |
| Other Products | 404 | 338 | 332 | 361 | | | | |
| Equity-linked Contracts | 6252 | 6964 | 6570 | 7071 | 477 | 524 | 575 | 608 |
| Instrument-wise: | | | | | | | | |
| Forwards and Swaps | 2574 | 2903 | 3210 | 3299 | 160 | 184 | 197 | 228 |
| Options | 3678 | 4061 | 3360 | 3772 | 317 | 340 | 378 | 380 |
| Commodity Contracts | 1,671 | 1,762 | 1,862 | 2,133 | 204 | 171 | 189 | 207 |
| Credit Derivatives | 10,103 | 9,967 | 9,578 | 8,582 | 301 | 307 | 313 | 238 |
| Other Derivatives | 100 | 112 | 137 | 164 | 6 | 9 | 8 | 9 |

*Source:* BIS Statistics

*Table 8.2* Exchange traded derivatives market worldwide

*Global Exchange Traded Derivatives Market*

| Exchange Traded Derivatives Instruments | Total Value Traded (USD Millions) | | |
|---|---|---|---|
| | H1 2017 | H2 2017 | H1 2018 |
| Stock Options | 1684278747 | 1728514493 | 1988640153 |
| Single Stock Futures | 488622935 | 523875602 | 851617852 |
| Stock Index Options | 1574322585 | 1791116620 | 1981451470 |
| Stock Index Futures | 1210961580 | 1245544826 | 160570873 |
| Interest Rate Options | 377481499 | 315260968 | 388050824 |
| Interest Rate Futures | 1650998971 | 1491130662 | 1747665722 |
| Commodity Options | 110874389 | 106989316 | 116610839 |
| Commodity Futures | 2583315002 | 2825555942 | 2575672798 |
| Currency Options | 388030244 | 426310098 | 525679214 |
| Currency Futures | 952822368 | 995672325 | 1158131584 |

*Source*: World Federation of Exchanges

again mark a significant growth, possibly around more than 50% from the last financial year (2016–17).

Even if the equity derivatives market in India continues to mark its significant presence in the worldwide derivatives market, the same may not be true for other derivative contracts available on other asset classes like interest rates, currencies, and commodities. The following table exhibits a mixed growth in the annual turnover in exchange traded derivatives contracts available on these few asset classes. As far as the interest rate futures market in India is concerned, it has again a long history, starting with the notional bond futures contract and also with physical settlement in 2003, followed by the long waited single bond futures contract and Treasury bill futures contract with cash settlement introduced in 2014, after a series of amendments from the regulators and the exchanges. Even if the exchange traded futures market on interest rates and currency products are at a nascent stage in India, the same is expected to experience a reasonable growth in the near future. The same is the case with commodity futures contracts as well, which will also develop, especially in the presence of institutional investors/traders like banks and other NBFCs.

*As far as the OTC derivatives market in India is concerned, the following table (*Table 8.4) exhibits the growth of interest rate products (IRS) over the years. Being the most important product in the IRS market in India, capturing more than 85% of the total notional volume in the year 2017–18, the overnight MIBOR swap market has experienced a tremendous growth almost by 78% (both in terms of number of trades and outstanding notional volume) during the year 2017–18, giving an indication of substantial future growth and developments in the OTC interest rate derivatives segment in India. Even if the interest rate swap on the long-term GOI benchmark rate,

*Table 8.3* Growth of exchange traded derivatives market in India

Growth of Exchange Traded Derivatives Market in India

| Year/ Month | Equity Futures & Options (NSE & BSE) | | Currency Futures & Options (NSE) | | Interest Rate Futures (NSE) | | Commodity Futures at (MCX, NCDEX & NMCE) | |
|---|---|---|---|---|---|---|---|---|
| | No. of Contracts Traded | Turnover (INR Million) | No. of Contracts | Turnover (INR Million) | No. of Contracts | Traded Value (INR crore) | Volume ('000 Tonnes) | Turnover (INR Crore) |
| 2010–11 | 1034217685 | 292483751 | 749602075 | 34497877 | N.A. | N.A. | 1229392 | 11470515 |
| 2011–12 | 1237268289 | 321582088 | 9733344132 | 46749899 | N.A. | N.A. | 1334788 | 17675650 |
| 2012–13 | 1393910784 | 386965220 | 959243448 | 52744647 | N.A. | N.A. | 1382974 | 16656617 |
| 2013–14 | 1570064538 | 474308423 | 660192530 | 40125135 | 1502148 | 30173 | 833932 | 9910596 |
| 2014–15 | 2342520000 | 759691939 | 480664694 | 30239077 | 20587036 | 421558 | 683082 | 6123810 |
| 2015–16 | 2204819789 | 693008426 | 673583164 | 45018856 | 26056481 | 526425 | 1133994 | 6683150 |
| 2016–17 | 1399869667 | 943772410 | 712451439 | 48570759 | 14807039 | 307809 | 917811 | 6490955 |
| Apr.–Sep 2017 | 880902663 | 732545499 | 361465366 | 23686128 | 7324149 | 150096 | 609773 | 4326340 |

*Source:* Indian Securities Market Review, NSE, 2018; SEBI Handbook of Statistics, *SEBI, 2018*

*Table 8.4* Outstanding value in interbank IRS trades in India

Outstanding Value in Interbank IRS Trades (INR Crores)

| Period | MIBOR | | MIFOR | | INBMK | | Total | |
|---|---|---|---|---|---|---|---|---|
| | Trades | Notional Volume | Trades | Notional Volume | Trades | Notional Volume | Trades | Notional Volume |
| 2007–08 | 61665 | 3655595 | 16528 | 611566 | 368 | 13690 | 78561 | 4280852 |
| 2008–09 | 23732 | 1394018 | 11803 | 468045 | 461 | 18715 | 35996 | 1880778 |
| 2009–10 | 29853 | 1748787 | 8201 | 326852 | 450 | 20385 | 38504 | 2096024 |
| 2010–11 | 43197 | 2645709 | 6357 | 270080 | 542 | 26910 | 50096 | 2942699 |
| 2011–12 | 27613 | 1975121 | 6402 | 296491 | 520 | 25910 | 34535 | 2297521 |
| 2012–13 | 20958 | 1554242 | 6017 | 294937 | 489 | 24845 | 27464 | 1874024 |
| 2013–14 | 17782 | 1447259 | 5566 | 276349 | 445 | 22420 | 23793 | 1746028 |
| 2014–15 | 17279 | 1495595 | 6222 | 326724 | 387 | 19320 | 23888 | 1841640 |
| 2015–16 | 16858 | 1368453 | 6171 | 349766 | 272 | 13585 | 23301 | 1731804 |
| 2016–17 | 19901 | 1417357 | 6452 | 368613 | 161 | 8460 | 26514 | 1794430 |
| 2017–18 | 35414 | 2521244 | 7098 | 390259 | 138 | 7135 | 42650 | 2918638 |

*Source*: CCIL Factbook, *2018*

known as the Indian Benchmark (INBMK), swap is also available in India, such contracts lose their popularity over the years, as experienced from the following table.

Other than interest rate futures and swaps, presently available in India, there may be a possibility that Indian market will also experience interest rate options contracts soon.

## Participants in financial derivatives market

There are three broad categories of participants involved in the derivatives market. These are trading participants, intermediary participants, and institutional framework. Hedgers, speculators, and arbitrageurs are the three major participants directly involved in the trading activities in the derivatives market. At the same time, brokers and market makers are involved in intermediary activities. Lastly, the institutional framework includes exchange, clearing house, etc. These are discussed in the following section.

### Hedgers

Hedgers intend to reduce or hedge their risks associated with the prices of different underlying assets by taking positions in the derivative market. Market participants are exposed to unfavorable price movements against which they would like to hedge their underlying position. Thus, a hedger is an entity whose basic objective to enter into the derivative market is to reduce the risks in their underlying position/portfolio.

## Speculators

Speculators wish to anticipate and accordingly bet on the future movements in the prices of underlying assets, and therefore are expected to increase the potential gains in their speculative venture. By taking a position in the market, speculators want to consciously take risks, hoping to make a profit from subsequent price changes. When a market player wants to hedge their risks, there has to be someone who is ready to take the risks; they are treated as speculator. Therefore, they provide the hedgers an opportunity to manage their risks by assuming the same. Speculators are essential to all the markets because they can provide the market a desired level of trading volume and also the high liquidity by their active participation in the market, and therefore are commonly known as *Market Maker*.

## Arbitrageurs

Arbitrage entails the locking in of a costless and riskless profit by simultaneously entering into transactions into two or more markets. Therefore, arbitrageurs expect to take the advantage of any discrepancy between the prices in two different markets – derivative and underlying markets – by taking some offsetting positions in both the markets. When the markets are imperfect, it is possible to make riskless profits by buying in one market and simultaneously selling in another. Arbitrageurs are always on the lookout for such price differences. Though in a perfect market situation, it is difficult to enjoy any arbitrage benefits, in a real life scenario, this does not happen, and arbitrage opportunity exists at least for a short period of time.

## Brokers

A broker performs an important function of bringing buyers and sellers together in exchange of a fee called brokerage. A member of a stock exchange plays the role of a broker. Membership in the exchange confers the broker the right to conduct transactions on behalf of the trading participants. In his role, a broker conducts all transactions and is also responsible for final settlement and delivery. Though a broker won't take any positions in his own account, he is open to the risks of his clients' defaulting. Therefore, the brokerage fee also includes a default risk premium.

## Exchange

An exchange provides the buyers and sellers of a derivative contract the infrastructure needed to execute the trading. In an open outcry system, there is supposed to be a trading floor in the exchange in which the members and their representatives assemble during a fixed trading period and carry out transactions. At the same time, in an online trading system, the exchange provides its members with real-time access to information online and also allows them to execute their orders through online trading platforms.

### Clearing house

A clearing house clears transactions executed in a derivative exchange. It may be a separate company or a part of the exchange. Transactions are conducted between the member and the clearing house and the clearing house ensures the solvency of the members of the exchange. This boosts the confidence of the people in those exchanges.

## Application of financial derivatives

Financial derivatives have achieved their growing popularity for their identical features, and therefore some important advantages to the market. The benefits of derivatives do not equally apply to all derivatives instruments. The application of derivatives instruments can be described as follows:

### Market completeness

In the theory of finance, a complete market is a market in which any and all identifiable payoffs can be obtained by trading the securities available in the market. Financial derivatives play a valuable role in financial markets through bringing completeness in those markets. A financial market, with various derivatives instruments, allows traders to adjust their portfolio as per the risk and return of the portfolio, and thereby increasing the welfare of traders involved in that market.

### Speculation

It is undoubtedly true that the financial derivatives instruments are assumed to be risky, but especially in the hands of uninformed traders. However, those risky derivatives instruments have proved to be a very powerful means for knowledgeable or informed traders who can properly expose themselves, with a complete understanding, to the risks with the hope of earning a higher profit. This is known as speculation. Therefore, an informed trader, by taking a position in one or more derivative market, can enjoy the benefits of a careful and artistic speculation due to an expected change in the value of any underlying asset. Though serving as a speculative tool is not the most important use of derivatives, it helps the financial market to become nearly complete.

### Risk management

Trading in the financial derivatives market helps individuals and firms to reduce their risks faced in the financial markets. Therefore, managing and controlling a certain level of risk in the financial market is one of the important applications of different derivative instruments traded in the market. Though financial derivatives themselves are risky in the sense that their prices are subject to substantial change, they themselves can prove to be a powerful tool limiting risk associated with the underlying. The derivatives market helps to transfer risks from the risk averter to the risk taker or risk lover.

## Trading efficiency

Traders can use a single or a number of financial derivatives products as a substitute for a position in the underlying asset because of a certain trading efficiency in the derivatives market. These may include lower transaction costs, market liquidity, etc. Most often, the transaction costs associated with trading of different financial derivatives products are found to be lower than the cost of trading in the underlying market. At the same time, financial derivatives might be more attractive than the underlying asset because of their greater liquidity. A liquid derivative market with enough trading activity will allow traders to easily trade their asset at almost the true market price. Because of these cost and operational advantages, traders might prefer to enter into the futures and/or options market rather than trading in the underlying cash market.

## Price discovery

Price discovery represents the revealing of information about the future price of different underlying assets, such as equity, interest rate, currency, etc. through their prices in the derivatives market. In the derivatives market, the price that people expect to prevail for an underlying at some delivery date is specified in the derivatives contracts. By using the information contained in today's prices of derivatives, market observers can estimate the expected price of an underlying at a specific time in the future. Therefore, financial derivatives play a very important role in discovering the future prices of underlying assets. Forecasts of future prices drawn from the futures market are quite accurate comparative to the other types of forecasts.

Since versatility is one of the important features of derivative products, it can be used either for hedging, speculation, or for arbitrage. But this versatility may cause a severe problem for the trading entity if there is no proper control in the trading of derivative products. It is quite natural that the strategy of hedging risk or doing some arbitrage may be converted into speculation. This sort of practice may prove to be a serious problem for the trading entity. Therefore, it is expected both for financial and non-financial institutions to have some control in the trading of derivatives and also to make sure that the derivatives are being used only for their intended purpose. It is also mandatory to set up some limit of risk exposure and the day-to-day activities of the trader should also be monitored to ensure that risk exposure is under the specific limit.

## Self-learning exercise

1  How do you define a financial derivative? How are these instruments/ contracts different from underlying assets?
2  How is an over-the-counter derivative product different from an exchange-traded contract? As a user of such a contract, which type of contract would you prefer and why?
3  Even if financial derivatives are named as "*weapon of mass destruction*", why is there a significant market worldwide for such instruments? Do you really believe this? Justify your answer.
4  How do you differentiate between forwards, futures, and options contracts? Can they be invariably used just depending on their availability in the market? If not, explain why.
5  How is the payoff structure, both for buyers and sellers, different between a futures and an option contract. Looking at the payoff, which instrument do you prefer and why? Justify your answer.
6  Differentiate between call and put options. Name a few possible users for these contracts and briefly discuss their requirements that can be fulfilled through these contracts.
7  What are in-the-money, at-the-money, and out-of-the-money options? Out of these, what types of options are costlier for the user and why?
8  How can a derivative transaction be settled? Which method of settlement is most popular and why? Do you support that there has to be only one method of settlement across the markets and products? Justify your answer.
9  Why is the growth of the financial derivatives market in emerging economies like in India relatively very poor? Discuss a few reasons and justify their validity.
10  How are different types of financial derivatives useful for the development of our economy, especially for the commercial banks? Briefly discuss.

## Bibliography

Chance, D. M., and Brooks, R. (2014). *An Introduction to Derivatives and Risk Management* (9th edn.). Cengage Learning, Boston, MA.

Choudhry, M. (2001). *The Bond and Money Markets*. Butterworth-Heinemann, Oxford, UK.

Das, S. (2004). *Swaps/Financial Derivatives: Products, Pricing, Applications and Risk Management* (3rd edn.). John Wiley & Sons, Inc., Hoboken, NJ.

Dubofsky, D., and Miller, T. W. (2007). *Derivatives: Valuation and Risk Management* (2nd edn.). Oxford University Press, Oxford, UK.

Hull, J. C., and Basu, S. (2016). *Options, Futures, and Other Derivatives* (9th edn.). Pearson Education, India.

Janakiramanan, S. (2011). *Derivatives and Risk Management* (1st edn.). Pearson Education, India.

Kolb, R. (2000). *Futures, Options and Swaps.* Blackwell Publishing, Oxford, UK.

Srivastava, R. (2014). *Derivatives and Risk Management* (2nd edn.). Oxford University Press, Oxford, UK.

Whaley, R. E. (2006). *Derivatives: Markets, Valuation and Risk Management* (1st edn.). John Wiley & Sons, Inc., Hoboken, NJ.

# 9 Interest rate futures

**Key learning outcomes**

At the end of this chapter, the readers are expected to answer:

- What is an interest rate futures (IRF) contract, and how does it work?
- What is the history and current status of IRF contracts in India?
- What are the important features of an IRF contract?
- How are single bond futures different from notional bond futures contracts?
- What types of IRF contracts are presently available in an emerging market like India?
- What type of financial institution/entities can use an IRF contract, and how does this contract benefit them?
- How are IRF contracts prices, valued, settled, and prematurely closed?
- How are IRF contracts used for hedging, arbitrage, speculation, and for asset liability management?
- How is the hedge effectiveness of an IRF portfolio ensured?

## Interest rate futures contract: meaning & product structure

Like a simple futures contract, irrespective of the underlying, interest rate futures, short term or long term, are a contract or an agreement between two counterparties, the exchange being the immediate/nearest counterparty to both the buyer and seller, to buy or sell an interest bearing instrument as the underlying asset as on a specific future date at a pre-decided price or rate. The underlying here may be a short-term money market rate (like a 91-day Treasury-bill rate), or a long-term debt instrument/bond. The debt instrument/bond again may be: notional or actual/single. In case of short-term interest rate futures contract, the underlying may be different T-bill rates, like 91 days, 182 days, etc. Similarly, in case of long-term bond futures, the underlying may be any security within a basket of few central government/Treasury bonds, or a single government security traded in the government securities market.

### How does an interest rate futures contract work?

- An interest rate futures (IRF) contract allows the buyer to lock in a future investment rate. IRF are based on an underlying security, which is a debt obligation and moves in value as interest rates change.
- When the interest rate increases, the buyer of a futures contract needs to pay the seller an amount equal to that of the benefit received by investing at a higher rate versus the rate as specified in the futures contract.
- When interest rates fall, the seller of a futures contract is required to compensate the buyer for the lower interest rate at the time of expiration.
- Therefore, in the regime of rising (falling) interest rates, short (long) positions in the IRF contract allow the hedger or trader to hedge their existing underlying position or to make money.
- In bond market, both the prices of the underlying bond and the bond futures move inversely with the movement of interest rates. Any rise (fall) in the rate of interest leads to fall (rise) in the prices of these instruments. Therefore, in order to hedge from the fall in price due to any abnormal rise in the interest rates, a bond holder may like to short the required amount of IRF contract.
- Similarly, a fixed rate lender (borrower) is expected to incur an opportunity loss due to the rising (falling) rate of interest. Therefore, lenders may prefer to enter into a short IRF position if the interest rate increases, whereas borrowers may opt for long IRF positions if they expect the interest rate to fall.
- The benefit of an IRF contract to a trader, i.e. if the contract is not used for hedging an underlying exposure, depends on the correctness of the interest rate view of the trader/users.
- Since IRF is an exchange traded product, the user (buyer or seller) needs to enter into such a contract with the stock/derivatives exchanges, like NSE/BSE/MCX, where buyer's/seller's nearest counterparty is the exchange, not the actual counterparty (buyer/seller of the IRF). Irrespective of the position (buy/sell), both the users need to oblige the contract if the same is hold till the maturity.
- Trading in IRF is a fully automated, screen-based trading, supporting an anonymous order driven market, which operates on a time priority/ strict price basis.
- The trading platforms used for trading in IRF are: NEAT and NOW. NEAT is a lease line/VSAT based platform, whereas NOW is web-based platform.
- User need to deposit an initial margin that act as a good faith deposit to ensure that the counterparties will oblige their contract even if the

market does not move in their favor. Initial margin requirements depend upon the volatility of the underlying price, and therefore the value of the futures contract, as predefined in the contract specification.

- Exchanges send consolidated positions at the end of the day, with day buy/sell figures and final closing position and closing rates for each contract and expiry individually.
- Daily MTM profits/losses are estimated as the difference between the trade or settlement price of the previous day with that of the current day. The clearing members (CMs) who have suffered a loss are required to pay the mark-to-market loss amount to the clearing corporation of the concerned exchange (NSCCL in the case of NSE), which is passed on to the other CMs who have made a profit. MTM profit/loss is cash settled on a T+1-day basis by crediting/debiting the clearing accounts of CMs with the respective clearing bank.
- In order to ensure robust risk management, clearing members, in addition to initial margins, would be subjected to extreme loss margins. Besides these, as a risk containment measure, the clearing corporation may also require clearing members to make payment of additional margins as may be decided from time to time.
- Accordingly, participants in IRF need to maintain sufficient balance in their account maintained with the clearing bank, otherwise a *Margin Call* (if any) may need to be duly honored without fail.
- During the expiry month, IRF contracts are expected to be finally settled either by cash or through physical delivery of deliverable grade securities, depending upon the nature of the contract. In case of notional bond futures contract earlier available in India, they used to be settled through delivery of the deliverable grade securities on the last business day of the delivery month, where the short position holder holds the right to decide which security to be delivered from the deliverable basket. In case of single bond futures, as presently available in the Indian market, they follow cash settlement, where the final settlement profit/loss is computed as the difference between trade price or the previous day's settlement price, as the case may be, and the final settlement price on the last trading day, as defined by the exchange.

### Interest rate futures market in India

Most of the global markets worldwide trade futures on underlying securities of two broader maturity levels: short term (up to 1 year), and medium term (say 10 years and above). Contracts on the long end of the yield curve are known as long bond futures and futures at the short end of the yield curve are generally called T-bill futures.

IRF products available in the Indian market till very recently, in line with the international practices on the interest rate derivatives, are futures on long bond (10-year 7% notional government securities) and on T-bills (91 days notional). But due to some very important developments in the Indian interest rate derivatives market, introduced in January 2014, an individual/ single bond futures contract, i.e. interest rate futures on various benchmark or liquid securities, changes from time to time. Even if the outstanding market volume for the notional bond futures contract in India completely disappeared after few months of its reintroduction in September 2009, the market has regained its faith in this single bond futures contract and is experiencing a sizable volume, with a very first day volumes (at NSE) of Rs. 3081.49 crores, with open interest of 16,057 contracts. Notional value of per IRF contract is Rs.2 lakhs consisting of 2000 units. Tenors of the contract presently permitted in the market are 3 months (March), 6 months (June), 9 months (September), and 12 months (December). The 10-year notional bond futures contract is settled through physical delivery, whereas the 91-day T-bills contracts, and the recently introduced single bond futures contract, follow cash settlement. Every contract is market-to-market on a daily basis and finally get settled based on T+1 basis.

The interest rate futures contract in India was initially issued in the year 2003, with a very poor market share just after a few months from the time of introduction, followed by almost a dead status. Thereafter, IRF contracts, with some significant modifications in the product structure and other related issues, were reintroduced in the year 2009 when the 7% 10-year notional bond futures was launched. This product, even though it got some initial response, failed to become popular in the Indian market. In response to this failure, and the actual demand from market players, the Indian futures market, since January 2014, started experiencing single bond futures contracts, with a sizable trading volume and a reasonable growth in the IRF market, as exhibited from the following figures (Figure 9.1 and Figure 9.2).

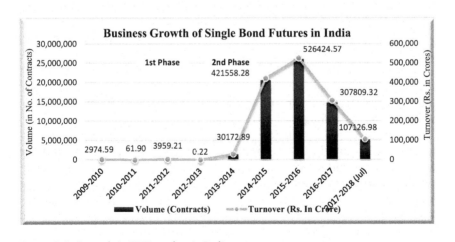

*Figure 9.1* Growth in IRF market in India

*Figure 9.2* Secondary market trading in IRF market in India

## Important features of IRF contract

### Underlying instrument (actual or notional)

The underlying bond of an IRF contract can be real or notional. A notional bond does not exist in reality but may have several characteristics (maturity, coupon) and varies from market to market. Use of a notional bond allows the market to use different bonds against a single IRF contract and brings more flexibility. The underlying for bond futures in India, during the initial phase, used to be a notional 10-year government bond with a coupon payment of 7% p.a. A 7% 10-year notional bond in this context simply referred to an equivalent bond issue, with a coupon rate of 7% and maturity of 10 years. The purpose to set the maturity at a level of 10 years and the coupon rate at a level of 7% per annum was basically due to the fact that the government mostly issues a 10-year bond and such security generally offers a coupon of 7%. Due to these facts, there would not be much difference in yield between the delivered security as per the futures contract and the notional issue. On the other hand, a futures contract can be on some single security of various maturity, outstanding in the market, commonly known as *Bond Futures* or *Single Bond Futures*.

If futures were to be introduced on each of the government bonds outstanding in the market, then the bond market like in India, having large number of outstanding securities, would experience a large number of interest rate futures contracts trading on each bond. As a result, the liquidity for most of the bond futures contracts may become poorer. But strong liquidity for the benchmark bonds led the Indian market to experience single bond futures contracts at least on a few benchmark securities. But lack of many such contracts, especially on illiquid securities, can be duly taken care off through the IRF on notional bonds, where a series of bonds, known as *Deliverable Basket*, are eligible for delivery at the maturity of the contract after being adjusted with a factor called *Conversion Factor*, which brings that bond at par with the notional bond available for trading. A notional bond futures contract is very active in many developed markets, where underlying bonds of various maturities are sufficiently liquid, leading to a greater liquidity almost for all the bonds within the deliverable basket, which is a major concern in a market like India, leading to the unpopularity of erstwhile notional bond futures in India.

### Deliverable basket

In case of a IRF on a notional bond having a physical settlement, the seller of the IRF contract at its maturity is supposed to deliver a bond which does not exist in the market. In such cases, the exchange may designate a list of all possible bonds actually outstanding in the market, which would be acceptable for delivery in lieu of a specific interest rate futures contract, and the short IRF holder is allowed to deliver either of the bonds listed in that basket. This basket of bonds is known as *Deliverable Basket*, and all bonds eligible for delivery are known as *Deliverable Bonds*. The composition of the deliverable basket is updated by the exchange at a certain time interval, say monthly, based on a certain mechanism. But the futures exchange takes care of the liquidity issue of all the deliverable assets by defining standard grade, deliverable grade, and price conversion factor. Existence of different deliverables creates a delivery option for the sellers of futures contracts.

### Conversion factor

If there is some mismatch between the actual underlying asset as specified in the interest rate futures contract and the deliverable asset as designated by the exchange, some adjustment needs to be expected to give a fair treatment to both the buyer and the seller of the futures contract. Suppose, as per an IRF contract, the buyer is expected to be delivered Rs.1,000,000 par value of a 7% 10-year Treasury bond by the seller at the maturity of the contract. Now, in the absence of exactly the similar asset, the seller may need to deliver either of the deliverable bonds. Suppose two similar bonds from the deliverable basket with exactly the same maturity but with different coupons are available – one is with a 6% coupon and the other is with an 8% coupon. Accordingly, the prices of such assets will be different from the price of the 7% 10-year Treasury issue. The price of 6% (8%) 10-year Treasury bond will be lower (higher) than the price of the actual bond as per the contract. In such case, if the asset with lower – 6% (higher – 8%) coupon is selected for delivery, there will be an injustice to the buyer (seller) of the futures contract. Therefore, the question is how to solve this problem so that both the counterparties get a fair treatment.

Here, the possible solution is to adjust the price of the IRF contract expected to be settled at the maturity after the delivery of the asset. The price of the IRF contract paid by the long IRF holder at maturity is not the price actually agreed upon while entering into the IRF contract, but a price adjusted with a factor known as *Conversion Factor*. Such a conversion factor is determined normally by the exchange before the trading of a specific contract with a specific underlying and a specific settlement date. The conversion factor, when multiplied with the contractual price of the futures contract (whose underlying is the notional bond), translates to the actual delivery price for a given deliverable security. The price actually paid by the buyer to the seller of the IRF contract is known as the *Invoice Price* and can be derived such that:

$$Invoice\ Price = Contract\ Size \times [Futures\ Settlement\ Price$$
$$\times Conversion\ Factor] + Accrued\ Interest \qquad (9.1)$$

P.N.: Here, contract size is the lot size, decided by the exchange, say 2000 units per futures contract in India; and accrued interest is the coupon due in the deliverable bond between its last coupon payment date and the maturity of the futures contract.

### Implied repo rate

The calculation of the implied repo rate can serve the purpose to select the deliverable asset which is cheapest-to-deliver. The implied repo rates of all the eligible securities in the deliverable basket are compared and the issue with the highest rate, giving the highest return to the holder, is selected as the CTD issue, which the short IRF holder is expected to carry till the maturity and deliver the same at maturity. The calculation of the implied repo rate depends on the cash flows in terms of:

- Cost of investment required to finance the bond issue purchased at the beginning of the short-term investment process, i.e. purchase price (clean price plus AI) of the bond issue.
- Coupon payments expected to be received until the delivery of the futures contract.
- Reinvestment income expected to be realized on the coupon payments till the delivery of the futures contract.
- Converted price of the deliverable bond issue plus the accrued interest expected to be received upon its delivery to satisfy the short position in the IRF contract.

All of the above elements are known to the investor except the rate of reinvestment of the coupon payments, which is perhaps a small part of the total return earned from the deliverable asset till the delivery of the futures contract. Therefore, the implied repo rate is almost expected to be certain and can be calculated as:

$$implied\_repo\_rate = \frac{Rupee\_return}{Cost\_of\_Investment} \times \frac{360}{Actual\_Days} \qquad (9.2)$$

Where, the Rupee return is nothing but the difference between the total proceeds received from the short-term investment, which is nothing but the sum of Converted Futures Price, Accrued Interest, Interim Coupon received on underlying, and Return on Reinvesting Interim Coupons; and the cost of such investment, which is again the price of the bond issue including the accrued interest. Again, the reinvestment return can be calculated by assuming *Term Repo Rate* as the reinvestment rate of interest applicable to the interim coupon payments expected to be reinvested, such that:

$$Reinvestment\_Interest = Interim\_Coupon \times Term\_repo\_rate$$
$$\times (Actual\_Days/360) \qquad (9.3)$$

The term repo rate is not only the borrowing rate for an investor who wants to borrow in the repo market, but also the rate which an investor can get from his short-term investment. The implied repo rate, as calculated from the above formula, represents the annualized rate of return, which is derived by following the convention available in the money market, i.e., Actual/Actual.

*Example: implied repo rate to identify CTD*

Calculate the implied repo rate for a hypothetical issue that is deliverable for a Treasury bond futures contract, assuming the details given in the following table (Table 9.1) for the deliverable issue and the futures contract:

*Table 9.1* Necessary details of IRF and deliverable securities

| Details of Deliverable Issue | | Details of Futures Contract | |
| --- | --- | --- | --- |
| Price of the Bond Issue (INR) | 107.00/- | Futures Price (INR) | 96.00/- |
| Coupon Rate (%) | 10% | Days to Delivery (30/360) | 82 Days |
| *Other Information* | | Conversion Factor | 1.1111 |
| No. of Days between Coupon Received and Delivery of Futures Contract (30/360) | 42 Days | | |
| 42-Day Term Repo Rate | 3.8% | | |

*Source*: All tables in this chapter are created by the author unless otherwise stated.

*Table 9.2* Estimation of implied repo rate of deliverable issue

| | |
|---|---|
| Total Proceeds Received | = Interim Coupon Payment(s) + Return on Reinvesting Interim Coupon + Futures Invoice Price |
| Cost of Investment | = Clean Price of Bond Issue + Accrued Interest |
| ***Details of Cash Inflows:*** | |
| Semiannual Coupon Received 40 Days (82–42) after Entering into the IRF contract | 5 |
| Reinvestment Income (Actual/365) | = 3.8% × Rs.5 × (42/365) = Rs.0.0219/- |
| AI Received at Futures Settlement Date (Rs.) (30/360 Convention) | = 10%/2 × Rs.100 × (42/180) = Rs.1.1667/- |
| Futures Invoice Price | = (96 × 1.1111) + 1.1667 = Rs.107.8323 |
| Total Cash Inflows till Futures Maturity | = 5 + 1.1667 + 107.8323 = Rs.112.8541/- |
| ***Details of Cash Outflows:*** | |
| Actual Price of the Underlying Bond | 107 |
| Accrued Interest Paid to Subscribe the Bond | = 10%/2 × 100 × (180–40)/180 = Rs.3.8889/- |
| Total Cost of Investment | = 107 + 3.8889 = Rs.110.8889 |
| Rupee Return for a Period of 82 Days | = 112.8541–110.8889 = Rs.1.9652/- |
| Implied Repo Rate (Actual/365) | = 1.9652 / 110.8889 × (365/82) = 7.8887% |

*Solution*

Solution of the above example may be seen from the Table 9.2.

*Cheapest-to-deliver issue*

The sellers of IRF contracts are allowed to decide which security out of the predefined deliverable basket they would like to deliver to the IRF buyers at the maturity of the contract. The sellers would prefer to choose that bond from the basket which leads to maximum profit or minimum loss to them. That particular security is known as the cheapest-to-deliver (CTD) bond, because it is the least expensive bond in the whole deliverable basket. Sellers of the IRF may ideally need acquire bonds of their choice to deliver them to the buyers, and the cost of acquiring such bonds is the quoted price of the security plus the accrued interest due on the same. On the other hand, when they deliver these bonds to the buyers of the IRF, what they receive is the invoice price, i.e. the adjusted futures price (original futures price × CF) plus the accrued interest (if any, depending upon the maturity of the IRF). The difference between these two values accounts for the profit/loss of the seller of futures contract. When the difference between the invoice price of the IRF to be received at maturity of the contract and the actual/implied cost of acquiring the security to be delivered is positive, the IRF seller books a profit, and vice versa. Being a linear product, the profit (loss) booked by the seller of an IRF becomes the loss (profit) of the buyer of the contract. The cheapest to deliver the bond is identified by calculating the profits/losses applicable to all the securities under the deliverable basket, termed as *Implied Repo Rate*, as shown in the previous section, and choosing that bond which maximizes the profit, i.e. with the highest positive implied repo rate (in case there is at least one profit making deliverable bond) or minimizes the loss, i.e. with the lowest negative implied repo rate (in case all deliverable bonds are loss making).

## Interest rate futures contract: product structures in India

The Indian market has a mixed experience in terms of the IRF product structure: notional and single bond futures contracts. Presently, interest rate futures contracts in India can be taken on:

- 91-Day Treasury Bills.
- Govt. of India Treasury Bonds (Benchmark Security).

### T-bills futures contract in India

Interest rate futures contracts, taken on short-term T-bills offered by the government, are known as Treasury bills (T-bills) futures contracts, the value of which changes due to any change in the concerned T-bill (91 days, 182 days, 364 days) rate available in the market. In India, such T-bill futures contracts are available only on 91-day T-bills. At any point of time, the total number of T-bill futures contracts available in the market for trading are: three serial monthly contracts followed by one quarterly contract of the cycle (i.e. either of March/June/September/December). Therefore, say in the month of July, the total number of such T-bill futures contracts available are 91-day T-bill futures contracts, maturing in the month of July (91DTB 270716), August (91DTB 310816), September (91DTB 280916), and December (91DTB 281216). Like forward rate agreement (FRA), available in the OTC derivatives market, a T-bill futures contract can be used to hedge an underlying exposure for a relatively shorter period of time, say for 3 months, or to use for market making with a short-term interest rate view. Since T-bills are always issued at a discount to the face value, and redeemed at the face value at maturity, the price quotations for T-bills are generally mentioned in terms of *Discount Yield*, the rate of interest per annum at which the discount is given on the face value or redemption amount. All necessary details towards the NSE T-bill futures are explained in Table 9.3, describing the contact specifications.

*Table 9.3* NSE 91-day t-bill futures: contract specifications

| | |
|---|---|
| Symbol | 91DTB |
| Market Type | N |
| Instrument Type | FUTIRT |
| Unit of Trading | One contract denotes 2000 units (Face Value Rs.2 lakhs) |
| Underlying | 91-day Government of India (GOI) Treasury Bill |
| Tick Size | 0.25 paise i.e. INR 0.0025 |
| Trading Hours | Monday to Friday (9:00 a.m. to 5:00 p.m.) |
| Contract Trading Cycle | Three serial monthly contracts followed by one quarterly contract of the cycle March/June/September/December |
| Last Trading Day | Last Wednesday of the expiry month at 1.00 pm<br>In case last Wednesday of the month is a designated holiday, the expiry day would be the previous working day |
| Price Quotation | 100 minus futures discount yield; e.g. for a futures discount yield of 5% p.a. the quote shall be 100–5 = Rs.95 |
| Contract Value | Rs.2000 * (100–0.25 * y), where y is the futures discount yield. e.g. for a futures discount yield of 5% p.a. contract value shall be 2000 * (100–0.25 * 5)= Rs.197,500 |
| Quantity Freeze | 7,001 lots or greater |
| Base Price | Theoretical price of the first day of the contract. On all other days, quote price corresponding to the daily settlement price of the contracts. |
| Price Operating Range | +/-1 % of the base price |
| Position Limits | **Clients** **Trading Members** |
| | 6% of total open interest or Rs. 300 crores whichever is higher |
| | 15% of the total open interest or Rs.1000 crores whichever is higher |
| Initial Margin | SPAN ® (Standard Portfolio Analysis of Risk) based subject to minimum of 0.1% of the notional value of the contract on the first day and 0.05% of the notional value of the contract thereafter |
| Extreme Loss Margin | 0.03% of the notional value of the contract for all gross open positions |
| Settlement | Daily settlement MTM: T + 1 in cash. Delivery settlement: Last business day of the expiry month. |
| Daily Settlement | Mark to Market (MTM): T + 1 in cash |
| Daily Settlement Price & Value | Rs. (100–0.25 * yw) where yw is the weighted average futures yield of trades during the time limit as prescribed by NSCCL. In the absence of trading in a prescribed time limit, the theoretical futures yield shall be considered. |
| Daily Contract Settlement Value | Rs.2,000 * daily settlement price |
| Final Contract Settlement Value | Rs.2,000 * (100–0.25 * yf) where yf is the weighted average discount yield obtained from weekly auction of 91-day T-bill conducted by RBI on the day of expiry. |
| Mode of Settlement | Settled in cash in Indian Rupees |

*Source*: National Stock Exchange of India Ltd.

*Example: discount yield and price of T-bill futures contract*

For example, if the price of a 91-day T-bill with 90 days remaining to maturity is quoted as 98.25, the concerned discount yield on the 3-month T-bill is 7% on the face value, such that: Discount Yield = {(100–98.25)/100 × (360/90)} = 7%. But the actual yield, considering the actual investment and the alternative day count convention used for money market instruments (i.e. Actual/365), may be different, such that:

$$\text{Actual Yield} = \{(100\ 98.25)/98.25\ (365/90)\} = 7.2236\%.$$

Suppose 91DTB270716 is a 91-day T-bill futures contract traded in NSE, where the underlying asset is a 91-day T-bill, issued by the GOI, and the futures contract matures on 27 July 2016. As per this futures contract, the seller, as on 27 July 2016, is required to deliver a T-bill maturing in next 91 days thereafter. In case of a T-bill futures contract, the price is quoted on the basis of the discount yield. Accordingly, the price of a September 2016 91-day T-bill futures contract (i.e. 91DTB 280916, as listed in NSE) in the month of July, quoted as Rs.93.7725/-, implies that the 3-month or 91-day discount yield likely to prevail in September is 6.2275% (i.e. 100–93.7725). Therefore, the discount yield on the 91-day T-bill futures contract maturing on 28 September 2016 (i.e. 91DTB 280916 Futures Contract), quoted at a price of Rs.93.7725/-, is 6.2275%. Given the discount yield, the invoice price of a single 91-day T-bill futures contract, with a lot size of 2000, is given as:

$$\text{Invoice Price} = (100 - 6.2275/4) \times 2000 = 98.4431 \times 2000$$
$$= \text{Rs.}1,96,886.25/-.$$

Therefore, the buyer of this 91DTB 280916 futures contract on its expiry, i.e. as on 28 September 2016, would pay Rs.196,886.25/- to the seller of the contract and receive a 91-day T-bill, maturing in 91 days thereafter, worth Rs.200,000/- of face value (i.e. Rs.100 × 2000).

### Single bond futures contract in India

During the second phase in the history of interest rate futures market in India, futures contracts are now available on single fixed coupon bearing benchmark government of India securities, falling under certain maturity ranges, as decided by the exchange. Securities eligible for NSE bond futures may be broadly of three maturity segments:

- 6-year (benchmark security with a residual maturity within 4–8 years).
- 10-year (benchmark security with a residual maturity within 8–11 years).
- 13-year (benchmark security with a residual maturity within 11–15 years).

Presently (as on 3 August 2017), NSE bond futures contracts are available on the following 10 government of India benchmark dated securities, eligible under different buckets:

- *679GS2027*: 6.79% GOI Security, Maturing on 15 May 2027 (10 Years Bucket).
- *679GS2029*: 6.79% GOI Security, Maturing on 26 Dec 2029 (13 Years Bucket).
- *684GS2022*: 6.84% GOI Security, Maturing on 19 Dec 2022 (6 Years Bucket).
- *697GS2026*: 6.97% GOI Security, Maturing on 06 Sep 2026 (10 Years Bucket).
- *759GS2026*: 7.59% GOI Security, Maturing on 11 Jan 2026 (10 Years Bucket).
- *759GS2029*: 7.59% GOI Security, Maturing on 20 Mar 2029 (13 Years Bucket).
- *761GS2030*: 7.61% GOI Security, Maturing on 09 May 2030 (13 Years Bucket).
- *768GS2023*: 7.68% GOI Security, Maturing on 15 Dec 2023 (6 Years Bucket).
- *772GS2025*: 7.72% GOI Security, Maturing on 25 May 2025 (6 Years Bucket).
- *788GS2030*: 7.88% GOI Security, Maturing on 19 Mar 2030 (13 Years Bucket).

As far as the maturity of a NSE bond futures contract on various eligible securities are concerned, there are contracts with 6 trading cycles: 3 serial months and 3 quarter ends. Accordingly, in the month of August 2017, there are six futures contracts against every eligible security, maturing at the end of August 2017, September 2017, October 2017 (serial months contract); followed by December 2017, March 2018, and June 2018 (quarter end contract). All necessary details towards the NSE bond futures are explained in Table 9.4, describing the contract specifications.

*Table 9.4* NSE bond futures in India: contract specifications

| Attributes | 6 Year | 10 Year | 13 Year |
|---|---|---|---|
| Underlying | GOI Securities with 4–8 years of residual maturity | GOI Securities with 8–11 Years of residual maturity | GOI Securities with 11–15 Years of residual maturity |
| Symbol | The symbol shall denote coupon, type of bond, and maturity year. Example – 7.72% central government security maturing on 25 May 2025 shall be denoted as 772GS2025 | | |

(*Continued*)

*Table 9.4* (Continued)

| Attributes | 6 Year | 10 Year | 13 Year |
|---|---|---|---|
| Instrument Type | FUTIRC | | |
| Unit of Trading | 1 Lot – (1 lot is equal to 2000 bonds with notional bonds of FV Rs. 0.2 million or 2 lakhs) | | |
| Quotation | Price based (derived from underlying clean price) | | |
| Contract Value | 1 Contract shall be equal to quoted price * 2000 | | |
| Tick Size | Rs.0.0025 | | |
| Quantity Freeze | 1251 lots | | |
| Trading Hours | Monday to Friday: 9:00 a.m. to 5:00 p.m. *(The trading hours aligned with underlying market in case of market extension)* | | |
| Trading Cycle | Three serial monthly contracts & three-quarter end contracts (Mar, Jun, Sep, & Dec) | | |
| Expiry Day | Last Thursday of the month. In case the last Thursday is a trading holiday, the previous trading day shall be the expiry/last trading day. | | |
| Base Price | Theoretical price on the 1st day of the contract. On all other days, daily settlement price of the contract | | |
| Price Operating Range | +/- 3% of the base price. (Whenever a trade in any contract is executed at the highest/lowest price of the band, exchange may expand the price band for that contract by 0.5% in that direction after 30 minutes after taking into account market trend. Price band may be relaxed only 2 times during the day.) | | |
| Exchange Level Overall Position Limit | Overall open interest in IRF contracts on each underlying shall not exceed 25% of the outstanding of underlying bond. | | |
| Initial Margin | SPAN Based Margin (Min 1.5%) | | |
| Extreme Loss Margin | 0.5% of the value of the gross open positions | | |
| Daily Settlement | Daily MTM settlement on T+1 in cash based on daily settlement price | | |
| Daily Settlement Price | Volume weighted average futures price of last half an hour or theoretical price | | |
| Final Settlement | Final settlement on T+1 day in cash based on final settlement price | | |
| Final Settlement Price | Weighted average price of the underlying bond based on the prices during the last two hours of the trading on NDS-OM. If less than 5 trades are executed in the underlying bond during the last two hours of trading, then FIMMDA price shall be used for final settlement | | |
| Spread Trading | Facility for spread trading. Margin Rs.1500 for a one month spread, Rs.1800 for two months and Rs.2100 for three months spread and Rs.3000 for greater than 3-month spread. | | |

*Source*: National Stock Exchange of India Ltd.

## Pricing of interest rate futures

In case of any futures contract, the price at which the contract is expected to be settled at maturity or expiry date is fixed and is decided at the initiation of the contract. This price is known as the original *Futures Price*. But in case of the interest rate futures contract, the price at which the IRF contract is expected to be settled depends on the security expected to be delivered under the same contract. Therefore, the actual settlement price depends on the conversion factor of the deliverable security. In case of single bond futures, there is no conversion factor, or the value of the conversion factor will be 1. The original futures price adjusted with the conversion factor is known as adjusted or converted futures price. The adjusted futures price, if again readjusted with the accrued interest (if any), is termed as *Invoice Price*.

The arbitrage-free fair price of an IRF contract can be based on a pricing model that incorporates the carrying cost of the security to be delivered with the current spot price. This pricing model is known as *Cost-of-Carry* model. Carrying costs are those costs which are the incidental costs incurred on holding the underlying asset, for example, the interest foregone on cash tied up for holding the asset, storage costs, and insurance costs for commodities. Therefore, the fair price of an IRF on a specific bond can be derived from the following information:

- Current price of the underlying bond issue in the cash market (P); current yield (Rupee coupon/spot price) of the underlying issue (c).
- Time of settlement/maturity (t) of the futures contract.
- Short-term *Financing Rate* (r) till the settlement date of the futures contract.

Given the above information, and with two important assumptions, no interim cash flows and no transaction cost, the fair price of an IRF contract can be derived as:

$$F = P + \left[ P \times (r - c) \times t \right]; \text{Or } F = P\{1 + (r - c) \times t\} \tag{9.4}$$

The moment the market price of the same futures contract is different (higher or lower) than this price, there will be an arbitrage opportunity, either through cash-and-carry or through reverse cash-and-carry described in the following sections, that further forces the market to get the futures contract traded at the arbitrage-free price. The net financing cost is also known as *Carry*, which can be positive or negative. If the current yield on the bond is higher (lower) than the funding cost, there will be *Positive (Negative) Carry*, causing the futures contract to be traded at a discount (premium), i.e. at a price below (above) the spot price. The cost of carry related to a single bond futures contract is basically a function of the present yield curve. In an upward-sloping yield curve scenario, the current yield from the bond is expected to be higher than the short-term funding cost (say short-term repo rate), leading to a positive carry and the futures contract to be traded at discount, i.e. at a price lower than the spot price of the underlying bond, and vice versa.

On the other hand, in physical settlement of an IRF contract, the short IRF holder gives one of the bonds from the deliverable basket in exchange for the contractual value received from the IRF buyer. When futures are traded, they are generally quoted at the clean price; accrued interest is subsequently with the traded futures price, and therefore the dirty price is taken into consideration at the time of settlement. Thus, on any given day, the settlement price of an IRF multiplied with the conversion factor gives the clean price of the deliverable bond for that day, which, after adding the accrued interest, gives the invoice price of the bond to be delivered. The buyer has to pay this price to the seller for getting delivery of the bond. Therefore, the invoice price of an IRF contract is such that:

$$Invoice\ Price = (Futures\ Settlement\ Price\ x\ Conversion\ Factor)$$
$$+ Accrued\ Interest \qquad (9.5)$$

### Example: pricing of IRF contract

Suppose a trader, as on 05 July 2016, may like to buy a 7.59 GS 2029 single bond futures contract maturing on 29 September 2016. The underlying security (759GS2029), currently traded at a price of Rs.100.09/-, will mature on 20 March 2029. The futures trader may like to know the arbitrage-free price of the futures contract as on 05 July 2016, and also may like to estimate the invoice price of the futures contract, which they need to settle as on the expiry of the futures contract. It may be assumed that the trader, as a commercial bank, has the option to borrow from the repo market at a rate of 6.50% p.a. The day count convention followed here may be 30/360.

### Solution

The available details required to estimate the arbitrage-free price and invoice price of the single bond futures contract are as exhibited in the following table (Table 9.5):

With the aforesaid details, the arbitrage-free price of the single bond futures contract, as on 05 July 2016 can be estimated, as given hereunder:

$$Futures\ Price = Spot\ Price \times \{1 + (r\ c) \times t\}$$
$$= 100.09 \times \{1 + (6.50\% - 7.58\%) \times (84/360)\}$$
$$= \textit{Rs.99.8370 / -}$$

*Table 9.5* Details available to estimate price of IRF contract

| | |
|---|---|
| Trade Date of the Futures Contract | 05 July 2016 |
| Maturity Date of the Futures Contract | 29 Sep 2016 |
| Maturity Period (Actual/Actual) | 26 Days in July + 30 Days in Aug + 28 Days in Sep = 84 Days (or 84/360 = 0.2333 Yr.) |
| Spot Price of the Underlying Bond as on 05 July 2016 | Rs.100.09/- |
| Maturity of the Underlying Bond | 20 Mar 2029 |
| Coupon Rate and Current Yield (c) | 7.59%; and 7.58% (= 7.59/100.09) |
| Semiannual Coupon Payment Dates | Sep 20 and Mar 20 |
| Last Coupon Payment Date before Expiry of the Futures Contract | 20 Sep 2016 |
| No. of Days between Last Coupon Payment Date and the Futures Maturity Date | 20 Sep 2016 to 29 Sep 2016 = 9 Days |
| Actual No. of Days in the Coupon Payment Period (20-Sep-16 to 20-Mar-17) | 11 + 30 + 30 + 30 + 30 + 30 + 19 = 180 Days |
| Short-Term Funding Rate or Repo Rate(r) | 6.50% p.a. |
| Time Period for Funding (t) | 84 Days |

[P.N.: *The actual settlement price of the same futures contract in NSE platform as on 05 July 2016 is Rs.99.9525, which is very close to the arbitrage-free price, calculated above, exhibiting the fact that there is hardly any arbitrage opportunity in the Indian bond futures market]*

It may be seen here that the current yield on the underlying bond (7.58% p.a.) is higher than the cost of financing (6.50% p.a.), leading to a positive carry, causing the futures contract to be traded at discount (i.e. at a price lower than the price of the underlying security on the trade date).

The invoice price of the 7.59 GS 2029 single bond futures contract maturing on 29 September 2016 to be settled at maturity after adjusted with the accrued interest is such that:

$$\text{Futures Invoice Price} = \text{Futures Price} + \text{Accrued Interest}$$
$$= 99.8370 + \{\text{Rs.}7.59 \div 2 \times (9 / 180)\}$$
$$= 99.8370 + 0.1898 = \textbf{\textit{Rs.100.0268 / -}}$$

## Method of settlement

Being an exchange traded product, all IRF contracts are settled through a *Central Counterparty (CCP),*[1] for example *National Securities Clearing Corporation Limited* (NSCCL), the clearing and settlement agency of the National Stock Exchange (NSE) where IRF in the Indian market is traded. Central counterparties (CCPs) are structures that help facilitate the clearing and settlement process in financial markets. The presence of such a central counterparty like NSCCL for Exchange traded products and Clearing Corporation of India Ltd. (CCIL) for OTC products, makes the clearing more robust and almost risk-free to the customers. Such CCP clearing allows the exchange to deliver operational and financial efficiencies to market participants, while reducing the risk inherent in trading activities. The role of the CCP broadly includes:

- Robust transaction processing.
- Post trade management functions.
- Financial management of members' collateral deposits.
- Final settlement of outstanding obligations through financial payment or physical delivery.
- The overall risk management of market participants.
- A financial guarantee of performance of its contracts.

Settlement of an IRF contract is done at two levels: MTM settlement which is done on a daily basis and physical/cash settlement which is done during the expiry month. Daily MTM of an IRF contract takes care of the daily price variation of the concerned IRF contract both for the buyer and seller of the contract, whereas the contract is finally settled at maturity either by way of physical delivery or through cash settlement.

### Mark-to-market (MTM) settlement

Since IRFs are standardized contract, they are marked-to-market on a daily basis by the exchange to cover the default risk. Market-to-market settlement in case of IRF is the process of adjusting the margin balance in an investor's account every day for the change in the value of the contract from the previous day. This process helps the clearing corporation in managing the counterparty risk of the futures contracts by adjusting the loss incurred by either of the counterparty due to adverse price movements with the margin account on a daily basis. In other words, the counterparty incurring loss due to adverse price movement needs to pay the clearing corporation the margin money to cover for the shortfall in the margin account. To ensure a fair mark-to-market process, the clearing corporation computes and declares the official price of IRF contract for each day for determining daily gains and losses. This price is called the "daily settlement price", computed through a certain mechanism, and represents the closing price of the futures contract for a given day. Daily MTM settlement in cash happens on T+1 basis.

The *Daily Settlement Price* (DSP) in India is the volume weighted average futures price (VWAP) of the trades in the last 30 minutes of trading. In case it is difficult to calculate the DSP due to lack of sufficient trading, the price considered will be a theoretical price [(Clean Price + Accrued Interest) or (FIMMDA Spot Price + Financing cost – Income on cash position)].

*Final settlement*

During the expiry month, an IRF contract is expected to be finally settled either by cash or through physical delivery of deliverable grade securities, using the electronic book entry system of the existing depositories (NSDL and CDSL) and public debt office (PDO) of the RBI. The notional bond futures contract in India used to be settled by delivery of the deliverable grade securities on the last business day of the delivery month. In case of single bond futures, following cash settlement, the final settlement prices is the weighted average price of the underlying bond based on the prices during the last 2 hours of the trading on NDS-OM platform. If less than five trades are executed in the underlying bond during the last 2 hours of trading, then the FIMMDA price may be considered as the final settlement price. Accordingly, the final settlement profit/loss is computed as the difference between the trade price or the previous day's settlement price, as the case may be, and the final settlement price on the last trading day, as defined by the exchange. Final settlement is also done on T+1 basis.

## Market participants

Futures market participants are typically divided into two categories: hedgers and speculators. Hedging refers to a futures market transaction made as a temporary substitute for a spot market transaction to be made at a later date. The purpose of hedging is to take advantage of current prices in future transactions. In a money market, hedgers use interest rate futures to fix future short-term borrowing and lending rates. Speculation in the futures market involves considering either a short- or long-futures position solely to profit from the change in the price of the futures contract caused by change in interest rates.

Interest rate is the most crucial element while doing financial planning, whether it is corporate, retail, or individuals. It affects everyone. Debt markets in India comprise sovereign and corporate, which are primary and secondary markets.

Banks, insurance companies, primary dealers, and provident funds bear the maximum hit on interest rate fluctuations due to exposure to the government securities. Savings by households and housing loans both bear the maximum hit on interest rate fluctuations within the household sector, which significantly drives the growth of many corporates. Hence, it is imperative that a hedging mechanism is derived since betting on the outlook of the society, especially during rising inflation, invariably leads to a rise in interest rates. This is possible through trading in derivatives which are listed on stock exchanges and, hence, tradable to provide liquidity for easy buy-sell, called as exchange-trade interest-rate derivatives.

Accordingly, following are the broader participants in the interest rate futures market:

## Banks

Banks, having large exposure in debt instruments, including investment in government securities (fixed rate and floating rate), market borrowing, lending to customer and to the financial market, may require necessary hedging from unfavorable movements in interest rates, and may therefore need to enter into suitable (long or short) position in the interest rate futures contract. Banks may also use such derivatives contracts for arbitrage, view based or speculative trading, adjusting (increase or decrease) the duration of their fixed income or bond portfolio, managing assets and liabilities, etc.

## Primary dealers

Primary dealers (PDs) also hold a significant volume of fixed income portfolios, and therefore are exposed to significant amount of interest rate risk. Besides using IRF contracts for hedging against such interest rate risk, PDs can also use such contracts almost for all other purposes, such as stated above, other than for asset-liability management.

## Foreign portfolio investors (FPIs)

*Foreign Portfolio Investors (FPIs)*[2] in India can make use of IRF contracts, especially for hedging their existing exposure, and also for a limited or restricted level of trading

## Mutual funds

Mutual funds, especially debt oriented funds, investing heavily in fixed income or debt instruments (government and non-government securities), are quite vulnerable to unfavorable movements or rise in interest rates, causing their net asset value (NAV) per unit to fall, exhibiting a poor performance, leading to a fall in the demand for such funds among investors (institutional and retail). Such an adverse situation for the fund manager can be managed if the interest rate risk of the fund's investment is hedged through the available IRF contracts. Mutual funds may also use IRF contracts to earn trading profit to improve the performance of the funds and appreciation of its NAV.

## Insurance companies

Insurance companies (ICs) mostly need to protect or hedge their long-term fixed rate liabilities, resulting from a fall in the rate of interests. As a result,

ICs may prefer to enter into long positions in the required number of IRF contracts to hedge its long-term fixed commitments. Since ICs mostly need to take long positions in the IRF, called *Long Hedge*, whereas banks mostly need to go for the short hedge in the IRF market, there is a greater possibility for banks and ICs to participate together in the IRF market to hedge their respective exposures, which will further help the market to develop faster. But the existing stringent regulations in the insurance sector in India may not allow the ICs to enter into the IRF market, causing insufficient players in the market, and therefore lack of sufficient development in terms of product range, price discovery mechanism, etc.

## Corporates

The treasuries of large corporate houses are now actively involved in the financial market, issuing debt instruments (fixed or floating) for their necessary financing, having good investments in various debt instruments, and also undertaking a limited amount of trading activities subjected to the fulfillment of necessary regulatory norms. Therefore, IRF contracts can also be used by such corporates, especially to hedge against the interest rate risk of their debt issuance or the investments. If a corporate issues a fixed (floating) rate bond, the issuer is exposed to the risk of a falling (rising) rate of interest, which can be duly hedged through the long (short) positions in the concerned IRF contracts. Similarly, investments in fixed (floating) rate bonds, issued by the government or non-government entities, may be exposed to the rising (fallng) rate of interest, which can be managed by entering into short (long) positions in the IRF market. As far as view-based trading activity in the IRF market is concerned, corporates in India are strictly controlled to undertake such activity.

## NBFCs

NBFCs can also use an IRF contract, basically to hedge their interest rate-related underlying exposures. They may also like to undertake some trading activity in the IRF market, subject to the regulations within which they operate.

## Individuals

Apart from institutional players (financial, non-financial), retailers, or individuals may also need to enter into IRF contracts to meet their diverse needs: protection from rising borrowing cost, protection from a fall in return or earnings from floating rate investments, safeguarding the value of fixed rate investments from rising interest rates, etc. Suitable (long or short) positions in the IRF contracts may help the individuals to hedge their exposures from rising or falling rates of interest. Availability of a smaller lot size for per unit of IRF contract, 2,000 units of underlying or INR 2 lakhs, in India gives an incentive to the retailers or individuals to participate in the IRF market and to increase the participant's base.

## Advantage/usefulness of IRF contract

Interest rate futures contracts can be used by different groups of market participants, stated hereunder in the next section, to satisfy their various requirements, arises specially due to interest rates movements. Some of the important advantages or usefulness of IRF contracts are discussed below:

### Hedging underlying exposure

Short-term interest rate futures contracts or Treasury-bill futures contracts (91 DTB, 182 DTB, 364 DTB) can be used to hedge against the future rising (falling) cost of borrowing/liability (return from asset). Accordingly, the required number of T-bill futures contracts, depending upon the value of exposure, lot size per futures contract, etc., may be sold (bought). Therefore, a borrower (investor), required to borrow (invest) for a short-term period but at a future date, may get exposed to the rising (falling) rate of interest, which can be duly (perfect or imperfect) hedged by entering into short (long) T-bill futures contracts (91 DTB / 182 DTB / 364 DTB Futures Contract), depending upon the tenor of borrowing (investment). Here, the market player may select the right T-bill futures contract of various maturities available in the market at any point of time.

### Example: hedging through T-bill futures contract

Suppose the Bank of Baroda, as on 28 June 2016, has decided to go for a short-term (91 days) borrowing from the market in an amount of INR 100 crore, but at a future date (say, as on 28 September 2016). Suppose the 91-day borrowing cost, supposed to be paid by the bank, is referenced to a 91-day Treasury bill rate which is likely to increase in next few months, causing a matter of concern for the bank to end up with a higher borrowing cost.

In order to hedge this risk of a possible rise in the future borrowing cost, the Bank of Baroda may like to enter into the short-term interest rate futures contracts, available in the National Stock Exchange (NSE). Accordingly, the bank has decided to immediately sell the required numbers of 91-day T-bill futures contract, preferably maturing in the month of September, followed by buying back the same at the right time in the future, preferably at the time of actually borrowing the fund from the market, and thereby locking in the borrowing cost applicable to the T-bill futures market today (i.e. 28 July 2016). Since there is a 91 DTB futures contract, with a maturity date of 28 September 2016 (i.e. 91 DTB 28092016) available in NSE, the bank has decided to take a short position with a required number, given the fact that the lot size per unit of the futures contract is 2000, and therefore the face value of single unit of such contract is Rs.200,000/-.

Suppose the price of the 91-day T-bill futures contract, maturing on 28 September 2016, as on 28 July 2016, is Rs.93.7725/-, representing a discount yield of 6.2275%. Show the hedge effectiveness of the use of the T-bill futures contract under different circumstances of change in interest rates, say 5.50%, 6.50%, and 8%.

*Solution*

Necessary details towards hedging and hedged positions are summarized as given in the following table (Table 9.6).

The amount received/paid during final settlement of a short T-bills futures position (if required to be held till maturity), or amount received/paid for premature offsetting of a short position by taking a subsequent long T-bill futures position, and the actual borrowing cost, all under different scenarios of rising or falling interest rates, can be described in the following table

*Table 9.6* Necessary details of hedging and hedged positions

| | |
|---|---|
| **Details of Underlying Exposure as on Day t:** | |
| Trade Date | 28 June 2016 |
| Nature of Exposure | Short-term Borrowing |
| Value of Exposure | 1000000000 |
| Starting Date for the Exposure | 28 Sep 2016 |
| Tenor of Exposure | 90 |
| Maturity of Exposure | 27 Dec 2016 |
| Present 90-Day T-Bill Rate | 6.2275% |
| | |
| **Details of 91 DTB Futures Contract (91DTB 28092016) as on Day t:** | |
| Trade Date | 28 June 2016 |
| Nature of Futures Contract | 91 DTB 28092016 |
| Yield on T-Bill Futures | 6.2275% |
| Maturity of Futures | 28 Sep 2016 |
| No of Days Remaining till Maturity | 90 |
| | (3 + 30 + 30 + 27; assuming 30/360 Convention) |
| Price of 91 DTB 28092016 as on Trade Date | 98.4431 |
| Lot Size of T-Bill Futures | 2000 |
| Face Value of One T-Bill Future | 200000 |
| Current Market Price of One Futures Contract | 196886.25 |
| | |
| Total No. of Futures Contracts Required to be Sold | 5000 |
| Contractual Value (to be Received) for Short T-Bill Futures Contract | 984431250.00 |
| No of Days Remaining till Maturity | 90 |

(*Continued*)

*Table 1.2* (Continued)

| | (3 + 30 + 30 + 27; assuming 30/360 Convention) |
|---|---|
| Price of 91 DTB 28092016 as on Trade Date | 98.4431 |
| Lot Size of T-Bill Futures | 2000 |
| Face Value of One T-Bill Futures | 200000 |
| Current Market Price of One Futures Contract | 196886.25 |
| Total No. of Futures Contract Required to be Sold | 5000 |
| Contractual Value (to be Received) for Short T-Bill Futures Contract | 984431250.00 |

*Table 9.7* Post-hedge payoffs under various scenarios

| Payoffs (Cash Inflow/Outflow) | Scenario 1 | Scenario 2 | Scenario 3 |
|---|---|---|---|
| Future Possible 91-Day T-Bill Rate | 5.50% | 6.50% | 8.00% |
| 90-Day Borrowing Cost at Current Rate | 15568750.00 | 15568750.00 | 15568750.00 |
| 90-Day Revised Borrowing Cost at New Rate in Future | 13750000.00 | 16250000.00 | 20000000.00 |
| Gain/(Loss) due to change in Borrowing Cost | 1818750.00 | −681250.00 | −4431250.00 |
| New Futures Price as on Settlement Date (at New Rate) | 98.6250 | 98.3750 | 98.0000 |
| Net Gain/Loss on Final Settlement of Futures Contract | −1818750 | 681250 | 4431250 |
| Overall Impact of any Change in Future Borrowing Rate with Short 91 DTB Futures Contract | 0.00 | 0.00 | 0.00 |

(Table 9.7). The financials under different scenarios clearly demonstrate that the Bank of Baroda, after entering into the short-term T-bill futures contract, can lock-in its short-term borrowing cost at the current 90-day T-bill rate, irrespective of the actual cost at the future date, when the bank is actually supposed to borrow from the market.

From the above example, a short-term T-bill futures contract is found to be hedge-effective for a borrower is required to protect from a future rise in borrowing cost. Similarly, such a contract can also be used by investors, who require protection from a future fall in the interest rates, and therefore a return on investment.

Like short-term T-bill futures contracts, long-term bond futures contracts, including notional bond futures or single bond futures, can also be used or shorted to hedge against the long position in the underlying debt securities. While estimating the number of futures contracts to be shorted is decided, the portfolio manager needs to take care of the risk of the assets to be hedged and the risk of the hedging asset, alternatively, the IR sensitivity of the underlying security/portfolio and that of the futures contract (CTD or the single bond against the bond futures). This hedge can be again an imperfect hedge or can be a so-called *Perfect Hedge*. But it is practically difficult to ensure a *Perfect Hedge* in the presence of *Basis Risk*. The risk of unpredictable change in the relationship between the prices of underlying securities and the futures contract, both when the hedge has taken place (i.e. at the time of entering into the IRF contract) and when the same is lifted (i.e. at the maturity of the IRF contract), is known as basis risk.

Basis risk may be substantially significant in case of *Cross Hedging*. Cross hedging reflects the dissimilarity between the security(s) required to be hedged and the security underlying the futures contract, i.e. either the CTD in case of a notional bond futures, or the single bond in case of a single bond futures contract. Any cross hedging, using a notional bond futures contract, involves two price relationships: prices of the underlying to be hedged and the CTD; and price of CTD and the futures. Whereas, any cross hedging using a single bond futures contract involves only one price relationship: the prices of underlying to be hedged and that of the single bond under the bond futures.

The key factor in the case of cross hedging is the selection of the correct *Hedge Ratio (HR)*. Hedge ratio needs to be selected in such a way so as to match the volatility of the underlying security and that of the futures contract (single bond under single bond futures or CTD under notional bond futures). Alternatively, HR helps to identify the number of futures contracts required to be entered into (i.e. shorted) to hedge the volatility in the underlying position.

The calculation of the hedge ratio again depends on the use of a specific (notional or single) bond futures contract, and the respective price relationship(s). Therefore, depending on the price relationship among the instruments, relative volatilities can be captured, which can further be used to get the hedge ratio matching the relative volatilities.

Accordingly, the hedge ratio, in case of notional bond futures with a given CTD can be estimated as:

$$HR = \text{Relative Volatility between Underlying Bond and CDT}$$
$$\times \text{Relative Volatility between CTD and Futures Contract}$$
$$= Vol._{Bond/CTD} \times Vol._{CTD/Futures} = (\Delta P_{Bond} / \Delta P_{CTD}) \times (\Delta P_{CTD} / \Delta P_{Futures})$$
$$= \{(M.D._{Bond} \times P_{Bond}) \text{ or } PV01_{Bond} /(M.D._{CTD} \times P_{CTD}) \text{ or } PV01_{CTD}\}$$
$$\times \{\Delta P_{CTD} /(\Delta P_{CTD} / CF_{CTD}\}$$
$$= \{PV01_{Bond} / PV01_{CTD}\} \times CF_{CTD} \tag{9.6}$$

Where: Vol. => Volatility; $\Delta P$ => Change in Price or Price Sensitivity; M.D. = > M-Duration

Whereas, the hedge ratio, in case of a single bond future, capturing the relative volatility only between the underlying bond to be hedged and the single bond behind the futures contract, can be estimated as:

$HR = Relative\ Volatility\ between\ Underlying\ Bond\ and$

$\qquad Bond\ under\ Futures$

$\qquad = Vol._{Bond/Bond\ under\ Futures} = (\Delta P_{Bond} / \Delta P_{Bond\ under\ Futures})$

$\qquad = \{(M.D._{Bond} \times P_{Bond})\ or\ PV01_{Bond} /$

$\qquad (M.D._{Bond\ under\ Futures} \times P_{Bond\ under\ Futures})\ or\ PV01_{Bond\ under\ Futures}\}$

$\qquad = \{PV01_{Bond} / PV01_{Bond\ under\ Futures}\}$ (9.7)

Therefore, the more volatile the hedged security than the CTD/bond under single bond futures is, the more would be the value of the HR and the required number of the IRF to be shorted. The hedge ratio can be calculated either by considering the m-duration or the PV01. But it may be more realistic to consider the PV01, capturing the current market scenario by linking the interest rate sensitivities with the current market prices.

Once the hedge ratio is estimated and is adjusted with the value of the underlying portfolio to be hedged and the value of every IRF contract, the required number of IRF to be used ($N_{IRF}$) can be calculated, such that:

$N_{IRF} = HR \times (Value\ of\ Security\ or\ Portfolio\ to\ be\ Hedged$

$\qquad \div Value\ of\ Single\ Lot\ of\ IRF)$ (9.8)

As far as the above value of the security/portfolio to be hedged and the value of the IRF to be considered is concerned, the portfolio manager may consider the face/par value or the market value, depending upon the perspective of the hedger.

To derive the correct HR and accordingly the required number of IRF, it is very important to consider the right estimate of interest rate volatility or PV01 of both the security/portfolio to be hedged and the CTD/single bond under the IRF. Here, the concern for a hedger could be the selection of the right time: the time of entering into such hedging agreement, or the time of lifting or executing the hedge (i.e. at the maturity of the IRF contract), when the interest rate sensitivity of both the asset to be hedged and the hedging asset needs to be captured. A hedger may be interested in locking in a price or rate only at that point of time when the hedge is lifted. Accordingly, the volatility of the bond issue to be hedged and that of the CTD/single bond should be its m-duration or PV01 on that date when the hedge is expected to be lifted, not at any other point of time. The effectiveness of such a hedge largely depends on regular monitoring of the HR, and therefore a regular rebalancing in the required number of IRF. Accordingly, the calculation of the hedge ratio should be based on the PV01 of both the hedged (spot) and hedging (futures) positions, and the required number of futures contracts to be entered into should also be based on the market values of both the positions. This may further require periodic adjustments in the number of futures lots required to ensure the necessary hedging, depending upon the change in interest rate sensitivity of both the positions. This periodic adjustment of the HR, and therefore the requirement of futures contracts, ensures that any loss arises due to periodic (daily, monthly, or quarterly) market-to-market of the underlying positions gets closely offset by the periodic MTM gains from the opposite position in the futures contract. The effectiveness of such a hedge also depends on the presence of convexity and the shifting of yield curve.

*Example: imperfect hedge with single bond futures*

On 13 June 2015, XYZ bank wants to hedge a part of its total government security portfolio for 2,000 units of a specific GOI security (7.72 GS 2025), the spot and futures price of which are mentioned hereunder:

Trading Date: 13 June 2015
Spot price of 7.72 GS 2025: Rs.102.10/-
Futures price of 7.72 2025 IRF: Rs.101.90/-

The Treasury head anticipates that the interest rate will rise in the near future. Therefore, to hedge the exposure in the underlying market, they may sell August 2015 interest rate futures contracts currently traded at Rs.101.90/-.

Suppose as on 24 July 2015, due to a rise in interest rates, the spot and futures prices of the concerned GOI security are respectively Rs.100.85/- and Rs.100.6819.

Calculate the net gain or loss on the portfolio of 2000 underlying government securities.

*Solution*

The Treasury head decides to hedge the interest rate risk by taking a short position in the interest rate futures.

On 24 July 2015 due to increase in interest rate:

Spot price of GOI security: Rs.100.85/-
Futures price of IRF contract: Rs.100.6819/-
Loss in underlying position will be (100.85/ – 102.10/-)*2000 = Rs.2500/-
Profit in the futures contract will be (101.90/ – 100.6819/-)*2000 = Rs.2436.20/-
**Net Position with Imperfect Hedge: Net Gain (Net Loss) = Rs.(2500–2436.20)/- = (Rs.63.80/-)**

When a portfolio manager intends to hedge their whole portfolio with the help of a notional or single bond futures contract, an effective strategy is to match the m-duration of the underlying portfolio and the futures contract to arrive at the required number of IRF (notional or single) contract to be entered into, as exhibited in the following exercise.

## *Example: hedging with notional bond futures*

The bond portfolio manager in the State Bank of India plans to use the September 2015 single bond futures contract available on 7.72% GS 2025, a 3-month single bond futures contract, maturing on 24 September 2015, offered by the National Stock Exchange of India Ltd., to hedge their bond portfolio worth of INR 10 crore with a portfolio m-duration of 5. The futures price as on 01 July 2015, the date of transaction is Rs.99.15/-, and each futures contract comes with a lot size of 2,000 bonds (i.e. par value of a futures contract is Rs.2,00,000/-). The underlying bond under the single bond futures (or the bond that is expected to be cheapest to deliver, in case the futures contract is notional bond futures) has a duration of 6.8060 years.

a   What position in such single bond futures contracts does the bank need to hedge the IR risk on the part of its government security portfolio?
b   Suppose if the bank is dealing with notional bond futures and the bond 7.72% GS 2025 is the CTD, with a conversion factor of 1.001, what adjustments to the hedge are necessary if after one month, the bond that is expected to be cheapest to deliver changes to one with a duration of 6.5 years and a CF of 0.99?
c   Suppose that all rates increase over the 3 months, but long-term rates increase less than short-term and medium-term rates. What is the effect of this on the performance of the hedge?

## *Solution*

(a) The total number of single bond futures contract to be shorted is:

$$N_{IRF} = \{MD \text{ of the bond to be Hedged} / MD \text{ of the Bond under the Futures}\} \times \{Par \text{ Value to be Hedged} / Par \text{ Value of an IRF}\}$$
$$= \{5.00 / 6.8060\} \times \{10,00,00,000 / 200000\} = 367.30$$

Rounding to the nearest whole number, 368 contracts should be shorted.

   (b) In case, the futures used is a notional bond futures, with a CTD (CF = 1.001, and M-Duration = 6.8060), the required number of futures contracts to be shorted is:

$$= \{5.00 / 6.8060\} \times 1.001 \times \{10,00,00,000 / 200000\} = 367.69$$
$$= 368 \text{ contracts}$$

But if the futures used is a notional bond futures, and in the event of change in CTD with a m-duration of 6.5 and a conversion factor of 0.99, the revised number of futures contracts to be shorted is: = {5.00 / 6.50} × 0.99 × { 10,00,00,000 / 200000} = 380.77 = 381 contracts.

As a result, due to the in the CTD under the notional bond futures contract, the bank needs to short 13 (i.e. 381–368) more futures contracts to take care of any futures losses in its bond portfolio.

(c) Since the bank holds the underlying portfolio, with a portfolio m-duration of 5, we may assume more concentration of short- and medium-term securities in the bank's portfolio, the value of which is expected to be affected by the movement of short-term and medium-term interest rates. At the same time, if we consider the interest rate futures (notional or actual) contract, and the same is assumed to be long term, the value of the same is expected to be driven by the movement in the long-term rate of interests. Now if we assume, short- and medium-term interest rates to rise more than the long term, the loss on the underlying bond portfolio (of short and medium term) is likely to be more than the gain on the short futures position (of long term). Duration-based hedging assumes that the movements in interest rates of all tenors (short, medium, and long) are the same, and therefore still possess the yield curve risk.

A bond portfolio can be hedged through IRF either by matching the m-duration of the portfolio or by matching the m-duration of each of the underlying securities with the m-duration of the IRF contract. The problem in matching the m-duration of the underlying portfolio, as shown in the previous example, is that it ignores the unequal changes in the interest rates of different tenors, commonly known as an unparallel shift in the yield curve. As a result of this, the underlying portfolio, even if after hedging, may get exposed to yield curve risk. This problem may be partially addressed by matching the sensitivity of each of the underlying secjurities in the portfolio with the sensitivity of the CTD (in case of notional bond futures) or of the underlying of the single bond futures contract, assuming the bond(s) to be hedged and the CTD bond of a notional IRF or the single bond(s) under the single bond futures are almost of similar maturities. Hedging a bond portfolio of several bonds of different maturities using a single bond futures contract, and thereby still exposed to some amount of yield curve risk, is discussed in the following example.

*Example: hedging with single bond futures*

An investor holds a portfolio of 5 GOI Treasury securities as on 29 July 2015, as given in the following table (Table 9.8). The nominal value of the bonds in the portfolio is Rs.20 crore, and the market value of the portfolio, excluding accrued interest, as on that date is Rs.19.95 crore (Rs.199,454,350/-). In order to hedge the whole portfolio, the investor wants to short the required number of September 2015 interest rate futures contracts (772GS2025

NSE bond futures maturing on 24 September 2015), currently traded at Rs.98.7975/-. From the given information, calculate the number of IRF contracts required to hedge each of the five long positions, and therefore the whole portfolio, assuming that the par value of each IRF contract is Rs.200,000/-.

*Solution*

In order to hedge the whole portfolio of five GOI securities, the investor or portfolio manager may like to match the sensitivity (here m-duration or PV01) of each of the underlying positions with that of the single bond futures contract. Accordingly, the required number of such bond futures to hedge the IR risk of individual position is calculated as:

$N_{IRF}$ = *(M-Duration of the Bond to be Hedged / M-Duration*
*of the Bond under the Futures) × (Value of Security to be*
*Hedged ÷ Value of Single Lot of IRF)* (9.9)

Now, there may be some ambiguity in terms of considering the value of the security and that of the IRF contract of each lot (i.e. 2,000 units) while estimating the required number of futures contracts to be entered into. One option is to consider the face value of both the underlying position and that of the IRF (i.e. Rs.2 lakhs per lot). The other option could be to consider the market value of both the position, considering the current market price of the underlying position to be hedged, and that of the single bond futures contract. Under such scenario, PV01 of the underlying and the IRF may be considered instead of m-duration. The major difference between these two approaches, face value vs. market value, is that the first approach is a static approach, ensuring a hedge against the face value, which may not be perfect and need not to be adjusted more frequently. But the second approach, considering the market value of the underlying and IRF positions, is a dynamic approach, which may give a perfect or close to perfect hedge, and also may require to be rebalanced on a continuous basis depending on the change in market prices of the underlying and IRF positions.

The required number of IRF to hedge all the five underlying positions, and therefore the whole portfolio, is extracted in the following table (Table 9.9), under both the aforesaid approaches.

As the above table suggests, the investor needs to short a total number of 924 772GS2025 NSE bond futures contracts, maturing on 24 September 2015, to cover the losses in the original bond portfolio (with a face value of 20 crore) that arises out of a rise in interest rates. The requirement for the similar IRF contracts may undergo a change just by considering the market value/prices of the underlying positions and that of the IRF contract, along with the PV01 as the interest sensitivity measure. Under the second approach, the required number of IRF contracts to be taken is 933 contracts

Table 9.8 Details of government security portfolio required to hedge with IRF contracts

Trade Date
**29 July 2015**

| Bond | Face Value (INR) | Market Price | Market Value (INR) | Coupon Rate | Yield | Maturity | Duration | M- Duration |
|---|---|---|---|---|---|---|---|---|
| 07.83 GS 2018 | 12,000,000 | 99.96 | 11,995,200 | 7.83% | 7.84% | 11 Apr 18 | 2.4312 | 2.3395 |
| 07.28 GS 2019 | 5,000,000 | 98.2 | 4,910,000 | 7.28% | 7.83% | 3 Jun 19 | 3.3807 | 3.2534 |
| 08.27 GS 2020 | 38,000,000 | 101.305 | 38,495,900 | 8.27% | 7.94% | 9 Jun 20 | 4.0623 | 3.9073 |
| 07.72 GS 2025 | 100,000,000 | 99.42 | 99,420,000 | 7.72% | 7.80% | 25 May 25 | 6.9588 | 6.6975 |
| 07.88 GS 2030 | 45,000,000 | 99.185 | 44,633,250 | 7.88% | 7.98% | 19 Mar 30 | 8.6656 | 8.3333 |
| **Portfolio** | **200,000,000** | | **199,454,350** | | **7.87%** | | **6.4213** | **6.1781** |

Table 9.9 Estimation of required no. of IRF to hedge underlying portfolio

| Bond | Face Value (in Crore) | Price (Rs.) | Maturity Date | Duration (Years) | M-Duration (%) | PV01 (for every single unit of bond) (in Rs.) | N-IRF based on MD & Book Value | N-IRF based on PV01 & Market Values |
|---|---|---|---|---|---|---|---|---|
| 07.83 GS 2018 | 12,000,000 | 99.960 | 11-Apr-18 | 2.4312 | 2.3395 | 0.0234 | 20.9586 | 21.3204 |
| 07.28 GS 2019 | 5,000,000 | 98.200 | 3-Jun-19 | 3.3807 | 3.2534 | 0.0319 | 12.1441 | 11.9225 |
| 08.27 GS 2020 | 38,000,000 | 101.305 | 9-Jun-20 | 4.0623 | 3.9073 | 0.0396 | 110.8448 | 115.8130 |
| 07.72 GS 2025 | 100,000,000 | 99.420 | 25-May-25 | 6.9588 | 6.6975 | 0.0666 | 500.0000 | 503.1504 |
| 07.88 GS 2030 | 45,000,000 | 99.185 | 19-Mar-30 | 8.6656 | 8.3333 | 0.0827 | 279.9554 | 280.3891 |
| **Portfolio** | **200,000,000** | | | **6.4213** | **6.1781** | | **923.90** | **932.60** |

of 2,000 lot size, 9 IRF contracts more than the number of IRF required under the first approach, especially to address the actual price volatility in the underlying securities and futures market, which is subjected to a regular change, causing the required number of IRF contracts to be rebalanced on a regular basis.

### Use of arbitrage opportunity

The short-term price differential in the underlying bond market and the IRF market can also provide an opportunity to arbitragers. If the futures are expensive compared to the underlying, then the arbitrager can make profit by taking a long position in the underlying market by borrowing funds and taking short positions in the futures market. This kind of strategy is known as *Cash and Carry Arbitrage*. On the other hand, if the futures are found to be cheaper than the underlying market, after considering the cost-of-carry, then the arbitrage opportunity can be enjoyed by taking a long position in the IRF and short position in the underlying market. Such a strategy is called as *Reverse Cash and Carry Arbitrage*. How such a price difference between the underlying security and the IRF contract creates an arbitrage opportunity for the market player, leading to implementation of the required strategy is explained through the following examples.

### Example: arbitrage opportunity in IRF

Suppose, as on 28 July 2015, a trader buys 7.72% GS 2025 at the current market price of Rs. 99.4039. The coupons are paid semiannually on November 25th and May 25th. The trader has accordingly shorted the August 2015 7.72% GS 2025 bond futures, as on the same date, traded at Rs.100.25/-

The short-term borrowing and lending rate, let's say 1-month MIBOR as on 28 July 2015, is 7.62% p.a.

Suppose, as on 27 August 2015, the trader wants to give a notice of delivery to the exchange, assuming that the settlement price of the futures contract remains at Rs.100.25/-.

Within this specific period (28 July 2015 to 27 August 2015), examine whether there is any opportunity for the trader to make some arbitrage project. If so, how is the same maximized within a given period?

### Solution

The strategy that a trader is supposed to follow to make the arbitrage profit depends upon the possibility for the futures contract to be mispriced as on the trade date. If the price of the futures contract, arrived at through the *Cost-of-Carry* process, is less than the actual market price, then the arbitrage profit can be made by taking a long position in the underlying and short in the futures, known as *Cash and Carry Arbitrage*. Similarly, if the market price of the futures contract is less than the price arrived at through the cost-of-carry mechanism, then the right strategy would be to be short in the underlying position and long in the futures, known as *Reverse Cash and Carry Arbitrage*. The above example can be broadly addressed by looking at the following steps:

Step 1 – Short the 15 August futures at the current price of Rs.100.25/-

Step 2 – Fund the bond by borrowing up to the delivery period (assuming the borrowing rate is 7.62% p.a.)

Step 3 – On 25 August, 2 days prior to the expiry of the futures, give a notice of delivery to the exchange

Step 4 – Deliver the security on the expiry date and receive the settlement price.

Under the strategy, the bank has earned a return of:

$$= (100.25 \quad 99.4039) \ / \ 99.4039 * 365 \ / \ 30 = 10.36 \ \%$$

(Note: For simplicity, accrued interest is not immediately considered for calculation.)

Therefore, the result found from this trading is that, against a funding cost of 7.62% (borrowing rate), the trader would able to earn a risk-free gross return of 10.36% p.a., leading to a net arbitrage profit of 2.74% p.a. (10.36% – 7.62%).

This example exhibits how a market player makes use of the futures market to generate an arbitrage profit by taking suitable positions in the underlying security and IRF contract.

### Directional trading

Since there is an inverse relationship between interest rate movement and underlying bond prices, the futures price also moves accordingly with the underlying bond prices, but not necessarily by the same amount.

If one has a strong view that interest rates will rise in the near future and expects to benefit from the rise in interest rates, one can do so by taking short position in IRF contracts and benefit from the falling futures prices. Similarly, a view towards a fall in the future rates of interest may benefit the trader if a long position in IRF contract is taken. Trading in the IRF market, based on these directional (upward or downward) movements of the interest rates is known as directional trading or speculative trading, where the trader takes a call to go for a long or short position only in the futures contract, based on their interest rates views.

*Example: directional trading*

A trader expects a long-term interest rate to rise. The decide to sell interest rate futures contracts as they shall benefit from falling futures prices. Below are some necessary trade and price information as given in the following table (Table 9.10):

*Table 9.10* Trade and price information on IRF contract

| Trade Information | | Daily Settlement Price of Futures Contract between 27 to 30 June 2015 | |
| --- | --- | --- | --- |
| Trade Date | 27 June 2015 | 27 June 2015 | Rs.100.2600/- |
| Underlying Security | 7.72 GS 2025 | 28 June 2015 | Rs.100.4625/- |
| Future Contract | 7.72% 2025 | 29 June 2015 | Rs.100.3025/- |
| Expiry Date | 30 June 2015 | 30 June 2015 | Rs.99.9685/- |
| Current Futures Price | Rs.100.30/- | | |

Strategy – Trader sells 250 7.72% 2025 single bond futures contracts (with a lot size of 2,000) at a price of Rs.100.30/-

[* Daily Settlement price shall be the weighted average price of the trades in the last half hour of trading]

Calculate the total profit or loss made by the trader on this directional trading at the end of 30 June 2015, considering the daily MTM gains or losses.

*Solution*

Daily MTMs due to change in the futures price are tabulated (Table 9.11) below

*Table 9.11* Estimation of daily MTM gains or losses on IRF contract

| Date | Daily Settlement Price (Rs.) | Calculation | MTM (Rs.) |
| --- | --- | --- | --- |
| 27-Jun-2015 | Rs.100.2600/- | - 250*2000*(100.2600–100.30) | 20000 |
| 28-Jun-2015 | Rs.100.4625/- | - 250*2000*(100.4625–100.2600) | (1,01,250) |
| 29-Jun-2015 | Rs.100.3025/- | - 250*2000*(100.3025–100.4625) | 80,000 |
| 30-Jun-2015 | Rs.99.9685/- * | - 250*2000*(99.9685–100.3025) | 1,67,000 |
| Total MTM Gain (Loss) | | | 1,65,750 |

Therefore, the net cumulative MTM gain made by the IRF trader as on 30 June 2015, out of their directional trading in the IRF market is Rs.165,750/-

*Alternatively, Total Profit on the trade = – 250 * 2000 (99.9685–100.30) = Rs.165,750/-; as applicable in case of a forward contract where the price difference is not settled on daily basis, or MTM is not followed.*

It may be noted here that the sign for the 250 units of IRF in all the calculations is negative, because the trader has taken a short position in the IRF, or has sold 250 units of IRF contract, causing a MTM gain (loss) when the daily settlement price falls (rises) in comparison with the last settlement price.

### Asset-liability/duration management

It is quite common in many banking and non-banking financial institutions to have a mismatch, in terms of the average maturity, between the assets and liabilities, leading to a significant concern in asset-liability management. Say for commercial banks, the average maturity of liabilities is relatively smaller than the average maturity of their assets, exposing the bank to interest rate risk on its overall balance sheet and causing a significant problem in their asset-liability management exercise. The best option to settle this issue is to change the nature of the bank's assets and liabilities and bring them into a common maturity structure. But this may not be feasible in reality, and banks and other FIs need to operate with this problem. One way to address this issue is to enter into the required number of interest rate futures contracts, short or long, depending upon the actual requirement. Such IRF contracts also help to manage the duration of the bond portfolio held by banks and other FIs.

If the interest rate is expected to rise, and the average maturity of bank's liabilities is lower than that of its assets, the bank will end up with interest rate risk, i.e. more interest expenses than interest incomes. Similarly, as the bonds with longer maturities are more sensitive to interest rate changes, a bond portfolio with longer m-duration will be more exposed to the vulnerability of the movement in interest rates. These problems may be addressed, either by reducing the average maturity of a bank's asset portfolio or by reducing the m-duration of the bond portfolio, to a targeted level as set by the bank.

Say, if the values of the bond portfolio is 5 crore, and the m-duration of 6.4%, a rise in the interest rate of 1% may cause a significant loss, leading to a requirement of reducing the portfolio m-duration level let's say at 4.5%, which may be adjusted not by reducing the duration of the asset portfolio by way of swapping long-term securities to short-term securities, but through short positions in the necessary number of IRF contracts.

Now, the question is, how many IRF contracts need to be shorted to reach the targeted level of m-duration? Due to a 1% rise in the interest rate, the value of 1 short futures contract will increase by m-duration of the bond futures × price of 1 futures contract).

Therefore, the total number of futures contracts required to be shorted is:

Total Loss in Asset Portfolio ÷ Profit in 1 Short Futures contract
Total Loss in Asset Portfolio (due to 1% rise in IR)
= (Targeted M-Duration − Actual/Initial M-Duration) × Portfolio Value
   Profit in 1 Short Futures (due to 1% rise in IR)
= M-Duration of IRF contract × {Original Price of an IRF × Lot Size of an IRF}

The approximate number of interest rate futures or bond futures (BF) contracts which need to be entered into to achieve the desired m-duration is given by:

$$N_{IRF} = \frac{\left(M\text{-}Duration_{Targeted} - M\text{-}Duration_{Initial}\right) \times Value_{Portfolio}}{\left(M\text{-}Duration_{BF} \times Price_{BF} \times Lot\_Size\right)} \qquad (9.10)$$

$$N_{IRF} = \frac{\left(MD_T - MD_t\right) \times V_P}{\left(MD_{BF} \times P_{BF}\right) \times LS}$$

*Example: asset-liability or duration management*

Suppose the size of a bond portfolio of a small bank is Rs.5 crore as on 28 July 2015. The portfolio has a modified duration of 6.4. The modified duration needs to be revised to 4.5 by using an interest rate futures contract. Suppose the m-duration of the August 2015 single bond futures contract available on 7.72% GS 2025 is 6.6975.

How many futures contracts will be required to modify the duration and should one buy or sell the required number of futures contracts?

*Solution*

A certain number of bond futures contracts can be used to modify m-duration of portfolio.

Target M-Duration = 4.5
Initial M-Duration = 6.4
Value of the Portfolio = Rs.5 cr. (Rs.50,000,000)
M-Duration of the Bond to be Delivered under the IRF = 6.6975
Price of the Single Bond Futures = Rs.99.41
Permissible Lot Size per unit of futures contract = 2000 units of underlying issue

Given the above information, the appropriate number of single bond futures contracts required to reduce the portfolio m-duration to the targeted level can be calculated as:

$$N_{IRF} = \left\{\left(MD_T - MD_I\right) \times V_P\right\} / \left\{MD_{IRF} \times P_{IRF} \times Lot - Size\right\}$$

$$N_{IRF} = \frac{\left\{(4.5 - 6.4) \times 5,00,00,000\right\}}{\left\{6.6975 \times 99.41 \times 2000\right\}} = -71.34 = -72$$

So, the number of contracts required to reach the targeted duration is 72. Since the number is negative, 72 bond futures contracts need to be sold. Alternatively, the bank needs to take 72 units of short position in the August 2015 single bond futures contracts available on 7.72% GS 2025.

## Hedge effectiveness of bond futures contracts in India: a case

### Background

Suppose the Bank of Baroda (BoB), one of the large, public sector commercial banks in India, out of its total investments of INR 1,214 billion in India (as per RBI Data), has invested roughly INR 1,110 billion in government securities (government of India – GOI bonds, T-bills, and state government securities – SDL) as on 31 March 2017. Out of this total investment in government securities, the bank has further classified its investment in held till maturity (HTM), available for sale (AFS), and held for trading (HFT). The majority of the bank's investments in government securities are part of HTM, especially in the event of a continuous rise in the risk-free bond yield in India and also subjected to the prudential limit set by the central bank towards classifying investment in government securities as a part of HTM. The bank has an experience of holding 60 – 80% of its total investment in government securities in HTM, depending on the prevailing interest rate scenario. Even if small, the bank still has a significant bond (government securities.) investment in AFS and HFT, ranging from INR 10,000 – 20,000 million in HFT (say with positions in 8 – 10 very liquid securities) and INR 300 – 400 billion in AFS (with positions in a wide range of securities), depending on the liquidity in the government security market in India and also the volatility in risk-free yields.

Suppose, BoB Treasury, as on 2 July 2018, has HFT trading positions in 10 very liquid GOI bonds with a face value of say INR 20,000 million, holding equal number of positions in all the securities. As per the internal investment norms, the Treasury may need to follow a daily market-to-market (MTM) to revalue its positions in HFT using the day-end values given by the Financial Benchmarks India Private Ltd (FBIL), a subsidiary of the Fixed Income Money Market and Derivatives Association (FIMMDA). Due to the current upward shift in the GOI risk-free yield curve in India, as exhibited in Figure 9.1, where the risk-free yields for any tenor on an average have gone up almost by 45 – 50 basis points (10-year FIMMDA par yield on 29 December 2017 and 29 June 2018 are respectively 7.63% and 8.14%) from December last year till June this year, the bank is expected to book regular MTM losses on its trading portfolios. Currently (as on 2 July 2018), the HFT portfolio (with 10 different positions) of INR 20,000 million (face value) held by the bank has a PV01 of close to INR 10 million.

Alternatively, as on 2 July 2018, for every single basis point rise in the risk-free yields (of any tenor), the bank is expected to book a MTM loss of close to INR 10 million. This sounded very risky to the bank's Treasury head, and therefore he/she has decided to explore the availability of a suitable hedging mechanism/instrument to hedge the market risk (more specifically, interest rate risk) losses expected to be incurred by the bank due to unfavorable movement in the risk-free yields.

The composition of the HFT government security portfolio (as on 2 July 2018) the bank intends to hedge against interest rate risk, with other necessary details, is given in the following table (Table 9.12):

The bank mostly prefers to keep the most liquid securities in its HFT portfolio, maybe with a restriction towards the m of the m-duration port-folio, as referred by the bank's investment policy document. Suppose the treasury's trading portfolio has got an m-duration limit of 6%. Due to uncertain movement in the risk-free yields across the tenors, the treas-ury head has decided to follow a ladder portfolio, where an equal propor-tion of investment is expected to be made in all the shortlisted positions across the yield curve. The composition may undergo a change any time depending on the view towards the movement of the yield curve.

**Possible way forward**

The treasury head has consulted the chief dealer (Rupee Treasury) and requested him/her to explore the suitability of *Single Bond Futures* con-tracts that gained more popularity than *Notional Bond Futures* contract initially offered in India. Bond futures is a financial contract between two counterparties to buy or sell a specific underlying security at a future date (i.e. maturity date) decided now and also at a contractual price, irrespective of the prevailing market price (high or low) during final set-tlement at the maturity. For example, as on 2 July 2018, if BoB takes a long position in a single bond futures contract (717GS2028 260718) offered by the NSE, maturing on 26 July 2018 (Thursday), on the current benchmark GOI bond (7.17 GS 2028), say at a contractual price of INR 95.03/-, the bank needs to take the delivery of the security on the matu-rity date at that contractual price, irrespective of the prevailing market price of the same security in the underlying cash market. Alternatively,

Table 9.12 Underlying positions held by the bank

Details of Underlying Positions Held by the Bank as on 2 July 2018

| | Security Description | Date of Maturity | Res. Mat. (Year) | Yield (%) | Market/ FIMMDA Price (INR) | Face Value (INR Million) | M-Duration (%) |
|---|---|---|---|---|---|---|---|
| 1 | 6.65% GS 2020 | 09-04-2020 | 1.77 | 7.55 | 98.52 | 2000 | 1.6132 |
| 2 | 8.27% GS 2020 | 09-06-2020 | 1.94 | 7.53 | 101.30 | 2000 | 1.7549 |
| 3 | 8.20% GS 2022 | 15-02-2022 | 3.62 | 7.94 | 100.78 | 2000 | 2.9931 |
| 4 | 8.08% GS 2022 | 02-08-2022 | 4.08 | 7.96 | 100.40 | 2000 | 3.3139 |
| 5 | 6.84% GS 2022 | 19-12-2022 | 4.46 | 7.96 | 95.87 | 2000 | 3.7491 |
| 6 | 7.59% GS 2026 | 11-01-2026 | 7.53 | 8.15 | 96.92 | 2000 | 5.4090 |
| 7 | 7.17% GS 2028 | 08-01-2028 | 9.52 | 7.91 | 95.10 | 2000 | 6.4839 |
| 8 | 6.68% GS 2031 | 17-09-2031 | 13.21 | 8.09 | 88.66 | 2000 | 8.1702 |
| 9 | 6.57% GS 2033 | 05-12-2033 | 15.43 | 8.12 | 86.52 | 2000 | 9.0543 |
| 10 | 7.06% GS 2046 | 10-10-2046 | 28.27 | 8.10 | 88.55 | 2000 | 11.0926 |
| | Portfolio | | | 7.9233 | | 20,000 | 5.2081 |

there may be a cash settlement as on the maturity date, based on the difference between the contractual price and the prevailing market price of the futures contract.

An alternative to this single and final cash settlement is nothing but the cumulative daily MTM settlement based on the daily market/settlement price of the futures contract. The treasury chief dealer made this very clear that the bank may prefer to go for a *Direct Hedge* where a particular position will be hedged by a bond futures contract with the similar security against it, wherever possible, depending upon the availability of the futures contract. Wherever such direct hedge is not possible, the bank may think of a *Cross Hedge*, where an underlying position will be hedged by a futures contract available on any other security other than the underlying one. While following a cross hedging, the bank may select those futures contracts where the *Price Correlations* (between spot and futures prices) are relatively higher, so that the losses in the underlying long positions, if not completely but significantly, are hedged by the gains from the short positions in the selected futures contracts. Therefore, while cross hedging, the bank may decide to look at the correlations between the price movement in the spot and futures market. The closer the residual tenor of the security behind the available futures contracts with the residual tenor of the underlying position, the greater would be chances to have a higher price correlation, and a better hedge, if not a *Perfect Hedge*.

Suppose, out of the given bond futures contracts available in NSE, the bank, based on its estimates of relatively higher price correlations, has decided to consider the following five single bond futures contracts, as included in the following table (Table 9.13), to hedge its underlying position in HFT portfolio.

**Concern towards hedge effectiveness**

Once the nature and value of a portfolio required to be hedged is identified, and the type of hedging instrument available in the market is explored, the treasury head requested the chief-dealer to verify to what extent such hedge is effective in taking care of the possible losses that the bank is likely to incur in its trading portfolio due to a rise in the GOI yields. Accordingly, different hedging methods, such as *Nominal Value Hedge, M-Duration/Sensitivity Based Hedge*, hedging at the *portfolio level with any single futures contract*, and *hedging individual positions*

Table 9.13 Details of single bond futures contract used

*Details of Single Bond Futures Contract (Near Month) Offered by NSE*

| 1 June 2018 | | | | | 2 July 2018 | | | |
| Security Description | Maturity of Futures | Market Price (INR) | M-Duration | | Security Description | Maturity of Futures | Market Price (INR) | M-Duration |
| --- | --- | --- | --- | --- | --- | --- | --- | --- |
| 684GS2022 280618 | 28-06-2018 | 96.258 | 3.7055 | | 684GS2022 260718 | 26-07-2018 | 95.885 | 3.7491 |
| 697GS2026 280618 | 28-06-2018 | 93.598 | 5.9974 | | 697GS2026 260718 | 26-07-2018 | 93.1575 | 5.9075 |
| 717GS2028 280618 | 28-06-2018 | 95.670 | 6.5756 | | 717GS2028 260718 | 26-07-2018 | 95.03 | 6.4839 |
| 679GS2029 280618 | 28-06-2018 | 90.225 | 7.4327 | | 679GS2029 260718 | 26-07-2018 | 89.1975 | 7.6095 |
| 668GS2031 280618 | 28-06-2018 | 89.365 | 8.2736 | | 668GS2031 260718 | 26-07-2018 | 88.72 | 8.1702 |

*either with the same futures contract (i.e. a futures with the same under-lying, referred to as direct hedging) if available, or with any other futures having a significant price correlation* (i.e. a futures with a different under-lying, referred to as cross hedging) are explored.

The result of such an exercise is nothing but to arrive at the *Hedge Ratio* that exhibits the number of *desirable (long or short)* positions the bank may require to take in single/multiple bond futures contracts *under different circumstances/methods*. It is also proposed to test the effectiveness of a *Static Hedge* and a *Dynamic Hedge*. In case of a static hedge, the bank just needs to take the short position on the required number of futures contracts, as suggested by the hedge ratio, and hold the same till they mature. But since the volatility of the underlying positions and that of the futures contracts keep changing, a hedger may need to rebalance his/her hedging positions, depending on the new hedge ratio required to be arrived at by a certain time interval, referred to as dynamic hedging. The bank may like to see the difference in the hedge effectiveness of a static hedge and also a dynamic hedge, say with a fortnightly rebalancing in the hedging portfolio.

In order to test the *Hedge Effectiveness* of different hedging methods, the chief dealer has taken the historical data on the same underlying trading portfolio required to be hedged and the bond futures (near-month) contract offered by the exchange in the month of June 2018. This one month of historical data on the concerned underlying positions and on selected bond futures contracts are used to analyze how effective these bond futures contracts would have been if the bank would have taken the required number of short positions, under different methods, as on 1 June 2018, to hedge its underlying trading positions till the maturity of the near-month futures contract (i.e. till 28 June 2018). Historical spot and futures (near-month) prices respectively for the concerned underlying securities (GOI Bonds) and selected bond futures contracts, during 1 to 28 June 2018, are given in the Annexure.

## Major aspects to be highlighted

- Bank's Hedging Requirement and Use of Single Bond Futures Contract
- Availability of Single Bond Futures in India, Their Structures, Mechanism, and Market Practices
- Different Possible Methods Available to Execute a Hedge

- Effectiveness of Nominal Value Hedge vs. Sensitivity-Based Hedge
- Effectiveness of Hedge at the Portfolio Level vs. Hedge at the Individual Security/Position Levels
- Effectiveness of Direct Hedge vs. Cross Hedge Based on Price Correlations
- Effectiveness of Static vs. Dynamic Hedge with Regular Rebalancing
- Critical Assessment of Different Hedging Methods and Final Recommendation

## Self-learning exercise

1 How does the nature of underlying, notional bond or single bond, against interest rate futures contracts play a role for the growth of the interest rate futures market in developing economies, like in India?

2 Why is it necessary to have conversion factors for a Treasury futures or notional bond futures contract? What price is the buyer of IRF supposed to pay to get the physical delivery of either of the securities from the deliverable basket at the maturity of the IRF, and how is the same calculated?

3 "When interest rate futures contracts are used to hedge the interest rate risk in the underlying exposure(s), and some cross hedging is initiated, it is always desirable to be over-hedged to get the desired protection". Do you completely agree with this statement?

4 An underlying bond position with a modified duration of 8% is hedged using an IRF contract with a CTD issue, having m-duration of 6.5%. What does this imply for the hedge that is put on?

5 Chief General Manager (CGM), Global Markets, State Bank of India has recently received authorization from the regulator to use a bond futures contract on GOI securities to hedge his exposure in GOI bonds, as well as for market making. The Treasury Head, therefore, advised his Chief Manager, recently shifted from the Credit Department and presently managing the Rupee Derivatives desk in the bank, to be sure to keep sufficient cash available to satisfy any contingency payments that must be made as a result of such positions in the interest rate futures market. The Chief Manager was not clear as to why any contingency payments must be made. You have some experience dealing in the IRF market and have recently joined the Domestic Treasury to assist him/her in managing the desk. Therefore, he/she has asked you to explain the necessity of such contingency payment in any position in the IRF. He/she is also confused about the viability of such exposure in the bank's business. What will be your response to him/her?

6 Is there any significant counterparty risk associated with an interest rate futures contract?

7 Do you agree with the following statement: *"Interest rate futures contracts and forward rate agreements expose the counterparties to the same degree of counterparty risk"*? Explain with justification.

8 How is an interest rate futures contract priced or valued? Explain with an example.

9 What are positive carry and negative carry, in the context of pricing interest rate futures contracts? How do these carries affect the price of an interest rate futures contract?

10 Explain how the market-to-market mechanism at a regular interval, say daily, in an interest rate futures contract affects both the counterparties.

11 How is an interest rate futures contract useful for a bank's asset liability management? Is there any alternative approach to do the same, dealing with the underlying market only? In the presence of both the alternatives, which one is easy and practically feasible to implement?

12 The Fund Manager of HDFC Mutual Fund, having expertise in the stock market, has got the role of managing a balanced fund, comprised of investment in both equities and bonds, created by the HDFC Mutual Fund. Therefore, in order to protect the NAV of the balanced fund, the fund manager would like to use a stock futures contract and Treasury bond futures contract, respective to managing the risk of equity and bond component of the fund. Since he/she is an equity expert, he/she does not have any problem dealing with the single stock futures contract. But he/she may not have sufficient expertise to deal with the Treasury bond futures contract. When he/she enquired from a broker about the IRF, he/she was told that the underlying for a Treasury bond futures contract is nothing but INR 2,00,000 par value of a 10-year 7% coupon Treasury bond. After enquiring in the market, the Fund Manager found that no such 10-year 7% Coupon Bond, issued by GOI, exists. The Fund Manager thought that the contract was probably a cash settlement contract because there is no deliverable. How should the broker respond to the understanding of the fund manager?

13 What is meant by *Basis Risk* in the context of establishing a hedge position on GOI bonds using NSE Bond Futures Contract?

14 What is cross hedging? How can notional bond futures and/or single bond futures be used to have different levels/types of cross hedging for an underlying bond portfolio consisting of securities of various maturities? Explain the benefits and limitations of such types of cross hedging.

15 What is the basis for any arbitrage opportunity to arise in the fixed income market? How are interest rate futures contracts useful to a fixed income trader to initiate an arbitrage under different market scenarios?

## Notes

1  A central counterparty clearing house (CCP) is an entity that facilitates trading in various financial market products. The primary function of CCPs as an intermediary in a transaction are: clearing and settlement. As counterparties to the buyers and the sellers, CCPs guarantee the terms of a trade – even if one party defaults on the agreement, and therefore bear the counterparty risk of both the buyers and sellers. Like a margining system required to be followed in case of exchange traded contracts, the CCP collects a certain amount, depending upon the value of exposure and open obligations, from both buyer and seller to cover the potential losses incurred due to the failing of either of the counterparty (buyer or seller).

2  Foreign portfolio investment, say in India, is investments made by non-residents in India in various securities (e.g. shares, bonds, etc.). Foreign portfolio investors (FPI) include investment groups of FIIs and qualified foreign investors (QFI). Besides several limits on FPI investments in India, as per circulars issued by the RBI and SEBI, a separate limit of INR 50 billion is allocated to FPIs for taking a long position in IRFs, especially to facilitate market development and to ensure that FPIs' access to bond futures. Unlike foreign direct investment (FDI), FPI is one of the common ways for investors (especially retail investors) to participate in an overseas economy without any direct ownership.

## Bibliography

Choudhry, M. (2010). *Fixed Income Securities and Derivatives Handbook: Analysis and Valuation* (2nd edn.). John Wiley & Sons, Inc., Hoboken, NJ.

Fabozzi, F. (ed.). (July 2017). *The Handbook of Fixed Income Securities* (8th edn.). McGraw Hill Education, New York.

Kishimoto, N. (1998). Duration and Convexity of Coupon Bond Futures. *Journal of Fixed Income*, 8(1), 79–83.

Kolb, R. W., and Chiang, R. (1981). Improving Hedging Performance Using Interest Rate Futures. *Financial Management*, 10, 72–79.

Kolb, R. W., and Chiang, R. (1982). Duration, Immunization and Hedging With Interest Rate Futures. *Journal of Financial Research*, 5(2), 161–170.

Rendleman, R. J. (1999). Duration-Based Hedging With Treasury Bond Futures. *Journal of Fixed Income*, 9(1), 84–91.

Senchak, A. J., and Easterwood, J. C. (1983). Cross Hedging CDs With Treasury Bill Futures. *Journal of Futures Markets*, 3, 429–438.

Sundaresan, S. (2009). *Fixed Income Markets and Their Derivatives* (3rd edn.). Elsevier India Pvt. Ltd., India.

Veronesi, P. (2011). *Fixed Income Securities: Valuation, Risk and Risk Management*. John Wiley & Sons, Inc., Hoboken, NJ.

# 10 Forward rate agreement and interest rate swaps

**Key learning outcomes**

At the end of this chapter, the readers are expected to be familiar with:

- What does an FRA or IRS structure look like?
- What is the current status of FRA and IRS Market in emerging economies like in India?
- How to simplify an FRA or IRS deal slip.
- Important IRS Structures available in emerging markets, and how do these derivative contracts practically work?
- What is the Theory of Comparative Advantage in the interest rate market, and how is it applicable to an FRA or IRS contract?
- How to price and value (market-to-market) these forward and swaps contracts.
- How are the payoffs due to regular (e.g. semi-annually) settlement and also settlement at maturity arrived at?
- What are different ways to prematurely cancel/unwind such a contract and arrive at the concerned payoff?
- What are the advantages and limitations of different methods of premature unwinding of such a deal?
- How are these contracts useful to various groups of market players?
- How is the hedge effectiveness of an IRS deal tested?
- What are the risks involved in FRA/IRS?
- What are the necessary documentations for FRA/IRS Deals?

## FRA & IRS: meaning & product structure

### Definition of FRA

Being an OTC financial derivative contract, a *Forward Rate Agreement* (FRA) is essentially a forward-dated loan dealt at an agreed rate. There is no exchange of principal, and therefore the principal becomes the *Notional Principal*. Only the interest differential between the contractual rate and the actual rate prevailing at the time of settlement, applicable on the notional principal, changes hands. In other words, an FRA is an agreement to borrow or lend a *notional* amount for a period of time, generally fixed up to 12 months, starting at any point over the next 12 months, at an agreed rate of interest (the FRA rate). The "Buyer" of an FRA is borrowing a notional sum of money while the "Seller" is the lender of the same. By trading today at an interest rate that is effective at some future point of time, FRAs enable banks, FIs, and corporates to hedge their interest rate exposures, but generally of shorter terms, say 3 to 12 months. FRAs may also be used to speculate on the level of future short-term interest rates.

### Example of FRA

Suppose a company may like to borrow an amount of INR 10 crores in three months' time for a subsequent period of 12 months. It can borrow funds today, say at MIBOR + 100 basis points, depending upon its creditworthiness in the market. Assuming that the MIBOR (currently prevailing at 8%) may possibly increase (say at 9%) over the next few weeks. Therefore, the company might be forced to borrow at a higher rate unless some hedging is initiated to protect the borrowing requirement. In order to hedge this interest rate risk, the company's treasurer decides to buy a suitable forward contract (say, 3 × 15 FRA) to cover risk in the coming 12-month period beginning 3 months from now. Suppose a bank quotes 8.5% for the similar FRA, which the company buys on a notional of INR 10 crores. Considering the fact that 3 months from now MIBOR indeed goes up to 9%, making the treasurer borrow funds from the market at 10% (the MIBOR plus fixed spread of 100 bps) and incurring a loss of INR 0.10 crore {(10% − 9%) × INR 10 crore} in his borrowing. However, he/she will receive a settlement amount equal to the difference between the rate at which the FRA was bought (i.e. 8.50%) and today's 12-month MIBOR rate (9%) as a percentage of Rs.10 crore, coming to INR 0.05 crore {(9% − 8.5%) × INR 10 crore}, which will compensate the treasurer, if not the whole but some of his additional borrowing costs.

### Mechanics of FRA

The *Buyer* of an FRA may be considered to be a notional borrower and becomes protected (fully or partially) for any rise in interest rates happening between the FRA traded date and the date when the contract comes into effect. On the other hand, if there is a fall in the reference interest rate, the buyer must pay the difference between the FRA and the actual rate prevailing on the effective date, as a percentage of the notional principal. The buyer of an FRA may use the contract either to hedge an actual exposure (e.g. an actual future borrowing) or may simply speculate on a rise in interest rates. As far as the *Seller* of the FRA is concerned, he/she is the notional lender of funds and has fixed the rate for lending funds. If there is any fall in the lending rates in spot market, the FRA seller will book a profit from this contract and could offset his/her losses (fully or partially) in actual lending (if any). On the other hand, any rise in lending rates makes the FRA seller book a loss in the FRA deal but may offset the loss with the additional earning from the higher interest income due in the lending exposure (if any). In case the FRA seller acts as a speculator, any rise (fall) in the reference rate makes the seller lose (gain).

The spot date is usually 2 business days after the trade date. The settlement date will be the time period after the spot date referred to by the FRA terms, for example a 3 × 6 FRA will have a settlement date 3 calendar months after the spot date, as shown in the above figure (Figure 10.1). The fixing date is usually 2 business days before the settlement date, assuming a T+2 settlement. The settlement sum, even if due at the maturity date, is normally paid on the settlement date. Since the amount is paid up front, at the start of the contract period, the calculated sum is the present value of the concerned amount, discounted at the prevailing rate of interest applicable for the period (settlement date to maturity date).

### Forward rate agreement: a sample deal

A forward rate agreement contract can be illustrated with a sample deal slip, as given in the following table (Table 10.1).

### FRA deal slip: simplified

* As per the above FRA deal, the bank (Bank of India) may be exposed to the risk of rising rates of interest in the near future, and therefore may like to hedge its fixed rate exposures by entering into this deal with Barclays

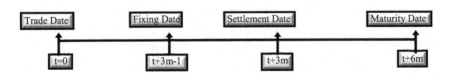

*Figure 10.1* Structure of a forward rate agreement

*Table 10.1* Forward rate agreement: a sample deal

| | |
|---|---|
| Bank of India<br>Treasury and International Banking Division<br>Mumbai | |
| Deal Number | FRA/****/**** |
| Type of Transaction | Hedging |
| Counterparty | Barclays Bank |
| Notional Amount | INR 25,00,00,000 (INR 25 Crore) |
| Trade Date and Time | 15 April 2015 / 15:40 |
| Start Date | 15 July 2015 |
| End/Maturity Date | 15 January 2016 |
| Fixing Date | Two Business Days Prior to Start Date |
| Settlement Date | 15 July 2015 |
| Fixed Rate Payer | Bank of India |
| Fixed Rate of Interest (FRA Rate) | 7.5% Per Annum |
| Floating Rate Payer | Barclay Bank |
| Floating Interest Rate | 3-Month INR-MIBOR |
| Day Count Basis | Actual/365 |
| Holiday Convention | Modified Following Business Day in Mumbai. |

*Source*: All tables in this chapter are created by the author unless otherwise stated.

Bank, where the BOI pays the fixed rate of 7.5% p.a. in exchange of the 3-month INR-MIBOR, received from the Barclays Bank.

- The deal is actually a 3 × 9 FRA, i.e. a 6-month forward contract 3 months hence, initiated/traded on 15 April 2015 for a future period of 6 months starting from 15 July 2015 and maturing on 15 January 2016 on a notional principal amount of INR 25 crores.
- The contract is expected to be settled on the starting date itself (i.e. on 15 July 2015), and therefore the date of fixing the floating rate of interest is just 2 days prior to the settlement date, i.e. on 13 July 2015.
- Accordingly, the present value, discounted for a period of 6 months as on 15 July 2015, of the interest differential on the notional principal amount is going to be settled by the concerned counterparty (BOI or Barclays Bank), depending on the prevailing 3-month MIBOR as on the fixing date.
- If the 3-M MIBOR is higher than 7.5%, Barclays bank needs to pay to the BOI, and vice versa.
- The interest differential will be calculated based on the Actual/365 day count convention.

### Definition of IRS

An interest rate swap (IRS), as shown in the following figure (Figure 10.2), is a contractual arrangement between two counterparties who agree to exchange payments based on two different rates of interest on a defined principal (notional) amount for a fixed period of time. Like FRAs, no exchange of the principal amount is also involved in IRS. In a standard IRS deal, having one fixed leg and another floating leg, the buyer of the contract pays a fixed rate and receives a floating rate, while the seller of IRS receives a fixed rate and pays a floating rate. In short, an interest rate swap (IRS) is a financial contract between two counterparties swapping *a Stream of interest payments* on a 'notional principal' amount at *Multiple Occasions* during a specified contractual period.

Interest rate swaps can be broadly categorized as: asset swap and liability swap. An asset swap is basically used to hedge the income stream generated from an asset, like loan or investment in bonds. A part or full fixed rate of interest received from the asset can be exchanged with a floating rate, as shown in the following figure (Figure 10.3).

Therefore, a fixed rate loan, or investment in fixed rate bonds, at a situation of rising interest rates, can be hedged with an asset swap. This helps a bank to match the interest rate exposure of short-term deposits and long-term loans. On the other hand, a liability swap is basically used to hedge the payment stream made for a liability, like the payment of fixed return to insurance policy holders. These fixed interest payments made by an insurance company to its liability holders can be exchanged with floating rates, possibly as depicted in the following figure (Figure 10.4).

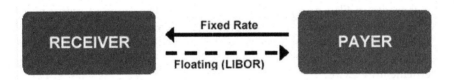

*Figure 10.2* Structure of a plain vanilla interest rate swap

*Figure 10.3* Structure of an interest rate swap (asset swap)

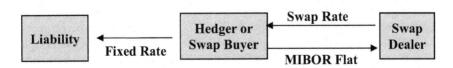

*Figure 10.4* Structure of an interest rate swap (liability swap)

Therefore, fixed rate liability, at a situation of falling rates, can be hedged with a liability swap. This helps an insurance company to match the interest rate exposure of fixed rate liabilities and floating rate investments.

## FRA and IRS market in India

OTC interest rate derivatives (FRAs and IRS) in India were introduced in 1999, enabling banks, PDs, and other financial institutions (FIs) basically to hedge their interest rate risk arising out of asset-liability mismatches. Further, to promote liquidity in the market, market making activities were also gradually permitted for eligible entities subject to internal prudential limits. Once the OTC derivatives market in India started gaining a foothold, RBI in the year 2007 decided to introduce a mechanism to ensure post-trade transparency and centralized trade processing, basically to promote efficient price discovery and ease of managing OTC trades in India. Accordingly, banks and PDs were mandatorily required to report all their inter-bank/PD deals in FRAs and IRS to the reporting platform developed by CCIL within 30 minutes of the execution of the trade. Necessary information (rates, notional amount, maturity, etc.) related to all the trades started getting disseminated to market participants through the CCIL platform. Subsequently, in November 2008, CCIL started offering settlement of the trades reported on its reporting platform on a non-guaranteed basis. Besides centralized settlement through CCIL, market participants (e.g. banks, PDs) started settling their trades in FRA and IRS bilaterally as well. The scope of reporting of OTC trades in interest rate derivatives was further extended to client-level (between banks/PDs with their clients) transactions as well. Further the non-guaranteed settlements in FRA and IRS has been upgraded to guaranteed settlement by CCIL.

In India, interest rate swaps are commonly traded on two benchmarks viz. Mumbai Interbank Outright Rate (MIBOR) and Mumbai Interbank Forward Offered Rate (MIFOR). Like MIBOR, the MIFOR is also a popular benchmark that has developed into a proxy for the AAA corporate funding cost in India. MIFOR is derived from the USD LIBOR and the USD/INR forward premium and is simply the Indian equivalent of USD LIBOR and the USD interest rate swaps market. Alternatively, this rate is the implied rupee yield for dollar liability hedged through the forward exchange market. Hence, a 6-month MIFOR denotes the implied rupee yield arrived by taking dollars at 6-month LIBOR and swapping for rupees in the dollar-rupee forward exchange market. There are a large number of Indian corporates who now regularly use this interest rate benchmark to actively manage the interest rate risk on their debt portfolios and access funding at better rates. MIFOR requires two market prices to be determined: the USD overnight LIBOR and the swap points of a USD-INR FX swap on the same maturity.

Even if the IRS in India is offered on three different benchmarks, viz. 1-year Indian benchmark rate (INBMK), Overnight Mumbai Interbank

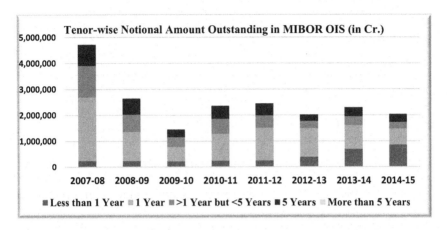

*Figure 10.5* Tenor-wise notional amount outstanding in MIBOR-OIS

Outright Rate (MIBOR), and Mumbai Interbank Forward Outright Rate (MIFOR), MIBOR-based contracts are more popular among market participants, accounting for almost 80% – 85% of the total trades in IRS in terms of notional amount. Another aspect of the market, which is not unique only to India, has been the concentration of market participants (share of foreign banks is about 80% of the total market volume with virtual absence of nationalized banks). Even if there is inconsistency in the popularity of MIBOR-OIS of various maturities, average trading activity in such contracts is mostly concentrated in the 1-year to 5-year deals, accounting for almost 41% and 59% of the total traded volume during 2017–18, respectively, for contracts of less than 1-year maturity, and more than 1-year till 5-year maturity, in comparison with the last year's (2016–17) figures that stands roughly at 45% and 55%. Contracts of more than 5 years maturity hardly experience any significant trades over the years. Tenor-wise, the share of MIBOR-OIS contracts over a period of the last 8 years is shown in the following figure (Figure 10.5), in support of the above statement.

## Pricing of forward rate agreement

FRAs are forward rate instruments and are priced using forward rate principles. Consider an investor who has two investment alternatives, either to invest for 6 months at 5% per annum or to invest for 1-year at 6% p.a. If the investor wishes to invest for 6 months and then roll over the investment for the subsequent period of 6 months, then the market may like to know the required rate of interest for the rollover period such that the final annual return comes out to be 6% available from the one-year investment. If the

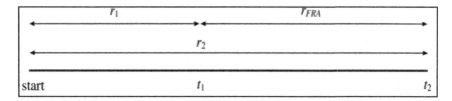

*Figure 10.6* Timeline in an FRA contract

FRA rate is viewed as the breakeven forward rate between the two periods, as shown in the following figure (Figure 10.6), we may simply solve for this forward rate, as discussed in the previous chapter, which could be considered as the approximate FRA rate.

The time period $t_1$ is the time from the dealing date to the FRA settlement date, while $t_2$ is the time from the dealing date to the FRA maturity date. The time period for the FRA (contract period) is $t_2$ minus $t_1$. Therefore, the FRA rate can be calculated, such that:

$$(1 + r_2 t_2) = (1 + r_1 t_1)(1 + r_f t_f); r_f = \frac{(r_2 t_2 - r_1 t_1)}{t_f \times (1 + r_1 t_1)} \tag{10.1}$$

### Example: pricing of FRA

A bank and a corporate enter into a 3 x 6 FRA on a notional amount of Rs.10 crore. Corporate pays the FRA rate and the bank pays the benchmark rate based on the 3-month CP issuance rate of the above corporate 3 months later.

Current 3-month and 6-month CP rates for the corporate are respectively 7.5% and 8%.

What will be the rate of interest that the corporate is supposed to pay for 3 months after a period of 3 months from now at the time of initiating the contract?

### Solution

The bank has the option of:

(i)  Buying the 6-month CP (Option 1).
(ii) Buying the 3-month CP and selling a 3x6 FRA (Option 2).

The FRA rate would be the 3-month over 6-month roll-over rate, which would make the bank indifferent between the two options today.

Given the spot rates for two years or periods, it is possible to calculate the forward rate between the two periods, such that:

$$f_{m,n} = [\{(1 + z_n \times n) / (1 + z_m \times m) \square 1\} \times (1 / (n - m))] \quad (10.2)$$

Therefore, Principal + Int. accrued on Option 1 = Principal + Int. accrued on Option 2

$$=> 100 \times (1 + CP_6 \ \ 184 / 365) = 100 \times (1 + CP_3 \times 92 / 365)$$
$$\times (1 + 3 \times 6 \ FRA \times 92 / 365)$$
$$=> 3 \times 6 \ FRA = 8.34\% \ p.a.$$

Therefore, $3 \times 6$ FRA rate is *8.34% p.a.*

## Settlement of an FRA deal

- Once the deal is initiated, the same needs to be settled in due time, which is normally on the start date itself.
- The fixed rate, which is the FRA rate, gets decided on the trade date, whereas the floating rate gets frozen on the fixing date, which is normally 2 days prior to the start/settlement date.
- The settlement amount depends upon the difference between the FRA rate and the floating rate, on the contractual notional principal amount, applicable for the actual contract period, i.e. the period between the start date and the end/maturity date, following the Actual/365 day count convention.
- Accordingly, the interest differential, which is actually due on the maturity date, will be settled between the buyer and seller of the FRA, but on the start/settlement date itself after discounting the same.
- Therefore, the sum of settlement can be calculated, such that:

*Settlement Sum = {(Benchmark Floating Rate - Contractual FRA Rate)*
*$\square$ Notional Principal $\square$ (Actual No. of Days in the Contract Period / 365)}*
*$\square$ {1 / (1 + Benchmark Floating Rate $\square$ (Actual No. of Days in*
*the Contract Period / 365)}* (10.3)

### *Example: FRA settlement*

Suppose the Bank of Baroda has entered into the following 6-month FRA deal 3 months hence, with the Barclays Bank to pay an FRA rate of 7.50%, against the 3-month INR-MIBOR. Assuming the 3-month MIBOR (annualized) as on the fixing date is at 7.75%, the settlement amount can be calculated as follows:

- Notional principal: INR 25,00,00,000
- FRA trade date: 15 April 2015
- FRA start/settlement date: 15 July 2015
- FRA maturity date: 15 January 2016
- FRA fixing date: 13 July 2015
- Contractual FRA rate: 7.5%

Since the 3-month MIBOR as on 13 July 2015 is at 7.75%, and the Bank of Baroda pays the FRA rate, which is presently lower than the floating rate, and receives the 3-month MIBOR, it will have a net interest receivable from the Barclays Bank. The net interest receivable can be calculated as:

$$Net\ Interest\ Settlement = \{(7.75\% - 7.50\%) \times INR\ 25\ Crore$$
$$\times\ (184/365)\} \times \{1\ /\ (1+7.75\% \times 184/365)\}$$
$$= INR\ 3,15,068.49/- \times 0.9624$$
$$= INR\ 3,03,222.06/-.$$

Therefore, the fixed rate payer, i.e. the Bank of Baroda, will receive a sum of INR 303,222.06/- from the Barclays Bank, as the first and final settlement for the FRA deal as on the start date, i.e. on 15 July 2015. In case the 3-month MIBOR falls, the net settlement amount as per the above calculations will be a negative sum, representing the net settlement amount payable by the Bank of Baroda to the Barclays Bank.

## Different types of interest rate swaps

Being an OTC product, the IRS can be customized to a wide range of structures in terms of reference benchmark rates, maturity, notional principal, etc. to meet the specific needs of various counterparties. However, in the interbank market of an emerging economy like in India, a few standardized types of IRS, as discussed below, are commonly traded.

1  *Fixed to Floating Rate Swap (same currency)* – Under this agreement, one party pays the fixed rate and the other pays the floating rate in the same currency on a notional principal amount for a specified maturity. These types of swaps are used to convert fixed rate liability/asset to floating rate liability/asset and vice versa in the same currency.
2  *Fixed to Floating Rate Swap (different currency)* – As per this type of contract, one counterparty pays/receives the fixed interest in a particular currency to receive/pay the floating rate in some other currency on a notional principal at an initial exchange rate for a specified period. Fixed-for-floating swaps in different currencies are used to convert a fixed rate asset/liability in one currency to a floating rate asset/liability in a different currency, or vice versa.

3   *Floating to Floating Rate Swap (same currency)* – This is a swap con-
    tract between two counterparties, where one party pays/receives the
    floating interest linked to some benchmark to receive/pay the floating
    rate of interest only but linked to another benchmark on a pre-specified
    notional amount for a particular period in the same currency. These
    types of swaps are used to hedge against or speculate on the widening
    or narrowing of the spread between two benchmark rates.

4   *Floating to Floating Rate Swap (different currency)* – This type of swap
    contract makes one counterparty pay/receive the floating interest rate in
    one currency linked to some benchmark to receive/pay again the float-
    ing rate but linked to some other benchmark rate and also in another
    currency, on a notional amount, at an initial exchange rate during a
    specified period.

5   *Fixed to Fixed Rate Swap (different currency)* – This is a swap contract
    between two counterparties where one party pays/receives the fixed
    interest in one currency in exchange of receiving/paying the fixed rate
    only but in other currency for a specified period.

## Important structures of IRS in India

There are various types of interest rate swaps available in the Indian market.
Some of them are discussed hereunder:

### INBMK swap

INBMK swaps are an interest rate swaps contract, denominated in INR,
where the interest rate under the floating leg is benchmarked to the Indian
Benchmark Rate. 'INBMK' here refers to the page on which the GOI yields
are quoted daily by Reuters. The floating GOI tenor, by general market
convention, is taken as a 1-year GOI yield, as it appears on the Reuters
page under the heading 'Yield' as "0#INBMK=", as of 12:30 p.m., IST, on
the day, i.e. 1 Mumbai business day preceding that reset date. This kind of
swap contract is basically used by various market players, like banks, PDs,
insurance companies, corporates, etc., especially to hedge the interest rate
risk that arises out of their investments in GOI securities.

### Example: INBMK swap

The structure of an interest rate swap with a long-term benchmark, known
as INBMK swap in India, is shown in the following figure (Figure 10.7).

- INBMK refers to the yield on the benchmark 1-year government of
  India security.
- Bank pays 1-year INBMK, reset annually and payable annually, in INR
  on the notional principal of INR 50 cr. for 5 years.

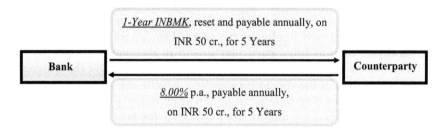

*Figure 10.7* Structure of an INBMK swap

- Counterparty pays (bank receives) 8.00% p.a., payable annually, in INR on the notional principal of INR 50 cr. for 5 years.
- No exchange of principal takes place between the counterparties at beginning or end.

This is also a plain vanilla pure INR interest rate swap, in which the bank as a counterparty of this contract does not carry any currency risk, but is exposed to the risk of any *rise in the 1-year benchmark yield*, and/or any *fall in the fixed rate*.

### Interest rate swaps (benchmark: INBMK): a sample deal

An interest rate swap contract can be illustrated with the following deal slip, as given in the following table (Table 10.2).

### IRS (INBMK) deal slip: simplified

- As per the above IRS deal, the bank (Indian Bank) may be exposed to the risk of rising rates of interest in the near future, maybe for a longer period, and therefore may like to hedge its fixed rate exposures by entering into this deal with the Standard Chartered Bank, Mumbai, where the Indian Bank pays the fixed rate of 7.54% p.a., payable semi-annually on 16 October and 16 April every year, commencing from 16 October 2015 till the maturity date 16 April 2020, in exchange of the 1-year INBMK rate plus a spread of 50 basis points, payable semi-annually on the same dates, received from the Standard Chartered Bank, Mumbai.
- The deal is actually a 5-year IRS deal, maturing on 16 April 2020, on a notional principal amount of INR 50 crores, linked to the long-term INBMK interest rate.
- Unlike FRA, even if the fixed rate of the IRS contract is fixed for the entire maturity at a level of 7.54% p.a., payable semiannually, the floating leg is expected to be reset every 6 months, more specifically one

*Table 10.2* Interest rate swap (INBMK): a sample deal

Indian Bank
Treasury Department
Mumbai

| | |
|---|---|
| Deal Number/ID | IRS-INBMK/****/**** |
| Type of Transaction | Hedging |
| Category | Hedging |
| Counterparty | Standard Chartered Bank, Mumbai |
| Trade Date and Time | 15 April 2015/15:40 |
| Effective Date | 16 April 2015 |
| Termination/Maturity Date | 16 April 2020 |
| Early Termination Clause | 2 Years from the Effective Date, i.e. 16 April 2017 |
| Callability | Not Applicable |
| Notional Amount | INR 500,000,000.00 (INR 50 Crore) |
| Amortization Schedule | Not Applicable |
| Fixed Rate Payer | Indian Bank |
| Fixed Rate of Interest (Swap Rate) | 7.54 % on Notional Principal Amount |
| Fixed Rate Payment Dates | 16 April and 16 October every year, commencing from 16 October 2015, till and including the termination date, subject to adjustment in accordance with the modified following business day convention |
| Fixed Rate Day Count Convention | Actual/365 |
| Floating Rate Payer | Standard Chartered Bank, Mumbai |
| Floating Interest Rate | 1-Year INBMK (reset and paid semi-annually) + 0.50% |
| Floating Rate Fixing Dates | One business day prior to the beginning of each interest calculation period |
| Floating Rate Payment Dates | 16 April and 16 October every year, commencing from 16 October 2015, till and including the termination date, subject to adjustment in accordance with the modified following business day convention |
| Floating Rate Day Count Convention | Actual/365 |
| Holiday Convention | Modified Following Business Day Convention in Mumbai |

business day prior to the beginning of each interest calculation period (16 April to 16 October), starting from 15 October 2015.

- Accordingly, the last reset of the floating leg of the IRS deal will be on 15 October 2019 one business day prior to the beginning of last interest calculation period (i.e. 16 October 2019 to 16 April 2020), followed by the last and final settlement on 16 April 2020.
- Unlike an FRA, since the interest differential in an IRS deal is settled in arrear, the same need not to be discounted, and all semi-annual

settlements take place at the actual amount. The interest differential may be received/paid by Indian Bank in all settlement dates till the maturity, depending upon the difference between the fixed and floating rate of interests.

- In case the 1-year INBMK rate, decided on any of the floating rate reset dates, is higher than the fixed rate minus the spread portion of the floating leg, i.e. 7.04% (7.54% – 0.5%), the Indian Bank will receive the interest differential on the notional principal of INR 50 crore for a period of 6 months, and vice versa.
- The interest differential during any of the settlement dates will be calculated based on the Actual/365 day count convention.
- In case any of the counterparties of the IRS deal would like to terminate/cancel the deal before the maturity, the same can be executed within 2 years from the effective date, i.e. within 16 April 2017. In such case, cancellation shall take place at the rate quoted by the counterparty, and the net interest accrued plus the MTM value of the IRS deal at the quoted rate need to be settled.

### MIBOR overnight index swap

Even though different types of IRS contracts are offered in India, the market which has taken off relatively well is the market for overnight index swaps (OIS). Benchmarks of tenor other than overnight have not become popular majorly due to the nonexistence of a vibrant inter-bank term money market.

A MIBOR overnight index swap (MIBOR-OIS) is a fixed/floating interest rate swap with the floating leg linked to an overnight inter-bank call money index. The term ranges from 1 week to 10 years, with an average maximum liquidity in a 1-year contract. The interest would be computed on a notional principal amount and settled on a net basis at maturity. On the floating rate side, the interest amounts are compounded on a daily basis based on the overnight index. The two parties agree to exchange the interest differential on the agreed notional amount either at maturity or at some intermediate settlement dates, depending on the maturity of the contract. In case of 1-year OIS, the interest differential is settled only at the maturity. Otherwise, for a long-term contract, settlement generally takes place every 6 months.

Settlement is based on the difference between interest accrued at the agreed fixed rate and interest accrued through geometric averaging of the floating index rate. Floating rate calculation replicates the accrual on an amount of rolling "principal plus interest" at the index rate every business day over the term of the swap. If cash can be borrowed by the swap receiver on the same maturity as the swap and at the same rate and lent back every day in the market at the overnight index rate, the cash payoff at maturity will exactly match the swap payout. Therefore, OIS acts as a perfect hedge for such a cash instrument. Economically, receiving (paying) the fixed rate in an MIBOR-OIS is like lending (borrowing) cash.

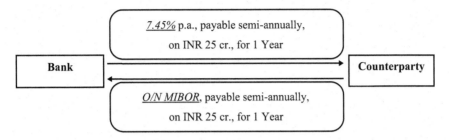

*Figure 10.8* Structure of an O/N Index swap

*Example: O/N MIBOR swap or overnight index swap*

The structure of an O/N MIBOR swap may be shown through the following figure (Figure 10.8).

1.  Bank pays 7.45% p.a. fixed, payable semi-annually, in INR on the notional principal of INR 25 cr.
    *   Counterparty pays (bank receives) *O/N MIBOR*, compounded daily but payable semi-annually, in INR on the notional principal of INR 25 cr.
    *   No exchange of principal takes place between the counterparties at beginning or end.
    *   This is a plain vanilla pure interest rate swap, in which the bank, as a counterparty of this contract, does not carry any currency risk but is exposed to the risk of any fall in the *Fixed Rate* and/or any fall in *O/N MIBOR*.

*Interest rate swap (benchmark: O/N MIBOR): a sample deal*

A MIBOR-OIS contract can be illustrated with a sample deal slip as exhibited in the following table (Table 10.3).

*IRS (MIBOR-OIS) deal slip: simplified*

*   As per the above MIBOR-OIS deal, the bank (Canara Bank) may have a view about the movement in the future rate of interest (O/N rate and/or the OIS rate), and therefore may like to enter into a pure trading deal, for a period of 9 months, with the HONGKONG & SHANGHAI BKG CORP., Mumbai, where Canara Bank pays the fixed rate (swap rate) of 7.54% p.a. on the notional amount of INR 50 crore for the specified period, payable only once, at the maturity (16 January 2016), because of its shorter tenor of less than 1 year.
*   In return, the HONGKONG & SHANGHAI BKG CORP., Mumbai, will pay based on the O/N MIBOR, compounded daily, on the same

*Table 10.3* Interest rate swap (O/N MIBOR): a sample deal

Canara Bank
Treasury Branch
Mumbai

| | |
|---|---|
| Deal Number/ID | IRS-OIS/****/**** |
| Type of Transaction | Trading |
| Category | Trading |
| Counterparty | HONGKONG & SHANGHAI BKG CORP., Mumbai |
| Trade Date and Time | 15 April 2015/15:40 |
| Effective Date | 16 April 2015 |
| Termination/Maturity Date | 16 January 2016 |
| Early Termination Clause | Not Applicable |
| Callability | Not Applicable |
| Notional Amount | INR 500,000,000.00 (INR 50 Crore) |
| Fixed Rate Payer | Canara Bank |
| Fixed Rate of Interest (OIS Rate) | 7.54 % on Outstanding INR Principal Amount |
| Fixed Rate Payment Dates | 16 January 2016 |
| Fixed Rate Day Count Convention | Actual/365 |
| Floating Rate Payer | HONGKONG & SHANGHAI BKG CORP., Mumbai |
| Floating Interest Rate | INR-MIBOR-OIS-COMPOUND |
| Floating Rate Fixing Dates | The Last Day of Each Calculation Period |
| Floating Rate Payment Dates | 16 January 2016 |
| Floating Rate Day Count Convention | Actual/365 |
| Holiday Convention | Modified Following Business Day Convention in Mumbai |

notional amount payable at the maturity. Interest differential may be received/paid by Canara Bank at maturity, depending upon the difference between the fixed rate and compounded O/N MIBOR.

- If the daily compounded O/N MIBOR, as on the maturity date, is higher than the 9-month OIS rate (7.54%) as agreed upon in the contract, Canara Bank will receive the interest differential on the notional principal of INR 50 crore for the specific period of nine months, and vice versa.
- The interest differential during any of the settlement dates will be calculated based on the Actual/365 day count convention.
- Since there is no specific early termination clause, the OIS contract can be prematurely unwound or terminated any time before the due date, subject to the settlement of proper dues to the concerned counterparty.
- Such a deal needs to be undertaken as per the treasury policy of the bank, duly approved by the board/competent authority from time to time.

### MIFOR overnight index swap

The other longer tenor benchmark that is available is the yield based on forex forward premiums, known as Mumbai Interbank Forward Offered Rate (MIFOR). MIFOR swaps have significantly grown in popularity in the Indian financial market. Preference of Indian corporates for external commercial borrowings, i.e. long-term foreign currency loans, to finance their projects becomes easier through MIFOR swaps. MIFOR swaps enable a domestic borrower to convert his/her floating rate (USD LIBOR) foreign currency loan into a fixed rate INR loan. The fixed rate of interest supposed to be paid in such a swap is the MIFOR. It is nothing but the LIBOR plus the annualized USD-INR forward premium for the same tenor. Since LIBOR is the standard international benchmark for corporate borrowing, and the forward premium reflects the view on change in the concerned currency (here USD-INR), this swap becomes very popular in India. In other words, hedging against interest rate risk as well as currency risk for an exposure of foreign currency borrowings makes the MIFOR swap an attractive option for Indian players. MIFOR swap is a fully hedged transaction at the cost of USD LIBOR plus the USD-INR forward premium. However, because of insufficient liquidity in the forward foreign exchange market in India beyond 1 year, it may be difficult to extract an FX forward premium for a MIFOR of more than 1-year maturity. In the Indian market, MIFOR swaps can be used to hedge long-term USD-INR currency swaps.

### Example: MIFOR swap

Structure of a simple MIFOR swap can be described through the following figure (Figure 10.9).

- MIFOR stands for Mumbai Interbank Forward Offer Rate.
- Bank pays 7.04% *p.a.*, payable semi-annually, on INR 25 cr. for 2 years.
- Bank receives *MIFOR*, reset and payable semi-annually, on INR 25 cr. for 2 years.

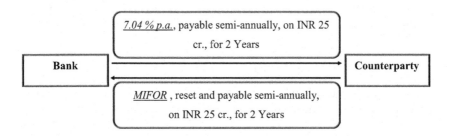

*Figure 10.9* Structure of an O/N MIFOR swap

- MIFOR = *6-month LIBOR* ± Annualized 6-month USD/INR forward premium/discount in %. Based on this formula, MIFOR is reset every 6 months.
- No principal exchange at inception or finish.
- Like the *O/N-MIBOR* swap, this is also an interest rate swap on INR, but on *6-month LIBOR*, adjusted with the 6-month USD/INR forward premium/discount to cover the USD/INR currency risk.
- Bank, as a receiver of MIFOR, is exposed to the risk of any fall in *6-month LIBOR* and fall (rise) in 6-month USD/INR forward premium/discount.

### Theory of comparative advantage in IRS

The possibility for two counterparties entering into an interest rate swap deal, paying a fixed (floating) rate of interest against the receipt of a floating (fixed) rate of interes, for a specific period of time on a notional principal amount, is supported by the *Theory of Comparative Advantage*[1] among both the counterparties involved. A pay fixed receive floating or receive fixed pay floating interest rate swap (IRS) contract can be used to serve this purpose, say converting a fixed rate loan to a floating rate loan, or vice versa.

For example, suppose the HDFC Bank, having the best credit rating of 'AAA', and United Bank of India, with a relatively poor credit rating of 'A', provided by a common credit rating agency, say CRISIL, may like to borrow INR 500 crore from the market for a period of 5 years by issuing tier II bonds. Now the concern for both the institutions is: whether to borrow the required amount at a fixed rate or at a floating rate; i.e. whether to issue fixed rate bond or to issue the floating rate bond. Details of both the institutions along with possible borrowing rates in both the markets are given hereunder:

| Institutions | Credit Rating | Fixed Rate Market | Floating Rate Market |
| --- | --- | --- | --- |
| HDFC Bank | AAA | 8% | 6-M MIBOR – 10 bps |
| United Bank of India | A | 10% | 6-M MIBOR + 100 bps |

It can be seen from the above details that the borrowing cost, irrespective of the fixed or floating rate market, is relatively higher for the United Bank of India (UBI), especially because of its relatively poor credit rating in comparison with the HDFC Bank (HDFC). But it may be noted here that the difference between the two fixed rates offered to both the banks (which is 2% or 200 basis points) is higher than the difference between the two floating rates at which they can tap the market (which is 90 bps). Alternatively, UBI has to pay 2% higher than what HDFC is supposed to pay in the fixed rate market, whereas UBI can manage paying just 90 basis points higher than whatever HDFC pays if the necessary funds are borrowed through the floating rate market. Therefore, *UBI seems to have a comparative advantage in the floating rate market*, while *HDFC enjoys a comparative advantage in the fixed rate market*. The reason for UBI to borrow funds from the floating rate market at a comparatively lower rate than the fixed rate market is just the fact that the borrowing cost, especially the spread above the market rate, can be duly adjusted in every reset period, whereas the fixed rate remains fixed for the entire borrowing period. Therefore, such flexibility for the lender to revise the lending rate as and when required, instead of getting stuck for the whole period, makes the floating rate market relatively favorable for a low rated or weak borrower. Therefore, this kind of comparative advantage is commonly seen in the market.

When two institutions or market players have comparative advantages in two different markets, they may initially tap the respective market and subsequently enter into an interest rate swap contract to change the nature of their exposures (fixed to floating or floating to fixed) after enjoying their respective comparative advantage. As per the previous example, HDFC and UBI have comparative advantage respectively in the fixed rate and floating rate market, but they may like to opt for the other market. In such case, HDFC will initially issue 5-year fixed rate tier II bonds at a rate of 8% p.a. payable semi-annually, whereas UBI will issue 5-year floating rate bonds at an interest rate of 6-month MIBOR plus 100 basis points, payable semi-annually, and subsequently enter into a IRS contract between them, where HDFC will receive a fixed rate from UBI and will pay a floating rate to UBI. This arrangement will finally lead HDFC to end up entering into the floating rate market and UBI to end up entering into the fixed rate market. Let's assume that the IRS deal between HDFC and UBI has taken place in the presence of the HSBC Bank as a dealing/brokering agent.

Suppose HSBC has structured the following IRS deal, as given in the following figure (Figure 10.10), for HDFC and UBI:

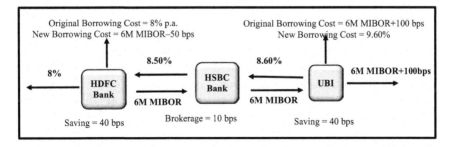

*Figure 10.10* Structure of an O/N MIBOR swap deal

As per the IRS deal, structured by the HSBC Bank to meet the requirements of both the HDFC Bank, having a comparative advantage in the fixed rate market, and UBI, having a comparative advantage in the floating rate market, the cash flows and the net savings for both the counterparties and the swap dealer are given hereunder:

### For HDFC bank

- Cash Outflow @ 8% p.a. as a cost of issuing tier-II bonds in the market.
- Cash Inflow @ 8.5% p.a. from the received fixed pay floating IRS contract.
- Cash Outflow @ 6-M MIBOR for the received fixed pay floating IRS contract.
- Net Cash Outflow @ 6-M MIBOR – 50 bps towards cost of market borrowing.
- Net Savings due to reduction in borrowing cost in preferred market.

$$= (6 \text{-} M \text{ MIBOR} \quad 10 \text{ bps}) \quad (6 \text{-} M \text{ MIBOR} \quad 50 \text{ bps}) = 40 \text{ bps.}$$

### For UBI

- Cash Outflow @ 6-M MIBOR + 100 bps as a cost of issuing tier-II bonds in the market.
- Cash Inflow @ 6-M MIBOR from the pay fixed receive floating IRS contract.
- Cash Outflow @ 8.60% p.a. for the pay fixed receive floating IRS contract.
- Net Cash Outflow 9.60% p.a. towards cost of market borrowing.
- Net Savings due to reduction in borrowing cost in preferred market.

$$= 10.00\% - 9.60\% = 40 \text{ bps.}$$

### For HSBC bank

- Net Savings of 10 bps, due to the two-way quote given to HDFC and UBI for the 5-year IRS at the rate of 8.60–8.50, against 6-M MIBOR.

The basic logic to create such an IRS structure is to ensure almost a similar net gain for both the counterparties with the comparative advantage in their respective markets, after setting aside a brokerage or commission for the IRS dealer. The net savings for both the HDFC Bank and UBI could have been 45 basis points each, in case the IRS deal could have been structured directly between both the counterparties, in absence of any dealer/broker. The total gain from this type of IRS arrangement is always the difference between the net differential among two fixed rates of interest faced by both the counterparties in the fixed rate market (noted as X), and the net differential among the two floating rates of interest faced by both of them in the floating rate market (noted as Y). In this example, X minus Y is such that:

$$(10\% - 8\%) - \{(6 - M\ MIBOR + 100\ bps) - (6 - M\ MIBOR - 10\ bps)\}$$
$$= 2\% - 1.10\% = 0.90\%$$

After keeping aside a small portion, say 10 basis points from the total gain of 0.90% or 90 basis points, the balance total gain of 80 basis points can be equally divided and passed on to both the counterparties of the IRS contract, making the same equally attractive for both of them. It may be noted here that there is a risk involved with this arrangement as well. The net gain from this kind of arrangement, availing the comparative advantage in the underlying market, supplemented by an IRS deal, may undergo a change (fall in the gain or turned out to a loss) for both the counterparties due to any change in their credit worthiness reflected through their credit ratings.

## Pricing and valuation of interest rate swap

At the time a swap contract is put into place, it is typically considered "at the money", meaning that the total value of fixed interest-rate cash flows over the life of the swap is exactly equal to the expected value of floating interest-rate cash flows. Alternatively, at the inception of the swap, the "net present value", or sum of expected profits and losses, should add up to zero.

### *Pricing of IRS*

The expected interest payments made by both the fixed interest payer and receiver till the maturity of the IRS contract should fundamentally be the same at the initiation of the IRS contract. Therefore, when an IRS contract settles, the contract needs to be priced. Here, pricing of an IRS means the derivation of the *Fixed* interest rate, also known as the *Swap Rate*, which ensures a zero valuation of the contract at its initiation, given a specific benchmark rate for the calculation of floating rate of interest, till the maturity of the contract.

Therefore, the initial pricing of an IRS contract needs to be done in such a way that the present values of the sum of interest payments, separately in the fixed and floating legs, are equal to each other so that neither of the counterparties lose anything based on the anticipation of the future movements on the reference rate of interest. But at the same time, the possibility of any change in the floating rate of interest from whatever is expected creates a value for the IRS contract, either to the fixed rate payer or receiver, depending on the direction of change. In short, the pricing of an IRS contract is to extract the swap or fixed rate at its inception. The swap rate can be derived through the following ways:

$$PV\_Floating\_Leg = Swap\_Rate$$
$$\times \sum_{t=1}^{n}\left[Notional\_Amount \times (Days_t/360) \times DF_t\right]$$

$$Swap\_Rate = \frac{PV\_Floating\_Leg}{\sum_{t=1}^{n}\left[Notional\_Amount \times (Days_t/360) \times DF_t\right]} \quad (10.4)$$

The pricing of MIBOR swaps, of different maturity, in India over last few quarters are given in the following figure (Figure 10.11).

### Example: pricing of IRS contract

A municipal issuer and counterparty agree to a Rs.10 crore "plain vanilla" swap starting in January 2015 that calls for a 3-year maturity with the municipal issuer paying the swap rate (fixed rate) to the counterparty and the counterparty paying the 6-month MIBOR (floating rate) to the issuer.

Calculate the swap rate by using the 6-month MIBOR "futures" rates, as given in the following table (Table 10.4), to estimate the present value of the floating component payments.

Payments are assumed to be made on a semi-annual basis (i.e., 180-day periods).

### Solution

Estimation of the swap rate through the iteration method may be shown in the following table (Table 10.5).

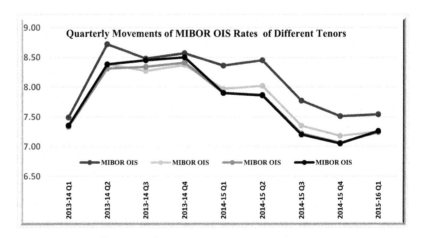

*Figure 10.11* Trend in MIBOR-OIS rates (%) of different maturity

*Table 10.4* Forward curve

| Date | Period | Forward Rates (Annual) |
|------|--------|------------------------|
| 1-Jan-15 | 1 | 8.00% |
| 30-Jun-15 | 2 | 8.25% |
| 1-Jan-16 | 3 | 8.50% |
| 30-Jun-16 | 4 | 8.60% |
| 1-Jan-17 | 5 | 8.75% |
| 30-Jun-17 | 6 | 8.90% |

*Table 10.5* Estimation of swap rate through iteration method

| Notional Value of the IRS Contract (Rs.) | | | | | 100000000 |
|------------------------------------------|--|--|--|--|-----------|

| Expected Fixed (Swap) Rate: Assumed at 10% but Needs to be Solved through Iteration | | | | | 8.48% |
|---|---|---|---|---|---|

| Date | Annual FR | Floating Rate Int. | Fixed Rate Int. | PV of Floating Rate Int. | PV of Fixed Rate Int. (Disc. at Floating Rate) |
|------|-----------|--------------------|-----------------|--------------------------|------------------------------------------------|
| 1-Jan-15 | 8.00% | 4000000 | 4238726.46 | 3846153.85 | 4075698.52 |
| 1-Jul-15 | 8.25% | 4125000 | 4238726.46 | 3804643.11 | 3909537.31 |
| 1-Jan-16 | 8.50% | 4250000 | 4238726.46 | 3751118.11 | 3741167.90 |
| 1-Jul-16 | 8.60% | 4300000 | 4238726.46 | 3633550.68 | 3581773.81 |
| 1-Jan-17 | 8.75% | 4375000 | 4238726.46 | 3531796.04 | 3421786.81 |
| 1-Jul-17 | 8.90% | 4450000 | 4238726.46 | 3426962.44 | 3264259.86 |
| | | | | **21994224.22** | **21994224.22** |

*Alternative solution*

Pricing of the interest rate swap, given in the above example, can alternatively be done using the equation described above and shown in the following table (Table 10.6).

*Example: valuation of IRS*

Bank X, having a plain vanilla interest rate swap contract with Bank Y with a residual maturity of 2 years wants to value the same as on 1 January 2013, where Bank X pays to Y an interest rate of 7.50% p.a., payable quarterly, on a notional principal of Rs. of 10 Cr. and in return Bank Y pays Bank X the 3-month MIBOR on the same notional principal.

Given the 3-month MIBOR (annual) for the future tenors, as given in the following table (Table 10.7), what would be the present value of the IRS contract to the payer of the fixed rate as on 1 January 2013?

*Table 10.6* Estimation of swap rate through pricing formula

| Date | Annual FR | Floating Rate Int. | Semi-annual DF | PV of Floating Rate Int. | PV of (Notional Principal * Period in Years) |
|------|-----------|--------------------|----------------|--------------------------|-----------------------------------------------|
| 1-Jan-15 | 8.00% | 4000000 | 0.961538 | 3846153.85 | 48076923.08 |
| 1-Jul-15 | 8.25% | 4125000 | 0.922338 | 3804643.11 | 46116886.13 |
| 1-Jan-16 | 8.50% | 4250000 | 0.882616 | 3751118.11 | 44130801.32 |
| 1-Jul-16 | 8.60% | 4300000 | 0.845012 | 3633550.68 | 42250589.29 |
| 1-Jan-17 | 8.75% | 4375000 | 0.807268 | 3531796.04 | 40363383.28 |
| 1-Jul-17 | 8.90% | 4450000 | 0.770104 | 3426962.44 | 38505196 |
| | | | | 21994224.22 | 259443779.10 |
| Theoretical Swap Rate (Fixed Leg) | | | | 8.48% | |

*Table 10.7* Estimation of discounting factor

| Dates | Jan 13 | Apr. 13 | July 13 | Oct. 13 | Jan 14 |
|-------|--------|---------|---------|---------|--------|
| MIBOR (%) | 7.25 | 7.73 | 7.78 | 8.00 | 8.15 |
| D.F. | 0.982198 | 0.962442 | 0.943848 | 0.923845 | 0.904068 |
| Dates | Apr. 14 | July 14 | Oct. 14 | | |
| MIBOR (%) | 8.25 | 8.46 | 8.75 | | |
| D.F. | 0.884714 | 0.863720 | 0.841042 | | |

*Solution*

The valuation of the IRS contract, as given in the above example, is shown in the following table (Table 10.8).

*Marked-to-market (MTM) of INBMK swaps*

Once an IRS deal is undertaken by the bank, irrespective of the type of transaction, hedging or trading/market making, the bank, as per the regulatory requirement, needs to follow a daily MTM valuation for the outstanding IRS, and the respective accounting entries, to capture the appreciation or depreciation in the value of the contract depending upon the movement in the long-term INBMK rates as on the valuation date, need to be passed.

Accordingly, the daily MTM process for an INBMK interest rate swap deal can be outlined as follows:

- The broader principal for the valuation of a contract, with fixed and floating legs, on any date, is to estimate the sum of present values of all future cash flows due in both the legs. Accordingly, the value of the contract is just the difference between the sums of present values of both the legs.
- As far as the future cash flows in both fixed and floating legs of an IRS contract are concerned, the periodical (semi-annual) cash flows in the

Table 10.8 Valuation of IRS to fixed and floating rate payers

| Date | Period | No. of Days in Quarter | Forward Rate (Annual) | Floating Rate Int. | Fixed Rate Int. | Quarterly DF (Using Spot Rate) | PV of Floating Rate Int. | PV of Fixed Rate Int. |
|---|---|---|---|---|---|---|---|---|
| 1-Jan-13 | 1 | 90 | 7.25% | 1787671.23 | 1849315.07 | 0.982198 | 1755846.51 | 1816392.95 |
| 1-Apr-13 | 2 | 91 | 7.73% | 1927205.48 | 1869863.01 | 0.962442 | 1854823.84 | 1799635.04 |
| 1-Jul-13 | 3 | 92 | 7.78% | 1960986.30 | 1890410.96 | 0.943848 | 1850873.64 | 1784261.22 |
| 1-Oct-13 | 4 | 92 | 8.00% | 2016438.36 | 1890410.96 | 0.923845 | 1862877.35 | 1746447.52 |
| 1-Jan-14 | 5 | 90 | 8.15% | 2009589.04 | 1849315.07 | 0.904068 | 1816804.54 | 1671906.02 |
| 1-Apr-14 | 6 | 91 | 8.25% | 2056849.32 | 1869863.01 | 0.884714 | 1819722.91 | 1654293.56 |
| 1-Jul-14 | 7 | 92 | 8.46% | 2132383.56 | 1890410.96 | 0.863720 | 1841783.31 | 1632786.63 |
| 1-Oct-14 | 8 | 92 | 8.75% | 2205479.45 | 1890410.96 | 0.841042 | 1854901.37 | 1589915.46 |
| Present Value of Interest Payments | | | | | | | 14657633.48 | 13695638.38 |

Value of the IRS Contract (to Fixed Rate Payer) = INR 9,61,995.10 (Gain)
Value of the IRS Contract (to Floating Rate Payer) = INR 9,61,995.10 (Loss)

fixed leg are derived from the fixed rate of the contract, and therefore remain fixed till the maturity; whereas, the semiannual cash flows in the floating leg, derived from some reference rate (here INBMK Rates) of interest prevailed as on the respective fixing dates, are different for different periods, and therefore the known component in the floating leg is just the floating interest till the next reset period.

- In order to estimate the future, subsequent to the next reset date, cash flows in the floating leg of the INBMK swaps, the Indian benchmark (INBMK) rates expected to prevail at different future points of time (fixing or reset dates) need to be projected.
- The present government securities benchmark rates of different maturity may be considered to arrive at the respective zero rates through methods like bootstrapping, available in Reuter/Bloomberg screen.
- Future benchmark rates for the required tenor, depending upon the reset schedule of the floating leg of the INBMK swap contract and semiannual settlements of net interest differentials, can be estimated through interpolation.
- These projected future benchmark rates for the concerned period can be used to estimate all the projected future cash flows due in the floating leg at the time of semi-annual settlements.
- Once all the future cash flows in both the legs are available, the same can be discounted at the relevant zero INBMK rates, as arrived at through the bootstrapping, to get the total present values of both the legs.
- Accordingly, the MTM value of the IRS contract can be arrived at by taking the difference between the PV of the fixed and floating leg of the contract.

The contract will have a positive MTM for the fixed rate payer buyer of the IRS) if the difference between the PVs (PV of Floating Leg – PV of Fixed Leg) is positive, and vice versa. If the contract shows a positive MTM for the fixed rate payer, the same will show a negative MTM with the same amount to the floating rate payer.

### Marked-to-market valuation of MIBOR-OIS

At the time a swap contract is put in place, it is typically considered "at the money", meaning that the total value of fixed the interest-rate cash flows over the life of the swap is exactly equal to the expected value of floating interest-rate cash flows. Alternatively, at the inception of the swap, the "net present value", or sum of expected profits and losses, should add up to zero. But as the time progresses and interest moves up or down, the value of the contract becomes positive or negative for counterparty. The buyer or seller of an MIBOR-OIS, irrespective of the type of transaction (hedging/trading), needs to capture this value on daily basis, known as daily MTM.

Unlike the valuation of INBMK swaps, or any IRS contract with a long-term benchmark rate, the MTM valuation of MIBOR-OIS may need not necessarily be arrived at by estimating the present value of both fixed and floating legs, and therefore the net present value of the swap contract. Since MIBOR-OIS is based on very short-term overnight rate, it may not be feasible to project all the future values of the O/N MIBOR till the maturity. Alternative methods to arrive at the MTM value of OIS at any valuation date may be simply based on:

- The difference between the original fixed (OIS) rate at which the contract is entered into and the current OIS rate for the concerned tenor/residual maturity of the OIS that prevailed as on the date of valuation.
- Replicating the MIBOR-OIS contract into fixed and floating legs and then separately capturing the PV of both the legs to arrive at the present MTM value.

The total MTM value of an OIS contract consists of:

(i) Net interest accrual between the fixed and floating leg till the valuation date, known as *Carry*.
(ii) Gain (loss) on future/remaining (unfixed) part of the trade, only linked to the fixed leg, due to change in the current OIS rate with the original contractual rate, called as *Roll*.

The sum of these two components (carry and roll) is considered as the mark-to-market value of the OIS contract. The first method can capture both the components separately, whereas the second method gives the final number. Counterparties (buyer or seller of an OIS) may like to know the final MTM (carry plus roll) to understand the situation (profit or loss) till the maturity of the contract and to estimate the carry to capture the net interest differential/payoff till the valuation date. One can follow the second method to calculate the final MTM and can capture the carry separately through the first method. Both the methods are described hereunder:

## MTM valuation method 1

The method of capturing carry and roll by considering the original OIS rate and the rate prevailed as on the valuation date consists of the following steps:

- Consider the *nature of the OIS position* (bought, pay-fixed/sold, receive-fixed), *notional amount* of the position, *original maturity* of the OIS contract, and the *original/contractual OIS rate*.
- Consider the *date of valuation* and the *MIBOR-OIS curve* as on the same date.

- Use the MIBOR-OIS curve, as on the valuation date, to extract the OIS rate for the residual tenor (valuation date to maturity date) of the existing contract. For example, an OIS contract with an original maturity of 12 months, valuing after 3 months, needs the extraction of the 9-month OIS rate as on the valuation date.
- Construct the zero swap curve, if possible, to extract the necessary zero swap rates to discount all future cash flows related to the swap contract. Accordingly, single or multiple discounting factors {1 / (1 + R)^t}, depending upon the nature of future interest settlements (single, in case of OIS with less than 1-year maturity; or multiple, in case of OIS >1-Year) can be estimated using the respective zero swap rates (R).
- Calculate the interest due on the fixed leg of the OIS since the origination or the last settlement date (in case the OIS is of more than 1-year maturity and has more than one settlement) till the valuation date, expected to be payable on the next settlement date or at maturity (in case of OIS less than 1-year maturity with only one and final settlement).
- Estimate the present value (PV) of the interest due on the fixed leg of the OIS till the valuation date, as computed above, by discounting the same with the respective discounting factor, depending upon the time length (valuation date to next settlement date or maturity date).
- Estimate the total interest accrual on the floating leg of the OIS contract by considering all the O/N MIBOR from the origination or last settlement date till the valuation date, following a daily compounding technique.
- In a market of 5 working days (Monday to Friday) in a week, the interest due in the floating leg gets compounded on daily basis for all the working days, but gets calculated on simple basis for the weekends (Saturday and Sunday) and other national holidays. In such case, calculation of simple interest is based on principal plus interest due as on the last working day (Friday).
- The absolute interest accrued in the floating leg of the OIS contract can be estimated on a daily basis and finally can be summed up to get the total interest till the valuation date; or daily compounded O/N rate (annualized) till the valuation date can also be estimated and can be straightway applied on the notional principal for the concerned period (origination or last settlement till the valuation date).
- Unlike the interest component in the fixed leg of an OIS, since the interest component in the floating leg is due on a daily basis but payable semi-annually or at the end of maturity depending upon the original maturity of the OIS, the total interest accrued in the floating leg till the valuation date need not to be discounted.
- Capture the difference between the actual amount of interest accrued and receivable (by the pay-fixed counterparty) in the floating leg and PV of interest accrued and payable (to the receive-fixed counterparty) in the fixed leg, as calculated in the above steps.

- The net interest differential, due as on the valuation date, is known as *Carry*. This carry can be positive to the swap buyer (pay-fixed counter-party) if the actual interest accrued in the floating leg is higher than the PV of the interest accrued in the fixed leg, and vice versa.
- Carry takes care of the net interest differential due as on the date of valuation. But the future (unfixed) part of trade, just due to change in the current OIS rate for the residual tenor of the OIS contract as on the valuation date, also needs to be captured.
- Accordingly, the difference between the current OIS rate for the residual tenor and the original OIS rate for the complete tenor need to be captured. This difference (positive or negative) shows whether the OIS contract is profitable (positive MTM) or loss making (negative MTM) to either of the counterparties.
- Positive (negative) difference indicates an opportunity gain (opportunity loss) to the swap buyer (pay-fixed counterparty), and vice versa.
- The amount of such opportunity gain (loss), alternatively termed as MTM gain (loss) of a future (unfixed) part of trade, as captured through the positive (negative) difference in the OIS rate, needs to be estimated by adjusting the difference with the original notional amount and for the residual tenor, such that *MTM Gain (Loss)* = *(OIS $_{Residual\text{-}Tenor}$ − OIS $_{Original}$) × Notional Principal × (No. of Days till the Maturity or Next Settlement / 365)*. In case there is more than one settlement due in the OIS contract, the same calculation needs to be done with the same OIS rates, but separately for different settlement periods.
- The actual MTM gain (loss), as calculated above, needs to be discounted back with the respective discounting factor, considering the timing (single or multiple) of settlement and the respective discounting rates (preferably zero swap rates).
- The PV of the actual MTM gain (loss) is called as *Roll*, which needs to be added with the *Carry*, as calculated above, to get the total MTM value of an OIS position.

*MTM valuation method 2*

- Calculate the notional principal plus the interest (single or multiple) due in the fixed leg till the maturity.
- In case the original maturity of the OIS is less than 1 year, there will be only one settlement throughout the maturity, and therefore there will be one principal and one interest. But if the maturity is more than 1 year, settlement generally takes place every 6 months, and therefore the total amount of interest in the fixed leg depends upon the total amount of settlement due during the residual maturity of the swap contract.
- Single or multiple cash flows (interest and principal) due in the fixed leg, at different future points of time, need to be discounted back by

adjusting them with the respective *Discounting Factor* arrived at from the *Zero Swap Curve*.

- Sum of all such PVs due in the fixed leg of the OIS is the present value of the fixed leg.
- Similarly, notional principal plus interest (daily compounded) due between the contract origination/last settlement date till the valuation date in the floating leg need to be estimated to get the PV of the floating leg of the OIS. Since interest in the floating leg of an OIS is due on a daily basis, the actual value as on any date itself is the present value. The total interest component in the floating leg can be estimated on a daily basis or through the daily compounded rate of interest as on the valuation date.
- The difference between the actual value of the floating leg and the present value of the fixed leg gives the market value or MTM value to the OIS buyer (pay-fixed counterparty).
- This method of calculating the MTM value of OIS, even if very simple, does not give the break ups, i.e. the carry and the roll.
- This method can be followed to estimate the total MTM, and carry can be estimated separately, which can be further deducted from the total MTM to arrive at the MTM of the future part of the trade or the roll.

## Settlement of periodical interest in IRS contracts

As far as the settlement of IRS is concerned, the same may be to settle the periodical interest, or it may be the final settlement at maturity or premature cancellation or unwinding. In case of a standard IRS or OIS, the periodical interest differential is settled every 6 months. But in case the original/residual maturity of such contract is less than 1 year, there is only one and final settlement, that takes place only at maturity. Therefore, if two counterparties enter into a 9-month OIS contract, there will be only one settlement, i.e. at the end of maturity. The settlement and interest reset dates of an IRS contract may or may not coincide with each other. For example, the floating leg of a MIBOR-OIS, say with a maturity of 5 years, gets reset over the night, but settlement happens only at the end of every 6 months. Settlement of periodical interest for two different types of IRS contract, available in India, are explained in the following section:

### Settlement of periodical interest in INBMK swaps

The process of periodical settlement of interest rate differential in the first settlement date on 16 October 2015, and thereafter at the end of every semi-annual period (i.e. 16 April and 16 October of every year) till the maturity or the early termination date, can be outlined as follows:

- 1-year INBMK rate as on 15 April 2015 may be assumed to set at 7.00%.

- Accordingly, the floating rate payer, here the Standard Chartered Bank, Mumbai, needs to pay to the Bank of Maharashtra (BOM) at a rate of 7.50% (7% plus a spread of 50 basis points) during the first semi-annual settlement on 16 October 2015.
- BOM will pay the fixed rate of 7.54% p.a. for every semi-annual settlement, including the first settlement on 16 October 2015.
- Interest settlement in both fixed and floating legs will be based on the Actual/365 day count convention.
- Accordingly, the fixed interest amount payable by the BOM on 16 October 2015, on the notional principal amount of INR 50 crores, following Actual/365 rule, will be INR 1,89,01,643.84/- *[INR 50 crore × 7.54% × 183/365]*.
- The first semi-annual interest component of the floating leg, receivable by the BOM on 16 October 2015, on the notional principal amount of INR 50 crores, following Actual/365 rule, will be INR 1,88,01,369.86/- *[INR 50 crore × 7.50% × 183/365]*.
- The net settlement amount for the BOM, towards the 1st semi-annual interest differential (floating – fixed) will be – (minus) INR 1,00,273.97/-, the net interest differential payable by the BOM as on 16 October 2015.
- The necessary accounting entries towards the payment/receipt of the semi-annual net interest differential are passed.
- One day prior to every reset of the floating leg, starting from 15 October 2015, the interest rate in the floating leg gets fixed based on the reference rate prevailing as on every fixation date.
- Accordingly, after the re-fixation of the floating rate as on every fixation date, the reset advice is generated by the payer of the floating rate (Standard Chartered Bank, Mumbai) and is sent to the fixed rate payer (BOM).
- If the 1-year INBMK, as on 15 October 2015 (the first floating rate reset date), is 7.10%, the interest component in the floating leg, payable by the Standard Chartered Bank, Mumbai, during the second settlement as on 16 April 2016, will be the reference rate prevailed on the fixation date plus the contractual spread of 50 basis points, i.e. 7.60% p.a., for a period of 6 months.
- The interest component in the fixed leg, payable by the BOM, remains the same at 7.54% p.a. on the notional principal of INR 50 crores, for a period of 6 months.
- Accordingly, the net interest differential can be calculated and will settled on 16 April 2016.
- Since the interest rate in the floating leg is higher than that of the fixed leg, in the second interest calculation period, the net interest differential will be paid by the Standard Chartered Bank, Mumbai, to the BOM.
- The same process will continue to calculate the net interest differential to be settled in the 3rd, 4th, 5th, till the last and final semi-annual settlement, payable/receivable by the BOM (fixed rate payer in this case).

- In case either of the counterparties, fixed rate payer or floating rate payer, would like to unwind the IRS contract any time before the maturity, the settlement takes place not only for the net interest accrual, but also for the MTM value, depending upon which counterparty the IRS has a positive value and the same is in-the-monehy.

### Settlement of periodical interest in MIBOR-OIS

The process of periodical settlement of interest rate differential in a MIBOR-OIS in every possible settlement date(s) till the maturity date or the early termination date can be outlined as follows:

- Even if the floating leg of OIS gets reset on daily basis, and the fixed leg remains fixed throughout the maturity, the settlement of net interest differential happens semiannually.
- The semi-annual interest on the fixed leg is just the simple interest on the notional principal amount for the 6-month period, following the necessary day count convention (Actual/365).
- The semi-annual interest on the floating leg is based on the O/N MIBOR during the entire interest calculation period, and therefore gets compounded on a daily basis.
- In case of weekends and any other holidays, when the market is closed and O/N rates are not available, the interest component in the floating leg of OIS is calculated on a simple basis, following the O/N rate on the previous business day.
- Suppose after the initiation of the OIS deal, as per the original deal slip explained earlier, as on 16 April 2015, the O/N MIBOR for next few days are found to be as follows:

  o 16 Apr. (Thu.) = 7.6832%; 17 Apr. (Fri.) = 7.6379%; 18 & 19 Apr. (Sat. & Sun.) = N/A

- Accordingly, one day interest on the floating leg as on 16 April 2015 would be INR 1,05,249.32 (7.6832% × INR 50 Cr. × 1/365).
- Due to daily compounding, the notional principal on the second day will no longer remain at INR 50 Cr., but the original principal plus the interest on the first day, i.e. INR 50,01,05,249.32 (INR 50,00,00,000 + INR 1,05,249.32).
- Therefore, the interest on the floating leg of the OIS as on the second day (17 April 2015) would be INR 1,04,650.79 (7.6379% × INR 50,01,05,249.32 × 1/365).
- Since the third and fourth days (18 April and 19 April) are respectively Saturday and Sunday, when the market is closed, the interest component in the floating leg will no longer be compounded, and therefore can be straightway calculated along with the interest due on the second day (i.e. 17 April).

- Accordingly, interest accrued on the floating leg of the OIS contract for the three days, 17 April to 19 April 2015 (Friday-Saturday-Sunday), would be INR 3,13,952.37/- (7.6379% × INR 50,01,05,249.32 × 3/365).
- The net interest accrual for the fixed rate payer during 16 to 19 April 2015 would be the difference between the floating interest for the a period of four days based on the O/N MIBOR, as shown above, and the fixed interest @7.54% p.a. on the notional principal of INR 50 Cr. for a period of 4 days.
- The interest due on the fixed leg during 16 – 19 April 2015 is INR 4,13,150.68 (7.54% × INR 50,00,00,000.00 × 4/365).
- Therefore, the net interest accrual between 16 – 19 April 2015 for the floating rate receiver would be:

  o INR (1,05,249.32 + 3,13,952.37) – INR 4,13,150.68 = INR 6,051.00/-

- This calculation shows that there will be a net interest receivable to the fixed rate payer for an amount of INR 6,051/-, payable by the floating rate payer.
- Likewise, the interest component on the floating leg gets recalculated following the daily compounding rule for rest of the business days and simple interest rule for the holidays till the end of 6 months (but for the entire period of nine months in this case).
- Once the total interest on both the fixed and floating legs for the concerned interest calculation period (6 months or total maturity) are arrived at, the net interest differential would be settled to the concerned counterparty.
- The same process will start for each of the interest calculation periods (if any) by restoring the notional amount at the original level (here INR 50 Cr.) as on the starting date of each of the 6-month interest calculation period.
- In case the OIS contract is terminated/unwound before the maturity, the net interest accrual is settled accordingly along with the MTM value of the contract, as on the early termination date.

*Example: payout in MIBOR-OIS as on settlement*

Suppose a bank (X) enters into a 7-day OIS with a corporation (Y), where X pays a 7-day fixed rate @ 8.50% and receives overnight MIBOR. Other terms and conditions of the OIS contract are given in the following table (Table 10.9).

Calculate the net payoff as on the date of settlement.

*Table 10.9* Details of a sample OIS deal and O/N MIBOR rates

| | |
|---|---|
| Trade Date | 23 August 2014 |
| Day Count Basis | Actual Number of Days/365 |
| Amount | INR 100 crores |
| Start Date | 24 August 2014 |
| End Date | 31 August 2014 |
| Fixed Rate | 8.50 % simple (Actual/365) |
| O/N Benchmark | NSE O/N MIBOR (Actual/365) |

Overnight MIBOR rates for the concerned period are:
Day 1 = 7.83%; Day 2 = 7.76%; Day 3 = 7.32%; Day 4 = 8.02%; Day 5 and
  6 = N/A; Day 7 = 8.22%

*Table 10.10* Estimation of daily payoffs in the floating leg of MIBOR-OIS

| *Day* | | *O/N MIBOR* | *Notional Principal (INR)* | *Accrued Interest (INR)* |
|---|---|---|---|---|
| Day 1 | Tue | 7.83% | 1,000,000,000 | 214,521/- |
| Day 2 | Wed | 7.76% | 1,000,214,521 | 212,648/- |
| Day 3 | Thu | 7.32% | 1,000,427,169 | 200,634/- |
| Day 4 to Day 6 | Fri-Sun | 8.02% | 1,000,627,803 | 659,592/- |
| Day 7 | Mon | 8.22% | 1,001,287,395 | 225,495/- |
| | | | | 1,512,890/- |

*Solution*

Overnight MIBOR for 7 days and interest due on floating leg may be shown in the following table (Table 10.10).

Therefore, total interest accrued in the floating leg (Corporate Y pays) = 1,512,890/-

Interest accrued in fixed leg (Bank X pays) = 1,000,000,000*8.50%*7/365 = 1,630,137/-

Net interest payment by Bank X on the settlement date = **Rs.117,247/-**

## Offsetting/premature unwinding/cancellation of FRA/IRS

The market value of an FRA/IRS contract fluctuates over time, depending upon the ongoing change in the interest rates. Accordingly, it is not necessary for the counterparties (buyer or seller) of an FRA or IRS contract traded in OTC to hold the position till the maturity, even if the same is not fetching a positive value. An IRS contract, fetching positive value to a counterparty, may also be considered for offsetting or premature cancellation just to book the current profit and get out of the contract, which otherwise may start fetching losses due to sudden unfavourable changes in the market rate of interest. The user of such a contract may like to opt for offsetting their existing position through either of the following two options:

- Booking a reverse contract (FRA/IRS).
- Premature cancellation/termination/unwinding of the outstanding position with the original counterpart.

According to the first option, i.e. through booking a reverse contract, the buyer of an FRA/IRS, i.e. FRA rate or fixed rate payer of the contract, may like to sell a similar FRA/IRS contract to any other counterparty for a period exactly similar to the residual tenor of the first contract as on the cancellation date and also on a revised notional principal, equal to the original notional principal of the first contract plus the interest accrued on the floating leg of the first contract till the cancellation date, or vice versa. This method replicates cancellation of the outstanding contract and the net settlement amount determined as per this option is equal to the amount determined by cancelling the swap. However, this method is credit and capital inefficient as it would involve booking extra credit limits for a reverse swap, and may not be the right choice for banks with limited capital support; whereas, cancellation of the outstanding swap would release counterparty credit limits, which can be further utilized for a better deal. Premature termination of such contract may occur based on a series of business, credit, legal, and financial events negotiated between both the counterparties.

An FRA/IRS contract can be prematurely cancelled/terminated/unwound at any time before its maturity by giving an advance notice to the counterparty agreeing to the necessary terms and conditions as per the contract and ISDA master agreement, and also agreeing to unwind the contract on the basis of *Market or Replacement Value*. Premature cancellation with the original counterparty largely depends upon the actual rate quoted by the counterparty, which can be the market rate, or may be at a bid and ask quote, with a narrower or wider spread. Most of the time, in a market like India, driven majorly by one group of players (like foreign banks), the counterparty intends to prematurely cancel such contract fails to execute the same at the market rate and gets a bid-ask quote from the original counterparty with a relatively wider *Bid/Ask Spread*, leading to a large amount of unpopularity of such contracts, especially to small players, who prefer to ensure a smooth and fare exit root before entering into any such contract. Premature cancellation or early termination of an IRS contract broadly depends upon the fixed rate of the original contract and the prevailing market rate for an IRS with similar terms. An early termination may also add a significant mark-up to the rate quoted for premature cancellation, which may eliminate any savings expected to be gained from the premature termination of the swap.

## Premature unwinding/termination of INBMK Swaps

As explained in the above section, an interest rate swaps can be unwound in two ways: entering into an offsetting swap or settling the net receipt or payment with the counterparty after marking the swap to market. Therefore, to unwind a 5-year swap with 4 years left, the first option is to enter into a 4-year swap, with receipts/payments opposite to the original swap, i.e. a fixed rate receiver of the original swap is entered into another pay fixed and receive floating swap, and vice-versa. Similarly, the same 5-year receive fixed (originally at 8% p.a.) pay floating swap, with 4 years to go under a falling (say at 7.5% p.a.) rate environment, can be unwound with the original counterparty (paying fixed and receiving floating) by collecting the present value of the swap rate differential (8% p.a. – 7.5% p.a.) on the notional amount for the residual maturity of 4 years, subjected to the counterparty's agreement and pricing at market rate. Here the fixed rate receiver may like to unwind the swap to en-cash the current opportunity and exit the market. Similarly, in a rising rate scenario, when the 4-year swap rate increases to 8.5%, the same fixed rate receiver, in order to reduce the MTM losses, may like to unwind the position by paying the suitable compensation, PV of the swap rate differential (8.5% – 8%) on the notional amount for the rest of the period, again subjected to the agreement of the fixed rate payer.

The process of premature unwinding/early termination of an INBMK swap can be outlined below:

- In case an INBMK swap is prematurely unwound, the MTM value of the contract, as on the unwinding date, can be settled between the counterparties.
- The MTM value of the INBMK Swap can be estimated through the existing Indian benchmark rates, available from the GOI securities market, as outlined in the MTM section above.
- But selection of the floating benchmark rates may differ between the processes of arriving at a normal MTM just for valuation and for estimating the settlement amount due to premature unwinding.
- The floating rate considered for premature unwinding can be any form of the benchmark rate: offer, MID (average of bid and offer), interpolated or extrapolated, as per the terms of the IRS contract, accepted by both the counterparties, on the trade date.
- Once the floating benchmark rates are finalized, the MTM can be arrived at as per the above procedure, and final settlement can be made by the concerned counterparty, fixed rate payer or floating rate payer, depending upon the difference between the single fixed rate and multiple floating rates for all future semi-annual settlement periods.

*Premature unwinding/termination of OIS*

- Any MIBOR-OIS contract can be prematurely unwound or terminated by any counterparty (fixed rate payer or receiver), either at the MTM rate or at the rate mutually agreed upon by both counterparties.
- Accordingly, the value settled between the counterparties in the event of premature unwinding will be the MTM value of the contract, not necessarily at the market rate, but at the mutually agreed rate, i.e. at the mutually agreed swap rate for the residual maturity of the swap contract, which may not be favorable to the counterparty who intend to terminate the contract.
- Therefore, in case the 5-year OIS rate declines, say at 7.25%, the fixed rate payers of a MIBOR-OIS contract with a residual maturity of 5 years and paying a relatively higher swap rate (say 7.50%), books an MTM loss, and therefore may like to unwind the contract with the counterparty (i.e. fixed rate receiver), preferably at a market rate of 7.25%.
- But the counterparty may agree to unwind the contract, not at the market rate, but at a slightly lower rate (say at 7.15%), with an expectation that the swap rate will fall further.
- Similarly, if the swap rate increases (say at 7.75%), the receiver of the fixed rate (say 7.50%) of an outstanding swap contract of similar maturity incurs opportunity losses, and therefore may like to prematurely unwind the contract.
- In such case, the counterparty (i.e. fixed rate payer) may agree to unwind the contract, but at a higher rate (say at 7.85%) comparative to the present market rate of 7.75%, assuming that the swap rate will increase further and the fixed rate payer will book more MTM profit.
- The major difference between MTM settlement and settlement due to premature termination of an OIS contract lies in the selection of the swap rate: the market rate or the mutually agreed rate.
- Therefore, the amount of premature settlement or unwinding is the MTM value of the OIS, but based on the mutually agreed OIS rate.
- Accordingly, if an OIS presently shows a negative MTM for a counterparty (fixed rate payer or recxeiver), the unwinding amount of the same will be slightly more unfavorable or more negative.
- But this costly unwinding may still be preferable for the loss-making counterparty, because it may protect the counterparty from booking more MTM losses in the future if the market continues not to be in his/her favor and he/she still holds the OIS position.

## Usefulness of FRA/interest rate swap

Even if the very basic purpose for using a derivatives contract is to hedge the risk of the underlying exposure(s), like other derivatives contract, FRA or IRS, can also be for many other purposes, as outlined in the following section:

## *Hedging*

Borrowers (lenders) are exposed to the risk of rising (falling) rates of interest. FRA/IRS contracts can be effectively used to ensure protection against fluctuation in interest rates for some short/medium/long duration exposures. The buyer (seller) of an FRA/IRS contract, used to hedge the interest rate risk, pays (receives) the FRA or fixed rate and receives (pays) the market rate, depending on the benchmark or reference rate of interest as per the contract. Therefore, borrowers or bond issuers (lenders or bond investors), under rising (falling) interest rate scenarios, will prefer to buy (sell) an FRA/IRS contract for a specified period depending upon the hedge requirement. An FRA/IRS contract enables the borrower (investor) to lock-in the borrowing rate (yield on investment) in advance. How such contracts are hedge effective irrespective of rise or fall in the rates of interest and allow the borrowers or investors to lock-in at a predetermined rate can be shown through the following example.

Banks, having major exposure to interest rate related instruments, can use FRA/IRS contracts to offset their interest rate risk in the following circumstances:

- An IRS enables the SLR investment and trading portfolios to be insulated from fluctuation in the interest rates. In effect, IRS enable banks to convert a fixed rate asset into a floating rate asset. Thus, even if interest rates rise, although the portfolio depreciates, the fixed leg of the swap appreciates (as the bank has contracted to pay a fixed rate before the rates rose). This offsets the fall in the value of the portfolio.
- A bank can use the IRS to freeze the profits on SLR bonds when yields are low, but it does not want to sell and lose the attractive coupons (by entering into a pay fixed, receive floating IRS).
- A bank can protect the interest spread in the fixed rate sector of the balance sheet by entering into an IRS (receive fixed, pay floating) in a falling interest rate environment.
- Balance sheet mismatches between fixed rate liabilities (assets) and floating rate assets (liabilities) can be adjusted through IRS. The higher duration of securities with longer maturity can be adjusted with the duration of the swap, so as to neutralize the impact of rising rates on the portfolio.
- A bank can have a significant amount of term deposits, which are fixed rate liabilities, loaded with higher cost of funds if interest rates fall. IRS (receive fixed and pay floating) offer the necessary protection against declining rates affecting the fixed rate liability of the bank.
- IRSs help a bank to resolve its basis mismatches, i.e. borrowing at a fixed rate and deploying at a floating rate or vice-versa. A bank,

accepting *FCNR* deposits carrying a floating rate of interest and investing in fixed rate bond or lending at a fixed rate, gets exposed to the risk
of rising *LIBOR* and thereby increasing the cost of liabilities. This can
be removed by swapping the fixed rate asset to floating. Here, the bank
may like to enter into a MIFOR swap, where it may elects to pay a fixed
and receive *LIBOR* ± *6-Month USD/INR Forward Premium/Discount*
in the swap. The presence of the forward premium/discount takes care
of the USD/INR currency risk in the swap contract.

*Example: use of FRA for hedging*

Investor X is expecting to invest INR 100 crores, expected to be available to
him/her after 3 months from another investment, for a period of 3 months.
The planned investment, currently giving a yield of 8.5%, is likely to offer a
lower level of yield, causing the investor to be concerned about low return
from the investment, when the same will be made after 3 months. Therefore, the investor is exposed to the risk of falling interest rates. Suppose the
State Bank of India at that point of time, offers a 2-way quote of "8.5% /
8.75% (Bid/Ask) for 3 Months" for a 3 × 6 M FRA (i.e. 3 months FRA 3
months hence), indicating the bank's willingness to buy the contract at an
FRA rate of 8.5%, paying 8.5% p.a. for 3 months against the market rate,
and to sell the contract at an FRA rate of 8.75%, receiving 8.75% p.a. for
3 months against the market rate. The market rate specified in the contract
is the 3-month MIBOR.

If the rate of interest really falls after 3 months, how can Investor X ensure
his hedge against the falling rate of interest? What would be the effective
return on investment under the following circumstances, assuming a similar
change in the yield on investment and 3-M MIBOR; and 30/360 day count
convention is followed:

(a)  3-Months MIBOR falls at 7.5%.
(b)  3-Months MIBOR rises to 9.5%.

Suppose another market player would like to speculate about the future
movements in the interest rates and would like to make a speculative gain
through a similar FRA contract. If the speculator is of the same view of
falling interest rates for the same 3-month period after 3 months, how is he
going to be benefited from this 3 × 6 M FRA contract. What if the future
interest rate rises? Alternatively, compute the expected profit (loss) due to
the similar change in interest rates as assumed above.

*Solution*

Since Investor X is expecting the 3-month rate to fall after 3 months when
he is going to make the investment, he may prefer to sell a 3 × 6 M FRA

contract to the State Bank of India on a notional amount of INR 100 crore, wherein he will receive the FRA rate and will pay the 3-month MIBOR. This will protect him from the fall in future rate of interest and to ensure a lock-in yield from his investment at a rate of 8.5%, the FRA rate offered by the SBI. The differential of the actual 3-month MIBOR and the FRA rate of 8.5% on the notional amount of INR 100 crore, discounted at the 3-month MIBOR, will be paid/received by Investor X after 3 months. If the 3-month MIBOR really falls (rises), leading to a subsequent fall (rise) in the yield on investment, as expected by Investor X, the investor will receive (pay) the discounted interest differential on a notional amount of INR 100 crore.

Therefore, the following section may describe the situation under two different circumstances of falling or rising rates of interest.

### (a) If 3-M MIBOR falls at 7.5% after three months

If the 3-M MIBOR, after a period of 3 months from the date of entering into the FRA contract, falls at 7.5% p.a., the State Bank of India, buyer of the $3 \times 6$ M FRA, and therefore supposed to pay the FRA rate of 8.5% on the notional amount of INR 100 crore, has to pay the interest differential of 1% (i.e. 8.5% – 7.5%) on the notional amount, discounted at the concerned rate. Accordingly, the discounted CF received by Investor X would be:

$$\{(8.5\% \quad 7.5\%) \quad 90/360 \quad INR\ 100\ cr.\} \quad \{1/(1 + 7.5\% \quad 90/360)\}$$
$$=> INR\ 25\ lakhs \quad 0.9816 => \textbf{\textit{INR 24.54 lakhs}}$$

The effective return for the next 3-month investment period:

3 - M Yield on investment at a rate of 7.5% p.a. = 7.5%  90 / 360   INR 100 Cr.

  = INR 1.875 cr.

Future value of Interest received from FRA   = INR 0.2454 cr.  (1 + 7.5%  90 / 360)

  = INR 0.2500 cr.

Net Interest Earned   = INR (1.875 + 0.25) cr. = 2.1250 cr.

Effective Yield on Investment   = 2.1250 / 100 × 360 / 90 = **8.50%**

### (b) If 3-M MIBOR rises to 9.5% after three months

If the 3-M MIBOR, after a period of 3 months from the date of entering into the FRA contract, rises at 9.5% p.a., the State Bank of India, the buyer of the $3 \times 6$ M FRA, and therefore supposed to pay the FRA rate of 8.5% on the notional amount of INR 100 crore, will receive from Investor X the interest differential of 1% (i.e. 9.5% – 8.5%) on the notional amount, discounted at the concerned rate.

Accordingly, the discounted CF paid by Investor X would be:

$$\{(9.5\% - 8.5\%) \quad 90/360 \quad INR\ 100\ cr.\} \quad \{1/(1+9.5\% \quad 90/360)\}$$
$$=> INR\ 25\ lakhs \quad 0.9768 => \textit{INR 24.42 lakhs}$$

The effective return after 3 months:

| | |
|---|---|
| 3-M Yield on investment at a rate of 9.5% p.a. = 9.5% | $90/360$   INR 100 Cr. |
| | = INR 2.375 cr. |
| Future value of Interest paid for FRA | = INR 0.2442 cr.   $(1+9.5\% \quad 90/360)$ |
| | = INR 0.2500 cr. |
| Net Interest Earned | = INR $(2.375 - 0.25)$ cr. = 2.125 cr. |
| Effective Yield on Investment | = $2.1250/100 \times 360/90 = \textbf{8.50\%}$ |

This ensures that, irrespective of the interest rate movements (fall or rise) after a period of three months, Investor X, by entering into a 3 × 6 M FRA contract, could lock-in his/her future investment at the desired yield prevailing at the time of entering into the FRA contract, not at the time of making the actual investment. It may be noted here that, the way Investor X is protected from any fall in the future interest rates, he/she also has to forego any opportunity gain due to a rise in future interest rates, and therefore the higher yield on his/her investment. This validates the fact that *hedging means: no profit, no loss, but always locked-in at a certain rate for any market movement.*

If an investor invests in a fixed coupon security, he/she is always exposed to the risk of rising rates of interest and accordingly the fall in the value of such security. In such circumstances, the investor can hedge his/her exposure from any change in the future rate of interest by entering into a pay-fix interest rate swap contract for a maturity similar to that of the actual exposure and also with a notional amount similar to the total value of such exposure. If the swap rate is assumed to be identical to the fixed coupon rate, then the investor can enjoy a perfect hedge for his fixed rate investment for any change in the prevailing market rate of interest. The loss (gain) in the underlying exposure, due to rise (fall) in the rate of interest, is expected to be totally offset by the gain (loss) in the pay-fix IRS contract. Here, the cash flows both from the fixed and floating legs of the IRS contract can be collectively compared with the cash flow from the fixed coupon security. If it is assumed that the market rate gets changed just after entering into the IRS contract, it is possible to ensure the hedge effectiveness of the IRS contract. The hedge effectiveness of such contract can be ensured both for the flat and uneven yield curve.

*Example: use of IRS for hedging*

Suppose an investor has invested in a 7.5% 5-year bond, traded at par, with a face value of INR 25 crore. The coupons are paid semi-annually. The investor has a fear that the interest in future periods is expected to rise, which will lead to a fall in the value of a fixed coupon security.

To hedge such risk of rising interest rate, the investor has decided to enter into a pay-fixed-receive-floating interest rate swap contract for 5 years with a notional amount of INR 25 crore, equal to the value of the actual exposure, and at a swap rate of 7.5%. The yield curve is assumed to be flat at 7.50% throughout the period.

How can it be ensured that the investor is perfectly hedged against any movement in the rate of interest by having such a pay-fixed IRS contract in his portfolio? Assume that the new yield, just after initiation of the swap contract, for all consecutive maturities has become 8.00% p.a.

*Solution*

Hedge effectiveness of the given IRS deal may be exhibited from the solution given in the following table (Table 10.11).

Hedge effectiveness of an IRS contract can also be explained through the following Diagram (Figure 10.12).

IRS contracts are used to manage the interest rate risk by altering the CF characteristics of an entity in order to match the CF characteristics of its assets and liabilities. If a bank sanctions a fixed rate loan (say at 11%), financed at floating rate of interest, say at 6-month MIBOR, and the floating rate at any period goes above the fixed rate, the bank is expected to suffer a loss. Therefore, the bank will try to lock in a spread over the cost of funds. Similarly, an insurance company may commit a fixed rate payment (say 8%) at some guaranteed investment over some future period of time and have an opportunity to invest the same at some floating rate, say 6-month MIBOR plus 60 basis points. If the floating rate of interest falls below the fixed rate plus the required spread, the insurance company faces a loss.

The risk arises due to these mismatches between the CFs from asset and liability, both for the bank and insurance company, and can be mitigated by swapping the fixed (floating) CFs from the asset (liability) with an equal number of floating (fixed) CFs from the swap contract. Through swapping these CFs, the risk of adverse movement of interest rates gets mitigated, but a required spread needs to locked-in. The above diagram clearly demonstrates that a bank and an insurance company, respectively being exposed to the risk of rising and falling interests, on their underlying exposure, can successfully hedge their risk by entering into an IRS contract, maybe through a swap dealer. Therefore, an IRS contract helps both counterparties to mitigate the interest rate risk after ensuring a locked in spread for both counterparties, and also for the swap dealer (if any).

*Table 10.11* Estimation of cash flows from underlying and hedging positions

### Cash Flows from the Fixed Coupon Bond

| SA Periods | Fixed CFs | DF (at 7.5% p.a.) | DF (at 8% p.a.) | PV of CFs at 7.5% | PV of CFs at 8% | Change in CFs |
|---|---|---|---|---|---|---|
| 1 | 9375000 | 0.963855 | 0.961538 | 9036144.58 | 9014423.08 | |
| 2 | 9375000 | 0.929017 | 0.924556 | 8709536.94 | 8667714.50 | |
| 3 | 9375000 | 0.895438 | 0.888996 | 8394734.40 | 8334340.86 | |
| 4 | 9375000 | 0.863073 | 0.854804 | 8091310.27 | 8013789.29 | |
| 5 | 9375000 | 0.831878 | 0.821927 | 7798853.27 | 7705566.63 | |
| 6 | 9375000 | 0.801810 | 0.790315 | 7516967.01 | 7409198.68 | |
| 7 | 9375000 | 0.772829 | 0.759918 | 7245269.40 | 7124229.50 | |
| 8 | 9375000 | 0.744895 | 0.730690 | 6983392.20 | 6850220.67 | |
| 9 | 9375000 | 0.717971 | 0.702587 | 6730980.43 | 6586750.65 | |
| 10 | 9375000 | 0.692020 | 0.675564 | 6487691.98 | 6333414.08 | |
| 10 | 250000000 | 0.692020 | 0.675564 | 173005119.52 | 168891042.21 | |
| | | | | 250000000.00 | 244930690.14 | −5069309.86 |

### Cash Flows from the Pay-Fixed Swap Contract: Fixed Leg (Payments):

| SA Periods | Fixed CFs | DF (at 7.5% p.a.) | DF (at 8% p.a.) | PV of CFs for Fixed Leg (at 7.5%) | PV of CFs for Fixed Leg (at 8%) | Change in CFs |
|---|---|---|---|---|---|---|
| 1 | −9375000 | 0.963855 | 0.961538 | −9036144.578 | −9014423.077 | |
| 2 | −9375000 | 0.929017 | 0.924556 | −8709536.943 | −8667714.497 | |
| 3 | −9375000 | 0.895438 | 0.888996 | −8394734.403 | −8334340.863 | |
| 4 | −9375000 | 0.863073 | 0.854804 | −8091310.268 | −8013789.291 | |
| 5 | −9375000 | 0.831878 | 0.821927 | −7798853.27 | −7705566.626 | |
| 6 | −9375000 | 0.801810 | 0.790315 | −7516967.007 | −7409198.679 | |
| 7 | −9375000 | 0.772829 | 0.759918 | −7245269.405 | −7124229.499 | |
| 8 | −9375000 | 0.744895 | 0.730690 | −6983392.197 | −6850220.672 | |
| 9 | −9375000 | 0.717971 | 0.702587 | −6730980.431 | −6586750.646 | |
| 10 | −9375000 | 0.692020 | 0.675564 | −6487691.982 | −6333414.083 | |
| | | | | −76994880.48 | −76039647.93 | 955232.55 |

*(Continued)*

*Table 10.11* (Continued)

**Cash Flows from the Fixed Coupon Bond**

| SA Periods | Fixed CFs | DF (at 7.5% p.a.) | DF (at 8% p.a.) | PV of CFs at 7.5% | PV of CFs at 8% | Change in CFs |
|---|---|---|---|---|---|---|

**Fixed Leg (Payments):**

| SA Periods | Floating CFs (at 7.5% Flat YTM) | DF (at 7.5% p.a.) | DF (at 8% p.a.) | PV of CFs for Floating Leg (at 7.5%) | PV of CFs for Floating Leg (at 8%) | Change in CFs |
|---|---|---|---|---|---|---|
| 1 | 9375000 | 0.963855 | 0.961538 | 9036144.578 | 9615384.615 | |
| 2 | 9375000 | 0.929017 | 0.924556 | 8709536.943 | 9245562.13 | |
| 3 | 9375000 | 0.895438 | 0.888996 | 8394734.403 | 8889963.587 | |
| 4 | 9375000 | 0.863073 | 0.854804 | 8091310.268 | 8548041.91 | |
| 5 | 9375000 | 0.831878 | 0.821927 | 7798853.27 | 8219271.068 | |
| 6 | 9375000 | 0.801810 | 0.790315 | 7516967.007 | 7903145.257 | |
| 7 | 9375000 | 0.772829 | 0.759918 | 7245269.405 | 7599178.132 | |
| 8 | 9375000 | 0.744895 | 0.730690 | 6983392.197 | 7306902.05 | |
| 9 | 9375000 | 0.717971 | 0.702587 | 6730980.431 | 7025867.356 | |
| 10 | 9375000 | 0.692020 | 0.675564 | 6487691.982 | 6755641.688 | |
| | | | | 76994880.48 | 81108957.79 | 4114077.31 |

Net Cash Flow from Fixed-Coupon Bond and Pay-Fix Swap, following a Certain Change in Yield:

Gain/Loss in Fixed Coupon Bond due to Change in Yield — 5069309.86

Gain/Loss in Fixed-Leg of the Pay-Fix Swap Contract due to Change in Yield   955232.55

Gain/Loss in Floating-Leg of the Pay-Fix Swap Contract due to Change in Yield   4114077.31

Net Position in the Portfolio of Bond and Pay-Fix Swap Contract, due to Yield Change   0.0000

Hedging Effectiveness of the Pay-Fix IRS Contract   Perfect Hedge

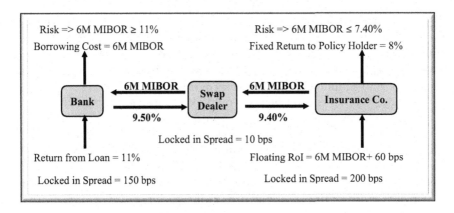

*Figure 10.12* Hedge effectiveness of IRS contract

### Arbitrage

Banks and other FIs may also have some possibilities to do some arbitrage between the cash (i.e. the underlying bond) and the IRS market and extracting a spread. If the swap rate, i.e. the rate of interest in the fixed leg of the IRS, is less than that in the cash market, such situation gives the market players more or less a risk-free opportunity to make an arbitrage profit. For instance, if the 5-year swap rate is 7.50% and the yield on GOI security of the same maturity is 7.80%, there is a clear 30 basis point spread, almost without any significant credit risk, which can be locked in by paying fixed on the swap (i.e. through pay fixed and receive floating IRS) and investing in the GOI security.

### Trading/market making

Users can also use (buy or sell) an FRA or IRS contract purely with a trading intention, or to make the market for others. Here, depending upon the possibility of a future rise (fall) in the rate of interests, users may like to buy (sell) an FRA/IRS contract, or may like to enter into a pay-fixed-receive-floating (receive-fixed-pay-floating) IRS contract. These positions may allow them to earn some trading profit, provided their view towards the movement in future rates of interest materializes. Banks can also enter into an FRA/IRS deal with its customer to manage their interest rate risk, short-term or long-term, or can structure a deal between two counterparties, and therefore can play the role of a market maker. Such trading activity in FRA/IRS is strictly subjected to the approval from the bpard/competent authority and also should be within the approved counterparty exposure limit.

*Example: use of FRA for trading/market making*

Consider the above example, investor X would like to sell a 3 × 6 M FRA contract to the State Bank of India on a notional amount of INR 100 crore, wherein he/she will receive the FRA rate (8.50% p.a. as per the above example) and will pay the 3-month MIBOR, expected to be falling at 7.50%, or rising at 9.50%, under two different scenarios.

Suppose another market player would like to speculate about the future movements in the interest rates and would like to make a speculative gain through the similar FRA contract. If the speculator is of the same view of falling interest rates for the same 3-month period after 3 months, how will he benefit from this 3 × 6 M FRA contract? What if the future interest rate rises? Alternatively, compute the expected profit (loss) due to the similar change in interest rates as assumed here above.

*Solution*

If a speculator enters into such a contract, he/she has nothing to hedge. His/her position at the end of the contract depends upon his/her speculating capability, i.e. strength of future prediction in terms of market interest rates. The speculator takes a position (buy or sell) in an FRA contract depending upon his/her prediction, and if the prediction truly materializes, he/she makes unlimited profit, or otherwise may suffer unlimited losses in the FRA contract.

If the speculator expects the 3-month interest to fall after 3 months, and accordingly sells the similar 3 × 6 M FRA contract to the State Bank of India at a rate of 8.5% p.a. for 3 months, on a notional amount of INR 100 crore, then the pay-off at the settlement date due to the speculator depends upon the actual 3-month MIBOR at the date of settlement.

If 3-month MIBOR falls at 7.5% after three months, the speculator's pay-off as on the settlement date will be:

$$\{(8.5\% - 7.5\%) \quad 90 / 360 \quad INR\ 100\ cr.\} \quad \{1 / (1 + 7.5\% \quad 90 / 360)\}$$

=> INR 25 lakhs   0.9816 => ***INR 24.54 lakhs***

(Positive, i.e. payable by the bank)

On the other hand, if the 3-month MIBOR rises to 9.5% after 3 months, the speculator's pay-off as on the settlement date will be:

$$\{(8.5\% - 9.5\%) \quad 90 / 360 \quad INR\ 100\ cr.\} \quad \{1 / (1 + 9.5\% \quad 90 / 360)\}$$

=> - INR 25 lakhs   0.9768 => - ***INR 24.42 lakhs***

(Negative, i.e. payable by the speculator)

## Managing liquidity

A bank can use IRS, specifically OIS contract, to manage its liquidity requirements more effectively. Term deposits may be raised at effectively floating overnight rates, improving liquidity ratios but without locking in the term interest rate. This involves paying the fixed rate on the term funds, then, through an OIS, receiving back the fixed rate and paying the overnight floating rate.

## Asset-liability management

A bank may have a maturity gap between its relatively longer-term fixed rate assets (fixed rate loan/advances, and fixed rate bonds) and liabilities (term deposits and short-term CDs) with relatively short maturity. Unfavorable movement in the interest rates may create severe losses for the bank having a gap between their assets and liabilities. Interest rate swaps provide an economic mechanism whereby the bank can benefit from a reduction in its balance-sheet gaps, and therefore can manage its assets and liabilities without altering the interest rate and maturity structure of its assets and liabilities.

The IRS contract can be used for ALM, depending on the view on the interest rate. Suppose a Bank/NBFC has a positive gap (RSA > RSL). A fall in the rate of interest leads to a fall in net interest margin (NIM), which can be possibly protected through and increase in fixed rate assets or reduction of rate sensitive assets (RSA), or increase in rate sensitive liability (RSL). Either of these three measure reshuffles the B/S and also are risky and may not be cost effective for the organization. IRS or OIS is relatively cost effective and helps an institution to manage its balance sheet. Now, selection of an IRS with a right notional principal and tenor depends on the tenor of the bucket the gap which needs to be managed. ALM mismatch (positive gap) for long-term exposure under a falling interest rate scenario can be managed through a receive-fixed pay-floating IRS contract. Similarly, when the interest rate rises, the problem occurs when there is a deterioration in the NIM, due to a negative gap (RSL > RSA). This ALM problem can be managed through a pay-fixed receive-floating IRS. Since Duration of an IRS is negative to the fixed rate payer, and is positive to the floating rate payer, inclusion of a pay-fixed-receive-floating IRS, in case of rise in interest rates, helps the IRS buyer (fixed rate payer) to reduce the portfolio duration or to manage the negative duration gap. Similarly, in case of a fall in interest rates, the portfolio duration can be increased, or a positive duration gap can be managed through a receive-fixed IRS contract.

## Risk in FRA/interest rate swap

Even if a forward rate agreement or interest rate swaps contract are used to hedge the interest rate risk of a user, the same is not free from subsequent amount of risk, discussed hereunder:

## Interest rate risk

The interest rate risks attached to a user in their FRA or IRS positions are the same as for on-balance sheet positions (assets and liabilities). Therefore, in any FRA/IRS position, where a user pays the fixed rate (and receives the floating rate), the risk is that interest rates falls after entering into the swap. Similarly, any fixed rate receiving (and floating rate paying) FRA/IRS position contains the risk of rising interest rates, after entering into the swap.

Incidentally, whether the bank or other FIs is a fixed rate payer or receiver (or floating rate payer or receiver) in an FRA/IRS position, it has a natural hedge against interest rate risk in FRA/IRS if the same position is used to hedge an underlying position. For example, any loss in the fixed rate paying (and floating rate receiving) FRA/IRS position due to a fall in the rate of interest, gets compensated by the appreciation in the value of fixed rate investment portfolio (e.g. fixed rate bonds). On the other hand, any fixed rate receiving (and floating rate paying) FRA/IRS position safeguards a bank or other FIs from the higher cost of fixed rate deposits, or other fixed rate liability or fixed rate funding, even at the time of a fall in interest rates.

In an FRA/IRS, the principal is not exchanged, and therefore does not attract any risk. But whether the loss (gain) in such a fixed rate paying (fixed rate receiving) contract is completely getting nullified (completely taking care off) by the value appreciation in the fixed rate investment portfolio (incremental cost of fixed rate deposits), is a matter of concern. If the user of such contract ensures a *Perfect Hedge*, and accordingly decides the notional volume of their FRA/IRS position (fixed rate paying or fixed rate receiving), maximum hedge effectiveness can be ensured. But at the same time, the movements in the rate of interest across all spectrums may not be exactly identical, and therefore may expose the FRA/IRS user to a certain extent of *Basis Risk*, the risk of un-identical movement in two different rates of interest, e.g. the 5-year swap rate and the 5-year government securities rate. *Market Risk Capital Charge (MRCC)*,[2] considering interest rate risk and basis risk, on such derivatives positions, discussed separately in the following chapter, may safeguard the user from incurring financial losses in such deals.

## Duration of IRS

Like the interest rate sensitivity measure for bonds and other fixed income instruments, the interest rate sensitivity of FRA or IRS can also be measured through duration or m-duration. Since an IRS contract can be considered as a combination of two cash market instruments, such as a fixed rate bond and a floating rate bond, the duration of an IRS contract can be expected to be a multiple of the bonds underlying the IRS contract. In case of a fixed rate payer of an IRS, the combination is long in a floating rate bond plus short in a fixed rate bond. The duration of a floating rate bond is normally small, just equal to the time till the next reset date, and the duration of the fixed rate bond is relatively large, based upon the residual maturity of the bond. Since the fixed rate payer of an IRS is long in a floating rate bond and short in a fixed rate bond, the duration of the floating leg and fixed leg are respectively a small positive number and a large negative number. Accordingly, the net duration of an IRS for fixed rate payer is negative. Similarly, the net duration of the same IRS for the fixed rate receiver, the difference between the duration of long in the fixed leg and short in the floating leg, is positive. As a result of these, the inclusion of an IRS contract helps the buyer of an IRS (i.e. fixed rate payer) to reduce the duration of his/her existing underlying portfolio. Similarly, the portfolio duration of the IRS seller (i.e. fixed rate receiver) increases roughly by the duration of underlying fixed rate bond.

### Credit risk

Since swaps contracts are OTC products, they always attract a certain amount of counterparty risk. The credit risk in an FRA/IRS contract is the possibility of the counterparty defaulting on its obligation for the payment of net interest differential on the interest exchange/settlement dates. Accordingly, the credit risk of the counterparty needs to be considered, which finally results into a higher capital charge. Setting counterparty exposure limits for all transactions, including derivatives deals and credit risk capital charges arrived at by adjusting the notional principal with the concerned credit conversion factor (CCF) may take care of the credit risk involved in such derivatives deals.

## Documentation for FRA/interest rate swap

Since OTC derivatives like FRA and IRS are mainly used to hedge the interest rate risk of underlying exposure (i.e. lending, borrowing, investments, etc.), besides the possibility to use the same for speculation or market making as well, it is very important to protect the interest of the counterparties throughout the tenor of the contract. Therefore, proper documentation, stating all possible financial and legal terms and conditions related to general understanding between the counterparties and dealing with specific issues, need to be undertaken before entering into such deals or contracts. This will ensure a legal obligation for both the counterparties to honour the contract, irrespective of the fact whether the same is favourable or not to either of them.

The International Swaps and Derivatives Association is the global trade association for the OTC derivatives market, offering a standard documentation service to the participants of such market. The ISDA Master Agreement is an internationally accepted standard-governing document, published by the International Swaps and Derivatives Association, Inc., that provides the necessary legal and credit protection to both the counterparties of an OTC derivative contract. Standard ISDA documentation consists of the following:

### ISDA Master Agreement

The ISDA Master Agreement, split into various sections, outlines the contractual relationship between the counterparties, stating the standard terms detailing the necessary course of action due to a default/bankruptcy of one of the counterparties out of a list of several standard *Events of Default*, followed by the termination of the OTC derivatives deal, within the purview of standard *Termination Events*. It is important to note here that the ISDA Master Agreement is a netting agreement, and all transactions under the master agreement depend upon each other. Accordingly, any default under one transaction is considered as a default in all other transactions, commonly known as *Close-out Netting*, resulting in the termination of all transactions without exception.

### A schedule

In order to supplement the standard Master Agreement, there is a schedule, which is subjected to negotiation between the counterparties, allowing them to add or to amend the standard terms of the Master Agreement. Therefore, a schedule to the Master Agreement captures what negotiators negotiate, causing a significant delay to finalize such Master Agreement between the counterparties before initiating such OTC derivatives deal.

### A Credit Support Annex (CSA)

Since OTC derivatives carry a large amount of risks, both the counterparties involved in such deals/contracts often prefer to maintain sufficient collateral as credit support for the trades. The requirements for such collateral are outlined in the Credit Support Annex, an integral part of the ISDA Master Agreement. A Credit Support Annex (CSA) is a legal document addressing the complexities of the pledge and transfer of collateral or some other form of credit support for OTC derivative transactions monitored on daily basis. It provides credit protection by setting forth the rules governing the mutual posting of collateral to ensure a good faith to honour the deal and/ or to mitigate the insolvency risks and potential losses associated with the derivative trades.

### Transaction(s) confirmation

OTC derivatives transactions are typically entered into verbally or electronically, followed by the preparation of a formal contract. The evidence of all the necessary terms and conditions of the transaction are contained in a transaction confirmation, alternatively known as *Trading Advice*. Confirmations are usually very short (except for complex transactions) and contain minimum transaction details like: dates, amounts, and rates, and are used to minimize the possibility of any dispute on the concerned T&C.

Even though signing the ISDA Master Agreement is very important for both the counterparties before entering into an OTC derivative transaction, the same may be postponed in certain transactions, especially due to the long time taken to negotiate between the counterparties and to finalize the schedule. Under such circumstances, transaction confirmation or trading advice need to include an undertaking between the counterparties that an ISDA Master Agreement will be negotiated and duly signed within a stipulated time, say 30/60/90 Days from the date of generating the trading advice. In the meantime, the standard ISDA Master Agreement without the schedule is deemed to apply. But the major limitation of such practice is that there is a lack of sufficient protection for both the counterparties of the OTC derivative deal.

## Overnight index swap: a case

### (Focus: MTM valuation, PV01, and premature cancellation)

### *Background*

Suppose the Treasury department of the State Bank of India, known as SBI Global Markets, Mumbai, has strengthened its derivatives desk and has decided to actively participate in the market making (trading) activities in the interest rate swap (IRS) market. An overnight index swap (OIS) is a popular IRS product in India, and the market is mostly dominated by the foreign banks, offering 2-way quotes to the other market players that include private and public sector banks, PDs, and other financial institutions. Accordingly, the bank enters into many such deals, either directly with other banks or a 2-way quote to other non-banking financial institutions or corporates.

Below is one such deal (OIS) entered into by SBI Global Markets with the HSBC Bank, Mumbai. The State Bank of India has entered into the MIBOR-OIS contract, pay-fixed-receive-floating OIS, with the HSBC, Mumbai, as on 1 February 2018, effective from 2 February 2018, the deal slip of which is given in the following table (Table 10.12).

*Table 10.12* A sample deal of MIBOR overnight index swap

| Deal Slip – MIBOR-OIS | |
| --- | --- |
| Deal Number/ID | IRS-OIS/****/**** |
| Type of Transaction | Trading/Market Making |
| Category | Trading/Market Making |
| Counterparty | HSBC, Mumbai |
| Trade Date and Time | 1 February 2018 / 15:40 |
| Effective Date | 2 February 2018 |
| Termination/Maturity Date | 2 February 2020 |
| Early Termination Clause | Not Applicable |
| Callability | Not Applicable |
| Notional Amount | INR 500,000,000.00 (INR 50 Crore) |
| Fixed Rate Payer | SBI Global Markets, Mumbai |
| Fixed Rate of Interest (OIS Rate) | 6.56% p.a. on Outstanding INR Notional Principal |
| Fixed Rate Payment Dates | 2 August and 2 February Every Year Till the Maturity |
| Fixed Rate Day Count Convention | Actual/365 |
| Floating Rate Payer | HSBC, Mumbai |
| Floating Interest Rate | FBIL INR-MIBOR-OIS-COMPOUND |
| Floating Rate Fixing Dates | The Last Day of Each Calculation Period |
| Floating Rate Payment Dates | 2 August and 2 February Every Year Till the Maturity |
| Floating Rate Day Count Convention | Actual/365 |
| Holiday Convention | Modified Following Business Day Convention in Mumbai |

## MTM valuation and estimation of PV01

Suppose a dealer working as a government securities dealer in the bank recently got shifted in the swap desk. He/she is trying to explore the economic relevance of holding the aforesaid swap deal in the bank's book. In this context, as on 29 June 2018, the OIS dealer may like to estimate the MTM value and the PV01 of the deal.

The dealer may like to see the movement of FBIL O/N MIBOR during the concerned historical period. As per the necessary market practices, the daily payoff in the floating leg may be estimated using the FBIL O/N MIBOR for the concerned historical/past period. Alternatively, the dealer may straightway look into the daily compounded FBIL O/N MIBOR applicable for the period from the start/last settlement date till the valuation. The daily compounded FBIL O/N MIBOR from the start/last settlement date till the valuation date comes out to be 6.1262% per annum.

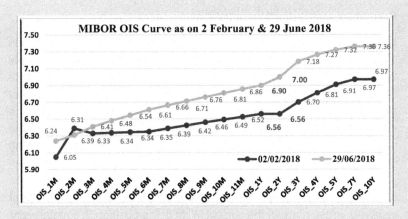

*Figure 10.13* Movement of MIBOR-OIS rates (of various tenors)

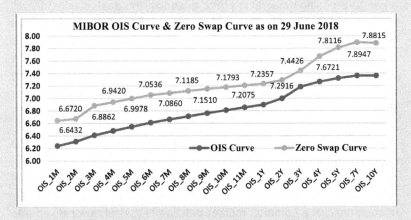

*Figure 10.14* MIBOR-OIS curve and ZC OIS curve as on 29 June 2018

The MIBOR-OIS curve as on the contract initiation date and on the valuation date, as exhibited in Figure 10.13, may be considered to estimate the MTM value of the swap contract.

As usually followed in the market, the dealer may like to use the zero swap curve, given by Thompson Reuters and exhibited in the following figure (Figure 10.14), to discount the future cash flows/payoffs involved with the swap contract to arrive at its MTM value and also to estimate the PV01 of the open swap position held in the swap book of SBI Global Markets.

### Premature unwinding/cancellation

Even if swap dealers enter into long-term swap contracts (say between 1 year to 5 years), a common trend in the market is to unwind the deal before maturity. The dealer in SBI Global Market is well aware that such deals can be prematurely unwound either by entering into a reverse swap in the market or unwinding with the original counterparty. The dealer may like to explore both the alternatives available to unwind the deal as on 29 June 2018, and the necessary payoffs to finally cancel the deal on the same date.

An outstanding OIS position may be prematurely unwound with the original counterparty by either of the counterparties (fixed rate payer or receiver), irrespective of the current MTM of the position. A counterparty, having a negative MTM in the OIS position, may prefer to cancel the contract to cut future losses. Similarly, a counterparty with a positive MTM on an OIS position may also prefer to cancel the deal, simply to book the current MTM profit and remove all possibilities to incur any future MTM losses on the same position due to adverse market conditions. But premature cancellation of any outstanding OIS position normally won't happen at the market rate, but at a rate quoted by the counterparty whom the interested counterparty approaches for cancellation. In such case, the quoted rate will definitely not be in favor of the counterparty approaching for premature cancellation.

While exploring for the second alternative (i.e. unwinding with the original counterparty), the dealer is aware of the fact that if one counterparty approaches the other for premature unwinding/cancellation of an OIS deal, the same may not happen at the prevailing market rate. In such case, the common market practice is that whoever (fixed rate payer or floating rate payer) approaches, gets an offer by the other counterparty (floating rate payer or fixed rate payer) at a rate slightly out of the market, adjusted by say 5 basis points. Under such situation, the dealer in SBI Global Markets may like to know the final amount of settlement (with the original counterparty) under both the following circumstances:

i.   SBI approaches HSBC to cut the future losses (if any) or to book the existing profit (if any) and unwind the deal; or
ii.  SBI is approached by HSBC under either of the aforesaid situations.

## Self-learning exercise

1 What is an interest rate swap (IRS)? How is it different from a forward rate agreement (FRA)? Explain with some simple examples.
2 A bank finds that its assets are not matched with its liabilities. It is taking floating rate deposits and making fixed rate loans. How can FRA and IRS be used to offset the risk?
3 How FRA or IRS can be used to make some speculative gains?
4 Two institutions, A and B, interested in borrowing a sum of INR 100 crore for a period of 6 years, have been offered the following rates per annum:

| Institutions | Fixed rate | Floating rate |
|---|---|---|
| A | 7.0% | LIBOR + 0.2% |
| B | 8.4% | LIBOR + 0.8% |

A needs to borrow at a floating rate of interest, whereas B prefers to tap the fixed rate market. Design an interest rate swap that will net a bank, acting as intermediary, 0.1% per annum and that will appear equally attractive to both the institutions.
5 How is the overnight index swap different from a standard IRS with a long-term reference rate? Explain the important operational aspects in which both the contracts differ from each other.
6 What is the basis of pricing an interest rate swap contract? How is the same valued once the contract is initiated?
7 How is the MTM value of an OIS deal arrived at. How does the residual tenor of an OIS plays its role in the valuation process?
8 How do you estimate the PV01 of an OIS deal outstanding in your book?
9 Why may a trader like to cancel an OIS deal before the maturity? How is such contract prematurely cancelled by a buyer or seller of the contract? If there are alternative methods to cancel an OIS deal, which method may a dealer like to choose and why?
10 How do you ensure that the interest rate risk arising from a floating rate borrowing can be duly hedged with the desired position in the IRS? What will you try to ensure to get a close to perfect hedge?
11 What makes an interest rate swap contract useful for duration management? How can the IRS be used to manage the duration of a bank's assets and liabilities under different circumstances?

## Bibliography

Bicksler, J., and Chen, A. H. (1986). An Economic Analysis of Interest Rate Swaps. *Journal of Finance*, 41(3), 645–655.
Brewer, E., Minton, B. A., and Moser, J. T. (2000). Interest-Rate Derivatives and Bank Lending. *Journal of Banking & Finance*, 24, 353–379.

Brown, R., In, F., and Fang, V. (2002). Modeling the Determinants of Swap Spreads. *Journal of Fixed Income*, 12(1), 29–40.

Chernenko, S., and Faulkender, M. (2011). The Two Sides of Derivatives Usage: Hedging and Speculating With Interest Rate Swaps. *The Journal of Financial and Quantitative Analysis*, 46(6), 1727–1754.

Choudhry, M. (2010). *Fixed Income Securities and Derivatives Handbook: Analysis and Valuation* (2nd edn.). John Wiley & Sons, Inc., Hoboken, NJ.

Corb, H. (2012). *Interest Rate Swaps and Other Derivatives*. Columbia Business School Publishing, New York.

Dynkin, L., Hyman, J., and Lindner, P. (2002). Hedging and Replication of Fixed-Income Portfolios. *Journal of Fixed Income*, 11(4), 43–63.

Fabozzi, F. (ed.). (July 2017). *The Handbook of Fixed Income Securities* (8th edn.). McGraw Hill Education, New York.

Gupta, A., and Subrahmanyam, M. G. (2000). An Empirical Examination of the Convexity Bias in the Pricing of Interest Rate Swaps. *Journal of Financial Economics*, 55(2), 239–279.

Jaffee, D. (2003). The Interest Rate Risk of Fannie Mae and Freddie Mac. *Journal of Financial Services Research*, 24(1), 5–29.

Purnanandam, A. (2007). Interest Rate Derivatives at Commercial Banks: An Empirical Investigation. *Journal of Monetary Economics*, 54(6), 1769–1808.

Sundaresan, S. (2009). *Fixed Income Markets and Their Derivatives* (3rd edn.). Elsevier India Pvt. Ltd., India.

Veronesi, P. (2011). *Fixed Income Securities: Valuation, Risk and Risk Management*. John Wiley & Sons, Inc., Hoboken, NJ.

## Notes

1  Suppose there are two financial institutions/NBFCs/corporates who are supposed to have some comparative advantage in terms of borrowing money from the market, depending upon their overall performance (say, financials, credit worthiness, etc.), as reflected from their credit rating offered by external rating agencies. Let's assume one institution/organization has a comparative advantage to borrow in the fixed rate market, while the other enjoys a comparative advantage borrowing in the floating rate market. Here, the comparative advantage among two institutions can be captured by looking at the differences between the two fixed rates and between both the floating rates, offered by the market to both the institutions, with different levels of performance or with different credit ratings, at a given point of time. As a result of this, institutions are supposed to consider that market where it has a comparative advantage. At the same time, even if there is a comparative advantage for institutions to borrow money from either of the markets (fixed or floating rate), the institutions may not find it suitable/reasonable, for any other ground, to tap the same, and may like to convert their exposure to the other market without losing the comparative advantage.

2  Commercial banks, as per the prescribed norms of Basel Committee and the respective central banks (RBI in India), need to keep the necessary capital for various types of risk that banks carry in their business. Accordingly, whenever a bank takes any position in FRA/IRS it is required to estimate the interest rate risk losses and counterparty risk losses on such position, followed by maintaining the required amount of capital charge as per the prescribed norms. This type of capital charge along with other capital charges on any trading positions are known as a market risk capital charge (MRCC).

# 11 Interest rate options and structured products

**Key learning outcomes**

At the end of this chapter, readers are expected to be familiar with:

- What do simple interest rate options (call and put) structures look like?
- How is the important vocabulary of options analyzed?
- What are interest rate caps, floors, and collars?
- How are these structures priced and valued?
- How are these contracts/products used to hedge IR risk?
- How are structured products used to reduce the cost of hedging?

## Interest rate options: meaning & structures

An option is a contract in which the *Writer* or the *Seller* of the option gives the options *Buyer* the *right but not the obligation*, in exchange of some price known as the *Option Premium*, to buy from or sell to the options seller or writer some *Underlying Instrument* at some specified price (*Strike Price* or *Exercise Price*) within a specified period of time (*Expiration Date*). Any option that gives the buyer (seller) the right to buy (sell) some designated instrument is known as the *Call* (*Put*) option. Similarly, other than the specified expiration date, any option which can (cannot) be exercised before the expiration date is known as American (European) option. At the same time, there may be an option which can be exercised before its maturity but only on some designated dates, known as *Bermudian Option*. There are four basic strategies adopted by the options trader. These are *Long Call*, *Short Call*, *Long Put*, and *Short Put*. The risk-return characteristic of an option trader depends on their trading strategies. The long call or long put holder enjoys the possibility of *Unlimited Upside Gain* with a *Limited Downside Risk* (equal to the option premium). Whereas, even with a limited possibility

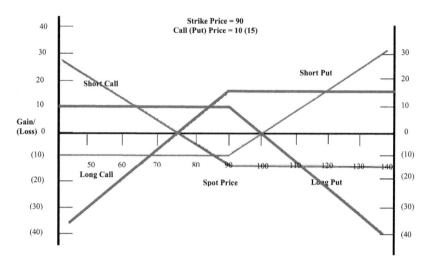

*Figure 11.1* Asymmetric risk-return profile in options contract

of upside gain, the short call or short put holder is exposed to the unlimited downside risk. Therefore, unlike in a forward or futures contract, the risk-return profile of two counterparties of an options contract is *Asymmetric*, as shown in the following figure (Figure 11.1).

The points on which futures and options contract can be differentiated are briefed in the following section:

- Status (Rights or Obligation) of the Buyer of Futures or Options.
- Nature (Symmetric or Asymmetric) of Pay Offs.
- Margin Requirements of Buyer and Seller.

In case of an interest rate option, the underlying instrument is nothing but the *Interest Rate*. Interest rate options can be traded both in *Recognized Exchanges* and in *Over-the-Counter* (OTC). The underlying instrument used for exchange traded interest rate options (IRO) may be of two types – fixed income security or interest rate futures contract. Accordingly, the interest rate options may be of *Options on Physicals* or *Futures Option*. Options on IRF or futures options are more active exchange traded interest rate options contracts than the options on physicals. Options on interest rate futures, or in short futures options, gives the buyer the right to buy from (sell to) the options seller a designated interest rate futures contract at a strike price at *any time* within the maturity of the option contract. Accordingly, the buyer (seller) of such call options contract is treated as the long (short) position holder in the underlying interest rate futures contract.

Similarly, the buyer (seller) of such put options contract is treated as the short (long) position holder in the underlying interest rate futures contract. The settlement price of the underlying IRF contract is also pre-specified in the futures option contract and is also known as the strike price. Since a futures option is an exchange traded option contract, it follows the marked-to-market system. Accordingly, the current futures price in everyday, until the option expiration date or the date of squaring off the option position, is compared with the strike price of the IRF contract and the payoffs are settled based on the difference between the strike price and the current price of the IRF contract and the type (call or put) of the futures option. As far as the margin requirement is concerned, an option on interest rate futures is similar to a simple option on some other underlying, like a bond, but only to the buyer of the futures option. The seller of such options contract needs to maintain a margin equal to the margin required on the IRF contract and the option premium received from the option buyer. The reasons for the higher popularity of the futures option in comparison with the options on underlying fixed income securities can be briefed as follows:

- Non-consideration of accrued interest in the pay offs of the option contract.
- Absence of issues related to delivery of the underlying instrument, or in other words, lowers chance of *Delivery Squeezes*.
- Easy availability of the futures price on an underlying bond issue rather the price of the underlying bond issue itself required to price the option contract.

## Pricing of interest rate options

The price paid by the options (call or put) buyer to enjoy the rights in an option contract mainly constitutes two components – one is the *Intrinsic Value* and the other is the *Time Value*.

### Intrinsic value

Intrinsic value of an option contract can be defined as its expected economic value that can be generated if the option contract is exercised immediately. In other words, an option contract is said to have an intrinsic value at any point of time if the holder of the option gets a positive payoff by exercising the option at the same point of time. If such payoff is found to be zero or negative, or in other words, if the exercise of the option does not result in any positive economic value, then the intrinsic value of the option contract is considered to be zero. Accordingly, intrinsic value can be simply defined as the difference between the current market price of the underlying instrument and the strike price of the option contract. If the current market price of the underlying instrument is greater (lower) than the strike or exercise price of the call (put) options contract, then the holder of such option may have some incentive to close or exercise their position on or before the maturity of the options. In such cases, the option has some intrinsic value and is said to be *In-the-Money* option. Similarly, if the current market price is lower (higher) than the strike price of a call (put) option, then there won't be any intrinsic value for such options contract and it is said to be an *Out-of-the-Money* option. An option contract is said to be *At-the-Money* if the current market price of the underlying instrument is just equal to the exercise price of the option.

### Time value

The time value of an option contract is the difference between the price of an option contract and its intrinsic value. An option buyer may expect that between the settlement and maturity of the contract, the price of the underlying instrument may increase, leading to a rise in the value of the rights given by the option writer. Therefore, the option buyer agrees to pay some premium over the intrinsic value of the option contract. This premium is nothing but the time value of such option contract. When an option contract is out-of-the-money or at-the-money, the price of such option is just equal to its time value, because of its zero intrinsic value.

### Factors affecting options' price

The price of an option contract, irrespective of the type of underlying instrument, broadly depends upon five different factors. Apart from these five important factors, one more important factor plays an important role in pricing an option on any fixed income instrument. But at the same time, if the underlying of an interest rate option is an interest rate futures contract, the factors affecting the option's price remains the first five, as like general options contract. The specific impact of each of these factors depends upon the type of the option, i.e. whether the option is call or put and whether the option is American or European. Assuming that the option is an American option (i.e. can be exercised on or before the maturity date), how all the six factors affect the price of a call or put option can be briefly described in the following section:

### i. Current market price of the underlying instrument

Any change in the price of the underlying instrument directly affects the price of an option contract. Holding all other factors constant, as the price of the underlying instrument increases, the intrinsic value, and therefore the price of the call (put) option increases (decreases). On the other hand, if the price of the underlying instrument is found to fall, the intrinsic value and therefore the price of the call (put) option tends to fall (rise). Therefore, there is a positive (negative) relation between the price of an underlying fixed income instrument and the price of a call (put) option on the same.

## ii. Strike price of the option contract

Assuming all other factors are constant, the higher the strike or exercise price, the lower (higher) would be the intrinsic value, and therefore the price of a call (put) option. Similarly, the lower (higher) the strike price, the higher (lower) would be the intrinsic value, and therefore the price of a call (put) option on a fixed income instrument. Therefore, the relation between the strike price and the value of an option is negative for a call option and positive for a put option.

## iii. Time to expiration of the option contract

Holding all other factors constant, the longer the time to expiration of the option contract, the higher would be the price of such options. Alternatively, for American options, as the time to expiration decreases, the time value of such options approaches zero and the option price approaches its intrinsic value. Therefore, the relation between the price of an option contract and its time to expiration, both for call and put options, is positive.

## iv. Short-term risk-free rate of interest over the life of the option

If the short-term risk-free rate rises, it is always preferable to make a short-term risk-free investment to gain the higher less risk return. Accordingly, in the regime of rising short-term risk-free interest rates, the expected buyer of an underlying asset would prefer to buy a call option on the underlying instrument and make a short-term risk-free investment for the amount equal to the difference between the price of the instrument and the option price. Therefore, the higher the short-term risk-free rate, the more attractive the call option is relative to buying the underlying instrument, and therefore the higher would be the price of such call option. On the other hand, if the short-term risk-free rate of interest increases, the holder of an underlying instrument would prefer to short the instrument in the cash market and invest the same at the risk-free rate, rather than buy a put option on such instrument. Therefore, as the risk-free rate of interest rises, the demand and the value of a put option falls. In short, the relation between the short-term risk-free rate of interest and the value of an option contract is positive for a call option and is negative for a put option.

## v. Expected interest rate volatility over the life of the option

The more unstable or volatile the price of a fixed income instrument, the higher would be the value of an options contract, irrespective of whether the option is a call option or a put option. Again, the price of an underlying fixed income instrument largely depends upon the interest rate. Therefore, keeping all other factors constant, the greater the expected interest rate volatility, the more volatile would be the price of a fixed income instrument, and accordingly, the higher would be the value of call and put options required to hedge the price volatility of underlying instruments. In short, there is a positive relation between the interest rate volatility and the price of an options contract.

*vi. Interim coupon payments over the life of the option*

Interim coupon payments on an underlying fixed income instrument make it more attractive for an investor to buy a call option on that underlying fixed income instrument. Therefore, the higher the amount of interim coupon payments, the lower would be the demand, and therefore the value, of a call option. On the other hand, interim coupon payments on a fixed income security make it more attractive to hold rather to sell in the market. Therefore, the holder of an underlying fixed income instrument would prefer to buy a put option on such instrument as the alternative to short the same in the cash market. Accordingly, the higher the amount of interim coupon payments, the greater would be the demand for the put option, and therefore the higher would be its value. Taking these altogether, the relation between interim coupon payments and the value of an option contract is negative (positive) for call (put) options.

## Pricing models for interest rate options

As it is clear, the price of an options contract has two components – intrinsic value and time value. The valuation of the first component can be done at any time without following any mathematical model. It can be valued just by considering the current market price or current reference rate and strike price of strike rate. The problem in valuing an option contract is its time value. Pricing models are basically used to derive the time value of an option contract. Two important models used to value an option on a fixed income instrument are:

- Black-Scholes Option Pricing Model.
- Arbitrage-free Binomial Option Pricing Model.

These two pricing models are generally used to price an option contract on a fixed income instrument. But as far as the pricing of an option on an interest rate futures contract (i.e. futures on a fixed income instrument) is concerned, a revised version of the Black-Scholes model, commonly known as the Black model, is used.

### Arbitrage-free binomial option pricing model

As far as the pricing of an option contract on an underlying of any fixed income security is concerned, the pricing model should be arbitrage-free and should incorporate the yield curve to reflect the change in the short-term rate of interest. The assumption of constant volatility can also be taken care off by considering different volatilities along with the consideration of the yield curve. A well-known arbitrage-free binomial option pricing model, widely used by the dealers in fixed income markets, is the *Black-Derman-Toy Model*.

The basic requirement of this model is to construct a *Binomial Interest Rate Tree* that would be arbitrage-free. The pricing of an option contract on a fixed income security can be done based on this interest rate tree.

### Construction of binomial interest rate tree

Following are the few points that need to be remembered before the construction of such arbitrage-free binomial interest rate tree:

i   A valuation lattice (in the form of a binomial tree), capturing the distribution of the interest rates over time, can represent a pricing model where the volatility can be assumed to be stationary or fixed.

ii  All the information required to value certain optionable interest rate products, such as cash flows across the life of the security, interest rates used to discount those CFs, etc., can be generated from the valuation lattice.

iii Since it is assumed that the interest rate can be realized as one of only two possible rates while moving from one period to another, the concerned lattice is known as the *Binomial Interest Rate Tree or Lattice*.

iv  If the current price or value derived from the interest rate lattice is equal to the current par value as per the par yield curve, the concerned lattice is treated as arbitrage-free and is known as fair lattice.

v   A binomial interest rate tree consists of a number of *Legs* and *Nodes*, where legs represent different 1-year intervals (or other periodic intervals) from year 0 to the maturity of the security, and nodes represent different possible interest rates at different periods or legs.

vi  Distribution of future interest rates in the binomial interest rate tree is represented by the nodes (N) at each time point with a combination of higher (H) and lower (L) on the tree relative to other nodes.

vii The root of the interest rate tree or the node at the root is denoted as N only where the interest rate ($R_0$) is certain and represented as the 1-year interest rate at today, which is nothing but the 1-year spot rate.

viii Since the distribution of the interest rate is binomial, the probability of occurring a specific interest rate (high or low) at any point in time and in each leg is 50%.

The binomial interest rate tree as explained above can not only be used to value an interest rate option, but also to value a fixed income security with or without any embedded options. Suppose the par Treasury yield curve is such that the YTM for 1-year, 2-year, 3-year, and 4-year maturities are respectively 3.5%, 4.2%, 4.7%, and 5.2% for a par value of Rs.100/-. Now the binomial interest rate tree for valuing such Treasury bond traded at par with a maturity of 4 years, assuming an interest rate volatility of 10%, can be exhibited in the following figure (Figure 11.2):

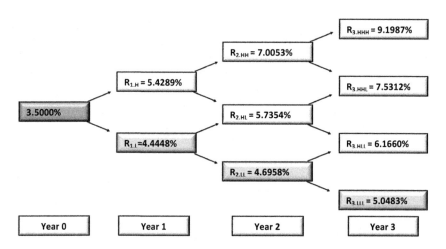

*Figure 11.2* Binomial interest rate tree used to value callable bond

The values of all the possible rates of interest on a coupon-bearing Treasury issue, calibrated to the current par yield curve, as depicted in the above binomial interest rate tree, have been derived by following the *Backward Induction Method*. The principal of this method is the interest rate at the lowest node of every leg (except the leg at year 0) is step wise, assumed at a certain level, and then calibrated to the par yield curve. That is how, given the interest rate at year 0, we can calculate the three other rates of interest at the lowest nodes of the other three legs of the interest rate lattice. After having all these three rates ($R_{1,L}$, $R_{2,LL}$, and $R_{3,LLL}$), interest rates at all other nodes can be calculated assuming certain interest rate volatility, such that: .

$$R_{1,H} = R_{1,L} \ e^{2\sigma}; R_{2,HL} = R_{2,LL} \ e^{2\sigma}; R_{2,HH} = R_{2,LL} \ e^{4\sigma};$$
$$R_{3,HLL} = R_{3,LLL} \ e^{2\sigma}; R_{3,HHL} = R_{3,LLL} \ e^{4\sigma}; R_{3,HHH} = R_{3,LLL} \ e^{6\sigma}$$

As soon as the binomial interest rate tree, calibrated to the par yield curve, has been formed, the valuation of a specific nth-year coupon-bearing Treasury security can be done by following the same method but by using

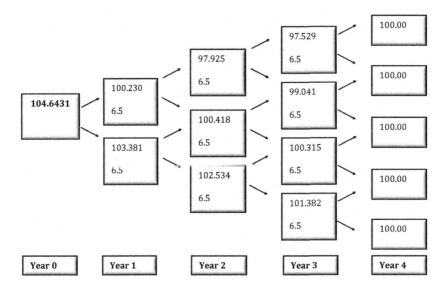

*Figure 11.3* Valuation of callable bond using binomial tree

the actual bond specific data on the bond's par value, maturity period, and coupon rate. The value of the bond derived through this method would be considered as arbitrage-free. The valuation of suppose a 4-year 6.5% Treasury coupon bond, derived through this binomial interest rate tree, can be shown in the following figure (Figure 11.3):

The above section has dealt with the formation of a binomial interest rate tree and the valuation of a 4-year 6.5% Treasury coupon bond based on this tree. Now the question is how this information can be used to value an interest rate option taken on such underlying bond issue? Suppose a European call option with a maturity of 2 (or 3) years and strike price of Rs.100.25/- has been taken on this 4-year 6.5% Treasury coupon bond. Now the value of such call option can be derived as follows:

While valuing the call option contract on the Treasury bond issue, we can consider the previous interest rate tree, only up to year 2 (or year 3), where the possible values of the treasury issue are considered in the last three (four) nodes of the third (fourth) leg, i.e. up to year 2 (year 3), along with the expected intrinsic value of the call option (if any), which is the positive difference between the bond's value at that node and the strike price in the option contract. After the calculation in the final (as per the option contract) leg, the same backward induction method is followed to get the final and arbitrage-free value of the option contract. In these lines, the arbitrage-free valuation of the aforesaid European interest rate option, both with

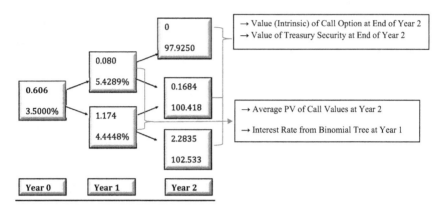

*Figure 11.4* Valuation of call option embedded in a 2-Y bond using binomial tree

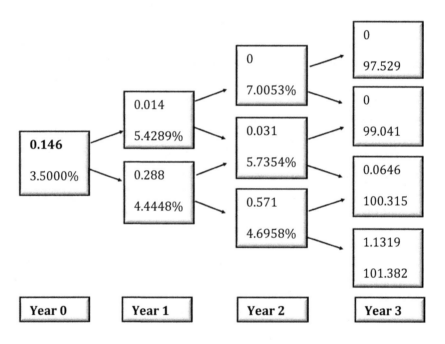

*Figure 11.5* Valuation of call option embedded in a 3-Y bond using binomial tree

2- and 3-years maturity, are shown in the following figures (Figure 11.4 and Figure 11.5).

The above calculation deals with the valuation of a European call option on a fixed income security. Similarly, a put option can also be valued in the same framework, except the calculation of the value (intrinsic) of a put option during the last year of its maturity, i.e. in the last leg of the binomial interest rate tree The required values of this leg would be the positive difference between the option's strike price and the current value of the fixed income security, otherwise zero.

## Interest rate caps, floors, and collar: meaning & structures

There may be some contractual agreement between two counterparties regarding some compensation resulting from the movement of some reference rate of interest beyond a certain pre-determined level known as the *Strike Rate.* The agreement is such that if the reference rate is different from the strike rate within a specific time period, one party, in exchange of an upfront premium, agrees to compensate the other party. The amount of compensation depends on the *Notional Value* of the contract and the difference between the actual level of reference rate and the strike rate. Such type of contract may be of two types – *Interest Rate Cap*, or simply cap, and *Interest Rate Floor*, or simply floor. If one party agrees to pay the other party if the reference rate exceeds (falls below) the strike rate, the agreement is referred to as interest rate cap (interest rate floor). The strike rate for the cap and floor is respectively known as the *Cap Rate* and *Floor Rate.* At the same time, if both these caps and floors are combined together to make a new contract, it is known as an *Interest Rate Collar* or simply collar. This contract is structured by buying an interest rate cap and selling an interest rate floor.

As far as the risk-return characteristic of such agreement is concerned, it is similar to an option contract, where the buyer of such interest rate cap (interest rate floor), in exchange of a limited downside risk equal to the upfront premium required to pay to the seller, enjoys the possibility of unlimited upside gains whenever the actual reference rate rises above (falls below) the strike rate. On the other hand, the seller of an interest rate cap (interest rate floor) needs to make an unlimited compensation to the buyer in the event of any rise (fall) of the reference rate above (below) the strike rate, only in exchange of a limited amount of premium, normally paid in upfront. At the same time, if the counterparty risk is taken into consideration, this agreement is similar to an option contract where the seller does not face any counterparty risk, but the buyers of such contract are exposed to unlimited counterparty risk.

Interest rate caps and interest rate floors can be represented as a package of interest rate options at different time periods, where each of the options comprising a cap (floor) are known as *Caplets* (*Floorlets*). As we know, the value of a fixed income instrument changes inversely with the change in the rate of interest. Accordingly, the value of a long call (long put) option on a fixed income instrument decreases (increases) with any rise in the rate of interest. Similarly, if there is a fall in the interest rate, the value of a long call (long put) option on a fixed income instrument tends to increase (decrease). The values of a short call or a short put on such instrument changes just in the opposite direction to the change in their respective long positions, both for the rise and fall in the rate of interest.

Caps and floors are respectively used to get the benefit of rising and falling rate of interest. Any customer or borrower, who wants to get the necessary protection from the possibility of rising interest rate, can buy a cap by paying some price. If there is an unexpected fall in the rate of interest, the customer can even save some money by incurring a lower interest cost. But buying a cap again involves some fixed cost, irrespective of the movement in the rate of interest. Suppose the customer is neither willing to suffer any loss due to an unexpected rise in the rate of interest, nor wants to make any gain from the unexpected fall in the rate of interest, but at the same time does not want to bear any fixed cost in such process. In other words, a customer, who opted for a floating rate interest payment on his/her loan, wants to set a minimum and maximum rate of interest that he/she wishes to pay on his/her loan obligation, irrespective of the prevailing market or reference rate of interest. Now, the question is, how is it possible? Buying a cap helps to protect from an interest rate rise in exchange for some fixed price; similarly, selling a floor restricts from getting any advantage from the falling rate of interest but makes it possible to get some price which can be used to compensate for the price required to be paid for buying the caps. This combination of long cap and short floor is known as the collar. Therefore, if a customer buys a collar to set a minimum and maximum rate of interest on his/her floating rate loan obligation, he/she is eligible to get the necessary protection if the interest rate rises beyond the strike rate of the cap, and is liable to forgo any benefits if the interest rate falls below the strike rate of the floor, without incurring any net cost, or maybe at a very lower cost, equivalent to the difference between the premium paid on the cap and the same received on the floor. Accordingly, even if the customer is in a floating rate obligation, the actual rate of interest applicable to him/her would be within a specific range with a maximum of the cap's strike rate and a minimum of floor's strike rate. Therefore, a collar can be treated as a costless instrument for acquiring a status of "neither risk – nor gain".

## Cost-effectiveness of interest rate derivatives: a case

Subject: Cost effectiveness among available interest rate derivative products to hedge interest rate risk.

Suppose a corporate entity wants to raise USD 100 million of a 3-year debt in the Indian market (where interest is quoted and paid on an annual basis). The alternatives available to the firm are:

1   A 3-year fixed rate note at a spread of 250 basis points over the 3-year Indian Treasury (say currently yielding 4.5%);

2   A 3-year floating rate note (FRN) on which it has to pay an annual interest of 1-year LIBOR plus 2% spread, where 1-year LIBOR currently yields 3.7%, leading to an interest payment of USD 5.7 million at the end of the 1st year.

However, the corporate wants to have a fixed rate liability for the entire 3 years.

Suppose the following instruments are also available to the corporate, proposed to be provided by say the State Bank of India, rated AAA as the counterparty.

**Instrument 1**

A 3-year swap contract with a pay-fixed rate of the current 3-year Treasury rate plus 30 basis points against receiving the floating rate of a 1-year LIBOR

**Instrument 2**

Combination of forward rate agreements –
FRA 1: 12/24 FRA with a pay-fixed rate of a 2-year Treasury (yielding 4.1%) plus 90 basis points against receiving a floating rate of a 1-year LIBOR
FRA 2: 24/36 FRA with a pay-fixed rate of a 3-year Treasury plus 150 basis points against receiving a floating rate of a 1-year LIBOR

**Instrument 3**

Combination of a 3-year cap and a 3-year floor contract, i.e. a 3-year collar contract, where the reference rate is a 1-year LIBOR. The premium for different cap and floror contracts with different strike rates are as follows:

| Strike Rate (Cap & Floor) | Cap Premium | Floor Premium |
|---|---|---|
| 4.00% | 2.23% | 0.18% |
| 4.80% | 0.70% | 0.70% |
| 5.00% | 0.49% | 0.90% |
| 6.00% | 0.08% | 3.22% |

**Out of the all available strategies, which strategy will enable the corporate to pay the lowest all-in fixed rate of interest?**
All rates are assumed to be quoted on an annual basis.

## Self-learning exercise

1　How can an options trader make use of interest rate call and put options?
2　How are interest rate call and put options different from interest rate cap and floor?
3　What are the standard option pricing models majorly used in the market? Can any of the models be useful to price interest rate options? Justify your answer.
4　How do you define the intrinsic value and the time value in the context of interest rate options? Can any of these components be zero at any point of time? Explain briefly.
5　Briefly explain the factors affecting the values of interest rate options.
6　What is the major shortcoming of buying an interest rate cap or a floor? How can the same be addressed through a position in interest rate collar? Briefly explain with examples. What is the drawback of an interest rate collar?

## Bibliography

Choudhry, M. (2010). *Fixed Income Securities and Derivatives Handbook: Analysis and Valuation* (2nd edn.). John Wiley & Sons, Inc., Hoboken, NJ.

Das, S. (2005). *Structured Products: Volume 1: Exotic Options; Interest Rates and Currency.* John Wiley & Sons, Inc., Hoboken, NJ.

Fabozzi, F. (ed.). (July 2017). *The Handbook of Fixed Income Securities* (8th edn.). McGraw Hill Education, New York.

Hull, J. C., and Basu, S. (2016). *Options, Futures, and Other Derivatives* (9th edn.). Pearson Education, India.

Jarrow, R. A. (2002). *Modeling Fixed-Income Securities and Interest Rate Options* (2nd edn.). Stanford University Press, Stanford, CA.

Sundaresan, S. (2009). *Fixed Income Markets and Their Derivatives* (3rd edn.). Elsevier India Pvt. Ltd., India.

Veronesi, P. (2011). *Fixed Income Securities: Valuation, Risk and Risk Management.* John Wiley & Sons, Inc., Hoboken, NJ.

# 12 Credit default swaps

Key learning outcomes

At the end of this chapter, the readers are expected to be familiar with:

- Meaning and history of credit default swaps, especially in light of 2008 US subprime crisis.
- Different types of credit default swaps, with special reference to emerging markets.
- Important features of credit default swaps, in line with RBI guidelines on CDS.
- Current scope of CDS in India and its future challenges.

## Meaning and definition of credit derivatives

*Credit Derivatives* are financial instruments designed to transfer the credit risk from one counterparty to another. In other words, a credit derivative is a *Privately Negotiated* contract the value of which is derived from the credit risk of a bond, a bank loan, or any other instrument with an exposure to credit risk. Credit derivatives can have the form of forwards, swaps, and options, which may be embedded in financial assets like bonds or loans or other investments with a credit risk exposure. Therefore, credit derivatives, on the one hand, allow investors or creditors to eliminate or reduce credit risk involved in their investment, and allow the counterparty to make some profit and leverage their position by assuming the credit risk in their own books of accounts. On the other hand, credit derivatives can be defined as arrangements that allow one counterparty (*Protection Buyer*) to transfer, in exchange of a certain price called *Premium*, the defined credit risk (full or in part), computed with reference to a notional value, of a reference asset(s), with or without its actual ownership, to another counterparty or counter-parties (*Protection Seller*).

There are different basic and complex or synthetic derivatives products or instruments used to mitigate the credit risk that a person or entity carries in their books of accounts. Broadly, credit derivative instruments are clas-sified into four categories: credit default swaps (CDS), total rate of return swaps (TRORS), credit spread products, and different synthetic structures. Again, credit spread products include credit spread forward/futures, credit spread options, credit spread swaps, etc. Similarly, credit link notes (CLN), collarized debt obligations (CDOs), etc. are some of the examples of syn-thetic credit derivatives instruments. All the above products may be simple in nature, or they may have a complex structure based on the type of the products. Apart from having a common purpose of hedging against credit risk exposure, different credit derivative products have some identical fea-tures that can differentiate one product from the other.

### Credit default swaps (CDS)

A credit default swap is a *bilateral* financial contract in which the *Protection Buyer* pays a *Periodic* or *Upfront Fee* in return for a *Contingent* payment by the *Protection Seller* following a *Credit Event* with respect to a *Reference Entity*. In other words, a CDS can be viewed as a put option on the reference obligation, the owner of which, i.e. the default swap buyer or the protection buyer, has the right so sell the reference obligation to the default swap seller or the protection seller in the event of a default in any future period of time. The payoff structure of a simple CDS contract would be as given in the fol-lowing figure (Figure 12.1).

CDS is essentially similar to any credit insurance product, except the fact that unlike in case of an insurance product, the CDS buyer need not

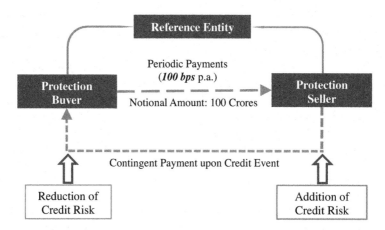

*Figure 12.1* Structure of a plain vanilla CDS contract

compulsorily hold the underlying asset and the buyer can trade on the CDS contract, i.e. the CDS contract can be sold before its maturity.

## History and growth of credit default swaps

It is very difficult to define a specific time period when credit derivatives emerged. The International Swaps and Derivatives Association (ISDA), in the year 1992, first uses the term "Credit Derivatives" to describe a new, exotic type of over-the-counter contract. The credit derivatives market begins to evolve in the year 1994. In 1997, JP Morgan developed a proprietary product called BISTRO (Broad Index Secured Trust Offering) that used CDS to clean up a bank's balance sheet. By March 1998, the global market for CDS was estimated at about USD 300 billion, with JP Morgan alone accounting for about USD 50 billion of this. In 2000, credit default swaps became largely exempted from regulation by both the U.S. Securities and Exchange Commission (SEC) and the Commodity Futures Trading Commission (CFTC). At the same time, there was a tremendous growth in the subprime mortgage market, leading to an exceptional growth in the market for mortgage backed securities (MBS). As a result, after 2000–01, there also has been a tremendous growth in the worldwide volume of different credit derivative products, especially for CDS. The market size for credit default swaps started growing more than double in size each year from USD 3.7 trillion in 2003. As a result, by the end of 2007, the CDS market had experienced a notional volume of USD 62.2 trillion. But following the breakdown in the market for subprime mortgages, and therefore the market for MBS, known as 2007–08 US subprime crisis, the CDS market started experiencing a drastic slowdown, and the notional amount outstanding had fallen by 38% to USD 38.6 trillion by the end of 2008, again falling to USD 25.9 trillion in December 2011, and to USD 24.3 trillion by the end of June 2013 (as per BIS Report).

### *Reasons for high growth in CDS market*

When we are talking about a faster growth of several credit derivative products, especially of CDS, all over the world, it is quite natural for us to explore the reasons or motivation towards this tremendous growth, especially comparative to other existing derivative products. In other words, why credit derivatives in general and credit default swaps in particular have become more popular as far as credit risk mitigation is concerned? Some of the possible answers can be derived from the following points:

### *Increasing bankruptcies*

If we look into the history of the last few decades, it would be clear that there were a large number of corporate and sovereign bankruptcies happening all over the world. Some of the important crises include the Latin American debt crisis in early 1980s, Asian financial crisis in 1997–98, Russian debt crisis in 1998, Argentina crisis in 2001, Enron bankruptcy in 2001, 2008 US subprime crisis, 2010 Greece debt crisis, etc. These bankruptcies not only ate up the capital of several banks and other financial intermediaries, but also caused major financial crises for a larger part of the economy. Credit derivative instruments, if used properly, can be used as a cushion for large credit exposures that lead to its faster growth all over the world.

### Improvement in technical and managerial ability

Any derivative contract, on one side, can be used to hedge against any risk exposure, and on the other side, can act as a boomerang if it fails to be valued and managed in a proper way. In other words, derivatives can be used to unbundle and remove the risk component from the return of an asset provided the derivative instruments are truly valued and properly managed. If it fails to do so, it invites different types of risk, even more than the risk that the investors are trying to hedge. Sufficient technical, managerial, and quantitative skills are required for a proper utilization of several derivative instruments. If we look into the last few decades, it would be clear that there was a lack of sufficient technical and managerial ability in banks and other financial organizations, which de-motivated them to use any sophisticated risk mitigation tools and techniques. But as far as the present scenario is concerned, people have become highly technical and they have the ability to properly value and manage the complicated risk management tools. This improvement in the quality of manpower in the banking and finance industry may also be attributed for the worldwide rapid growth of more advanced derivative products, including credit derivatives.

### Yield enhancement possibility

The purpose of entering into a credit derivative market, for a protection buyer, may be to hedge against the risk of credit exposure. But why is the counterparty selling the protection by assuming the same risk in its own books of accounts? What is the reason for being exposed to the credit risk transferred by the counterparty? The main reason behind selling protection and buying risk is to get some non-funded return, i.e. return without any investment. This may enhance the yield of the protection seller. By selling protection on low rated credits, insurance companies, asset managers, hedge funds, etc. can earn a higher return that boosts up their yield. Therefore, not only on the buyer side, but also on the seller side, there is a tremendous growth in selling protection against different risk exposure that significantly leads to faster development of different credit derivative products, including CDS.

*Exposure without actual lending*

Though the basic purpose of credit derivatives is to hedge against the credit risk raised due to some real credit exposure, they can be used even without any actual exposure, i.e. buying credit protection without giving any credit. In other words, credit derivatives allow investors to take exposure without actual lending. This may allow an investor (protection buyer) to protect against some of his/her parallel exposure, or the purpose of buying such protection might be simply to get the benefit of speculation and/or arbitrage.

*Regulatory & economic capital relief*

One of the important objectives for a protection buyer to buy protection against his/her credit exposure is to remove the credit risk from his/her own books of accounts. Since banks and other financial intermediaries need to keep aside a certain amount of regulatory capital based on the risk category of their assets of different credit quality, if the risk of a specific asset comes down, it will directly affect the total amount of regulatory capital needed to be maintained by them. Therefore, banks and other financial interme-diaries can reduce their regulatory capital; alternatively, theycan get some relief in regulatory capital if they protect themselves from different credit exposure(s). This will ultimately help the protection buyer to increase the volume of its business by utilizing the excess capital relieved by the regulator.

Regulatory capital is the part of capital needed to be maintained as per the requirement of the regulator, and the relief is related to the relief from the concerned regulator. At the same time, the amount of *economic capital* is based on the internal assessment of inherent risk of an individual bank, which it should maintain to cover its unexpected loss at any point of time. Therefore, if CDS leads to a significant reduction in the credit risk of banks and other financial intermediaries, it would ultimately help in reducing their economic capital as well.

# Different types of credit default swaps

*Binary or digital swaps*

In case of binary or digital swaps, the amount of protection expected to be paid in the event of a credit event is fixed in advance while entering into the contract. In such cases, the protection seller neither goes for physical settlement nor for cash settlement. Therefore, it is irrelevant to calculate the market value of the defaulted obligation. A binarhy default swap is nor-mally related to those standardized exposures where the losses arise due to any credit event and can easily be estimated in advance based on the past experience of the counterparties. Therefore, any costs involved in deriving the market value of a defaulted obligation can be ignored by entering into this type of swap contract.

### Basket CDS

A standard CDS, alternatively a single-name CDS, deals with only one reference obligation; whereas, in a basket CDS or multi-name CDS, the reference obligation consists of a basket of individual obligations. In this type of CDS contract, the protection buyer looks for the protection against the default of any one of the obligations of equal quality and of equal notional value in the whole basket. There are several types of basket CDS. In case of a first-to-default basket CDS, the protection buyer is compensated after the first default of any obligation in the basket, and thereafter the contract gets closed. In other words, this type of CDS protects only against the first default. Similarly, the basket CDS is known as second-to-default if the loss for the first default would be borne by the protection buyer himself/herself and the protection will be given for any loss related to the second default. Likewise, a nth-to-default basket CDS gives protection for the default of nth obligation in the whole basket. Basket CDS are useful for those protection buyers who can bear the loss of one or a few defaults, but only up to a certain level. The premium of a basket CDS is lower than the sum of the CDS premium on individual obligations, and therefore the protection buyer is hedged against the risk of more obligations at a comparatively lower cost. At the same time, the protection seller is also exposed to meet the compensation of only one obligation but receives a higher premium comparative to that of a single-name CDS.

### Portfolio CDS

A portfolio CDS is similar to a basket CDS in the sense that it also refers to a group of reference obligations. But unlike a basket CDS, the focus of a portfolio CDS is on covering a pre-specified loss amount, rather than protecting against a pre-specified number of defaults. In case of a basket CDS, the contract gets closed after the nth default. But a portfolio CDS contract works until the total amount of credit loss comes to the pre-specified amount of loss or compensation as per the contract. Here, the focus is on the amount, rather than the number of defaults. In case of a portfolio CDS, it is not necessary for all the obligations to possess the same quality and notional value as a basket CDS.

### Index based CDS

A simple CDS can be referenced to an individual asset or to a portfolio of assets. Similarly, a CDS can also be related to an index of some representative obligations or obligors, e.g. an index of high yielding bonds or an index of highly rated obligors. This type of swap contract allows a protection seller to synthetically invest in a broad index of obligations, which is otherwise impossible to generate in the form of cash.

## Cancelable default swap

A cancelable default swap is a default swap with the option to cancel the contract in certain situations. The buyer, the seller, or both the parties entertain the right to terminate the default swap. The default swap, in the hands of the buyer, is known as *callable default swap*; whereas, the same in the hands of the seller, it is termed as *puttable default swap*. The first type, i.e. the callable default swap, is quite common in trading practices. Suppose an investor owns a credit asset, e.g. a bond, and has bought credit protection by entering into a cancelable CDS contract on that asset. Now, in the case of termination or closure of that asset by its issuer, the investor need not get any protection anymore and is eligible to terminate the swap contract. Therefore, a person need not continue with a contract which has no worth to him/her.

## Contingent default swap

In case of a contingent default swap, the compensation payment is usually triggered by a simultaneous occurrence of the standard credit event and an additional credit event. In other words, settlement takes place not after the occurrence of a credit event related to an obligation, but after another credit event such as the default of another obligation. Therefore, the cost or the premium of such CDS is comparatively less, unless the two credit events are perfectly positively correlated. The buyer of such CDS may be motivated for the requirement of casual or weak protection on their credit exposure and/ or for a lower premium.

## Leveraged default swap

In case of leverage or geared default swap, the amount of compensation gets leveraged or geared after the occurrence of a credit event. In other words, the amount of compensation is a multiple of the amount of the actual loss. Whatever would be the payoff in case of a standard default swap, a certain percentage of the notional amount will be added to derive the final payoff of a leveraged default swap. Because of this added benefit, this type of swap is comparatively costlier than a standard default swap. In other words, the premium of a leveraged default swap is comparatively higher. Now, the question is, who will opt for this type of swap at a higher cost? Obviously, the answer is the speculators. A speculator, without a real credit exposure, can enter into a leveraged CDS and earn not only the amount equal to the notional value of the exposure, but also can enjoy a profit equal to the multiple of the notional amount and can easily leverage its earnings.

## Features of credit default swaps

### Protection buyer & protection seller

A party, with or without its actual ownership on the reference asset, who does not want to carry the risk of their credit exposure and wants to transfer the credit risk to another counterparty is known as protection buyer. On the other hand, a party, who wants to carry the risk in exchange of some rewards and is ready to give protection against the credit risk exposure, is called a protection seller. The protection buyer and protection seller are alternatively termed as the *risk seller* and *risk buyer* respectively. Commercial banks or other financial intermediaries, having exposure in credit assets, funded or unfunded, can buy protection to hedge against the credit risks inherent in the credit assets. At the same time, the role of the protection seller can be played by commercial banks, insurance companies, hedge funds, equity funds, investment companies, etc. Before getting into this business of buying and selling protection, it is mandatory to get the permission of the concerned regulators, e.g. in case of Indian banks, insurance companies, and pension funds/hedge funds, the permission has to be taken respectively from RBI, IRDA, and SEBI.

As per RBI guidelines on CDS, the concerned market players are broadly divided into two groups: users and market makers. Users can only buy protection, while markets makers are free to buy or sell protection. But there are clear cut norms specified for both these groups, such that:

- Users are permitted to buy credit protection only to hedge their underlying credit risk.
- Users are also not permitted to sell credit protection.
- Users can unwind their bought CDS positions with the original counterparty.
- Users can sell the underlying bonds only by assigning the CDS in favor of the buyer of the underlying bond.
- Market makers are allowed to buy or sell credit protection.
- Market makers can buy credit protection even without any underlying exposure.
- Market makers (banks) have to fulfill the eligibility criterion as set by the RBI: CRAR $\geq 11\%$ (or $15\%$ for NBFC & PD), Tier I Cap $\geq 7\%$ (Net Owned Fund $\geq 500$ Cr.); Net NPA $< 3\%$.

### Reference asset & reference entity

A CDS deal is made with reference to either a single credit asset or a portfolio of credit assets. These are known as reference asset or reference portfolio. It is not necessary for a protection buyer to actually own the reference asset, i.e. funded credit asset. Perhaps the protection buyer may use the CDS contract as a proxy to transfer some other risks or he/she may be interested to get the benefits of arbitrage or speculation. Irrespective of the motive to enter into a credit derivative contract, such a deal does not necessitate the holding of the reference asset by either of the counterparties. The bond can be considered as the most common type of reference asset because of its tradability in the secondary market. Apart from this, a bond price available in the market can be used as a basis to calculate the default swap premium. On the other hand, since loans are not usually traded in a secondary market, their prices are not directly observable and are derived from some financial and other factors of the company. Since it is difficult to price a loan, the pricing of the CDS also becomes difficult, especially with reference to loans.

CDS in India can be issued only on single and listed corporate bonds. Even if short-term instruments, with original maturity of less than 1 year (i.e. CPs, CDs, NCDs) were originally excluded, the same are now eligible as reference assets in CDS. CDS can also be written on unlisted but rated bonds, issued by infrastructure companies. Such infra bonds, eligible for CDS, may also be unrated if issued by the SPVs set up by infra companies. Other than on bonds issued by infrastructure companies, CDS is India can also be issued on any other unlisted but rated corporate bonds. Asset backed securities (ABS), mortgage backed securities (MBS), convertible bonds, any other structured products shall not be permitted as underlying in India.

## Asset and maturity mismatches

There may be some dissimilarity or mismatches as far as the value and residual maturity of underlying and reference assets in a CDS are concerned. Suppose a credit protection is bought for an amount of 100 crores on a reference asset with a residual value of 200 crores. In such case, there is an asset mismatch in the CDS contract, and the capital relief supposed to be availed by the protection buyer will be adjusted accordingly based on the part of the asset duly protected by the CDS. The investor will not get any relief for the unprotected portion of the asset. At the same time, an investor may have a credit asset, e.g. a bond, for 5 years, but a protection can be bought on that asset for a period equal to or less than the said period. Therefore, if the tenure of the CDS is less than the residual maturity of the underlying asset, or if the CDS is junior to the underlying, then it will be treated as a maturity mismatch. Like the case of asset mismatch, maturity mismatch is also considered and accordingly adjusted to derive the amount of capital relief given by the regulator. These mismatches do not affect the amount and time of protection given by the protection seller of a CDS. In case of asset mismatch, the following points need to be considered:

- Reference and underlying asset must be issued by the same obligor.
- Reference asset must be junior to the underlying asset.
- Cross-default and cross-acceleration clause between assets should be properly specified in the contract documents.

## Default swap premium

The premium for a CDS contract is nothing but the reward paid for assuming the unwanted risk of the reference asset that lies in the protection buyer's books of accounts. This premium is normally represented in annualized basis points and can be paid up front, i.e. while entering into the contract, or periodically such as quarterly. The payment of the periodic premium terminates in the event of a credit event or the completion of the tenure, whichever is earlier. Suppose the credit event takes place before a due date of a quarterly paid premium. In such case, the protection buyer has to pay the premium due for the period from the last premium paid date to the date of the credit event. The amount of premium or the price of a CDS depends mainly on the quality or risk of the reference asset or reference obligation. Apart from this, there are some other factors, such as tenure of the CDS, terms of settlement, risk of the protection seller, joint probability of default of the protection seller and the reference obligor or entity, number of credit events included in the CDS contract, exchange rate risk (if any) involved in the contract, etc., which are considered while pricing a CDS.

As far as pricing of a CDS or CDS premium in India is concerned, the guidelines suggest that there will be a daily CDS pricing curve published by FIMMDA in association with ISDA, subject to sufficient trading. Broadly, what is observed in the international market suggests that there may not be any consistent and robust method to price a CDS contract, and the same may be subjective up to a certain extent.

## Unwinding CDS position

A CDS buyer can unwind his/her position before the credit event or maturity. The unwinding can be possible either by taking an offsetting position or settling with the original counterparty or anybody else in the market. This exit route plays a very important role for the market player to get into any such contract. If the exit route, i.e. unwinding of a position, is easy, the market for that position is expected to experience a good volume and liquidity. Users in India, who at any point of time are not allowed to maintain a naked CDS position, are not permitted to unwind any CDS contract by entering into any offsetting contract. Any open contract can be unwound only with the original counterparty. Users are allowed to unwind their CDS bought position either with the original protection seller at a mutually agreeable price or at the price as arrived at by FIMMDA.

## Credit events

Credit events, in the context of a credit default swap, are the collection of different events or situations that define the type of risk against which the protection buyer has bought a protection from its counterparty, i.e. from the protection seller. Unlike some other credit derivative products, the settlement of a CDS contract is totally restricted to the occurrence of any one or more of the specific credit events. The type of credit events may be standardized or non-standard. Any credit event set out by some parent organization, such as ISDA in case of derivatives, and is common for all can be termed as a standard event. On the other hand, apart from the standard credit events, the counterparties are free to define their own credit events based on their own requirements. The scope of these events may depend upon the type of reference asset to capture the risks inherent in a specific reference asset.

Lists of credit events, as suggested by the Reserve Bank of India in its final CDS guideline released in May 2011, include: bankruptcy, insolvency, failure or inability of the obligor to pay its debts within the grace period, obligation acceleration, obligation default, restructuring approved under BIFR, and CDR Mechanism. The contracting parties to a CDS may include all or any of the approved credit events. Any issue related to a credit event will be addressed by the Determination Committee (DC). DC, formed by the market participants and FIMMDA, shall deliberate and resolve all CDS related issues. Decisions of the Committee would be binding on CDS market participants. At least 25% of the DC members should be drawn from the users.

### Compensation settlement

A CDS contract, in occurrence of a credit event, can be settled in any of the three ways. These are: physical settlement, cash settlement, and auction based settlement.

There may be different situations when a physical settlement is preferable comparative to a cash settlement. Suppose the reference obligation or asset cannot be properly valued after the credit event, or the protection seller is in a financial business and can easily manage to hold and recover the value of reference obligation. In such cases, physical settlement is preferable. If a CDS is expected to be physically settled, the protection buyer, after a credit event has taken place, has to deliver the reference obligation or a deliverable obligation to the protection seller in exchange of which the protection seller is obliged to settle the par value of the reference obligation.

In case of cash settlement, all the losses or compensation are settled in cash. Normally, if the reference obligation, after the occurrence of a credit event, can be properly valued and if the protection seller, such as an SPV, is not in a financial business so as to recover the true value of the reference asset, it is preferable to go for a cash settlement. In case of cash settlement, the protection buyer does not have to transfer any asset to the protection seller. Therefore, in case of buying a protection on an artificial exposure, i.e. buying a CDS other than hedging, the preferable settlement mechanism is a cash settlement. On the other hand, a cash settlement also prevents the protection buyer from the difficulty of delivering a pari passu asset, if it is difficult to transfer the reference asset, of a contracted notional amount.

Therefore, if a CDS is cash settled, the protection seller, after the occurrence of a credit event, is obliged to pay compensation equal to the difference between the notional value of the reference obligation and its market value.

A CDS can also be settled through an auction process where the same can be conducted by some specified committee, as decided by the domestic regulator, and also within the terms as set by the committee. The settlement amount is decided through the auction.

A CDS in India can be settled depending on the nature of the counterparty, users or market makers. Users always need to settle the CDS contract physically, while market makers can opt for any of the three settlement modes. Participants need to adhere to the provisions given in the master agreement for a CDS prepared by FIMMDA. Any settlement related issue needs to be resolved by the concerned committee, called the determination committee (DC).

## Current scope and future challenges for CDS in India

The economic growth of a country highly depends upon the credit flow that leads to increasing the productivity in several sectors, leading to a higher GDP. Two very important routes to channelize the credit flow in an economy are bank loans and corporate bonds. There is no doubt that being a bank dominated economy, Indian banks play a major role in channelizing credit to the economy to ensure a reasonable and sustainable growth in India. This is evident from the fact that the gross outstanding credits from scheduled commercial banks in India to its GDP is more than 50% during almost a decade, which is much higher in comparison to the size of the total outstanding in the corporate bond market to GDP in India. This very high level of dependency on the banking sector for the required credit is really a matter of concern for the Indian economy. Banks are not only exposed to the high level of credit concentration risk, they also face a huge problem in managing their assets and liabilities, leading to the problem of ALM mismatches, especially for their long-term priority sector exposure commitment for infrastructural growth in India. An important solution for this high credit concentration risk and ALM mismatches for Indian banks is to ensure a sufficient growth of the corporate bond market, so that the required credit can be channelized through the corporate bond rout. But at the same time, Indian corporates are also finding real difficulties in raising the required capital by issuing bonds in India, especially because of the lack of sufficient demand from investors, especially for the low rated bonds. Here, as major financial institutions in India, Indian banks have a very significant role to play for the growth of any segment of the financial market, and therefore for the corporate bond market as well. Since corporate bonds, depending on their credit rating, carry a significant credit risk, and the market is extremely illiquid for almost all securities, most of the

Indian banks are very much reluctant to invest in this market other than in very few securities issued by some specific entities like PSUs and some very good corporate bodies having a rating of AA and above. This lack of sufficient demand for the alternative channel for flowing credit to the economy has led to increased credit risk concentration within the banking sector and poses a serious systemic risk for the economy. Therefore, it is very important to provide a market that enables lower-rated companies to raise the capital required to finance their projects without depending heavily on bank loans and advances. The success of this alternative credit channel largely depends upon the availability of an efficient mechanism by which credit risk can be managed and distributed among a larger number of stakeholders. Credit default swaps, even if after their so called role as *"Weapon of Mass Destruction"* in the 2008 US subprime crisis, can be an important support to ensure a proper mitigation of the credit risk, leading to a significant growth in the corporate bond market in India. But the success of the CDS market in India again depends on the interest of major stakeholders and flexibility given to the market players to deal with the product.

Credit default swaps, even though they are very well-known and controversial financial products worldwide, are a new development in the Indian financial market. After the release of the final guideline by RBI in May 2011, the first trading happened on 7 December 2011, between two Indian banks, IDBI Bank and ICICI Bank. This was followed by very few deals in the first few months, and the same market could not experience any further volume till date, even after several discussions among the market players and several amendments in the RBI guidelines addressing the objection and further requirements from the market.

Besides the fact that India truly requires products like CDS to ensure an overall growth of the Indian financial market, Indian market players are equally concerned about some of the important issues that may affect the growth of this market, as evidenced from the insufficient deals after its opening ceremony during December 2011. Some of the future challenges for the growth of CDS market in India, especially in line with the RBI Guidelines, are highlighted in the following section:

- There is a lack of sufficient market makers to sell CDS contracts not only on low-rated bonds, but also on unrated infrastructure bonds, especially due to the possibility of an improper pricing mechanism available in India that can capture both the credit and liquidity risk of low-rated and illiquid corporate bonds.
- Even if market players appreciate the stringent RBI regulations to control the systemic risk that can arise due to excessive speculation, the incentive given to the speculators in market making plays a very important role to ensure sufficient liquidity in the CDS market.

- RBI concern on the possibility of offsetting an open CDS position only with the original counterparty, even if at a minimum price set by FIM-MDA, is really a matter of concern to the market players.
- Lack of sufficient clarity in terms of a credit event, triggering the settlement of compensation, may also pose an important challenge for the growth of the CDS market in India. Inclusion of cross default as a credit event and the presence of information asymmetry between the loan and bond market may cause some ambiguity to trigger a CDS settlement in the event of any cross default. Exclusion of loan restructuring from the credit event list may also cause some problems.
- Stringent capital requirements, especially for trading positions, may also pose an important challenge for the market makers to actively participate in the CDS market in India.

## Self-learning exercise

1 What is a credit derivative? How is a credit derivative contract different from other financial derivatives like interest rate futures and swaps?
2 What is a credit default swap (CDS)? How does a CDS contract work? Explain with an example.
3 Why do you think CDS contracts are important for the development of the financial market, especially the fixed income securities market?
4 How is a vibrant CDS market helpful for commercial banks in emerging economies like in India?
5 "It is not possible to take an insurance policy on someone else's house – because you would then have a financial interest to burning it down. But investors can do something similar with a CDS contract". Do you agree with this statement? Explain.
6 Briefly explain different types of CDS contracts with their advantages and limitations. What type of contract is suitable for an emerging economy and why?
7 Do you think commercial banks are the right entities to sell protection in a CDS contract, as defined by the Reserve Bank of India in its circular on CDS? Critically explain.
8 Even if CDS are allowed in India, what stops the market players from dealing with such contracts, causing almost a zero volume in the said market? Briefly explain your point of view.
9 In terms of complexity, how is unwinding and settlement of a CDS deal at maturity different from that of an interest rate swap deal? What kind of settlement mechanism is suitable for such contract? Briefly explain.
10 Suppose the Reserve Bank of India has constituted a committee for the revival of the CDS market in India, and you are supposed to chair the committee. Draw few points which you may like to emphasize upon, and therefore may like to suggest in your report to experience some volume in the market.

# Bibliography

Chacko, G., Sjoman, A., Motohashi, H., and Dessain, V. (2006). *Credit Derivatives: A Primer on Credit Risk, Modeling, and Instruments* (1st edn.). Wharton School of Publishing, Philadelphia, PA.

Choudhry, M. (2004a). *Structured Credit Products: Credit Derivatives and Synthetic Securitisation*. John Wiley & Sons, Singapore.

Choudhry, M. (2004b). The Credit Default Swap Basis: Analysing the Relationship Between Cash and Synthetic Markets. *Journal of Derivatives Use, Trading and Regulation*, June, 9–26.

Choudhry, M. (2010). *Fixed Income Securities and Derivatives Handbook: Analysis and Valuation* (2nd edn.). John Wiley & Sons, Inc., Hoboken, NJ.

Das, S. (2005). *Credit Derivatives: CDOs & Structured Credit Products* (3rd edn.). John Wiley & Sons, Inc., Hoboken, NJ.

Fabozzi, F. (ed.). (July 2017). *The Handbook of Fixed Income Securities* (8th edn.). McGraw Hill Education, New York.

Hull, J., Predescu, M., and White, A. (2004). The Relationship Between Credit Default Swap Spreads, Bond Yields, and Credit Rating Announcements. *Journal of Banking & Finance*, 28, 2789–2811.

Jarrow, R. A., and Turnbull, S. M. (1995). Pricing Options on Derivative Securities Subject to Credit Risk. *Journal of Finance*, 50, 53–58.

Parker, E. (2007). *Credit Derivatives: Documenting and Understanding Credit Derivative Products* (1st edn.). Globe Business Publishing Ltd., London.

Stulz, R. M. (2010). Credit Default Swaps and the Credit Crisis. *Journal of Economic Perspectives*, 24(1), 73–92.

Subrahmanyam, M. G., Tang, D. Y., and Qian, S. (2014). Does the Tail Wag the Dog? The Effect of Credit Default Swaps on Credit Risk. *The Review of Financial Studies*, 27(10), 2926–2960.

# 13 Trading and management strategies

**Key learning outcomes**

At the end of this chapter, the readers are expected to be familiar with:

- What are the issues required to be looked into by different types of investors to manage their fixed income portfolio?
- How are the setting of investment objectives/goals and development of necessary strategies to achieve the goals important?
- What are the different passive strategies bond traders or portfolio managers may like to follow to manage their fixed income portfolio?
- How are passive strategies like bond indexing, cash flow matching, and immunization effectively implemented to manage bond portfolios?
- How is an active portfolio manager different in his/her approach in bond trading and portfolio management?
- What is the role of yield curve shifts in the selection of a desired active trading strategy?
- What are the various strategies that a trader or portfolio manager may like to consider to actively manage their fixed income portfolio?
- What is the broader usefulness and limitations of both passive and active strategies?
- What is bond portfolio optimization? How can a bond portfolio manager achieve his/her objective, subjected to fulfilling the required set of constraints?

## Bond portfolio management: meaning

Whenever financial institutions, including banks, invest in various instruments in the financial market and create multiple portfolios, they are supposed to manage them to get the desired results. Therefore, managing the portfolio of the concerned asset class becomes very important, especially when the financial market is reasonably volatile and uncertain, and investors or portfolio managers have a variety of objectives to meet. In order to successfully manage an investment portfolio, financial institutions need to ensure:

- FIs need to set the specific investment objectives.
- Proper investment policy in line with the broader objectives needs to be established and circulated to the concerned department/person.
- Strategies need to be well defined to manage the portfolio.
- Portfolios need to be optimized by ensuring a proper assets mix.
- Performance of the portfolio needs to be measured and evaluated at regular intervals.
- The composition, both in terms of nature of securities/instruments and their respective proportion, of the portfolio needs to be rebalanced whenever necessary.

The above process of managing a portfolio of several assets is not a static event but is a dynamic and continuous activity for the financial institution. Bonds, being an important asset class, constitute the major chunk of the investment portfolio of various FIs, and therefore need to be successfully managed to meet the investment objectives. Whether the objectives will be met or not largely depends upon the strategies that portfolio managers adopt to manage their bond portfolio.

As defined by John Maginn and Donald Tuttle (2007), the investment management process for fixed income portfolios involves the following four major activities:

- Setting of the Investment Objectives.
- Development and Implementation of a Portfolio Management Strategy.
- Continuous Monitoring of the Fixed Income Portfolio.
- Implementation of Necessary Adjustment in the Portfolio, whenever required.

All the above 4major stages to manage a fixed income portfolio are described in the following section.

### Setting investment objectives

Management of any investments largely depends upon the single objective or a set of objectives behind making such investments. The broad objective behind any investment may be categorized as:

- *Return Objective*

When investors invest their money in some instrument or asset, the very basic purpose is to generate sufficient cash flows or returns from the investment till the time the investor's money is blocked in that asset. The role of a portfolio manager is to deploy the money, say in fixed income instruments, in such a way that the portfolio generates sufficient returns, but after fulfilling the necessary guidelines, predefined by the institutions in their investment policy. Return expectations can again largely depend upon the liability structure of the institutions or the source of such funds required to be invested. The source can be the institution's own money (i.e. owners' fund or share capital, and reserves and surplus) or can be borrowed funds. In most of the cases, institutions like banks, insurance companies, mutual funds, pension funds, etc. use their borrowed funds to make these investments. To keep the business viable, the minimum criteria to make such investments is to earn a return greater than the borrowing cost involved. Since the borrowing cost varies from institution to institution, the return expectations of different types of investors, even from similar investments, may vary, which may lead to following a different set of strategies to manage the investment portfolio. Even if the broad objective of such investors is to earn a positive spread, the difference between the return on investment and the borrowing cost, there may be a series of concerns from the investors, including: nature of their liabilities (source of funds), investment size, market perception, risk absorption capacity, regulatory environment, etc., some of which can be highlighted hereunder:

- In case of commercial banks, where the major source of funds are deposits of various maturities, or the liabilities are due on demand and as on some specific point of time, any investment, say in fixed income instruments or bonds, should happen in such a way that there will be *Sufficient and Timely* cash inflows to meet the liability as and when required, without any possibility of failure. There may be some liability, say tier-II floating rate bonds issued by a commercial bank, where the timing of all possible cash outflows, i.e. an annual/semi-annual coupon on the bonds issued, are certain, but not the amount of cash outflows. Therefore, an investment portfolio needs to be constructed and managed in such a way that the same generates sufficient future cash flows in the right time, as defined by the given liability structure.
- The primary concern to generate a positive spread, above the borrowing cost, may have a different impact on the investors, depending upon their cost of funds. A targeted return on investment, therefore, also depends on the cost of borrowing. Accordingly, managing investments, maybe with a slightly lower return, may be easier for those institutions having relatively cheaper funds available. At the same time, a small institution with a relatively higher cost of funds may find it more difficult and challenging to manage its investments with a desired rate of rreturn.
- For institutions like life insurance companies, the majority of their liabilities are fixed, both in terms of the cash outflows and also the timing of such outflows. Life insurance companies need to pay most

of their policy holders a fixed sum assured at a given point of time. Therefore, fund managers of such institutions need to invest the total proceed towards the insurance premiums collected from its huge pull of policyholders in such a way so as to generate at least a pre-decided rate of return within a given time horizon to settle the fixed future liabilities. At the same time, insurance companies may have certain liability, let's say a pure term plan of Rs.50 lakhs, where the amount of possible cash outflow is fixed but the timing of such outflow is completely uncertain, depending on the death of the person insured. There may be some insurance products, like most of the general insurance, where both the amount and timing of future cash outflows are uncertain, posing more challenges for the manager to manage the investments.

- The borrowed funds available should be invested in such a way that the market value of an investment, under any circumstance, should be at least equal to the actual investment, or the book value of the investment, so that the institution is completely immune from any unfavorable movements in the concerned risk factor(s). Accordingly, investments may be made till that period at which the values of the investments are protected and also get matched with the series of future liabilities.

- Managing investments with a return objective also depends upon the perception of the investors towards the market. The way an investor, having a strong feeling that market is always right and it is always better to be with the market, makes his/her investment decisions may be significantly different from another investor who has an expertise to capture market anomalies, and therefore tends to beat the market sometimes. These perceptions may be majorly driven by the investment environment within the institution, as reflected from their investment policy, the external environment imposed by the respective market regulators (like RBI, SEBI, IRDA, PFRDA), the expertise of the concerned investment managers, etc.

- An investor may have several constraints while meeting the return objective. The constraints may be in terms of institutional and regulatory guidelines towards a maximum permissible level of exposure to an individual sector/entity, a maximum exposure within various sub-portfolios, like a portfolio of money market instruments, dated securities issued by the central government or state government, various non-government entities, etc., sub-portfoliios based on maturity level of securities, etc.

- *Risk Objective*

Even though return is the most crucial factor for an institution to consider before finalizing an investment decision, the same needs to be equally supplemented by the institution's objective to deal with the risk(s) involved with such investments. The risk, in simple terms, can be defined as the chances of incurring financial losses. There is a very common theory in the financial world: "*The higher the returns, the great would be the risk*". Since most of these institutions use borrowed funds to make these investments, returns cannot be the sole objective to manage investments. All possible risk, arising out of any investments, needs to be duly taken care off. Accordingly, the risk objective of an institution could be to make investments in such a way that the risk can be minimized, or can be kept under a certain tolerable level set out by the institution depending upon its *Risk Absorption Capacity*, possibly reflected from its owner's fund (i.e. equity capital, and reserve and surplus). Some of the important risks involved in investments in a fixed income asset class include: interest rate risk (price risk and reinvestment risk), yield curve risk, basis risk, call risk, liquidity risk, credit risk, etc. For an institution or the investment portfolio manager, especially when the major concern in making investments is to match the cash flows from its assets and the same for its liabilities, the risk of its liabilities may also need to be taken into consideration. For financial institutions like commercial banks, the major risk of their liabilities could also be: interest rate risk, the risk of rising deposit rates, and therefore the borrowing cost, and the option risk, the risk of premature withdrawals of deposits, and therefore the amount and timing of future cash outflows. Similarly, if institutions like insurance companies prefer to match their investments with their fixed rate liabilities, there may be a risk of insufficient and untimely return from investments to meet their future liabilities as and when due. Accordingly, the risk related concerns or issues required to be addressed by an institution or a fixed income portfolio manager include:

- A reasonable and maximum level of interest rate risk that the institution may like to be exposed to under various circumstances, as defined in the internal (investment and risk) policies of the institution, is an important factor to manage investments.
- In case an institution needs to match its assets and liability structure, risk may arise due to any mismatches between the assets and liabilities. This falls in a specific bucket, like till 1 year, 1–3 years, 3–5 years, etc., may be in terms of amount and/or timing.
- Even if the asset and liability structure of an institution are broadly similar, i.e. both are linked to a floating rate of interest, there may be a possibility for the institution to still get exposed to some other form of interest rate risk: basis risk, unequal movements of borrowing and lending/investment rates, and yield curve risk, uneven changes within the yield on investments of different maturities. These risks are very difficult for an institution to address while managing their investments.
- Risk, if it materializes, leading to incurring financial losses on investments, needs to be taken care of through necessary provisioning and/or the owner's fund (reserve and surplus, and equity capital). Therefore, investors like commercial banks, before making investments, need to

ensure whether the concerned risk factors and the resultant market risk capital charge on the proposed investment(s) fall within the balance amount of capital available to take care of the market risk.

## Development and implementation of portfolio management strategy

Once the broad objective(s) are set, the second and most important stage to manage an investment portfolio is to develop the right mix of strategies in line with the internal investment and risk policy, external regulation, given constraints (internal and/or external), followed by a proper implementation of the same. The portfolio manager, at this level, decides the composition of the total investment portfolio and sub-portfolios and also the proportion of each single instrument within the portfolio/sub-portfolio. In case of a fixed income portfolio, the composition could be: government (central government security, state government security) vs. non-governmental instruments/securities (securities issued by PSUs, banks, NBFCs, private corporates); short-term money market instruments (T-bills, CPs, CDs) vs. long term dated securities (GOI bonds, corporate bonds, PSU bonds, bank bonds); exchange traded (interest rate futures, interest rate options) vs. OTC (FRAs, IRS) interest rate derivative contracts.

Development of a fare list of strategies and their successful implementation is very crucial for an institution to fulfill its expectation from its investments. An institutional investor may like to consider the following to develop and implement trading/investment strategies:

- Development of a robust investment strategy should start with the formulation of a proper investment policy, to be updated and revised at regular intervals, depending upon any change in institutional goals and objectives, and also due to a change in market conditions.
- Selection of financial instruments/assets under single or multiple asset classes, in the right proportion, and in line with the internal and external norms and constraints.
- Selection of necessary hedging instruments, like interest rate derivative contracts (IRF, FRA, IRS) to manage the risk of underlying securities and ensure its hedge effectiveness.
- Implementation of the right trading and management strategies, and passive and active strategies for the construction of an investment portfolio.
- Collection of necessary market inputs, like a change in economic, social, political conditions both in domestic and international markets, change in financial market variables like interest rates, exchange rates, etc., change in domestic and international regulations, expectations of other players in the market, availability of alternative investment channels fulfilling the broader objectives, etc., before the construction of an optimum portfolio.

*Portfolio monitoring and necessary adjustments*

After successful construction of a desired portfolio, following a robust strategy and with a right mix, the next challenge for the investment manager is to ensure a desired performance of the portfolio and to identify the deviation (if any) due to any change in the market conditions. Performance of the portfolio may be measured and the same may be evaluated under various possible scenarios to judge its relevance under different circumstances. The very basic purpose of monitoring the portfolio is to undertake necessary adjustments as and when required. Based on the performance of the existing portfolio and change in market conditions, a portfolio manager may decide to reconstruct the portfolio, maybe with a minor alterations or with significant changes. An institution may think of following a different set of trading and management strategies, depending upon the change in its investment objective and the policy guidelines to achieve the same.

## Passive management strategies

*Passive Portfolio Management* is a financial strategy in which an investor invests according to some pre-determined strategy that doesn't necessitate any forecasting of future market movements. The idea behind such a strategy is to minimize the transaction costs and avoid the adverse consequences of failing to correctly anticipate the future market movement. Over the years, passive portfolio management has gained increasing importance in asset allocations. Passive management can be attractive as it offers low management costs and allows highly diversified investments. Instead of relying heavily on a portfolio manager's skills and expertise in trading and portfolio management, this strategy believes in delivering the market returns which are appropriate for longer term investments. Followers of passive management believe in the efficient market hypothesis, where any market is expected to always incorporate and reflect all available information. In the context of bond investments, it is a simple strategy to buy-and-hold bonds with desired maturities, coupons, and quality ratings generally with the intent of holding them till maturity. Passive strategies require the formation of a portfolio with returns that broadly mirror the returns on a bond index.

A passive management strategy broadly involves:

- Making investments to meet the regulatory requirements.
- Investment of surplus funds in liquid assets.
- Holding of securities till their maturities.
- Presence of efficient market, ensuring market price of FI securities are fairly set.
- Focus of a portfolio manager to earn rather than to beat the market return.

A bond portfolio can be passively managed in various ways. Some of the important passive management strategies are:

- Bond Indexing
- Cash Flow Matching
- Classical Immunization

## *Bond indexing*

Bond indices are used to measure the performance of bond markets. An index can play the role of a benchmark against which investment managers measure their performance. It can also be used as a measure to compare the performance of different asset classes. The sovereign bond market is the most liquid segment of the bond market. The index can again be: broad index and liquid index. The broad (liquid) index in India, provided by CCIL, for a month would consist of the top traded 20 (5 mostly liquid) government securities traded during the previous month, as shown in the following table (Table 13.1). Some of the important bond indices are: Merrill-Lynch Composite Index /CCIL Broad (Liquid) Total Return/Principal Return Index, as

*Table 13.1* Composition of the CCIL broad & liquid index

*July 2018*

| SN.NO | ISIN NO | ISINDESC | Maturity |
|---|---|---|---|
| 1* | IN0020170174 | 7.17% G.S. 2028 | 8-Jan-28 |
| 2* | IN0020170042 | 6.68% G.S. 2031 | 17-Sep-31 |
| 3* | IN0020160050 | 6.84% G.S. 2022 | 19-Dec-22 |
| 4* | IN0020150093 | 7.59% G.S. 2026 | 11-Jan-26 |
| 5* | IN0020120054 | 8.12% G.S. 2020 | 10-Dec-20 |
| 6 | IN0020100015 | 7.80% G.S. 2020 | 3-May-20 |
| 7 | IN0020110071 | 8.19% G.S. 2020 | 16-Jan-20 |
| 8 | IN0020120013 | 8.15% G.S. 2022 | 11-Jun-22 |
| 9 | IN0020140029 | 8.27% G.S. 2020 | 9-Jun-20 |
| 10 | IN0020060037 | 8.20% G.S. 2022 | 15-Feb-22 |
| 11 | IN0020130012 | 7.16% G.S. 2023 | 20-May-23 |
| 12 | IN0020110022 | 7.80% G.S. 2021 | 11-Apr-21 |
| 13 | IN0020180017 | 6.65% G.S. 2020 | 9-Apr-20 |
| 14 | IN0020090034 | 7.35% G.S. 2024 | 22-Jun-24 |
| 15 | IN0020160019 | 7.61% G.S. 2030 | 9-May-30 |
| 16 | IN0020180025 | 7.37% G.S. 2023 | 16-Apr-23 |
| 17 | IN0020060318 | 7.94% G.S. 2021 | 24-May-21 |
| 18 | IN0020150010 | 7.68% G.S. 2023 | 15-Dec-23 |
| 19 | IN0020140060 | 8.15% G.S. 2026 | 24-Nov-26 |
| 20 | IN0020150028 | 7.88% G.S. 2030 | 19-Mar-30 |

*Source*: CCIL

* *Note:* Composition of the CCIL LIQUID INDEX for the respective month

*General Bond Indices*; Salomon Smith Barney's Global Government Bond Index, Dow Jones CBOT Treasury Index/Dow Jones Corporate Bond Index/Dow Jones Long-Term Inflation Index/CCIL's Tenor Specific Bond Index (0–5 Y, 5–10 Y, 10–15 Y, 15–20 Y, 20–30 Y), as *Specialized Index*; and indices offered by some investment companies to meet certain investment objectives, as *Customized Index*. Some of the other bond indices presently available in the Indian market are: the CCIL All Sovereign Bonds TR/PR Index, CCIL T-Bill Liquidity Weight/Equal Weight Index, and CCIL SDL TR/PR Index.

*Example: formation of CCIL liquid bond index*

Suppose the CCIL liquid bond index, consisting of the five most liquid GOI securities selected on a monthly basis as specified in the above table, is valued at Rs.2417.5782/- as on 2 July 2018. The issue sizes of all the five eligible securities forming the index, as on the first day of July 2018, remaining the same as on 3 July 2018, are given hereunder. Even if the issue sizes of the eligible securities change, due to reissuance of the securities, any time during a specific month, the same will not get reflected while calculating the index values during that specific month, but will be taken into consideration in the next month. The value of an index within a month changes due to a change in the prices of the eligible securities, not due to a change in the issue sizes (if any). Suppose we may like to estimate the value of the index as on 3 July 2018. The values of five eligible securities both as on the 2 and 3 July, along with the issue sizes, are given hereunder (Table 13.2):

Based on these values of the index as on 2 July 2018 and the individual market prices of the five eligible securities both on 2 and 3 July, and considering their respective issue sizes, assumed to be fixed during the month of July, the value of the index as on 3 July can be estimated as:

$$I = 2417.5782 \times (95.10 \times 680 + 88.66 \times 932 + 95.87 \times 990 + 96.92 \\ \times 1090 + 101.06 \times 760) \div (95.29 \times 680 + 88.75 \times 932 + 95.94 \times 990 \\ + 96.97 \times 1090 + 101.03 \times 760)$$

$$= 2415.7915$$

*Portfolio Rebalancing*[1] for any change in any of the issue sizes is done only on the first index calculation day of the next month.

*Bond Indexing* represents construction of a bond portfolio whose returns over time replicate the returns of a concerned bond index. In other words, bond indexing is the strategy of constructing a portfolio that mimics the index along several dimensions of risk and return on the portfolio. Indexing is a passive strategy, often used by investment fund managers who believe that actively managed bond strategies do not outperform bond market indices. A portfolio manager may also construct a portfolio to resemble the index in many ways, but through various active management strategies, hoping to

*Table 13.2* Details of securities eligible under CCIL liquid index

|  | 7.17% G.S. 2028 | 6.68% G.S. 2031 | 6.84% G.S. 2022 | 7.59% G.S. 2026 | 8.12% G.S. 2020 |
|---|---|---|---|---|---|
| 3 July | 95.29 | 88.75 | 95.94 | 96.97 | 101.03 |
| 3 July | 95.10 | 88.66 | 95.87 | 96.92 | 101.06 |
| Issue Size as on 3 July 2018 (Rs. Crore) | 68,000.00 | 93,251.70 | 99,000.00 | 1,09,000.00 | 76,000.00 |
| Issue Size as on 3 July 2018 (INR Billions) | 680 | 932 | 990 | 1090 | 760 |

*Source*: CCIL Trade Analysis; RBI Data on Outstanding Securities

consistently *outperform* the index. Bond indexing can be: *Pure Bond Indexing* and *Enhanced Bond Indexing* with different degree of mismatches.

In a pure bond indexing strategy, the manager replicates every dimension of the index. Every bond in the index is purchased and its weight in the portfolio is determined by its weight in the index. A manager, who feels he has no reason to disagree with the market forecasts, has no reason to assume that he can outperform an indexing strategy through active management. This approach of managing a bond portfolio is alternatively known as the *Do Nothing Approach*. This approach would result in a perfect correlation between the bond fund and the index. However, due to huge number of different bond issues in the typical bond index as well as the inefficiencies and costs associated with pure bond indexing, a pure bond indexing strategy is rarely implemented. Replication of an index consisting of say 500 bonds may lead to very high transaction costs to acquire all the bonds. Instead of perfectly replicating an index, an enhanced portfolio can be created with a different degree of *Mismatches* from the index. Enhanced indexing may include small tilts in the portfolio, intending to compensate for the administrative costs. This approach replicates the index's primary risk factors while holding only a percentage of the bonds in the index.

### Cash flow matching

*Cash flow matching strategy* encompasses construction a bond portfolio generating cash flows within a period or at a given point of time, say at the end of every 6 months, which match the cash outflows to meet the concerned liabilities at the same time. Cash flow matching is also referred to as a *Dedicated Portfolio Strategy*. One simple method of cash flow matching is to start with the final liability due at time T and then work backwards, based on the other due dates for liabilities to settle.

Buy-and-hold and bond indexing strategies allow generating a steady rate of return in a portfolio. But if investors expect their portfolios to generate a specific amount at a certain point in the future, they may prefer to follow a structured or dedicated strategy, essentially to meet the exact future liabilities.

How this cash flow matching strategy works can be explained through an example. Suppose a financial institution wants its bond portfolio manager to construct the portfolio in such a way to meet the future liabilities of Rs.30,000/- in year 1, Rs.40,000/- in year 2 and Rs.50,000/- in year 3. In order to meet these liabilities, the manager can invest the required fund in such a way so as to get the exact amount to settle the liabilities whenever due. Suppose three different bonds with maturities of 3, 2, and 1 year, and with different coupons, are available in the market. If the funds are invested in these three bonds, different sets of coupons and principals are expected to be due at the end of every year till the 3rd year. There will be three coupons and one principal, two coupons and one principal, and one coupon and one principal, respectively at the end of 1, 2, and 3 years. The portfolio manager can invest the required fund in all these three securities in such a way so that the inflows due at the end of every year are sufficient enough to meet the concerned liabilities. In such strategy, the most important part is the estimation of the right volume of funds to be invested in various securities available in the market. Any wrong estimation may lead to generation of insufficient fund to meet the liabilities. This strategy is known as cash flow matching because the manager just tries to match the inflow of cash from the asset with the outflow of cash for the liabilities.

Cash flow matching is a very simple and peaceful strategy for the investors. But the main vulnerability in this strategy is the assumption of no defaults in the payment of both coupon and principal in either of the investments. But as is almost always the case, the lower the quality of securities the investor purchases, the higher the risk those securities carry and the higher the possibility for a loss. Further, in case of callable bonds, if these securities are called before they mature, this can eliminate some of the expected coupon payments and may cause some risk for the investor or manager.

*Example: passive management – cash flow matching*

Suppose a fixed income portfolio manager wants to follow a passive strategy to manage its fixed income portfolio by following cash flow matching. The manager attempts to match the liabilities of USD 4 million, USD 3 million, and USD 1 million respectively due in years 3, 2, and 1 with 3-year, 2-year, and 1-year bonds each paying 5% annual coupons and selling at par. The details of assets (bonds) and liabilities are given in the following table (Table 13.3).

Calculate the actual amount of investment in these three bonds and show how the liabilities are settled in due time with the cash flows received from these three bonds.

*Table 13.3* Details of assets and liabilities held by the portfolio manager

| | Coupon Rate | Par | Yield | Market Value | Liability | Year |
|---|---|---|---|---|---|---|
| 3-Year | 9.00% | 100 | 9.00% | 100 | USD 4M | 3 |
| 2-Year | 8.00% | 100 | 8.00% | 100 | USD 3M | 2 |
| 1-Year | 7.00% | 100 | 7.00% | 100 | USD 1M | 1 |

*Source*: All tables in this chapter are created by the author unless otherwise stated.

*Table 13.4* Details of matching CFs from assets and liabilities

| Year | CFs from 1-Year Bond (USD) | CFs from 2-Year Bond (USD) | CFs from 3-Year Bond (USD) | Principle Payment (USD) | Total CFs (USD) | Liability to be Met (USD) | Ending Balance |
|---|---|---|---|---|---|---|---|
| Year 1 | 30,876.37 | 197,757.39 | 330,275.23 | 441,091.01 | 1,000,000 | 1,000,000 | 0 |
| Year 2 | 0.00 | 197,757.39 | 330,275.23 | 2,471,967.38 | 3,000,000 | 3,000,000 | 0 |
| Year 3 | 0.00 | 0.00 | 330,275.23 | 3,669,724.77 | 4,000,000 | 4,000,000 | 0 |

*Solution*

The USD 4 million liability at the end of year 3 is matched by buying USD 3,669,724.77 worth of 3-year bonds: [USD 3,669,724.77 = USD 4,000,000/1.09]

The USD 3 million liability at the end of year 2 is matched by buying $2,471,967.38 of 2-year bonds: [USD 2,471,967.38 = {USD 3,000,000 − (.09)(USD 3,669,724.77)}/1.08]

The USD 1 million liability at the end of year 1 is matched by buying USD 441,091.01 of 1-year bonds: USD 441,091.01={USD 1,000,000 − (.09)(USD 3,669,724.77) − (.08)(USD 2,471,967.38)}/1.07]

The following table (Table 13.4) ensures that the liabilities due in all the 3 years are matched with the cash flows due in the respective years from the three bonds:

### Classical immunization

Immunization is a bond portfolio management strategy basically designed to manage the interest rate risks, ensuring that the portfolio generates a sufficient yield to meet any liabilities as and when they are due. Any change in the market interest rates may lead to a subsequent change (rise or fall) in the portfolio yield, affecting the market value of the portfolio, and therefore its ability to satisfy the obligations in a timely manner. Effective immunization entails matching the portfolio's duration to the length of the investment horizon, ensuring the present value of the cash flows from the investments equal that of the future liability. Securities are generally purchased with different maturities, both lower and higher than the required time horizon, and therefore need to regularly rebalance at a specific interval (say semi-annually or annually) to keep the immunization strategy effective. This strategy may not be perfect due to its condition of a flat yield curve and parallel shifts in the term structure.

Immunization is a strategy used to minimize interest rate risk, and it can be used to fund either single or multiple liabilities. This portfolio management strategy has the features of both active and passive strategies. By definition, pure immunization implies that a portfolio is invested for a defined return for a specific period of time regardless of any outside influences, such as changes in interest rates. Similar to bond indexing, the opportunity cost of using the immunization strategy is giving up the upside potential of an active strategy for the assurance that the portfolio will achieve the desired return even under unfavorable market scenarios. The securities best suited for this strategy are usually high-grade bonds with distant possibilities of default. For high quality bonds, the purest form of immunization would be to invest in a zero coupon bonds and matching the duration, equal to the maturity, of the bond with the period when the liability(s) are expected to be due in the future. This enables the portfolio manager to even eliminate the reinvestment risk. This strategy is generally used by financial institutions, like insurance companies, pension funds, and banks, to match the time horizon of their future liabilities (such as fixed payment to insurance policy holders, fixed retirement benefits to individual, etc.) with structured cash flows from investment in fixed income securities.

Classical immunization is the process of structuring a bond portfolio that balances any change in the value of the portfolio with the return from the reinvestment of the coupon and principal payments received throughout the investment period. The goal of classical immunization is to form a portfolio so that:

- If interest rates increase, the gain in reinvestment income ≥ the loss in portfolio value.
- If interest rates decrease, the gains in portfolio value ≥ the loss in reinvestment income.

Even if classical immunization does not require any active involvement of the portfolio manager, it works for only a one-time instantaneous change in interest rates. In reality, interest rates fluctuate frequently, changing the duration of the portfolio, and therefore necessitating a change in the immunization strategy. Alternatively, classical immunization requires the bond portfolio to be rebalanced after every change in the rate of interest. To keep a portfolio immunized, it must be rebalanced periodically. Rebalancing is necessary to maintain equality between the duration of the immunized portfolio and the duration of the liability. Therefore, frequent rebalancing, especially when interest rates become more volatile, may make this strategy a little cumbersome and costly. Transaction costs associated with rebalancing must be weighed against the possible extent to which the terminal value of the portfolio may fall short of its target liability. Furthermore, the mere passage of time causes the duration of both the portfolio and its target liabilities to change, although not usually at the same rate. Immunization can be accomplished by equating the duration of assets and liabilities.

### Example: passive management – classical immunization

Suppose a fund has a single liability of *Rs.1392.21* due in 4.30 years (i.e. duration of liability $D_L$ = 4.30 years). Suppose the current yield curve is flat at 8.6130%. The fund manager, investing in bonds, wants to invest in the bond market in such a way so that its liabilities are immune irrespective of the change in the rate of interest. Show how the fund manager will invest in a bond to ensure classical immunization, irrespective of any change in the rate of interest. Suppose a 5-year bond, 8% annual coupon at YTM of 8.6130%, is currently traded at Rs. 975.92/-

### Solution

The present value of the future liability of *Rs.1,392.21*, due after 4.30 years and at a yield of flat 8.6130%, is:

PV of Rs.1,392.21 = 1,392.21 / (1 + 8.6130%) ^ 4.3 = Rs.975.92

Duration of the proposed 5-year 8% annual coupon bond, with a face value of Rs.1000/- currently yielding 8.6130% and presently traded at Rs.975.92/-, is *4.30 years.*

Therefore, if the fund buys this specific bond, the duration of which is matched with the duration of the liability, then any parallel shift in the yield curve in the very near future would have price and interest rate effects that exactly offset each other, and the fund will be immune from any interest rate risk in settling the claim towards its liability through the cash flows from its assets.

As a result, the cash flow or ending wealth at year 4.30, referred to as the accumulation value or target value, would be sufficient to cover the liability of Rs.1392.21/-, as exhibited in the following table (Table 13.5):

### Advantages and limitations of passive strategy

Some of the important advantages of adopting a passive strategy to manage a bond portfolio are:

- It is straightforward and easy to understand.
- A passive approach is also of good use if investors are engaging in premeditated asset allocation.

*Table 13.5* Immunization of CFs under any IR scenarios

| Time (Year) | Interest Rate = 8.6130% | Interest Rate = 9.00% | Interest Rate = 8.50% |
|---|---|---|---|
| 1 | $80(1.08613)^{3.3} = 105.08$ | $80(1.09)^{3.3} = 106.32$ | $80(1.085)^{3.3} = 104.72$ |
| 2 | $80(1.08613)^{2.3} = 96.74$ | $80(1.09)^{2.3} = 97.54$ | $80(1.085)^{2.3} = 96.51$ |
| 3 | $80(1.08613)^{1.3} = 89.07$ | $80(1.09)^{1.3} = 89.48$ | $80(1.085)^{1.3} = 88.95$ |
| 3.52 | $80(1.08613)^{0.3} = 82.01$ | $80(1.09)^{0.3} = 82.10$ | $80(1.085)^{0.3} = 81.98$ |
| 3.52 | $1,080/(1.08613)^{0.7} = 1,019.31$ | $1,080/(1.09)^{0.7} = 1,016.78$ | $1,080/(1.085)^{0.7} = 1,020.05$ |
| Target Value | 1,392.21 | 1,392.22 | 1,392.21 |

- It also ensures portfolio diversification.
- Portfolio managers are less bothered about significant decision-making.
- It matches the risk profile of the index, and therefore the return generated. By reducing the number of bonds in the portfolio and selecting the liquid bonds in each cell, transaction costs can also be reduced.
- Specific indices, such as tenor index, T-bill index, and SDL index, are helpful to match the performance of specialized bond portfolios, if separately created by the financial institutions.
- Enhanced indexing is another benefit, as it allows for an additional return pickup if an investor has some information about future returns that would allow them to slightly outperform the benchmark.
- The passive strategy approach also avoids problems associated with statistical models that rely on historical correlations. After the financial crisis, it is clear that these correlations are not always stable.

Even if passive strategy is simple and easy to implement, it also has some limitations, such that:

- Index funds can never outperform the market.
- Investor has the discretion as to the number and type of risk factors to focus on. An omitted risk factor may be a significant driver of index performance, leading to a significant tracking error between the performance of an index with that of the index fund.
- Passive strategies need to be monitored and rebalanced regularly so that the actual return does not deviate from the benchmark.
- In portfolio immunization theory, any changes in the yield curve are assumed to be parallel. But parallel shifts in the yield curve rarely occur. Therefore, equating the duration of the portfolio with the duration of the liability may not ensure complete immunization.

## Active management strategies

Active portfolio management is a strategy of managing assets by continuously repositioning portfolios to take advantage of most of the favorable opportunities. The main objective of such portfolio manager is to have their portfolios outperform the benchmark index. Alternatively, the primary objective of an active strategy is to realize returns more than what one would get from holding the securities in a passive mode, i.e. the normal returns from holding till maturity. The goal of active management is maximizing total return. Essential to all active strategies is specification of expectations about the factors that influence the performance of an asset class. In the case of active bond management, this may involve forecasts of future interest rates, future interest-rate volatility, or future yield spreads. In all active strategies, the investor is willing to make bets on the future rather than settle with what a passive strategy can offer. To generate such returns, positions must be taken that differ from the market consensus. The autonomy given to managers to take positions that deviate from the benchmark depends on the investor's risk tolerance. Active strategies are typically speculative. Active management strategies involve:

- Taking views on future interest rate movements.
- Anticipating future price movements.
- Investment of surplus funds not to earn but to beat the market return.
- Holding of securities just to have a good deal within the stipulated time.
- Reducing the loss in absence of a profitable deal.
- Managing interest rate risk.

Typically, there are two broad kinds of active management strategies. These are:

- Trading on *Interest Rate Predictions*, which is called *Market Timing*.
- Trading on *Market Imperfections*, which is called *Bond Picking*.

### Important news affecting interest rates and bond yields

The major driving force for bond portfolio managers to actively trade and manage their portfolio is the expected change in future rates of interest due to change in the economic/market/regulatory conditions, such as: demand and supply of securities, inflationary pressure, economic growth (e.g. GDP numbers), credit growth, liquidity concerns, global economy, sovereign status of the country (e.g. sovereign rating), FIIs movements, major exchange rates, etc. Therefore, it is very important for a trader/portfolio manager to properly analyze the change in such economic/market/regulatory conditions, as reflected through various news or information continuously flowing into the market. Some of the important news having a strong relationship with the interest rates are described below:

*News: reduction in budgetary deficit due to fall in international
oil prices*

- The fiscal deficit of a country fixes the issue of the securities to fill the deficit.
- The government, through the budget statement, determines how much of a fall in revenue will take place for the year and decides to issue the securities.
- Thus, the supply is decided in light of the budget or fiscal deficit. Hence, any news, such as fall in the crude oil prices, may lead to a fall in the deficit, and therefore a lower supply of securities.
- Due to a low supply and expected high demand of the instrument, the price may go high and the yields will fall.

*News: hike in international prices of crude oil*

- Higher oil prices lead to a rise in the prices of almost all commodities, and therefore a country's inflation figures. In order to control the inflation, the government may try to suck out the liquidity, resulting in a rise in policy rates or a rise in supply of government securities through fresh issue or OMO sale, and therefore rise in yields.

*News: announcement for an OMO purchase/OMO
sales by the RBI*

- Open market operation (OMO) is basically a liquidity adjustment mechanism used by the central bank of the country to control the market by way of injecting more liquidity in the system or sucking liquidity from the system whenever needed.
- Under these operations, the government may like to buy-back (i.e. OMO purchase) the existing government securities from the market and can inject more liquidity in the system, or the government may like to reissue the existing securities (OMO sale) from the market to absorb excess liquidity from the system, and therefore affect the demand and supply of government securities.
- These regulatory interventions may affect the interest rates as they get affected by normal demand and supply forces or may also remain stable if the market finds it suitable, even after the OMO announcements.

*News: rising inflationary expectation in the country*

- Expected future rate of inflation is a very crucial factor to determine any rate of interest. Any lender, expecting the rate of inflation to go high in the future, may prefer to lend at interest rates that are higher than the rate of inflation, and vice versa.

- Therefore, rising (falling) inflation signals a higher (softer) interest rate regime. Interest rate or yield on debt securities, therefore, largely depends upon the prevailing and future rate of inflation in that economy, as may be indicated by the wholesale price index (WPI), or consumer price index (CPI).
- Because of its higher importance, the market players always wait for the dates when these inflation numbers are released by the competent authority.

## *News: rise in expected growth estimates (e.g. GDP)*

- General economic condition or general growth of an economy plays a very crucial role in determining the level of interest rate in that economy.
- In an economy with an increasing growth rate, chances for more spending (institutional and retail) increases, leading to more demand of available funds to channelize credit, followed by rising inflation, and may finally lead to a rise in the rate of interest.
- Alternatively, higher growth enhances bank lending and reduces banks' investment in the debt market, thereby reducing the demand for debt securities, followed by a fall in the price and a rise in interest rates or bond yields.
- Higher growth may boost the confidence of the domestic as well as the international investor into the market of the country, causing an improvement in the sovereign rating, followed by a rise in FIIs inflows, which may finally bring the yields down and prices up due to more demand for the domestic securities.
- This situation holds when the economy tends to grow without any intervention from the central bank. On the other hand, if the higher growth rate is a result of intervention from the central bank, the high growth may be ensured by injecting liquidity in the system through OMO purchases or cutting the liquidity ratio (SLR), where the price of bonds, and therefore the bond yield, may or may not get affected.

## *News: insufficient credit growth in the economy*

- Whenever there is a less demand for credit, a fall in the GDP is expected in major sectors of the economy.
- The FII inflows will be questionable and FII outflows will be expected.
- Hence, reduced demand for government securities will fetch the price down and the yields to move up.
- Alternatively, lack of sufficient credit growth in the country will encourage the domestic institutional investors, like commercial banks, to invest more in the government securities, leading to a rise in the demand, and therefore the price, and a fall in the yield, and vice versa.

*News: downgradation of sovereign rating by international rating agency*

- Sovereign rating of an economy is adversely related to the risk-free yield in that economy.
- If the economy has a poor credit worthiness (say BB credit rating), even if there is no risk for a domestic investor to invest in the securities issued by the central government of that economy, any such investment will be risky for a foreign investors.
- Therefore, expectation of foreign investors, in terms of sufficient compensation depending upon the sovereign rating, may also play a significant role in deciding the rate of interest in government securities.
- Accordingly, downgradation of sovereign credit rating (say from A to BBB) by the international rating agencies, say Standard & Poor's or Moody's, will lead to raise the expectation of foreign investors to invest in the domestic market, making the yield to go up.

*News: change in policy rates (repo rate/repo reverse rate) by the RBI*

- Rates of interest which are part of the monetary policy issued by the central bank of an economy are known as policy rates. The Reserve Bank of India governs the monetary activities such as money supply, liquidity, and interest rates through its key policy rates: repo rate and reverse repo rate.
- Repo rate is the discount rate at which banks borrow from RBI. On the other hand, reverse repo rate is the rate at which RBI borrows money from the banks by depositing government securities with them.
- Liquidity can be controlled through these policy rates by the RBI within a system called liquidity adjustment facility (LAF) provided by the RBI to the banks. Therefore, any fall (rise) in the repo rate allow banks to get money at a cheaper (expensive) rate, thereby controlling the money supply and liquidity in the system.
- Policy rates and yield on debt securities are positively interrelated. Any expectation in the rise (fall) in repo rate may lead to a subsequent rise (fall) in the interest rates of debt securities as well.

*News: change in liquidity ratios (CRR/SLR) by the RBI*

- Liquidity ratios, like the cash reserve ratio (CRR) and statutory liquidity ratio (SLR), set by the central bank especially to control the liquidity in the system depending upon the economic condition, also play a crucial role in determining the risk-free rate of interest or yield on debt securities.
- CRR (presently at 4%) is the minimum proportion of a bank's total deposits that need to be kept or deposited with RBI in cash. Similarly,

SLR (set at 18.50% as in December 2019) is the minimum percentage of bank's deposits, called as net demand and time liabilities (NDTL), which the bank has to maintain internally in the form of gold, cash, or other approved securities defined by the RBI.

- A change in these policy/liquidity ratios is actually a regulatory move and may cause a change in the market rate of interest, or the interest rate may remain stable depending upon the reaction of the market and its impact on the demand of debt securities.
- Any rise in CRR may lead to a fall in the demand for debt securities, causing a fall in the prices of such securities, which may finally take the interest rate or yield at a higher level, and vice versa.
- On the other hand, if the SLR increases, maybe due to economic instability or a higher fiscal deficit, the demand for SLR approved securities, which are essentially the government securities, increases, causing the bond price to rise and yield to fall.
- Similarly, under a stable economic condition with a lower fiscal deficit, providing room to free liquidity for the private sector, the central bank may decide to cut the SLR, which may lead to fall in the demand for such bonds, and therefore the price falls and the yield rises.
- But under certain market conditions, even after a change in these policy ratios, the demand for such bonds may remain stable, and therefore there may not be any change in the rate of interest.

### News: change (rise/fall) in FII flows in the country

- Domestic rate of interest can get affected by the presence of foreign international investors (FIIs). There can be significant inflow and/or outflow of funds by the FIIs, which can affect the domestic market.
- Significant amount of such FIIs inflows, within the permissible limit, may increase the demand for domestic financial assets, including debts and equities, and therefore can push the prices up, which may finally lead the yield on debt security to fall.
- On the other hand, significant FIIs outflows from the domestic debt market may cause an oversupply of debt securities in the market, pushing the price to go down and the yield to go up.
- Therefore, movement of FIIs in the domestic debt market may play a short-term but crucial role in determining the rate of interest or yield on debt securities.

### News: change in global economic condition

- Not only has the economic condition in the domestic economy, but also the global economic condition, especially some of the economies like US, UK, Europe, Japan, etc., play a very crucial role in deciding the domestic rate of interest in India, including the yield on GOI debt securities.

- The higher the growth possibility for the global economies, especially the large economies, the greater would be the possibility for the foreign as well as domestic interest rates to rise.
- Growth, say in the US economy, may lead to a possible hike in the US Fed. Rate, making the US financial market more interesting for the FIIs, leading to a possible FII's outflow from the Indian market, causing a decline in the demand for securities and a rise in the yield.

### News: appreciation of INR against USD and fall in USD-INR rates

- Domestic rate of interest, if not monotonically, but up to a significant extent, depend upon the appreciation or depreciation of the domestic currency in comparison with the foreign currency, or alternatively the movement of the exchange rate.
- Suppose the Indian Rupee appreciates against the US Dollar, the USD-INR exchange rate (presently at a level of 62.67 as on 18 March 2015, meaning USD 1 is equal to INR 62.67) falls.
- Any appreciation of INR against at least some of the major currencies (e.g. USD, EUR, GBP, JPY, etc.) leading to a fall in the concerned exchange rate (e.g. USD-INR, EURO-INR, GBP-INR, JPY-INR), may finally lead to a fall in the domestic rate of interest, including the yield on debt securities, and vice versa. *Interest Rate Parity* theory, implying the equality of the expected return on domestic assets with the exchange rate-adjusted expected return on foreign currency assets, may be referred to understand the linkage between the domestic rate of interest and foreign exchange rate, to ensure a no interest arbitrage.

## Yield curve shifts and different types of active management strategies

Mangers' anticipation or predictions toward the future rate of interest, and/ or their capability to capture market imperfections, especially in terms of price, lead to the selection of a specific strategy to manage a bond portfolio. A bond portfolio manager may expect the yield curve to shift in various ways. Selection of an active management strategy essentially depends upon the possible type of shift in the yield curve. Three broader types of yield curve shifts are:

- No shift in the yield curve
- Parallel shift in the yield curve
- Unparallel Shift in the yield curve

*No shift in the yield curve: strategies*

If a trader or bond portfolio manager does not expect any change in the bond yields in the future, and therefore assumes that the yield curve will not shift at all, then the following strategy may be adopted.

1.  Riding the yield curve

The simplest strategy that a portfolio manager may like to follow is to invest in securities with a maturity equal to their investment horizon and hold them till the securities mature. In order to outperform this simple strategy, investors may purchase securities with maturities longer than the investment horizon and then sell them at the end of the horizon. This strategy is known as *Riding the Yield Curve*. If the term structure of interest rate is upward sloping and remains stable without any shift (upward or downward), this strategy will provide higher holding period returns than a simple buy-and-hold strategy. If long-term securities offer higher return, a portfolio manager, if they prefer to be on the higher segment of the yield curve, can successfully generate higher average return, provided there is a normal yield curve in the market and no change is expected. For example, suppose the 5-year and 10-year government security rates as on a specific date are 8% and 8.50%. An investor with an investment horizon of 5 years may prefer to invest in the 5-year security. But if it is assumed that the existing yield curve will remain upward sloping and unchanged in the future, the investor may gain more if they prefer to make the initial investment in the 10-year security and then selling the same after 5 years. This is called beating the market by riding or preferring the higher yield point of the normal yield curve.

Investors are exposed to the reinvestment risk if they choose a fixed income security with any maturity lower than the investment horizon. Therefore, investment can be made in a security having a maturity more than the investment horizon. Riding down the YC has been proved to be a profitable strategy for investors in different countries and in different circumstances. The amount of benefit from this strategy depends on the slope of the yield curve and the timing of purchases and sales. The steeper the slope of the yield curve, the higher would be the returns from such a strategy. But if future short-term rates are expected to rise, as assumed by expectations theory, then this strategy may fail to generate higher returns.

*Example: active management – riding the yield curve*

Suppose that at the end of 1 June 2012, the Treasury, non-callable yield curve was as given in the following table (Table 13.6):

Further suppose an investor invests Rs.100,000/- in a bond with the following characteristics:

*Table 13.6* Treasury yield curve as on 1 June 2012

| Maturity | Yield | Maturity | Yield | Maturity | Yield |
|---|---|---|---|---|---|
| 1 | 8.24% | 6 | 8.58% | 11 | 8.37% |
| 2 | 8.15% | 7 | 8.55% | 12 | 8.49% |
| 3 | 8.18% | 8 | 9.00% | 13 | 8.68% |
| 4 | 8.36% | 9 | 9.27% | 14 | 8.84% |
| 5 | 8.48% | 10 | 8.55% | 15 | 8.76% |

*Table 13.7* Details of treasury bond for investment at different times

| | Bond for Initial Investment | Bond for New Investment after 10 Years |
|---|---|---|
| Settlement Date | 1-Jun-12 | 1-Jun-22 |
| Maturity Date | 1-Jun-27 | 1-Jun-37 |
| Maturity (Years) | 15 | 15 |
| Yield | 8.76% | 8.76% |
| Price | 100 | 101.14 |
| Coupon | 8.76% | 8.902% |

Ten years later, on 1 June 2022, if interest rates remain the same throughout the yield curve, the investor could sell that bond at a price based on the fact that bonds with 5 years to maturity are priced to yield 8.48%. The proceeds of that sale could be used to purchase the new bond as shown in the following table (Table 13.7):

By selling the original bond for more than par, the investor would be able to buy a premium bond with a higher coupon. Finally, in the year 2027 (15 years after the original investment and five years after the bond swap), the new bond has a specific price (priced to yield 8.55% to maturity in 10 years). The investor or trader in the above example is always trying to be in the longer segment of the yield curve to get the benefits of the rising yield curve. Therefore, the trader may follow two strategies: buy and hold the bond for the full 15 years or buy and hold the bond initially for 10 years and again try to ride the yield curve thereafter.

Calculate the internal rate of return from these two strategies. What happens (impact on the IRR) if interest rates fall (rise) parallely by 0.50% sometime in the first 10 years after the bond was purchased and remained there for the remainder of the 15-year period?

Suppose, as on 1 June 2022, with different yield curve scenarios, the investor is expected to prefer any of the following three bonds, depending on the change in the yield curve, as shown in the following table (Table 13.8):

*Table 13.8* Yield curve scenarios and investor's preference

| Description | No Change in YC | Change in YC by -0.5% | Change in YC by +0.5% |
|---|---|---|---|
| New Settlement Date | 1-Jun-22 | 1-Jun-22 | 1-Jun-22 |
| Maturity Date | 1-Jun-37 | 1-Jun-37 | 1-Jun-37 |
| Maturity (Years) | 15 | 15 | 15 |
| Yield (New) | 8.76% | 8.26% | 9.26% |
| Price | 101.14 | 103.18 | 99.14 |
| Coupon | 8.902% | 8.638% | 9.157% |

*Solution*

Using the cash flows related to initial investment, the coupon income for the first 10 years and next 5 years from new investment, and final selling price at the end of 15 years for various scenarios of changing the yield curve, it is possible to compute the internal rate of return (IRR) on this investment. If the investor just held the original bond until it matured, the IRR would have been 8.764%, which is the yield at which the bond was purchased. Therefore, by selling the bond with 5 years remaining to maturity and reinvesting in another 15-year bond, the investor increases the return by 0.109%, as exhibited in the following table (Table 13.9).

*Parallel shift in the yield curve and desired strategies*

A parallel shift in the yield curve is a phenomenon that occurs when the interest rate on all maturities increases or decreases by the same number of basis points. For example: If the 10-year Treasury bond yield increases (falls) by 100 basis points, then the 3-month, 6-month, 1-year, 5-year, 20-yeare, and 30-year rates are expected to increase (fall) by the same 100 basis points, as shown in the following figure (Figure 13.1). In such case, a portfolio manager may outperform the market by swapping the existing bonds with other sets of bonds of required maturity, depending upon the anticipation of rising or falling rates of interest. This strategy is known as *Rate Anticipation Swaps*.

*Rate anticipation swaps*

If the yield curve is expected to experience a parallel shift, a portfolio manager may follow this strategy in which bonds are exchanged according to their current duration and predicted interest rate movements. Alternatively, rate anticipation swaps involve simultaneously selling and buying bonds with different durations. A rate anticipation swap is often considered to take advantage of the opportunities of investing in more profitable bonds, depending on the movement of interest rates. Rate anticipation swaps are

*Table 13.9* Future cash flows from different securities under different yield curve scenarios

| 2nd Settlement Date | 1 June 2022 | | |
|---|---|---|---|
| | No Change in Yield | Yield Change by -0.5% | Yield Change by +0.5% |
| Selling Price of Existing Bond | 101.14 | 103.18 | 99.14 |
| **Details of Reinvestment 10 Years Later:** | | | |
| Maturity Date | 1-Jun-37 | 1-Jun-37 | 1-Jun-37 |
| Maturity | 15 | 15 | 15 |
| Yield | 8.76% | 8.26% | 9.26% |
| Price | 101.14 | 103.18 | 99.14 |
| Coupon | 8.90% | 8.64% | 9.16% |
| Annual Income | 8902.08 | 8637.76 | 9156.80 |
| **3rd Settlement Date** | 1-Jun-27 | 1-Jun-27 | 1-Jun-27 |
| Selling Price of Existing Bond | 102.35 | 104.00 | 100.71 |
| **Cash Flows during 1 June 2012 to 1 June 2027:** | | | |
| | Cash Flows | Cash Flows | Cash Flows |
| Face Value of Initial Investment | −100000 | −100000 | −100000 |
| Coupon in 1st Year | 8764 | 8764 | 8764 |
| Coupon in 2nd Year | 8764 | 8764 | 8764 |
| Coupon in 3rd Year | 8764 | 8764 | 8764 |
| Coupon in 4th Year | 8764 | 8764 | 8764 |
| Coupon in 5th Year | 8764 | 8764 | 8764 |
| Coupon in 6th Year | 8764 | 8764 | 8764 |
| Coupon in 7th Year | 8764 | 8764 | 8764 |
| Coupon in 8th Year | 8764 | 8764 | 8764 |
| Coupon in 9th Year | 8764 | 8764 | 8764 |
| Coupon in 10th Year | 8764 | 8764 | 8764 |
| Coupon in 11th Year | 8902 | 8638 | 9157 |
| Coupon in 12th Year | 8902 | 8638 | 9157 |
| Coupon in 13th Year | 8902 | 8638 | 9157 |
| Coupon in 14th Year | 8902 | 8638 | 9157 |
| Coupon in 15th Year + Final Selling Price | 111253 | 112639 | 109865 |
| **IRR of the Above Investment Option** | 8.873% | 8.876% | 8.869% |
| **IRR of Original Investment (if Held till Maturity) 8.764%** | | | |

speculative in nature, since they depend on the outcome of the expected interest rate change. The nature of swaps depends on the upward or downward parallel shift in the yield curve.

• *Strategy: Rate Anticipation Swaps (Shortening Portfolio's Duration)*

When the yield curve is expected to have an upward parallel shift, the manager of a bond portfolio with longer duration may be expected to suffer

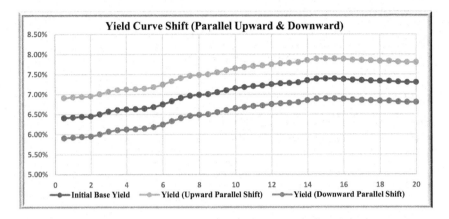

*Figure 13.1* A parallel upward and downward shift in the yield curve

severe losses. In such circumstances, managers can attempt to reduce the duration of their bond portfolio by swapping some of the higher duration bonds with some lower duration bonds. This strategy will ensure reduction of losses expected to be suffered by the portfolio manager due to a rise in interest rates. The objective of this strategy is to preserve the value of a bond.

- *Strategy: Rate Anticipation Swaps (Lengthening Portfolio's Duration)*

When the yield curve is expected to have a downward parallel shift, a portfolio manager is expected to enjoy the price gain in all the bonds irrespective of their duration. But the higher the duration, the greater would be the price gain due to the fall in interest rates. Therefore, in the event of falling interest rates, a portfolio manager could swap some of his/her lower duration bonds with some higher duration bonds, and thereby can increase the duration of the bond portfolio. This strategy is extremely sensitive to interest rate changes and as a result would subject the manager to a higher return-risk position, providing greater upside gains in value if rates decrease but also greater losses in value if rates increase.

### Unparallel shift in the yield curve

When the yield curve is expected to change, the change in the yield for various bonds with different maturities do not occur evenly. For example, given a yield curve for bonds with 1-year, 5-year, and 10-year maturities, the yield for the 1-year bond may increase by 50 basis points, the 5-year may stay the same, and the 10-year may increase or decrease by 20 basis points. This kind of shift in the yield curve is known as an unparallel yield curve shift. Historically, two types of unparallel yield curve shifts have been observed:

a)   Yield curve shifts with twists.
b)   Yield curve shifts with humpedness.

### Yield curve shifts with twists

Any twists in the yield curve may lead the curve either to be flatter or steeper. Flattening and steepening of the yield curve may be discussed in the following section.

- *Yield Curve Flattening*

Yield curve flattening means that the yield spread between the yield on a long-term and a short-term bond has decreased, as shown in the following figure (Figure 13.2). Such reduction in the spread between long- and short-term securities depends upon the state (*Bullish and Bearish*[2]) of the market and happens when:

- The market is bearish for the whole segment (long, medium, and short), but stronger for short-term securities and weaker for the long-term securities, leading to an upward shift of the whole curve, but it becomes flatter.
- The market is bullish for the whole segment (long, medium, and short), but stronger for long-term securities and weaker for the short-term securities, leading to a downward shift of the whole curve with flattening.
- The market is in a mixed (bearish and bullish) state, where it is bearish for the short-term securities and bullish for the long-term securities,

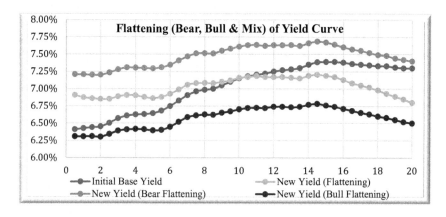

*Figure 13.2* Flattening of the yield curve

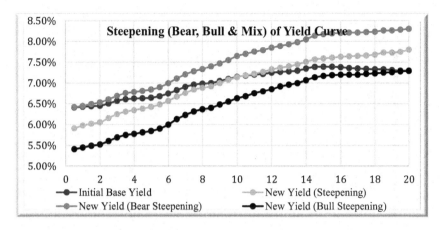

*Figure 13.3* Steepening of the yield curve

leading to a situation where the short-end of the yield curve goes up, and long-end comes down, making the curve flatter.

- *Yield Curve Steepening*

Yield curve steepening means that the yield spread between a long-term and a short-term bond has increased, as shown in the following figure (Figure 13.3). Such a rise in the spread between long- and short-term securities may happen when:

- The market is bearish for the whole segment (long, medium, and short), but weaker for short-term securities and stronger for the long-term securities, leading to an upward shift of the whole curve but it becomes steeper.
- The market is bullish for the whole segment (long, medium, and short), but stronger for short-term securities and weaker for the long-term securities, leading to a downward shift of the whole curve with steepening.
- The market is in a mixed (bearish and bullish) state, where it is bearish for the long-term securities and bullish for the short-term securities, leading to a situation where the long-end of the yield curve goes up, and short-end comes down, making the curve steeper.

### Yield curve shifts with humpedness

A shift with humpedness is a nonparallel shift in the YC in which short-term and long-term rates change by greater magnitudes than intermediate rates, known as *Butterfly Shifts*. It is the combination of a barbell (called the wings

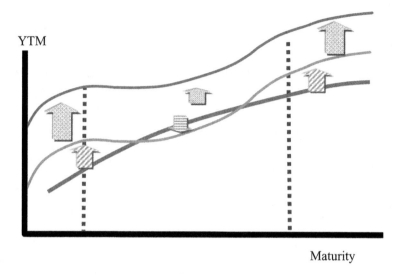

YTM

Maturity

*Figure 13.4* YC shift with humpedness: positive butterfly

of the butterfly) and a bullet (called the body of the butterfly). Depending on the nature of the shifts, this can be categorized as positive butterfly and negative butterfly.

• *Positive Butterfly:*

A positive butterfly refers to an increase in both short- and long-term rates relative to the intermediate rates, as shown in the following figure (Figure 13.4). For example, if short-term and long-term rates move upward by 100 basis points (1%) while medium-term rates remain the same, the convexity of the yield curve will increase. This yield curve shift is called a positive butterfly shift because it causes the curve to hump.

• *Negative Butterfly:*

In case of negative butterfly, both short- and long-term rates decrease more relative to the intermediate rates. Alternatively, negative butterfly is a kind of non-parallel yield curve shift in which long- and short-term yields decrease by a greater degree than intermediate rates, as exhibited in the following figure (Figure 13.5). This yield curve shift effectively creates a hump in the curve. For example, a negative butterfly shift can happen when short- and long term-rates decrease by say 60 basis points (0.60%), while intermediate rates decrease only by 50 basis points (0.50%). This kind of yield curve shift exhibits just an opposite picture of what we experience in

YTM

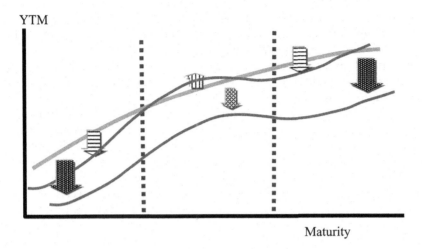

Maturity

*Figure 13.5* YC shift with humpedness: negative butterfly

case of a positive butterfly shift, in which short- and long-term rates increase more than intermediate rates.

### Unparallel shift in the yield curve: possible strategies

For any unparallel shift in the yield curve, the portfolio manager is supposed to construct his/her portfolio with a right combination of short-, medium- and long-term securities, depending upon the nature of the shifts. Based on this tenor-based combination of securities, the portfolio management strategy can be classified as:

- *Bullet Strategy:*

A bullet strategy is a fixed income strategy in which a portfolio is designed to have securities with maturities and/or durations that are highly concentrated at one point on the yield curve, preferably the intermediate points. Alternatively, bullet strategy is based on the acquisition of a number of different types of securities over an extended period of time, but with all the securities maturing around the same target date. One of the main benefits of the bullet strategy is that it allows the investor to minimize the impact of fluctuations in the interest rate, while still realizing better returns on the investments. A bullet strategy can be useful if prevailing interest rates for medium-term bonds are higher than either short-term or long-term. On the other hand, if the severity of the rise in interest rates is expected to be more both in the short and long end of the yield curve, it may be a good proposition to remain in the intermediate segment of the yield curve, where neither the gain due to fall in interest, nor the loss due to rise in interest are severe. Therefore, such strategy can ensure a moderate portfolio return at any circumstances, i.e. for any change in the future rate of interests. The main benefit of bullet strategy is that it sets off the possibility of higher opportunity loss (if interest rates increase) with higher opportunity gain (if interest rates fall), especially when it is difficult to predict the nature of shifts in the yield curve.

If the yield curve flattens, a portfolio manager may adopt a strategy of constructing a bullet portfolio by including more long date securities where the impact of rising rates is comparatively less, and therefore the potential loss may decline. Similarly, if the yield curve steepens, an investor may prefer short duration bonds compared to the long duration bonds, and therefore may adopt the bullet strategy, concentrating on the lower segment of the yield curve. If any humpedness is found in the yield curve, i.e. a shift in the yield curve with a twist where both the short and long end of the yield curve shifts upward, keeping the intermediate segment unchanged or shifting downward, (i.e. positive butterfly), the portfolio manager may prefer the bullet strategy with bonds of intermediate maturity or duration.

- *Barbell Strategy:*

A strategy of concentrating in both sides (long end and short end) of the yield curve is known as *Barbell Strategy*. With this strategy, a portfolio manager will prefer to buy only short-term issues and long-term issues, without purchasing anything in between. Securities with short-term maturities provide liquidity and help to reduce the market risk of the portfolio, while securities with longer maturities give higher yields and help to increase portfolio return. It is a strategy focusing both on the risk and return, not on achieving one at the cost of other. The higher amount of loss in long-dated securities due to a rise in rate of interest may partially get neutralized by the smaller loss amount incurred in short-dated securities. Similarly, a smaller price gain in short-dated securities due to a fall in interest may be expected to be widened due to a higher gain in long-dated securities for the similar movement in the rate of interest. Therefore, this strategy duly deals with the uncertain movement in the rate of interest and gives focus both on leveraging return and curtailing risk.

Barbell strategy is profitable when the yield curve is expected to shift but with a twist, where both the short and long end of the curve are expected to move downward, and the intermediate portion is expected to remain the same or moves upward (i.e. negative butterfly). In such case, a barbell portfolio, a combination of short- and long-dated securities, can experience a higher capital gain due to a fall in the interest rates, or can experience a lower potential loss due to a rise in interest rates throughout the segment but with different degree.

- *Ladder Strategy:*

According to the ladder strategy, a bond portfolio is constructed to have almost equal amounts of investment in securities of each maturity range within a given limit, basically to manage the interest rate risk under all possible interest rate scenarios. Alternatively, in a ladder strategy, after deciding the maximum acceptable maturity within the bond portfolio, the portfolio manager tries to evenly spread his investment across all the maturities. The face value of bonds maturing every year may be roughly equal. Following a ladder strategy, a portfolio manager may be in a position to capitalize on higher interest rates prevailing on long-term investments by taking exposure maturing at different times and reinvesting the proceeds of those bonds at varying intervals. Suppose a manager has purchased bonds maturing respectively in 2, 4, and 6 years. These are short-term bonds and typically will not provide with large returns. However, buying these bonds allows the manager to reinvest into longer-term, higher interest rate bonds at different intervals. When the 2-year bond matures, the proceeds can be invested into say a 10-year bond, and the same process can be repeated with the other bonds as well. This will allow the manager to leverage the portfolio yield. On the other hand, the ladder strategy can also enable the portfolio manager to reduce the overall portfolio duration and thereby the overall interest rate risk. Since the total investable fund is parked in all possible securities throughout the maturity ladder, the concentration risk gets diluted, and the portfolio manager can soften the portfolio loss in the event of rising interest rates. It is a kind of safe strategy to trade in an uncertain market, without taking any extreme positions. Some of the important advantages of a ladder portfolio are: higher average yield, more consistent return, lower expenses, less reinvestment risk, portfolio diversification, ongoing liquidity, etc. In a normal market, it is more common to see that a bond portfolio manager follows a ladder strategy, maybe with slight variation in the volume of investments made throughout the maturity ladder.

## Strengths and weaknesses for active management

Essential to all active strategies is specification of expectations about the factors that influence the performance of an asset class. In the case of active bond management, this may involve forecasts of future interest rates, future interest-rate volatility, or future yield spreads. Some of the important strengths and weaknesses of active bond portfolio management are briefed hereunder:

### Strengths

- Available funds can be ideally managed with the optimum returns.
- Portfolio manager can take the advantage of bond market inefficiencies.

- Portfolio composition can be adjusted whenever any opportunities arise due to change in market scenarios.
- Portfolio can be managed with respect to the tax consideration.
- Decision on asset allocation and portfolio composition can be undertaken with sectoral preferences and ensuring portfolio diversification at regular intervals.
- Any specific security or group of securities can be added to or removed from the portfolio whenever required, depending upon internal and/or external norms, rules, and regulations.
- Various risks can be ideally managed at regular intervals based on risk perception of the portfolio manager and the concerned risk appetite.

## Weaknesses

- Cost involved with active portfolio management may be relatively higher than passive management.
- Passive portfolios are also more tax efficient with their "buy and hold forever" approach result in low income tax costs.
- Active portfolio often attracts capital gains tax on the gains made on the regular trading of securities.
- If not managed properly, active portfolio management may lead to heavy losses in extreme market scenarios.
- Active portfolio management generally attracts higher risk, and therefore needs to be supplemented with a better risk appetite.
- Success of active bond portfolio management largely depends upon liquidity in both primary and secondary bond markets. Therefore, it is quite difficult to practically implement in the economies with illiquid bond markets.

## Bond portfolio optimization

*Portfolio Optimization* is a process through which an institutional portfolio manager tries to create/select the best portfolio for the institution, by way of creating a best possible composition of securities/assets depending upon the nature of the portfolio, out of a set of various portfolios with various possible compositions from the concerned asset classes according to some predefined set of objective(s). On the similar line, "Bond Portfolio Optimization" refers to the process of creating an optimum or best possible portfolio of various government and/or non-government debt securities, depending upon the objective towards the creation and maintenance of such portfolio. The main focus of such optimization process is to select the best possible combination of securities in the portfolio to get the desired results.

Needless to say, the most important objective, say for an institutional investor, for constructing and holding a bond portfolio is to get/earn a desired level of return or yield from the portfolio within a specific period of time. Accordingly, the portfolio manager may choose the securities out of all possible alternatives available and their respective weights in the portfolio. Selection of optimum weights of a particular security/position and also of various sub-portfolios depends upon the main objective of the investor/ portfolio manager, as defined through the *Objective Function*, which mostly remains unchanged till the investor changes his/her focus. Such objective could be either to maximize the portfolio yield or to earn a specific yield as per the predefined expectation. The portfolio manager may also set an objective to minimize the financial risk in his/her portfolio. Even if the first priority for the investor is to achieve the objective, the same may not be easily possible without facing some hurdles, which are known as *Constraints*, and are very important for any optimization process. For example, if it is targeted to maximize the bond portfolio yield without looking at anything else, it is obvious that the level of various types of risk, such as interest rate risk and credit/spread risk, automatically shoot up and may cause various problems for the institutional investor, who needs to operate strictly under the rules, regulations, guidelines, and policies set by the concerned regulatory bodies and also by the institution itself. In other words, investors need to strictly adhere to the internal *Investment Policy*[3] and also the norms set by the domestic regulators, before achieving their predefined objective. All such internal and external norms of a trade-off with the main objective need to be clearly defined as a list of constraints while optimizing the portfolio. Therefore, two very important aspects of portfolio optimization are:

i.   Clearly defining the objective function.
ii.  Carefully setting up the list of constraints and avoiding multiple trade-offs.

In case both the aspects are not clearly and carefully set, it may not be possible to successfully optimize the portfolio.

A typical bond portfolio manager may hold different types of debt securities, such as central and state government securities, non-government (bank, PSU, FI, NBFC, corporate) securities, securities of fixed and floating coupons, and also of various tenors, etc. If he/she intends to create an optimum bond portfolio, he/she may like to have the following objective function and a list of constraints:

### Objective function

*   Maximization of portfolio yield.
*   Minimization of portfolio risk (minimizing portfolio m-duration/convexity adjusted m-duration, portfolio VaR, general or total market risk capital change, etc.).

*List of constraints*

- *Portfolio M-Duration to be less than or equal to a particular limit as set by the institution in its investment policy (say, <= 5%)*: Basically, to keep the interest rate risk within a comfortable level, or to avoid wider asset liability mismatches, by ensuring an optimum mix of short-, medium-, and long-term securities.

- *Portfolio Convexity to be more than equal to a predefined limit (say, >= 25)*: Mainly to avail the benefits of lower price depreciation due to rise in yield and higher price appreciation due to fall in yield, leading to a slightly lower level of interest rate risk, again by ensuring a proper selection of securities with the desired maturity.

- *Market Risk Capital Charge (GMRCC+SRCC) under M-Duration or Convexity Adjusted M-Duration to be less than or equal to a predefined limit (say, <= 100 crores)*: Mainly applicable for a commercial bank to ensure that the total capital available to take care of the market risk is sufficient enough to support the interest rate (GMR) and spread risk (SR) assumed by the bank in its trading portfolio, possibly by selecting securities of desired maturity and also of desired issuer segment and credit rating.

- *Portfolio Yield to be more than or equal to a desired limit as set by the investor (say, >= 8%), applicable only when the main objective is minimization of portfolio risk*: Mainly to ensure that the investor doesn't deviate from the yield target even if focusing on risk minimization.

- *Various Sub-portfolio Limits (Maximum and Minimum Limits) to be more than or equal to and/or less than equal to a predefined number as set by the institution (say, 60% =< government security portfolio =< 70%)*: Mainly to ensure a desired composition, to avail the benefits of natural portfolio diversification and to avoid higher concentration risk in the whole portfolio.

- *Various Individual Position-wise Limits (Maximum and Minimum Limits) within Sub-portfolios to be more than or equal to and/or less than equal to a predefined number as set by the institution (say, 0.5% =< Position in Single Non-Govt. Security =< 5% of total position in non-government securities portfolio)*: Possibly to ensure a diversification within each sub-portfolio and to avoid concentration risk in each sub-portfolios.

This portfolio optimization can be easily done in MS-Excel, using an option called "**SOLVER**" available under the '**Data**' tab. Once the SOLVER window opens, the user needs to set the objective (maximizing or minimizing the number, or achieving a particular number), giving reference to the concerned cell (exhibiting portfolio return or risk) in MS-Excel, and also needs to set the list of constraints as per the predefined requirements, giving reference to the respective cell(s) in MS-Excel and setting a predefined value for each of the calls. Once the objective is set and the constraints are defined, simply by clicking the button "SOLVE", the user may get the result with an optimum portfolio composition.

## Self-learning exercise

1  What could be the investment objective of a bank and a pension fund to invest in fixed income securities?

2  What is a funded investment? What should be the primary objective of a funded investor to initiate such investment?

3  What is passive portfolio management? How is an active portfolio manager different in his approach from the passive portfolio manager in managing a fixed income portfolio consisting of Govtgovernment and non-government securities?

4  Suppose a portfolio manager of a mutual fund is following a benchmark index, say CCIL Broad Index, an index consisting of the 20 most liquid central government securities in India, as far as its investment in Treasury bond is concerned. Suppose the portfolio manager is outperforming the index but is still worried about not meeting the investment objective. Explain how such situation arises.

5  Liability structure is very important for an institution to decide the nature of its assets, more specifically investments. What are the two major dimensions of liabilities of an institution which are of grave concern for the manager of the investment portfolio of an institution? Is it always easy for institutions like banks and insurance companies to estimate their liability?

6  How are two bond portfolio managers, one following bond indexing and the other actively managing the portfolio, different in their approaches to manage their respective portfolios?

7  One bond portfolio manager is following bond indexing, with some mismatches in the primary risk factor, to manager his/her bond portfolio consisting of government and non-government securities. One of his/her counterparts in the industry manages his/her portfolio actively and is of an opinion that any deviation from an index is another form of active portfolio management. Do you agree with this perception?

8  In order to neutralize two opposite positions against a small parallel shift in the yield curve, the interest rate sensitivities of both the positions need to be matched. Is it sufficient enough just to match the m-durations of both the positions? Explain.

9  What is the objective of a bond immunization strategy? What is the basic underlying principle in an immunization strategy?

10  A portfolio manager is anticipating the implication of an immunization strategy. He/she believes that this is nothing but a buy-and-hold strategy, and the great advantage of such strategy is that it requires no management of the portfolio once the initial portfolio is constructed.

Do you agree with the portfolio manager's assessment of the immunization strategy?

11   Can a portfolio manager immunize his/her bond portfolio simply by investing in zero-coupon bonds? Explain.

12   In the situation of steepening of the yield curve, what kind of bond portfolio, bullet or barbell, having almost the same PV01, performs better?

13   Why is a ladder portfolio preferable to the bullet or barbell portfolio?

14   "Suppose, a portfolio manager holds a fixed income portfolio of 1000 crores, consisting of Treasury bonds of various maturities, a few 10-year state government securities, and some AAA/AA rated PSU and bank bonds of maturities less than 5 years. Suppose he/she is expecting that the economy is doing well, and the interest rates are expected to increase in the near future. Accordingly, the portfolio manager is giving a proposal to replace the long-term (say beyond 15 years), if any, and some of the medium-term (say close to 10 years) securities, with some short-term Treasury bonds. As far as positions in non-government securities are concerned, the manager is of an opinion not to change the composition." What kind of strategy is the portfolio manager trying to follow, and how the same will be benefitted for his/her institution?

15   Suppose a fund manager is managing a barbell portfolio of INR 5000 crore, consisting of government securities of medium-term (say 10 years) and long-term (say 20–25 years) maturities. Due to the present economic boom when high growth is expected, the market may be of a view that the central bank will increase the policy rates to control future rise in inflation, even at the cost of a slight impact on the economic growth. The fund manager, even though he/she has a similar feeling, believes that the interest rate may start rising but after few months. Therefore, he/she has decides to swap most of his/her long-term securities with medium-term bonds, but not immediately. Since the market starts experiencing a temporary fall in the long-term yields, the fund manager decides to swap some of his/her positions in medium-term bonds with long-term securities to tap the immediate benefits of falling long-term interest rates. The fund manager may prefer to rebalance the portfolio, as per the decision taken, before the interest rate starts rising. What kind of strategy the is portfolio manager expected to follow under the prevailing situation? Is there any temporary deviation from the original decision taken?

16   Is it practically feasible to follow a bond swap strategy by a portfolio manager to rebalance the portfolio m-duration when the market expects a parallel shift (upward or downward) in the yield curve?

17   How may an active bond portfolio manager like to construct his/her portfolio expecting butterfly shifts in the yield curve? Explain.

18   What are the two major dimensions of liabilities of an institution which are of grave concern for a portfolio manager? Is it always easy to estimate the liability of an institution, like banks or insurance companies?

19  Trustees of a pension fund are discussing with the fund's consultant the fund's bond portfolio to meet future liabilities. They understand the two possibilities for structuring the portfolio: multi-period immunization and cash flow matching. Which strategy has less risk of not satisfying the future liabilities and why?

## Bibliography

Ang, S., Alles, L., and Allen, D. (1998). Riding the Yield Curve: An Analysis of International Evidence. *Journal of Fixed Income*, 8(3), 57–74.

Barrett, B., Gosnell, T., and Heuson, A. (1995). Yield Curve Shifts and the Selection of Immunization Strategies. *Journal of Fixed Income*, 5(2), 53–64.

Choudhry, M. (2001). *The Bond and Money Markets: Strategy, Trading, Analysis*. Butterworth-Heinemann, Oxford, UK.

Choudhry, M. (2002). *Professional Perspectives on Fixed Income Portfolio Management*. John Wiley & Sons, Chichester, UK.

Choudhry, M. (2004). *Advanced Fixed Income Analysis* (1st edn.). Elsevier Butterworth-Heinemann, Oxford, UK.

Choudhry, M. (2005). *Corporate Bond Markets: Instruments and Applications*. John Wiley & Sons, Singapore.

Choudhry, M. (2010). *Fixed Income Securities and Derivatives Handbook: Analysis and Valuation* (2nd edn.). John Wiley & Sons, Inc., Hoboken, NJ.

Dolan, C. P. (1999). Forecasting the Yield Curve Shape, Evidence in Global Markets. *Journal of Fixed Income*, 9(1), 92–99.

Dyl, E. A., and Joehnk, M. D. (1981). Riding the Yield Curve: Does It Work? *Journal of Portfolio Management*, 7(3), 13–17.

Fabozzi, F. (ed.). (July 2017). *The Handbook of Fixed Income Securities* (8th edn.). McGraw Hill Education, New York.

Fabozzi, F. J., Martellini, L., and Priaulet, P. (eds.). (2006). *Bond Portfolio Management: Best Practices in Modeling and Strategies*. John Wiley & Sons, Inc., Hoboken, NJ.

Grieves, R. (1999). Butterfly Trades. *Journal of Portfolio Management*, 26(1), 87–95.

John, L. M., Tuttle, D. L., McLeavey, D. W., and Pinto, J. E. (eds.). (2007). *Managing Investment Portfolios – A Dynamic Process* (3rd edn.). John Wiley & Sons, Inc., Hoboken, NJ.

Jones, F. (1991). Yield Curve Strategies. *Journal of Fixed Income*, 1(2), 43–51.

Mann, S. V., and Ramanlal, P. (1997). The Relative Performance of Yield Curve Strategies. *Journal of Portfolio Management*, 23(4), 64–70.

Martellini, L., Priaulet, P., and Priaulet, S. (2002). Understanding the Butterfly Strategy. *Journal of Bond Trading and Management*, 1(1), 9–19.

Sorensen, E. H., Miller, K. L., and Samak, V. (1998). Allocating Between Active and Passive Management. *Financial Analysts Journal*, September-October, 18–31.

## Notes

1 Portfolio rebalancing is the process of realigning the concentrations or weights of individual securities/assets/positions in a portfolio. Such rebalancing is done by way of buying and/or selling the desired amount/volume of securities, basically to

maintain a desired level of asset allocation and/or desired level of risk. For example, if a portfolio manager holds an equal amount of positions in short-, medium-, and long-term securities, the portfolio, in the interest rate rising scenario, may need to rebalance, especially to keep the interest rate risk at the portfolio level up to a desired extent. In such case, the portfolio can be rebalanced by selling some long-term securities and investing more in short- and medium-term bonds. In case of bond portfolio, such rebalancing is mainly done based on interest rate view. Portfolio rebalancing may safeguard an investor from being overly exposed to undesirable type and/or volume of risks, and also ensure that the portfolio exposures remain within the manager's area of expertise. The success of portfolio rebalancing largely depends upon the frequency of rebalancing the portfolio composition. Even if there is no optimum frequency, a portfolio manager may decide the frequency of rebalancing his/her portfolio, maybe annually/semi-annually/quarterly, depending upon its cost-benefit analysis.

2 The terms "bullish" and "bearish" market are used to describe the general trend in the securities market in terms of appreciation or depreciation of market values/prices of securities, and therefore investors' sentiments as well. A bullish market refers to a situation where the price of securities is on a rising trend and investors carry a faith that the uptrend will continue in the long run, possibly implying a strong economy. On the other hand, when the securities market is on a declining trend, prices of securities start dropping, and investors continue to have a feel of downward trend, such condition is referred to as a bearish market. In case of bond market, the market is expected to be bullish when the bond yields are expected to fall, and vice versa. Whether a bond market will be completely bullish or bearish depends upon the shift (upward or downward) in the entire yield curve.

3 An investment policy is a document prepared by say an institutional investor outlining the general rules towards creation and management of an investment portfolio held by the investor. This document provides the general investment goals and objectives of the investor and describes the strategies that a portfolio manager, managing the investment portfolio on behalf of the institutional investor, should undertake to meet these objectives, keeping in mind the asset allocation, risk tolerance, and liquidity requirements, as per the institution's internal norms and guidelines of concerned regulatory bodies. It acts as a guidance for informed decision-making and also serves both as a roadmap to successful investing and a firsthand protection against potential mistakes. Well-documented policy, with clear investment objectives subjected to the available constraints, complete clarity about the roles and responsibility of portfolio managers, etc., plays a very important role in the successful management of an investment portfolio.

# 14 Risk management (focus: market risk)

**Key learning outcomes**

At the end of this chapter, the readers are expected to be familiar with:

- Overview of risk management practices, especially market risk, applicable for banks and other financial institutions.
- Identification of major risks in fixed income securities, with special reference to the fixed income market in emerging economies.
- Methods or approaches (standard and advanced) to quantify the interest rate risks affecting investment in fixed income securities to a large extent.
- Use of different methods (VCV, HS, MCS) to estimate the value at risk (VaR), especially of a bond portfolio.
- Impact of using sensitivity-based measures (m-duration, PV01) verses simulation-based measures (value at risk – VaR, expected shortfall – ES) in quantifying the interest rate risk of a bond portfolio.
- Conducting back testing and stress testing exercises to ensure a robust risk measurement and management system.
- Regulatory approach, in the context of commercial banking, to manage the major risks in a fixed income portfolio by way of estimating the necessary capital charges, depending on the selected risk measurement techniques, and their impact on the overall business of the concerned institution.

## Risk management and Basel accord: an overview

Needless to say, banks play a critical role in the development of an economy. The nature of their business has changed considerably over the last few decades. Even if taking deposits and giving credit continue to be the key business lines for commercial banks, they have expanded into many other areas, including investment banking, trading, insurance, mutual funds, brokerage, etc. This variety of exposures has not only led to enhance the size of their business into many folds, but also exposed them to domestic and international financial markets, making them more sensitive not only to the risk of their own domestic market but also to the market disturbances worldwide.

In light of widening and internationalization of banks' exposure, the *Basel Committee on Bank Supervision* (BCBS) started disseminating guidance on *Critical Issues* to ensure healthy banking systems across the world. One such issue is the regulation of *Bank Capital*, especially under any abnormal circumstances like the 2008 US subprime crisis. Capital adequacy standards promulgated by the BCBS over more than the last two decades, and supposed to be implemented by the national regulators, are collectively known as the *Basel Accords*, suggesting *Capital Ratio*, expressed as *Capital/Risk-weighted Assets Ratio (CRAR)*.[1] BCBS has produced three such accords, Basel III (2010) being the most recent Accord. Basel I finalized and approved by the BCBS in 1988, established four risk categories or "buckets" with risk weights of 0%, 20%, 50%, and 100%. An inappropriate risk-weighting system in Basel I finally led the BCBS to release a Three-Pillar Basel II approach. Instead of altering Basel I's definition of capital, Basel II altered the approach of arriving at the denominator of the capital ratio, i.e. the calculation for risk-weighted assets. Without replacing Basel II, Basel III focuses mainly on the numerator of the capital ratio, i.e. quantity and quality of capital held by banks. In order to maintain the required CRAR in banking, as stipulated in Basel norms and also by the national regulators, banks need to ensure a proper and effective *Risk Management*[2] System.

As per Basel norms, risk in banking can be broadly categorized as: credit risk and market risk, jointly known as financial risk, and operational risk or non-financial risk. *Credit Risk* is the possibility of losses associated with changes in the credit profile of borrowers or counterparties. These losses may arise due to the outright default or the actual or perceived deterioration in credit quality of the counterparty. *Market Risk* is represented as the risk of losses arising from movements in market conditions which affect the value of financial transactions hold by the bank/organization. *Operational Risk* is the risk of direct or indirect losses resulting from inadequate or failed internal processes, people, and systems or from other external events.

### Market risk

Depending on the nature of banks' investments in Treasury products, exposed to changes in market conditions, market risk again can be classified as:

- *Interest Rate Risk*: Change in the value of the *Fixed Income Portfolio* on account of changes in the interest rates, e.g. money market yield curve, goverfnment security curve, swap curve, etc. Interest rate risk may again be comprised of price risk, reinvestment risk, basis risk, yield curve risk, option risk, gap/mismatch risk, etc.

- *Exchange Rate Risk*: Change in the value of the *FX Portfolio* due to change in the exchange rate – appreciation/depreciation of one currency against another.
- *Equity/Commodity Prices Risk*: Change in the value of the *Equity Portfolio* due to change in the price of a stock or commodity.
- *Volatility Risk*: Change in the value of *Options Portfolio* due to change in the implied volatility.

### Interest rate risk

Fluctuation of different rates of interest affect banking business (both assets and liabilities) in general, and Treasury operations in particular, in different ways, and therefore becomes risky for the bank. This interest rate risk broadly comprises:

- *Price Risk*: Risk arises due to the possibility of securities being sold at higher yields/interests, and therefore at lower prices, before their maturities.
- *Reinvestment Risk*: Risk arises due to uncertainty with regard to interest rates at which future cash flows could be reinvested.
- *Yield Curve Risk:* Risk arises due to the possibility of different movements in yield curves having a bearing on the benchmarks used in pricing of the assets/liabilities.
- *Option Risk*: Risk arises due to the possibility of customers exercising their option of prepayment of loan, pre-redemption of bonds, and premature encashment of deposits in the wake of changes in market interest rates.
- *Basis Risk*: Risk arises due to the possibility of interest rates of different assets/liabilities/off-balance sheet items changing in different magnitude.
- *Gap or Mismatch Risk*: Risk arises due to holding of assets/liabilities/off-balance sheet items with different principal amounts/maturity dates.
- *Net Interest Income Risk*: Risk arises due to difference in the size of interest payment on liabilities and interest earning on assets, affected by market interest rates, thereby impacting the net interest income/margin.

### Liquidity risk

The Treasury of a commercial bank may face the liquidity risk due to: the possibility that the Treasury fails to convert an asset held in its book into cash when needed; the scarcity of funds to borrow, either from the market or from the RBI; lack of sufficient lenders due to the bank's poor credit worthiness; etc. Such risk can be mitigated through:

- Higher proportion of investments in liquid securities.
- Higher proportion of investments in near-maturity high-quality/rated instruments.
- Maintain credit rating, reputation, and image.

Apart from maintaining sufficient liquidity in the investment, a bank also needs to manage the liquidity risk arising out of the possible mismatch between its assets and liabilities. Therefore, the bank needs to fix multilayer tolerance levels and to evolve strategies and contingency plans for liquidity mismatches. As far as the negative mismatches between the bank's assets and liabilities under different buckets are concerned, the same need to be within the prescribed tolerance level, as set by the bank.

### Credit risk

Credit risk in Treasury activities may arise out of: the possibility of the issuer of a debt instrument being unable to honor his/her interest payments and/or principal repayment obligations; possibility for a company, in which the Treasury has made some investment, not to perform well; and non-performance by a counterparty in a variety of off-balance sheet contracts such as forward contracts, interest rate swaps, and currency swaps in the inter-bank market. Therefore, some of the investment proposals are subject to the same appraisal and standards as credit proposals. In order to capture the credit risk in non-SLR investments, a bank may like to follow a rating mechanism, involving various financial and non-financial factors/information, compiled from the final accounts of past few years.

### Non-financial or operational risk

Non-financial or operational risk may arise from the entire range of the transaction cycle from dealing to custody. Some of the important and common sources of such risk includes:

- System deficiencies to capture the complete process of a deal.
- Non-compliance with laid-down procedures and authorizations for dealing, settlement, and custody.
- Fraudulent practices involving deals and settlement.
- IT risk involving software quality, bugs, and hardware uptime.
- Legal risk arising from inadequate definitions and coverage of covenants and responsibilities of the bank and counterparty in contracts and agreements.

## Measuring risk in fixed income securities

Investments in fixed income securities are broadly exposed to two important risk factors. These are: interest rate risk and spread risk, depending upon the nature of the security. Government securities carry only the first risk factor, whereas investments in non-government securities are exposed to both the risk factors. As far as the measurement of interest rate risk is concerned, there are two broad measures: duration/m-duration based sensitivity measures and advanced *Value at Risk* (VaR) and *Expected Shortfall* measure. Spread risk can be measured with the techniques used to measure the counterparty credit risk, mainly by using the credit rating information.

If we consider the Basel II accord and RBI Guidelines on Risk Measurement, banks can follow two different approaches or methods to measure market risk for their fixed income portfolio. As per the Basel and RBI guidelines, overall market risk, in terms of capital charge calculations, can again be categorized as: general market risk (GMR) and specific risk (SR). Accordingly, risk in a fixed income portfolio is also of two types: general market risk, which is nothing but interest rate risk, and spread risk represented as the specific risk. Here, GMR captures all possible risk factors affecting the risk-free interest rates or yield on central government securities. On the other hand, SR captures the risk of adverse price movements caused by any issuer related factor affecting the spread beyond the risk-free yield.

Depending upon the measurement techniques used, there may be two broader approaches that commercial banks may follow to estimate the market risk in general, and interest risk in particular:

• Standardized Duration Based Approach.
• Internal Model Approach (IMA).

*Standardized approach*

The standardized approach allows calculating the market risk (GMR and SR) separately for various trading positions. Interest rate risk (GMR) on FI portfolio is calculated through the well-known interest rate sensitivity measure: modified duration. Actual m-duration of all securities in the trading portfolio are calculated and then supplemented by the expected change in yield of different tenors, based on several time bands, as suggested by the regulator and given in the following table (Table 14.1). It is well known that even if interest rates of all tenors or maturity are volatile, the extent of such volatility or fluctuation are not expected to be the same among all tenor points, say 1 month to 40 years. In general, short- and/or medium-term rates are expected to be more volatile than the long-term rates. Therefore, markets need to have their own expectations in terms of expected future change in the yield for different tenor points, which are required to be adjusted with

*Table 14.1* Time bands and prescribed yield shock under standardized duration method

| Time Bands | Prescribed Yield Shock | Time Bands | Prescribed Yield Shock |
|---|---|---|---|
| **Zone 1:** | | **Zone 3** | |
| 1 Month or Less | 1.00 | 3.6 to 4.3 Years | 0.75 |
| 1 to 3 Months | 1.00 | 4.3 to 5.7 Years | 0.70 |
| 3 to 6 Months | 1.00 | 5.7 to 7.3 Years | 0.65 |
| 6 to 12 Months | 1.00 | 7.3 to 9.3 Years | 0.60 |
| **Zone 2:** | | 9.3 to 10.6 Years | 0.60 |
| 1.0 to 1.9 Years | 0.90 | 10.6 to 12 Years | 0.60 |
| 1.9 to 2.8 Years | 0.80 | 12 to 20 Years | 0.60 |
| 2.8 to 3.6 Years | 0.75 | Over 20 Years | 0.60 |

*Source*: Basel and RBI Document on Capital Adequacy

the m-duration of different securities. This gives an estimate of interest rate risk, and accordingly, the required capital charge, for all bonds held in the trading portfolio.

Similarly, specific risk on banks' exposures in fixed income securities can be captured as default risk, credit migration risk, credit spread risk, and incremental risk. Standard method for market risk does not suggest any specific measure to capture the specific risk in fixed income securities. Banks in India, following the standard method of market risk, are supposed to maintain the required capital for specific risk, not by measuring the same, but as per the standard norms set by the Reserve Bank of India. RBI straightway indicates the requirement of such capital for a variety of fixed income securities (e.g. central and state government securities, foreign government securities, bank bonds, corporate bonds, securitized debts, etc.) under HFT portfolio, depending on their maturity and/or rating grade. However, for an AFS portfolio, the debt securities that are held for a longer period attract a higher specific risk and may need to be covered either by a separate heading of specific risk or by combining with general market risk and giving a total risk estimate.

Even though measuring interest rate risk (GMR and SR) on fixed income securities under the standard approach is simple and easy for banks to follow, this risk measurement approach has certain important limitations. It is true that interest rate risk (GMR) on fixed income securities is estimated based on their respective m-durations. But the final risk is calculated after incorporating the tenor-wise yield shock along with the m-duration figures. These estimates for yield shocks are pre-specified and may not vary with the actual volatility of the concerned tenor point. SA follows a fixed adjustment to deal with the basis risk (risk of different price movement for different instruments following a general movement in interest rates) and yield curve risk (risk of uncorrelated interest rate movements across maturities, i.e. risk of unparallel shift in yield curve) while calculating the market risk capital charge. This risk measurement method also neglects any diversification possibilities across market risks – within each category and across different categories.

### *Internal model approach (IMA)*

In order to address the limitations of the standard method of measuring market risk, and to capture the risk more realistically, investor or portfolio managers may like to follow an advanced market risk measurement approach, known as internal model approach (IMA). It is a risk management system that is supposed to be developed by the users (e.g. banks, other FIs) themselves to analyze the overall risk position, to quantify risks, and to determine the economic capital required to safeguard their business from those risks. The main building block of the internal model approach is *Value at Risk (VaR)* and/or *Expected Shortfall (ES)*.

Specification of an appropriate set of market risk factors is an integral part of banks' internal risk measurement system. Risk factor is any variable which affects the value of the bank's trading position, both on and off balance sheet. A VaR model, as the risk measurement system under IMA, should sufficiently capture all the risk factors inherent in a bank's portfolio. The absence of any market risk factors in the VaR model need to be reported along with a risk estimate and need to be captured within a reasonable time. Granularity and comprehensiveness of the risk factors should match with the complexity of the risks assumed by the bank.

### Value at risk: a risk measurement tool

Value at risk (VaR) is defined as "The *Maximum* amount of money that one could expect to lose over a *Specific Period* of time at a given *Confidence Level* under *Normal Market* conditions". Alternatively, "VaR is the *Maximum Loss* over a *Target Horizon* such that there is a low, but *Pre-specified Probability* that the actual loss may be Larger" (Jorion, 2009). VaR gives us a number, in terms of *Money*, which can be aggregated across risks and positions. Even if VaR is a maximum estimate, it does not measure the worst possible loss because that is not quantifiable. The strength of this loss estimation largely depends upon a few parameters, like time period, level of confidence, normality, etc. A VaR at 95% level of confidence represents that there is a 5% probability for actual losses being greater than VaR. Alternatively, losses will exceed VaR only on 5 out of 100 "normal" trading days. This means that VaR is the smallest amount that could be lost on those 5 exceptional days. The higher the level of confidence, the wider would be the future loss projection, and therefore the higher is the VaR estimate. The time horizon is specified to account for the maximum period needed for orderly portfolio liquidation once the portfolio starts incurring losses. The portfolio is expected to be frozen for the time horizon.

Market risk exposures in general, and risk in fixed income securities in particular, can be measured through the VaR method, which again may follow either of the following approaches:

- Variance-Covariance (VCV) Approach.
- Historical Simulation (HS) Approach.
- Monte-Carlo Simulation (MCS) Approach.

The basic method, as developed by JP Morgan, is the VCV method, well known as *Risk-Metrics*. HS is a non-parametric approach and gives more practical Information. MCS is the sophisticated version of HS.

### Variance-covariance (VCV) approach

VCV assumes that all risk factors and asset returns are normally distributed. As the portfolio return is a linear combination of normal variables, it is also normally distributed. This measure gives the financial institution an idea about the estimated *Potential Loss* under adverse circumstances over the next day or a period of few (5 or 10) days, assuming that the asset return follows specific statistical behavior, called *Normal Distribution*. Some of the important features of a financial asset following normal distribution are:

- Securities are assumed to be *Liquid* and can realize *all possible prices*.
- Because of higher volatility, all kinds of trading gains and losses (large, moderate, small) are possible.
- Large gains or losses, even if possible, are of very *Lower Probability*.
- Neither losses nor gains are *clustered*.
- Investors *frequently adjust* their well-diversified portfolios.
- Investors can *quickly sell-off* those securities which might make large losses and *buy* the ones which make smaller losses.
- *Sudden market crashes* do not occur.

The daily VaR, commonly known as daily earning at risk (DEAR) after the same was published by J P Morgan, can be represented as:

$$DEAR = Position's\ Market\ Value \times Price\ Sensitivity$$
$$\times Potential\ Adverse\ Move\ in\ Return \qquad (14.1)$$

The measure of price sensitivity depends on the type of position. Accordingly, the price sensitivity measure for any fixed income security, foreign currency, or equity positions are respectively the bond's return volatility, exchange rate volatility, and stock return volatility. Different measures, such as standard deviation (SD), exponentially weighted moving average (EWMA), and generalized autoregressive conditional heteroscedasticity (GARCH), can be used to capture the volatility or sensitivity of the financial variable. Standard deviation of past daily returns captures the average return variation, giving equal weights to all the past days. Whereas the EWMA method gives different weights to the past variable that varies exponentially, highest weight to the latest variable, second highest to the immediate previous, and so on, the weights are declined by a factor called *Decay Factor* ($\lambda$ => Lambda), the value of which, as set by J P Morgan to estimate VaR, was 0.94. As per this weighting system, the weight for older values is expected to decay rapidly, and data older than say 100 days get weighted almost equal to zero. The GARCH method captures the conditional volatility, both for short term and long term. Selection of the potential adverse move in the return depends upon the level of confidence, assuming normality in the return movement. Under normality, a 95%, 97.5%, 99%, 99.9% (one tailed) level of confidence respectively assume a value of 1.64, 1.96, 2.33, and 3.09. Accordingly, the maximum losses in any position, in adverse circumstances, will be the average loss times the value of level of confidence.

DEAR on each of the individual positions can be added together, subject to the co-movements between the positions, to arrive at the daily market risk measure at the aggregate level. Such daily aggregate measures can again be converted into a loss measure for T days, through the square root of time principal, such that VaR for 10 Days = (1-Day VaR × $\sqrt{10}$).

*Steps followed to estimate portfolio (bond, equity, & FX) VaR under VCV technique*

- First of all, historical prices/rates of all the concerned securities/positions need to be collected, roughly for the last year (250 historical observations).
- Historical prices of equities and the exchange rates can be straightway obtained from the concerned sources.
- But historical prices of the GOI securities cannot be obtained as is due to the property of *Maturity Reduction* in the case of fixed income security. Therefore, *Model Prices* of all the debt securities during the historical period need to be recalculated using the concerned *Spot Rates or Zero Coupon Yield* extracted from the past zero coupon yield curves (ZCYC) that prevailed on all those historical dates using the NSS parameters of constructing ZCYC, as provided by the CCIL.
- Past actual/model prices/rates need to be used to estimate the historical daily returns (logarithmic price/rate change).
- Historical daily returns are used to estimate the average daily variation (daily standard deviation) in the prices/rates of all the securities/positions.
- Daily standard deviations are multiplied with the current market value of each of the positions, to arrive at the daily average loss in all such securities/positions.

- Assuming all security/position returns follow the normal probability distribution, the daily average losses in all individual securities/positions are adjusted with the value of 99% level of confidence derived from the cumulative normal pdf, as available in Excel {*NORMSINV(99%)*}.
- Accordingly, daily maximjum loss or 1-day VaR for each of the securities/positions are estimated through {*1-Day VaR = S.D. × Market Value × NORMSINV(99%)*}.
- Once security/position daily maximum loss is estimated, then the daily maximum loss in the sub-portfolio or whole portfolio can be captured by simply summing up the daily security/position wise losses or incorporating the correlation factor between the returns of all possible pairs of securities/positions while estimating the daily portfolio loss.
- If the daily VaR on each security/position is simply added to arrive at the portfolio VaR, then any possibility for the diversification of profits/losses among the securities/positions are ignored, and therefore is termed *Undiversified Value at Risk*.
- In order to ensure the natural diversification between the profits/losses of various securities of different types (bond, equity, FX), the correlation between the securities/positions needs to be incorporated to arrive at the portfolio loss. Such portfolio VaR is called *Diversified Value at Risk*.
- In order to estimate the portfolio diversified VaR, the pairwise correlation between the securities/positions needs to be calculated separately, which needs to be finally incorporated into the calculation of portfolio variation, such that the VaR for a portfolio of three securities/positions is:

$$VaR_{Portfolio,99\%,1D} = \sqrt{\begin{array}{c} VaR_{Bond}^2 + VaR_{FX}^2 + VaR_{Equity}^2 + 2r_{BF}VaR_{Bond}VaR_{FX} \\ +2r_{BE}VaR_{Bond}VaR_{Equity} + 2r_{FE}VaR_{FX}VaR_{Equity} \end{array}}$$

(14.2)

- When there are various types of securities/positions in the portfolio, some of the pair of securities/positions are expected to be negatively correlated, which leads the diversified VaR to be lower than the udiversified VaR. This difference is treated as the *Diversification Benefit*.[3]
- Pairwise correlations among the securities/positions within the sub-portfolios (bond, equity, and FX) and also across the sub-portfolios or within the whole portfolio may be estimated over the period of the last year.
- Security/position wise daily VaR, along with the estimated correlations are fitted in the aforesaid function to estimate the diversified portfolio VaR.

EXAMPLE (VAR ON BOND POSITION)

Suppose an investor hold 5000 units of 8.83-GS-2023 bond yielding 8.7922% as on March 06 2014 at a current market price of Rs.100.22/-, leading to a total market value of Rs.501,100/-. The daily return volatility (standard deviation), captured from the historical prices, of this security is found as say 0.23%. Assuming normality, the investor may like to estimate the 10-Day VaR on this position at 99 per cent level of confidence.

Daily Price volatility = (SD) × (Potential adverse change in return)
= (0.2320%) × (2.3263) = 0.5398%

DEAR or 1-Day VaR = Market value of position × Daily Price volatility
= Rs.501,100/- × 0.5398% = *Rs.2,705/-*

Accordingly, 10-Day VaR = 1-Day VaR × $\sqrt{10}$ = *Rs.8,553/-*

## *Historical simulation (HS) approach*

The variance-covariance approach of calculating VaR, even if it evolved as the first measure to estimate VaR and is easy to calculate, there are some major flaws of this approach that may lead to pose a question mark on the reliability of the VaR estimate derived through this method. Critiques normally point out the following against the VCV method:

- VCV or risk-metrics method is based on the assumption of normal distribution that asset returns are expected to follow, which may not be true in reality.
- Estimation of VaR for a portfolio of many securities is extremely cumbersome due to separate estimation of correlations among securities within the portfolio.
- During abnormal circumstances, there may be a major breakdown in the correlation estimates that may lead to quite different losses than the estimated VCV VaR.

In order to develop a VaR model which is free from any statistical assumption, easy to understand, and more close to real market movements, the historical simulation approach has evolved. This approach predicts the future changes in the value of current exposures by considering the current market portfolio of several assets and revalues them on the basis of actual returns that prevailed on those assets yesterday, the day before, and so on. Alternatively, the HS method calculates the loss estimate by revaluing the portfolio based on actual distribution of past returns, only with the assumption that past changes are reliable guides to project future changes in the value of the asset. In simple terms, historical or back simulation answers the question, "If future returns are just as they were in the past, how much loss is a financial institution or investor expected to incur on its current portfolio".

### Steps followed to estimate VaR under historical simulation technique

Value at risk under the historical simulation approach can be simply estimated by linking the current market value of existing positions with the historical price movements of the same. The following steps can be followed to estimate the VaR number:

- Past actual/model prices/rates need to be used to estimate the historical daily returns (logarithmic price/rate change), as described in the above section of estimation of VaR through VCV method.
- Unlike using the historical daily returns to estimate the average loss in the case of the VCV method, historical simulation techniques try to capture all possible profits/losses on all the securities/positions by incorporating each of the historical returns on the present market value of all the securities/positions.
- This security/position wise of all possible profits/losses, based on historical market movement, is considered to capture the maximum loss under a 99% level of confidence by using the *PERCENTILE(1%)* Excel function on the security/position wise series of profits/losses.
- Accordingly, daily VaR on each of the securities/positions at a 99% confidence level needs to be estimated.
- Daily VaR on the whole portfolio, under the historical simulation method, can be estimated not by combining the security/position wise daily VaR, adjusted with the pairwise correlation factors, but before arriving at any VaR estimate.
- After estimating the possible profits/losses on each of the securities/positions within the portfolio, all such day-wise profits/losses are combined together to arrive at portfolio-level possible profits/losses.
- This portfolio-level possible profits/losses series can then be considered to arrive at the portfolio VaR using the same process as used to estimate the security-wise VaR.
- Historical simulation method does not capture the correlation between the securities/positions separately to arrive at the portfolio-level maximum loss. The correlation is embedded while estimating the portfolio-level possible profits/losses through the security-wise possible profits/losses.
- Therefore, portfolio value at risk under the HS method can be simply calculated in Excel just by adding one more column in the estimation exercise.

Because of its simplicity, the absence of stringent assumptions close to the actual market movement, historical simulation becomes an important and widely applicable method to estimate VaR. Some of its specific strengths can be highlighted below:

- HS does not assume normality or serial independence.
- No average measures, like standard deviation and correlation, are used to calculate the HS VaR.
- HS-VaR for different percentiles (e.g. 95% and 99%) are not constant multiples of each other since it is no longer assumed that market shocks are just multiples of average volatility.
- Multi-day VaR does not need to follow the square root rule: 10-day HS VaR may not be a multiple of 1-day HS VaR.
- Co-movements in returns are implicit in daily data and do not need to be captured separately, leading to easy aggregation of individual risk estimates to get a portfolio view.

### Monte-Carlo simulation (MCS) approach

The major limitation of the historical simulation approach, even if it is widely applicable to estimate the VaR, lies with its main assumption that *History Repeats*. Accordingly, this approach may fail to cover any scenario which the market has not experienced in the recent past. If an asset becomes extremely volatile and may experience a future shock, totally different from the past scenarios, the historical simulation method may fail to capture the extent of that future shock. In such cases, the Monte-Carlo simulation (MCS) approach can be followed to get a better and more realistic result. MCS focuses on arriving at VaR on current positions, not as expected through the limited past return movements, but by considering the huge number of possible price movements which are random in nature but maintain the distribution of actual past returns. This is similar to the historical simulation but uses random numbers to simulate future losses. This approach first estimates the statistical distribution and parameters from historical data, and then generates random numbers to simulate future possible loss, as is done in the HS approach. The MCS approach is expected to perform better than the HS approach, especially if applied on highly volatile assets, where correct prediction of future losses is more challenging.

### Special treatment for bond VaR

Value at Risk for any financial asset is generally calculated based on its historical market prices. Even if this is true for assets like equity, foreign currency, commodity, etc., the same may not be the case for bonds. Market prices of a bond cannot be used to calculate its past returns. Since the maturity of a bond after its primary issue, reduces over a period of time, the total number and/or present values of CFs changes in different periods, and therefore also affect the price. A 10-year bond today was an 11-year bond 1 year ago and 12-year bond 2 years ago. Therefore, comparing such prices, even if of the same security but of different maturity, may not capture the bond price sensitivity exclusively due to interest rate changes. In such case, the market price of such bonds, over a specific historical period, becomes different both due to interest rate change and change in the residual maturity of the bond. Therefore, this *Maturity Reduction* creates an invalid return estimate if derived from the past market prices of a bond. Therefore, while comparing the past prices of a bond, the maturity needs to be frozen at the level of current residual maturity. As a result, instead of taking the past market prices, the historical daily spot rates for the required tenors during the past period need to be collected. The fixed tenor specific spot rates that prevailed during all the past dates can be derived through the past daily ZCYC curve, as reported by CCIL in India, known as *NSS ZCYC*. This practice allows having different prices of a bond not due to any change in many parameters, but only due to change in the spot rates. This price series can be termed as *Model Price*. Past returns can now be calculated by considering the past theoretical or model prices of the bond. The VaR on a whole bond portfolio can also be calculated through mapping the entire future cash flows due from similar securities of different maturities. This process allows investors to avoid calculating the past model prices of several securities separately and focuses only on the change in the present values of the entire cash flows due from all securities till their maturities, with respect to the changes in interest rates.

## Expected shortfall: a risk measure beyond VaR

Even if value at risk (VaR) is a very important tool to measure the risk of a financial asset, the same may be misleading under certain contexts and may provide a false sense of security that "the maximum possible loss is estimated and therefore managed". Even if consciously we understand the true meaning of VAR, subconsciously the 99% confidence may lead to a false sense of security. But in reality, 99% confidence is very far from 100% certainty and this small distance may prove to be a very crucial element to successfully manage. A VaR that focuses on the manageable risks near the center or, up to a certain extent, from the center of the distribution, could possibly ignore the tails. Tails exhibit situations where the chances of a bigger deviation from the center is very small, but the magnitude or impact is so big that it may cause a worst possible loss. VaR does not measure such worst possible losses. Ninety-nine percent VaR does not say anything about the size of losses within 1% of the trading days which is beyond the predefined confidence. VaR is compared to "an airbag that works all the time, except when there is a car accident".

VaR and expected shortfall (ES) are associated to each other. Whatever is ignored in VaR, the tail risk, gets captured in ES. ES, also known as conditional VaR (CVaR) is defined as the average of all losses which are greater than or equal to the VaR. Alternatively, ES is the average loss in the worst (1-p)% cases, where p is the confidence level. Where VAR asks the question, "How bad can things get?", ES asks, "If things really go bad, what is the outcome?". ES gives the answer for the question, "What is the expected loss if the value at risk threshold is breached?" Therefore, the method required to estimate the expected shortfall largely depends upon the method used to estimate the VaR. From the quantification or measurement point of view, the only difference between estimating VaR and ES is that, once the possible gains or losses are estimated based on the daily historical scenarios applicable on the current market value of the concerned position/portfolio, VaR is estimated from the 99% (with 99% LoC) of the possible values, whereas the ES is estimated from the rest 1% of the numbers, exhibiting an extreme situation. Therefore, estimation of ES is just one step extension of VaR estimation.

### Example (VaR and ES on bond and equity portfolio)

Suppose an institutional investor holds a trading portfolio consisting of five securities: three central government securities and two equities, the market values of which (as on 7 December 2018) are given in the following table (Table 14.2). The investor may like to estimate the market risk – interest rate risk and price risk applicable to that portfolio with the help of VaR and ES measures, and also may like to compare the loss estimates arrived at under different methods available under both the measures. Suppose 100 days historical data are used to arrive at the respective loss estimates.

A 1-day VaR and ES need to be estimated using both the VCV and HS methods, assuming a 99% level of confidence, and market information for last 100 days.

*Table 14.2* Sample portfolio of dated securities

*Portfolio of 5 Securities Held as on 7 December 2018*

| Sl. No. | Security Description | Date of Maturity | Residual Maturity (Years) | Market Price (INR) | Market Value (in INR Cr.) |
|---------|---------------------|------------------|---------------------------|--------------------|---------------------------|
| 1 | 7.17% GS 2028 | 8 January 2028 | 9.2528 | 98.30 | 491.50 |
| 2 | 7.5% GS 2034 | 10 August 2034 | 15.8417 | 98.37 | 295.11 |
| 3 | 7.37% GS 2023 | 16 April 2023 | 4.5250 | 100.11 | 100.11 |
| 4 | HDFC | N.A. | N.A. | 1951.35 | 50.74 |
| 5 | RELIANCE | N.A. | N.A. | 1133.80 | 49.89 |

*Source*: All tables in this chapter are created by the author unless otherwise stated.

*Table 14.3* Price co-movements of different securities

*Coefficient of Correlation between Pair of Positions as on 7 December 2018 (Using 100 Historical Days)*

|  | 7.17% GS 2028 | 7.5% GS 2034 | 7.37% GS 2023 | HDFC | RELIANCE |
|---|---|---|---|---|---|
| 7.17% GS 2028 | 100.00% |  |  |  |  |
| 7.5% GS 2034 | 98.07% | 100.00% |  |  |  |
| 7.37% GS 2023 | 96.99% | 92.82% | 100.00% |  |  |
| HDFC | 7.22% | 9.95% | 3.99% | 100.00% |  |
| RELIANCE | 16.15% | 21.06% | 13.06% | 29.33% | 100.00% |

### Solution

Considering the market values of all the five securities/positions, sub-portfolios, whole portfolio, historical (last 100 days) market prices of both the stocks, historical model prices of all the three GOI bonds arrived at using the NSS ZCYC curve of all the historical dates, freezing the residual maturity, and the coefficient of correlation between the historical market and/or model prices of all the positions, as given in the following table (Table 14.3), the daily value at risk (using both VCV and HS methods) and the expected shortfall, at 99% confidence level, for all the individual positions, sub-portfolios, and the whole portfolio are estimated as per the methods described in the above sections.

The VaR and ES estimates, both in absolute and relative terms, for all the individual positions, sub-portfolios, and the whole portfolio are summarized in the following table (Table 14.4).

## Back testing and stress testing of risk measurement tools

Even if several models can be used to estimate the risk of various financial assets, including fixed income securities, it is very crucial to validate the outcome of such models and also to estimate the possible outcomes under various critical/stress market conditions. These testing procedures ensure the reliability of the risk measurement tool/model and also make the users confident about their sustainability even during the period of financial stress/crisis. Therefore, back testing and stress testing are two very important exercises that portfolio managers or risk managers need to undertake to successfully manage the financial risk.

### Back testing VaR & ES estimates

Back testing represents the process of verifying the efficacy of a risk management model by comparing the series of predictions (VaR or ES numbers)

Table 14.4 Estimation of VaR and expected shortfall

*Estimates of VaR and Expected Shortfall Using Different Methods*

| Positions/ Portfolio | Market Value (in INR Cr.) | VaR: VCV Method | | VaR: HS Method | | Expected Shortfall | |
|---|---|---|---|---|---|---|---|
| | | Absolute Loss (in INR Cr.) | % of Market Value | Absolute Loss (in INR Cr.) | % of Market Value | Absolute Loss (in INR Cr.) | % of Market Value |
| 7.17% GS 2028 | 491.50 | 2.5123 | 0.5112% | 2.2320 | 0.4541% | 2.5725 | 0.5234% |
| 7.5% GS 2034 | 295.11 | 2.0186 | 0.6840% | 1.8281 | 0.6195% | 2.1870 | 0.7411% |
| 7.37% GS 2023 | 100.11 | 0.2964 | 0.2961% | 0.2586 | 0.2583% | 0.3115 | 0.3112% |
| HDFC | 50.74 | 2.1141 | 4.1669% | 2.3274 | 4.5874% | 3.4435 | 6.7871% |
| RELIANCE | 49.89 | 2.4206 | 4.8521% | 3.3762 | 6.7677% | 3.5533 | 7.1227% |
| G-Sec. Portfolio | 886.72 | 3.5273 | 0.3978% | 4.3187 | 0.4870% | 5.0710 | 0.5719% |
| Equity Portfolio | 100.62 | 3.3285 | 3.3079% | 4.5399 | 4.5118% | 5.4058 | 5.3724% |
| Whole Portfolio | 987.34 | 4.7427 | 0.4803% | 5.6832 | 0.5756% | 9.1663 | 0.9284% |

*Source:* (Solved in MS Excel)

made by the model with the actual outcome. Alternatively, back testing is a process of evaluating and calibrating risk measurement models. The essential element is to measure the accuracy of the model prediction against actual changes in portfolio value, and to ensure that the model estimates the risk consistent with the desired level of confidence. Banks should perform back testing of their VaR/ES models for each of the major risk categories separately, and also of their overall VaR/ES

Back testing is supposed to be based on daily VaR/ES at 1% level of significance. In order to verify the model assumptions, back-testing may also be performed at 2%, 5%, and 10% levels. Actual losses are back tested with the predicted VaR/ES number for a period of 250 days. Back testing may assume that one exception per month (i.e. 12 p.a.) can be tolerated, leading to a selection of 95% level of confidence for 250 days of data. Exceptions captured in back testing need to be accounted for at least on a quarterly basis, but preferably on monthly basis.

Bank regulators play an important role in back testing by deciding a *Scaling Factor*, a combination of *Multiplication Factor* (M) and a *Plus Factor* (P), required to decide the market risk capital charge. The multiplication factor depends on the quality of banks' risk management system, with a floor level of 3 under Basel II. Banks decide the value of plus factor, depending on the results of back testing their VaR model, and it generally ranges from 0 to 1. The plus factor takes a value of 0.40, 0.50, 0.65, 0.75, 0.85, and 1 respectively for the number of exceptions of 5, 6, 7, 8, 9, and 10 or more.

### Stress testing VaR & ES estimates

Stress testing is a valuable risk management tool which tries to quantify the size of potential losses under certain stress events. Stress testing is the process of validating the extent of pressure the VaR/ES model can withstand from a sudden future extreme adverse movement in the market. VaR/ES numbers reflect expected losses under normal market conditions. Stress testing is designed to estimate potential losses in abnormal markets. Abnormality can be defined in terms of occurrence of extreme events and presence of fat tails.

Identifying events or influences that could greatly impact banks is a key component of a bank's assessment of its capital position. Stress scenarios need to cover several factors causing for extraordinary losses or gains in banks' trading portfolios. Banks that propose to use an advanced risk management approach for capital calculations should have in place a rigorous and comprehensive stress testing programme to capture such potential stresses. There may be a set of risk factors, not included in the normal VaR/ES model, that need to be modelled separately under the stress testing programme.

# Market risk capital charge on fixed income portfolio of a bank

Once the market risk on a trading portfolio is measured, after adjusting for the hedging positions (e.g. forward, futures, swaps, options contracts), banks need to maintain the required market risk capital charge to finally manage the market risk. Under the market risk capital charge (MRCC), banks are required to provide the necessary capital separately for different types of trading positions (fixed income securities, foreign currency, equity, commodity, and derivatives). The MRCC pertaining to the interest rate of related instruments needs to be maintained both for fixed income securities included in trading book (HFT and AFS) and for interest rate derivative (IRD) contracts entered into both for hedging and trading. This calculation of MRCC for a fixed income portfolio including IRD again depends upon the method or approach followed to capture the market risk. Therefore, MRCC on a fixed income portfolio may vary between the SMM and IMA approach to capture interest rate risk.

## Market risk capital charge under SMM

The capital charge for interest rate related instruments would apply to the current market value of all securities in a bank's trading book. Since banks are required to maintain capital for market risks on an ongoing basis, they are required to mark-to-market their trading positions on a daily basis. The current market value will be determined as per the existing RBI guidelines on the valuation of investments. The minimum capital requirement for market risk is segregated into two different components:

- General Market Risk Capital Charge (GMRCC): To capture the risk of loss in a trading portfolio due to a change in the market rate of interest.
- Specific Risk Capital Charge (SRCC): To protect against adverse price movements of individual security (long and short) owing to factors, termed as spread risk, event risk, and default risk, related to the individual issuer.

## MRCC on fixed income portfolio under SMM

The GMRCC for all trading positions (HFT and AFS) in interest rate related instruments can be estimated through their m-duration measures adjusted with the expected interest rate shocks, as suggested by the national regulator, followed by some more adjustments to the account for the basis risk and yield curve risk in a fixed income portfolio. On the other hand, SRCC needs to be calculated separately for HFT and AFS positions based on their maturity and/or credit worthiness, as indicated by the regulator. Steps that need to be followed to calculate GMRCC are:

- Calculate the m-duration of each instrument separately.
- Apply the assumed yield change to the modified duration of each instrument between 0.6% and 1.0%, depending on their maturity.
- Slot the resulting capital charge measures into a maturity ladder with the 15 time bands (falls under three time zones) pre-specified by the regulator.
- Subject long and short (only in derivatives) positions in each time band to a 5% *Vertical Disallowance* designed to capture the basis risk.
- Carry forward the net positions in each time-band for the 2nd round of offsetting subject to the concerned Disallowances (*Horizontal Disallowance*) to capture the yield curve risk.

For debt securities held under the AFS category, in view of the possible longer holding period and presence of higher specific risk, banks shall hold total MRCC as the higher of the following:

- SRCC, computed notionally for the AFS securities treating them as held under the HFT category, plus the GMRCC.
- Alternative total capital charge for the AFS positions computed notionally, depending upon maturity and/or credit rating of different positions, treating them as held in the banking book, and following the respective numbers given by the national regulator.

EXAMPLE

Suppose a commercial bank in India, in its HFT portfolio, as on 31 March 2017, holds a few GOI dated securities, details of which are given in the following table (Table 14.5).

The bank follows the standard measurement method to estimate the market risk (general market risk) in all its trading positions and the resultant capital charges.

Given the basic details of all the securities/instruments held by the bank in its trading portfolio and the standard approach (in terms of prescribed yield shock for different types of securities based on their residual maturities) suggested by the Reserve Bank of India, estimate the market risk capital charges the bank is supposed to maintain as on 31 March 2017.

SOLUTION

Estimation of general market risk capital charge on the portfolio of 10 government of India dated securities are shown in the following table (Table 14.6).

*Table 14.5* Composition of government security portfolio (HFT) as on 31 March 2017

| Sr. No. | Security | Maturity Date | Res. Mat. | Yield | Coupon Rate | Market Price | Market Value |
|---|---|---|---|---|---|---|---|
| 1 | 7.49% G.S. 2017 | 16-Apr-17 | 0.04 | 5.8589% | 7.49% | 100.06 | 100063444.71 |
| 2 | 8.07% G.S. 2017 | 03-Jul-17 | 0.26 | 5.9663% | 8.07% | 100.51 | 100505611.16 |
| 3 | 6.25% G.S. 2018 | 02-Jan-18 | 0.76 | 6.2412% | 6.25% | 99.99 | 99994401.59 |
| 4 | 7.83% G.S.2018 | 11-Apr-18 | 1.03 | 6.2412% | 7.83% | 101.56 | 101558853.99 |
| 5 | 8.12% G.S. 2020 | 10-Dec-20 | 3.69 | 6.6684% | 8.12% | 104.67 | 104668977.44 |
| 6 | 8.08% G.S. 2022 | 02-Aug-22 | 5.34 | 6.8288% | 8.08% | 105.51 | 105505273.71 |
| 7 | 7.35% G.S. 2024 | 22-Jun-24 | 7.23 | 6.9897% | 7.35% | 102.00 | 102001829.42 |
| 8 | 6.97% G.S. 2026 | 06-Sep-26 | 9.43 | 6.6582% | 6.97% | 102.15 | 102151821.71 |
| 9 | 6.79% G.S. 2029 | 26-Dec-29 | 12.74 | 7.0310% | 6.79% | 97.98 | 97979019.35 |
| 10 | 8.24% G.S. 2033 | 10-Nov-33 | 16.61 | 7.3745% | 8.24% | 108.20 | 108198907.51 |
| | Portfolio | | | 6.5930% | | | 1022628140.58 |

Table 14.6 Estimation of general market risk capital charge under standard duration approach

*Estimation of General Market Risk Capital Charge under Standard Duration Approach*

| 1 | 2 | 3 | 4 | 5 | 6 | 7 | 8 | 9 | 10 |
|---|---|---|---|---|---|---|---|---|---|
| Sr. No. | Security | Res. Mat. | Market Value (INR) | M-Duration (%) | Convexity | Convexity Adj. M-Duration (in %, for 1% Rise in IR) | Assumed Change in Yield (BPS) | GMRCC (M-Duration) (Rs. in Lakhs) | GMRCC (Convexity Adj. M-Duration) (Rs. in Lakhs) |
| | | | | | | $(5-6\times1\%^2)$ | Given | $(5\times4\times8)$ | $(7\times4\times8)$ |
| 1 | 7.49% G.S. 2017 | 0.04 | 100063445 | 0.0432 | 0.0020 | 0.0432 | 1.00 | 0.4321 | 0.4319 |
| 2 | 8.07% G.S. 2017 | 0.26 | 100505611 | 0.2509 | 0.0660 | 0.2502 | 1.00 | 2.5212 | 2.5146 |
| 3 | 6.25% G.S. 2018 | 0.76 | 99994401 | 0.7180 | 0.4419 | 0.7136 | 1.00 | 7.1796 | 7.1354 |
| 4 | 7.83% G.S.2018 | 1.03 | 101558854 | 0.9459 | 0.7222 | 0.9387 | 0.90 | 8.6458 | 8.5798 |
| 5 | 8.12% G.S. 2020 | 3.69 | 104668977 | 3.0998 | 6.1716 | 3.0381 | 0.75 | 24.3341 | 23.8496 |
| 6 | 8.08% G.S. 2022 | 5.34 | 105505274 | 4.2706 | 11.4488 | 4.1562 | 0.70 | 31.5403 | 30.6947 |
| 7 | 7.35% G.S. 2024 | 7.23 | 102001829 | 5.4530 | 19.1065 | 5.2619 | 0.65 | 36.1538 | 34.8870 |
| 8 | 6.97% G.S. 2026 | 9.43 | 102151822 | 6.8381 | 29.7337 | 6.5408 | 0.60 | 41.9114 | 40.0890 |
| 9 | 6.79% G.S. 2029 | 12.74 | 97979019.4 | 8.2371 | 46.3739 | 7.7734 | 0.60 | 48.4238 | 45.6976 |
| 10 | 8.24% G.S. 2033 | 16.61 | 108198908 | 9.0110 | 61.3129 | 8.3979 | 0.60 | 58.4991 | 54.5187 |
| | **Portfolio** | | 1022628141 | 3.9205 | 17.7407 | 3.7431 | | 259.6411 | 248.3983 |
| | | | 102.2628 Crores | 400.92 Lakhs | | 382.78 Lakhs | | | |

*Source:* (Solved in MS-Excel)

The interest rate sensitivity measures of the debt portfolio are as follows:

Market Value of the Debt Portfolio (HFT) = INR 102.2628 Crores
M-Duration of the Debt Portfolio = 3.9205%
Convexity Adjusted Portfolio M-Duration = 3.7431%

Accordingly, the portfolio loss due to a change in general market conditions, i.e. due to a rise in the interest rate (of all tenors) by 1%, is estimated to be INR 400.92 lakhs, as per the simple m-duration approach, considering a linear change in the bond values due to a change in interest rates. But if the non-linearity in the price-yield relationship is considered, and therefore the m-duration is adjusted with the convexity, the portfolio loss is estimated out to be INR 383.7786 lakhs. But in either of these cases, it is assumed that the interest rates for all tenors are going to change by the same 1%, resulting to a parallel shift in the yield curve.

Since the yield curve is not expected to shift parallel (up or down), the yield shock for different tenors is prescribed. According to the prescribed yield shock (for different time bands under three time zones), the general market risk capital charge (GMRCC) due to change in risk-free interest rates is estimated out to be:

- INR 259.6411 lakhs (considering security-wise m-duration).
- INR 248.3983 lakhs (considering security-wise convexity adjusted m-duration).

*MRCC on interest rate derivative positions under SMM*

The measurement of the capital charge for market risks should include all interest rate derivatives (e.g. FRA, IRS, IRF), currency derivatives (e.g. FX forward, currency swaps, currency futures, and currency options), and credit derivatives (e.g. CDS) in the trading book and also derivative contracts entered into for hedging trading book exposures reacting to the concerned risk factors.

- Any interest rate derivatives may be converted into positions in relevant underlying and be subjected to GMRC and SRCC. Positions in FRA/IRS/IRF are treated as a combination of a long and a short position in notional government security(s), where maturity of such positions will be the delivery/exercise period of the contract and life of the underlying instrument.
- Long and short derivative positions may offset each other in case of identical instruments and MRCC is applicable on net positions.
- No offsetting is allowed between positions in different currencies. Opposite positions in the same category of instruments, if perfectly matched, may be allowed to offset fully.

- GMRCC applies to any derivative exposures (replicated as two cash positions of concerned maturity) in the same manner as for the cash positions, subject to necessary offsets.
- IRS, FRAs, and IRFs (other than futures on bond/bond-index) will not be subject to any SRCC.
- However, a specific risk charge will apply especially on OTC derivative products according to the credit risk of the issuer.
- Because of their off-balance sheet nature, the notional principal amount of each instrument needs to be multiplied by the *Credit Conversion Factor (CCF)*, as shown in the following table (Table 14.7) to get an *Adjusted Value*. The CCF again depends on the maturity of the contract, such that:

*Table 14.7* Credit conversion factor for Off-B/S items

| Original Maturity | Credit Conversion Factor |
|---|---|
| > One Year | 0.5% |
| ≥ One Year; < Two Years | 1.0% |
| For Each Additional Year | 1.0% |

*Source*: BIS and RBI

- The adjusted value, after multiplying the CCF with the notional amount, needs to be multiplied by the counterparty's risk weight: 20% for banks/all India financial institutions and 100% for all others (except government). PDs/NBFCs need to maintain additional capital at 12% (15%) of RWA towards specific (credit) risk on interest rate contracts.

### Specific risk capital charge for HFT and AFS securities

Estimation of credit risk on different types of investments, alternatively known as *Specific Risk*, broadly depends upon the market risk management practices followed in the bank. As per the Basel norms, a bank may follow standard, or basic, approach or advanced approach to estimate its credit and/ or market risk, and accordingly the resulting capital charges. In its market risk management system, if a bank follows the standard approach, known as standardized duration approach, the bank can estimate the specific risk capital charge on its HFT securities as per the standard RBI Circular on Capital Adequacy. In case of securities kept under AFS having a relatively higher risk due to a longer holding period, a bank, apart from the general market risk, needs to separately estimate the specific risk and total risk, as per the RBI guideline, and accordingly needs to maintain the capital charge.

### Limitations of standardized method to estimate MRCC

Standardized sensitivity measures, proposed by the Basel Committee and approved and implemented by the domestic regulator, may be simple enough to estimate the market risk and resultant capital charge on various trading positions (e.g. fixed income security/bonds, equities, foreign currencies, etc.) of banks and other FIs. But these measures/processes are not free from some severe limitations in terms of capturing the true level of risks of various positions before estimating the market risk capital charge required to be maintained to safeguard the business. Some major limitations of the standardized method may be described in the following section:

### Limitation of proposed sensitivity measures

Under the standardized duration method, the interest rate risk in fixed income securities/portfolios is captured through m-duration/PV01. Even if these measures capture the sensitivity of the concerned position(s) to any change in interest rates, the estimated change in the value(s) of such positions may be different from the actual price change followed by any change in interest rates, especially due to the asymmetric behavior of change in bond price due to a change in interest rates. Alternatively, m-duration assumes a symmetric/linear price-yield relationship, due to which the magnitude of change in a bond's value is the same for both the rise and fall in interest rates. Therefore, the rise in a bond's value due to a fall in interest rates is more than the fall in a bond's value due to a similar rise in interest rates, at least for plain vanilla (option-free) securities. This feature, commonly known as convexity, is not captured in the existing m-duration-based sensitivity measure to estimate the capital charge, leading to an overestimation of losses, and therefore the required capital charge due to any rise in interest rates. Therefore, duration-based sensitivity measures, if adjusted with the respective convexity features, are considered to estimate the interest rate risk and required capital charges. The same will be more robust and meaningful.

### Pre-specified rate shocks across various maturities

The interest rate risk losses at a portfolio level broadly depend on the change in interest rates for different tenors, alternatively, the expected shift in the yield curve. The yield curve shift may be parallel or non-parallel, where the interest rate for different tenors changes with different magnitudes. The possibility of non-parallel shift in the yield curve, which may be more realistic, is dully considered while capturing the interest rate risk losses at a portfolio level, and thereby estimating the capital charge for interest risk by considering various yield shocks, depending upon the maturity band of the individual security/position. But there may be a possibility for some disagreement with regard to the magnitude of the interest rate shocks prescribed for different maturity bands. Even if the interest rate shocks, prescribed by the domestic regulator, range from 60 to 100 basis points, depending upon the residual tenor of the security, there may be some possibility of disagreement towards the association between maturity level and prescribed yield shock, and also the magnitude of yield shock at various maturity levels. Even if the prescribed yield shock is negatively associated with the maturity, with a minimum and maximum shock of respectively 60 and 100 basis points, as prescribed, the interest rate volatility may be positively associated with the residual tenor or there may not be any significant association at all. Even if there is some strong association, positive or negative, the same need not be fixed across the markets or periods. These possibilities may lead to a requirement to capture the historical interest rate volatility separately for various tenors and also, on an ongoing basis, to capture the actual market situation under various scenarios without generalizing the same across the markets and under all possible scenarios. Yield shocks for various maturities arrived at under this mechanism may be more robust and realistic before the same are prescribed to estimate the interest risk losses, and therefore the interest risk capital charge.

### Pre-specified adjustments to arrive at MRCC for IR risk

While netting off between long and short (in government securities and derivatives) positions, while estimating the market risk losses, and therefore the required capital charge, there may be some possibility to ignore the risk that arises due to netting-off between non-identical long and short positions under various time bands (i.e. basis risk), and also the risk for netting-off between net long and net short positions within and across various time bands (i.e. yield curve risk). These possibilities of incurring additional market risk losses due to the basis risk and yield curve risk get adjusted with the estimated market risk capital charge through some pre-specified adjustments, known as vertical disallowances (for basis risk) and horizontal disallowances (for yield curve risk). There is no doubt that these risks arise while estimating portfolio losses after duly netting-off between long and short positions, but such adjustment is again based on some pre-specified numbers given by the domestic regulator. Unless these numbers are robust and are derived after considering the actual market scenario, there may be a possibility for improper (higher or lower) estimation of market risk losses, and therefore total market risk capital charge.

### Simple risk aggregation within and across asset classes

Once the risk in different positions or sub-portfolios (debt, equity, FX) are separately estimated and the required market risk capital charges under various heads are arrived at, the total market risk capital charge at the whole trading portfolio level, under the standardized approach, is arrived at through a simple summation process. Alternatively, the total market risk capital charge on the trading portfolio, under the standardized approach, is just the simple sum of market risk capital charges in debt, equity, and FX portfolios. This process of simple risk aggregation among various asset classes to arrive at the portfolio risk in terms of the market risk capital charge on the whole trading portfolio completely ignores the co-movement (possibly negative) among various segments of the financial market. If these major segments (debt, equity, FX) in the financial market are expected to be negatively associated, as may be captured through negative correlation, simple risk aggregation among various asset classes may lead to ignoring the natural diversification among various asset classes, which may possibly overestimate the portfolio losses, and therefore the required market risk capital charges.

### Market risk capital charge under IMA

Calculation of the market risk capital charge on a fixed income portfolio under the internal market approach is purely based on value at risk estimates under different circumstances: normal and stressed. Normal VaR represents the maximum of the previous day's VaR and an average of the daily VaR of the last 60 business days multiplied by a *Multiplier (K)*. Similarly, a stressed VaR represents the maximum of the latest S-VaR and an average of S-VaR over the last 60 business days multiplied by a *Multiplier (K)*. The value of K depends on two individual factors: multiplication factor ($M_C$ and $M_S$) and plus factor ($P_C$ and $P_S$). $M_C$ and $M_S$ are supposed to be set by the RBI on the basis of their assessment of the quality of the bank's risk management system, subject to a floor of 3. Whereas values of the *Plus Factor* ($P_C$ & $P_S$) range from 0 to 1, depending on the back testing results of a banks' VaR model. Treatment of normal VaR and stressed VaR in calculation of MRCC is such that:

$$MRCC = [ \, Max \, \{ \, VaR_{t-1} \, ; (K \times VaR_{Avg.} ) \, \}$$
$$+ \, Max \, \{ \, S\text{-}VaR_{t-1} \, ; \, (K \times S\text{-}VaR_{Avg.} ) \, \} \, ] \qquad (14.3)$$

Where $K = (M_c + P_c)$ or $(M_s + P_s)$; M and P are respectively the multiplication factor and plus factor.

Specific risk (or IRC for IR risk) in India as of now needs to be captured as per SMM. However, in due course, banks should attempt to model specific risk and IRC.

### Steps followed to estimate GMRCC under the IMA using the VaR numbers

- Other than estimating the daily portfolio VaR as on the concerned estimation date, following either of the two (VCV, HS) VaR methods, the same VaR numbers need to be estimated also for the last 60 working days using the same method.
- The daily portfolio VaR on all the last 60 working days needs to be used to arrive at the 60-day daily average portfolio VaR.

- These daily portfolio VaRs, both the latest and the past 60-day average VaR, are then converted into 10-day VaR, as suggested by the RBI, by multiplying the daily VaR with the square root of the specified number of days (i.e. $\sqrt{10}$).
- Accordingly, we arrive at the latest 10-day portfolio VaR ($VaR_{P,\,t-1}$) and the 60-day average 10-day portfolio VaR ($VaR_{P,\,Avg.}$) under *Normal Market Condition*.
- The same process as described above can be followed to arrive at the same VaR estimate, latest and 60-day average, on the same portfolio but by assuming a stressed market situation reinforcing the concerned data that prevailed during 1 year of stressed market conditions, as suggested by the RBI.
- Accordingly, in case of a bond VaR, model prices of the concerned securities need to be re-estimated, not by using the spot rates of the latest 1 year period, but by using the same, let's say during the 2008 crisis period. Similarly, the equity VaR can be estimated by using the security-wise/market returns during the same 2008 crisis period. The FX VaR again can be estimated by using the concerned FX rates that prevailed during the same stressed period.
- Capturing the normal market situation and the stressed situation separately, we can separately estimate the GMRCC under both the conditions, the sum of which will be the total GMRCC on all the trading positions held by the bank.
- GMRCC may be estimated under normal market conditions, assuming the value of multiplication factor equals 3.
- SRCC may be estimated separately under the SMM method and then may be added with the GMRCC to arrive at the total market risk capital charge on the HFT portfolio, both under the normal and stressed market condition.

## Case study: estimation of MRCC on FI portfolio under advanced (VaR) method

As per the internal model approach, suppose the Bank of Baroda is supposed to capture the market risk, especially the general market risk, following to the value at risk method, and accordingly needs to estimate the general market risk capital charge (GMRCC). The bank may capture the specific risk as per the standard approach suggested by the RBI or by following the internal rate based (IRB) approach as followed by the bank (if at all) to capture the credit risk in its credit portfolio.

This GMRCC, as per the VaR method under IMA, can again be estimated only on those trading positions which are liquid enough with sufficient trading history, so that VaR for all such positions can be estimated based on their historical price information. Therefore, as suggested by the RBI, banks in India can implement the IMA on their HFT portfolio, consisting of sufficiently liquid securities, and can still follow the standard approach to capture the market risk of the AFS portfolio, consisting of relatively fewer liquid securities.

Accordingly, the Treasury mid-office may like to apply the VaR method to capture the market risk on its HFT portfolio, consisting of say 10 highly liquid GOI securities and 10 equity shares, and open trading positions in four important foreign currencies, say: USD, EURO, GBP, and JPY, as on 5 December 2014, as exhibited in the following table (Table 14.8).

*Table 14.8* Details of securities/positions under HFT portfolio of the bank as on 5 December 2014

| Sl. No. | Security Name | Category | Residual Mat (in Yr.) | No. of Securities Hold ('000) | Current Price (Rs.) on 5 Dec. 2014 | Market Value (Rs. in Crore) on 5 Dec. 2014 |
|---|---|---|---|---|---|---|
| 1 | 08.08 GS 2022 | G-Sec. | 7.66 | 11000 | 100.14 | 110.154 |
| 2 | 08.13 GS 2022 | G-Sec. | 7.80 | 5000 | 100.37 | 50.185 |
| 3 | 07.16 GS 2023 | G-Sec. | 8.46 | 5000 | 94.65 | 47.325 |
| 4 | 08.20 GS 2025 | G-Sec. | 10.81 | 30500 | 100.98 | 307.989 |
| 5 | 08.33 GS 2026 | G-Sec. | 11.60 | 500 | 102.01 | 5.1005 |
| 6 | 08.24 GS 2027 | G-Sec. | 12.21 | 500 | 101.47 | 5.0735 |
| 7 | 08.26 GS 2027 | G-Sec. | 12.67 | 5000 | 101.51 | 50.755 |
| 8 | 08.83 GS 2023 | G-Sec. | 8.98 | 5000 | 105.12 | 52.55875 |
| 9 | 08.40 GS 2024 | G-Sec. | 9.65 | 13000 | 103.04 | 133.952 |
| 10 | 08.28 GS 2027 | G-Sec. | 12.80 | 5000 | 101.87 | 50.9325 |
| | **G-Sec. Portfolio** | | | | | 814.02525 |
| 1 | ICICIBANK | Equity | N/A | 279 | 1794.1 | 50.06 |
| 2 | SBIN | Equity | N/A | 1575 | 317.55 | 50.01 |
| 3 | INFY | Equity | N/A | 242 | 2070.3 | 50.10 |
| 4 | AXISBANK | Equity | N/A | 1003 | 498.55 | 50.00 |
| 5 | RELIANCE | Equity | N/A | 522 | 957.35 | 49.97 |
| 6 | HDFC | Equity | N/A | 448 | 1114.85 | 49.95 |
| 7 | TCS | Equity | N/A | 194 | 2578.95 | 50.03 |
| 8 | YESBANK | Equity | N/A | 666 | 750.6 | 49.99 |
| 9 | TATAMOTORS | Equity | N/A | 952 | 525.35 | 50.01 |
| 10 | MCDOWELL-N | Equity | N/A | 176 | 2837.3 | 49.94 |
| | **Equity Portfolio** | | | | | 500.07 |
| 1 | USD/INR | FX | N/A | 8084 | 61.8535 | 50.00 |
| 2 | GBP/INR | FX | N/A | 5169 | 96.7265 | 50.00 |
| 3 | EURO/INR | FX | N/A | 6533 | 76.5313 | 50.00 |
| 4 | JPY/INR | FX | N/A | 9707 | 51.51 | 50.00 |
| | **FX Portfolio** | | | | | 200.00 |

We may consider the following trading positions (government security, equity, and foreign currency) for which the bank needs to calculate the VaR and the resultant capital charge under the IMA.

Estimate the market risk capital charge of the bank's HFT portfolio under the IMA using the value at risk method, both through the VCV technique and historical simulation method.

## Self-learning exercise

1  What is market risk in banking? What are the major risk factors that banks/FIs in India are exposed to in their investments?

2  What are the important sensitivity measures that capture all the major risk factors that come under the broader category of market risk?

3  How are the interest rate sensitivity measures, generally used to capture the interest rate risk, different from each other in terms of their usefulness and limitations?

4  How is the yield curve shift important for estimating the interest rate risk in the bond portfolio? Explain with example.

5  "Convexity, if adjusted with modified duration while estimating the interest rate risk losses, and therefore the resultant capital charge, allows banks/FIs to save some capital." Explain.

6  What motivates a risk manager to think for an alternative to the sensitivity-based measure to capture the interest rate risk in a bond portfolio?

7  What is value at risk? Explain various methods used to estimate VaR. Highlight the advantages and limitations of different methods.

8  What is expected shortfall (ES)? How is this risk measure different from the VaR measure? Do you agree that the ES measure always gives a more reliable loss estimate than the VaR measure?

9  "Historical market prices are one of the major inputs to estimate the VaR of a portfolio consisting of various bonds". Do you agree with this statement? Explain.

10  What is general market risk (GMR) and specific risk (SR)? How are these risks for different debt securities estimated?

11  What is meant by basis risk and yield curve risk? While estimating the market risk at the portfolio level, how are presence of these risks taken care of?

2  What is back testing? How is this important in the context of risk measurement and management?

13  Even if VaR is generally used to estimate the losses under normal market conditions, how are abnormal market movements as experienced during financial crisis captured in the risk measurement framework?

14 How is the market risk capital charge, under the standardized approach, on a whole trading portfolio consisting of various positions estimated? Is there any limitation in this process of arriving at the portfolio level losses and required capital charge?

## Bibliography

Alexander, C. (2008). *Market Risk Analysis: Value-at-Risk Models.* John Wiley & Sons, Inc., Hoboken, NJ.

Allen, L., Boudoukh, J., and Saunders, A. (2004). *Understanding Market, Credit, and Operational Risk: The Value at Risk Approach.* Blackwell Publishing Ltd., Hoboken, NJ.

Bessis, J. (2006). *Risk Management in Banking.* John Wiley & Sons, Inc., Hoboken, NJ.

Choudhry, M. (2006). *An Introduction to Value-at-Risk* (4th edn.). John Wiley & Sons, Inc., Hoboken, NJ.

Das, S. (ed.). (1998). *Risk Management and Financial Derivatives: A Guide to the Mathematics.* McGraw-Hill, India.

Dowd, K. (2002). *An Introduction to Market Risk Measurement.* John Wiley & Sons, Inc., Hoboken, NJ.

Esch, L., Kieffer, R., and Lopez, T. (2005). *Asset Risk and Management.* John Wiley & Sons, Inc., Hoboken, NJ.

Golub, B., and Tilman, L. M. (2000). *Risk Management: Approaches for Fixed Income Markets.* John Wiley & Sons, Inc., Hoboken, NJ.

Hull, J. C. (2013). *Risk Management and Financial Institutions* (3rd edn.) John Wiley & Sons, Inc., Hoboken, NJ.

Jorion, P. (2009). *Value at Risk* (3rd edn.). McGraw Hill Education, New York.

Ramaswamy, S. (2004). *Managing Credit Risk in Corporate Bond Portfolios: A Practitioner's Guide.* John Wiley & Sons, Inc., Hoboken, NJ.

Veronesi, P. (2011). *Fixed Income Securities: Valuation, Risk and Risk Management.* John Wiley & Sons, Inc., Hoboken, NJ.

## Notes

1 Capital to risk-weighted asset ratio (CRAR), or in-short capital adequacy ratio (CAR), is a measurement of a bank's available/required capital expressed as a percentage of its risk-weighted exposures/assets. As per Basel, and therefore the domestic regulator's capital adequacy norms, banks are expected to maintain a minimum CRAR or CAR, which is again subjected to necessary changes depending upon the revisions in the capital adequacy norms. This minimum CRAR carries a lot of importance for the solvency of a bank, especially in a worst market scenario. The CRAR is calculated as: *(TierI Capital + Tier II Capital)/(Risk Weighted Assets).* Accordingly, a bank taking a more risky exposure and/or investing in risky assets, causing a rise in risk weighted assets due to a rise in the applicable risk weights if not the assets, would need to maintain a higher capital to ensure that the minimum CRAR is maintained. At the same time, a bank having less amount of capital may need to take a less risky exposure and/or invest in less risky assets, therefore leading to lower risk-weighted assets, even if the asset size

remains the same, allowing the bank to maintain the minimum CRAR without raising any fresh capital.

2 Risk management is a collective and continuous process that begins with the identification of risks, followed by measuring, managing, and finally monitoring the same to ensure the sound existence of the business. Failure in any of these four stages would lead to a failure in the whole risk management system. Basel capital adequacy norms applicable to banks are basically to ensure a robust risk management system in banking to protect the banking system from financial difficulties or any financial stresses.

3 Diversification is basically a portfolio or risk management strategy in which a variety of assets with various risk-return characteristics are selected in the portfolio. This ensures that, due to some negative co-movements in the values of a few pairs of assets, losses in a few assets are naturally offset by the gains in a few other assets. This benefit is commonly known as the diversification benefit, which can only be ensured whenever there is negative correlation, if not perfectly negative, between a few pairs of assets. In a portfolio of various securities (e.g. bonds, equities, mutual funds, commodities, etc.), due to negative correlation between the prices of say bond and equity or equity and commodity, the portfolio will be treated as a well-diversified portfolio. Even if such diversification is a very common risk management strategy, the same is true only under normal circumstances. In case of extremely abnormal market scenarios, there may be a correlation breakdown and all diversification possibility may disappear.

# Glossary

**Accrued interest:**  The coupon income that accrues from the last coupon date to the valuation/settlement date of the transaction.

**Actual/360:**  A day/year count convention taking the number of calendar days in a particular period and in a year assumed to be of 360 days.

**Actual/365:**  A day/year convention taking the number of calendar days in a particular period and in a year of 365 days.

**Actual/Actual:**  A day/year count convention taking the number of calendar days in a particular period and in a year equal to the actual number of days in that particular year, considering the leap year (if any)

**American option:**  An American option is one which may be exercised at any time during its life.

**Amortization:**  A process where the principal amount decreases during the life of a deal, or is repaid in multiple instalments during a loan.

**Annuity:**  An investment providing a series of equal amount of future cash flows.

**Appreciation:**  An increase in the market value of a security or positions.

**Arbitrage:**  The process of buying securities or taking positions in one country, currency, or market and selling identical securities/positions in another to take the short-lived advantage of price differences/imperfections, and thereby making a risk-free transaction.

**Arbitrageur:**  Someone who undertakes arbitrage transaction/deals.

**Ask price:**  The price which a trader or a market maker quotes to sell a security/position.

**Asset & liability management (ALM):**  The process of matching the term structure of interest rates and cash flows (inflows and outflows) of an organization due from (to) the portfolio of assets (liabilities) to maximize its net returns and to minimize the risk.

**Asset allocation:**  Distribution of surplus/investable funds within an asset class or across a range of asset classes with an objective of maximizing the portfolio return and diversifying the portfolio risk.

**Asset securitization:**  The process whereby loans, receivables, and other illiquid assets in the balance sheet are packaged into interest bearing securities that offer attractive investment opportunities.

**Asset swap:**   An interest rate swap or currency swap used in conjunction with an underlying asset such as a bond investment.

**Asset-backed security (ABS):**   A type of debt security that is based on pools of assets or is collateralized by the cash flows from a specified pool of underlying assets.

**At-the-money (ATM):**   An option is at-the-money if the current value of the underlying is equal to or very close to the strike price.

**Auction:**   A process of issuing bonds where institutions submit their bids to the issuer in terms of a price or yield.

**Available for sale (AFS):**   A sub-classification of an investment portfolio where investors may like to keep securities/positions (mostly semi-liquid) for trading, but without any restriction on the maximum holding period as applicable in the case of HFT.

**Back testing:**   A process of verifying the efficacy of a risk management model by comparing the series of predicted losses suggested by a model with the actual losses that an institution has actually incurred.

**Backwardation:**   The situation when a forward futures price of an underlying is lower than its spot price.

**Barbell position:**   A long position in a portfolio of two types of debt securities: very shorter term and longer term, need not be of exactly equal proportions.

**Base yield curve:**   Graphical presentation of risk-free yields (i.e. yields on central government securities) on a given date with respect to their time to maturities, alternatively known as risk-free yield curve (e.g. government of India yield curve).

**Basis risk:**   A form of market risk that arises whenever one kind of risk exposure is hedged with an instrument that behaves in a similar, but not necessarily identical way. Such risk normally arises when the risk of an underlying position is hedged by a hedging instrument, say a futures contract, where the price movements of underlying and futures are similar, but not identical.

**Basis swap:**   An interest rate swap where both legs are linked to two different floating rates of interest, basically used to hedge the basis risk.

**Benchmark bond:**   A preferably risk-free bond whose terms set a standard for the market. The benchmark usually has the greatest liquidity, making it more expensive with the highest turnover and most frequently quoted.

**Benchmark rate:**   The yield applicable to the most liquid risk-free security of a particular time to maturity (e.g. the yield on recently issued and therefore most liquid GOI bond).

**Bid price:**   The price that a trader or market maker quotes to buy a security.

**Bid-ask spread:**   The difference between the prices at which a trader buys an asset from a seller (i.e. the bid price) and sells the same to a buyer (i.e. ask/offer price), often representing the liquidity of a market.

**Bilateral netting:** The ability to offset amounts owed to a counterparty under one contract against amounts owed to the same counterparty under another.

**Binomial tree:** A mathematical model to value option contracts based on the assumption that the value of the underlying can move either up or down a given extent over a given short period of time. This process is repeated many times to give a large number of possible paths, known as the "tree", which the value could follow during the option's life.

**BIS (Bank for International Settlements):** Known as the central bank for central banks, an international organization situated in Basel, Switzerland, which acts as the central bank for sovereign entities, producing capital adequacy norms for banks through various "Basel accords".

**Black-Scholes:** A widely used option pricing model developed by Fischer Black and Myron Scholes.

**Bootstrapping:** A method of deriving the term structure of interest rates from market prices and yields using successive bonds to calculate the spot rate or zero coupon yields along the maturity term structure.

**Broker/dealers:** Members of the stock/derivative exchange who may intermediate between customers and market makers and/or transacting business with customers from their own holdings of stock.

**Bullet security:** A debt security that just pays coupons and matures on a specific date with no call features.

**Butterfly strategy:** A strategy in which security with an intermediate maturity is sold (bought) and two securities for which maturities straddle the intermediate maturity are bought (sold).

**Calendar spread:** The spread arises due to simultaneous purchase/sale of a futures contract for one date and the sale/purchase of a similar futures contract for a different date.

**Call date:** The possible date(s) a debt security may be called by its issuer.

**Call option:** The right but not any obligation to purchase an underlying or an instrument at a pre-decided price on a future date.

**Call price:** The price at which the issuer or call buyer can call back a bond.

**Callable bond:** A bond which provides the borrower with an option to redeem the issue before the original maturity date, preferably with some prior details such as the date after which the bond is callable and also the redemption price.

**Cap:** An agreement where one party agrees to pay the other party if the reference interest rate exceeds the strike interest rate on multiple occasions.

**Capital adequacy:** System of maintaining an adequate amount of capital to be held by banks and other financial institutions to meet the necessary statutory requirements, generally defined by international and domestic regulatory authorities.

**Capital market:** A segment of the financial market where several long-term financial products/instruments are issued or traded with a minimum original maturity of more than 1 year.

**Carry:** Carry in an IRS position is the net interest accrual between the fixed and floating leg till the valuation date.

**Cash-and-carry arbitrage:** A situation in the financial markets when the price at which an investor can sell a bond in the futures market (at the maturity date of the futures contract) is higher than the cost of financing the bond for delivery; i.e. an arbitrage opportunity through buying in the cash market (long in bond market) and selling in the futures market (short in futures market).

**CDS spread:** The premium paid by the protection buyer to the protection seller under the CDS contract.

**Certificate of deposit (CD):** A money market instrument issued by a bank of up to 1 year's maturity that pays a bullet interest payment on maturity.

**Cheapest to deliver (CTD):** In a notional bond futures contract, the one underlying bond among all the deliverable securities which is the most price-efficient for the seller to deliver at maturity.

**Clean price:** The price of a bond, generally quoted in the market, arrived at by deducting the accrued interest/coupon from the dirty price.

**Clearing house:** The body that settles trades executed on a trading platform/exchange, and which acts as the counterparty to every transaction, offering a guaranteed settlement.

**Collar:** The simultaneous sale of a put (or call) option and purchase of a call (or put) at different strike price/rates.

**Collateralized debt obligation (CDO):** A debt obligation backed by pools of corporate bonds, bank loans, and so on.

**Commercial paper:** A money market instrument issued by a non-banking entity of up to 1 year's maturity that pays a bullet interest payment on maturity.

**Competitive bid:** A bid in which bidders specify the quantity that they would like to buy and the price at which they would like to buy.

**Compound interest:** Interest payments to an investor where he/she can earn interest on interest, depending upon the frequency of interest payments (e.g. semi-annually, quarterly, daily).

**Concave yield curve:** A yield curve where, in the event of an upward-sloping (downward-sloping) curve, interest rates/yields increase (decrease) as maturity increases, but at a decreasing (increasing) rate.

**Contango:** The situation when the forward or futures price for an underlying/instrument is higher than the respective spot price.

**Conversion factor (CF):** In a bond futures contract, a factor to make each deliverable bond comparable with the contract's notional bond specification. The price payable against the delivery of a particular security within the deliverable basket is the futures settlement price times the conversion factor.

**Convex yield curve:** A yield curve where, in the event of upward-sloping (downward-sloping) curve, interest rates/yields increase (decrease) as maturity increases, but at a increasing (decreasing) rate.

**Convexity adjustment:** An adjustment used to make the change in price due to a given change in yield as estimated through the m-duration measure closer to the actual price change, making the m-duration-based symmetric price-yield very close to the actual and asymmetric price-yield curve.

**Convexity:** The curvature of the price-yield curve, the second order differentiation of the bond price function with respect to the yield and the non-linearity or asymmetricity in the price-yield curve of an underlying bond, that makes the rise in price due to a fall in yield different from the fall in price due to a similar rise in yield, against the similar price change as claimed by the modified duration.

**Correlation:** A degree of association between a pair of variables, as captured by the well-known Karl Pearson's measure of coefficient of correlation, possibly indicated by a scatter plot.

**Cost of carry:** The net running cost of holding a position, for example, the cost of borrowing cash to purchase a security less the coupon earned on that security while holding the same. Cost of carry may be positive or negative, depending upon the short-term borrowing rate and the coupon rate of the respective security.

**Coupon:** The contractual regular interest payment(s) made by the issuer of security to the holders, based on the coupon rate and the face value.

**Covered bond:** Debt securities issued by banks or mortgage institutions that are fully collateralized by residential or commercial mortgage loans or by loans to public sector institutions and typically have the highest credit ratings.

**Credit default swaps (CDS):** A bilateral financial contract in which the protection buyer pays a periodic or upfront fee in return for a contingent payment by the protection seller following a credit event with respect to a reference entity.

**Credit derivatives:** A privately negotiated financial contract the value of which is derived from the credit risk of a bond, a bank loan, or any other instrument with an exposure to credit risk.

**Credit event:** The collection of different events or situations that define the type of risk against which the protection buyer of a CDS deal has bought a protection from its counterparty, i.e. from protection seller.

**Credit risk:** The risk of financial losses due to non-payment of the necessary dues (interest and/or principal) by the respective counterparty of a deal/transaction in a timely manner due to financial distress, reorganization, workouts, or bankruptcy.

**Credit spread:** The difference between yields of two debt securities of almost identical nature except for their credit quality as exhibited by the credit rating. Normally, the spreads of a credit-risky debt are estimated with respect to a risk-free benchmark such as a Treasury bond or interest rate swap rates.

**Cross hedge:**   Hedging an underlying position using a derivative contract having some different underlying, causing a different change in the value of the derivatives for a given change in the value of the underlying expected to be hedged, and therefore may fail to completely offset each other, causing an imperfect hedge.

**Current yield:**   The yield/return on a bond estimated with respect to its current market price, arrived at by an annual coupon amount divided by the current market price.

**Curvature risk:**   The risk of realizing losses due to changes in the shape of the yield curve.

**Day count:**   The convention used to calculate the accrued interest on bonds using various conventions. For government securities in India, the day count convention used is 30/360.

**Dealer:**   An institution that handles transactions for its customers and purchases securities for its own account, selling them to customers.

**Deep discount bond:**   Bonds offering a deep discount to the subscriber in the beginning itself as a compensation for not earning any regular coupons from debt instruments till the maturity; otherwise known as zero coupon bond.

**Default:**   Any missed or delayed disbursement of contractual obligations (interest, sinking funds, or principal), bankruptcy, receivership, or distressed exchanges.

**Deliverable bond:**   One of the bonds which is eligible to be delivered by the seller of a bond futures contract at the contract's maturity, according to the specifications of that particular contract.

**Delivery versus payment (DvP):**   A method of simultaneous exchange of securities and cash while settling a transaction through a clearing house. There are three important DvP systems used in Indian market.

**Delta ($\Delta$):**   The change in an option's value relative to a change in the underlying's value.

**Dirty price (invoice price):**   For bonds, the sum of all discounted future cash flows including the accrued interest. For exchange traded bond futures contracts, the price received by the short futures position holder, calculated as (futures price × conversion factor) + accrued interest.

**Discount rate:**   The rate of interest used to arrive at the present value(s) of a single or multiple future cash flows. Discounting factor that is used to apply with the future cash flows to arrive at the PV, may be arrived at by: $DF = 1/(1 + r)^t$.

**Duration (or Macaulay duration):**   A measure of the weighted average life of a bond or other series of cash flows using the present values of the cash flows as the weights.

**Effective duration:**   A duration measure applicable to a debt security where the number of future cash flows are uncertain, as in the case of bonds with some embedded options (call and/put) where the option can be exercised any time before the maturity, making the total number of future cash flows uncertain.

**European option:** An option that may be exercised only at the date of expiry.

**Extrapolation:** The process of estimating a price or rate for a particular value date/period from other known prices/rates when the value date/period required lies outside the period covered by the known prices.

**Face value:** The principal amount of a security generally redeemed at maturity on which the coupon amounts are calculated.

**Flight to quality:** A state of financial markets in which investors liquidate their investments in assets that are perceived to be too risky and "flee" to "safer" assets such as Treasury securities.

**Floating rate:** An interest rate set with reference to an external index or reference rate and is re-fixed at regular intervals depending upon the respective convention.

**Floor:** An agreement where one party agrees to pay the other party if the reference interest rate falls below the strike interest rate on multiple occasions.

**Forward contracts:** A contract to buy (sell) a specific underlying asset at a pre-decided price and at a specified future time, traded in the OTC market.

**Forward price:** The price agreed today for an asset that will be delivered to the buyer at maturity.

**Forward rate agreement (FRA):** An agreement to borrow or lend a *notional* amount for a period of time lasting up to 12 months, starting at any point over the next 12 months, at an agreed rate of interest (the FRA rate).

**Forward rates of interest:** Rate of interest applicable for a future period in time, e.g., 6-month rate 6 months from now, denoted as $FR_{6,12}$.

**Future value:** The amount of money to be received in the future by investing a given amount of money now and includes the interest at a specific rate and also due at specific interval(s), normally estimated as: $FV = V \times (1 + r/k)^{kt}$, k being the interval/frequency of interest payments.

**Futures contracts:** A contract to buy (sell) a specific underlying asset at a pre-decided price and at a specified future time, traded in recognized exchanges.

**FX risk:** The risk of realizing financial losses due to adverse movements in the exchange rate.

**Gamma ($\gamma$):** The change in an option's delta relative to a change in the underlying's value.

**Gap ratio:** Ratio of interest-rate sensitive assets to interest-rate sensitive liabilities; used to determine changes in the risk profile of an institution with changes in interest rate levels.

**Hedge ratio:** The process of matching the volatility of the underlying position to be hedged and that of the hedging instrument, especially in case of cross hedging, in order to decide the required number of futures contracts to be entered into (long or short) to ensure an optimal hedge.

**Hedging:** Protecting the value of the underlying position against the risks that arise due to potential adverse market movements in exchange rates, interest rates, or other variables.

**Held for trading (HFT):** A sub-classification of an investment portfolio where investors may like to keep securities/positions (mostly liquid), not to hold for a longer time or till the maturity, but just to trade in the market within a stipulated time period (within 90 days applicable to banks in India).

**Held till maturity (HTM):** A sub-classification of an investment portfolio where investors may not have any trading intentions and just like to hold securities/positions till they mature.

**Historical simulation:** Method of calculating value-at-risk (VaR) using historical data to assess the likely effect of market movement on a portfolio.

**Horizontal disallowance:** A larger proportion of the matched positions across different time-bands to be added while estimating the market risk capital charge on matched (net of long and short) positions across different time bands to take care of yield curve risk.

**Humped yield curve:** A yield curve where, unlike consistent rise or fall in the yield as maturity increases, there is a change in the slope of the curve, i.e. the yield may rise till a certain maturity. and thereafter it may fall for the rest of the maturities or may start rising again beyond some maturity point.

**Immunization:** This is the process by which a bond portfolio is created that has an assured return for a specific time horizon irrespective of changes in interest rates, which can be further utilized to settle the pre-defined liabilities, basically allowing the portfolio manager to offset interest-rate risk and reinvestment risk.

**Implied repo rate:** The internal rate of return associated with the strategy of selling T-bond futures and borrowing and buying an eligible T-bond and delivering it to the futures market at maturity.

**Inflation indexed bond:** Securities where the coupon is linked to some inflation index, basically to safeguard investors against an adverse macroeconomic situation, such as rising inflation.

**Interest rate parity:** A theory in which the interest rate differential between two countries is equal to the differential between the forward exchange rate and the spot exchange rate, playing an important role in foreign exchange markets, connecting interest rates between two economies, spot exchange rates, and foreign exchange rates.

**Interest rate swap:** A financial contract between two parties exchanging or swapping a stream of interest payments for a "notional principal" amount on multiple occasions during a specified period.

**Internal rate of return:** The yield or rate of interest required to discount a series of future cash flows (inflows and outflows) to make the net present value (NPV) equal to zero. Alternatively, a yield or a discounting rate making the sum of PVs of all future CFs due from a bond equal to its current market price.

**Interpolation:** The process of estimating a price or rate for a particular value date/period from other known prices/rates when the value date/period required lies within the period covered by the known prices/rates.

**In-the-money:** A call (put) option is in-the-money if the underlying is currently more (less) valuable than the strike price.

**Intrinsic value:** The amount by which an option is in-the-money, arrived at by comparing the current market value and the strike price/rate.

**Inverse floater:** A floating rate note/bond structured in such a way that its coupon falls as interest rates rise, and vice versa.

**Inverted yield curve:** A yield curve where, unlike a standard scenario, the rate of interest or bond yield falls as the maturity increases, projecting a downward-sloping curve.

**Investment-grade debt:** A debt instrument that comes with a better credit rating (preferably BBB and above), exhibiting a better credit worthiness and is least likely to default.

**Junk bonds:** Bonds offering higher yield but with lower credit rating, and therefore higher counterparty risk.

**Leverage:** The ability to control large amounts of an underlying variable for a small initial investment.

**Liability swap:** An interest rate swap used in conjunction with an underlying liability such as a borrowing.

**Liquidation:** Any transaction that closes out or offsets an existing position in a futures or options contract.

**Liquidity adjustment facility (LAF):** A tool used by the central bank of a country in its monetary policy allowing banks to borrow money through repurchase agreements and respond to liquidity pressure.

**Liquidity measure:** A measure capturing the ability of a trader or investor to buy or sell large amounts of a security easily without any adverse price reaction, generally captured by bid-offer spread, number and volume of trades, etc.

**Liquidity risk:** The risk that arises from the difficulty of selling or buying an asset in a timely manner and also at a right price.

**Liquidity:** A word describing the ease with which one can undertake transactions in a particular market or instrument. A market where there are always ready buyers and sellers willing to transact at competitive prices is regarded as liquid.

**Long position:** Holding/buying an underlying asset/position, buying a futures contract, paying a fixed rate of interest in an IRS deal.

**Maintenance margin:** The lowest balance of funds that traders are required to maintain with the exchange even after the daily MTM.

**Margin call:**   A request following mark-to-market of a transaction for the initial margin to be reinstated by depositing the required amount of cash.

**Margin:**   An amount that is set aside to ensure that the investor has sufficient equity to meet any adverse price moves.

**Market risk capital charge (MRCC):**   The capital that an institution is supposed to maintain to take care of any abnormal losses caused by a change in market conditions in its trading positions.

**Market risk:**   Risk of financial losses on the market value of investments that arises due to a change in market conditions as reflected through the adverse movement of interest rate, exchange rate, equity price, etc.

**Market-maker:**   Market participant who is committed to offer two-way (bid and ask) quotes/prices at all times, irrespective of the exact requirement (buy or sell) of the counterparty.

**Mark-to-market:**   The process of revaluing securities/positions to the current market values.

**Maturity date:**   The date on which the bond matures and is paid off in full.

**Modified duration:**   The percentage change in price of a debt security for 1% (100 bps) change in yield of the security, also defined by the slope of the price-yield curve as captured through the first order differentiation of the bond price function w.r.t the yield.

**Money market:**   A segment of the financial market where several short-term financial products/instruments issued or traded are of original maturity less than or equal to 1 year.

**Mortgage-backed security (MBS):**   Bond that is secured or backed by a portfolio of underlying mortgage loans.

**Moving average:**   Refers to a statistical technique used to analyze a set of data points by creating an average of subsets, known as rolling window, out of the full data set, especially to filter out the short-lived noise in the data set.

**Multiple price auction:**   An auction in which all the winning bidders are required to pay different prices based on whatever they have quoted in the auction.

**Naked:**   A naked position, preferably in a derivative contract (futures, swap, option), is one not protected by an offsetting position in the underlying.

**Non-competitive bid:**   A bid in which bidders can specify the amount that they would like to buy but do not specify the price.

**Notional bond futures:**   A bond futures contract where the underlying security is not specific, but can be any security from the deliverable basket, as decided by the exchange.

**Offer price:**   The price at which a market maker sells bonds, also known as the ask price.

**Off-market:**   A price/rate which is far beyond (higher or lower) the current market price/rate.

**Offset:** In the futures market, taking an equal amount of position (long or short) in the same futures contract opposite to the existing position (short or long), basically to close out the position, i.e. to have a net position equal to zero.

**Off-the-run security:** Securities which are not recently issued by the issuer, and therefore are relatively less liquid in the market.

**On-the-run security:** Securities which are recently issued by the issuer, and therefore attract a very high level of liquidity in the market, making them benchmark securities.

**Open interest:** The quantity of futures contracts (of a particular specification) which have not yet been closed out by reversing. Either all long positions or all short positions are counted, but not both.

**Open market operation (OMO):** An operation conducted by the central bank of a country, basically to manage the liquidity in the banking system, where the central bank may like to buy (sell) securities from (to) the commercial banks to inject (suck) more (surplus) liquidity to (from) the system, known as OMO purchase (OMO sale).

**Operational risk:** Risk of incurring financial losses due to inadequate systems and control, human error, management failure, etc.

**Opportunity cost:** Value of an action that could have been taken if the current action had not been chosen.

**Optimal hedge:** The number of derivative contracts required to be bought or sold in order to hedge the value of the overall portfolio.

**Option:** The right but not the obligation to buy or sell securities at a fixed price within a specified period.

**Option-adjusted spread (OAS):** An additional spread (beyond the risk-free yield) that is required to equalize the average present value across all simulated paths (in a binomial framework) due in a bond with some embedded option to its observed market price.

**Out-of-the-money:** A call (put) option is out-of-the-money if the underlying is currently less (more) valuable than the strike price, making the option contract less attractive to exercise by the option buyer.

**Over-the-counter (OTC):** .A trading system where transactions are not conducted on a registered stock exchange but via telephone and/or other media of communication, where unlike exchange traded transactions, each counterparty is aware about the other counterparty with a possibility of better customization but possibly with a higher amount of counterparty risk.

**Overnight index swaps (OIS):** An overnight index swqp (MIBOR-OIS in India) is a fixed/floating interest rate swap with the floating leg linked to the O/N MIBOR (Mumbai Interbank Outright Rate), derived from the overnight inter-bank call money rates.

**Par yield curve:** The relationship between the yield to maturity and time to maturity of bonds traded at par value (i.e. at INR 100) or close to par value.

**Perfect hedge:** A mechanism through which the loss (gain) in an underlying asset/instrument is completely offset by the gain (loss) in a derivatives contract.

**Perpetual bond:** Bond or debt instrument without any pre-defined maturity date, and therefore sometimes treated as equity but with a specific coupon, unlike in the case of equity, and sometimes issued with a provision of redemption after a particular period (i.e. with call option).

**Physical delivery:** Physical transfer of the underlying asset/instrument at the contractual price/rate as on the maturity/delivery date, applicable to a derivatives contract.

**Policy rate:** The rate of interest used by the central bank through its monetary policy to control the economy, basically refers to the repo and reverse repo rate.

**Present value:** The amount of money which needs to be invested now to achieve a given amount in the future with the interest component.

**Price value of a basis point (PVBP):** See **PV01**.

**Price value of 01 (PV01):** The price change in a debt security for one basis point or 0.01% change in interest rates.

**Primary debt market:** A market where borrowers issue debt securities to raise capital.

**Probability of default:** The statistical measure of how likely it is that an institution will default on its debt obligations over a specific future period of time (e.g. in the next year), normally derived from the transition of credit rating over a period of time.

**Protection buyer:** A party, with or without holding a reference asset, who does not want to carry the risk of its credit exposure and wants to transfer the credit risk to another counterparty in exchange of a price.

**Protection seller:** A party who wants to carry the credit risk of others in exchange of some rewards and is ready to give protection against the credit risk of an exposure.

**Put option:** A contract that gives the buyer a right but not the obligation to sell an underlying asset/instrument at a pre-agreed price/rate on a future date.

**Reference asset:** A single asset/underlying or a portfolio of assets on which a protection buyer takes a protection from protection seller.

**Reinvestment rate:** The rate at which the periodic interest received during the life of an investment is reinvested to earn interest-on-interest.

**Reinvestment risk:** The risk of earning lesser interest on interest due to adverse changes in the future rate of interests.

**Repo agreement:** A contract in which a security is sold with an agreement to repurchase the security at a higher price on a future date as specified in the contract.

**Repo rate:** The rate at which the central bank of a country (RBI in case of India) lends money to commercial banks in the event of any shortfall of funds against specified securities as collateral.

**Residual Maturity:** The remaining time from the trade/settlement/valuation date till the final maturity date, applicable to debt instruments.

**Reverse cash-and-carry arbitrage:** A situation where the price differences in the cash and futures market is such that an arbitrage is possible by taking a long position in the futures market (i.e. buying an underlying through a futures contract) and a short position in the cash market (i.e. selling the underlying).

**Reverse repo rate:** The rate at which commercial banks, in the event of surplus funds with them, park the funds with the central bank of a country (RBI in case of India), but against specified securities as collaterals.

**Reversed repo agreement:** A contract in which a security is borrowed with an agreement to replace the security at a higher price on a future date as specified in the contract.

**Risk management:** A collective and continuous process, started from the identification of the risk, followed by measuring, managing, and finally monitoring the same to ensure the sound existence of the business.

**Risk-free return:** The rate of interest that an investor is expected to earn for a particular period (say 10 years) form his/her investment in a completely risk-free (free from counterparty risk) asset/instrument (like securities issued by the central government of a country)

**Roll:** Gain (loss) on the future/remaining (unfixed) part of an IRS deal, only linked to the fixed leg, due to a change in the current swap rate with the original contractual rate.

**Secondary debt market:** A market in which securities are traded after they are initially issued in the primary market.

**Securitization:** The process of raising finance, via a framework in which liquid or illiquid assets of an institution are transformed into a package of debt securities backed by these assets.

**Settlement date:** A date, usually on the trade date (T+0), or 1/2/3 days after the trade is executed (i.e. T+1 / T+2 / T+3), when the buyer and seller exchange cash and security as per the terms agreed upon on the trade date.

**Settlement risk:** The risk that occurs due to non-simultaneous exchange of securities and the concerned value.

**Settlement:** The simultaneous process of transferring securities from seller to buyer and arranging the corresponding movement of funds from buyer to seller.

**Short hedge:** A short (sell) position taken in the futures market to hedge the existing long position in an underlying asset.

**Short position:** Selling an underlying asset/position, selling a futures contract, receiving fixed rate of interest in an IRS deal.

**Simple interest:** An interest on an investment which is paid directly at maturity or not reinvested to earn interest on interest.

**Specific risk:** Risk of incurring any financial losses in trading positions (bond, foreign currency, equity, etc.) only due to a change in issuer specific conditions.

**Speculation:** A deal (buy or sell) undertaken by a dealer purely based on his/her view (need not be completely correct) about the future favourable movement of the concerned market/factor with a view to book a profit.

**Spot price:** The price of an underlying asset/instrument for delivery today or at the earliest possible delivery date.

**Spot rate of interest:** The yield to maturity on a zero coupon (deep discount) bond, also known as zero coupon yield (ZCY).

**Stress testing:** A valuable risk management tool which tries to quantify the size of potential losses that an institution is expected to incur under certain stress events.

**Strike price/rate:** The price or rate at which the holder of an option (call or put) can insist on the underlying transaction being fulfilled.

**Swap rate:** The single rate of interest applicable to the fixed leg of an interest rate swap deal that the fixed rate payer is supposed to pay at the end of every settlement period (say in every 6 months).

**Swap spread:** The difference between the fixed rate on an interest rate swap and the risk-free yield of the Treasury benchmark security with the similar maturity.

**Treasury bill:** A short-term government paper of up to 1 year's maturity, sold at a discount to principal value and redeemed at maturity at par.

**Underlying:** The underlying of a futures or option contract is the commodity or financial instrument on which the contract depends. The underlying for a bond future is the bond; the underlying for a short-term interest rate futures contract is typically a short-term risk-free rate (like 91-day T-bill rate).

**Uniform price auction:** An auction in which all the winning bidders are required to pay exactly the same price, irrespective of the price (higher or lower than the cut-off price) which they have quoted in the auction.

**Unsecured Bond:** Securities that are not backed by any collaterals, and therefore attract settlement (in the event of winding up of the institution) only after any payment made to the secured bond holders but before the holders of preference shares.

**Value-at-risk (VaR):** The maximum amount of loss that an investor/trader is likely to incur on a particular asset/investment, over a specific time horizon (say 1 day), under a given level of confidence (like 99% or 95%), but only under normal circumstances.

**Vertical disallowance:** A small proportion of the matched positions in each time-band, to be added while estimating the market risk capital charge on matched (net of long and short) positions in different time bands, to take care of basis risk.

**Yield curve:** Graphical representation of the rate of interests with respect to their maturities, where the interest rates are measured in the vertical axis whereas the horizontal axis captures the time to maturity.

**Yield spread:** The difference between the yields on a non-government security (corporate bond) of a particular maturity and that of the risk-free security (central government security) of similar maturity.

**Yield to maturity (YTM):** The average rate of return (yield) that an investor is supposed to earn from his/her investment in a particular security, provided the security is held till the maturity and the reinvestment of interim cash flows happens at the same rate. Alternatively, it is the discounting rate at which the present value of all future promised cash flows is exactly equal to its market price, again commonly known as the internal rate of return (IRR) of the debt security.

# Index

Note: Page numbers in *italic* indicate a figure and page numbers in **bold** indicate a table on the corresponding page; Page numbers followed by 'n' denote notes.

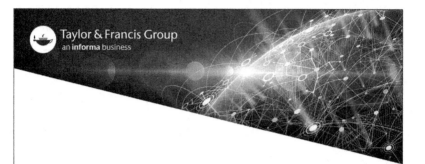

Printed in the United States
by Baker & Taylor Publisher Services